Korris R B

S0-CJE-763

Louis & Brigitte Bell

For historians ought to be precise, truthful, and quite unprejudiced, and neither interest nor fear, hatred nor affection, should cause them to swerve from the path of truth, whose mother is history, the rival of time, the depository of great actions, the witness of what is past, the example and instruction of the present, the monitor of the future.

MIGUEL DE CERVANTES, 1547–1616

For

Daniel R. Burns, 1956–1972

who started it all

Episodes in American History

An Inquiry Approach

ROBERT E. BURNS

The Great Seal of the United States

The design for the cover of this book (found on the greenback of every one dollar bill in circulation since 1935) is taken from the reverse side of the Great Seal of the United States. Designed in 1782, it depicts an unfinished pyramid, built upon 13 layers of stone, symbolizing the nation's 13 original colonies and its future growth.

In a triangle over the pyramid is the eye of Providence surrounded by rays of "glory" or a sunburst. At the base of the pyramid is the date 1776 when the Union was begun. The motto Annuit Coeptis means "He (God) has favored our undertakings." Novus Ordo Seclorum, "A new order of the ages," refers to the fact that the United States was the first civilization in recorded history to have a democracy within a republic.

The face of the Great Seal is our nation's symbol of sovereignty and consists of the national coat-of-arms— the familiar American bald eagle with its shield breastplate and the motto E Pluribus Unum, "From Many, One." It is used on the official documents of the land, and over the entrances of U.S. diplomatic offices abroad. It is the basis for other seals and coats-of-arms such as those used by civil and military authority, and in the colophon on the back of this book. The Great Seal is kept in the U.S. Department of State, Washington, D.C.

Episodes in American History

An Inquiry Approach

ROBERT E. BURNS

LEE R. BOYER • JAMES R. FELTON

PHILIP GLEASON • JOHN J. LYON

JAMES E. O'NEILL • CHARLES J. TULL

GINN AND COMPANY
A XEROX EDUCATION COMPANY

XEROX

About the Authors

Robert E. Burns, senior author, earned his B.A. at Northeastern University, and his M.A. and Ph.D. in History at Harvard University. He is affiliated with Notre Dame University where he serves as Associate Dean, College of Arts and Letters, Professor of History, and a member of the board of Notre Dame Journal of Education. For three years, he directed the Experienced Teacher Fellowship Program at Notre Dame University, under the U.S. Office of Education.

Lee R. Boyer, currently on the history faculty of Eastern Michigan University, received his B.A. degree from Mount Union College in Ohio, and his M.A. and Ph.D. in History from the University of Notre Dame. Dr. Boyer has served as secondary school instructor and curriculum author for several Ohio schools, and as a staff member of the Notre Dame Experienced Teacher Fellowship Program in History.

James R. Felton earned his B.A. in Secondary Education with a History Major at Xavier University in New Orleans, and his M.A. from Notre Dame University. He taught history for a number of years at L. B. Landry Junior-Senior High School in New Orleans. In 1969, the Board of Education transferred him as the first black teacher to Benjamin Franklin Senior High School in New Orleans, an accelerated learning center.

Philip Gleason is chairman of the History Department at Notre Dame University where he has been on the faculty since 1960. Dr. Gleason received his B.S. in Education from the University of Dayton, and his M.A. and Ph.D. from Notre Dame University. He taught high school in Xenia, Ohio, and is the author of numerous articles on American intellectual and cultural history. He has three books to his credit, including: *The Conservative Reformers: The German-American Catholics* and the *Social Order.*

John J. Lyon is associate Professor in the General Program of Liberal Studies at Notre Dame University, and a specialist in the history of the Civil War and Reconstruction. He received his B.A. and M.A. degrees from Notre Dame, and his Ph.D. in History from the University of Pittsburgh. He taught high school in Ohio for five years and then joined the faculty of Duquesne University's History Department. Dr. Lyon's articles and reviews have appeared in many scholarly journals.

James E. O'Neill is Deputy Archivist of the United States. He received his B.A. and M.A. from the University of Detroit, and his Ph.D. in History from the University of Chicago. Dr. O'Neill has taught at Notre Dame University, University of Chicago, Loyola University in Chicago, and George Washington University, served in the Library of Congress as Specialist in American History, and was Director of the Franklin D. Roosevelt Library at Hyde Park, New York.

Charles J. Tull is a professor of History at Indiana University, South Bend, and a specialist in history of the Twentieth Century. He received his B.S. from Creighton University, his M.A. and Ph.D. in History from Notre Dame University. He has taught at Notre Dame, St. Vincent College, Latrobe, Pennsylvania, and De Paul University, Chicago. Dr. Tull is the author of several historical articles and publications, including *American History Since 1865* and *Father Coughlin and the New Deal.*

© Copyright, 1973, by Ginn and Company (Xerox Corporation)
All Rights Reserved
Lexington, Massachusetts 02173
0–663–20787–8

Contents

Chronologies, Charts, and Graphs

MAP and PICTURE CREDITS

All maps were drawn by the Richard Lufkin Co. Graphs, diagrams and pictographs are by Magnuson & Larson, Inc. Drawings on pages A18, A20, A22, A43, A79, A80 (top), A81, A149, B28 and B172 were made by Brendan Lynch. Those on D50–52 are by Ron Carreiro/Graphic Design Associates, and on D141 by Joseph Patti. The drawing of archaic corn on A24 is from P. Mangelsdorf and C. E. Smith, "New Archaeological Evidence on Evolution in Maize," Harvard University Botanical Leaflets, Vol. 13, No. 8, March, 1949, by permission.

The illustrations are reproduced by courtesy of the sources listed.

Page

ii   (top to bottom) American Museum of Natural History; Virginia State Chamber of Commerce; Maryland Historical Society; *Life* magazine, © 1972, Time, Inc.; Library of Congress; Ford Archives, Henry Ford Museum, Dearborn, Michigan

iii   The Smithsonian Institution; The Boeing Company; NASA

Unit One

A15 National Park Service

A21 Arizona State Museum

A25 Museum of the American Indian, Heye Foundation

A26 Smithsonian Institution Anthropological Archives, Bureau of American Ethnology Collection

A32 University Museum, Philadelphia

A33–35, 37 Redrawn by permission of the Indiana Historical Society

A49 (left) Library of Congress; (right) The Huntington Library, San Marino, California

A50 Rare Books Division, The New York Public Library, Astor, Lenox and Tilden Foundations

A53 Culver Pictures

A60 The New York Public Library

A67 The Bettmann Archive

A68 Museum of the American Indian, Heye Foundation

A72 Ewing Galloway

Unit Two

A81 Virginia State Chamber of Commerce

A86 (left) Wide World; (right) UPI

A92 (left to right) National Maritime Museum (1); © National Portrait Gallery, London (2), (3), (4); Rare Books Division, The New York Public Library, Astor, Lenox and Tilden Foundations

A98 The Governors of Dulwich College Picture Library

Page

A99 Rare Books Division, The New York Public Library, Astor, Lenox and Tilden Foundations

A100 Massachusetts State House, George M. Cushing photo

A101 Plimoth Plantation

A102 (top) Enoch Pratt Free Library; (bottom) National Portrait Gallery, London

A103 Stokes Collection, The New York Public Library

A104, 105 The Bettmann Archive

A106 © National Portrait Gallery, London

A115 Historical Pictures Service, Chicago

A123 Essex Institute, Salem, Massachusetts

A125 (top) The Library of Congress, photo by T. Waterman; (right) Virginia State Library

A126 From the original in the Henry E. Huntington Library, San Marino, California

A127 Library of Congress

A129 enjamin Franklin Collection, Yale University Library

A135 (left) Mark Sexton; (right) The Peabody Museum of Salem (Mark Sexton photo)

A137 Library of Congress

Unit Three

A141 Wide World, New Haven Historical Society

A142 Werner Forman

A143 © British Museum

A146 Bibliothèque Naitonale, Paris

A150, 152, 153 © British Museum

A158 (top) Cornell University Libraries; (middle) Library of Congress; (bottom) National Maritime Museum, Greenwich

A159 (top) Library of Congress; (left) Musée de la Marine, Nantes, France (photo Madec); (right) Library of Congress; (bottom) The New York Public Library

A162 British Museum

A164 The Peabody Museum of Salem

A165 Library of the Religious Society of Friends, London

A166 (left) Hull Museums Copyright

Page

A169 American Antiquarian Society

A174 © National Portrait Gallery, London

A178 Historical Pictures Service, Chicago

A180 The Historical Society of Pennsylvania

Unit Four

B8 (left) The New York Public Library, Emmet Collection; (right) Historical Pictures Service

B9 New Hampshire State Historical Society

B11 (right) Massachusetts Historical Society

B12 Historical Society of Pennsylvania; Newport Historical Society; Historical Pictures Service; The New-York Historical Society

B17 Smithsonian Institution

B24 (both) Massachusetts Historical Society

B25 Detail of Paul Revere's engraving of "The Bloody Massacre," The American Antiquarian Society

B27 Massachusetts Historical Society

B32 Photo by George M. Cushing

B33 (left) Independence National Historical Park Collection; (middle, right) The New York Public Library, Astor, Lenox and Tilden Foundation; (right) NYPL, Emmet Collection

B35 Independence National Historical Park Collection

B37 Rare Book Division, The New York Public Library, Astor, Lenox and Tilden Foundation

B40 National Geographic Photographer George F. Mobley, courtesy U.S. Capitol Historical Society

B49 Independence National Historical Park Collection

B53 © National Portrait Gallery, London

Unit Five

B69 Virginia Museum of Fine Arts

B72 Shelburne Museum, Inc., Shelburne, Vermont

Page

B74 (left) Independence National Historical Park Collection (right) The New-York Historical Society
B75 Culver Pictures
B78 The Mount Vernon Ladies' Association, Mount Vernon, Virginia.
B88 Culver Pictures
B90 Field Museum of Natural History
B91 (left) The Bettmann Archive; (right) Essex Institute, Salem, Mass.
B96 (left) Library of Congress; (right) The New-York Historical Society
B98 Brown Brothers
B99 Art Commission of the City of New York
B101 (top) American Antiquarian Society; (bottom) Library of Congress
B121 Tennessee State Library and Archives, from the Andrew Jackson Papers in the Manuscript Unit
B122 The St. Louis Art Museum (*The County Election*, 1852, by George Caleb Bingham)

Unit Six
B146 Fruitlands Museum, Harvard, Mass.
B147 Collage: (background photo) Jim Jowers, Nancy Palmer Photo Agency; (left and middle) Steve and Joel Axelrad; (right) Wide World
B148 (left) The Bella C. Landauer Collection, New-York Historical Society; (right) George M. Cushing photo, courtesy Boston Athenaeum
B149 George M. Cushing photo, courtesy Boston Athenaeum
B151 Franklin Wing (right) Wide World (bottom)
'B153 George M. Cushing photo, courtesy Boston Athenaeum
B157 D. B. Morrisson
B170 (right) Wide World
B174 New York State Historical Association, Cooperstown
B185 The Bettmann Archive
B187 UPI

Unit Seven
C1 The New York Public Library
C3 The Governing Body of Christ Church, Oxford
C5 (top) Missouri Historical Society; (bottom) The Bettmann Archive
C7, C10, C11, C12 Library of Congress
C14 Charles Bird King: John C.

Page

Calhoun, Corcoran Gallery of Art, Washington, D.C.
C18 (bottom) Library of Congress
C19 Prints Division, The New York Public Library, Astor, Lenox and Tilden Foundation
C20 (top) Culver Pictures; (middle) *Frank Leslie's*; (bottom) Chicago Historical Society
C24, C25 Library of Congress
C30 (left) C31 U.S. Signal Corps photo in the National Archives (Brady Collection)
C33 The New-York Historical Society
C34 The Sophia Smith Collection, Smith College
C44 U.S. Signal Corps photo in the National Archives (Brady Collection)
C48 The New-York Historical Society
C50 Jay Leviton—Black Star
C54 The National Archives
C56 (1860) Library of Congress; (1864) New-York Historical Society; (1868, 1872, 1876) Ohio Historical Society Library

Unit Eight
C65 Southern Pacific and The Association of American Railroads
C80, C81 The New-York Historical Society
C90 The Kansas State Historical Society, Topeka
C91 (top) Library of Congress; (bottom) *Harper's Weekly*
C94 Culver Pictures
C96, C98, C99 Library of Congress; background photo on C98–C99 from International Harvester Co.
C101 Culver Pictures
C102, C104 Library of Congress
C105 Jacob A. Riis photo, The Jacob A. Riis Collection, Museum of the City of New York
C108 AFL–CIO
C109 The Bettmann Archive
C111 Culver Pictures
C125 U.S. Department of Transportation
C126 Metropolitan Life Insurance Co.
C128 Museum of the City of New York
C133 The New York Public Library
C136 Jacob A. Riis photo, The Jacob A. Riis Collection, Museum of the City of New York
C139 Library of Congress

Unit Nine
D1 (Harding, Coolidge) Keystone

D3 Library of Congress
D4 U.S. Signal Corps photo, The National Archives
D12 (left) Bostwick-Fohardt Collection, KMTV, Omaha; (right) © Old "Life" Magazine; (bottom) Library of Congress
D14 Photograph by Jacob A. Riis, The Jacob A. Riis Collection, Museum of the City of New York
D16 Doubleday & Co., Inc.
D18 l. to r., Culver, Brown Brothers, Theodore Roosevelt Association
D23 Brown Brothers
D24 Brown Brothers; © The New York Times Company
D30 Culver
D31 Sy Seidman
D32 UPI
D34 The National Archives
D36 © Old "Life" Magazine
D37 (bottom) Reprinted with permission from *The Saturday Evening Post*, © 1919, The Curtis Publishing Company
D40 Library of Congress
D42 Reprinted, courtesy of the Chicago Tribune
D56 Underwood & Underwood
D59 University of Hartford: DeWitt Collection
D62, D63 UPI
D69 All Wide World except TVA (bottom)
D72 Wide World
D75 UPI
D76, D83 The National Archives
D89 U.S. Army
D94 U.S. Air Force
D98 UPI
D101 Wide World-AP
D104 (top) Ernst Maria Lang, Süddentsche Zeitung
D105 (top) With permission of Robert Speller & Sons, Publishers, Inc.
D106 Wide World
D107 UPI
D112 Library of Congress; Brown Brothers
D114 Wide World
D115 UPI
D119 Pictorial Parade
D121, 123 Wide World
D129 UPI
D130 Cornell Capa, Magnum
D131 Wide World
D132 UPI
D134 UPI
D135 George Ballis from Black Star
D136 UPI
D137 The New York Times, by George Tames
D138 UPI
D141, 143 NASA

In the case of some material for which acknowledgment is not given, we have earnestly endeavored to find the original sources and to procure permission for its use, but without success.

To the Student

Episodes in American History is a new kind of textbook. It is different from most of the history or social studies textbooks that you may have studied in the past—different in both organization and subject matter.

This book is composed of nine units of instruction arranged into seventy-four assignments. Each assignment is divided into sets of readings and audio-visual exercises. Some assignments can be completed in one class period but most will require two or three. Your teacher will tell you exactly how many sets of readings are required for homework. Since most of your class work will be discussion of what you have read, you must try very hard to complete your homework assignments on time.

In this book you will read brief historical narratives, examine charts and graphs of historical facts, analyze paintings and cartoons, read historical dramatizations, and study the actual words and statements of people who made history. You will also try to learn about the past by making comparison with the present, and you will read what eminent historians have said about the specific subject or problem you have examined.

Episodes is organized in such a way that while studying American history you will also be trained to think systematically. As you proceed you will be asked—and you will ask—a great many questions about historical problems and issues. Thinking systematically requires learning how to perform intellectual tasks such as recognizing relationships between sets of facts, asking the kinds of questions that clarify and inform, and discovering what historical facts suggest as well as what they say.

Performance of such intellectual tasks involves learning skills. In the course of your study you will learn how *to use concepts, draw inferences, analyze testimony, form hypotheses, test hypotheses,* and *make judgments.* These terms may appear baffling to you now, but as you proceed you will learn what they mean and how to perform the intellectual skills they describe. In this book task performance and skill development are important learning objectives. For this reason, every assignment carefully explains precisely what tasks and skills are required to complete it. While studying the past you will be learning intellectual tasks and skills that are useful in the present.

The history of the American people is a fascinating story. History writing, however, must be a process of selection. Everything about the past cannot be known; everything that is known cannot be told. There is simply not time enough or printed pages enough to tell it all. The authors of this book believe that American history is the history of American people. They have tried to present for your study and analysis vital episodes from the historical traditions and experiences of all the American people—Red, White, and Black. By knowing from whence we came, we may better know who we are and where we are going.

ROBERT E. BURNS

xvi

UNIT ONE
First Americans

The grass which grows out of the earth
is common to all.
(AN ANONYMOUS DELAWARE INDIAN, 1777)

1 History as detection

The Nature of Historical Inquiry

Introduction

Do you find it exciting to read detective stories or watch great detectives practice their arts on television? Would you enjoy being in their shoes? If you would, you will probably enjoy studying history the way it is presented in this book.

The arts and skills of detectives and historians are much alike. Detectives and historians both approach their work in a systematic way and both are framers of probing and inquiring questions rather than seekers of *yes* or *no* answers. In a word, detectives and historians are both *inquirers*. Inquiry involves the use of skills that can be taught and learned.

As inquirers, detectives and historians must know *how to distinguish facts from opinions*. Successful detectives and historians separate facts from opinions by evaluating testimony or evidence. Evaluation simply means making judgments about what can be believed in testimony or evidence, and what cannot. To make judgments, the detective or historian establishes criteria (standards) of *credibility** by putting questions of a probing nature to the evidence at hand. For example:

Credibility is the worthiness or capacity for being believed.

1. Is the record of testimony or evidence at hand an accurate representation of what the witness actually reported?

2. Does the person testifying have any personal or party interests to protect or advance by giving evidence?

3. Was the person testifying in a position to have seen, heard, or known the testimony with certainty?

4. Are there unstated assumptions or omissions in the testimony that may cause doubt of its credibility?

5. Can the testimony or evidence be corroborated from other sources?

6. Are all of the circumstances described in testimony or evidence sufficiently probable to remove all causes for doubt?

Questions of this kind or others like them enable detectives and historians to judge whether or not a given piece of testimony or evidence is probably factual or probably opinion.

Problem Recognition

When at work, successful detectives and historians must do much more than ask questions in order to establish credibility criteria. They must know what kinds of evidence to seek. To know this, detectives and historians must be able to recognize in a situation or in testimony that a problem exists. The process of recognizing such a problem and identifying it takes the form of noting relationships between facts and developing the implications of them by asking inquiring questions.

For example, a detective may note that two tickets to Acapulco, Mexico, were found on the body of a reported male suicide who fell from the eighteenth floor of a New York office building. Examining the facts, the detective asks: Why would a man intending suicide have purchased two tickets to Acapulco?

Or take the case of a historian studying early times in America. He notes that the Dutch traders in colonial New York supplied the Mohawk Indians with guns, but traded none to the Mahicans. These facts lead him to inquiring questions such as why the Dutch behaved as they did.

In both cases, observed relationships between facts were transformed into the kinds of problems that could be investigated or researched.

Hypothesis Formation

Once a problem is recognized and identified, detectives and historians continue their investigative procedures by suggesting a tentative solution called a hypothesis. A hypothesis is a possible explanation or solution to a problem assumed to be true for the sake of giving direction to an investigation. The process of hypothesis-making is much like that of problem-recognition. It consists of asking inquiring questions.

For example, the detective concerned with the problem of the male suicide with two tickets to Acapulco might ask who was the intended user of the second ticket. One of several hypotheses suggested by that question might be that the man was involved in a romantic triangle and was killed because of it.

A historian concerned with the problem of why the Dutch supplied guns to the Mohawks but traded none to the Mahicans might ask what special benefit the Dutch derived from that kind of arrangement. One of several hypotheses suggested by that question might be that the Dutch were under the protection of the Mohawks, who insisted on denying guns to the Mahicans.

Hypothesis Testing

After formulating a hypothesis, detectives and historians proceed to gather as much factual testimony and evidence bearing upon it as possible. As facts accumulate, both detectives and historians may have to refine, modify, or totally reject their original hypothesis.

For example, after inquiring into the personal life of the reported male suicide with two tickets to Acapulco, a detective may discover that the victim

Acrophobia is a morbid dread of being at a great height.

was happily married, was part owner of a hotel in Acapulco, and suffered severely from *acrophobia*.* These facts shed a different light on the nature of his death.

After inquiring into the nature and conditions of trading with Indians in seventeenth-century colonial New York, a historian may discover that the Mahicans bought guns from English traders which were less expensive than Dutch guns. These facts give us new reasons why the Dutch traded with Mohawks instead of Mahicans.

In the case of these two examples, the original hypotheses are not consistent with the known facts. Therefore they must either be changed so they are consistent, or rejected and replaced by new ones and the entire process repeated. A hypothesis is not a firm solution or explanation of a problem until it is consistent with all of the known facts.

Inferences

In the course of their investigations, even the hardest-working detectives and historians may not discover much factual testimony and evidence on their subjects. However, what is available may be used in different ways. Successful detectives and historians are able to recognize what facts *suggest* as well as what they *say* about a subject. Such recognition is called a *probability statement* or *inference*.*

An **inference** is a probability statement derived from facts, objects, principles, ideas, or observations.

When inferences are drawn from facts and are not contradicted by other facts, they are extremely useful tools of inquiry. Inferences may be used by both detectives and historians at all stages of inquiry, namely:

Problem recognition

Hypothesis formation

Hypothesis testing

Recall the examples used so far. The inference that a reported male suicide intended to visit Acapulco with another person was drawn from the fact that he possessed two tickets to that resort. Similarly, the inference that there were practical reasons for the Dutch to trade with the Mohawks but not with the Mahicans was drawn from the known facts of Dutch trading policies. In each case, these inferences suggested the kind of inquiring questions which led to problem-recognition and hypothesis-formation.

In the process of hypothesis-testing when factual testimony and evidence are incomplete, inferences drawn from known facts may be used to support, modify, or reject the hypotheses. For example, a detective may infer from the size of a footprint the height, weight, and sex of a suspect which could change the entire direction of his investigation. A historian may infer from the discovery of clay pipes in Indian burial mounds that those particular Indians knew how to cultivate tobacco and work clay. This inference could lead the historian to a search for other evidence of Indian agricultural activities and ceramic culture.

A4

The Historian—Judge and Jury

Like asking probing or inquiring questions, the ability to make sound inferences comes from experience and knowledge. These abilities are skills that successful detectives and historians must have, and they are skills that students can learn.

There is a point, however, where the similarities between the work of detectives and historians end. Both groups use probing and inquiring questions to establish criteria for distinguishing facts from opinion. They both use probing and inquiring questions and inferences to recognize problems, to form hypotheses, and to test hypotheses. However, a detective's work is over when his investigation is completed. Judge and jury render final verdict on the case he has investigated.

Unlike a detective, a historian does not end his work with completion of his investigation. The historian is judge and jury, as well as investigator. As judge and jury, the historian must decide whether men and events of the past have been successful or unsuccessful, right or wrong, good or bad. *Judgments** of this kind rarely agree, and different historians frequently judge the same historical person or event in different ways.

Though agreement about what is truth in history may be hard to achieve, honesty is not. Historical judgments or judgments of any kind are generally honest not so much for what they say or for how much agreement they may command, but because they have been honestly obtained. An honest judgment is one based upon testimony and evidence that have been systematically and carefully evaluated.

> **Judgment** is the mental or intellectual process of forming an opinion through evaluation of testimony or evidence.

Objective

The overall objective of this book is to increase your ability to make judgments based on systematic and careful *evaluation** of testimony and evidence. We have not set this objective because we want to train you to become good detectives or good historians; we have set it because we believe *inquiry* is the key to all learning, as well as the key to understanding and appreciating America's past.

Studying American history as a process of inquiry rather than as a selection of facts and conclusions to be remembered has implications for your education that range far beyond understanding and appreciating America's past. Learning a method of inquiry and acquiring the skills to use it will enable you to expand your knowledge after your days in school are over. You can do this by asking important and meaningful questions and making reasoned judgments based on evaluated testimony and evidence.

Simply stated, inquiry skills are useful intellectual tools for living and working in modern America. Well-developed inquiry skills are especially vital today if one is to gain any balanced understanding of the many conflicting charges and counter-charges that swirl around the crime, drugs, pollution, poverty, war, race, and minority problems we face in America.

> **Evaluation** is the examination of worth, quality, significance, amount, degree, or conditions for the purpose of making a judgment.

1   TO BE AN INQUIRER

Objectives of this assignment are to:

—Describe the process of distinguishing fact from opinion.

—Describe the process of inquiry.

—Describe an inference and its functions in the process of inquiry.

—Recognize and identify the process of inquiry in two detective stories.

You have just read a description of how some detectives and historians function as inquirers. One of the best ways to learn how to be an inquirer yourself is to watch an expert do it. Read the short story below very carefully and try to discover how Inspector Thomas inquires into this strange incident. While reading the story, keep the following questions in mind:

How and where in the story does Inspector Thomas:

1. *Decide that part of the agent's testimony may be questionable?*

2. *Recognize and identify a problem to be solved?*

3. *Form a hypothesis?*

4. *Propose to test his hypothesis?*

Two Thousand Shoes for Left Feet

Some years ago Paul Thomas, an inspector in the U.S. Customs Service, made a number of routine inspections of east coast ports of entry. When Thomas reached New York City, he made his formal inspection of customs facilities during the early part of the day. Late in the afternoon, he dropped in on a group of customs officers taking a coffee-break.

Some of the agents were old friends and they were behaving now exactly as they had the last time Thomas visited them—they were complaining about their jobs.

"We are underpaid and overworked," lamented one agent, "and the American public is inconsiderate and doesn't appreciate our services."

"Would you believe," remarked another agent to Thomas, "two thousand heels in three days! Have you ever heard of such a thing?"

Thomas turned quickly and asked, "What are you talking about?"

"The owner of a shoe store imported a thousand pairs of men's shoes. Then he refused to pay the duty on them. He claimed two thousand dollars for duty was too much. He said for all he cared we could dump the shoes in the river and jump in after them," explained the agent, adding morosely, "So there we were—another citizen offended."

"That's life," observed Thomas.

"Wait a minute," replied the first agent, "that's not the end. We confiscated the shoes and advertised them for sale at public auction. Would you believe it—when we opened the boxes, every single shoe was for the left foot!"

The second agent broke in, "Chief Michael McGinnis thought he smelled a rat and played Sherlock Holmes. We had to examine every single shoe. We checked each one for a hollow heel filled with diamonds or dope. Two thousand heels we pried off, and two thousand heels we tapped back on!"

"Then what?" questioned Thomas.

"Then? We found nothing, absolutely nothing in any of the heels. We repacked the boxes and put them up for auction."

The second agent commented, "Yeah, but how many people want two thousand left-footed shoes with heels ripped off and replaced? Believe me, not many!"

"We sold 'em, though," remarked the first agent. "We were lucky to get two hundred dollars from a shoe store owner in Manhattan. He said he had a lot of one-legged left-footed customers. So he bought the shoes."

Thomas was incredulous. "You believed him? Look, maybe two hundred dollars for merchandise owing a duty of two thousand dollars is a good deal. But why would anyone in his right mind pay even two hundred dollars for two thousand left-footed shoes?"

"There are people in this world who'll buy anything," the agent responded.

Thomas scratched his nose. "Maybe yes and maybe no. No matter how cheap they were, I'd buy two thousand left-footed shoes only if I knew where there were two thousand right-footed ones. Where would a guy look for something like that?"

The agent's neck turned red. He looked at Thomas and began to shout angrily, "What's the matter with you? You may be an inspector, but don't smile at me that way, and stop scratching your darn nose! Believe me, with Chief McGinnis playing Sherlock Holmes and looking over our shoulders every minute, we were very conscientious. We checked everything. There wasn't a single right-footed shoe in the entire shipment!"

Thomas scratched his nose again and smiled, "I don't doubt that you were thorough as far as you went. The rat that Chief McGinnis smelled was there all right, but you fellows didn't know where to look for it. Two thousand shoes for left feet! Incredible!"

"Thomas, you're not communicating," fumed the agent.

"Okay," answered Thomas, "I'll try to make it simple. Can't you see that someone may be trying to defraud the United States government of its legal customs duty?"

Then Thomas stopped smiling and scratching his nose. He left the group and hurried to a telephone in Chief McGinnis's office where just before the door closed he was heard to say, "Operator, this is Inspector Thomas. I want to make several calls. Would you please connect me first with . . ."

2   MAKING INFERENCES

You have seen how historians and detectives use *inferences*. If you tried to guess how Inspector Thomas intended to test his hypothesis in the case of the left-footed shoes, then you yourself made an inference. Beyond saying he would make several telephone calls, Inspector Thomas told you nothing directly about how he proposed to test his hypothesis. Whom he intended to call, where he intended to call, is not given in the story. That information must be inferred from Thomas's actions and from other facts.

You already know how to make inferences, and most likely you have been making them all of your life. The best way to improve a skill that you already have is to watch an expert use it. In the last reading, the customs agent mentioned one of the most skillful inference-makers of all time, the greatest detective in English literature, Sir Arthur Conan Doyle's incomparable Sherlock Holmes.

In the following example of Holmes's extraordinary inference-making ability, try to discover how he does it. As you read the account related by his friend, Doctor Watson, keep in mind these questions:

1. *What hypothesis does Holmes make about the messenger with the blue envelope?*

2. *What facts and what inferences drawn from them suggested Holmes's hypothesis?*

3. *How does Holmes use the inquiry process to form his hypothesis?*

4. *How was Holmes's hypothesis tested?*

How in the World Did You Know That?

After having lost another friendly argument with Holmes, I walked over to the window and stood looking out into the busy street. "Holmes may be very clever," I thought to myself, "but he is also extremely conceited." Though still somewhat annoyed at my friend, I thought it best to change the subject.

"I wonder who that fellow is and what he's looking for?" I asked, pointing to a plainly dressed husky man who was walking slowly down the other side of the street, looking carefully and deliberately at house numbers. He had a large blue envelope in his hand, and was evidently the carrier of a message.

"It's difficult to guess," said Holmes after looking out of the window, "but I'll wager half a crown that he's a retired sergeant of Marines."

"Oh no, not again," I thought, "Holmes knows I can't check out his guess."

The thought had hardly passed through my mind when the man whom we were watching caught sight of the number on our door and quickly crossed the street. We heard heavy steps climbing the stairway and then a loud knock on our door.

"For Mr. Sherlock Holmes," he said, stepping into the room and handing my friend the large blue envelope.

Here at last was a chance for me to get the better of my conceited friend. "May I ask," I said to the man, "who do you work for?"

"I'm a courier for the Midland Bank, sir," he replied.

"And what did you do before that?" I asked with a quick look at Holmes.

"A sergeant, sir; Royal Marine Light Infantry. Twenty-five years of service, sir."

He clicked his heels together, saluted smartly, and was gone.

"How in the world did you know that?" I asked, turning to Holmes.

"Know what?" he smiled.

"Why, that he was a retired sergeant of Marines."

"Ordinarily, I don't give explanations, but in your case I will. You really were not able to see that our late visitor was a sergeant of Marines?"

"No, indeed."

"It is easier to know it than to explain *why* I know it. If you were asked to prove that two and two make four, you might find some difficulty, but nonetheless you are quite sure that two and two do make four. Well, even across the street I could see a large blue anchor tattooed on the back of the fellow's hand. That suggested some connection with the sea. He walked erect, just like a drill instructor, and with that regulation hair-cut we have a marine. He was a man of self confidence and used to responsibility. You must have observed how carefully he examined the house numbers. He was middle aged. All of these facts led me to believe that he had been a sergeant. In sum, what else could he have been but a retired sergeant of Marines?"

"Amazing!" I replied.

Sir Arthur Conan Doyle, **A Study in Scarlet** (simplified and adapted by Robert E. Burns by permission of the Sir Arthur Conan Doyle Estates) published by Ward Lock Ltd., London and Sydney.

2 Early man in North America

Sources of Knowledge for
North American Prehistory

Introduction

In your previous assignment you observed Inspector Thomas and Sherlock Holmes asking probing and inquiring questions, drawing inferences, and forming hypotheses in order to solve problems. Testing Holmes's hypothesis was easy. Holmes's friend simply asked the courier what was his former employment. Testing Inspector Thomas's hypothesis took more time but was also simple to accomplish. All Thomas had to do was make several telephone calls.

The present assignment is concerned with hypothesis-testing of a more difficult kind. There are no eyewitnesses to question, no written records to examine, and no memories to jog about an event that occurred many thousands of years ago.

Latin words: **homo-erectus** means a man who walks in an upright position: **homo-sapiens** means a man with sense and knowledge.

The question of *how* man came to North America and *where* he came from is not a new one. Anthropologists and archaeologists tell us that man did not originate in the western hemisphere, but came here from somewhere else. After more than a hundred years of archaeological and anthropological investigations in both North and South America, no evidence of *homo-erectus*,* or primitive, man has been discovered. Only skeletal remains of *homo-sapiens*,* or modern thinking man, have been found anywhere in the Americas.

Therefore, the most ancient of all Americans must have come from somewhere in the Old World (Asia, Europe, or Africa) where man in primitive as well as modern forms existed for hundreds of thousands of years.

If early man came to the Americas from elsewhere, we have identified our problem: *Where did the original American come from and how did he get here?* The other sets of facts suggest a hypothesis.

First set of facts: Columbus and other early European explorers who followed him called the original inhabitants of North and South America *Indians* because they thought they had discovered the East Indies. But the peoples of the New World did not resemble physically the inhabitants of the Asian sub-continent of India.

American Indians were beardless, with skins ranging from dark brown to yellow to near white, with black or brown eyes, black or brown hair, straight or wavy, and noses that were Roman, snub, or flat. Some American Indians had physical characteristics that resembled Asian people of Mongol stock. Others had characteristics that resembled European or Mediterranean stock.

Second set of facts: The closest point of contact between the Old World and the New is the Bering Strait where only fifty-six miles separate northeast Asia from Alaska.

A Spanish priest, **Father José de Acosta,** was the first to pose the land bridge theory in an article he wrote in 1590 which was translated into English in 1604.

By asking how these two sets of facts relate to the problem of how man came to North America and where he came from, we have a hypothesis to test: *The first men to discover and inhabit North America (the ancestors of American Indians) migrated via the Bering Strait from Asia to Alaska long ago.**

Since no factual evidence of any kind has survived bearing directly on when, where, or why the first migration occurred, our hypothesis must stand or fall on inferences drawn from factual information gathered thousands of years after the event. To get such information, put probing and inquiring questions to your hypothesis. For example:

1. What was the Bering Strait like ten, twenty, or thirty thousand years ago?

2. Was a migration across the Bering Strait possible? Was such a migration possible for men only, or was it possible for women and children as well?

3. Are there any measurable physical characteristics of living American Indians from which an ancient Asian connection can be inferred?

Questions like these suggest examination of facts dealing with composition, form, and history of the earth and with man's physical characteristics. The sciences which collected these facts are archaeology, paleontology and physical anthropology.

A10

Map labels:

Point Barrow   50
24   32   31   28   25
Wrangell Island
30   27   22
CHUKCHI
27
30   26
SEA
27
27
U.S.S.R.   Kotzebue Sound
U.S.A.
(ALASKA)
Bering Strait
35   22
Gulf of Anadyr   Norton Sound
32   22   12
43
50   St. Lawrence Island
20   Cape Navarin   22
65   BERING   23
75
46   Nunivak Island
50   42
1765   SEA   27   22
1363
Bristol Bay
52   44
77   50
1745   Unimak Island   3005
1205

N

BERING AND CHUKCHI SEA

Soundings in Fathoms
1 Fathom = 6 Feet
0   100
Scale of Miles

3   TESTIMONY OF GEOLOGY

The science of geology is concerned with the composition, form, and history of the earth. Information collected by geologists about changes in landforms and land and sea levels has been very useful to historians and archaeologists. From the testimony of geology, historians and archaeologists can draw inferences about the geologic history of the Bering Strait region in order to test a hypothesis about how man first came to North America.

While examining the map above and reading the selection on ocean levels and icecaps, keep the following questions in mind:

1. What determines worldwide sea levels?

2. What happened to the oceans during the Ice Ages? How do we know?

3. Why was the Bering Strait a likely point of entry for the first men to discover and inhabit North America?

Objectives of this assignment are to:

—Draw inferences from readings to test the hypothesis presented here.

—Evaluate (make credibility judgments about) such inferences.

—Make a judgment on the basis of evaluated testimony whether the hypothesis tested is probably true or probably untrue.

A11

Ocean Levels and Ice Caps

At any point in time or place in the world, the sea level depends not only on the height and depth of the land, but also on the volume of water in the oceans. If at any time in the past the amount of water in the oceans was less than it is today, the sea level would have been lower and the amount of dry land in the world would have been increased.

During the thousands of years of the Ice Age, the volume of water in the oceans of the world was probably much less than it is today. Ice can imprison enormous quantities of water. Take the Greenland and Antarctica icecaps, for instance. The first is more than one mile deep, and the second is at least three miles thick. If these icecaps thawed rapidly, worldwide ocean levels would rise as much as 300 feet and completely submerge most of the world's coastal cities.

It is clear from geological evidence that the great glaciers of the Ice Age were thousands of feet thick and covered nearly all of what is now Canada and part of the northeastern United States. The quantities of water locked up in these enormous icecaps could have reduced ancient sea levels as much as 500 feet.

We know that worldwide ocean levels were actually reduced by several hundred feet in ancient times. This fact is borne out by the evidence of coral atolls in tropical seas. The coral organisms that built these atolls will not live at depths greater than 300 feet. Yet the coral structures of these islands go down several thousand feet into the ocean depths. If in the past, ocean levels had not been much lower than they are today and had not remained that way for a very long time, those coral structures could not have been made.

Furthermore, samples of formerly living matter from a land environment have been recovered by off-shore drillers on the continental shelf in the Gulf of Mexico 30 miles from the nearest shore. These samples have been radio-carbon dated as being 40,000 years old.

The maximum depth in the Bering Strait is about 30 fathoms (180 feet). Only 56 miles wide, the Strait is dotted with large and small islands that appear to aerial observers as stepping stones between Asia and Alaska.* Migrations probably moved over these stepping stones from Asia to North America.

The Bering Sea lies south of the Strait. Its floor slopes no more than three or four inches to the mile, and is probably one of the smoothest terrains of the undersea world. The Bering Sea runs from Unimak Island in the Aleutians to Cape Navarin on the Asiatic shore, plunging from 450 feet to a depth of 13,000 feet to the ocean bottom.

North of the Bering Strait is the Chukchi Sea with depths varying from 20 fathoms (120 feet) to 30 fathoms (180 feet). Shoals reduce the depths in some places to a mere 8 fathoms (48 feet). About 200 miles north of Wrangel Island along an east-west line, the sea floor drops sharply several thousand feet. Soundings of the Bering and Chukchi seas reveal a large shallow underwater plain—about 1300 miles at its widest point, north to south.

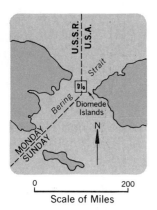

0   200
Scale of Miles

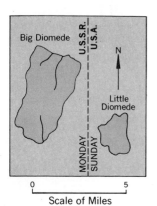

0   5
Scale of Miles

The **Diomedes** in the Bering Strait: The U.S.—U.S.S.R. boundary and the International Date Line run between Little Diomede on the American side and Big Diomede on the Russian side. By foot over the ice in winter, by umiak (open Eskimo boat) in summer, one can leave Big Diomede on Monday and a few minutes later reach Little Diomede, where it is Sunday.

MAXIMUM EXTENT OF GLACIATION

Shallow Areas of Continental Shelf

Outer Limits of Pack Ice at Annual Maximum

(Glaciated Areas Appear as White)

0   2200
Scale of Miles

Glaciation in the Southern Hemisphere was limited to Antarctica and those portions of the Andes Mountains south of 40° latitude.

4   TESTIMONY OF PHYSICAL ANTHROPOLOGY

Physical Anthropology is that branch of the science of anthropology concerned with the study and classification of human physical characteristics and variations. There are many different kinds of measurable characteristics used by physical anthropologists to differentiate and classify mankind. Only two kinds, blood types and ear wax types, are used in this assignment. Others such as skin color, skull shape, and structure of teeth are not considered here.

Physical anthropology: specialized branch of the science of anthropology concerned with human biology, racial differences, changes in human bodies over generations, and classification of human physical characteristics and variations.

Anthropology: scientific study of man and his physical, mental, cultural characteristics and history, his geographical distribution, racial classifications, and group relationships.

Archaeology: scientific study of extinct peoples and cultures through skeletal remains, fossils, and objects of human workmanship such as monuments, inscriptions, tools, utensils.

Blood types and ear wax types are both inherited characteristics, and their distribution varies among people of different racial stocks. People are as distinguishable by blood and ear wax types as they are by skull shape or skin color. Like skull shape and skin color, specific blood and ear wax types tend to predominate among people who are racially alike.

For instance, white skin color indicates European ancestry and black skin color African ancestry. In the same way, the predominance of one blood or ear wax type indicates the possibility of past connection with other people of the same predominance.

From the testimony of physical anthropology, historians can draw inferences about the possibility of an ancient connection between American Indians and Asians and test a hypothesis about how man came to North America. While examining the charts at the end of this lesson, keep these questions in mind:

1. What blood types ought to predominate among living American Indians if their ancient ancestors originated in Asia?

2. What ear wax type ought to predominate among living American Indians if their ancient ancestors originated in Asia?

Blood Types

Dr. Karl Lansteiner's discovery of certain blood substances in the early years of this century made possible the classification of human blood into types. Antigens are substances in human blood that can be identified and used to differentiate one type of blood from another. There are several different schemes currently in use for classifying human blood into types, but only two are used in this assignment: the classical blood types of O, A, B, AB and the factors of Rh positive and Rh negative.

In the 1930's, Dr. William C. Boyd, a physical anthropologist, made a study of blood groups and types as a system for classifying men. The distribution and frequency of blood types among various groups tested is shown here.

Distribution of Blood Types

BLOOD TYPE	O	A	B	AB	Rh POSITIVE	Rh NEGATIVE
NON-INDIAN GROUPS						
Europeans	45	40	10	5	85	15
NE Asians	28	27	39	6	100	0
Africans	45	25	25	5	92½	7½
AMERICAN INDIANS						
Blackfeet	45	50	2½	2½	100	0
Navajos	70	30	0	0	100	0
Sioux	85	10	5	0	100	0

All figures expressed in percentages

Compiled from W. C. Boyd "Blood Groups," Tabulae Biologicae, Vol. 17 (The Hague, Netherlands: Dr. W. Junk, Publishers, 1939) pp. 113–240.

Ear Wax Types

Researchers led by Dr. Nicholas L. Petrakis of the University of California Medical Center at San Francisco, developed during the late 1960's the use of human ear wax as a physical characteristic for differentiating and classifying men.*

Doctor Petrakis tested certain Indian tribes in North and South America, as well as non-Indians (Caucasians, Negroes, Chinese) living in San Francisco to find out the distribution and frequency of dry and moist ear wax.

Some results from the Petrakis ear wax study appear below:

ETHNIC ORIGIN OF PEOPLE STUDIED	FREQUENCY OF TYPE	
	DRY	MOIST
European	1	99
African	0	100
Northeast Asian	58	42
American Indian Tribes with little inter-marriage with Caucasian or Negro	75	25

(All figures expressed in percentages)

The **Petrakis** study sampled a number of American Indian tribes. It showed a wide range of **dry ear wax** among them— from 3.3 percent to 76.7 percent, with the highest frequency appearing among isolated "full blood" tribes. Indian stock mixed with White or Negro showed higher frequency of **moist ear wax**— from 23.3 percent to 96.7 percent.

3 Cultures of Prehistoric North America

History as a Culture Record

Introduction

Man's history in North America before 1500 as a record of past events is impossible to reconstruct because no written record has been preserved. Except for a few examples of picture writing, North American Indians neither wrote nor kept written records. After 1500 there is an abundance of written historical information about North America and its many different people.

What can be reconstructed of man's history in North America before the age of European explorations is the record of how men lived and worked during the thousands of years they inhabited this continent. Reconstruction of that kind of historical record requires historians to draw upon the factual information, inferences, and hypotheses of archaeologists and anthropologists. When reconstructed, the focus of that record will be on *objects* rather than on great men and great events. It will be a history without precise dates. It will be history as a culture record.

Sometimes skeletons were found alongside artifacts in the caves.

A15

5　CULTURE STAGES OF ABORIGINAL NORTH AMERICA

The concept of culture stages aids the study of the vast information on aboriginal* North America. Concepts can be many things: ideas, thoughts, notions, *mental models,** approaches to problems, questions to be answered, or as in this case, a classification scheme. When archaeologists, anthropologists, historians, and other scholars refer to culture stages, as they do in this essay, this term is a concept.

During the last hundred years, archaeologists and anthropologists collected such a vast quantity of factual information that organizing it was a problem. Scholars and scientists divided this material on the prehistory of North America into segments, periods, or areas. Then, recently, archaeologists and anthropologists came up with a concept to classify the information better. They suggested that the segments of prehistory be called culture stages. Man's culture record in prehistoric North America is uneven. Early Americans did not change or improve their ways of living and working at the same time or to the same extent. Thus, thinking about North American prehistory in terms of stages instead of periods or areas has two important advantages.

First, because the concept of culture stages is not limited by geographic and time dimensions, people of different culture levels living in the same region at the same time can be more easily distinguished from one another.

Second, by comparing the traits and characteristics of one culture stage with those of another culture stage, culture change through time and across distance can be described.

Three Culture Stages

In this essay the prehistory of North America has been divided into three culture stages: Paleo-Indian, Archaic, and Formative.

The *Paleo-Indian** culture stage was the oldest and least known culture stage of prehistoric North America. It was a stage where people made and used simple stone tools and lived in small isolated social groups.

Archaic describes a culture stage that was richer in content and shorter in time than the Paleo-Indian. Stone tools were more complicated and more skillfully made. People lived in larger and less isolated groups.

During the *Formative* culture stage new economic patterns appeared, enabling the formation and support of larger and more complex social groups than had previously existed.

Each culture stage had its own distinguishing traits and characteristics. Although these culture stages followed one another, no law or natural course of events required all North American cultures to pass through these three stages. We cannot say, for example, that an Archaic culture stage will positively develop into a Formative culture stage. Some Archaic culture stages in both North and South America have lasted even into the twentieth century.

Aboriginal means native inhabitants of a region or area.

Mental Model is an idea or perception resulting from the orderly arrangement of facts, impressions, or thoughts.

Culture: term used to describe man's inherited and invented tools, goods, customs, ideas, and patterns of religious, social, political, economic, and artistic behavior.

Culture stage: concept developed by archaeologists to reconstruct the culture history of ancient North America.

Paleo-Indian: most ancient peoples of North and South America.

Paleolithic: combination of Greek words meaning **ancient** and **stone.**

A16

In the following essay, try to recognize and identify the most important culture facts and inferred traits and characteristics of each culture stage in prehistoric North America. While reading the essay, keep the following questions in mind:

1. *What factual information does the author use as a basis for his inferences about the importance of* Clovis *points?*

2. *Why was stone boiling so important for the prehistoric inhabitants of North America?*

3. *Why was the development and spread of organized agriculture so important?*

Objectives of this assignment are to:

—Describe what concepts are and how they are used as explained.

—Describe the concept of culture stages.

—Identify the most important culture facts and inferred traits and characteristics of three prehistoric North American culture stages.

Identify the culture stages of North American **artifacts*** presented in the filmstrip or photographs.

—Draw inferences from artifacts and drawings in the filmstrip about the ways people of each North American culture stage lived and worked.

6   PALEO-INDIAN CULTURE STAGE

Archaeological sites in places as far apart as Alaska, Texas, and the extreme tip of South America have yielded information suggesting that man has inhabited the American continents for a very long time. Guessing how long man has been here can be an interesting pastime.

Charcoal taken from what may have been a cooking fire and campsite of the most ancient men in North America has been *radiocarbon dated** as about 37,000 years old. Charred mammoth bones, perhaps the remains of the oldest dinner party ever given in North America, have been recovered from a site on Santa Rosa Island, California, and given an age of about 33,000 years. Stone implements of undoubted human manufacture found with camel bones in Sandia Cave in central New Mexico may be 20,000 years old.

Sites in Clovis, and Folsom, New Mexico, have indicated that men were hunting game in those areas between 15,000 and 10,000 years ago. At another site, Palli Aike Cave near the Straits of Magellan in southern Chile, stone spear points, scrapers, and burned sloth bones were found. Radiocarbon dating of these items revealed that man reached this most southern point of South America no later than 8000 years ago.

What were North America's first migrants like? No positive answer can be given. The physical and cultural characteristics of these earliest people, the first hunter-discoverers of America, are unknown. But we do have some facts which allow us to make an interesting hypothesis about them.

For instance, geological evidence at archaeological sites in Alaska and northwestern Canada, such as Kogruk, Naiyuk, Anaktuvuk Pass in north central Alaska, and British Mountain at the head of the Firth River delta in Yukon Territory, Canada, tell us certain things. Stone tools and implements found in those places have been dated at 13,000 years.

Some of the *artifacts* found there show a striking resemblance to artifacts recovered from paleolithic sites in central Asia, Siberia, and elsewhere in

Radiocarbon dating: Carbon 14 is a radioactive isotope present in every living organism and it disintegrates at a known rate after death of the organism. Measurement of the remaining Carbon 14 in an archaeological specimen yields a time of death accurate within a few hundred out of many thousand years.

Artifact is any object made by human hands, such as weapons, pottery, and utensils.

A17

North and South America. But many other items uncovered in these Alaskan and Canadian finds, however, are unlike any found in Asia and other American sites.

The Link between Two Worlds

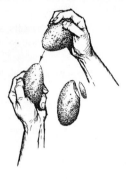

If we concentrate on the similarities, we can conclude that there was a common sharing of important tool forms and tool-making techniques between Asian and American paleolithic centers. It would then seem that Kogruk, Naiyuk, and British Mountain peoples were the link between the Old World and the New.

According to this hypothesis, a group of hunting-oriented people developed efficient stone tools for successful hunting of smaller Ice Age animals. They began expanding out of paleolithic locations near Lake Baikal, the upper Lena River, and elsewhere in central Asia, into areas where that type of game was more abundant.

The tool-making techniques of these hunters were based on a method known as percussion flaking, that is, shaping and chipping stone implements by using a hammer stone. Percussion flaking produced stone blades and points that were effective in killing smaller grazing animals.

When these movements out of central Asia began is uncertain, but they may have been as early as 20,000 years ago. The wanderers appear to have followed two directions: east to the Sea of Okhotsk in the Pacific, and north to the Arctic shore.

Descendants of either or both groups of these wanderers probably crossed the Bering-Chukchi plain between Siberia and Alaska between 15,000 to 11,000 years ago and became the first *effective* inhabitants of North America. Some of them reached Kogruk, Naiyuk, and British Mountain.

Clovis Point—Ancient Breakthrough

Percussion flaking—large pieces of flint were struck with a hammerstone to split off flakes. Then the tool was chipped to refine the edges. The finished tool and a cross section are shown at bottom.

Once in Alaska, these people probably moved east through the Alaskan foothill country and then south, following the major hunting trails. With game abundant in the foothills, our hunters tried to make the most of a favorable situation. Perhaps the men of Kogruk, Naiyuk, and British Mountain were driven by a desire to include larger Ice Age animals·in their regular diet.

By drawing upon flaking techniques derived from Asia, these ancient peoples of North America developed a new tool which produced a major revolution in the condition of human life in America. That tool, which was used to hunt and kill big game such as mammoths, great ground sloths, and camels, was the *Clovis* fluted stone point.

Called the Clovis point because it was first discovered near Clovis, New Mexico, in 1932, these points have been found in sites scattered throughout Canada, the United States, and South America. (At a site near Dent, Colorado, a *Clovis* point was found lodged between the ribs of an extinct mammoth.)

A18

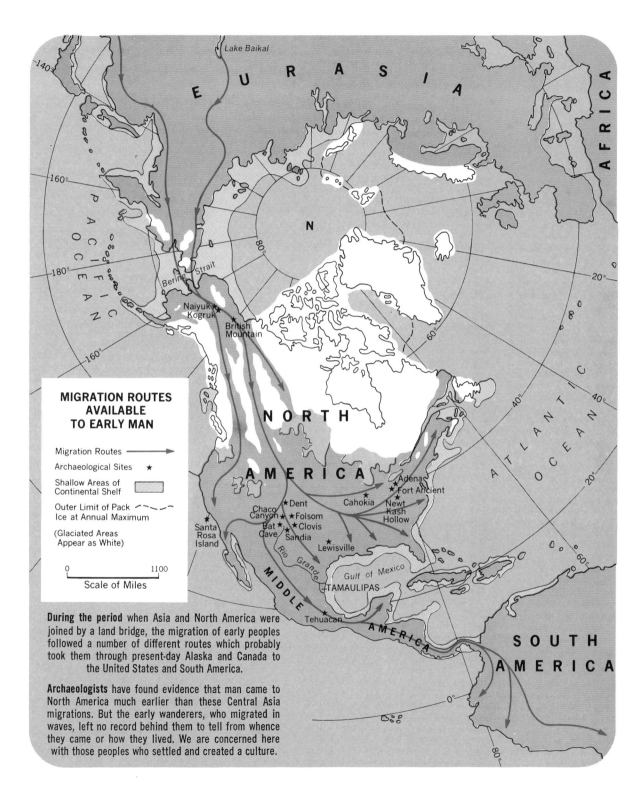

**MIGRATION ROUTES
AVAILABLE
TO EARLY MAN**

Migration Routes ———→

Archaeological Sites ★

Shallow Areas of
Continental Shelf

Outer Limit of Pack – ⌒ ‿
Ice at Annual Maximum

(Glaciated Areas
Appear as White)

0   1100

Scale of Miles

Lake Baikal

EURASIA

AFRICA

PACIFIC OCEAN

Bering Strait

Naiyuk
Kogruk
British
Mountain

N

NORTH

AMERICA

ATLANTIC OCEAN

Adena
Fort Ancient
Cahokia
Newt
Kash
Hollow
Chaco
Canyon
Dent
Folsom
Bat
Cave
Clovis
Sandia
Santa
Rosa
Island
Lewisville

Rio Grande

MIDDLE

Gulf of Mexico

TAMAULIPAS

Tehuacan

AMERICA

SOUTH
AMERICA

During the period when Asia and North America were
joined by a land bridge, the migration of early peoples
followed a number of different routes which probably
took them through present-day Alaska and Canada to
the United States and South America.

Archaeologists have found evidence that man came to
North America much earlier than these Central Asia
migrations. But the early wanderers, who migrated in
waves, left no record behind them to tell from whence
they came or how they lived. We are concerned here
with those peoples who settled and created a culture.

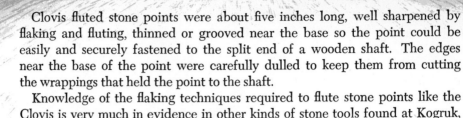

Clovis fluted stone points were about five inches long, well sharpened by flaking and fluting, thinned or grooved near the base so the point could be easily and securely fastened to the split end of a wooden shaft. The edges near the base of the point were carefully dulled to keep them from cutting the wrappings that held the point to the shaft.

Knowledge of the flaking techniques required to flute stone points like the Clovis is very much in evidence in other kinds of stone tools found at Kogruk, Naiyuk, Anaktuvuk Pass, and British Mountain. Stone flakes that may have been produced by the fluting process and a few roughly fluted points have been uncovered there.

Although we know very little about the culture stage that archaeologists and anthropologists have named Paleo-Indian, the Clovis fluted stone point is the most important culture fact, and big game hunting is the most important culture trait of that culture stage.

Clovis points actually embedded in the bones of extinct mammoths, sloths, and camels have been recovered from archaeological sites scattered across North America. Once he invented the Clovis point, ancient man could hunt big game and greatly expand his food supply.

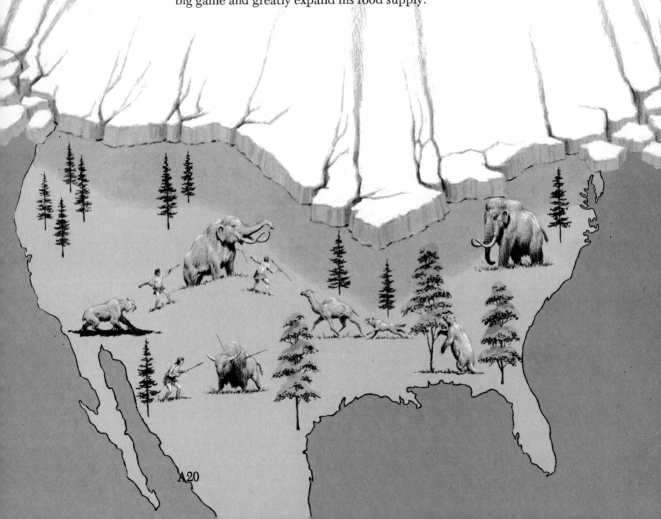

During the period 13,000 B.C. to 7000 B.C., the technique of big game hunting spread. With more food to eat, Paleo-Indian people lived longer. Life became more secure, and the sparse human population of America multiplied. The people created a culture—ways of living, working, thinking, and feeling—that was different from what their ancestors had known and experienced in Asia.

Clovis point—made and used by hunters about 12,000 years ago.

What Did Paleo-Indians Look Like?

Our knowledge of the physical characteristics of the Paleo-Indian people is very limited. The number of skeletal remains uncovered is small. We can't be certain about skin color, languages, customs, or beliefs of the people of Paleo-Indian America.

Nearly all that is known about the Paleo-Indian culture stage must be inferred from the stone artifacts unearthed by archaeologists and from the kinds of work and activities that men could undertake with them. These included stone spear points, stone blades, cutting tools, stone scraping and digging implements, and fire.

Paleo-Indian men were both food gatherers and hunters. As food gatherers they collected seeds, dug for roots, and consumed them along with edible parts of the wild vegetation growing around them. As hunters, they set fire to the grass and forests to drive out game. They set snares and traps, dug pits, and sometimes stampeded animals into swamps or off cliffs for easier killing.

In that harsh world of endless search for food, weaklings and fools could not survive. To succeed as hunters, speed and endurance, sharp eyes, a powerful spear arm, and excellent coordination were essential qualities. Men had to run down much of their game on foot and match their intelligence against the speed of the dire wolf and the might of the mammoth.

If these hunters had shelters, the shelters must have been very crude because no traces have survived. They left behind no evidence of having made pottery, cultivated plants, or domesticated animals. Judged by our standards, however, the hunters were wise in the ways of nature, highly athletic, and shrewd—far shrewder than the animals around them. Proof of this is that Paleo-Indian man survived in North America; the mammoth, dire wolf, great ground sloth, and camel did not.

During the thousands of years when the cold winds from the glaciers still blew south from Canada, the climate of most of North America was cool and moist. Lush vegetation supported large herds of grazing animals which Paleo-Indian man hunted.

However, by 7000 B.C. the glaciers had retreated, the cold moist winds no longer blew, and the climate became warmer and drier. The face of the land changed, and Paleo-Indian man adapted to changed conditions.

Sometime between 7000 B.C. and 3000 B.C. the Paleo-Indian culture stage in many parts of North America was succeeded by what archaeologists and anthropologists have called the *Archaic* culture stage.

A21

7 ARCHAIC CULTURE STAGE

Atlatl—a device used by archaic man to kill animals for food. The atlatl held a 6- to 9-foot spear which the hunter launched to make his kill.

What distinguishes the Archaic culture stage in North America from the Paleo-Indian one is the quantity and quality of its surviving stone artifacts and tools. Archaic man not only made more things and made them better than his Paleo-Indian ancestors, but he made them for new and different reasons. His artifacts and tools were concerned not with survival alone, but also with efficiency and comfort.

Stone tools of all kinds were polished and more skillfully made. Hunting techniques improved, and what may have been the first machine ever used in America, the *atlatl* or spear thrower, found widespread use. The spear thrower extended the reach of the human arm, and increased its power by fifty percent.

Archaic hunters were probably the first to use the bow and arrow in America, and in areas where fishing was possible, they developed a variety of bone hooks and points so that fish could be added to their diets.

The number of awls, needles, and scrapers recovered indicates that Archaic man probably dressed himself in clothing made of animal skins. He used shells as beads, cut geometric designs on bone and shell ornaments, and made head dresses, combs, spoons, and cups out of antler bone.

Although not much is known about Archaic-culture-stage housing except that floor areas were often clay covered, this housing probably consisted of adequate but impermanent lean-to structures, dome-shaped wigwams, or tepee-like shelters.

Perhaps even more important than Archaic man's improved stone tool technology was his increased attention to food gathering and food preparation. He became more systematic about the collection of edible parts of weeds, wild plants, bushes, and trees than had been his Paleo-Indian ancestors. He fashioned stone food preparation dishes like stone mortars with hand-stones for grinding food, and discovered a method of boiling food with hot stones.

Not having pottery or metal to make utensils that could heat water directly over open fires without burning, Archaic man boiled water in vessels made of bark, skins, and wood, by dropping hot stones into them. Stone Boilers were excellent basket makers, a widespread art during the Archaic culture stage. Since pottery was unknown, closely woven baskets set in holes or smeared with clay may have served as primitive cooking pots.

Stone boiling also led Archaic man to the making of soup and the cooking of food. Meat and vegetables were put in the cooking pot, water was poured on top of them, and a few boiling stones did the rest. No longer did people have to eat food raw. The very young, the aged, and the sick had tasty nourishment in soups easy to digest. And everyone could enjoy cooked foods.

Stone boiling improved living standards, increased the population of North America, and helped develop a new form of social organization.

Unlike the small, isolated, closely related family groups of his ancestors, Archaic man lived in larger bands of 30 or 40 persons who ranged across a specific food-gathering and hunting territory. Several of these bands may have gathered at food-rich locations and engaged in trade. There is some evidence that raw materials were carried several hundred miles from their source to locations where they were made into finished tools and implements.

Finally, Archaic man paid more attention to burials and burial ceremonies than his ancestors. *Cremation** was practiced in some parts of the continent, but burials were much more common and burial practices more ceremonial.

Cremation is the practice of burning human corpses.

For example, in the Great Lakes region red stone beads, copper beads, and shells have been found with human bodies, and in some Archaic-culture-stage sites dogs were intentionally buried with humans.

As we have seen, it is extremely difficult to set time limits to the *Archaic** culture stage. At the earlier end of the time scale there were overlaps with Paleo-Indian culture. At the later end there was overlapping with what archaeologists and anthropologists call the *Formative* culture stage.

On rare occasions, Archaic culture sites have yielded the unusual find of a drinking cup made out of a human skull.

The Food Revolution

However, by 1000 B.C. hunting and food gathering in much of North America was succeeded by food production in organized agriculture. The discovery that cultivated plants could yield more food was as revolutionary in its effects upon man in North America as the development of the Clovis point and the spread of stone boiling.

Exactly when some of the hunting and food gathering people of North America turned to agriculture and became food producers is unknown. We know more about *how* it happened than *when* it happened.

For example, sunflower, giant ragweed, and pigweed, all have edible parts and grow wild near Newt Kash Hollow, Menifee County, Kentucky. Hunting and food gathering people in that region gathered such plants and wild seeds and planted them in sheltered spots near their dwellings. Some of the seeds recovered by archaeologists from excavations at that site are larger than those of the wild species, and botanists tell us that the enlarged size of those seeds means that they had been cultivated.

Although we do not know when the inhabitants of Newt Kash Hollow began to practice gardening, the enlarged seeds recovered from that site have been radiocarbon dated as harvested in 600 B.C. Possibly, the people of Newt Kash Hollow had been gardening much earlier than 600 B.C. and had learned how to do it from somewhere else.

When most of eastern North America was still in the Archaic culture stage, events of extraordinary importance were occurring in the region that archaeologists called *Nuclear America*—Mexico to southern Peru. In that region has been found not only the earliest evidence of agriculture, but its most intensive development and the most complex and elaborate Indian cultures of the New World. In both agriculture and building, the peoples of the plains and woodlands of North America had continuous inspiration from the South.

Excavations in caves in Tamaulipas, Mexico, have revealed something about the nature of that inspiration. Radiocarbon dating of debris found

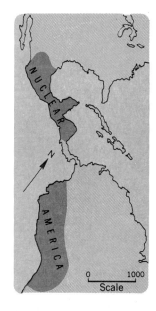

Nuclear America—Mexico to Peru
This area nurtured the growth and development of native America's highest civilizations.

A23

there discloses that between 7000 B.C. and 5000 B.C. the inhabitants of that site passed from being food gatherers to food producers.

Up to 5000 B.C. they were almost entirely gatherers of wild plants which they dried and stored in baskets. They cultivated gourds for use as containers, and chile peppers and pumpkins for food.

8   FORMATIVE CULTURE STAGE

After 5000 B.C., a major event—the discovery of corn—revolutionized the way these people lived and worked. The importance of that discovery cannot be overestimated. Corn was the foundation for the great Indian *civilizations** of Mexico, Central and South America, and for the beginning of the *Formative* culture stage of the people of the North American woodlands.

Corn came into North America from the South after it had become the chief plant food of Mexico. Excavations at a site in the valley of Tehuacán, southeast of Mexico City, have uncovered tiny cobs of wild corn, less than one inch long, which have been dated as picked about 5000 B.C. For about one thousand years the people of Tehuacán were content with wild corn.

By 3500 B.C. something had happened. Corn cobs that are longer and thicker than the wild type appear in debris for that period and seem to be the result of cultivation. After 3000 B.C. the cultivated corn of Tehuacán was produced in quantities sufficient to support a large population. By 2000 B.C. corn was well established in Mexico and Central America and was spreading rapidly into South America.

Radiocarbon dating has placed cultivated corn in Bat Cave, New Mexico, as early as 3500 B.C., but for reasons which are not clear it spread much more slowly to the north than to the south. By 400 B.C. cultivated corn had spread throughout most of North America.

As corn spread to the north, another discovery from the south spread with it. Need for storage vessels and further experiments in food preparation led to the discovery and use of pottery. Hand-made pottery was used in the more advanced Mexican villages as early as 2000 B.C., and pottery appeared north of the Rio Grande about 100 A.D. The earliest samples of North American pottery are heavy, thick, and coarse, built up by coiling, shaped by paddles made of loose cord-wrapped sticks, and then set by firing at low temperatures.

Skill in working clay and knowledge of firing techniques were quickly applied to uses other than making storage vessels and cooking utensils. Along with pottery, archaeologists have found in sites in Ohio and elsewhere in the east a large number of tubular and elbow clay pipes and quantities of tobacco. Invariably pipes are found with evidence of corn cultivation and pottery making. In the eastern woodlands, pipe-and-tobacco use was the most important trait of the Formative culture stage after corn and pottery.

Civilization is a term often used interchangeably with **culture,** but more properly, civilization means a highly developed culture.

At Bat Cave, New Mexico— a drawing of a reconstructed primitive ear of cultivated corn found by archeologists was dated several thousand years before the birth of Christ.

Building in Ancient America

In the Americas as in the rest of the prehistoric world, protection, religion, and comfort inspired men to build when they ceased wandering and had crops to harvest. Nothing built in North America during the long pre-Columbian period compares with the great forts, temples, pyramids, and cities of Mexico, Central America, and Peru. However, beginning about 300 A.D. the mound builders of the Ohio, Cumberland, and Tennessee valleys built on a scale that still compels admiration.

For example, the *Adena* burial mound in Ohio is a monument to the important members of the community of families living in the area. At *Fort Ancient*, Ohio, the mound builders moved 600,000 cubic yards of earth to build walls and embankments of a fort.

The *Cahokia* mound in Illinois is 100 feet high and covers sixteen acres of ground. In the Mississippi Valley, overlooking plazas and town squares, are great pyramidal mounds upon which the important buildings of the community were erected. Finally, in the west, the Pueblo builders of *Chaco Canyon*, New Mexico, built housing complexes capable of accommodating 1,000 persons.

The quality and extent of building in North America suggest that three things happened after hunters and food gatherers took up agriculture. First, the overall population increased; second, forms of social organization changed; and third, relations between different groups became more complicated and opportunities for inter-group conflict increased.

Great Serpent Mound, Hillsboro, Ohio—some Indian mounds were **effigy** mounds built in the shape of animals. Great Serpent is one of the best and largest effigy mounds in the world. Its sinuous body is more than ½ mile long and 2 feet high, uncoiling in seven curves. It was probably a religious emblem of the Adena people about 1000 B.C. to 700 A.D.

Pueblo Bonito, Chaco Canyon, New Mexico—restoration of ancient ruins shows one of the oldest communal dwellings (called **pueblos**) built by Indians for perhaps 1,000 dwellers. Made of stone and adobe, at least five stories high, the pueblo faced a central plaza. Outside walls were finely made of sandstone blocks; inside walls were plastered with adobe.

The simple fact of building indicates that there were sufficient people to occupy or use what was built. Moreover, the erection of buildings that were clearly public and ceremonial suggests that political authority had passed from the small bands of the Archaic culture stage to a larger body, the tribe.

So many fortified places, and the amount of time and labor expended upon massive protective embankments and ditches, indicate that the tribes of North America paid the costs and took the risks of intertribal warfare. Furthermore, the unexplained disappearance of the mound-building people from the face of North America suggests just how fierce that warfare must have been.

Anthropologists tell us that when the French, English, and Dutch explorers arrived in North America at the beginning of the seventeenth century, there were an estimated 840,000 to 1,000,000 inhabitants living in more than 600 distinctive tribal societies. They answered to more than 2,000 tribal names, and spoke nearly 300 different languages.

Population density refers to the number of people living in a specific unit or area of land.

Indian *population densities** were heaviest on the Pacific Coast, in the Pueblo villages of Arizona and New Mexico, in Wisconsin, and on the Atlantic Coast. The distribution of tribes across the length and breadth of North America defies description. Languages spoken on the banks of the Delaware were more like some of those spoken on the western plains than in the nearby Hudson Valley.

Some eastern tribes were so distinctive from one another by 1600 that even today when one looks at seventeenth-century European prints and paintings of the period, it is easier to distinguish a Mahican from a Mohawk than an Englishman from a Dutchman.

Algonkin: derived from Indian words meaning "at the place of spearing fish and eels," most likely the bow of a canoe. Originally applied to a small tribe on the Gatineau River in what is now Quebec, the name later included all eastern seaboard Indians.

When the Europeans reached North America in the early seventeenth century, they first encountered the *Algonkin*-speaking* Wampanoag, Pequot, Narraganset, and Massachuset in New England, the Lenni-Lenape (Delawares) in the New York-Pennsylvania area, and the Powhatans in Virginia.

A26

ARCTIC OCEAN

NORTH

AMERICA

PACIFIC OCEAN

ATLANTIC OCEAN

Gulf of
Mexico

Population
Density
High
Medium
Low

0   650
Scale

INDIANS OF
NORTH AMERICA,
1500 A.D.

Selected
Language Groups

Iroquoian

Algonquian

0   575
Scale of Miles

Hudson
Bay

ESKIMO

HAIDA
BELLA BELLA
SHUSWAP   BLACKFOOT
LILLOOET
NOOTKA
CHIPEWYAN
CREE
MONTAGNAIS
BEOTHUK
OJIBWA
(CHIPPEWA)
PASSAMAQUODDY
CHINOOK   SPOKANE
PENOBSCOT
YAKIMA
TILLAMOOK   WALLA
WALLA   OTTAWA
CROW   MANDAN   HURON
COOS   MAHICAN   MASSACHUSET
CAYUSE   NEZ PERCE   SAUK   MOHAWK   SWAMPANOAG
KLAMATH   FOX   ONEIDA   NARRAGANSET
WINNEBAGO   ONONDAGA PEQUOT
SHASTA   POTAWATOMI   CAYUGA   MOHEGAN
YUKI   DAKOTA   KICKAPOO   SENECA
POMO   SUSQUEHANNA
CHEYENNE   PAWNEE   LENI LENAPE
PAIUTE   (DELAWARE)
SALINAS   UTE ARAPAHO   POWHATAN NANTICOKE
Colorado River
NAVAHO   SHAWNEE
MOHAVE   HOPI   TUSCARORA
ZUÑI PUEBLO   APACHE   CHEROKEE
APACHE   Mississippi River
COMANCHE   CHOCTAW
Rio Grande   NATCHEZ   APALACHEE
SEMINOLE
YAQUI
PACIFIC OCEAN
ATLANTIC OCEAN
PERICU
TAMAULIPEC   Gulf of
Mexico

A27

Although these tribes did not build on the scale of the Mississippi Valley or Pueblo tribes, their place in the history of North American Indians is secure for another reason. They developed a form of picture writing on bark and sticks. Although they made only limited use of it, the pictographs were an effective way of preserving some of their history, legends, and folklore for future generations.

In other ways, however, the Algonkin were typical of the eastern woodland tribes; their housing was simple but comfortable. Their dome-shaped structures, called wigwams, were covered with slabs of bark or woven mats. Most of their utensils were wood; their tools were polished stone and bone.

The Algonkin grew corn, squash, pumpkin, peppers, and beans. They gathered wild rice and made popcorn and maple sugar.* Deer was the principal food animal, and when available, fish and shellfish were consumed in large quantities. The Algonkin also made baskets and pottery.

Women shredded fibers from bark and twisted them into thread and twine for bags and straps. Clothing was simple and made of animal skins. Even in winter men went about in moccasins, leggings, breechcloths, and robes. Women wore skirts and jackets of sewn skins.

The eastern Algonkin-speaking tribes were the first to welcome the French, English, and Dutch, and were the first to shed blood in conflict with them. Nearly all of the most famous individual Indians celebrated in the early history of the English colonial settlements in America were Algonkin: *Pocahontas,** *Massassoit,** *Squanto,** and King Philip. Furthermore, it was an unknown Algonkin-speaking Lenape whose pictographs recorded that historic moment when strange-looking vessels with strange-looking people on them appeared off shore. He wondered what kind of people these strangers were. Were they friendly? Had they come to stay?

The Indians poured hot maple syrup over the popcorn for a delicious sweet. The French, first Europeans to taste it, called it **snow food.** Today we know it as caramel corn.

Pocahontas: daughter of a Powhatan chief, best known for saving the life of Captain John Smith, became a Christian, took the name of Rebecca, and married John Rolfe, a prominent member of the Jamestown Colony.

Massasoit: Wampanoag chief who visited the Pilgrims at Plymouth in 1621 and made a treaty of peace with them that lasted almost 40 years. His son, King Philip, became chief in 1662 and led the Wampanoags in war against the English settlers in 1676.

Squanto: a Wampanoag, was captured by Captain Thomas Hunt in 1614 and sold in Spain as a slave. He escaped and made several voyages from England to the New World. He was on hand to greet the Pilgrims in 1621 at Plymouth, taught them how to raise corn, and served as an interpreter. He died in 1622.

4 Oral traditions of the Delawares

History as a Record of the Remembered Past

Introduction

Archaeology has revealed much about how North American Indians—a people without written records—lived and worked. But archaeology can tell us little about their great men or their great events. To learn these things, we have to turn to *oral traditions*.

Nearly all social groups have accounts, explanations, stories, songs, and legends about the past transmitted by word of mouth from generation to generation. Such oral traditions are part of a specialized branch of anthropology called *folklore*, and they can be collected from living people.

In the absence of written records, oral tradition can tell us about the great men or the great events in the life of a people. Oral tradition may contain both fact and fiction and may rarely ever provide a basis for dating men and events. Nevertheless, it is a record of what people believed to be true about themselves, their heroes, their misfortunes, and their enemies.

When the testimonies of oral tradition and archaeology are brought together, great events and great men become part of a people's known culture record. This record tells not only how man has lived and worked, but also makes possible inferences and hypotheses about what man has done and why he did it.

Lenni-Lenape

In this present assignment you will read two samples of the oral tradition of the *Lenni-Lenape** or Delaware Indians. The Delawares were an Algonkin-speaking confederation inhabiting the entire basin of the Delaware River in Delaware, eastern Pennsylvania, southeastern New York, and all of New Jersey. The Algonkins also included the Powhatans of the Virginias and the Shawnees of South Carolina.

The main body of Delawares consisted of three tribes: *Unami*, in the central region; *Munsee*, in the north; and *Unalachtigo*, in the south. Although each of the main tribes had its own territory and dialect, they all regarded themselves as part of the same people.

In addition to the main body, Algonkin-speaking tribes of the Atlantic seaboard (Nanticoke, Mahican, Shawnee), all recognized the Delawares as *Grandfather,** claimed a close connection with them, and preserved a common oral tradition.

Nearly all of the Algonkin-speaking tribes from Virginia to New England, and several as far west as the Mississippi River, claimed kinship with the Delawares and were their war allies at different times in their long history.

The Delawares were one of the two most powerful confederations of Indian tribes in eastern North America. Much of Delaware oral tradition is concerned with the other great eastern confederation, the Iroquois-speaking *Five Nations* (Seneca, Cayuga, Onondaga, Oneida, and Mohawk) who inhabited the Mohawk Valley and Finger Lakes region of New York.* (The Five Nations later on became the *Six Nations* when the Tuscaroras of North Carolina were taken into the confederacy.)

The Delawares and the Six Nations were bitter enemies and fought against each other many times. A near-permanent state of hostility between the Delawares and the Six Nations was the central political fact of eastern North American history. What follows is the Delaware version of how their mutual hostilities began.

Delawares, most important of the Algonkin, called themselves **Lenape** or **Leni-Lenape,** meaning original people, real men, or native, genuine men. The English called them **Delawares** from the name of their principal river. The French called them **Loups** (wolves).

The title **Grandfather** accorded to the Delawares by all Algonkin tribes meant they had priority and rank in the home territory.

Hayenwatan (the historic Hiawatha of Longfellow's beautiful poem) founded the **Iroquois Confederacy** in the 1500's after a bloody war with the Algonkins and Hurons of lower Canada. The Confederacy had an unwritten constitution, an elected representative body. Votes were cast by tribes; disputes were arbitrated.

Objectives are to:

—Analyze samples of Delaware oral tradition for meaning, agreement, and disagreement.

—Recognize and identify statements that suggest a hypothesis for an unresolved historical problem studied in the previous assignment.

—Make a hypothesis for that unresolved historical problem.

—Summarize the advantages and disadvantages of using oral tradition as a source of historical information.

9   WANDERINGS OF THE DELAWARES

This sample of Delaware oral tradition is taken from a large collection of stories and legends prepared by Reverend John Heckewelder, a white Protestant minister of the Moravian Church. Heckewelder was an active missionary to the Delawares and other Indian tribes in western Pennsylvania, Ohio, and Indiana, from 1762 to 1810. During his many years of living among the Delawares, he learned their language and as much of their history and traditions as was known by any other white man of his day.

Heckewelder greatly admired the Delawares, and they trusted him. Everything that Heckewelder wrote about the Delaware traditions, customs, and culture was written from the point of view of an admirer and trusted friend. He presented the past of the Delawares as they remembered it.

When reading the selection below, keep in mind the following questions:

1. What did the Delawares believe was worth remembering about the Talligewi?

2. How does the Heckewelder sample of Delaware oral tradition explain the origin of hostility with the Iroquis?

Tale of the Delawares

According to accounts handed down from generation to generation, many years ago the Lenni-Lenape, or Delawares, lived in a very distant country in the western part of the American continent. The Delawares became unhappy and decided to migrate to the east. After a very long journey they arrived at the Mississippi River (*Namaesi Sipu*, or *river of fish*, in the Lenapi language) where they fell in with the Iroquois, who had also migrated from a distant country. The object of the Iroquois was the same as that of the Delawares; they were moving east to find a country that pleased them.

Scouts sent ahead by the Delawares reported that the country east of the Mississippi was inhabited by a very powerful nation. This nation had built many large towns on the great rivers flowing through their land. Many wonderful things were told about these famous people, who called themselves *Talligewi*: they were tall; there were giants among them; they built huge forts and dug deep trenches; they were fierce warriors.

The Delawares sent a message to the Talligewi requesting permission to settle near them. The Talligewi refused, but they gave the Delawares permission to pass through their country and settle farther to the east. However, when the Delawares began crossing the river, the Talligewi attacked them and threatened to destroy all who dared cross.

Not being prepared for conflict but unwilling to let the enemy think they were cowards, the Delawares held a great council to decide what action to take. The Iroquois, who had been watching from a distance, offered to join the Delawares in attacking the Talligewi on condition that the conquered

Delaware Migration Routes
The map above shows how the Delaware nation crossed the continent to the Delaware and Hudson rivers and the Atlantic Ocean.

Migration Route

0   1450
Scale of Miles

country be shared between them. The Iroquois proposal was accepted, and the two nations resolved to conquer or die.

Great battles were fought in which hundreds of warriors fell on both sides. The Delawares and Iroquois stormed many forts and crossed many embankments. No quarter was given; none was asked. The dead were buried in holes or laid together in heaps and covered over with earth. Finally, the Talligewi realized they would all be destroyed if the war continued, so they abandoned their country and fled down the Mississippi, never to return.

During the long war with the Talligewi, the Delawares lost many more warriors than the Iroquois, who would always hang back, leaving the Delawares to face the enemy. In the end, however, the victors divided the country between themselves. The Iroquois chose lands near the Great Lakes, and the Delawares took lands to the south. For many hundreds of years, the Delawares and Iroquois lived in peace and increased their populations.

Delaware hunters and warriors crossed the great mountains and followed streams to the great Bay River (Susquehanna) and then to the great Bay itself. They travelled by land and by water and eventually reached the great Saltwater Lake which they called the Sea. They discovered the great river named after them—the Delaware, and explored further east to the country now called New Jersey. They arrived at another great stream, now called the Hudson.

When these far-ranging hunters returned across the mountains with stories about the wonders of the eastern lands, small groups of the Delawares began migrating toward the great rivers and Saltwater Lake of the east. At last they settled on the four great rivers (Delaware, Hudson, Susquehanna, and Potomac) making the Lenapewihittuck (meaning stream of the Lenape, or what we call the Delaware) the center of their possessions.

Not all the Delawares migrated east, however. Some never crossed the Mississippi, and others did not cross the mountains. Only half of the total nation settled on the lands of the four rivers. In time, those Delawares who had crossed the mountains divided themselves into three tribes called *Unami*, *Unalachtigo*, and *Munsee*.

From these three tribes came the people the Europeans called Delawares. From these three tribes also sprang several other peoples. The Mahicans along the Hudson River and the Nanticokes along the Potomac acknowledged the Delawares as their *Grandfather*. The great Delaware family prospered and multiplied.

Meanwhile the Iroquois who had settled near the Great Lakes moved north to the St. Lawrence River and became neighbors of several Delaware tribes. The Iroquois looked upon their southern neighbors with jealous eyes, afraid of their growing power and prosperity. They first sought to embroil the Delawares in wars with distant tribes. When this treachery was discovered, the Delawares openly declared war on the deceitful Iroquois.

The war was carried on with such vigor that the Iroquois found themselves no match for the Delawares, who had a powerful connection of related tribes ready to join them when needed. Until this time, each tribe of the Iroquois

Munsee: meaning "at the place where stones are gathered together"; the northern Lenni-Lenape, one of the three principal divisions of the Delawares. Munsee dialect was so different from that of the other two Delaware divisions (Unami and Unalachtigo) that the Munsees were regarded as an entirely different tribe.

Unalachtigo: means people who live near the ocean; the southern Lenni-Lenape, who lived along both sides of the Delaware River. Most of the Unalachtigo villages were in what is now Burlington, New Jersey.

Unami: the central Lenni-Lenape, occupying the Pennsylvania side of the Delaware River.

had acted independently, but now they decided to create a confederacy to unite all tribes in common causes and against a common enemy.

The restless and warlike Seneca joined with the Cayuga, Onondaga, Oneida, Mohawk (and later, the Tuscarora) against the Delawares. Bloody wars were waged for a long time between the confederated Iroquois and the Delawares. The Delawares were aided by their allies and generally came away from the fighting victorious. Such was the state of affairs between the Delawares and the Iroquois when the Europeans arrived.

Adapted from Reverend John Heckewelder's **History, Manners, and Customs of the Indian Nations,** New and Revised Edition (Philadelphia: Historical Society of Pennsylvania, 1876).

10   WALAM OLUM—A PAINTED RECORD

This sample of Delaware oral tradition is taken from the *Walam Olum.* In the Delaware language, the words *Walam Olum* mean *painted record.* The Walam Olum is a painted record of Delaware tribal history and is an excellent example of the kind of picture writing developed by the eastern Algonkin-speaking tribes. This tribal history was preserved by story tellers and singers. It was transmitted from generation to generation in the form of symbols painted on sticks and kept in order by bundles.

These pictorial symbols served as *mnemonic** devices for the story tellers. No one could read the history from the picture writing alone. Story tellers had to learn the history by hearing it told or sung by someone else. Once the history had been learned, the symbols were used by story tellers to jog their memories.

Mnemonic is a term derived from two Greek words meaning to be mindful or to remember. Describes an object or system intended to assist memory.

The complete Walam Olum consists of five books or 183 statements relating the tribal history of the Delawares from the creation of the world to the arrival of Europeans in North America. Each pictorial symbol represents one statement.

None of the original painted sticks has survived into our time. However, 150 years ago Constantine S. Rafinesque,* a botanist and historian, obtained a collection of the painted sticks, and a written version of an oral recitation of the Walam Olum story. He prepared an English language text that included copies of the picture symbols. A new interpretation of Rafinesque's work was published by the Indiana Historical Society in 1954.

We have selected 39 statements from the original 183 that make up the Walam Olum. When reading them in the following assignment, keep in mind these questions:

Rafinesque taught botany and natural history at Transylvania University, Lexington, Kentucky, from 1819 to 1825. His handwritten original manuscript was completed in 1833 and is now in the museum of the University of Pennsylvania.

1. What did the Delawares believe was worth remembering about the Talligewi wars?

2. How does the Walam Olum explain the origin of hostility with the Iroquois?

Excerpts from the Oral Tradition of the

WALAM OLUM

. . . the Northerners were of one mind and the Easterners were of one mind: it would be good to live on the other side of the frozen water.

Ten thousand men went upstream, went right on upstream during a single day, upstream to the eastern lands of Snake Island: every man kept going along.

By the good hills and along the plains, buffalo were beginning to graze.

All of them said they would go together to the land there, all who were free . . .

When Handsome One Feather was chief, he became possessed with hate and wanted to go away . . .

. . . because he was angry; he called for an emigration toward the east, but some went off secretly.

Those at Snow Mountain were happy and made One Who Is Beloved chief.

When Opossum Face was chief, he worried about the destruction of things belonging to others.

Now when daylight came, he spoke three times: "Let those going east be many."

They separated at a river; the ones who were lazy returned to Snow Mountain.

Some of the **pictographs** plainly represent sun, moon, mountains, celestial arch, similar to those of ancient Egyptians, Chinese, Cretans, Babylonians. However, other Delaware symbols are unique in representing abstract ideas such as peace, peril, chief, prosperity.

A33

When Lean-to-Man was chief, the Talligewi were in possession of the east.

> When some infiltrated into the east where the Talligewi were, some were killed.

In right-minded indignation, all said: "Let us despoil! Let us destroy!"

> The Iroquois, their northern friends, then arrived; and all was explained to them.

It was while Long Bread was chief that they went along the road and on the river to the other side of the water.

> That was good, for they killed many there in the Talega country.

When One Who Has A Resonant Voice was chief, they were exceedingly powerful in the Talega country.

> When Go Between was chief, all the Talega habitations were in the south.

When One Who Preserves What Is There was chief, all the men enjoyed living.

> The Snow Mountain men were now south of the lakes; and while their Iroquois friends were north of the lakes . . .

. . . these were incapable of remaining friends, for they went about to forbidden places when Snow Blizzard was Chief.

> When Truth-Telling Man was chief, the Iroquois had already destroyed things.

When Upright Nature was chief, the Iroquois trembled.

> Road Man was chief there along the middle reaches of the White River.

When One Who Paddles was chief, they traveled on many rivers.

 When they were along the Susquehanna, River-Bird Man was chief.

All the hunters were approaching the large body of water where the sun rises from the water.

 When Red Arrow was chief, they were so far downstream that tides could be felt.

 When Red-Paint Soul was chief, they were at the mighty water.

When One Who Makes Himself White was chief, they were at the shore near the water.

 They wanted to divide into three divisions with each of the three to follow its own customs, dating from the time that each was created . . .

❋ ❋ ❋

 All the Seneca and the Disgusting Wildcats trembled.

When One Who Fails At Water's Edge was chief, they destroyed things belonging to the Seneca.

When Friendly One was chief, he played with the Seneca.

When One Who Takes Things By Accident was chief, there came from yonder . . .

 . . . persons floating in from the east: the Whites were coming.

When Hawk was chief, they were looking at an expanse of water . . .

  . . . where persons floating in from the north and from the south: the Whites . . .

. . . friendly people with great possessions: who are they?

Selected and adapted from **Walam Olum: The Migration Legend of the Lenni Lenape or Delaware Indians,** by permission of the Indiana Historical Society, Indianapolis, published 1954, pp. 3–216.

A35

5 Interpreting Algonkin picture writing

Culture Empathy

Introduction

Knowing how Algonkin-speaking Delawares tried to communicate information, ideas, emotions, and values will enable you to understand what one generation was trying to say to the next, and why they said what they did. Your problem in this assignment is similar to that of Constantine S. Rafinesque when he interpreted the Walam Olum in 1833.

Rafinesque relates that he obtained bundles of sticks with painted Algonkin picture symbols in 1820, and two years later was given a written version of an oral recitation of the Walam Olum story. Next, Rafinesque matched each picture symbol with the appropriate statement in the written version of the Walam Olum. We have no way of knowing what inquiry processes Rafinesque used, or how much time he gave to preparing his text of the Walam Olum. All that we know about Rafinesque's procedures is that he had to learn the Delaware language and that it took him twelve years to complete his text.

Your task in this assignment is much simpler than the one undertaken by Rafinesque. You are asked to match up only eight Algonkin picture symbols with the appropriate statements from a written version, whereas Rafinesque had to match up 183. Furthermore, you are familiar with and can follow the inquiry model that has been studied in previous assignments.

In previous assignments, you learned that the process of recognizing and identifying problems in testimony and evidence consisted of noting relationships between facts and developing the implications of them by asking probing and inquiring questions. This same process applied to our present problem will enable you to interpret these eight Algonkin picture symbols and to discover meaning in them that you had not suspected was there.

Objectives are to:

—Apply the first stage of our inquiry model (noting relationships between facts and discovering meaning from them by asking probing and inquiring questions).

—Match eight Algonkin picture symbols with appropriate statements from a written version of the Walam Olum.

—Recognize and describe the cultural achievements of the eastern woodland American Indian tribes.

—Express personal reactions to Delaware social and moral values and Delaware attitudes toward Europeans.

11 EXAMINING ALGONKIN PICTURE WRITING

While examining the picture symbols and statements from the Walam Olum presented here, keep in mind the following questions:

A36

1. *Which of the symbols are similar? How are they similar?*

2. *How would you classify the symbols so that similar ones are grouped?*

3. *Which statements are similar in content? How are they similar?*

4. *How would you classify the statements so that similar ones are grouped?*

Random Order of Symbols and Statements from Algonkin Picture Writing

1.    1. When Upright Nature was chief, the Iroquois trembled.

2.   2. When Lean-to-Man was chief, the Talligewi were in possession of the east.

3.    3. When Truth-Telling Man was chief, the Iroquois had already destroyed things.

4.   4. The Iroquois, their northern friends, then arrived; and all was explained to them.

5.    5. Persons floating in from the east: the Whites were coming . . .

6.   6. When Handsome One Feather was chief, he became possessed with hate and wanted to go away . . .

7.    7. That was good, for they killed many there in the Talega country.

8.    8. . . . friendly people with great possessions: who are they?

Selected and adapted from
Walam Olum: The Migration Legend of the Lenni Lenape or Delaware Indians, pp. 3–216.

A37

6 Life style of the Delaware Indians
Values and Social Attitudes

Introduction

In your last assignment you applied our inquiry model to the problem of analyzing and interpreting eight Algonkin picture symbols taken from the Walum Olum. You learned how the Delawares preserved their oral traditions and how they tried to communicate information, ideas, and emotions in a visual form. The present assignment is concerned with the information, ideas, and emotions they chose to preserve and communicate. It examines the values or culture standards, the social attitudes and cultural differences by which the Delawares decided what was important or unimportant, good or bad, right or wrong.

Values

Values: an anthropological and sociological concept used to identify commonly accepted cultural standards of a people against which behavior, attitudes, desires, and needs can be compared and judged. For example, youth is a value (cultural standard) of contemporary American culture, and old age is a value (cultural standard) of traditional Chinese culture.

The concept of values was developed by anthropologists and sociologists to make it easier to recognize and identify culture standards of a group. All cultures, peoples, and groups have traits commonly accepted as culture standards, such as honesty, equality, independence, loyalty, generosity, success.

How or when a *culture trait* becomes a *culture standard* is difficult to discover. The origin of specific values is usually lost in time. Some values such as charity may have originated in an ancient or recent religious experience and are sanctioned and perpetuated from generation to generation by religion.

Others such as affluence may have originated in some ancient or recent adjustment to new or changed conditions in the natural environment. Still others such as marrying only one wife may have originated in simple usefulness and common-sense experience. Some culture traits like honesty are highly valued in virtually all human groups; others like equality are not.

Not only may values differ from people to people, or culture to culture, but they may vary even within groups. For example, culture traits like success or generosity may be highly valued by some members of a group, and be of only slight importance to others.

Data means facts, figures, and general information from which inferences can be drawn, hypotheses formed, and hypotheses tested.

Knowing what the principal values of a particular group are, knowing the standards by which individual or group action are judged, knowing what acts and desires people believe are important or unimportant, good or bad, right or wrong, worth sacrificing or even dying for, is extremely useful information. It is *data** for inquiring into why events and actions occurred.

A38

Values affect emotions, and aroused emotions lead to actions. Knowledge of values enables anthropologists, sociologists, and historians to describe and explain how a social system works, to tell how and why a people live, work, and behave the way they do. Knowledge of values may help one group of citizens understand the inner feelings and aspirations of another.

Without a knowledge of values, we can describe, infer, and hypothesize *descriptions*. With a knowledge of values, we can describe, infer, and hypothesize *explanations*.

Social Attitudes

The concept of social attitudes was developed by psychologists and sociologists to help explain why individuals and groups behave toward each other as they do. Social attitudes are based on moods and feelings that cause a person to act favorably or unfavorably toward individuals, groups, or objects. Social attitudes are derived from experience and values; they are taught and learned.

Anything that is taught and learned can be changed. For example, in the ten years preceding World War II, the moods and feelings underlying American social attitudes toward the Germans and the Japanese were highly unfavorable. Words like tyrannical, cruel, despotic, and ruthless describe some of the feelings that predisposed Americans to act unfavorably toward them. Those feelings, as well as the social attitudes they formed, resulted from our actual experience with the behavior of the German and Japanese governments from 1931 to 1941, and the value judgments we made upon that behavior.

In the two decades following World War II, the moods and feelings underlying American social attitudes toward Germans and Japanese changed dramatically. Words like friendly, industrious, democratic, and cooperative describe some of the feelings that predisposed us to act favorably toward them.

Again, those feelings as well as the social attitudes they formed resulted from our actual experience with the behavior of the postwar governments of Germany and Japan and value judgments made upon that behavior. In the 1930's many Americans refused to buy goods of German or Japanese manufacture; in the 1970's Volkswagens and Toyotas are everywhere.

Like knowledge of values, knowledge of social attitudes adds another dimension to our study of history. Knowledge of social attitudes is extremely useful to historical inquirers. With this knowledge, political and economic facts become more meaningful. Skilled inquirers are able to recognize relationships between such political and economic facts, identify problems, and hypothesize explanations.

Take as an example the history of the relations between the eastern woodland tribes of North America and the Europeans who settled among them in the seventeenth and eighteenth centuries. Indian social attitudes towards Europeans and their culture were mixed. Knowing how and why they were mixed is essential for reconstructing and explaining the political history of North America during the seventeenth and eighteenth centuries.

Objectives are to:

—Describe the concepts of **values** and **social attitudes** as presented in the introduction.

—Recognize and identify in the readings culture traits of the Delaware Indians accepted as **values.**

—Make value judgments on actions according to Delaware culture standards.

—Recognize and identify value conflicts in Delaware culture as presented in a recording and in readings.

—Use knowledge of Delaware values as a basis for hypothesis explaining Delaware actions.

A39

12 OBSERVATIONS ON THE CUSTOMS AND MANNERS OF THE EASTERN TRIBES

The first reading in this assignment is taken from Reverend John Hecke-welder's recollections of his life among the Delaware Indians. The second reading is an adaptation of Heckewelder's translation of a Delaware song.

According to Heckewelder, Indian songs—like European songs—are useful sources of information about beliefs and feelings. However, Indian singers perform quite differently from European singers. Indian songs are not sung all the way through from beginning to end. Songs are sung in detached parts, in short sentences, and singers feel no compulsion to finish a song. They sing as much of a song as the occasion, their feelings of the moment, or time permits. According to Heckewelder the total effect of words and music upon listeners is moving and unforgettable.

While reading the selections, keep in mind the following questions:

1. Which culture traits of the Delawares described in the readings would you recognize and identify as culture standards or values?

2. According to the values you have identified, which actions described or inferred from the readings should be judged good or right?

3. According to the values you have identified, which actions described or inferred from the readings should be judged bad or wrong?

Advice to Travellers Westward Bound

Like the other eastern woodland tribes the Delawares consider themselves to be the creation of an all-powerful, wise, good, and great *Mannitto* or *Great Spirit*. All that Indians possess, everything they enjoy or use, all skills and abilities, every success and good fortune, was given to them by the Great Spirit. Owing so much to the Great Spirit, they believe very strongly in an obligation to worship him and they do so with enthusiasm and regularity.

Not content with simply being grateful for all of the wonderful things that the Great Spirit has provided for his people, the Delawares try to regulate their lives according to how they imagine the Great Spirit wants them to live.

They believe that the Great Spirit would be greatly angered if they neglected those whom he has protected and permitted to attain old age. For children to neglect parents or grandparents is unthinkable. Aged parents and grandparents receive their share of the family's hunt and harvest as a matter of right and are frequently given first choice out of what is available.

The respect that the Delawares and neighboring tribes show for their aged parents and grandparents extends far beyond their own immediate families. Among the Delawares and other eastern tribes aged persons, whether relatives or not, command a degree of respect that is unmatched anywhere else in the world.

Aged people receive full shares of food and clothing from their own family's resources. They are also supplied by families unrelated to them, simply because they are old and may need help. From infancy Delawares are taught to be kind and attentive to aged persons and never let them suffer for lack of comforts or necessities.

Furthermore, the company of the aged is sought out by the young; the aged are listened to even when their talk may seem endless and irrelevant. Senility and other infirmities attendant upon some persons in old age are never subjects of ridicule and laughter among Indians.

Respect for old age is so strong that joking about it is as unthinkable as neglecting one's own parents. On every occasion and in every situation in life, age takes the lead among the Delawares. The oldest in any group, even among small boys, will be recognized and accepted as the spokesman for the group.

If the word respect best describes how the Delawares treat their own parents and all aged persons, the word politeness best describes how they treat each other. Delawares are extremely careful to avoid giving offense by either words or actions.

Importance of Friendship

Friendship is one of the most important relationships that the eastern Indians know. For example, the word *friend** to the ear of a Delaware does not convey the same vague and indefinite meaning that it does to Europeans. The word friend is not a mere complimentary or meaningless social expression; among the Delawares friends are important enough to fight for and to die for.

The Delaware word for "my friend" is **nittis** (pronounced neé teés).

When a Delaware suspects that someone may have evil designs against a friend, he may avert bloodshed by saying emphatically, "This is my friend. I will punish anyone who tries to hurt my friend."

Since Indians are so serious about friendship and never offer it except totally and completely, they know the meaning of that language. It means that a friend will stand with a friend, and a threat to one is a threat to the other.

In most situations Delawares are not quarrelsome people and are moved to violence only when insulted beyond what an apology can repair. They believe that fighting is only for dogs, wild animals, and enemies. However, it is an undoubted principle with them that evil can not come out of good; that no friend will injure another friend; no friend will steal from another friend; and that whoever wrongs or does harm to another is an enemy.

Like the other eastern tribes, Delawares do not forgive or forget very easily. The passion of revenge is so strong in them that they will sacrifice themselves and all that they possess to avenge wilful injuries, insults, and contemptuous treatment. As it is with individuals, so it is also with tribes, nations, or groups. Against enemies, punishment and revenge is as natural as respect for a father or love for a wife. When taken, revenge is frequently cruel and rarely ever swift.

A41

The Delawares are great warriors, but they have an unusual mixture of pride and modesty in their warlike activities. Rarely ever do singers or dancers recite details about ancient heroes or ancient battles. The Delawares are always uncomfortable when talking about the dead and the past.

Occasionally, they meet in a circle to recount the warlike exploits of living men. The oldest warrior recites first, followed by the next in order of age. After each has made a short recital in his turn, they begin again in the same order and continue as before until each one has concluded.

On these occasions great care must be taken not to give offence by bragging or belittling another's accomplishments, because each warrior must live up to his reputation. If insulted, each warrior is ready to show by action that he can still do what he claims to have done in war. I well remember an incident when an insulted warrior stepped out of the circle and struck dead an impudent boaster who had offended him.

Hospitality among Indians

Dignity and respect are extremely important to North American Indians. There is probably not a people anywhere in the world more sensitive and careful about paying common courtesies to one another, and there is certainly no people anywhere who are more hospitable.

For example, when visiting the house of an Indian, even if one is a perfect stranger, the first words spoken are, "Sit down, my friend."

As a matter of fact, the most common form of greeting to a person totally unknown and met for the first time is the word for *friend*. No one is ever left standing; seats are provided for all and the tobacco pouch is handed around. Next, food is offered.

Without a single word passing between man and wife, the wife will prepare and serve food to the visitors. After serving food, she will retire to a neighbor's house and inform the neighbors that her husband has been honored with a visit. She will never once grumble because food prepared for her own family has been eaten by her husband's visitors.

For Delawares and other eastern tribes, hospitality is not something that good men ought to practice; it is a strict duty. They believe that the Great Spirit has made the earth and all it contains for the common good of mankind. When the Great Spirit stocked the eastern lands with game and the eastern rivers with fish and when he made the corn grow out of the earth, it was for the benefit of all, not just a few.

Consequently, rarely ever will you find a Delaware making excuses for not giving and sharing. They freely supply their neighbors' needs from their own resources and will share even their last morsel of food with each other and with strangers.*

Delawares would rather suffer the pangs of empty stomachs themselves than be thought neglectful of the needs of the sick and the poor. Far better for one's own family to eat nothing than to have friendly strangers go away with bad impressions of Delaware hospitality.

The main duties of Indian women were child care, cutting firewood, growing corn, baking bread, and making clothes. Housework was not demanding —only one pot or kettle to scrub, and very few clothes to wash. Indian women rarely complained and performed their family duties cheerfully and well.

Delawares are not only hospitable to their friends, they are also generous. As we have noted, they cannot long endure seeing the sick and aged suffer from lack of food, clothing, or personal attention. They give freely of their own goods and time to such people.

With others, however, when Indians give presents, they usually expect something of equal value in return. Frequently, the receiver of a gift from a Delaware is informed precisely what is expected in return. When a gift has been presented to a stranger, Delawares are usually content to receive some trifle or token of remembrance; if no gift of any kind is offered to them, they become offended. Wise and prudent travellers through their country avoid giving unnecessary offense.

Adapted from Reverend John Heckewelder's **History, Manners, and Customs of the Indian Nations.**

13   A DELAWARE WARRIOR'S LAMENT

Oh poor me!
Who leaves to fight the enemy,
And knows not when I shall return,
To enjoy the love of wife and child.

Oh unfortunate man!
Whose life is not his own to live,
Who goes where he is told to go
And does what he is told to do.
For we are right and they are wrong
And tribal honor does require,
Revenge by blade, by blood and fire.

Oh Great Spirit high above!
Take pity on my wife and son,
Let them not mourn on my account!
Grant me success in this attempt
That I may slay my enemy,
And homeward come with scalps of war,
To please my father and my friends
That we may all rejoice together
And know that honor is avenged.

If I am to return again,
I need your courage to overcome
Those dogs and beasts that walk like men.
Pity me, preserve my life.
And the best of theirs I'll sacrifice.

Adapted from Reverend John Heckewelder's translation of "The Song of Delaware Warriors Going Against the Enemy," **History, Manners, and Customs of the Indian Nations.**

A43

7 Indian culture and European trade goods

Technology and Culture Change

Introduction

From the earliest moments of contact, North American Indians discovered that Europeans possessed many fine tools and luxury goods of every description. Indians also discovered that many of these new and wonderful things were readily available to them. They had great bargaining power and were quick to learn how to use it.

Indians not only kept the first European settlers from starving while adjusting to a new environment, but they had control over a major economic resource—fur. Fur-bearing animals abounded in the forests and along the rivers and lakes of North America and brought high prices in Europe. *Beaver skins** for hats, coats, and other kinds of clothing were in great demand in London, Paris, and Amsterdam.

Indians exchanged their animal skins and furs for the products of seventeenth- and eighteenth-century European technology and industry. The demand for furs by Europeans and the demand for European goods by Indians created a flourishing transatlantic trade in which Indian hunters and trappers became essential parts.

During the 1650's the Dutch shipped an average of **55,000 beaver skins** to Amsterdam each year.

Organizing the Fur Trade

As the fur trade developed during the seventeenth century, an increasing number of Indians became involved in it. As a result, the actual exchange of furs for European goods became more organized and more complicated. For example, the Huron and Iroquois Indians established themselves as middlemen between European traders on the Atlantic Coast and Indian hunters and trappers of the Great Lakes region. By trade and by warfare, the Hurons and Iroquois collected furs from their Indian neighbors, transported them to a central location, and exchanged them for European goods.

The Hurons generally traded with the French, while the Iroquois traded with the Dutch and English. So intense became the competition for furs between the two tribes that in 1643 the Iroquois obtained more than five hundred guns from the Dutch and attacked their more lightly armed Huron rivals. Firearms prevailed over bows and arrows. After six years of fierce fighting, the Iroquois eliminated the Hurons from the fur trade and destroyed them as an organized tribe.

Elsewhere in North America the fur trade developed along different lines. For example, in those parts of Pennsylvania where the power of the Iroquois did not extend, European traders established a chain of trading posts in Indian country where European goods were exchanged for furs which were collected at the trading posts and transported east by canoe or pack train for shipment to Europe. Though risky, such trading operations were extremely profitable. By the early eighteenth century, trading posts and *itinerant** European traders were patronized by nearly all the eastern woodland tribes.

Here was trade that linked together in a common economic network lonely Algonkin-speaking hunters on the banks of the Susquehanna with gentlemen merchants in the shadow of London Bridge. It was a trade that sent thousands of Indians from all of the eastern tribes in pursuit of beavers and otters.

This trade, which drove the Iroquois to destroy the Hurons and sent hundreds of European traders into the American wilderness, greatly changed the lives of the eastern woodland tribes involved in it. When two dozen beaver skins could be traded for a brass kettle, three woolen shirts, three pounds of glass beads, and a half keg of rum, many Indians became dissatisfied with clay pots, deerskin shirts, shell beads, and spring water.

Itinerant means traveling from place to place.

14 WHAT THE INDIANS WANT

In 1746 when England and France were at war, a group of Indians traveled from the Ohio country to Philadelphia. There they complained about the Provincial Government of Pennsylvania's lack of concern for the wants and needs of Indians in the Ohio region. The Indians warned that unless the Pennsylvania Government changed its policies and sent gifts of trade goods to the Indians, French influence in the area would probably increase.

The Provincial Council of Pennsylvania considered the seriousness of the political situation in the Ohio country. It decided to heed the warning and take the advice of the visiting Indians. The Council agreed to send the Ohio Indians a free gift of the trade goods requested by them, hoping to satisfy Indian needs and insure Indian loyalty for the duration of the war with France.

While examining the following list of trade goods sought by the Ohio Indians, keep in mind these questions:

1. What items on this list are in greatest demand?

2. How many different categories of goods did the Indians want? How would you classify them?

3. What inquiring questions are suggested by the way you have classified the goods on this list?

Objectives are to:

—Examine given data on Indian requests for European trade goods and form a hypothesis about the effect of European trade goods on Indian culture.

—Examine other data and test your hypothesis with inferences drawn from it.

—Test and modify your hypothesis as your data and inferences require.

—Decide whether your tested hypothesis stands as a judgment or a conclusion.

A45

Gifts to the Ohio Indians Provided by the Pennsylvania Provincial Council, 1747

AMOUNT	ARTICLE	COST		
18 barrels	Gunpowder	£ 171		
2000 pounds	Bar Lead	43	10s	
40	Guns	60		
26 pieces	Blanket and Cloth	265	1	7d
50 dozen	Knives	24	5	
6,500	Flints	4	11	6
341	Shirts, with Thread	105	12	1
100 pieces	Fine Cloth	29		
20 gross	*Gartering**	25	5	
15 pounds	Vermillion Face Paint	11	16	10
112	Looking Glasses	7	11	
30	Brass Kettles	11	2	
20 dozen	Hatchets	18		
18 gross	Rings, Medals	16	10	
2 gross	Drilling Blades (for beads)	2		
35 pieces	Ribbon	29	2	
2½ pounds	Beads		15	
58	Dutch Pipes	2	11	
1 dozen	Toy Dolls		15	
		£ 822	126s*	24d*

Converting shillings and pence into pounds (£), we have . . .

£ 828*   8s   - - d

(*£ comes from the Latin word for pound, **libra**. *d means pence and comes from the Latin word, **denarius**. *Twenty shillings equal one pound; 12 pence equal one shilling.)

Gartering means bands or straps which held up the knee-length stockings commonly worn by men in the eighteenth century.

In 1747, £828 was a lot of money. For example, a school teacher earned £31; a brick-layer, £48. Land sold at £3 for 100 acres; a horse for £4.

Adapted from **Minutes of the Provincial Council of Pennsylvania** (Harrisburg: Theodore Fenn and Co., 1851), Vol. V, p. 197.

15   TESTIMONY OF CONTEMPORARIES

By the middle of the eighteenth century, many people were aware that traditional Indian ways of living and working were being changed by the desire for, and the use of, European goods. European painters of Indian portraits were perhaps the most aware of all. Some painters represented the observed facts of Indian culture change as creative and noble. Other painters saw it as destructive and *grotesque*.*

Grotesque is something absurd, ugly, fantastic, departing from the normal.

Most contemporary men of affairs simply recorded what they saw. Others thought more seriously about what was happening to the Indian way of life and wondered whether the changes were desirable, whether the gain was worth the loss. While reading the statements of contemporaries presented here, and examining the two eighteenth-century portraits of the Mohawk Indian chief, Old Hendrick, keep in mind the following questions:

A46

1. What European trade goods do these commentators see Indians as wanting and using the most?

2. What inferences about the effect of European trade goods on the ways Indians lived and worked are suggested by these samples of contemporary comment?

3. What inferences about the effect of European trade goods on the ways Indians lived and worked are suggested by the two eighteenth-century portraits of the Mohawk chief, Old Hendrick?

Proclamation of the Provincial Council of Pennsylvania, February 17, 1747

Whereas, complaints made from time to time that irregularities and abuses have been committed by traders in Indian country *trafficking** in rum and other strong liquors contrary to law . . .

Whereas, many Indians, being intoxicated and drinking to excess, are not only grossly cheated in their bargains but are inflamed to such a degree as to destroy their own lives and endanger the lives of others . . . for the future prevention of such disorders . . . we give full power and authority to any Indian or Indians to whom rum or other strong liquors be offered for sale contrary to law . . . to stave and break the casks or vessels in which rum or other strong liquors are contained.

Trafficking means carrying on an illegal trade or commerce.

Adapted from **Minutes of the Provincial Council of Pennsylvania,** Vol. V, pp. 195–196.

Benjamin Franklin to James Parker, March 20, 1750

Everyone must approve the proposal of encouraging a number of sober blacksmiths to reside among the Indians. They would doubtless be of great service. The whole subsistence of the Indians depends upon keeping their guns in order; and if they are obliged to make a journey of two or three hundred miles to an English settlement to get a flint lock mended, it may cause the loss of their hunting season.

Adapted from **The Writings of Benjamin Franklin,** Albert H. Smyth, ed. (New York: The Macmillan Co., 1905), Vol. III, pp. 44–45.

Sir William Johnson, Superintendent of Indian Affairs for the Northern District, to an Aide, July 22, 1755

You are ordered to travel to the Seneca Country by the first of August next and you shall repair their arms, axes, and tools in the best manner you can.

Adapted from **The Papers of Sir William Johnson,** James Sullivan, ed. (Albany: The University of the State of New York, 1921), Vol. 1, p. 765.

George Washington to Colonel Joshua Fry, May 23, 1754

All the Indians that come to our camp expect presents . . . if you want one or more for any particular service . . . they must be bought. The Indian that accompanied me down the river would go no further than . . . about ten miles, till I promised him a ruffled shirt, which I must take from my own, and a *matchcoat.**

Matchcoat is an Indian coat made of blanket-like material.

Conversation with an Aged Delaware Indian, 1771

Adapted from Rev. John Hecke-welder, **History, Manners and Customs of the Indian Nations,** pp. 202–203.

Europeans are ingenious. They make many wonderful things that we need and use, but our forefathers did without guns, brass kettles, and woolen shirts, and we have never heard that they were the worse for it. Our forefathers were ingenious, too. They made axes of stone, arrow points from flint, and hoes and shovels from shoulder blades of elk and buffalo. They were not in want for anything. Game was abundant and tame. Arrow shots did not frighten game then as gun shots now do. We had everything we required. We were happy.

Journal of a Fur Trader among the Indians on the North Shore of Lake Superior, 1778

From George Irving Quimby, **Indian Life in the Upper Great Lakes, 11,000 B.C. to A.D. 1800.** © 1960 by The University of Chicago Press, Published 1960, p. 154.

I traded for their skins and furs and gave them some rum, with which they had a frolic which lasted three days and nights; on this occasion five men were killed, and one woman dreadfully burned.

On Indian Dress in the 1780's

In ancient times the dress of Indians was made of animal skins and feathers. This type of clothing was not only warmer but lasted longer than any of the woolen goods they have since purchased from Europeans. They made coats of fur and petticoats, shirts, leggings, and shoes of deerskin. The present dress of Indians consists of blankets, shirts, leggings, and petticoats all made of cloth purchased from Europeans. Some of the shirts are plain and some are ruffled. Women line their petticoats and blankets with choice ribbons of various colors.

Adapted from Rev. John Hecke-welder, **History, Manners and Customs of the Indian Nations,** pp. 191–192.

16   TESTIMONY OF ARCHAEOLOGY

Archaeological data illustrating the culture state of Indians of the Upper Great Lakes during the seventeenth and eighteenth centuries has been recovered from sites throughout the region. Remains of European trade goods and Indian artifacts are usually found together in seventeenth and early eighteenth century excavations. George I. Quimby's description of archaeological remains recovered from late eighteenth century Upper Great Lakes Indian burial mounds reveals a thoroughly changed situation.

While reading this summary of archaeological findings, keep in mind the following questions:

A48

Old Hendrick, or Tiyanoga, was a fashion-conscious Chief of the Mohawks who was known to the English as "Emperor of the Six Nations." He is shown here in his Indian attire and in the modish colonial garb which he enjoyed wearing.

1. How many different kinds of archaeological remains have been found in the burial mounds described in this reading? How would you classify them?

2. What inferences about the effect of European trade goods upon the ways Indians lived and worked are suggested by your classification?

Burial Customs

Burial customs among the Upper Great Lakes Indian tribes during the period 1760 to 1820 were essentially the same as they had been in earlier periods. The deceased were placed in both extended and flexed positions either in graves dug into sandy knolls and ridges or in graves dug into existing ancient burial mounds. What was most different about these late eighteenth century burials was the fact that most of the weapons, tools, utensils, and ornaments placed in the grave with the deceased had been purchased from European traders.

A man, for example, would be buried with his loaded flintlock gun; a beaded pouch of bullets; extra gun flints; an iron ax; white clay tobacco pipes made in Scotland; silver armbands, *gorgets,** and ear ornaments made in London or Montreal; a glass bottle of peppermint oil for his stomach; a flint and steel (strike-a-light) and *punk** for starting fires; pewter dishes of food; powdered vermillion face paint; and any other thing that might be useful to him in the world of spirits.

An Indian woman might well be buried with her brass kettles; silver brooches; necklaces of colored beads; Chinese blue and white porcelain or Staffordshire china from England; an iron ax for chopping wood; a hand mirror; a *jew's harp** and other furnishings believed necessary in the spirit world.

Gorgets were large ornaments worn around the neck by men or women.

Punk is an Algonkin word used to describe decayed, dried wood, which served as tinder wood to start fires.

Jew's harp is a small lyre-shaped instrument which, when placed between teeth, gives tones when struck by the finger.

From George Irving Quimby, **Indian Life in the Upper Great Lakes, 11,000 B.C. to A.D. 1800,** pp. 156–157.

A49

8 Indians and great power conflicts, 1607–1713

Patrons and Dependents

Introduction

When the Europeans came to eastern North America, three different groups arrived at approximately the same time, and one group came later. This assignment examines the roles that Indians and Europeans played in each other's politics. Under Captain John Smith, the English founded Jamestown in 1607. Under Samuel de Champlain, the French explored the St. Lawrence River and founded Quebec in 1608. And under Henry Hudson, the Dutch entered the river bearing his name and explored its length for more than one hundred miles in 1609. The Swedes arrived on the Delaware and established Fort Christina in 1633.

Within forty years of the Jamestown foundation, these modest beginnings grew into a chain of permanent settlements and trading posts of approximately 55,000 persons. They extended from the St. Lawrence River in the north to the James River in the south.

Four European groups had come to North America to stay, but they did not come in equal numbers. By 1650 there were about 45,000 Englishmen and 1,000 Africans in Virginia, Maryland, and New England; 5,000 Dutch and 500 Africans in New Netherlands or what came to be New York and New Jersey; 3,000 French in Quebec and other settlements along the St. Lawrence; and perhaps 200 Swedes on the Delaware.

This battle, fought near what is now known as **Lake Champlain**, marked one of earliest uses of guns in an Indian war.

Early Indian-European Relations

During the first forty years of settlement, European relations with the Indians developed slowly and painfully. At first these relations were determined largely by the way the Indian tribes got along together politically. For example, tribes at war with each other were often friendly and helpful to the Europeans, hoping that the white men with powerful weapons would become their allies and crush their enemies.

Examples of inter-tribal politics affecting European relations with Indians are Champlain's celebrated participation in a Huron raid* against the Iroquois in 1609, and the Pequot War in New England in 1637. When Champlain used his guns against the Iroquois, he took sides in an existing Indian quarrel, and those few shots were answered by much fire and bloodshed in the years that followed.

The circumstances of the Pequot War were somewhat different, but the war itself was no less a consequence of differences and resentments among Indians. The English settlers of the Connecticut Valley attacked the Pequots and were enthusiastically assisted in the destruction of that tribe by the Mohegans and Narragansets. These two tribes had suffered at the hands of the Pequots in the past, and they marched with the English settlers against their common enemy.

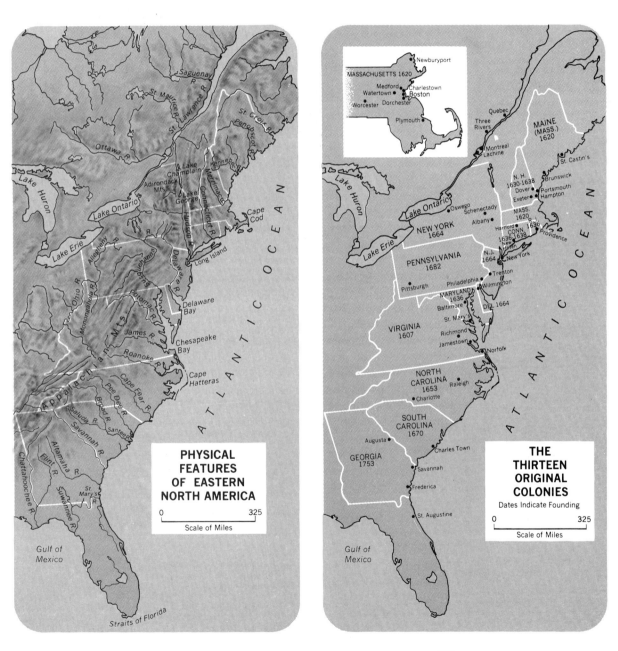

PHYSICAL FEATURES OF EASTERN NORTH AMERICA

0 — 325
Scale of Miles

THE THIRTEEN ORIGINAL COLONIES

Dates Indicate Founding

0 — 325
Scale of Miles

Changed Relations

Later, Indian-European relations were determined largely by the ways the Indians reacted to European behavior and to the expansion of foreign settlements. Indian reactions occurred most frequently in the coastal regions. As more Europeans arrived and as more land was fenced and more fishing sites taken over, the feelings of the Indians changed from those of tolerance and curiosity to hatred and violence.

One example was Chief Opechancanough's massacre of 350 Virginians in 1622. That attack was followed by twenty-two years of intermittent but fierce warfare, ending with Opechancanough's death and the displacement of most of the Indians from coastal Virginia.

Another example of Indians reacting to European behavior followed Dutch Governor Willem Kiefft's massacre of eighty Raritan Indians on Long Island in 1643. That attack resulted in two years of warfare that forced many Dutch settlers to return to Holland. It almost destroyed the entire province of New Netherlands.

Incidents like those two massacres and the wars that followed them convinced many Europeans and Indians that relations between them as *individuals* could be either good or bad. But relations between *groups of Europeans* and *groups of Indians* were best only when there were many miles of distance between them.

During the second forty years of settlement, group hatred and violence continued generally to characterize Indian-European relations. Important exceptions were William Penn's Quaker settlements in New Jersey and eastern Pennsylvania.

Elsewhere in North America, inter-tribal politics and Indian resentment of European encroachment upon hunting and trapping grounds led to full-scale war. In the north, the French paid dearly for their friendship and aid to the Hurons. One after another, French outposts and missions fell to the Iroquois, who had turned against the French after crushing the Hurons. Montreal itself was threatened, and raiders came within a short march of Quebec. Not until 1665, when 1,000 battle-hardened regular troops of the crack French Carignan-Salières regiment were sent to Canada, were Iroquois raids checked. These disciplined veterans of many European wars invaded and ravaged Iroquois lands for two years before the tribes made peace and allowed French exploration and expansion into the interior.

In New England, Wampanoag warriors under their gifted chief, King Philip, tried to preserve what remained of their hunting grounds and fishing sites in southern Massachusetts. Starting in 1675, they tried to drive the English into the sea. Joined by neighboring tribes, the Indians escalated the conflict, and soon full-scale war raged from Maine to Rhode Island. Farms were destroyed, towns were burned, and ten percent of the entire European population of New England were casualties. *

Finally, by the summer of 1676, English firepower and organization prevailed. King Philip was trapped and killed. Captured Indian leaders, in-

The **turning point** of the war was the wholesale massacre of Indians by the English at the Great Swamp Fight in Rhode Island on Sunday, December 19, 1675.

A52

In August, 1676, King Philip was trapped in Assowamset Swamp near Mount Hope, Massachusetts, by an Indian named Alderman, who betrayed him to Capt. Benjamin Church. Alderman killed Philip, and Church ordered the head and hands cut off and the body quartered. Philip's head hung on a pole in Plymouth, his hands were sent to Boston. His men were either killed or captured and sold into slavery. Indian power in southern New England was ended forever.

cluding Philip's wife and son, were sold and exported to the West Indies as slaves. Broken remnants of defeated tribes were moved onto special tracts of land where they could be watched and controlled.

By 1690, the European presence in North America had changed and grown enormously. The Dutch had displaced the Swedes in 1655, and the English had displaced the Dutch in 1664. The English had established settlements along the Atlantic coast as far north as the Kennebec River in Maine, and as far south as Charleston, South Carolina. French forts overlooked all of the Great Lakes, and French explorers had penetrated deep into the Mississippi River valley.

During the second forty years of settlement, the population of the European settlements increased sharply, but most of the increase was English and African. In 1690, there were about 195,000 Europeans and 15,000 Africans in English America, and only 10,000 Europeans in French America.

Anglo-French Relations

The same years that witnessed so much strife between Indians and Europeans in North America also saw a decisive change in political relations between England and France. From 1660 to 1680, relations were generally good. French cultural influences were strong in England, and both countries fought successful wars separately and together against the Dutch. However, a political revolution broke out in England in 1688, and the English Crown was given to the ruler of Holland, William of Orange. England and France then went to war.

This change of policy in 1688 proved to be a permanent one. In the course of the next seventy-five years, England and France fought four major wars. The first two of these wars—King William's War (1689–1697) and Queen

Anne's War (1702–1713)—were fought largely over European issues. The last two—King George's War (1744–1748) and the Seven Years' War (1756–1763)—were fought mainly over American issues. In each of these wars, whether American issues were directly involved or not, battles were fought in North America, and Indians participated in them.

The Indian Role in the Great Power Struggle

Great Power politics was the struggle between England and France for trade and territory in North America.

After 1688, relations between Europeans and Indians ceased being merely matters of trade advantages and local security arrangements. Instead, they became major questions of *Great Power politics** that were brought before the heads of European states for decision.

Issues and military requirements of Great Power politics brought crowned heads and Indian chiefs together as patrons and dependents. Kings acknowledged the Indians as their adopted children. Indians recognized the monarchs of France and England as their adopted fathers. However, the relationship between patron and dependent was a delicate one, and during the next seventy-five years it is difficult to be sure who did the commanding and who did the obeying. Some Indians fought for the French, some fought for the English. Others fought for both sides, and some did not fight at all. Many Indians died for King William of England or King Louis of France.

Knowing why the Indians chose to participate in Great Power conflicts at all, and knowing how they decided whom to fight and when to fight, is important. Those decisions helped determine the political future of North America.

Objectives are to:

—Examine given testimony on Indian participation in Great Power conflicts and draw inferences from it.

—Form a hypothesis from your inferences about why Indians chose to participate in Great Power conflicts.

—Examine given testimony on late seventeenth century Iroquois relations with England and France, draw inferences from it, and form a hypothesis about when and how the Iroquois decided which country to support.

—Make additions or modifications to your hypothesis as other given testimony and inferences drawn from it may require.

17   KING WILLIAM'S WAR, 1689–1697

In October, 1688, war broke out in Europe as France fought against an alliance of England, the Netherlands, several German states, and Sweden. King Louis XIV of France hoped to carve out more territory for his country from Germany. When the war spread to America, it was known as King William's War.

The first North American actions of King William's War began in the summer of 1689. On behalf of the French, tribes of the Abnaki confederation of northern New England burned Dover, New Hampshire, and captured Fort Pemaquid in Maine. On behalf of the English, an Iroquois war party destroyed the French village of La Chine, near Montreal. A few months later Schenectady, New York, and Salmon Falls, New Hampshire, met the same fate as Dover.

Except for an unsuccessful naval attack on Quebec by New Englanders in 1690, the war in North America settled down to eight years of raids and counter-raids on frontier communities. The fighting contributed very little toward a meaningful victory for either side.

While reading the accounts of military actions and statements of Indian leaders presented below, keep in mind the following questions:

1. *Which Indians supported the French? Why?*
2. *Which Indians supported the English? Why?*
3. *What inferences about Indian participation in Great Power conflicts are suggested by these accounts and statements?*

Account of a French Expedition against the Iroquois, October 15–23, 1687

We burned the village and the remainder of the day was spent burning corn. We destroyed the grain of a small village. By noon we finished destroying Indian corn in four villages and estimated it would amount to many thousands of bushels. We can infer from what we have done that suffering of these villages from this devastation shall be very great.

Adapted from **Documents Relative to the Colonial History of the State of New York** (Albany: Weed, Parsons and Company, 1851), Vol. X, pp. 367–368.

Account of the Surrender of Pemaquid Fort in Maine to the Eastern Indians, August 3, 1689

With relief being hopeless, Lieutenant Weems agreed to negotiate with the Indians on conditions of life. Weems found that the Indians were all well armed with new French *fusees*,* waist belts and cutlasses, and most of them with bayonet and pistol, grey and black hats on their heads, and some of them with colored wigs.

The Indians said the English governor was a great rogue and had nearly starved them last winter, that they hated New England people, and shall have their country by and by.

Fusee: A flintlock firearm used by infantrymen before the invention of the rifle.

Adapted from **Calendar of State Papers, Colonial. 1689–1692**, His Majesty's Stationery Office (London, 1901), pp. 114–115.

Speech of an Iroquois Chief to English Agents at a Meeting in Albany, New York, September 25, 1689

We have a hundred and forty men scouting about Canada; it is impossible for the French to attempt anything without being discovered and harassed by these parties. If the French attempt anything in this region, we will come to your assistance. Brothers, we are but one, and we will live and die together. The Great God of Heaven knows how deceitful the French have been to us. Their arms can have no success. The Great God has sent us signs in the sky to confirm this. Take courage, brothers; all we require to destroy the French is courage, courage, courage.

Adapted from Cadwallader Colden, **The History of the Five Nations** (New York: New Amsterdam Book Company, 1902), Vol. I, p. 126.

Answer of the Iroquois to the Governor of New York at Albany, June 1, 1691

We beg that traders may be ordered to enlarge bags of powder, so that ammunition may be had at a reasonable price. We asked for this before, but no

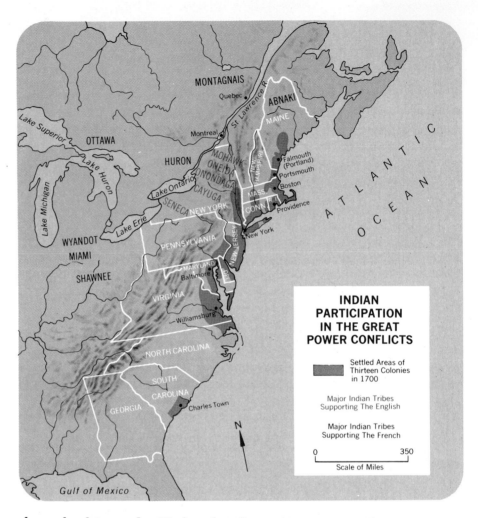

INDIAN
PARTICIPATION
IN THE GREAT
POWER CONFLICTS

Settled Areas of
Thirteen Colonies
in 1700

Major Indian Tribes
Supporting The English

Major Indian Tribes
Supporting The French

0   350
Scale of Miles

change has been made. We beg that if our squaws come without money for rum for our captives and soldiers, it may be supplied to them. Our blacksmith at *Onondaga*° has left us, and we want another to help keep our arms mended. We will prosecute the war with all possible vigor, as you order us, and will keep Canada in perpetual alarm. We are but a weak people without you; pray write to the Great King to send great ships with great guns to take Canada, and then we can all live in peace. We are surprised you say nothing of the help that we may expect from New England, Virginia, and Maryland.

Onondaga: Upstate New York in the Syracuse area.

Adapted from **Calendar of State Papers, Colonial, 1689–1692,** pp. 460–461.

Answer of the Delaware Indians to the Governor of Pennsylvania, May 10, 1693

We desire peace with all of the Indians that belong to any English plantation in America and desire your Excellency to persuade the Iroquois from doing us harm in our hunting as was done last summer. We will be one heart and true to the English and to one another.

Adapted from the **Minutes of the Provincial Council of Pennsylvania,** Vol. I, pp. 372–373.

18   KING WILLIAM'S PEACE

The war ended in 1697, but it proved to be only a truce. In both Europe and North America the political situation at the end of the war was virtually the same as it had been in 1688. All of the participants in the war expected an early renewal of hostilities. As principal combatants in the North American phases of the war, the Iroquois suffered heavy casualties.

The prospect of another war in which Iroquois warriors would again do much of the actual fighting encouraged a re-thinking of Iroquois policy toward the Great Powers. Between the end of King William's War in 1697 and the outbreak of Queen Anne's War in Europe in 1702, the Iroquois reexamined their relations with France and England.

While reading the following statements of Indian leaders presented below, keep in mind the following questions:

1. What persuaded the Iroquois to reexamine their policy of fighting the French?

2. What words would you use to describe Iroquois policy toward the French and English in 1700 and 1701?

3. What inferences about Iroquois relations with the Great Powers are suggested by these statements?

Answer of an Iroquois Chief to an English Agent, 1696

You set us on daily to fight and destroy your enemies and bid us go with courage, but we see not that you do anything yourselves. Neither do we see any great strength you have to oppose the enemy. We hear of no great matter being done at sea. The war must be hotly pursued on your side. What do our neighbors in New England and the other English do? They all stay at home and set us on to do the work.

Adapted from L. H. Leder, ed., "The Livingston Indian Records, 1666–1723," **Pennsylvania History,** XXIII (January, 1956), p. 165.

Answer of the Iroquois to the Governor of New York at Albany, August 27, 1700

We are firmly determined to hold fast to the covenant made with the English, and that if the Great King of England will defend us against the *Twightwees** and other nations over whom the French have an influence and who murdered several of our people since the peace, we will have nothing to do with the French.

Adapted from **An Abridgment of the Indian Affairs, Contained in Four Folio Volumes, Transacted in the Colony of New York, from the Year 1678 to the Year 1751,** by Peter Wraxall; C. H. McIlwain, ed. (Harvard University Press, 1915), pp. 33–34.

Answer of the Iroquois to the Governor of New France at Montreal, September 3, 1700

We now tell you that there is not anyone on the warpath, nor desirous to go on it, we have laid all hatchets aside. You and the English have made peace,

Twightwees, original tribal name for the Miamis, who inhabited the Midwest and were of Algonkin linguistic stock.

and you have told us we should oppose all who violate it. The English seem desirous of creating disturbances. They forbid us to listen to your words, yet we have come to Montreal.

We should like to take a blacksmith back with us to Fort Frontenac and should like you to send some goods there to be sold at Montreal prices.

The English Governor is becoming ill-humored, he may indeed create disturbances. We would therefore wish to have the protection of your guns at Fort Frontenac.

Adapted from **Documents Relative to the Colonial History of the State of New York**, Vol. IX, p. 716.

Conveyance of a Tract of Land Claimed by the Iroquois to King William III, July 19, 1701

This tract is eight hundred miles long and four hundred miles wide and runs northwest by west of Albany and includes all of the land between the Lakes called by the Christians Erie, Huron, and Michigan.

Our ancestors conquered these lands from the Hurons, and we have been sole masters of them for sixty years. Lately, the Governor of Canada has encouraged some Hurons to return and has sent a strong force to Detroit, the principal pass commanding the said lands, to build a fort without our permission. The French and the Hurons will possess themselves of that excellent country and shall deprive us of our livelihood.

We freely and voluntarily surrender and deliver up unto our Great Lord and Master the King of England these lands provided we have free hunting for us and our descendants forever and provided that we are protected from all others in our hunting rights by the Crown of England.

Adapted from **Calendar of State Papers, Colonial, 1701,** pp. 454–455.

19   QUEEN ANNE'S WAR, 1702-1713

In 1702 war broke out again in Europe between France and the Grand Alliance of the Holy Roman Empire, England, Holland, and others. The first North American actions in the war did not begin until the summer of 1703 when an Abnaki war party led by a few Frenchmen attacked the coastal village of Wells, Maine. Unlike the previous war, there was no immediate counterattack upon French settlements by Indians friendly to the English.

Next, the exposed Connecticut Valley town of Deerfield, Massachusetts, was attacked by Indians in the autumn of 1703 and destroyed in February 1704. Once established, the pattern of silent approach, sudden attack, and destruction by fire was repeated all over New England.

Apart from some vigorous fighting in Maine in 1704, English offensive military activities in North America were undistinguished and generally unsuccessful. The war was won on the battlefields of western Europe largely through a series of brilliant victories by England's Duke of Marlborough.

Deerfield Massacre—Indians launched a surprise attack on the town of Deerfield in 1703 and burned it to the ground. A few days later a company of ninety settlers were ambushed while attempting to save the town's grain supply. Only eight men out of the entire company escaped. The rest were either killed or taken into captivity.

Fighting ended with the signing of the Treaty of Utrecht in 1713. For North America the results were minimal. The treaty transferred what is now Nova Scotia, Newfoundland, and the Hudson Bay region from French to English rule and recognized the English protectorate over the Iroquois. But French power remained formidable, and relations with the Indians after almost twenty years of conflict continued as uncertain as ever.

While reading the selections from English dispatches on Indian relations during the early part of Queen Anne's War, keep in mind the following questions:

1. *How did Iroquois neutrality in the war affect New York?*
2. *How did Iroquois neutrality in the war affect New England?*
3. *How did the policy of neutrality affect the Iroquois?*

A59

Dispatch from Albany to London, August 10, 1703

The advantages attending Her Majesty's plantations in North America from the steadiness and firmness of the Iroquois have been many. They have fought our battles for us and have been a constant barrier of defense against the French. But the late long war and the great losses they suffered in it has dispirited them. The French have used all of their ingenuity to gain them to their side or to terrify them into inaction by fear of French power.

The French make ill impressions on their minds and entice them to their forts for trade. Our Indian trade has fallen to a fifth part of what it was formerly.

We have had no mischief from the French or from their Indians in this region since the war was proclaimed, but it is every day expected.

Dispatch from Boston to London, July 13, 1704

It has been customary for this province once in a few years to conciliate and confirm our friendship with the Iroquois, and accordingly have provided a present of about £500 which is necessary to keep them steady.

Dispatch from Boston to London, October 10, 1704

We have messengers in treaty with the Iroquois and hope that they will continue steady, if we cannot prevail with them to take up the hatchet against the French as they call the war.

Dispatch from Albany to London, July 8, 1705

Fifty *Fusiliers** must be sent to Albany for defense of the frontier for one year. This is absolutely necessary at this time because we have received an account of a design of the Wauwaughtanees Indians and other nations friendly to the French to attack the Iroquois. If the Iroquois see that we are unwilling or unable to defend them against their enemies, the more easily they will be persuaded to go over to the French.

Dispatch from Boston to London, May 3, 1708

This province and New Hampshire has borne the brunt of this war because New York has in no measure joined our assistance against the common enemy. Nor has New York encouraged the Iroquois to hostility against the French. Instead New York trades with the French Indians of Canada and with those of the eastern parts who have made bloody incursions upon us. The governor of New York refused to support our efforts to move the Iroquois to take up arms against the French. We humbly request the Queen to direct him to do so, otherwise this province shall be in great danger of being ruined.

Fusiliers: Soldiers armed with fusils.

Adapted from the **Calendar of State Papers, Colonial, 1702–1708.**

9 Pontiac's war

Deciding for War

Introduction

The end of the war in 1713 was followed by thirty years of uneasy peace in North America during which time European settlements expanded at an unprecedented rate. By 1760 the population of English settlements grew to 1,267,000 Europeans, and 325,000 Africans. French settlements increased only to 70,000. Steady European encroachment upon Indian hunting grounds all along the frontiers of English North America forced most of the eastern tribes into more complicated political arrangements with the Great Powers. Again the Iroquois took the lead. They continued to seek trade advantages and military assistance from the English, while allowing the French to build a fort at Niagara in Seneca country.

In 1744 France and England were facing one another in war in Europe for the fourth time in half a century. Except for some occasional Indian raids, major North American actions were not undertaken in King George's War until 1745 when the New Englanders captured the great French fortress of *Louisbourg** on Cape Breton Island. The French and their Indian allies retaliated by burning Saratoga and spreading terror throughout the northern Hudson Valley. The Abnaki returned to coastal Maine and destroyed the villages of Waldoboro and Kennebec.

The Iroquois remained neutral until late 1746 when they were persuaded to move against the French. They did so unenthusiastically and slowly. However, events in America did not affect the outcome of King George's War. It ended in Europe in 1748, and the Treaty of Aix-la-Chapelle restored Louisbourg to the French and a temporary peace to the northern frontier of English America. Nothing had been settled; nothing had changed; no one doubted that war would come again very soon.

For North America, Aix-la-Chapelle proved to be nothing more than a brief truce. Four years later (1752), a French-led Indian attack on an English trading post at Pickawillany on the Miami River reopened hostilities in North America. The next year, a French military expedition began building a chain of barrier forts running from Lake Erie to the Forks of the Ohio River against further English penetration of the Appalachians.

In 1754 a strong French force drove away a group of Virginians from the Forks of the Ohio River and constructed a wilderness stronghold at that strategic point, which they named Fort Duquesne. Later in the year, the Virginians returned to the Forks with a small force under Colonel George Wash-

The town and fort of **Louisbourg** was constructed by the French in 1720 and was regarded by Englishmen and Frenchmen alike as being the key to North America. The fortress was destroyed by the English in 1758 and is presently being restored by the Canadian Government as a historical monument.

ington. They were defeated and forced to withdraw. Everywhere along the frontier, Englishmen reported Indians were showing hostile signs.

The Albany Conference

Representatives from New York, Pennsylvania, Maryland, and New England met in Albany in June, 1754, to develop plans for inter-colonial unity and cooperation against their common enemies and to improve relations with the Iroquois.* On both counts, the Albany Conference failed. First, a plan to unite all colonies of English America under a president appointed by the king was presented and rejected. Second, discussions with Iroquois chiefs failed to budge them from their policy of neutrality.

In 1755 the wisdom of Iroquois policy appeared confirmed when General Edward Braddock led a force of 2,000 English regular troops and colonial militia against French positions on the Ohio River. Within ten miles of Fort Duquesne, Braddock ran into a well prepared force of 950 French, Ottawas, Shawnees, Delawares, and Wyandots who decisively defeated the English force. Braddock's defeat was the beginning of a fierce French and Indian campaign against the frontier settlements of Pennsylvania and Virginia. Hundreds of families had to abandon their farms and seek protection in the east.

By 1756, eight years after Aix-la-Chapelle, the Seven Years' War broke out in Europe. But it did not alter the course of events in America. French military victories followed one another in rapid succession. A French and Indian force burned *Fort Oswego** on the Great Lakes in 1756; Fort William Henry on Lake George fell in 1757; and as late as July, 1758, French arms turned back a major English assault against Fort Ticonderoga between Lakes Champlain and George. However, by 1758 William Pitt's appointment as war minister and English naval superiority began to change the conduct and outcome of the war. Reinforcements, military supplies, and trade goods were cut off from the French, but flowed in ever-increasing quantities to the English.

As the number of English victories at sea increased and supplies of trade goods in the interior of North America diminished, the Iroquois were persuaded to reexamine their policy of neutrality. Bands of Mohawks participated in English campaigns on a regular basis in 1758. More important than Iroquois military actions against the French was their influence on other tribes. At a meeting near Easton, Pennsylvania, in October, 1758, the Iroquois claimed a right to dictate policy to the Delawares and proclaimed an end to Delaware hostilities with the English. After Easton, Indian support in Pennsylvania shifted from the French to the English.

By the end of 1758 the English had retaken Louisbourg and Fort Frontenac. The French abandoned Fort Duquesne to the English, who renamed it Fort Pitt. Fort Niagara surrendered to a force of English and Iroquois in 1759. Ticonderoga and Crown Point were abandoned, and finally in September, 1759, Quebec itself fell into English hands. The subsequent downfall of Montreal and the surrender of all Canada followed in due course. The war ended with the Treaty of Paris, 1763.

A62

At the **Albany Conference** an Oneida chief suggested to the colonial delegates that they use the Iroquois Confederation as a model for inter-colonial unity.

Oswego, on Lake Ontario, was an important trading center on the Great Lakes in colonial days.

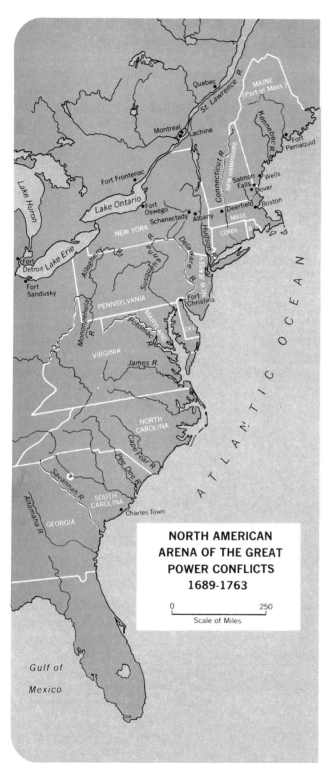

NORTH AMERICAN ARENA OF THE GREAT POWER CONFLICTS 1689-1763

0   250
Scale of Miles

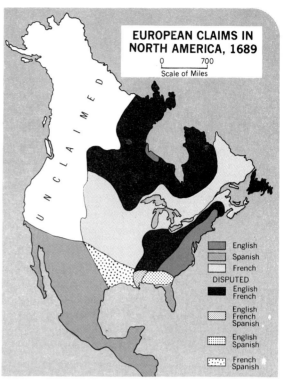

EUROPEAN CLAIMS IN NORTH AMERICA, 1689

0   700
Scale of Miles

English
Spanish
French
DISPUTED
English French
English French Spanish
English French Spanish
English Spanish
French Spanish

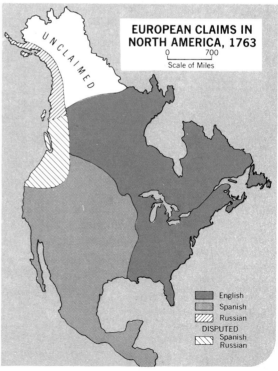

EUROPEAN CLAIMS IN NORTH AMERICA, 1763

0   700
Scale of Miles

English
Spanish
Russian
DISPUTED
Spanish Russian

To the Indians who had fought for the French in this war and in King George's War, or who knew the history of the earlier wars of King William and Queen Anne, the collapse of French power in 1759 was a profound shock. The French were gone. The Ottawas, Chippewas, Wyandots, Miamis, Potawatomis, Delawares, and even Senecas wondered about their future with only one set of European neighbors, the English. With the end of the Great Power conflicts in North America, they had lost the opportunities to advance their economic and political interests.

The Rise of Pontiac

The period of shock and wonder was brief. If the prospect of the new age was uncertain and unwanted, why shouldn't the Indians join together and fight to restore the old? The ink on the treaty between England and France ending the war was scarcely dry in May, 1763, when nearly every Indian tribe north of the Ohio River made war against the English. Suddenly and without warning, approximately 7,000 warriors, more than had ever fought for the French, attacked every English fortified outpost between the Mackinac Straits and the Susquehanna River.

The success of those attacks was astonishing, but even more astonishing was the report that one Indian leader was directing them all. His name was Pontiac, and for six years he was North America's most celebrated person. Settlers feared him; soldiers fought him; statesmen sought to appease and content him.

Knowing why so many Indians decided to challenge the greatest military and naval power in the world, knowing why this war broke out when and where it did, is historically important knowledge. Knowledge of Pontiac's War is important, also, for what it reveals about the ways great leaders persuade men to wage war.

Objectives are to:

—Draw inferences about Indian politics and war aims from a chronology of events for May and June, 1763, and from a map of the battle areas.

—Form a hypothesis from your inferences about why so many tribes decided to war against the English in 1763.

—Make additions or modifications to your hypothesis about why so many Indian tribes decided to war against the English.

20 BATTLE AREAS AND TACTICS IN PONTIAC'S WAR

The extent of Indian attacks on English outposts and settlements in North America at the outset of Pontiac's War surprised and frightened the civil and military officials responsible for the government and defense of the interior of North America. The map of outposts and settlements and the chronology of events for the months of May and June, 1763, presented here suggest reasons for that surprise and fright. While examining this map and chronology, keep in mind the following questions:

1. What inferences about Indian politics are suggested by the number of tribes participating in the attacks on English forts?

A64

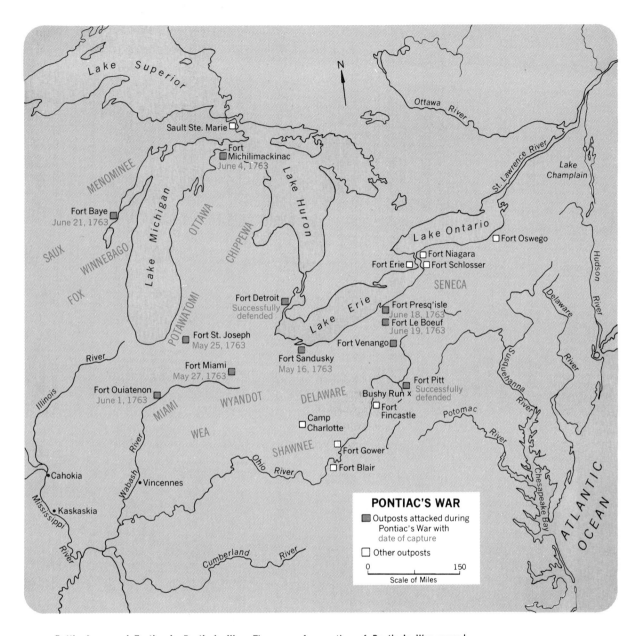

Map labels:
Lake Superior
Ottawa River
N
Sault Ste. Marie
Fort Michilimackinac June 4, 1763
MENOMINEE
Lake Huron
CHIPPEWA
OTTAWA
Fort Baye June 21, 1763
SAUX
WINNEBAGO
FOX
POTAWATOMI
Lake Michigan
Lake Ontario
St. Lawrence River
Lake Champlain
Fort Oswego
Fort Niagara
Fort Erie
Fort Schlosser
SENECA
Hudson River
Fort Detroit Successfully defended
Lake Erie
Fort Presq'isle June 18, 1763
Fort Le Boeuf June 19, 1763
Delaware River
Fort St. Joseph May 25, 1763
Fort Venango
Fort Sandusky May 16, 1763
Fort Miami May 27, 1763
River
Fort Ouiatenon June 1, 1763
MIAMI
WYANDOT
DELAWARE
Fort Pitt Successfully defended
Bushy Run x
Fort Fincastle
Susquehanna River
Potomac River
WEA
Wabash River
Camp Charlotte
SHAWNEE
Ohio River
Fort Gower
Fort Blair
Cahokia
Vincennes
Mississippi River
Kaskaskia
Cumberland River
ATLANTIC OCEAN
Chesapeake Bay
Illinois

PONTIAC'S WAR
- Outposts attacked during Pontiac's War with date of capture
- Other outposts
0 ——— 150
Scale of Miles

Battle Areas and Tactics in Pontiac's War—The area of operation of Pontiac's War ranged through the Great Lakes region and extended from the Mississippi to New York and Pennsylvania.

2. *What inferences about military preparations are suggested by the tactics and timing of the attacks?*

3. *What inferences about Indian war aims are suggested by the locations of the places attacked?*

Chronology of Events for May and June, 1763

	ATTACKED OR BESIEGED	CAPTURED	TRIBES	TACTICS
Fort Detroit	May 7, 1763	Successfully defended	Ottawas Chippewas Potawatomis Wyandots	Infiltration of fort by Indians with concealed weapons. Not captured.
Fort Sandusky	May 16, 1763	May 16, 1763	Wyandots	Infiltration of fort by Indians with concealed weapons. Christopher Pauly,* garrison commander, the only survivor.
Fort St. Joseph	May 25, 1763	May 25, 1763	Potawatomis	Infiltration of fort by Indians with concealed weapons. Only 4 of a 14-man garrison survived.
Fort Miami	May 27, 1763	May 27, 1763	Miamis	Fort commander enticed out of fort on pretext of aiding sick Indians. Only 1 survivor.
Fort Ouiatonon	June 1, 1763	June 1, 1763	Weas Miamis	Surrender on condition that lives of garrison be spared.
Fort Michilimackinac	June 4, 1763	June 4, 1763	Chippewas Fox	Infiltration of fort during a game of lacrosse. Only 13 of a 95-man garrison survived.
Fort Presqu'isle	June 15, 1763	June 18, 1763	Ottawas Delawares Senecas	Direct assault followed by surrender of garrison. Only 3 of the 27-man garrison survived.
Fort LaBaye	June 16, 1763	June 21, 1763	Sauk Fox Winnebago Menominee	Surrender on condition that lives of garrison be spared.
Fort LeBoeuf	June 19, 1763	June 19, 1763	Senecas Delawares	Direct assault of fort abandoned by garrison; 1 killed; 12 escaped.
Fort Venango	June 19, 1763	June 19, 1763	Senecas	Infiltration of fort by Indians presumed to be friendly. No survivors.
Fort Pitt, formerly Fort Duquesne	June 22, 1763	Successfully defended	Delawares Shawnees Wyandots	Negotiation for surrender followed by direct assault. Not captured.

21 PONTIAC—OTTAWA WARRIOR

Pontiac—Ottawa Chief

Englishmen who saw and heard Pontiac, the Ottawa Chief, at Detroit in 1763 described him as about fifty years old, vigorous and imposing in appearance, and a skillful and experienced warrior. He had fought against General Braddock in Pennsylvania in 1755, and raided English settlements as far east as Lake Champlain in 1757. All accounts agree that Pontiac was a brilliant orator, a talent highly valued by Indians and one absolutely indispensable for persuading different Indian tribes to act together against a common enemy.

Pontiac demonstrated his oratorical talents on many occasions. Some of the more memorable ones were recorded in a diary of a French Catholic priest present at a series of war councils held by Ottawas, Potawatomies, Wyandots, and Objibwas shortly before the attack on Detroit.

According to this diary, Pontiac began his speeches by referring to a prayer attributed to a Delaware prophet who dreamed he had traveled to heaven and talked with the Great Spirit. He ended them with a ringing call to arms against the English. While reading these selections from Pontiac's speeches, keep in mind the following questions:

1. According to Pontiac, how are the English different from the French?

2. According to Pontiac, why should the war council decide for war against the English?

3. Why do you think Pontiac included Wolf's* prayer in his speech?

Pontiac's plan to capture **Fort Detroit** (chronology, opposite page) was betrayed to Major Henry Gladwin, the fort commander, by an Indian woman.

Wolf was the name of the Delaware prophet.

Pontiac and the Delaware Prayer

Brothers, remember the prayer which the Great Spirit commanded our brother, Wolf, to teach to all of the Indians.

Do not drink more than once, or at most only twice, a day.
Have only one wife and do not run after the wives of others or after the girls.
Do not fight amongst yourselves.
Do not sell to your brothers what the Great Spirit has put on earth for food.
Drive off your lands those dogs clothed in red.
Do not talk with evil spirits.
Be good and your needs shall be met.
When you meet one another, exchange greetings and offer the left hand, which is nearest the heart.

Brothers, these are the words of the Great Spirit as revealed to our brother, Wolf.

Brothers, it is important that we drive from our lands this *nation** which seeks only to destroy us. You can see as well as I that we can no longer supply our needs from our brothers, the French. The English sell us goods at

Lieutenant Christopher Paully, commander of **Fort Sandusky,** (chronology, opposite page) was spared on the plea of an Indian woman who wanted to adopt him in place of her fallen husband. Paully later escaped from his Indian spouse.

This nation means the English.

Wampum: Shells colored and designed into beads and belts; served as records of ceremonies and laws; used by orators so their words would be remembered. As ornaments, an indication of wealth and power. Shown here is an Iroquois Five Nations war wampum belt.

twice the price asked by our French brothers, and their goods do not last. Scarcely do we buy one blanket before we must think about getting another. When we wish to set out for our winter camps, the English do not give us credit the way our French brothers used to do.

Brothers, when I go to the English comander at Detroit and say that some of our comrades are dead, instead of bewailing their death as our French brothers did, he laughs. If I ask for something for our sick, he refuses with the reply that he has no use for us.

Brothers, from all this you can clearly see the English are seeking our ruin. We must all swear their destruction and wait no longer. Nothing prevents us from destroying them. All the nations who are our brothers attack them—why should not we attack? Are we not men like them? Have I not shown you the *wampum belts** from our father in France? He tells us to strike them.

Remember what the Great Spirit told our brother, Wolf, to do. That concerns us as well as others. I have sent wampum belts and messengers to our brothers, the Chippewas of Saginaw, and to our brothers, the Ottawas of Michilimackinac. They will not be slow in coming, but while we wait let us strike anyway. There is no time to lose. When the English are defeated we shall see what there is left to do, and we shall block their routes and trails so they may never again come upon our lands.

Adapted from **Journal of Pontiac's Conspiracy, 1763,** translated by R. Clyde Ford (Detroit: published by Clarence Monroe Burton, under the auspices of the Michigan Society of Colonial Wars, 1912), pp. 28–32; 38–40.

22 ROYAL PROCLAMATION OF 1763

An attack on Fort Detroit in May, 1763, signalled the start of Pontiac's War. A series of attacks on the Great Lakes frontier posts followed one another. Lord Jeffrey Amherst, head of British military forces in North America, was caught by surprise. But he was quick to react; so was the British government.

Lord Amherst ordered counter-attacks by Colonel Henry Bouquet. King George III issued a Royal Proclamation designed to cool Indian anger.

In August Colonel Bouquet defeated and routed an Indian war party at Bushy Run, a few miles east of Fort Pitt, and relieved the fort. Though Pontiac failed at Detroit and was forced to lift his siege in November, 1763, nearly all the Great Lakes posts fell for a time to the Indians.

Heavy fighting continued into 1765 and 1766, but the great danger was over by 1764 when English officers and Iroquois warriors raided Delaware villages. In July of that year, the Senecas, expecting the same kind of punishment, asked for peace and forgiveness.

Pontiac himself appeared at Fort Oswego in 1766 to negotiate a final peace. Trade arrangements satisfactory to the Indians were offered. Pontiac promised loyalty and peace, and loaded with presents and trade goods, he retired to the west. Three years later, Pontiac was murdered at Cahokia, Illinois, by a <u>Kaskaskia</u> Indian allegedly in the pay of an English trader.*

Pontiac's followers took such violent vengeance for his assassination that they nearly wiped out the **Kaskaskias.**

A68

The peace settlement of 1766 was made possible as much by the Royal Proclamation of 1763, as by vigorous military action in 1764 and 1765. This document had been prepared by Lord Shelburne, the Secretary of State, as early as June, 1763, but was not formally issued in London until October 7, 1763. While reading the selections from the Proclamation of 1763 and studying the map, keep in mind the following questions:

1. *What reasons does the king give for issuing the Proclamation?*
2. *What Indian grievances are recognized in the Proclamation?*
3. *What remedies for Indian grievances does the Proclamation propose?*

0   400
Scale of Miles

The Proclamation Line of 1763
The Proclamation Line established the Appalachian Mountains as a barrier between European settlements and Indian country.

King George's Document

We have taken into our royal consideration the extensive and valuable lands secured to our Crown by the late definitive treaty of peace. Being desirous that all our loving subjects, in England as well as in our colonies in America, may avail themselves of the great benefits and advantages which must *accrue** to their commerce and manufactures, we have thought fit, with the advice of our *Privy Council,** to issue this, our Royal Proclamation.

Whereas it is just and reasonable, and essential to our interest and the security of our colonies, that the several nations or tribes of Indians with whom we are connected and who live under our protection should not be molested or disturbed in the possession of such parts of our dominions and territories as are reserved to them for their hunting grounds; we declare it to be our royal will and pleasure that no Governor or Commander-in-Chief or anyone else in any of our colonies in America shall grant warrants of survey for any lands beyond the source of any of the rivers which flow into the Atlantic from the west or north west; or upon any lands, whatever, which are reserved to the said Indians.

We do further declare it to be our royal will and pleasure, for the present to reserve all the land and territories lying to the westward of the sources of the rivers which fall into the sea from the west and northwest; and we do hereby strictly forbid all our loving subjects from making any purchases or settlements whatever, or taking possession of any of the lands above reserved, without our special leave and license. We do further strictly require all persons whatever, who have seated themselves upon any lands which are still reserved to the said Indians, forthwith to remove themselves from such settlements.*

Whereas, great frauds and abuses have been committed in the purchasing of lands from the Indians, and in order that Indians may be convinced of our justice and determination to remove all reasonable cause of discontent; we strictly enjoin and prohibit any private person from purchasing lands from Indians within those parts of our colonies where settlement is allowed. If at any time, any of the said Indians should be inclined to dispose of the said lands, the same shall be purchased only for us, in our name, at some public meeting or assembly of the said Indians.

Accrue means to increase naturally without unusual or special efforts.

Privy Council—principal advisers to the king.

As early as 1761 Colonel Henry Bouquet had **prohibited European settlement** west of the Allegheny Mountains. But surveys and lobbying for grants in Indian hunting territory continued.

George III, House of Hanover, was king of England during this time, reigning from 1760 to 1820.

Adapted from "The Proclamation of 1763," Annual Register, 1763, 208ff.

And we do declare that trade with the said Indians shall be free and open to all subjects, whatever, provided that traders do take out a license from the Governor and give security to observe such regulations as we shall at any time think fit to direct and appoint for the benefit of the said trade, and take special care that such license shall be void and the security forfeited in case of refusal or neglect of our regulations.

Given at our Court at St. James's 7 October, 1763. *

10 What historians have said

Analyzing Historical Judgments

Introduction

The present assignment concludes your work on Indians and Europeans in early North American history by examining selections from the writings of two well-known professional historians on some of the issues and problems you have just studied.

Objectives are to:

—Analyze two given historical selections for differences in interpretation.

—Decide which of the selections is most convincing.

—Change or expand their content as your studies in previous assignments may require.

—Make inferences about the nature of history and history writing from what you have studied so far about Indians and Europeans in North America.

23 FRANCIS PARKMAN ON INDIANS AND INDIAN CHARACTER

Francis Parkman was born in Boston in 1823, and was educated at Harvard College and Harvard Law School. In 1846 he made a trip through Indian-occupied lands of the Far West which he recorded in a journal and published in 1849. Never a person of robust health, the strains of that western trip left Parkman a semi-invalid for the rest of his life. Despite this, Parkman wrote eight exciting volumes about the Anglo-French struggle for domination of North America, and established himself as the leading American historian of his time. His books were published between 1851 and 1892, and he died in 1893.

A70

Parkman's work is characterized by careful use of original source materials, a powerful and distinctive writing style, with many vivid passages describing Indian life in the primitive North American wilderness. His books are recognized today as classic works in American history. The selection below is taken from Parkman's first book in his series on Anglo-French conflict in North America, The Conspiracy of Pontiac, first published in 1851. While reading this selection, keep in mind the following questions:

1. *According to Parkman, what lies at the basis of Indian character?*
2. *What does Parkman infer about Indians from their use of language?*
3. *How does he account for the defeat and displacement of the Indians?*

Parkman Assesses the Indian

Of the Indian character, much has been written and foolishly and *credulously** believed . . . The shadows of his wilderness home, and the darker mantle of his own inscrutable reserve, have made the Indian warrior a wonder and a mystery. Yet to the eye of rational observation, there is nothing unintelligible in him.

It is true that the Indian is full of contradiction. He deems himself the center of greatness and renown; his pride is proof against the fiercest torments of fire and steel; and yet the same man would beg for a dram of whiskey, or pick up a crust of bread thrown to him like a dog, from the tent door of a traveller.

At one moment, he is wary and cautious to the verge of cowardice; at the next, he abandons himself to a very insanity of recklessness; and the habitual self-restraint which throws an impenetrable veil over emotion is joined to the unbridled passions of a madman or a beast . . .

Revenge is an overpowering instinct in him; nay, more, it is a point of honor and a duty. His pride sets all language at defiance. He loathes the thought of coercion; and few of his race have ever stooped to discharge a menial office. A wild love of liberty, an utter intolerance of control, lie at the basis of his character, and fire his whole existence.

Yet in spite of this haughty independence, he is a devout hero-worshipper; and high achievement in war or policy touches a chord to which his nature never fails to respond. He looks up with admiring reverence to the sages and heroes of his tribes; and it is this principle, joined to the respect for age . . . which beyond all others, contributes union and harmony to the erratic members of an Indian community. Love of glory kindles into a burning passion in him; and to allay its cravings, he will dare cold and famine, fire, tempest, torture, and even death itself . . .

Over all emotion he throws the veil of an iron self-control, originating in a peculiar form of pride, and fostered by rigorous discipline from childhood upward. He is trained to conceal passion, and to subdue it. Wrangling and quarreling are strangers to an Indian dwelling. A Roman senate might have

Credulous—easy to persuade, believing on very slight evidence.

taken a lesson from the grave solemnity of an Indian council. In the midst of his family and friends, he hides affections under a mask of icy coldness; and in the torturing fires of his enemy, the haughty sufferer maintains to the last his look of grim defiance . . .

Among all savages, the *powers of perception** preponderate over those of reason and analysis; but this is more especially the case with the Indian. An acute judge of character, at least of such parts of it as his experience enables him to comprehend; keen in all exercises of war and the chase, he seldom traces effects to their causes, or follows out actions to their remote results.

His curiosity, abundantly active within its own narrow circle, is dead to all things else. He seldom takes cognizance of general or abstract ideas. His language has scarcely the power to express such ideas, except through the medium of figures drawn from the external world, and often highly picturesque and forcible. The absence of reflection makes him grossly *improvident,** and unfits him for pursuing any complicated scheme of war or policy.

Some races of men seem moulded in wax, soft and melting, at once plastic and feeble. Some races, like some metals, combine the greatest flexibility with the greatest strength. But the Indian is hewn out of rock. You can scarcely change the form without destruction of the substance. Races of inferior energy have possessed a power of expansion and assimilation to which he is a stranger; this fixed and rigid quality has proved his ruin. He will not learn the arts of civilization, and he and his forest must perish together.

The stern, unchanging features of his mind excite our admiration for their very *immutability;** we look with deep interest on the fate of this irreclaimable son of the wilderness, the child who will not be weaned from the breasts of his rugged mother. Our interest increases when we discern in the unhappy wanderer the germs of heroic virtues mingled among his vices, a hand as bountiful to bestow as it is rapacious to seize, and even in the extremest famine, imparting its last morsel to a fellow sufferer; a heart which, strong in friendship as in hate, thinks it not too much to lay down life for its chosen comrade; a soul true to its own idea of honor, and burning with an unquenchable thirst for greatness and renown.

Powers of Perception—knowing by instinct, knowing without inquiring.

Improvident—wasteful, not providing for the future.

Immutable—never changing or varying.

Quoted from Francis Parkman, **The Conspiracy of Pontiac and the Indian War after the Conquest of Canada,** 10th edition, revised with additions (Boston: Little, Brown, and Company. 1913), Vol. I, pp. 42–44.

A72

24 RANDOLPH C. DOWNES ON THE INDIAN POINT OF VIEW

Randolph C. Downes was born in Connecticut in 1901 and was educated at Dartmouth College, the University of Wisconsin, and received his doctorate in history from Ohio State University in 1929. He has taught American history for many years at the University of Pittsburgh, Smith College, and the University of Toledo. Professor Downes has written many books and articles on Ohio history. He has also served as a consultant for the Association of American Indian Affairs.

The next selection is taken from Downes's Council Fires on the Upper Ohio, published in 1940. While reading this selection, keep in mind the following questions:

1. According to Downes, what was the basis of conflict between Indians and Europeans?

2. What does Downes infer about Indians from their use of language?

3. How does Downes account for the defeat and displacement of the Indians?

Downes Compares Indian and White

The story here narrated is one of a conflict between two civilizations, between two methods of living, one based on hunting and fishing, the other on farming and commerce. This conflict, grim and unceasing . . . was nourished by the profound conviction of each race that *its* ways were superior to those of the other. In the white man this conviction was aggressive and militant and justified the displacement or extermination of the Indian. In the Indian it was defensive and heroic and gave strength, in the face of despair and overwhelming force, for resistance against the hated conqueror . . .

Yet in all sincerity, the Indians believed themselves to be a chosen people in the sight of God. This belief was justified, in their opinion, by the fact that the whites were a race of mongrels, while they themselves were thoroughbreds. The uniformity of their physical characteristics revealed them as a race of aristocrats among the races of men . . .

The Indians were quite conscious that they were more skilled in certain arts than the white men. These were the arts of hunting, trapping, and fishing, all of which required a *versatility** and a craftsmanship of a type superior to that of the farmer, the trader, and the mechanic. In contrast with wild game, the plants, tools, and domestic animals of the white men were tame and easily controlled . . .

Their lives stood the daily test of direct comparisons with nature and natural forces. The sincerity with which they lived according to their beliefs is evidenced in their spoken language, in which there were no abstractions, but

Versatile—having many different aptitudes and skills, doing many things well.

A73

Ideology—manner and content of thinking that is characteristic of an individual or group.

in which natural objects and forces were used to create *ideologies** and definitions. Their leaders were "wise and beloved men"; other tribes were brothers, nephews, cousins or grandfathers; the whites might be elder brothers or great fathers . . .

To make friends was to "take by the hand"; to confer was to "smoke together"; to pray was to entrust the spoken word to the rising smoke. To trade was to "keep the road open," and when trade was interrupted, "trees and branches had fallen across the road." When there was friendship between nations, "the council fire burned brightly . . ."

In times of peace, "the tomahawk was buried," but in war it was "taken up, brightened, and made sharp." Treaties or conferences were invariably begun by the ceremony of wiping tears from the eyes and dust from the faces, opening the ears, cleansing the hearts, and covering the bones of those killed in conflict . . .

Knowing only the simpler arts needed to sustain a small population . . . they were no match for those whose arts were capable of . . . sustaining large units of population . . . Even though in the days of conflict the Indians were not greatly outnumbered by the actual frontier invaders, there were always the legions of white people to the east who could be hired to crush the red man.

Unable to make a gun or to repair it and supply it with powder and bullets, lacking horses and wagons needed to move them quickly to battle, and facilities to sustain a siege, Indians were forced to rely on foreign allies and on bush fighting. Unfortunately, they chose the wrong allies, the French. As for their methods of fighting, . . . the American frontiersman . . . soon learned not only ways in which to defend himself, but also ways by which the Indians could be deprived of their main source of sustenance, their hunting grounds.

Reprinted from **Council Fires on the Upper Ohio** by Randolph C. Downes, pp. 3–15, by permission of the University of Pittsburgh Press. © 1940 by the University of Pittsburgh Press. Renewed 1968 by Randolph C. Downes.

Additional Reading

American Heritage Pub. Co., *The American Heritage Book of Indians.* New York: Simon & Schuster, 1961.

Baldwin, Gordon C., *America's Buried Past: The Story of North American Archaeology.* New York: E. P. Putnam, 1962.

Callan, Eileen T., *A Hardy Race of Men: America's Early Indians.* New York: Harcourt, Brace & World, 1970.

Carpenter, Frances, *Pocahontas and Her World.* New York: Alfred A. Knopf, 1957.

Collier, John, *Indians of the Americas.* New York: W. W. Norton, 1947.

Hibben, Frank C., *Digging Up America.* New York: Hill and Wang, 1960.

Jacobson, Daniel, *Great Indian Tribes.* New Jersey: Hammond Incorporated, 1970.

LaFarge, Oliver, *Pictorial History of the American Indian.* New York: Crown Publishers, 1956.

Leland, C. G., *Algonquin Legends of New England.* Boston: Houghton, Mifflin & Co. 1884.

Marriott, Alice, and Rachlin, Carol K., *American Epic.* New York: New American Library, 1969.

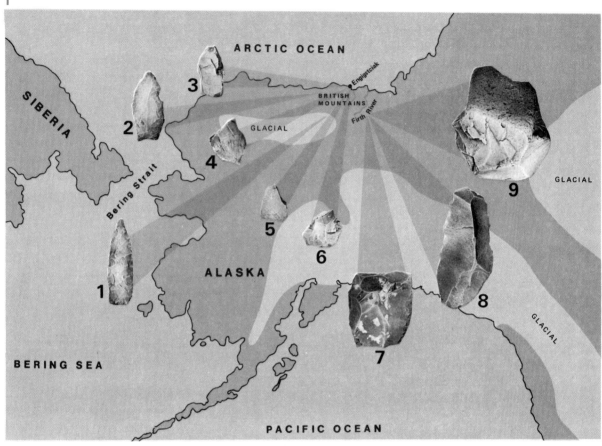

Artifacts, Courtesy National Museums of Canada, Ottawa

Artifacts of Prehistoric North America

The artifacts in the picture above and in the pictures that follow may also be presented in a filmstrip. These artifacts illustrate aspects of the different North American culture stages that you have been studying.

Examine the pictures carefully so that you can *make inferences* about the use to which these artifacts were put, and the skills possessed by the people who made them. After inferring what could be done with these tools, you will be asked to make a judgment about which culture stage produced them.

2

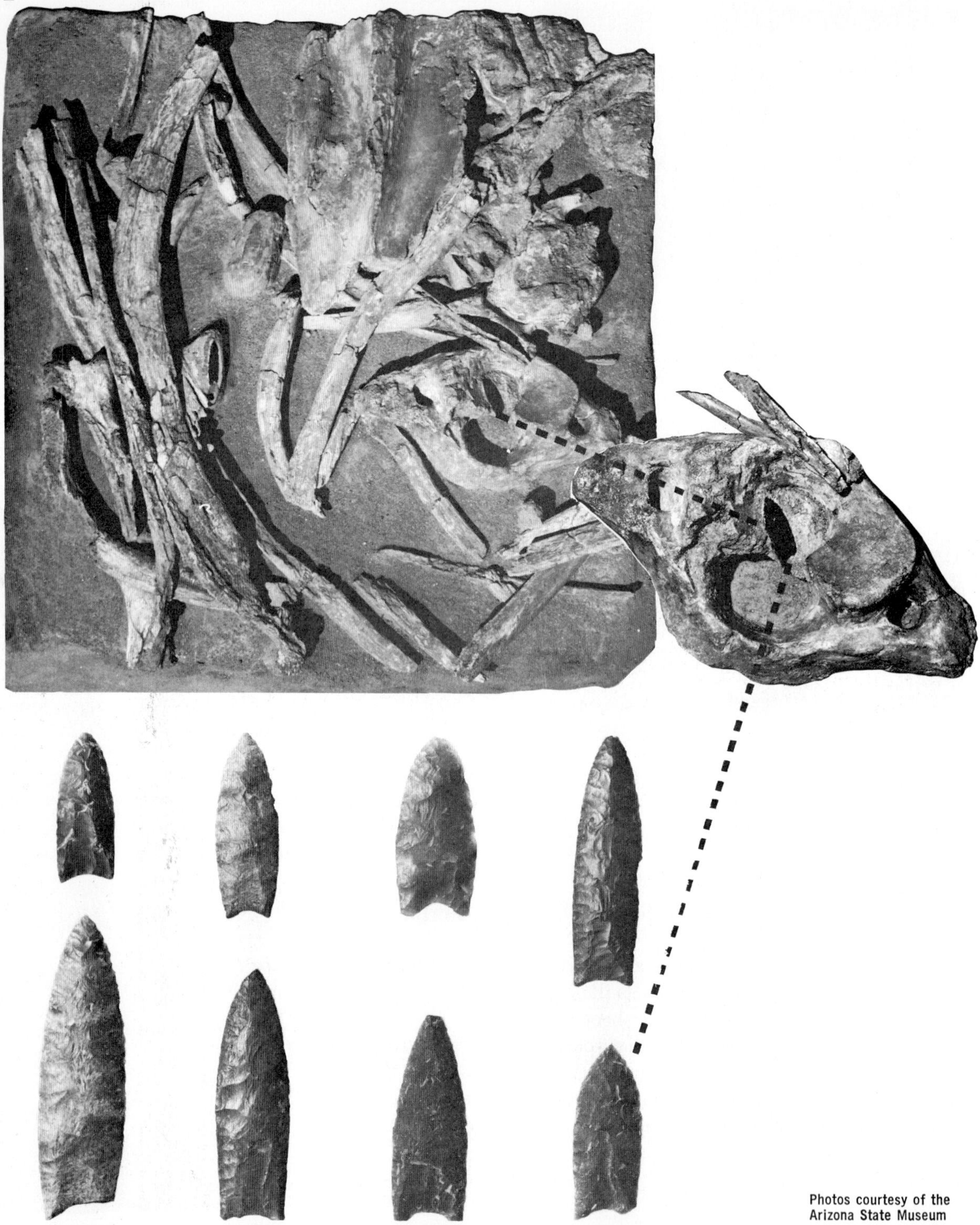

Photos courtesy of the
Arizona State Museum

A76

3

Left—Peabody Museum

Right—The Smithsonian
Institution

Below—Reproduced from THE
ARCHAEOLOGY OF NEW YORK
STATE by William A. Ritchie,
Copyright 1965, 1969 by
William A. Ritchie. Used by
permission of Natural History
Press and Doubleday & Company,
Inc.

4

5

Courtesy of Illinois State Museum

6

Left—The Ohio Historical Society   Right—Museum of the American Indian, Heye Foundation

A78

7

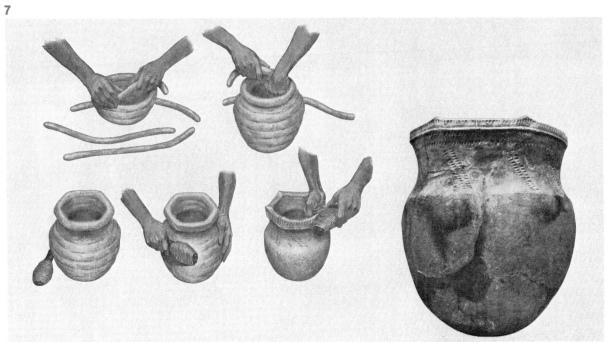

Photo, courtesy of the Rochester Museum and Science Center

8

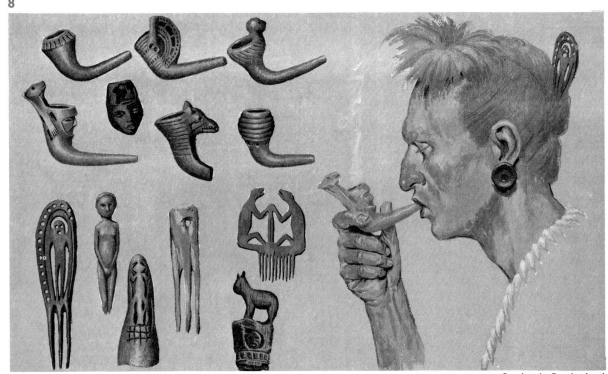

Drawings by Brendan Lynch

A79

9

Drawing by Brendan Lynch

10

Painting by Arthur A. Jansson, Courtesy of The American Museum of Natural History

Euro-Americans

O my America! My new-found land.
(JOHN DONNE, 1669)

1 What can you believe?

Frame of Reference

Introduction

When you began your studies you learned that historians were inquirers and that inquiry was a set of intellectual skills that could be taught and learned. As inquirers, you asked probing and inquiring questions, drew inferences, recognized problems in testimony and data, and made hypotheses. You tested your hypotheses and decided whether they were judgments, conclusions, or whether they remained hypotheses. As inquirers, you used facts. The certainty of your inferences, hypotheses, and judgments have depended totally upon the accuracy of the facts used in the making of them.

As inquirers, historians are users of facts. The quality of any historical work stands or falls on the accuracy of the facts appearing in it. However, facts of any kind, especially historical facts, are *elusive.** This is because most historical facts come to us through the medium of others. They are observations made, recorded, or remembered by someone in the past and relayed to us. In other words, historical facts are largely witnesses' impressions of past events.

As inquirers, historians make credibility judgments about testimony of such witnesses; they decide what can be believed in it and what cannot. They establish standards of credibility by putting probing and inquiring questions to the testimony under examination. These questions and the standards by which such judgments are made come out of what social scientists call a *frame of reference.*

Frame of Reference

Frame of reference means a person's background of values, attitudes, knowledge, and experience. A historian's frame of reference affects how he reads the testimony and what parts of it he accepts as facts. Because of different frames of reference—different values, attitudes, knowledge, and experience—one historian may accept as facts certain statements in testimony. Another historian may not.

Frames of reference, however, are not unique to historians or to scholars and scientists. Everyone has a frame of reference. For example, because of different frames of reference two eyewitnesses to an argument disagree about who started it and who won it. Because of different frames of reference, one television viewer sees professional football as an extraordinary display of tactics and skills. Another viewer sees it as a boring way to spend a Sunday afternoon. Even beauty, since it lies in the eyes of the beholder, is a matter of frame of reference.

Elusive—tending to escape notice, to evade.

A82

Courtesy of The Museum of Modern Art

Landscape by Mathieu
Merian (1593–1640)
Oil on panel, 12½″ x 16¼″
Private Collection

This assignment makes it possible for you to discover something about your own frame of reference and to make the kind of credibility judgments that historians have to make.

What Do You See?

Social science concepts as complex as frame of reference are sometimes more clearly illustrated by the work of people who are not themselves social scientists. As a rule, artists are neither historians nor social scientists, but they are inquirers and communicators of ideas. Frequently, a work of art communicates in a visual form immediately and clearly ideas whose complexity would require many carefully written pages to explain. The paintings presented in the text and on film were not painted specifically to illustrate the concept of frame of reference. Nevertheless, a careful examination of them will enable you to discover what a frame of reference is and how it functions.

A83

Objectives are to:

—Count the figures and describe the actions present in a filmstrip and pictures of Merian and Dali paintings.

—Draw inferences from your examination of the paintings about the effect of frame of reference on what you see.

—Distinguish between facts and opinions in conflicting testimonies and make judgments on what can be believed in them.

—Draw inferences about the effect of your own frame of reference on your judgment from the reasons you presented to support it.

The landscape on page 83 is the work of a Swiss artist, Mathieu Merian (1593–1640), and was created in the early seventeenth century. It follows the tradition of an Italian artist, Guiseppe Arcimboldo (1527–1593). The slave market, the fruit dish on a beach, and the three ages, were painted by the well-known contemporary Spanish artist, Salvador Dali.

While examining the paintings in the text and on film, keep in mind the following questions:

1. How many human figures has Merian scattered about his Landscape and what are they doing?

2. How many human figures has Dali placed in his painting of the Slave Market and what are they doing?

3. How do the titles of the paintings of the Landscape and the Slave Market and the actions of the human figures in them affect the way you see and interpret the paintings?

The Slave Market by Salvador Dali
Reproduced by permission of Mr. and Mrs. A. Reynolds Morse, Cleveland, Ohio.

13

Draeger Frères

14

Apparition by Salvador Dali

Wadsworth Atheneum, Hartford, Conn.

The Three Ages by Salvador Dali
Reproduced by permission of Mr. and Mrs. A. Reynolds Morse,
Cleveland, Ohio.

Draeger Frères

15

1 WHAT HAPPENED IN CHICAGO?

The demonstrations and disturbances during the Democratic National Convention in Chicago, August 24–28, 1968, were witnessed by millions of television viewers, and by hundreds of newspaper reporters and television commentators from all over the world. Even though the Convention and demonstrations received greater newspaper and television coverage than any other political event of the twentieth century up to that time, there were fundamental disagreements in the published accounts about what actually happened.

Eyewitnesses disagreed about when and how the demonstrations became disturbances. Reporters disagreed about the behavior of demonstrators and about the conduct of the police. Nearly everyone had an opinion about who was responsible for the situation. Reporters observing and writing about the same incidents did not see the same things.

While reading these two conflicting accounts published less than three weeks after the events occurred, keep in mind the following questions:

1. *According to* The Battle of Chicago, *who started the rioting?*

2. *According to* The Hilton Hotel Incident, *who started the rioting?*

3. *How would you distinguish facts from opinions in these two accounts?*

Riots in Chicago During Democratic National Convention—this montage shows some of the Grant Park and Conrad Hilton incidents.

The Battle of Chicago—And the Consequences

Controversy seethed throughout the U.S. and around the world in the aftermath of the bloody "battle of Chicago."

Attempts of thousands of youthful radicals to disrupt the Democratic National Convention brought the city to the edge of anarchy.

The climax came on the night of August 28, 1968, in a wild struggle that pitted police and National Guardsmen against an estimated 10,000 demonstrators.

Mayor Daley of Chicago described the mob as "terrorists" who came to Chicago "to assault, harass, and taunt the police into reacting before television cameras." The mayor said he had intelligence reports of an assassination plot against all the presidential candidates and himself.

The week's total of arrests mounted into the hundreds. So did the total of injuries. Casualties included at least 50 policemen and 20 newsmen.

Night of Bloodshed. This was the scene on the night of August 28, as Mr. Humphrey looked on from his suite on the 25th floor of the Conrad Hilton.

Marchers by the thousands marched in Grant Park. Then shouting taunts and obscenities, the youths—many of them bearded, dressed for "shock effect" in tattered dungarees, brandishing antiwar signs—surged in flying wedges against police lines.

From the mob came barrages of bottles and stones. Lye was thrown and cleaning fluid was squirted at the police. The police counter-attacked and the fray was on. Patrolmen clubbed and seized youths by the dozens, jamming them into patrol wagons. Tear gas was used as was the antimob material, Chemical Mace.

As clubbed youths fell or were collared, others moved forward to take their places. Bystanders were caught in the onslaught. Some were crushed against the window of the Haymarket Inn, a restaurant in the Conrad Hilton. They fell backward through the shattered glass. The Hilton lobby, permeated with tear gas, was turned into an emergency ward for some of the injured.

As the tempo of violence heightened, police pursued fleeing youths through the lobby. All the while TV cameras ground and demonstrators chanted, "The whole world is watching."

Violence subsided gradually when National Guardsmen—at first with fixed bayonets, then with bayonets sheathed—moved into action.

Deep Sadness. In his acceptance speech to the Convention, Mr. Humphrey expressed "deep sadness" at the bloodshed, but said it taught the lesson that "violence breeds counterviolence and it cannot be condoned, whatever the source." He said that the nation should resolve that "never, never again shall we see what we have seen."

However, Tom Hayden, a leader of the Mobilization Committee to End the War in Vietnam, threatened more and greater violence. Addressing a rally in Grant Park, he urged youths to go home and create "one, two, three hundred Chicagos." Hayden cried: "If they want blood to flow from our heads, the blood will flow from a lot of other heads around this city and around the country. We must take to the streets, for the streets belong to the people. It may well be that the era of organized, peaceful, and orderly demonstrations is coming to an end and that other methods will be needed."

Hayden's audience, some waving Vietcong flags and the black banners of anarchy, cheered and shouted, "The streets belong to the people!"

Reprinted from **U.S. News & World Report** (September 9, 1968) pp. 42–43. Copyright 1968 U.S. News & World Report, Inc.

The Hilton Hotel Incident

Blitzkrieg—lightning war conducted with great speed and force.

The unprovoked *blitzkrieg** police attacks on the pacifist crowd and bystanders in the front of the Conrad Hilton Hotel on the third day of the Democratic convention can adequately be compared only to the Nazi use of Blackshirts during Hitler's rise to power in Germany.

In the Hilton assault it is significant to report that the victims included guests of the hotel, elderly bystanders, women, and children who had the misfortune to be standing behind police barriers outside the picture window of the Haymarket Inn. After first assaulting the pacifist demonstrators, the police turned on this group of witnesses, and pressed their club-wielding attack so severely that, in panic, the bystanders pressed back until they crashed through the window.

But the glass-spiked bloody escape route was cut off inside when the police flanked them by running around into the restaurant and beating the people who had fallen through the window. At this point, one young man was dragged through the revolving doors of the hotel and beaten until his face turned into an unrecognizable mass of loose pulp. Another victim was forced into a partially opened section of the revolving door and beaten through the crack until he fell into a heap on the floor. He was then swept out of the hotel by a man pushing the door around.

In Chicago, the law-and-order standard became particularly ironic when the great majority of the crowd that were being assaulted by the police remained true to their credo of nonviolence. In the heat of the rape, even veteran newsmen lost their cool and began screaming at the police from the safety of an awning that hung over the scene in the street. But even after the first line of protesters had been peeled off—by clubbings and knees to the groin—the next row remained firm and refused to defend themselves, with what few weapons the street is able to provide.

Still the police pressed forward with their sticks, their well-practiced karate chops, and their boots, until they themselves fell back exhausted with the efforts of their administered beatings. Soon afterward the Chicago police were replaced by the National Guard. Remarkably, the uniformed soldiers were cheered.

If they did this while the whole world was watching, what might they have done if they had been off camera? If their unprovoked attacks were carried out with the intention of triggering a violent response from a nonviolent crowd, to what lengths might they have gone if the crowd had responded with violence, or even if they had defended themselves?

By Thomas W. Pew, Jr., **The Nation** (September 16, 1968) p. 229.

A88

2 English explorations

The Founding of Virginia

Introduction

English interest in the New World began much earlier than the seventeenth century. As early as 1488 Bartholomew Columbus, on behalf of his brother Christopher, visited the court of King Henry VII in London. He sought financial support for an exploratory and trading voyage westward across the Atlantic to China.

Although it is not clear why these negotiations with Columbus in 1488 failed, the idea of a westward voyage from England was not forgotten. Negotiations were resumed a few years later. However, by the time Henry VII was ready to take action, it was too late. Christopher Columbus had already concluded an agreement with Spain in 1492.

Cabot's Exploration

England lost Columbus, but she had other explorers at hand. John Cabot (Giovanni Caboto), a Venetian, had settled in the port of Bristol as early as 1490. Through the influence of the merchant community in that port, Henry VII agreed to support a westward voyage of exploration. Cabot sailed from Bristol on May 2, 1497, with a small ship and a crew of only eighteen. His first sighting of North America was *Cape Breton Island,** now part of Nova Scotia, on June 24, 1497.

Cabot sailed south and west as far as Maine, making sure he had discovered a continent and not a group of islands. On returning to England, he passed the Grand Banks of Newfoundland where he saw an abundance of cod, haddock, and other edible fish. Back in Bristol by August 6, 1497, John Cabot reported his discovery of rich fishing grounds off a continent he mistakenly believed was Asia. England's claims to lands in North America rested on this voyage across the Atlantic in the summer of 1497.

John Cabot made a second voyage to North America with a small fleet of five ships in 1498 and sailed as far south as Delaware. His ship was lost at sea with all hands, and accurate details about where the small fleet went or how long it stayed is unknown. The English had looked for traces of Chinese civilization, but Cabot's voyages turned up only evidence of an aboriginal culture. After 1498, English maps and charts referred to North America as the *New Found Land*, never again as China or Asia.

Realizing that North America was a barrier to westward sea routes to Asia, explorers begin to search for a northwest passage around it.*

Cabot Strait, named in the explorer's honor, lies between Cape Breton Island and Newfoundland and links the St. Lawrence River with the Atlantic Ocean.

Roald Amundsen, noted Norwegian explorer, took three years to make the first Northwest Passage. He sailed his vessel, Gjoa, from Europe to Nome, Alaska, going from the Atlantic to the Pacific between 1903 and 1906.

A89

MAJOR VOYAGES
OF EXPLORATION
TO AMERICA
1492-1609

- — — — Spain
- — — — Portugal
- —·—·— France
- ········· France
- — — — England
- ———— Netherlands

0   1100
Scale of Miles

Davis Strait

GREENLAND

Hudson Bay

Davis

Frobisher

LABRADOR

Sebastian Cabot

John Cabot

Hudson

NEWFOUNDLAND

Cartier

Champlain 1613-1616

Champlain 1603

Champlain 1604

NORTH AMERICA

ATLANTIC

de Soto

FLORIDA

de Verrazano

Narvaez
Gulf of
Mexico

Columbus

Ponce de Leon

Raleigh's Expedition

Cortez

Cabrillo

Mexico

PACIFIC OCEAN

Caribbean   Sea

OCEAN

Balboa

SOUTH AMERICA

Pizarro PERU

Cabral

— · — Drake
— — Magellan

In the summer of 1969, the S.S. Manhattan, assisted by ice breakers, was the first commercial vessel to sail around the North American continent by a **northwest passage** from the Atlantic Ocean to Prudhoe Bay, Alaska.

The last significant English exploration of the early sixteenth century was a search for such a northwest passage. In 1509, Sebastian Cabot, son of John Cabot, sailed from Bristol with two ships past the southern tip of Greenland into the Davis Straits, then west around the north shore of Labrador into Hudson Bay. Cabot tried to pass the North American barrier to Asia* by sailing around its northern end. Threatened by drifting ice, Cabot's crew forced him to turn back.

After exploring the North American coast to the south, Sebastian returned to England to find that his patron, Henry VII, had died. He lingered a while in England, but the new king, Henry VIII, was less interested in exploration and overseas ventures. So Sebastian Cabot entered the services of the king of Spain and abandoned his search for a northwest sea route to Asia.

Cabot's departure for Spain ended English exploration of North America for almost seventy years. Although some English fishermen visited the Newfoundland Banks on a regular basis during this period, exploration of North America was left to the Spanish and French. Not until the 1570's did English expeditions, now commanded by Englishmen rather than foreigners, return to North America. Between 1576 and 1587 *Martin Frobisher** and *John Davis** each made three voyages in search of a northwest passage. In 1578 *Sir Humphrey Gilbert** received a license from Queen Elizabeth for exploring and colonizing lands in North America.

Colonizing—An English Idea

Gilbert's license to colonize lands in North America marked a change in English thinking about their Atlantic ventures. The colonizing idea as developed by the English in the sixteenth century was new. Neither the Portuguese, Spanish, nor French had been interested in transporting men, women, and children overseas for purposes other than trade and profit.

There were no precedents for founding plantations or permanent settlements of colonists in distant lands in which homes were built, farming begun, and family life encouraged. The plantation idea was English in origin and was developed first in Ireland as a means of securing English control over that country. Subsequently it was applied to North America. Many of the same persons promoting and managing plantation schemes in Ireland were among the first promoters of plantations in North America.

Although Gilbert made a voyage to North America shortly after obtaining his royal license for colonizing in 1578, he was unable to raise funds for a plantation project until 1583. In that year, Gilbert sailed with a fleet of five ships and 260 men to claim Newfoundland as an English possession. However, bad luck and insufficient funds plagued the expedition from the start. Only four ships reached Newfoundland. Another was wrecked near Cape Breton Island, and the prospective colonists remained on shore for only two weeks. On the return voyage to England, Gilbert lost his life in a sea accident.

*Sir Walter Raleigh,** Gilbert's half brother and a member of his expedition, obtained a renewal of Gilbert's license in 1584. Raleigh's idea of locating a plantation differed from that of Gilbert. Raleigh intended to work farther south in warmer latitudes where colonies might be expected to produce wines and fruits. He sent out an exploring venture in 1584; his captain reached what is now Albemarle Sound on the North Carolina coast and landed on Roanoke Island. The region was reported as perfect for a plantation. The climate was warm, the soil fertile, and the Indians friendly. Raleigh named those newly discovered lands *Virginia.*

John Davis (1550–1605) first searched for a northwest passage in 1585, and again in 1586 and 1587. He served against the Spanish Armada and captured several Spanish ships in 1589 and 1590. Davis wrote several books on navigation and seamanship, and the straits between Greenland and Labrador bear his name. He was killed by the Japanese in the Straits of Malacca in 1605.

(*See page 92.)

(*See page 92.)

Martin Frobisher (1535–1594) made several voyages to the African coast in the 1550's, fought against the Spaniards, served in Ireland with Sir Humphrey Gilbert. His first search for a northwest passage was in 1576; his second and third in 1577 and 1578.

Sir Walter Raleigh (1552–1618), writer, adventurer, soldier of fortune in France and the Netherlands, fought the Spanish in the late 1570's, and tried to colonize in Ireland, Newfoundland, and Roanoke Island. He was executed in England in 1618.

Richard Grenville (1540–1591) became a soldier of fortune at an early age, fought against the Turks in Hungary during the 1560's, and went to sea in the 1580's. After his voyage to Roanoke Island, he fought the Spanish until he died in a sea battle against them in 1591.

Sir Humphrey Gilbert (1539–1583) served as a soldier in the Netherlands and in Ireland. In 1567, he unsuccessfully tried to found a plantation of English colonists in northern Ireland.

John White's map of Secotan shows the arrival of the English at Roanoke in 1585. White's records included watercolors of Indian life, maps of North America, and descriptions of native inhabitants. His granddaughter, Virginia Dare, born August 18, 1587, was the first English child born in the New World.

The following year Raleigh dispatched *Richard Grenville** to Roanoke Island with a small party of colonists. Arriving in June, 1585, Grenville spent two months there. After promising to return within one year with supplies, he left a military force rather than a plantation settlement on the island and returned to England. True to Grenville's promise, supply ships were sent out in 1586. When they arrived at Roanoke Island, they found the settlement deserted. Offered transportation home by a fleet of English warships that had put into Albemarle Sound, the colonists had abandoned their settlement.

(*See opposite page.)

The Lost Colony

Undaunted by these failures, Raleigh in 1587 sent another expedition to Roanoke Island under *John White** who had been with Grenville earlier. This expedition had more of a settler, rather than a garrison, mentality. Some men brought along their wives and children. Arriving in July, the settlers immediately established themselves as a permanent plantation with White as governor. After two months, White reluctantly left his daughter, granddaughter, and a hopeful and promising colony to return to England for supplies.

Supply ships were fitted out a year later, but were prevented from sailing because of the outbreak of war with Spain. White was unable to return to Roanoke Island until five years later—August, 1591. By that time the Roanoke colony had disappeared without a trace, leaving a single word **Croatan** carved on a tree. In 1602 Raleigh sent a final expedition in a futile search for survivors. The mystery of the lost Roanoke colony was never solved.

In 1603 the war with Spain was over, and during the next four years English captains made several voyages to North America. The most important was George Waymouth's exploration of Nantucket and the coast of Maine in 1605. Waymouth brought five Indian captives back to England.* The accounts of this voyage and the first Indians ever seen in England aroused great interest.

One of the Indians enticed on board Captain Waymouth's ship may have been the famous Wampanoag Indian, **Squanto**, who greeted and assisted the English settlers at the Plymouth colony fifteen years later.

WHAT HAPPENED TO THE "LOST COLONY"?

Three hundred years later, **Croatan** oral tradition related this story. Croatan Indians lived on Roanoke Island when the English settlers landed in 1587. The English became part of the tribe when John White did not return in the promised time. The Indians, in turn, kept the English alive and adopted the white man's language, religion, and laws.

After a couple of years, the Indian-English community moved to North Carolina, where they eventually settled near the Lumber River in Cumberland County.

There, in 1709, a group of Huguenot settlers was astonished to find Indians with Anglo-Saxon speech and customs, with farms and roads, and other evidence of English culture.

And there, in the 1880's, Hamilton McMillan, a North Carolina historian, researched the Croatan oral history and wrote a book offering a possible solution to Sir Walter Raleigh's lost colony of Roanoke.

A93

Sir Ferdinando Gorges (1565–1647) served as a soldier in the Netherlands, as governor of the port of Plymouth, and as governor of New England. His last years were spent developing the province of Maine.

Sir John Popham (1531–1607), an able lawyer and Chief Justice, helped found the Virginia and Plymouth Companies and helped colonize Maine.

A council of 13 members was appointed by the company to act as the governing board in each colony. A royal council of 14 members residing in England was appointed over the colonial councils by the king.

Sagahadoc colony, set up on the Kennebec River near the present town of Popham Beach, Maine, failed due to disagreements, inadequate preparations, severe weather. Abandoned September, 1608.

LAND GRANTS 1606-1607

PLYMOUTH COMPANY
Sagadahoc Colony
Plymouth
NEUTRAL ZONE
Long Island
Jamestown
Chesapeake Bay
Roanoke Island
LONDON COMPANY
Cape Fear
0   200
Scale of Miles

Among those Englishmen interested in Waymouth's voyage were *Sir Ferdinando Gorges** and *Sir John Popham,** who educated the Indian captives. Popham representing London, and Gorges representing the western ports of Bristol and Plymouth, joined with several others in petitioning King James I for a license to form two companies for colonizing and trading in North America. The license was granted in April, 1606.

London and Plymouth Companies

The London Company was authorized to colonize the region between what is now New York City and North Carolina, and the Plymouth Company was assigned lands located between the Potomac River and northern Maine. Neither company was to settle within 100 miles of the other.*

This arrangement created a neutral zone between the regions assigned to the two companies. Each company was allowed to incorporate and sell shares of stock to raise money for the necessary shipping, supplies, and equipment. Each company was empowered to govern its own colony and share in all future profits from trade, mining, and land sales.

The Plymouth Company acted first. In August, 1606, the company sent a ship to explore the coasts of the region covered in its license. Contrary to orders, the ship sailed too far south and was captured and detained by the Spaniards near Puerto Rico. A second ship sailed out to the coast of Maine in October, 1606, and brought back glowing reports about the excellence of that country for a plantation. Encouraged by these reports, the Plymouth Company prepared an expedition of 120 men and two ships to leave in the spring of 1607 and establish a plantation on the coast of Maine.*

Meanwhile, the London Company had been preparing an expedition of its own. Under the command of Captain Christopher Newport, three ships—Sarah Constant, Goodspeed, and Discovery—left England for southern Virginia on December 20, 1606. Newport's small fleet passed into Chesapeake Bay on April 26, 1607, entered the James River shortly thereafter, and on May 24, 1607, landed at a site which they called Jamestown. Immediately, the 105 colonists established the first permanent English settlement in North America by building a fort, a church, and some houses.

When viewed against England's record of disappointment and disaster in previous North American ventures, the decision in 1606 to found two colonizing companies might appear unrealistic. Yet investors were willing to risk their money, and men their lives, in order to try again where Raleigh, Grenville, and White had failed.

Similarly, when viewed against the background of early seventeenth-century foreign policy, the decision to go to Virginia might appear positively dangerous. One ship already had been captured for intruding into regions claimed by Spain. Another English expedition to Virginia would challenge Spain and threaten the peace. King James I was committed to a policy of peaceful relations with Spain. Yet he did not check private activities of his subjects, such as the Virginia expedition, that might lead to renewal of war.

A94

Major Voyages of Exploration to America 1492–1609

1492	Christopher Columbus discovered America for Spain
1497	John Cabot explored Newfoundland for England
1500	Pedro Cabral discovered Brazil for Portugal
1509	Sebastian Cabot explored the Hudson Bay area for England
1513	Juan Ponce de León discovered Florida for Spain
1513	Vasco Nuñez de Balboa discovered the Pacific Ocean for Spain
1519–1521	Ferdinand Magellan sailed around the world for Spain
1519–1521	Hernando Cortes conquered Mexico for Spain
1523	Giovanni da Verrazano explored the east coast of North America for France
1528	Pánfilo de Narváez explored the gulf coast of Florida for Spain
1531	Francisco Pizarro conquered Peru for Spain
1534–1542	Jacques Cartier explored Newfoundland and Canada for France
1539–1542	Hernando de Soto explored the Mississippi River for Spain
1542	Jean Francois de Roberval explored the St. Lawrence for France
1542	Jean Rodriguez Cabrillo explored the California coast for Spain
1576–1578	Martin Frobisher searched for a Northwest Passage for England
1577–1580	Sir Francis Drake sailed around the world for England
1578–1579	Sir Humphrey Gilbert explored North America for England
1583	Sir Humphrey Gilbert sent out a colonizing expedition to Newfoundland for England
1584	Sir Walter Raleigh's expedition discovered Virginia for England
1585	Sir Walter Raleigh sent out Sir Richard Grenville to Virginia for England
1585–1587	John Davis searched for a Northwest Passage for England
1587	Sir Walter Raleigh sent out John White to Virginia for England
1602	Sir Walter Raleigh sent out an expedition to search for survivors of the Roanoke Colony
1602	George Waymouth explored the Hudson Bay area for England
1603–1616	Samuel de Champlain explored Canada for France
1605–1606	George Waymouth explored Nantucket and the Maine coast for England
1607	**Christopher Newport*** landed English colonists at Jamestown
1609	Henry Hudson explored the Hudson River area for the Netherlands

Christopher Newport (1565–1617) made five voyages to Virginia between 1606 and 1611. He entered the services of the East India Company in 1614 and made three voyages to the Far East. He died on board ship in Java in 1617.

2 GOING TO VIRGINIA: A SPANISH VIEW

On the basis of discoveries, explorations, and international treaties, Spain claimed possession of the American continent as far north as the present state of Maine. Early in the sixteenth century, the English seemed to accept those Spanish claims. However, as time passed, and especially after war broke out between England and Spain in the 1570's, Englishmen paid less and less attention to Spanish claims to North America.

Objectives are to recognize and
identify:

—Reasons for Spanish concern
over an English expedition to
Virginia.

—King James's reasons for allowing an expedition to go to
Virginia.

—Reasons why Englishmen
ought to go to Virginia.

—Analyze the reasons you have
recognized and identified for
their value, attitude, and
knowledge assumptions.

—Make two historical hypotheses about the Virginia expedition from the results of your
analysis.

As the European power most firmly established in the New World, Spain was vitally interested in England's intentions in North America. The king of Spain instructed his ambassador in London to discover all he could about English voyages and plantation schemes and to report his findings as soon as possible. While reading the following selections from Spanish state papers, keep in mind these questions:

1. Why were the Spaniards so concerned about the prospect of an English expedition to Virginia? What were their reasons?

2. Which of their reasons do you think were expressions of attitudes *about the English?*

3. Which of their reasons do you think were value judgments?

4. What does the Spanish ambassador think is the real purpose of the expedition to Virginia?

Coded Message from the Spanish Ambassador in London to Philip III, King of Spain, March 6, 1606

The English propose to send 500 or 600 men, private individuals of this kingdom, to colonize Virginia which lies close to our settlement in Florida. In years past they have sent small groups of men there.

Some months ago, they brought back several natives who have been taught the English language and have been trained to say how good that country is for people to go and live in. The principal leader in this business is the Chief Justice, Sir John Popham, who is a very great Puritan and an enemy of Spain. The Chief Justice tells everyone that Virginia is a perfect place to send the misfits, thieves, and traitors that abound in this country.

Adapted from Alexander Brown, Editor, **Genesis of the United States: A Narrative of the Movement in England, 1605–1616,** 2 vols. (Boston: Houghton Mifflin, 1890), Vol. I, pp. 45–46.

Instructions from Philip III, King of Spain, to his Minister of State, May 7, 1607

Our ambassador in England has informed us of certain plans the English have of going to Virginia. That country which they call Virginia lies 35 degrees from Florida in the direction of Newfoundland and is contained within territories belonging to the Crown of Spain. From England, Virginia lies 1,200 *leagues** and from Spain, it lies only 1,000. This consideration, in addition to others, requires us to find ways of preventing execution of this plan of the English.

A league varies from 2.4 to 4.6 miles.

Being a discovery and possession of the Crown of Spain and being located so near our Indies, the country of Virginia is most important to us. An English presence there shall require increased vigilance over our commerce in that part of the world. This increased vigilance is all the more necessary if they should establish in Virginia the religion and liberty of conscience which they profess and which of itself obliges us to defend that country against them.

Adapted from Brown's **Genesis,** Vol. I, p. 100.

Coded Message from the Spanish Ambassador in London
to Philip III, King of Spain, September 22, 1607

I have reported to your Majesty how there had come to Plymouth two of the ships that went to Virginia. Captain Newport makes haste to return there with more people.

I have found a confidential person, through whom I shall find out what shall be done in the *Council*° (which they call the Council of Virginia). They are in a great state of excitement about that place and very much afraid that your Majesty should drive them out of it.

There are so many here, and in other parts of the kingdom, who speak of sending people to Virginia, that it is advisable not to be too slow. They will soon be found there with large numbers of people, whereupon it will be much more difficult to drive them out.

The Royal Council, appointed by King James I and located in London, supervised the resident Colonial Council and the region from North Carolina to Maine.

Coded Message from the Spanish Ambassador in London
to Philip III, King of Spain, October 5, 1607

A man has told me today, a man who usually tells me the truth, that the English are in great fear that your Majesty will give orders to stop the colony.

It appears clearly to me now that it is not their intention to plant colonists, but to send out pirates from there since they take no women to Virginia, only men.

Adapted from Brown's **Genesis,** Vol. I, pp. 116–119.

3 GOING TO VIRGINIA: TWO ENGLISH VIEWS

There's very little factual information about the thinking, actions, and intentions of the persons managing the early seventeenth-century English expeditions to America. No accurate accounts of the money raised, the number of colonists recruited, or the locations selected for settlement were made public at the time. All such information was closely kept to themselves by the managers of the London and Plymouth companies, who had been sworn to secrecy.

Information on why the English decided to go to Virginia, and why they were allowed to go when they did, must be gathered from public and private statements of persons close to the project, but not sworn to secrecy. While reading the following selections, keep in mind these questions:

1. How did King James view the expedition to Virginia? What were the reasons for his views?

2. *Which of his reasons do you think were based on <u>knowledge and experience</u>?*

3. *Which of his reasons do you think were based on <u>values</u>?*

4. *Why did the preachers of the sermons insist that Englishmen ought to go to Virginia? What were their reasons?*

5. *Which reasons were based on <u>knowledge and experience</u>?*

6. *Which of their reasons do you think were based on <u>values</u>?*

King James I

Adapted from Brown's **Genesis**,
Vol. I, pp. 120–124.

An Account of the Spanish Ambassador's Conversation With His Majesty, King James I, about Virginia, October 8, 1607

The King stated he had not particularly known what was afoot about Virginia, but declared that prevention of further sailings or recall of his subjects already there would be interpreted as acknowledging the Spanish Crown's claim to lordship over that entire region.

The King did not believe that Spain or any other country had any claims to Virginia. Existing peace treaties prohibited his subjects from going to the Indies, not to Virginia.

The King observed that all those going to Virginia went at their own risk and if some of them should turn up in the Indies, neither he nor they could complain if the Spaniards punished them.

He did not see advantages of any kind coming to him from these expeditions to Virginia.

The King expressed his opinion that the soil of Virginia was very sterile and that those of his subjects who expected to find great riches there had been sadly deceived.

He said he would seek information about allegations of intended piracy made against the Virginia Company and would take whatever action was appropriate.

The King admitted that two ships had recently left English ports for the Indies, but he insisted that those who had gone were terrible people and he was very much embarrassed by their departure.

Sermons on Going to the Virginia Plantation, 1608–1609

Let the honorable expedition now intended for Virginia attract cheerful and worthy persons. In this most difficult of times when our country is so overcrowded, God favors us with a territory so large and spacious as Virginia.

Yet the happiness that delights us the most is the glorious thought of replacing superstition and brutish incivility among the poor savages with religion and humanity. With such honorable and religious intentions to the enterprise, what glory, what honor, to our King! What comfort to us to see a New Britain established in another world.

❂   ❂   ❂   ❂   ❂

If there be any of you that have opposed actions tending to the glory of God and the saving of souls, let him know he is a persecutor and an enemy of Christ.

When the discovery of the Indies was offered to that learned and famous prince, Henry VII, some idle and unworthy sceptics persuaded the king not to get involved in such expensive futile adventures. We know now our loss was the Spaniards' gain.

Yet some among us still counsel against the present voyage. It is likely to be the most worthy voyage ever undertaken by Christians. That country shall rival India for gold, Persia for oils, Arabia for spices, and Babylon for corn, besides the abundance of mulberries, minerals, rubies, gems, grapes, deer, fowl, timber, fish, and whatever commodities England lacks.

Philosophers praise the climate; politicians extol our opportunity; and clergymen count the souls for conversion. The natives desire us to come; the Spaniards desire us far away. Yet some among us—lazy, drowsy, barking countrymen—condemn our efforts. Heed them not.

Go on! Go on! Make a savage land a sanctified country. Save souls. Enlarge both the bounds of England and the bounds of heaven. Go and possess the land, a land flowing with milk and honey. God shall bless you for it.

Adapted from Brown's **Genesis**, Vol. I, pp. 256, 313–315.

3 English colonization of North America, 1607–1700

Causes of Migration

Introduction

Although King James viewed the Virginia expedition through a frame of reference different from that of the promoters, he allowed a succession of new plantation schemes. Early in 1616, a small group of *Separatists** from the Church of England, who had emigrated to Holland in 1608, negotiated with the Virginia Company for a charter to found another plantation within its territory. After three years this group, known later as **Pilgrims**, obtained financial support from some hard-headed London merchants who exploited them unmercifully for years.

Separatists—Seventeenth-century English Protestants who separated themselves from the Church of England. They were known as Independents in England, and Congregationalists in America.

(*See opposite page.)

Under their leader, *William Brewster,** thirty-five Pilgrims left Holland for Plymouth, England in July, 1620. There they joined sixty-nine emigrants from London and Southampton, including *Captain Miles Standish,** their military leader. The group sailed for Virginia on the ***Mayflower,*** and fifty-six days later—on November 9, 1620—reached Cape Cod. Even though this was outside the territory of the Virginia Company, the Pilgrims decided to land and search for a plantation site.

The Mayflower Compact

Because their charter was for Virginia, not New England, the Pilgrim leaders feared that uncooperative members of their party might become rebellious when ashore. Therefore, in the cabin of the Mayflower, they drafted a preliminary plan of government, chose *John Carver** to be their governor, and selected the future site of Plymouth, Massachusetts, for their settlement. (Carver died five months later, and William Bradford became governor.) The Mayflower Compact was signed by forty-one male members of the party, who agreed to obey all laws enacted by the group for the general welfare.

Although Plymouth colony has occupied a major place in the history of America's past, its importance as a colony was short-lived. It was never significant either for population growth or economic development and was quickly outstripped by Massachusetts Bay.

Under the leadership of *John Winthrop,** the Massachusetts Bay Company sent out a fleet of eleven ships to New England in 1630 where settlements were established at the future sites of Boston, Charlestown, Medford, Watertown, and Dorchester. Most of the promoters of the company, including Winthrop, were **Puritans** who came to New England to establish a new way of life. Puritans were sixteenth- and seventeenth-century English Protestants who were dissatisfied with the rituals and organization of the Church of England and were determined to create a society in the New World which was more firmly based on their own vision of Christianity and the Bible than was possible in England.

Between 1630 and 1640, a migration of more than 20,000 Puritans and non-Puritans came to New England and planted basic political, religious, and social ideas that have affected American history profoundly from that day until the present.

Massachusetts Bay was extremely important in another respect: it became the severe mother of the other colonies. The leaders of Massachusetts Bay did not tolerate dissent from the Puritan life style which they had traveled so far to create. If one did not love Massachusetts Bay, one had to leave it. For example, *Roger Williams** came to Massachusetts in search of religious toleration and did not find it. He was banished from the colony in 1636, moved south, and founded a settlement at Providence which in time became the colony of Rhode Island. Other migrations from Massachusetts led to the founding of both Connecticut and New Hampshire.

John Winthrop (1588–1649) was the son of a successful lawyer and landowner. A deeply religious man, he joined the Massachusetts Bay Company in 1629 and quickly became its leader. He became New England's first elected governor in 1630 and remained active in Massachusetts affairs for the rest of his life.

Roger Williams (1604–1683) was the son of a London merchant. He became a minister in 1629, and arrived in New England in 1631. Williams believed that civil government should have no authority whatever over the conscience of men.

A100

Mayflower II, replica of the original ship.

In ye name of god Amen. We whose names are underwriten
the loyall subiects of our dread soueraigne Lord King Iames
by ye grace of god, of great britaine, franc, & yreland king
defendor of ye faith, &c

Haueing vndertaken, for ye glorie of god, and aduancemente
of ye christian faith and honour of our king & countrie, a voyage to
plant ye first colonie in ye Northerne parts of Virginia. Doe
by these presents solemnly & mutualy in ye presence of god, and
one of another, Couenant, & combine our selues togeather into a
ciuill body politick; for ye bettor ordering, & preseruation & fur=
therance of ye ends aforesaid; and by vertue hearof to enacte,
constitute, and frame shuch iust & equall Lawes, ordinances,
Acts, constitutions, & offices, from time to time, as shall be thought
most meete & conuenient for ye generall good of ye Colonie: vnto
which we promise all due submission and obedience. In witnes
wherof we haue hereunder subscribed our names at Cap=
odd ye .11. of Nouember, in ye year of ye raigne of our soueraigne
lord king Iames of England, franc, & yreland ye eighteenth
and of Scotland ye fiftie fourth. An: dom. 1620.]

Governor Bradford's copy of the **Mayflower Compact**

William Brewster (1560–1644), a postal officer in Scrooby, England became one of the leaders of the Pilgrim migration to Holland. In Holland and later in America, Brewster served as the ruling elder in the church and acted as both preacher and teacher.

Miles Standish (1584–1656), a soldier of fortune, became a convert to the Pilgrim Church after joining the expedition. As the only man with practical experience in camping, he was the mainstay of the Plymouth Colony during its early years and founded Duxbury in 1631. There is no historical basis for the story of John Alden's proposal to Priscilla Mullins on Standish's behalf as related in Henry Wadsworth Longfellow's poem **The Courtship of Miles Standish**. Standish was happily married and had six children.

Replica of a Pilgrim village of the 1620's as it appears today at Plimouth Plantation.

John Carver (1575–1621) was a deacon in the Pilgrim Church in Holland. He negotiated the agreement with the London merchants for the Mayflower voyage and, shortly before his death in 1621, negotiated a treaty with Indian chiefs.

Lord Baltimore (1580–1632) died before the charter was issued. However, the plantation was taken over by his son, Cecilius Calvert (1605–1675), and the charter was issued in his name.

Joseph West served as governor of Carolina, 1670–1685. He was a friend of Lord Shaftesbury, one of the eight men rewarded by King Charles II with the Carolina land grant.

The **Duke of York**, brother of King Charles II, was the future King James II, reigning 1685–1689.

James Oglethorpe (1696–1785), a former army officer, became a philanthropist committed to social reform after a close friend died of smallpox in a London debtors' prison.

Creation of Maryland

In 1632 George Calvert (*Lord Baltimore*),* a recent convert to Catholicism, sought a charter from King Charles I to colonize territory north of the Potomac River. He called his colony Maryland and intended it to be a refuge for English Catholics, who were unwelcome in either Virginia or Massachusetts. The first group of approximately 200 settlers—including both Catholics and Protestants—arrived in Chesapeake Bay in early 1634 and founded the town of St. Mary's.

The Maryland foundation ended the <u>first phase</u> of English colonial expansion. The outbreak of Civil War in England in 1642 was followed by the execution of Charles I in 1649. The abolition of monarchy, experiments with other forms of government, and the eventual restoration of monarchy in the person of King Charles II in 1660, left Englishmen with little time for colonizing projects.

After Charles II's restoration, the <u>second phase</u> of English colonial expansion began. The king rewarded some of the men who had fought for his father, and remained loyal to him in the civil war, with large grants of land in the American south. In 1670 *Joseph West** led a party of colonists from England to the region known as Carolina and founded the town of Charleston. Meanwhile, peaceful English penetration of Dutch settlements around the Hudson River continued until the outbreak of war with Holland in 1664. In that year, the *Duke of York** captured the port of New Amsterdam, renamed it New York, and carved out the new English colonies of New York, New Jersey, and Delaware, from territories attached to it.

Pennsylvania and Georgia

The last of the mainland colonies founded by the English in the seventeenth century was unique. William Penn, son of a prominent English admiral, and friend of the Duke of York, became a Quaker in 1666. In exchange for cancellation of a debt of £16,000 which King Charles II had owed his father, Penn obtained a charter in 1681 to a large tract of land west of the Delaware River. Penn intended his colony to be not only a place where Quakers would be welcome, but where men of all religions could live in peace and harmony.

In addition to being a man of high ideals, Penn was also an extremely talented promoter. Pamphlets describing the wonders of the region he called Pennsylvania were translated into German, French, and Dutch, and circulated throughout western Europe. Farmers everywhere, especially in Germany, were attracted by his promises of religious toleration and rich farm lands. Pennsylvania was unique among seventeenth-century English colonial foundations for its devotion to religious toleration and its appeal to non-English immigrants.

With the founding of Pennsylvania, English colonization of North America was complete except for Georgia. Chartered in 1732, Georgia was planned by *James Oglethorpe,** partly as a philanthropic enterprise, and partly as a frontier outpost against the Spanish in Florida.

During the course of the seventeenth century approximately 150,000 Englishmen undertook the risks of a transatlantic crossing and the uncertainties of life in a new world. Why were so many willing to leave their country and their friends, and take such risks?

Objectives are to:

—Analyze given economic data and make inferences about economic conditions in 17th-century England.

—Analyze given statements about religious conflict and make inferences about religious life.

—Make a hypothesis about the influence of economic conditions and religions on English emigration to America.

—Analyze additional contemporary testimony and make additions or modifications to the hypothesis.

Thirteen English Colonies in North America 1607–1733

COLONY	SETTLEMENT	ORIGIN	LEADERS
Virginia	Jamestown	England, 1607	John Smith
Massachusetts	Plymouth	England, 1620	William Bradford William Brewster John Carver Miles Standish
	Boston Charlestown Dorchester Medford Watertown	England, 1630	John Winthrop
New Hampshire	Portsmouth Dover Hampton Exeter	England and Massachusetts, 1630–1638	John Mason John Wheelwright
Rhode Island	Providence	Massachusetts, 1636	Roger Williams
Connecticut	Hartford New Haven	Massachusetts, 1636–1638	John Hooker John Davenport
Maryland	St. Mary's	England, 1634	Lord Baltimore
New York	New York	Captured from the Dutch, 1664	Duke of York
New Jersey	Scattered settlements	Captured from the Dutch, 1664	Lord Berkeley George Carteret
Delaware	Wilmington	Captured from the Dutch, 1664	Duke of York
Pennsylvania	Philadelphia	England, 1682	William Penn
North Carolina	Albemarle	Virginia, 1653	Group of settlers
South Carolina	Charleston	England, 1670	Joseph West
Georgia	Savannah	England, 1733	James Oglethorpe

4 ECONOMICS AND POLITICS AS CAUSES OF EMIGRATION

The desire to emigrate is not one that comes easily to most men. Ties of home and family, love of familiar things, distrust and fear of the unknown have tended to make men reluctant to turn away from their native country. Yet one of the important facts of American history is that the United States is a nation of immigrants. These two circumstances suggest that emigrants are not born; they are made by conditions in their native country.

While examining the following charts and chronology of economic and political conditions in seventeenth-century England, keep in mind these questions:

1. How would you describe political conditions in seventeenth-century England? Economic conditions?

2. In what time periods were general economic conditions good? In what periods were they bad?

3. In what time periods was the gap between food prices and wages greatest? What did this mean for most Englishmen?

Political Events and Economic Fluctuations in England
1600–1700

Mass burials during the **London Plague.**

1600–1605	Plague, 34,000 deaths in London.	1603 — James I accession (Anglican).
		1603 — Puritans petition James for changes in the Church.
		1604 — Peace with Spain.
1605–1610	Revival of trade after depression. Prosperity.	
1610–1615	Business failures and bankruptcies increase.	1611 — King James version of the Bible completed.
1615–1620	Partial recovery.	
1620–1625	Catastrophic depression of trade. Bad harvests, riots, plague, 36,000 deaths in London.	1625 — Charles I accession (Anglican).
		1625 — War with Spain.
1625–1630	Slight recovery of trade, then renewed depression. Continuing bad harvests.	1626 — War with France.
		1628 — The King's counselor, Buckingham, assassinated.
		1630 — Peace with Spain.
		1630 — Peace with France.
1630–1635	Slight recovery of trade, then stagnation; plague, 11,000 deaths in London.	1633 — Archbishop Laud (Anglican) prosecutes Puritans for slandering bishops.
1635–1640	Depression of trade.	
1640–1645	Depression of trade.	1642 — Outbreak of Civil War.
		1645 — Archbishop Laud executed by Puritan-dominated Parliament.

A104

1645–1650	Bad harvests.	1646 — Abolition of Anglican Church.
		1649 — Abolition of Monarchy.
		1649 — Execution of Charles I.
1650–1655	Recovery and prosperity.	1652 — 1st Dutch War begins.
		1653 — Military dictatorship of Oliver Cromwell (Puritan) begins.
		1654 — 1st Dutch War ends.
1655–1660	Excellent harvests.	1658 — Military dictatorship of Oliver Cromwell ends with his death.
		1660 — Restoration of monarchy with return of Charles II.
1660–1665	Bad harvests.	1664 — 2d Dutch War begins.
1665–1670	Plague, 69,000 deaths in London. Fire of London. Financial panic.	1667 — 2d Dutch War ends.
1670–1675	Peace. Building boom in London. Partial recovery.	1672 — 3d Dutch War begins.
		1674 — 3d Dutch War ends.
1675–1680	Bad harvests, bankruptcies, depression.	
1680–1685	Recovery.	1685 — Charles II dies (Anglican).
		1685 — James II accession (Catholic).
1685–1690	Recession.	1688 — Revolution and deposition of James II.
		1689 — William III and Mary accession (Anglican).
		1689 — War with France.
1690–1695	War. Bad harvests. Recession.	
1695–1700	Recession.	1697 — Peace with France.

The Great London Fire, which started in September, 1666, and lasted six days, destroyed St. Paul's Cathedral.

Food Prices and Skilled Laborers' Wages in England from 1590 to 1700

Oliver Cromwell (1599–1658), Puritan, member of Parliament was military commander of the Parliamentary Army in the English civil war. After execution of King Charles I, Cromwell became Lord Protector and military dictator of England until his death in 1658. Cromwell's Puritan revolution closed theaters, forbade amusements, enforced strict Sabbath observance, and made life drab.

Adapted from Lucy Hutchinson, **Memoirs of the Life of Colonel Hutchinson** (London: H. G. Bohn Co., 1846), pp. 80–81.

Adapted from statements in the **House of Commons Journal** (London: March 19, 1604); **Diary of John Manningham,** ed. by Ed. J. Bruce (London: Camden Society, 1868), p. 156; **The Miscellaneous Works of Sir Thomas Overbury,** ed. by E. F. Rimbault, 1890, p. 262.

5   RELIGION AS A CAUSE OF EMIGRATION

Seventeenth-century England was a Protestant state. The Church of England, or Anglican Church, had been established by law about a hundred years earlier as the official church of the country. The vast majority of Englishmen were Anglicans. Among the Anglicans was a large group known as Puritans who were determined to change its rituals and organization.

In addition, groups of Protestants, known as Separatists, had separated themselves from the Anglican Church and founded their own religious organizations. Finally, there were a few Catholics whose church was illegal in England, but who managed to retain their own services and traditions with the help of priests smuggled into the country from abroad.

Throughout the seventeenth century, religion in England was far more than a set of personal beliefs; it was an outward sign of a person's political and social attitudes. Englishmen identified and grouped themselves in religious categories rather than in geographic or political ones. To change the English Church was to change all of English society. While reading the following accounts of religious controversies and of governmental actions on religious matters, keep in mind these questions:

1. What do the seventeenth-century definitions of Puritanism suggest about the relations between religious groups in England?

2. Which religious groups in seventeenth-century England suffered discrimination or persecution?

3. Which religious groups used the power of the state to discriminate or persecute?

Two Seventeenth-Century Definitions of Puritanism

If any were grieved at the dishonor of the kingdom or the complaints of the poor, or the unjust oppression of the King's subjects in a thousand ways, he was a Puritan. If any showed favor to godly, honest persons, or protected them from violent and unjust oppression, he was a Puritan. If any stood up for his country and maintained the good laws of the land, he was a Puritan. In short, all that ran against the views of needy courtiers, proud and encroaching priests, thievish entrepreneurs, the lewd nobility, and gentry, all these were Puritans.

Puritans love God with all their souls but hate their neighbors with all their hearts. They are naturally close with their purses and liberal with their tongues.

Puritans are a sect rather than a religion—ever discontented with the present government and impatient to suffer any superiority. To any well governed Commonwealth, this sect is unendurable.

Anglican Judges Condemn a Puritan Author in the Court of Star Chamber,* 1634

Mr. Prynne has compiled and published a voluminous libel, a scandalous and seditious book. The intention of this book is to promote disobedience to the King, to the State, to the Church, and a general dislike of all government. He would have a new church, a new government, a new king. He would make all people discontented and offended with all present things. It is high time to deal firmly with those who have made such distraction in this kingdom.

Therefore, we condemn Prynne to be deprived of all University degrees, to be fined £5,000, to stand in the pillory at Westminster wearing papers declaring his offences, to have his ears cut off, and to be imprisoned for life.

The Court of Star Chamber, made up of the king's advisers and two judges, sat in a room with stars painted on the ceiling. No jury. Condemned accused almost before cases heard. Court abolished in 1641.

Adapted from S. R. Gardiner, Documents Relating to the Proceedings Against William Prynne (London: Camden Society, 1876), pp. 16–18.

A Puritan Argues in the House of Commons for Abolishing All Anglican Archbishops and Bishops, 1641

One of the main ends of church government is to advance and perfect religion. This House has already voted that Episcopal Church government contradicts that end. This House has already voted that Episcopal Church government is prejudicial to the civil state. If we desire a peaceful reformation, the growth of our religion, and the good of our civil state, we must pull down Episcopal Church government now, or it will fall about our ears within a few years.

Adapted from W. A. Shaw, History of the English Church Under the Commonwealth (London: Longmans Green, 1900), Vol. I, p. 86.

Instructions from a Puritan Committee of the House of Commons, 1643

This committee requires you to take away and demolish every altar or table of stone within your church and remove all candlesticks. You are required to demolish all crucifixes, crosses, and all images or pictures of any one or more persons of the Trinity or the Virgin Mary, inside or outside of your church, before the twentieth day of March next.

Adapted from W. H. Hutton, The English Church from the Accession of Charles I to the Death of Anne (London: Macmillan and Co., 1903), p. 126.

Oliver Cromwell* on Liberty of Conscience for Catholics, 1649

I meddle not with any man's conscience. But if by liberty of conscience, you mean a liberty to exercise the Catholic Mass, I judge it best to use plain dealing, and to let you know, where the Parliament of England has power, that will not be allowed.

Adapted from Thomas Carlyle, Letters and Speeches of Oliver Cromwell (London: Methuen and Co., 1904), Vol. I, p. 493.

George Fox* Describes the Difficulties of Being a Quaker, 1650

After I was set at liberty from the Nottingham jail, where I had been kept in prison for a long time, I travelled as before in the work of the Lord. Coming to Derby, I was moved by the Lord to go into the Steeple-house and speak to those assembled there about what the Lord has commanded.

Then came an officer and took me by the hand and said I must go before the

George Fox (1624–1691) was the son of a well-to-do Puritan weaver. He became the founder of the Society of Friends, or Quakers.

Adapted from the book **Journal** by George Fox. Rev. by Norman Penney. Intro. by Rufus M. Jones. Everyman's Library Edition. Published by E. P. Dutton & Co., Inc. and used with their permission, p. 30.

magistrates. When they had wearied themselves in examining me, they committed me to the House of Correction in Derby for six months as a blasphemer.

The Test Act Sets New Qualifications for Public Office, 1673

Adapted from **Statutes of the Realm**, Charles II, London, V. 782: 25, c.2.

Be it enacted that every person that hold any office, civil or military, or that shall receive any pay, salary, fee, or wages by reason of service to his Majesty, or have a command or place of trust or serve in the Navy, shall subscribe before a magistrate in open court that he has received the sacrament of the Lord's Supper according to the usage of the Anglican Church.

An Anglican Bishop Discusses Irish *Presbyterians,** 1696

Presbyterians were English, Scottish, or Irish Protestants who advocated a form of church government that did not include bishops.

Adapted from William King's letter to John Norman, November 13, 1697, **William King's Letter Book**, National Library, Dublin, Ireland.

In Ireland we have no *Test Act,** and from the lack of it, there is a design to exclude all Anglicans from the government of the city of Londonderry and admit only Presbyterians to civil office. Moreover, Presbyterian tradesmen take only those apprentices who agree to go to church with them. They neither employ nor trade with those who are not of their own sort if they can help it. When they serve on juries, they are more interested in favoring Presbyterians than rendering justice.

Parliament passed the Test Act to keep from public office any one who did not accept the Anglican Church or take Communion according to its custom.

6 TESTIMONY OF CONTEMPORARIES

In one hundred years' time, thousands of Englishmen and their families left their homeland for the opportunities and risks of a new life in North America. The minds of most of these courageous emigrants are closed to us; their thoughts were never recorded. However, the minds of some of the prominent leaders of the colonizing movement are open to us. Leaders like John Winthrop, William Penn, and the proprietors of Carolina wrote extensively about their thoughts, motives, and reasons. Also, there were prominent persons like Archbishop William King who were not colonists, but who were amazed by the dimensions of the colonizing movement, and recorded their accounts of it.

While reading the testimony of leaders of the seventeenth-century colonizing movement, and an observer of it, keep in mind these questions:

1. *What economic conditions encouraged English emigration to America?*
2. *What religious ideas encouraged English emigration to America?*
3. *What else encouraged English emigration to America?*

John Winthrop's Reasons for Undertaking a Plantation in New England, May, 1629

1. It will be an important service to the Church to carry the Gospel into those parts of the world and raise up a barrier against the kingdom of anti-Christ that *Jesuits*° are trying to establish there.

2. All other churches in Europe are brought to desolation. For our sins the Lord already frowns upon us and evil times may be coming. Who knows but that God has provided this place to be a refuge for those he wants to save out of a coming general calamity? The Church has no better place to fly than into the wilderness.

3. This land grows weary of her inhabitants so that man, who is the most precious of all creatures, is here more vile and base than the earth we walk on, and of less value than a horse or a sheep. Authority forces masters to take care of servants and parents to support their children. All of the towns complain about the burden of their poor. Children, servants, and neighbors, especially if they are poor, are counted as great burdens, while if times were right they would be our greatest earthly blessings.

4. The whole earth is the Lord's garden and he has given it to the sons of men with a general commission: Genesis I:28: Increase and multiply and replenish the earth and subdue it. Why, then, should we stand striving here for places to live? Many men spend as much labor and money to obtain or keep an acre or two of land here as would buy many acres in another country. Why allow a whole continent so fruitful and convenient for the use of man to lie wasted without any improvement?

5. We have grown so intemperate that no man's income is sufficient to keep up with society. And he who fails to keep up, lives in scorn and contempt. For this reason, all arts and trades are carried on in such deceitful ways that it is almost impossible for a good and upright man to make a decent living.

Jesuits (Society of Jesus) were a Catholic religious order founded in 1540 in Spain and approved by the Vatican. They were active missionaries in French and Spanish America throughout the seventeenth century.

6. The fountains of learning and religion are corrupted in England. Despite the great expense of their education, most children are corrupted and utterly overthrown by the poor education and by so many evil examples before them. The licentious government of the schools consists of men who strain at gnats and swallow camels. Dignities and formalities are strictly observed, but ruffian-like behavior and all kinds of disorders are allowed to pass uncontrolled.

7. What better work can an honorable Christian undertake than to join with a company of faithful people to raise and support an infant church into strength and prosperity?

8. If Godly men living in wealth and prosperity in England shall forsake all of that to join with this church and risk hardship and deprivation, it will be a great example for encouraging others to join in the plantation.

Adapted from Robert C. Winthrop, **Life and Letters of John Winthrop** (Boston: Ticknor and Fields, 1864), pp. 309–310.

9. It appears to be a work of God for the good of his Church in that he has disposed the hearts of so many of his wise and faithful servants to interest themselves in the plantation.

William Penn's Letter to the Delaware Indian Chiefs, 1681

My friends, there is one great God and power that has made the world and all things. This great God has written his law in our hearts by which we are taught to love, help, and do good to one another. Now this great God has been pleased to make me concerned in your part of the world. The king of the country where I live has given unto me a great province, but I desire to enjoy it with your love and consent, that we may always live together as neighbors and friends.

I am very sensible of the unkindness and injustices that has been too much exercised toward you by people from my part of the world. But I am not such a man. I have great love and regard towards you and I desire to gain your love and friendship by a kind, just, and peaceable life. The people I send are of the same mind and shall in all things behave themselves accordingly.

Adapted from **Memoirs of the Historical Society of Pennsylvania,** (Philadelphia, 1858), Vol. VI, pp. 251–252.

Life in Carolina, 1666

There is full and free liberty of conscience granted to all, so that no man is to be molested or called into question for matters of religion.

Every man and woman that transport themselves shall have for himself and each member of his family 100 acres of land forever by paying at most ½d* per acre per year.

If any maid or single woman have a desire to go over, they will think themselves in a Golden Age. Men pay a *dowry** for their wives. If single women be but civil and under 50 years of age, some honest men will purchase them for their wives.

d means pence and comes from the Latin word, denarius. Half a pence was the pittance paid annually on 100 acres of land in the colonies.

Tract by the Proprietors of Carolina, **Historical Collections of South Carolina,** edited by B. R. Carroll (New York, 1836), Vol. II, pp. 10–18.

Dowry is either money or property that a bride brings to a husband in marriage, or a gift of property by a man to or for a bride.

An Anglican View of Presbyterian Emigration
from Ireland to America, 1717

Some would say that Presbyterians leave Ireland because of uneasiness over religious matters. That is a mistake. Presbyterians have never been more content on that point than they are now. They never thought about leaving the country till oppressed by excessive rents.

After the revolution in 1688, much of the country suffered during the war that followed. At the time, landlords were desperate for tenants and let lands out for long leases at easy rents. Now these leases have expired and tenants are obliged to pay what was paid before the revolution which, in most cases, is double or triple what they have been paying during the last twenty-five years.

Charles Simeon King, **A Great Archbishop** (London: Longmans Green, 1906), pp. 301–302.

A110

4 Political and economic development of English America, 1660–1760

Ties of Dependence

Introduction

The last assignment pointed out that complex historical movements involving many people over long periods of time usually have more than one cause. It also taught you:

> Economic conditions, religious idealism, and social pressures were all causes of English emigration to America.

> Religious intolerance in Puritan Massachusetts Bay led to the foundation of other colonies in New England.

> Pennsylvania was unique for its commitment to religious toleration and for its appeal to non-English emigrants.

This present assignment is concerned with the political and economic development of the colonies in the century after they were founded. It examines the nature of the political and economic ties that bound England and her colonies together.

Three Kinds of Colonies

Incorporated Colonies

The legal basis of colonial government in seventeenth-century English America took three forms: corporate, royal, and proprietary. The earliest colonies were founded by incorporated trading companies whose stockholders elected a governor and an advisory resident council. The governor and council were charged with day-to-day management of the colony.

Today both houses of the Massachusetts legislature are known as the **General Court.**

Important policy decisions were made at periodic meetings of the company's stockholders called Great and General Courts.* These Courts were prohibited from enacting any laws for the colony that were contrary to the laws of England. Such was the substance of the Virginia Company's charter. In 1619 the company created an elected legislature for Virginia. Later, the other colonies followed Virginia's example.

Although the charter of the Massachusetts Bay Company was modeled after that of Virginia, its Puritan stockholders acted in a highly original way. By join-

A111

In order to prevent **Connecticut's Charter** from being surrendered to King James II's representative in 1687, Captain Joseph Wadsworth hid the charter in a large oak tree in Hartford. Known as the **Charter Oak,** this historic tree survived until 1856 when it was blown down in a storm.

ing the colony themselves, they moved the meetings of the company's Great and General Court to America, where it evolved into a two-house legislature for the colony.

The Great and General Court elected the governor and his council, but only church members were allowed to vote in elections for Court representatives. This charter and its political arrangements remained the basis of Massachusetts government until it was annulled by court action in 1684. In 1691 the King granted a new charter, appointed a governor and other officials for the colony, and abolished the voting requirement of church membership.

Although founded by refugees and emigrants from Massachusetts Bay rather than by a trading company, the legal bases for government in Rhode Island and Connecticut were also charters of incorporation. The King recognized these colonies as corporations with governing authority vested in a governor and members of the corporation, who were free men of the colony. The business of the corporations of Rhode Island and Connecticut* was government, not trade. These two colonies elected their own governors and were self-governing throughout the entire colonial period, except briefly between 1686–1688 when all the colonies north of Pennsylvania were combined under a single government called the Dominion of New England.

Royal Colonies

Virginia was not only the first incorporated colony; it was also the first royal colony. (See chart on page 118 for other royal colonies.) By 1624 the Virginia Company could no longer meet its financial obligations. It went into bankruptcy; its charter was revoked, and the Crown took over administration of the colony. Under royal control, the elected legislature remained, but the king appointed the governor and other officials. The governor, in turn, appointed his council. In later years, the constitutional settlement of Virginia became the model for other royal colonies.

Proprietary Colonies

The first successful proprietary colony in America was Maryland. Holders of proprietary charters for large land grants were like kings of their own domain. Proprietors could grant land, confer titles of nobility, appoint all officials, create courts, command armies, establish churches, and make laws. The only limitation on the power of the proprietors of Maryland, New York, and Carolina was that laws passed and taxes levied had to have the consent of the free men of the colony.

The proprietary charter of Pennsylvania was not quite so extensive. Inhabitants had rights of appeal to the Crown, and all acts of the Pennsylvania legislature had to be submitted to the Crown for approval within five years. The proprietary charter of Georgia was limited still further. Its life was only twenty years, after which time the colony reverted to the Crown.

Whatever the basis of government in the colonies—corporate, royal, or proprietary—by 1700 the executive and legislative framework of government was much the same everywhere. In all the colonies except Connecticut and Rhode Island, governors were appointed. Similarly, *appointed councils** composed of a colony's leading men were common to most of them. There were also elected assemblies in each colony. In those assemblies—called by different names such as House of Representatives in Massachusetts, House of Burgesses in Virginia, and House of Commons in South Carolina—representation was apportioned sometimes by population and sometimes by wealth. Some kind of property qualification was necessary for voting.

In Massachusetts the members of the **Governor's Council** were not appointed. They were elected by the General Court subject to the Governor's veto.

Political Relations between the Colonies and England

In contrast to the similarity of *institutional** development in the colonies, there was no such corresponding development in English colonial administration. There was in England no single authority to whom colonial officials were obliged to report. There was no formal agency responsible for supervising colonial affairs until 1675. In that year, a committee of the King's closest advisors, called the Lords of Trade and Plantation, was established to provide overall direction to English colonial policy. The job quickly proved to be bigger than the men assigned to it.

Institutional refers to offices or agencies of government such as the governor, the legislature, and the courts.

In 1696, under pressure from Parliament, King William III created a new body, the Board of Trade and Plantation.* In time, this board also became ineffective and declined in importance. Other agencies such as the Secretary of State, Treasury Board, Customs Board, and Admiralty all had some responsibilities for colonial affairs. Consequently, colonial officials in America were responsible to many different agencies and offices in England. The result of this division of responsibility and lack of direction was often confusion, inefficiency, and sometimes, injustice.

Composed of fifteen members, the Board of Trade's most famous member was **John Locke,** the political philosopher.

Throughout the entire colonial period, governments in both England and America were greatly concerned over economic development. Their concerns were the same, but their frames of reference were not. When disputes arose between the elected assemblies in America and the elected House of Commons in England, they were usually caused by differences over the objectives and operation of economic development.

The ties binding England and her American colonies together had both economic and political strands. Understanding how England's relations with her American colonies changed between 1660 and 1760 requires knowledge of all the strands that bound them together. Economic disputes between the Mother Country and the colonies quickly became political ones. Economic issues were increasingly argued in political terms. Economic policies justified in England as best for the Empire were denounced in America as acts of tyranny and political injustice. Changing economic relations inevitably affected how the king's subjects in England and America thought and felt about one another.

Objectives are to:

—Recognize and identify in given testimony and data the objectives of English laws regulating colonial trade and manufacturing.

—Analyze the effect of such laws on the economic relations between England and colonial America.

—Recognize, identify, and analyze the effects of points of political disagreement between colonial assemblies and colonial governors.

—Summarize your analysis of economic and political relations between England and colonial America.

A113

7 ENGLAND AND COLONIAL AMERICA: THE ECONOMIC TIE

England's economic policy toward her American colonies was characterized by regulation and encouragement. This policy began in 1621 with a royal proclamation requiring shipment of <u>all</u> Virginia tobacco to England and prohibiting tobacco planting and cultivation in England. The Navigation Acts of 1660–1696 and other legislation enacted in the early eighteenth century were much more comprehensive and ambitious. You can best identify and understand the objectives of England's economic policy toward her colonies by examining legislation that expressed them most clearly. While studying the following extracts from English laws, customs information, and population statistics, keep in mind these questions:

1. What were the reasons given by the English Parliament for enacting laws regulating colonial trade and industry?

2. Who do you think benefited most (and who benefited least) from the laws regulating colonial trade? Which groups in what countries?

3. How did colonial America's economic importance to England change between 1700 and 1760?

Excerpts from Navigation Laws, 1660–1696

For the increase of shipping and encouragement of the navigation of this nation wherein under the good providence and protection of God, the wealth, safety, and strength of this kingdom is so much concerned, be it enacted that:

No goods or commodities shall be imported into, or exported out of, territories or plantations belonging to his Majesty except in ships that have been built in the British Isles or in the said territories or plantations. The said ships must be wholly owned and captained by British subjects, and be manned by crews of whom three quarters must be British subjects.

No sugars, tobacco, cotton, wool, ginger, indigoes, and *dyeing-wood** of the growth, production, or manufacture of any English plantation in America, Asia, or Africa, shall be shipped anywhere except to another English plantation or to the British Isles.

No commodity of the growth, production, or manufacture of Europe, except salt for the fisheries and wines from Madeira and the Azores, shall be imported into any English territory or plantation except that which has been laden and shipped from the British Isles in English-built shipping. Colonial governors are required to swear an oath that they shall enforce all of the clauses of all laws enacted by Parliament affecting trade or navigation.

All laws enacted or to be enacted in the plantations that conflict with any of these provisions shall be null and void.

A **special kind** of wood from which color is extracted to use in dyeing materials.

Adapted from Danby Pickering, ed., **Statutes At Large**, VII, 452ff; VIII, 161ff; 398ff; IX, 428ff.

Importance of wool to England's economy is symbolized by members of the House of Lords sitting on sacks of wool. Symbolic wool sacks are still used in Parliament today.

Woollen Act, 1699

Since wool and woollen manufactures are the greatest and most profitable commodities of this Kingdom on which the value of lands and the trade of this Kingdom do chiefly depend; and since great quantities of such manufactures have been of late made in Ireland and in the English plantations in America, and are exported from those places to foreign markets up to now supplied from England, the trade of England will be ruined and the value of lands will sink if this be continued.

For the prevention of this situation and the encouragement of the woollen manufactures of this Kingdom be it enacted that no wool or woollen manufactures being the product of or manufacture of Ireland or any of the English plantations in America shall be exported out of Ireland or from one plantation to another or to any other place whatsoever.

Naval stores consist of tar, pitch, turpentine, hemp, masts, yardarms (cross piece on the mast), and bowsprits (pole for sails and rigging, extending forward over bow of ship)

Naval Stores Act,* 1703

Since the wealth, safety, and strength of this Kingdom so much depends on naval stores which are now brought in from foreign parts to the discouragement of the trade and navigation of this Kingdom; and since her Majesty's plantations in America were settled with a design to render them useful to England, and profitable to themselves, trade in naval stores ought to be encouraged.

Be it therefore enacted that anyone directly importing naval stores from any of her Majesty's plantations in America in ships that may lawfully trade with the plantations shall receive a reward or premium according to rates set forth below.

Adapted from Danby Pickering, **Statutes at Large**, X, XI.

The official **value of hats** exported from England in the years <u>before</u> and <u>after</u> passage of the Hat Act in 1732 were:

1731	£105,000
1732	£116,500
1733	£118,000

Adapted from Danby Pickering, ed., **Statutes at Large**, XVI, 304ff.

*Hat Act,** 1732

Since the art and mystery of hat-making in Great Britain has arrived to great perfection, and considerable quantities of hats in the past have been exported to his Majesty's plantations in America, and since great quantities of hats have of late years been made in the American plantations and exported to foreign markets up to now supplied from Great Britain, be it enacted that no hats or felts, finished or unfinished, shall be transported from one plantation to another, or shipped to any other place, whatsoever.

Economic Importance of Colonial America to England, 1700–1760

Year	Exports to America	Percent	Imports from America	Percent
1700	£354,345	5	£395,025	6.5
1720	£319,706	4.5	£468,191	7.5
1740	£806,385	8.5	£520,419	10.5
1760	£2,611,567	16.5	£761,102	8.0

Adapted from **Customs 3, Public Records Office, London, 1700–1760.**

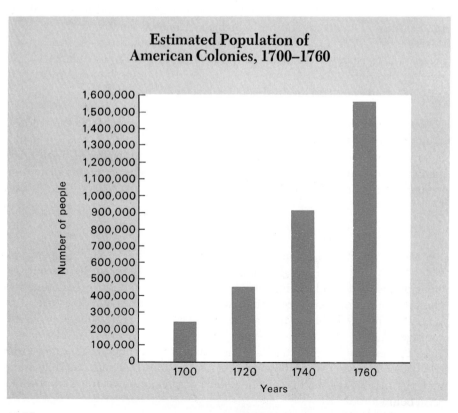

Estimated Population of American Colonies, 1700–1760

8 ENGLAND AND COLONIAL AMERICA: THE POLITICAL TIE

During the seventeenth century England's internal political difficulties greatly influenced how her colonial policy developed. Political relations with the American colonies assumed a trial-and-error character. However, after the Revolution of 1688 stabilized English politics, relations with the colonies became more regular and more predictable. Englishmen on both sides of the Atlantic could devote attention to describing what the political relations between England and her American colonies actually were and speculating about what they ought to be. While studying the following chart of political relations and selections from governmental officials and a political theorist, keep in mind these questions:

1. Which English colonies permanently changed their legal status between 1607 and 1760? Which English colonies did not?

2. What complaints did colonial assemblies have against colonial governors?

3. What complaints did colonial governors have against colonial assemblies?

4. What was the major political issue between England and her American colonies in the 1760's?

Complaints against the Colonial *Governor** of Virginia, 1702

To speak of the governor's injustices, oppressions, and insolences to individuals would require a large volume, so we shall limit our observations to his behavior toward the members of our General Assembly.

Formerly the General Assembly was called for sittings at appropriate times. The present governor calls frequent Assemblies at unseasonable times of the year, and at great trouble and expense to the inhabitants. Furthermore, his behavior toward the Upper House of the Assembly has been arbitrary and outrageous. For example:

> He has taken upon himself the right to preside over this body and limit debate.
> He states the questions, and overrules in an arbitrary and threatening manner.
> He threatens and abuses all who speak anything contrary to his opinions.
> He endeavors to encourage bad understanding between the two Houses, by siding sometimes with one House, and sometimes with the other.
> He makes entries to that purpose in the books of the Assembly.
> He meets privately with members and uses all of the arts of cajoling and threatening for his own ends.
> His behavior constitutes intolerable encroachments upon the liberties of both Houses.

The governer was **Francis Nicholson** (1655–1728). He served as Lieutenant Governor of the Dominion of New England, 1688–1689, Lieutenant Governor of Virginia, 1692, Governor of Maryland, 1694–1698, Governor of Virginia, 1698–1705, and Governor of South Carolina, 1720–1725.

Adapted from "A Memorial Concerning the Maladministrations of His Excellency Francis Nicholson, Esq.," printed in **The Virginia Magazine of History and Biography**, III (1895–1896), pp. 373–382.

Political Relations between England and Colonial America, 1607–1760

COLONY	ORIGINAL STATUS	CHANGES IN STATUS	STATUS IN 1760
Virginia	Chartered as an incorporated company in 1606.	Company bankrupt in 1623, Charter revoked, and Royal Colony set up.	Royal
Massachusetts	Chartered as an incorporated company in 1629.	Charter annuled 1684. Dominion of New England, 1685–1688. Massachusetts, Maine, Plymouth united. Massachusetts a Royal Colony, 1691.	Royal
New Hampshire	Part of Massachusetts, 1638–1680.	Separated by Royal Commission, 1680. Dominion of New England, 1685–1688. Royal government, 1686. Royal Colony, 1692.	Royal
Rhode Island	Chartered as a self-governing corporate colony by Parliament, 1644.	Charter reissued by Charles II in 1663. Dominion of New England, 1686–1688. Charter reconfirmed 1693.	Corporate Charter
Connecticut	Self-governing community without a charter, 1636–1662.	Self governing corporate colony, 1663. Dominion of New England, 1687–88. Charter reconfirmed, 1690.	Corporate Charter
Maryland	Chartered as a proprietary colony in 1634.	Parliament assumed control and suspended proprietary governor in 1652. Calvert family restored as proprietors in 1662.	Proprietary
New York	Captured from the Dutch and granted to James, Duke of York, as proprietor in 1664.	Became a Royal Colony when Duke of York became King James II in 1685. Dominion of New England, 1687–1688. Royal Colony in 1691.	Royal
New Jersey	Captured from the Dutch and granted by Duke of York to Lord Berkeley and Sir George Carteret as proprietors.	Dominion of New England in 1688. Proprietors restored, 1692; surrender authority to Queen, 1702. Royal Colony set up.	Royal
Pennsylvania	Chartered as a proprietary colony in 1681.	King assumed control over the colony in 1692. William Penn reconfirmed as proprietor in 1694.	Proprietary
Delaware	Captured from the Dutch in 1664.	Given to William Penn in 1682. Same governor rules in both Pennsylvania and Delaware.	Proprietary
North Carolina	Chartered as a proprietary colony in 1663.	Governor set up, 1712. Charter surrendered to king, 1729. Royal Colony set up.	Royal
South Carolina	Chartered as a proprietary colony, 1663.	Governor appointed, 1721. Charter surrendered to king, 1729. Royal Colony set up.	Royal
Georgia	Chartered as a proprietary colony for 21 years in 1732.	Charter surrendered, 1752. Royal Colony set up.	Royal

A Colonial *Governor** Complains about the Massachusetts General Assembly, 1723

Samuel Shute (1662–1742), a former soldier and governor of both Massachusetts and New Hampshire, 1716–1723, made this complaint.

Upon arrival in Massachusetts Bay I soon called the General Assembly together. I found the House of Representatives, who are chosen by annual elections, possessed of all of the same powers of the English House of Commons, and some greater. They have the power of nominating once a year the persons that constitute your Majesty's council, and also of giving the salary of the governor and lieutenant-governor for six months, rather than for a full year.

The House of Representatives also provides the salary of the treasurer once a year, and thereby gains sole authority over that important office. They use their authority thus obtained to intimidate the treasurer from obeying proper orders for issuing money, if such orders are not agreeable to their views. By all of this, the House of Representatives is, in a manner, the whole legislative and in a good measure, the executive power of this province.

Presently, three persons that I have negatived for nomination to the Council have been elected to the House as representatives for the town of Boston. This practice is so notorious and so widely justified in this town that it is a common maxim that a negatived councilor makes a good representative.

Thus constituted, and unsatisfied with the many uncommon privileges they enjoy, the House of Representatives for some years past has been making attempts to usurp the few rights of government remaining to the Crown.

Adapted from Cecil Headlam, et al., **Calendar of State Papers, Colonial Series, America and West Indies, 1722–1723** (London: Her Majesty's Stationery Office, 1934), pp. 324–330.

An Inquiry into the Rightful Relations between the King and the American Colonies, 1765*

Full uncontrolled independent rights of debate as concerns the framing of bills, the passing of them into law uncontrolled by any power of the Crown or governor is essential to the very existence of a free legislature.

The point at issue here is whether the colonial legislatures are free or are subordinate and can be instructed, restricted, or controlled by the king or governor in the act of legislation. The colonists constantly deny it. The king's ministers affirm it.

Thomas Pownall (1722–1805) first published **The Administration of the Colonies** in 1765. An experienced administrator, he served as Lieutenant Governor of New Jersey in 1755, and Governor of Massachusetts from 1757–1760.

After all the confusion and obstruction which this point has caused, it is time, surely, that in some way or another, it be determined:

Whether in fact or deed the people of the colonies have a right to a whole legislative power.

Whether the people of the colonies are entitled to the same full and free unrestrained powers and legislative will in their several assemblies under their respective charters and royal commissions as the people of Great Britain enjoy in their Parliament under its constitution and the Great Charter.

Adapted from **Thomas Pownall, The Administrations of the Colonies,** 4th edition (London, 1768), pp. 70–80.

5 Life styles of colonial America

Cultural Diversity

Introduction

This present assignment is concerned with one aspect of colonial American cultural history. It examines the *social* frames of reference out of which different life styles in colonial America developed.

From the very beginning of English colonization of North America, non-English elements were present. A few Poles and Germans were in Jamestown as craftsmen as early as 1608. Africans were brought to Virginia in 1619. Several Frenchmen also appear in the records of the Virginia Company in 1619, and a few Italians arrived in 1625. The Dutch arrived in significant numbers after the settlement of New Amsterdam in 1624, and Dutch continued to be spoken in Albany as late as 1750. Small numbers of Scots, Irish Catholics, French Protestants, and Jews came during the seventeenth century. Yet by 1700 the vast majority of the inhabitants of the American colonies were English by birth or descent, and Anglican or Congregationalist in religion. In the next sixty years this situation changed.

Colonial population increased rapidly after 1700. Much of that increase came from enslaved blacks imported from the West Indies and Africa, and from *indentured servants** imported from largely Protestant northern Ireland and from the Protestant parts of Germany. By 1760 only half of the people inhabiting colonial America were English or of English descent.

Indentured servants—persons who contracted to work for a specified number of years in exchange for passage from Europe to colonial America.

Estimated Ethnic Composition of Colonial America in 1760

British		
English and Welsh	49.0%	
Scots	6.5	
Protestant Irish	4.8	
Catholic Irish	3.2	
Total British		63.5%
African		20.0
German		7.2
Dutch		2.3
French		1.5
Unassignable		5.5
		100.0%

Colonial Religions Quarrel and Split

During the same sixty years the religious composition of colonial America also changed significantly. All accounts agree that in 1760 colonial Americans were overwhelmingly Protestant and remarkably denominational. Church records indicate that Congregationalists, Presbyterians, Baptists, and Anglicans were the largest sects, followed by Quakers, German and Dutch Reformed. Lutherans, Catholics and Jewish congregations were few in number and small in size.

Some striking social effects resulted from this ethnic diversity and religious denominationalism. Many Germans spoke their own language and separated themselves from the English-speaking majority. Some blacks, even when freed, were segregated from white society by law or by custom. Protestant denominations were quarrelsome. Individual churches frequently split over points of religious doctrine or over the personalities of ministers and lay leaders. When that happened, some members withdrew from the church, abandoned social relationships of long standing, and sought new ones elsewhere.

Varied Life Styles

Catholics and Jews were usually regarded as being so different from the rest of society that they could not be changed. Therefore, sometimes they were treated as outsiders. Yet for all of its denominationalism, English Protestantism and the English language had extraordinary *assimilative** power. Cultural diversity and the variety of life styles in colonial America came more from the natural conditions of life in the American environment than from ethnic and religious differences transported from Europe. Attitudes towards blacks and the legal status of slavery imposed on them were the exceptions.

Assimilative: Capable of absorbing or bringing together; making people similar.

Land was abundant in America; labor was scarce. Wages were twice what they were in England. For white men society was far more open than in Europe. More than one indentured servant served out his contract, prospered in business or farming, married a planter's daughter, and won a place for himself among the ranks of land-owning gentlemen.

Conditions were not the same everywhere, and men had to work in different ways in order to make a living. But everywhere men had to work at something. And everywhere there was some form of the Protestant religion. It was a powerful, all-enveloping, seven-days-a-week influence. Religious beliefs were almost as varied then as now, but men clung to their beliefs much more staunchly then than they do today.

What men did for a living and how intensively they did it, what men believed and how intensively they believed it, inspired the different life styles of colonial Massachusetts, colonial Virginia, and colonial Philadelphia. To understand the cultural history of colonial America, we must recognize and identify the social frames of reference out of which different life styles of that culture developed.

Objectives are to:

—Recognize and identify in given readings expressions of values and social attitudes.

—Reconstruct from the values and attitudes identified three representative colonial American life-styles.

—Analyze a filmstrip of five colonial American women and decide to which life-style they belong.

A121

9 MASSACHUSETTS: THE DIARY OF A JUDGE, 1696-1703

By 1700 the power of the Congregational Church over the public and private lives of the people of Massachusetts was much less than had been the case earlier. Wealthy merchants challenged Congregationalist ministers for the social leadership of the colony.

Nevertheless, in the early eighteenth century Congregationalist ministers and prominent laymen in the church were still powerful. They influenced the government and the economy, and dominated social and cultural life. They established the social values and expressed the social attitudes that most other men accepted. The frame of reference of the godly man was the basis for the Massachusetts life-style.

Samuel Sewall (1652–1730) was one of the most prominent public figures of his day. Though educated for the ministry and active in church affairs all of his life, he chose a career of public service. He served in both Houses of the Massachusetts Assembly, was appointed a judge of the Superior Court in 1692, and Chief Justice in 1718. Sewall was a very complicated man and his diary has become a classic of early American literature.

On the one hand, as one of the judges at the witchcraft trials at Salem in 1692, Sewall shared the responsibility for the execution of twenty persons. On the other hand, Sewall was one of the first public officials to speak out and write against the horror and injustice of Negro slavery. While reading the following selections from Samuel Sewall's diary, keep in mind these questions:

1. How many of Judge Sewall's values can you recognize and identify?

2. How many of Judge Sewall's social attitudes can you recognize and identify? What kinds of social behavior do you think he would favor or disfavor?

Museum of Fine Arts, Boston

Samuel Sewall

Samuel Sewall's Diary, 1696–1703

February 7, 1696

My brother spoke to me about finding another occupation for my son, Sam. He mentioned to me Mr. Wadsworth's sermon against idleness which he said was a great affliction with Sam. He said Sam's *calling** was an idle one and that he did more at home than he ever did at work. Sam overheard him and complained about the difficulty of his job.

* * *

Calling—a job, vocation or purpose in life. Sewall's complaining brother was a merchant for whom Sam worked as a clerk.

February 10, 1696

I am very sorrowful by reason of the unsettledness of my son. Good Lord, give me Truth and give rest to my dear Samuel and put him to some calling.

* * *

The John Ward House in Salem, Massachusetts, was built in the 1680's. The second-story overhang and the casement windows are characteristic of many 17th-century houses copied from medieval English architecture.

February 26, 1696

I prayed with Sam alone that God would direct our way as to a calling for him.

❊   ❊   ❊

April 8, 1698

I visited Mr. Morton. He was asleep, but I went in. He awoke, stretched out his hand, and tried to speak. I asked him how he did in such a long illness. He at first said, *that which can't be cured must be endured.* Then he

The Ward House kitchen with its homemade furniture is dominated by a huge fireplace used for cooking, heat, and light. Sprays of herbs hang from the beams.

corrected himself and said, *I desire patiently to submit to the hand of God.* When I took my leave, he said, *I wish you well and all of your family.* I told him I doubted not but that I should fare better for his blessing.

He died between two and three o'clock.

❖ ❖ ❖

June 10, 1701

Having heard last night that Josiah Willard had cut off his hair (a very full head of hair) and put on a wig, I went to him this morning. I asked him what extremity had forced him to cut off his own hair and put on a wig. He answered, none at all. But he said that his hair was straight, and he did not like how it parted. He argued that men might as well shave hair off their heads as off their faces. I answered that God ordained our hair as a test to see whether we are content with his creation. If disliked, we do not cut off skin and nails. Pain and danger restrain us. And they that care not what men think of them care not what God thinks of them.

He said he would leave off his wig when his hair was grown. His father thanked me and said if he had known of his intention, he would have forbidden him. His mother had heard him talk of it but was afraid to forbid him, lest he should do it and be more at fault.

❖ ❖ ❖

January 6, 1702

Through my wife's many illnesses, especially after her fall upon the stairs five weeks ago, she has kept to her rooms. From her fears about what the issue would be, and from the misgivings of our unbelieving heart, God has been wonderfully merciful to us in her comfortable delivery of our daughter. This is the thirteenth child that I have offered up to God in Baptism.

❖ ❖ ❖

December 19, 1702

Captain Croft died last night. He is buried in the new burying place. For debauchery and irreligion, he was one of the vilest men that has ever set foot in Boston. 'Tis said he refused to have any minister called to pray with him during his sickness which lasted more than two weeks.

❖ ❖ ❖

February 22, 1703

This morning I was praying alone. I was much affected to think how concerned and inquisitive I was in my travelling about, whether I was going right or not. Yet not so constant and inquisitive am I, whether I be on the right or wrong way to Heaven. May He who is the Way, the Truth, and the Light, bring me into and always keep me on the right way.

❖ ❖ ❖

Adapted from **Samuel Sewall's Diary**, edited by Mark Van Doren (New York: Macy-Masius Publishers, 1927), pp. 131–133, 149–150, 161–166, 169–170. By permission of Vanguard Press.

A124

At left is **Westover,** the elegant Georgian mansion, built in the 1730's by William Byrd II of Virginia (below). It was one of the first of the great Virginia plantation homes.

10 VIRGINIA: THE SECRET DIARY OF A PLANTER, 1712

During the eighteenth century large plantations using slave labor were the outstanding social fact of colonial life in Virginia. This does not mean that most colonial Virginians were large plantation owners and masters of many slaves. The opposite was true. Most white Virginians owned small farms and few, if any, slaves. Nevertheless, it was the large plantation owners who dominated economic life, ran the government, established social values, and expressed the social attitudes which most white Virginians accepted. The *planter* frame of reference was the basis of the Virginia life-style.

William Byrd II (1674–1744) of Westover was one of the most famous and celebrated gentlemen planters of his day. Though his properties were large, much of his life was spent in public service. He served in both Houses of the Virginia Assembly and on several occasions was chosen to represent the interests of Virginia in England. The secret diary which he kept during much of his life was clearly intended for his eyes alone. He wrote it in a primitive version of shorthand which scholars only recently have learned how to decipher. While reading the following selections from William Byrd's secret diary, keep in mind these questions:

1. How many of William Byrd's <u>values</u> can you recognize and identify?

2. How many of William Byrd's <u>social attitudes</u> can you recognize and identify? What kinds of <u>social behavior</u> do you think he would favor or disfavor?

A125

William Byrd's Secret Diary, 1712

A few entries from William Byrd's Diary, which he wrote in shorthand so that it could not be deciphered by his contemporaries, appears here.

April 2

I rose about 7 o'clock and read nothing. However I said a short prayer and ate some potato and milk for breakfast. Then we played at cards and I lost 10 shillings . . . . About 2 o'clock we went to dinner, about 17 of us, and I ate some roast beef for dinner which was very fat and good . . . . In the evening I went home with Colonel Bassett . . . . We had a supper but I ate only some milk. Colonel Hill lay with me and snored terribly so that I could not sleep and I wouldn't wake him for fear his head should ache. I neglected to say my prayers but had good health, good thoughts, and good humor, thank God Almighty.

* * *

April 3

I rose about 6 o'clock but neglected to say my prayers. However I had some chocolate for breakfast . . . . About 10 o'clock we took our leave and the Colonel went with us to the store . . . . where I bought a maid to look after my spinners. Here we saw the salt works. About 12 Colonel Hill and I went away home and by the way I called at Drury Stith's and let him know that the Governor had promised his brother to be sheriff . . . . Then I went home and found every body well there . . . . At night I ate some cold roast beef for supper. I neglected to say my prayers but had good health, good thoughts, and good humor, thank God Almighty . . . .

Lucian (120 A.D.–200 A.D.)— Greek writer of satires.

The people and boys mentioned here, and the maid who was bought, were probably enslaved blacks.

Byrd here refers to men of the Virginia Militia sent to aid the English settlers in North Carolina against the Tuscarora Indians. After their defeat the Tuscaroras moved to New York and joined the Iroquois Confederation as the sixth nation.

April 5

I rose about 6 o'clock and read a chapter in Hebrew and some Greek in *Lucian.** I said my prayers and ate boiled milk for breakfast . . . . I settled several accounts till dinner, and then I ate some fish. In the afternoon I read a little English and then took a walk to [see] my people at work. It continued to rain by fits. In the evening I took a walk about the plantation and found some of my boys going to burn some of my hogshead staves, for which I beat them* . . . . At night I wrote two letters to my officers to choose men to go to Carolina.* I said my prayers and had good health, good thoughts, and good humor, thank God Almighty . . . .

April 9

I rose about 6 o'clock and read a chapter in Hebrew and some Greek in Lucian. I said my prayers and ate boiled milk for breakfast . . . . The weather was clear and warm which tempted me to go . . . as far as Colonel Hill's . . . . About 2 o'clock we went to a very indifferent dinner and I ate some bacon and peas but the Colonel would give me no wine, notwithstanding he had it in the house. In the afternoon we went to see the ships that were building and stayed there about an hour . . . . Then I took leave and went home and found all well. I said my prayers and had good health, good thoughts, and good humor, thank God Almighty. My wife had Moll whipped for not letting the people have what was ordered them.

Quoted from **The Secret Diary of William Byrd of Westover, 1709–1712**, edited by Louis B. Wright and Marion Tinling (Richmond, Va.: The Dietz Press, 1941), pp. 509–513.

❉   ❉   ❉

11 PHILADELPHIA: ADVICE ON HOW TO SUCCEED

By 1760 Philadelphia had become the largest and most prosperous city in North America. The leading characters in Philadelphia's success story were merchants and businessmen. Mostly Quakers, the merchant and business community ran the city government, dominated economic life, established the values, and expressed the attitudes that most Philadelphians accepted. The merchant frame of reference was the basis for the Philadelphia life-style.

This view of the southeast corner of Third and Market Streets in Philadelphia about 1799 depicts the prosperous development of the city.

Benjamin Franklin wrote and circulated **Poor Richard's Almanack** (Americanized maxims, proverbs and epigrams of the old world). Though he attended school only briefly, Franklin founded the Academy of Philadelphia in 1751 which later became the University of Pennsylvania, and established a circulating library. He printed currency for Pennsylvania, New Jersey, Delaware, and Maryland; founded a debating club; Philadelphia's first fire company; and found time to be postmaster.

Though not a Quaker, Benjamin Franklin (1706–1790) was Philadelphia's most celebrated citizen. Franklin's personal success story paralleled that of his beloved city. Born into a poor family, Franklin ran away at the age of 17. In the course of a long and adventurous life, he achieved astonishing success in colonial America as a businessman, inventor, journalist, publisher, philosopher, and politician. He achieved worldwide recognition as a scientist and diplomat. Franklin's writings summarized what the merchant community believed was success and how anyone, no matter how disadvantaged by humble beginnings, could obtain it. While reading Benjamin Franklin's *Formula for Success*, keep in mind these questions:

1. How many of Benjamin Franklin's <u>values</u> can you recognize and identify?

2. How many of Benjamin Franklin's <u>social attitudes</u> can you recognize and identify? What kinds of <u>social behavior</u> do you think he would favor or disfavor?

Benjamin Franklin's Formula for Success, 1728

Those who write of the art of poetry teach us that if we would write what may be worth reading, we ought always before we begin, to form a regular plan and design of one piece. . . . I am apt to think it is the same as to life . . . let me therefore, make some resolutions, and form some scheme of action, that henceforth I may live in all respects like a rational creature.

1. It is necessary for me to be extremely frugal for some time, till I have paid what I owe.

2. To endeavor to speak truth in every instance, to give nobody expectations that are not likely to be answered but aim at sincerity in every word and action—the most amiable excellence in a rational being.

3. To apply myself industriously to whatever business I take in hand, and not divert my mind from business by any foolish project of growing suddenly rich, for industry and patience are the surest means of plenty.

4. I resolve to speak ill of no man whatever, not even in a matter of truth; but rather by some means excuse the faults I hear charged upon others, and upon proper occasion speak all the good I know of every body.

Adapted from "Plan for Future Conduct," Benjamin Franklin's Autobiographical Writings, edited by Carl Van Doren, (New York: Viking Press, 1945), pp. 25–26.

The Way to Wealth, 1758

If time be of all things the most precious, wasting time must be . . . the greatest *prodigality;** since . . . lost time is never found again; and what we call time enough, always proves little enough. . . . *Sloth** makes all things difficult, but industry all easy . . . while laziness travels so slowly, that poverty soon overtakes him . . . and early to bed, and early to rise, makes a man healthy, wealthy, and wise.

So what signifies wishing and hoping for better times? We make these times better, if we bestir ourselves. . . . There are no gains without pains. . . . Work while it is called today, for you know not how much you may be hindered tomorrow . . . one today, is worth two tomorrows . . . be ashamed to catch yourself idle . . . .

If you would be wealthy . . . think of saving as well as of getting . . . . Beware of little expenses; a small leak will sink a great ship . . . and moreover, fools make feasts, and wise men eat them . . . .

If you would know the value of money, go and try to borrow some; for he that goes a-borrowing goes a-sorrowing; and indeed so does he that lends to such people when he goes to get it in again. . . . This doctrine, my friends, is Reason and Wisdom; but after all, do not depend too much upon your own Industry, Frugality and Prudence, though excellent things, for they may all be blasted without the blessings of heaven. . . . Ask that blessing humbly.

Prodigality—extravagance or wasteful spending.

Sloth—indolence or laziness.

The Autobiography of Benjamin Franklin and Selections from His Other Writings (New York: Random House, Inc. [Carlton House], 1932), pp. 206–207, 211–214.

The two medallions shown here are examples of how Franklin's adages worked their way into the art of the times.

16

Ann Pollard
Anonymous oil, 1721

Photo by Sandak, courtesy of
The Massachusetts Historical Society

17

Alice Grymes Page (1723–1746),
first wife of Mann Page II, and
one of her infants.
Original painting attributed to
Charles Bridges

Photo courtesy of the College
of William and Mary,
Williamsburg, Virginia

A130

18

Mrs. Seymour Fort, 1776
by John Singleton Copley
Reproduced by permission of the Wadsworth Atheneum, Hartford, Connecticut

19

Irish Peasant Woman
Watercolor, late 17th century
Artist unknown
Photo © British Museum

20

The Cook
Courtesy, Library of Congress

A132

6 What historians have said

Analyzing Historical Interpretations

Introduction

You have learned that cultural diversity was very much a fact of colonial American life. This assignment is concerned with the political consequences of the cultural diversity you have just studied and with the concept of frame of reference that you have been using. Your work on the European colonization and settlement of colonial America ends with selections from the writing of well-known professional historians on colonial American politics.

In the past thirty years, historians of colonial American politics have been very busy. They have collected many new facts and have rethought older interpretations in the light of these new facts. As yet, no one interpretation finds general acceptance. Historians seem to be much more certain about what the issues and realities of colonial American politics *were not,* rather than what they *were.* While reading the selections that follow do not expect to find agreement, but try to discover *why* agreement has been so difficult to obtain.

Objectives are to:

—Analyze two selections on colonial American politics for differences in interpretation.

—Analyze historical research on mid-18th century colonial America's political frame of reference.

—Recognize and identify statements and assumptions that suggest a modern frame of reference.

—Make inferences about the nature and writing of history from this research material.

12 MERRILL JENSEN ON COLONIAL AMERICAN POLITICS

Merrill Jensen was born in Iowa in 1905 and was educated at the University of Washington and the University of Wisconsin. He received his doctorate in American history from the University of Wisconsin in 1934. Professor Jensen taught American history for many years at the University of Washington, the University of Wisconsin, and served as a Visiting Professor of American history at Oxford University, the University of Tokyo, and the University of Ghent in Belgium.

During the past thirty years, he has written numerous books, articles, and essays on many aspects of American colonial and early national history. Professor Jensen's work emphasizes social, economic, and sectional conflicts as the basis of early American politics.

The selection below is taken from Professor Jensen's edition of *American Colonial Documents to 1776,* published in 1955. While reading this selection, keep in mind the following questions:

1. Who were the colonial aristocrats and what was the basis of their <u>economic</u> power?

2. What was the basis of the colonial aristocracy's* *<u>political</u> power and how was it exercised?*

3. What were the outstanding characteristics of colonial American society and their political consequences?

Aristocracy—small group of wealthy and privileged persons who managed to control political and economic life.

Struggle for Democracy in Colonial America

Social discontent of various sorts was a constant factor in the history of the American colonies. . . .

However, the most important causes of political and social tensions, which at times led to outright rebellions, are to be found in two basic facts of colonial life: the constant expansion into frontier areas . . . and the development of indigenous colonial aristocracies that exercised an extraordinary amount of control over the political and economic life of most of the colonies. Although men of wealth and family were to be found in the colonies from the outset, the majority of the members of the colonial aristocracies gained their wealth within the framework of colonial society.

By the eighteenth century, the aristocracy tended to become an hereditary one. . . . Basically, it was an aristocracy founded on wealth: wealth in the form of land, slaves, ships, stores, and goods, rather than on ancestry. The acquisition of wealth made one a member; the loss of wealth meant the loss of social and political importance.

As the colonies developed, wealth and political power concentrated in the seaport towns of the north, and the plantations of the tidewater south. The rising merchant classes in the northern towns—as importers and exporters, as creditors, and increasingly as speculators in unsettled lands—had a tight economic grip on the vast majority of the people who were made up of artisans, shopkeepers, and small farmers. The planters of the southern tidewater played a similar role as creditors, and, above all, as speculators in land.

Geographically, the aristocracy was centered along the coast. . . . It was the fact of concentrated settlement along the coast during the seventeenth century and the rapid expansion away from it during the eighteenth century that helps to explain the political control exercised by the colonial aristocracies. The early governments provided for representation of townships, counties, and cities in colonial legislatures. But the creation of new townships and counties did not keep pace with the rapid expansion of population.

The aristocracies in control of the older areas and hence of the colonial legislatures, refused to create new areas of representation, or if they did so, they were so large as to be politically meaningless. Hence by 1763 the great majority of back country farmers had little direct influence in colonial legislatures. The policy was a deliberate one on the part of the colonial ruling classes . . . .

Coupled with the refusal to grant adequate representation of new areas was the imposition of a property qualification for the suffrage—an effective

In a colonial aristocracy based on wealth, Elias Hasket Derby amply qualified for influence. Son of merchant Richard Derby, who gave him this house as a wedding gift in 1761, he carried on a thriving trade in the West Indies before the Revolution. Later he developed a world-wide merchant empire and became the nation's first millionaire. Several of Salem's famous captains and merchants obtained their early training on Derby's ships.

means of keeping the poorer inhabitants of the towns from voting. Most of the colonies had no property qualification to begin with, but all of them had adopted one by the eighteenth century. Thus while the colonies as a whole had won effective self government from Great Britain by 1763, it was not extended to the ever-growing population within the colonies. . . . The colonial aristocracies thus fought a battle on two fronts: against increasing British control, and against . . . demands for what amounted to more self government within the colonies. . . .

Each of the colonies . . . was characterized by political and social cleavages which . . . more than once resulted in popular rebellions against the established political order in the colonies. In the years after 1763 there was a growing demand by farmers and the citizenry of the towns for what amounted to more political and economic democracy.* Yet at the same time, many of the outstanding popular leaders, who were willing in the end to lead a war for independence, wanted no change in the internal political and economic structure of the colonies, although most of their support came from people who wanted such change.

Jensen refers to risings of back country people known as **regulators** in North and South Carolina in 1764–1771, and to outbursts of violence by frontiersmen known as the **Paxton Boys** in Pennsylvania in 1763–1764.

From **English Historical Documents: American Colonial Documents to 1776,** edited by Merrill Jensen. Reprinted by permission of Oxford University Press, Inc. (New York: 1955), pp. 575–576, 622, and Eyre & Spottiswood (Publishers) Ltd., London.

13 ROBERT E. BROWN ON COLONIAL AMERICAN POLITICS

Robert E. Brown was born in Kansas in 1907, and was educated at the University of Washington and the University of Wisconsin, from which he received his doctorate in 1946. Professor Brown taught American history for many years at the University of Washington and at Michigan State University. He has written three major books and several articles and essays on colonial American politics with special attention to Massachusetts and Virginia. His work emphasizes the democratic character and absence of sharp social and economic divisions in early American politics.

The next selection is taken from Professor Brown's *Middle Class Democracy and the Revolution in Massachusetts, 1691–1780*, published in 1955. While reading this selection, keep in mind the following questions:

1. What assumptions have led some historians to interpret colonial American society as undemocratic?

2. What was the actual state of representation and voting rights in colonial Massachusetts?

3. What were the outstanding characteristics of colonial American society and their political consequences?

Middle Class Democracy in Colonial Massachusetts

Thesis—an argument, proposition, or point of view.

For the past fifty years or more a *thesis** has been current in the teaching and writing of American history . . . [that colonial America] was not a democratic society. . . .

The concept of an undemocratic society is based on two major assumptions: One, that property qualifications for voting eliminated a large proportion of the free adult male population from participation in political affairs; the other, that inequitable representation heavily favored the older aristocratic commercial areas along the seacoast at the expense of the more recently settled inland agricultural areas. Hence it followed naturally that colonial political and economic life was dominated by the upper economic classes. . . .

To understand what happened we must have a clear picture of Massachusetts society. Economically speaking, it was a middle class society in which property was easily acquired and in which a large proportion of the people were property-owning farmers. There was undoubtedly more economic democracy for the common men then than there is now. A large permanent labor class was practically non-existent: men could either acquire land and become farmers or work for themselves as skilled *artisans.** . . . There

Artisan—skilled worker or handicraftsman.

was nothing approaching the spread between the rich and poor that Europe had at that time and that we have at present; a much larger proportion of society owned property then than now. . . .

Economic opportunity, or economic democracy, in turn contributed to political democracy. While it is true that property ownership was a *pre-requisite** for province and town voting, it is also true that the amount of property required was very small and that the great majority of men could easily meet this requirement. . . . It makes a tremendous difference in our understanding of colonial society whether 95 percent of the men were disenfranchised or only five percent. Furthermore, representation was apportioned in such a way that the farmers, not a merchant aristocracy, had complete control of the legislature. . . .

Prerequisite—something necessary to know or to do beforehand.

The number of men who *could* vote in the colony must not be confused with the number who *did* vote. These are certainly different problems, for the fact that there was much indifference on election day did not mean that many men could not participate. . . .

In addition to economics and politics, there were other manifestations of democracy in colonial Massachusetts. The system of education was, for its day, the best provided for common people anywhere. . . . Many democratic practices were used in the operation of the Congregational Church . . . education and political office were open to those who were not Congregationalist . . . there was little dissatisfaction with religion to contribute to internal conflict. Even the colonial militia was democratic in its organization and in the influence which it exerted on politics.

In brief, Massachusetts did not have a social order before the American Revolution which would breed sharp internal conflicts. . . .

It is not necessary to explain whatever conservatism existed in colonial times in terms of limited electorate. There is implied in this approach an assumption that universal suffrage will result in increased liberalism, but this is not necessarily so. The elections of 1920, 1924, 1928, and even 1952, when women as well as men had the vote, should convince us that the "people" can and do vote for conservatism. . . .

This study of Massachusetts raises some rather serious questions about our interpretation of colonial society. . . . Were the other colonies as undemocratic as we have supposed them to be? Was their economic and social life dominated by a coastal aristocracy of planters in the South and merchants in the North? How was property distributed? These are questions for which we need well-documented answers before we interpret the colonial . . . period with any assurance of accuracy.

Evidence which has turned up in the course of this study suggests that Massachusetts was not fundamentally different from the other colonies and states. If so . . . we might be forced to make some drastic revisions in our interpretation of American history. . . .

Reprinted from Robert E. Brown: **Middle-Class Democracy and the Revolution in Massachusetts, 1691–1780,** pp. 401–408. © 1955 by the American Historical Association. Used by permission of Cornell University Press.

14 ROBERT E. BURNS ON INTERPRETING COLONIAL AMERICAN POLITICS

Robert E. Burns was born in 1927, and was educated at Northeastern University and Harvard University. He received his doctorate in British history from Harvard University in 1961, and has taught British history at The University of Notre Dame since 1957.

Professor Burns's main interests are in eighteenth-century Anglo-American constitutional and political history. He has examined what eighteenth-century Anglo-Americans thought, said, and read about politics. His work attempts to recognize and identify the assumptions, values, and attitudes underlying Anglo-American political thinking and political behavior.

While reading this selection, keep in mind the following questions:

1. How is representation supposed to function today?

2. How was representation supposed to function in mid-eighteenth century colonial America?

3. How can the confusion about colonial American political ideas be cleared away?

4. What does this selection from Burns suggest to you about Jensen's interpretation of colonial American politics? About Brown's interpretation of colonial American politics?

A138

Reconstructing the Political Frame of Reference
of Colonial America

Finding agreement about the essential qualities of democracy in our own time is difficult. But applying concepts of modern democracy to colonial American society is even more difficult, and creates problems of definition such as: what does democracy mean? More problems than definition are involved, however. Trying to interpret colonial American society by the values we use today such as one man, one vote, majority rule, minority rights, religious freedom, educational opportunity, and racial equality limits, rather than advances, our understanding of that early period.

To be sure, the word *democratic* was part of the eighteenth-century Anglo-American political vocabulary. Writers and politicians on both sides of the Atlantic used the word in familiar ways. For example, eighteenth-century Anglo-American writers and politicians sometimes referred to their legislatures or assemblies as the "democratic branches" of their constitutions. Twentieth-century American writers and politicians have made numerous similar statements about their own representative (legislative bodies) institutions. But are such statements made two hundred years apart saying the same thing? Should we expect them to be saying the same thing?

By describing representative institutions as the "democratic branches" of their constitutions, eighteenth-century commentators were being very precise. They were distinguishing the democratic branch of the constitution (representative assembly) from the aristocratic branch (upper house) and the monarchical branch (king). They were pointing out how each branch of the constitution was made up. For instance, kings inherited their positions. Membership in upper houses was by inheritance or appointment. Membership in representative assemblies was by election. Representative assemblies were democratic because of the way they were chosen (election by the people), not because of what they did or were expected to do.

Today, the monarchical and aristocratic branches are gone. With the exception of the judicial branch, all branches (executive and legislative) of our constitution are chosen by election. When twentieth-century commentators speak about representative assemblies being democratic, they mean they are the places where the will of the people is expressed in politics. Representative assemblies are democratic because of what they do or are expected to do, not because of the way they are chosen.

The eighteenth-century definition of *democratic* (chosen by the voters) is as irrelevant to us as our modern definition (citizen participation in government) would have been to them. These definitions are so different because they have come out of different *frames of reference*. Until historians are more imaginative about reconstructing the eighteenth-century Anglo-American *political* frame of reference, confusion about colonial American political ideas will remain. Until the *values* and *assumptions* underlying colonial American political thought have been identified and clarified, we will not know what colonial Americans believed about the role of the common people in government. If colonial Americans differed from us in their understanding of how ordinary people should participate in government, then historians will have to reconsider such things as the meaning of property qualifications for voting, and the apportionment of representation as practiced in colonial times.

Today, the institution of representation is the principal means through which the mass of people participate in politics. Within the context of our political values and assumptions, elected representatives are expected to conform to the views of their constituents: to represent voters' will and express voters' feelings on political and legislative issues. Candidates are even expected to take positions on political questions as pre-conditions for election.

The modern view of representatives functioning as servants of their constituents was unacceptable to most colonial Americans. Colonial representatives were elected because they were outstanding individuals: wiser, more talented, better educated than their constituents. They were elected to consider, determine, and decide what was best for the country as a whole. If colonial representatives were obliged to express what their constituents had already decided, they would have considered the purpose of representation lost.* The country would have lost the benefit of a representative's wisdom and judgment. Requiring candidates to promise support or opposition for certain measures as pre-conditions of election was considered improper. Such promises were inconsistent with the Anglo-American idea of free legislatures. They regarded representatives as no longer free if major issues were determined by the voters. To be sure, eighteenth-century voters could, and often did, refuse reelection to representatives who betrayed the people's best interests. But representatives were never turned out of office because they had disobeyed instructions from their constituents.

The value of representation to colonial Americans and their assumptions about it are far removed from those of modern America. As understood in the eighteenth century, representation was not a means for expressing the will of the common people in politics. It was a means of protecting the country from government by self-seeking and self-interested men, and a means of choosing the best qualified men to govern.

Edmund Burke (1729–1797), famous Anglo-Irish statesman, and advocate of the doctrine that representatives should act according to their own independent judgment, rather than according to instructions from their constituents.

Additional Reading

Billington, Ray Allen, ed., *The Reinterpretation of Early American History.* New York: W. W. Norton & Co., 1968.

Bradford, William, *Of Plymouth Plantation,* ed. by Samuel Eliot Morison. New York: Knopf, 1952.

Morison, Samuel Eliot, *Builders of the Bay Colony.* Cambridge, Massachusetts: Houghton Mifflin Co., 1963.

Van Doren, Mark, ed., *Samuel Sewall's Diary.* New York: Vanguard Press, Inc. [Macy-Masius Publishers, 1927].

Wright, Louis B., *Everyday Life in Colonial America.* New York: Putnam, 1966.

Wright, Louis B., and Tinling, Marion, eds., *The Secret Diary of William Byrd of Westover, 1709–1712.* Richmond, Virginia: The Dietz Press, 1941.

UNIT THREE

Afro-Americans

*I have a dream that one day this nation will rise up
and live out the true meaning of its creed....*

(MARTIN LUTHER KING, 1963)

1 Atlantic slave trade

Origin and Expansion

Introduction

No one knows for certain when the first Africans arrived in the New World. Men of African descent recruited in the Canary Islands may have sailed with Columbus in 1492. Others may have struggled with Balboa through the steaming Panama jungles to reach the Pacific shore in 1513, and still others may have marched with Cortez in his conquest of Mexico in 1519.

However, most of the Africans coming to the New World in the early sixteenth century did not come as seekers of gold and glory or as servants of God. They were brought to the West Indies in the holds of Spanish ships as slave laborers. Forced African labor made possible the Old World's cultural conquest and economic development of the New World.

The Portuguese were the first Europeans to take slaves out of Africa. During the fifteenth century they established forts and trading stations along the West African coast from which they captured, bought, or traded for slaves. The Portuguese shipped their human cargoes to Lisbon where they were sold to Italian merchants, who resold them to Spaniards for shipment to the West Indies.

By 1517 the transatlantic slave trade was under way. Spanish, French, Dutch, and English ships all participated in this exchange of trade goods for people which brought millions of Africans to the Americas. It was a Dutch ship that brought the first Africans to Jamestown in 1619.

Who Invented Slavery?

Neither the institution of slavery itself nor the exchange of trade goods for people was invented by the Portuguese or Spanish. Slavery is as old as man himself. The Bible records the sons of Jacob selling their brother, Joseph, into slavery in ancient Egypt. The Greeks enslaved each other; and the Romans enslaved many peoples. All of the great African kingdoms of Ghana, Mali, Songhai, and *Benin** practiced it. Slavery existed in parts of the Arab world, and the economy of the Turkish empire was heavily dependent on it. A thousand years ago Swedish merchants were selling Slavic war prisoners to buyers in Constantinople.

During the thirteenth century Venetian merchants operated trading stations and slave depots along the shores of the Black Sea, much like the ones established by Europeans on the West African coast in the sixteenth and seventeenth centuries. Both Europeans and Africans either had known

The **Kingdom of Benin** was especially noted for its bronze sculpture. Metal casters in Benin cast heads and figures with great artistic and technical skill and during their best period—15th and 16th centuries—their art was outstanding.

A142

slavery in the past or were currently practicing it when Portuguese ships went slave hunting along the African coast. Nevertheless, the slave trade that developed after 1517 was unlike anything that Europeans or Africans had experienced before. The Atlantic trade in African slaves was something unique in world history.

Benin—capital of the Kingdom of **Benin** was within the boundaries of what is now the modern African state of **Nigeria**. Located inland, for two hundred years it was a trading and cultural center.

Why the Atlantic Slave Trade Was Different

There are five principal reasons why the Atlantic slave trade was such a unique historical experience for the millions of people whose lives were changed by it. First, the trade developed at a time when slavery as an institution had disappeared from the Christian countries of western Europe. There were forms of bondage, but in western Europe Christians no longer bought and sold other Christians. Second, the enslaved Africans lost their personal freedoms and property rights. They were removed from the comforts and consolations of their religion and culture by being transported thousands of miles across the sea to strange places without hope of return.

Third, the trade was a racist enterprise in which the only persons bought and sold were black Africans, not white Europeans. Fourth, cruel and inhuman treatment in the slave trade was routine. Fifth, the trade flourished for more than four hundred years, directly affecting the lives of at least *nine and a half million Africans* and indirectly affecting the lives and culture of uncounted millions more.

Knowledge of the Atlantic slave trade is important because black Americans are important and because so much of our cultural history, recognized and described as typically American, has African roots.

Objectives are to:

—Identify groups of Europeans and Africans participating in the Atlantic slave trade.

—Summarize your findings on why some Europeans traded for African slaves.

—Summarize your findings on why some Africans traded slaves to the Europeans.

A143

1 NUMERICAL, GEOGRAPHICAL, AND TIME DIMENSIONS OF THE ATLANTIC SLAVE TRADE

The exact number of Africans enslaved and transported to the Americas in the course of four hundred years is unknown. The necessary records for an accurate accounting are missing or were never kept. Nevertheless, a kind of direct evidence exists in records. These are: records of slaves imported through a particular port or into a given colony over a period of years; shipping records covering destinations and cargoes of ships; contemporary estimates by ships' captains, traders, and travelers; and population estimates of colonies importing slaves. Together, these form a basis for estimating the numerical and time dimensions of the Atlantic slave trade.

The statistics presented here are estimates based on the examination of such evidence.

While examining the statistics and studying the maps accompanying them, keep these questions in mind:

1. *During what period was the Atlantic slave trade heaviest?*
2. *What regions in the Americas imported the most slaves?*
3. *What coastal regions in Africa exported the most slaves to North America?*

Estimated African Slave Imports into the Americas, 1451–1870

REGION	1451–1600	1601–1700	1701–1810	1811–1870	TOTAL	PERCENT
British North America	—	—	348,000	51,000	399,000	4.5
Jamaica	—	85,100	662,400	—	747,500	7.5
Barbados	—	134,500	252,500	—	387,000	4.4
Other British Caribbean	—	44,100	486,400	—	531,000	5.6
French Caribbean	—	155,800	1,348,400	96,000	1,600,200	18.0
Dutch Caribbean	—	40,000	460,000	—	500,000	5.5
Danish Caribbean	—	4,000	24,000	—	28,000	0.2
Spanish America	75,000	292,500	578,600	606,000	1,552,100	17.5
Brazil	50,000	560,000	1,891,400	1,145,400	3,646,800	36.8
Total	—	1,290,000	6,051,700	1,898,400	9,566,100	100.0

From Philip D. Curtin, **The Atlantic Slave Trade: A Census** (Madison: The University of Wisconsin Press; © 1969 by the Regents of the University of Wisconsin), p. 268.

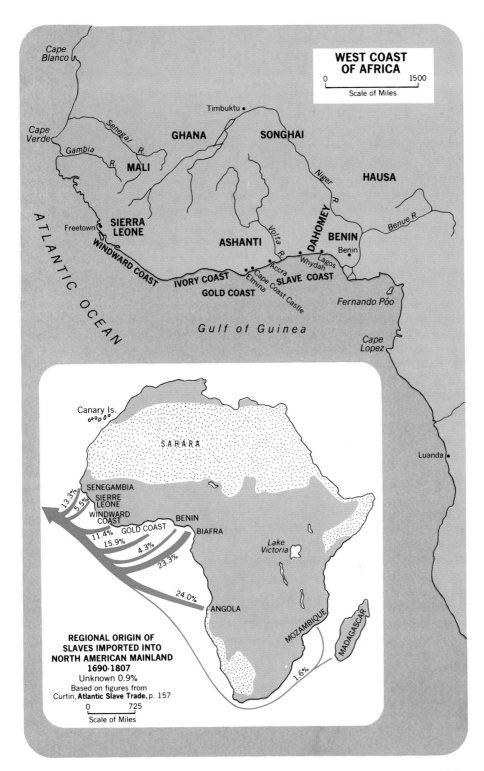

WEST COAST OF AFRICA

Scale of Miles
0   1500

Cape Blanco

Cape Verde

Timbuktu

GHANA

SONGHAI

Senegal R.

Gambia R.

MALI

HAUSA

Niger R.

Benue R.

ATLANTIC OCEAN

SIERRA LEONE

Freetown

WINDWARD COAST

ASHANTI

Volta R.

DAHOMEY

BENIN

Benin

Lagos

Whydah

Accra

IVORY COAST

Elmina

Cape Coast Castle

SLAVE COAST

GOLD COAST

Fernando Póo

Gulf of Guinea

Cape Lopez

Canary Is.

SAHARA

Luanda

SENEGAMBIA 13.3%

SIERRE LEONE 5.5%

WINDWARD COAST 11.4%

GOLD COAST 15.9%

BENIN 4.3%

BIAFRA 23.3%

Lake Victoria

ANGOLA 24.0%

MOZAMBIQUE

MADAGASCAR 1.6%

REGIONAL ORIGIN OF SLAVES IMPORTED INTO NORTH AMERICAN MAINLAND 1690-1807
Unknown 0.9%
Based on figures from
Curtin, **Atlantic Slave Trade,** p. 157

Scale of Miles
0   725

Prince Henry of Portugal (1394–1460), known as Prince Henry the Navigator, most renowned patron of explorers of his day, dispatched many expeditions along African coast.

Nuño Tristam, a young sea captain in Prince Henry's service, made several voyages along the northwest African coast between 1441 and 1446. Tristam was killed by a poisoned arrow while attacking an African village in 1446.

Adapted with the permission of Carnegie Institution from Gomes Eannes de Azurara, "The Chronicle of the Discovery and Conquest of Guinea, 1453," by Elizabeth Donnan, **Documents Illustrative of the History of the Slave Trade to America** (Washington, D.C.: Carnegie Institution, 1930), Vol. I, pp. 23–25.

Lagos, a port in southwestern Portugal. Use the maps on pages 145 and 147 to locate the other places mentioned here.

Jeronimite—a member of Roman Catholic religious order of St. Jerome.

Adapted from Sir Arthur Helps, **The Spanish Conquest in America** (London: John Lane Co., 1902), Vol. II, pp. 11–12.

2 WHY DID EUROPEANS TRADE FOR AFRICAN SLAVES?

Many in both Europe and America favored the development and expansion of the Atlantic slave trade. This trade in human beings, like any other form of trade, existed because there were people who were willing to buy and people willing to sell. While reading the comments of Europeans engaged in or interested in the buying of African slaves, keep in mind the following questions:

1. What was the role of European governments in developing and expanding the Atlantic slave trade?

2. What classes of people in Europe can you identify as favoring expansion of the Atlantic slave trade?

3. What classes of people in America can you identify as favoring expansion of the Atlantic slave trade?

Fifteenth-Century Account of *Nuño Tristam's** Voyage to Africa, 1443

And in the year of Christ 1443, *Prince Henry** caused another ship to be armed and bade embark in it that noble knight, Nuño Tristam. Pursuing their voyage along the African coast, they arrived at *Cape Blanco.** And coming from an island of *Arguin,** they saw in twenty-five canoes a number of people all naked. They were well able to take them and but for the smallness of their boat they would have captured more than fourteen. Upon Tristam's return to *Lagos,** prominent persons doubted whether any profit would result from all of his toil and expense. However, they changed their minds when second and third cargoes were landed with so little trouble shortly thereafter. Their greed increased as they saw the houses of others full to overflowing with male and female slaves. Prominent persons thought about the whole matter and began to talk among themselves.

Letter from the *Jeronimite** Priests in *Hispaniola** to the King of Spain, 1518

Wherefore here it is agreed that your Highness should command us to grant *licences* to send armed ships from this island to fetch heathen Negroes from *Cape Verde** or *Guinea,** or that it may be done by some other persons to bring them here. Your Highness may believe that if this is permitted it will be very advantageous for the future of the settlers of these islands, and for the royal revenues; and also for the Indians who will be cared for and eased in their work, and can better cultivate their souls' welfare, and will increase in number.

Letter from Jamaica Planters to the Lords of Trade and Plantation, London, 1680

The inhabitants of Jamaica beg that the *Royal African Company** be encouraged to honor its commitments to provide plentiful supplies of Negro slaves at moderate rates. As to quantity, it is supposed that three or four thousand Negroes would sell here now, and every year thereafter more and more.

Wherefore it is hoped that his Majesty will regulate the Negro trade so that the planters may not be ruined.

Royal African Company— founded in 1672 with exclusive rights from Charles II to trade on the African coast. English traders who were not employees of the Company were considered interlopers subject to punishment by the Company.

Adapted from Donnan, **Documents**, Vol. I, p. 265.

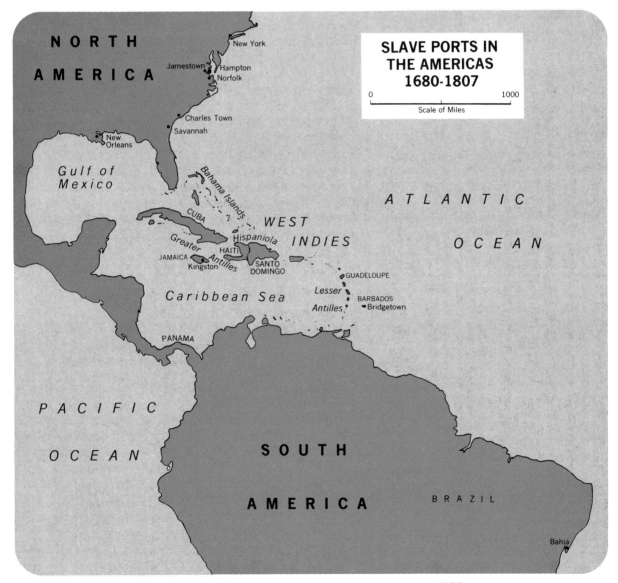

SLAVE PORTS IN THE AMERICAS 1680-1807

Minutes of the *Spanish Council of the Indies,** 1685

Spanish Council of the Indies was founded in 1524 to supervise and administer the government of Spanish America.

By a decree of July 5, 1685, his Majesty was pleased to order the Council of the Indies to inform him at once concerning the advantages of having Negroes in America and what damage would follow if they could not be had.

Complying with this order, the Council sought responses to the following question: What is the advantage America derives from the fact that Negroes are brought there, and what are the damages that would follow if they did not have them?

The introduction of Negroes into America is not only desirable, but absolutely necessary. The fatal consequences which would result from not having Negroes are easily deduced. Because Indians cannot be forced to render personal services, Negroes are the only ones who cultivate the *haciendas.** The food needed for the support of the whole kingdom would cease to be produced; the landed properties, the main wealth of which consists chiefly of Negro slaves, would be lost, and America would face absolute ruin.

Hacienda—a large estate or plantation in Spanish America.

Representation of the State of the African Trade Presented to Their Majesties' *Privy Council,** London, 1693

Privy Council—principal advisers to the crown, in this instance to King William III and Queen Mary.

That the great part of the trade to Africa is for Negro servants which are sent to the English plantations by whose labor all the West India commodities as sugar, indigo, cotton, ginger, and tobacco are produced.

That the plenty and cheapness of Negroes would enable the English colonies to produce the said commodities cheaper as to outdo the other nations.

That the plantations have brought great riches to this kingdom by not only furnishing sugar, indigo, cotton, ginger, and tobacco for our own consumption, which was formerly brought in from abroad, but by supplying great quantities for export to other nations.

Petitions to the English House of Commons, 1694–1696

A petition of the clothiers in and about Witney, Oxfordshire, was presented to the House and read: That by reason of the great difficulties occasioned by illegal traders in Africa, the Royal African Company of England has been discouraged in their trade there. Whereby the petitioners, who have their chief dependence upon the Company, are so much impoverished that unless relief is given they cannot subsist in their several employments. The petitioners pray that the trade of the Company be protected in such a manner as the House shall determine.

A petition of the *weavers** in Worcestershire who have their chief dependence upon the African Company must go abegging in case the trade of Africa is not secured to the Company from illegal traders. The petitioners pray that this trade will be preserved to the Company.

Cloth-weaving was a significant part of Britain's economy. Cloth was an important trade item in bartering for African slaves.

Adapted from Donnan, **Documents,** Vol. I, pp. 346–418.

A148

Caravel—Portuguese sailing ship, 14th century, especially manageable in changing winds and shallow water.

3   WHY WERE AFRICANS ENSLAVED AND TRADED TO EUROPEANS?

The development and expansion of the African slave trade was not accomplished by Europeans alone. Europeans were willing buyers, but some Africans were willing sellers. While reading the comments of a sixteenth-century African king and several Europeans engaged in slave trading on the West African coast about why Africans were enslaved and traded to Europeans, keep in mind the following questions:

1. *Who traded for slaves on the West African coast?*
2. *What roles were played by African kings in the slave trade?*
3. *What was traded for slaves on the West African coast?*

Alvise *Cadamosto's** Account of his Voyage to the Gambia River, 1456

When we had cast anchor, I sent one of the interpreters with Negroes to King Batti Mansa, bearing a handsome *Moorish** dress as a present, who told him we had come from the Christian King of Portugal to make a treaty. Batti Mansa received our messengers favorably and sent some of his people to the *caravel.** A treaty was made, and European goods were exchanged for slaves and gold. But the quantity of gold was not at all equal to what we had expected. The Negroes value their gold as highly as do the Portuguese, but they showed how much they admired the European goods by their willingness to give a large price for them.

Letter from *Affonso,** King of the Congo, to the King of Portugal, 1526

Sir, Your Highness of Portugal should know how our kingdom is being lost in so many ways that it is convenient to provide for the necessary remedy. This condition is caused by the excessive freedom given by your merchants who are allowed to come to this kingdom to set up shops with goods and many things prohibited by us. Your merchants spread their goods throughout our Kingdoms and Domains in such an abundance that many of our *vassals,** who we had in obedience, no longer obey us because they have these goods in greater abundance than we ourselves. And it was with these things that we had them content and under our jurisdiction.

And we cannot reckon how great the damage is. Everday the mentioned merchants are taking away our natives, sons of the land, sons of our noblemen and vassals, and even our relatives. Thieves and men of bad conscience

Cadamosto was a Venetian sea captain who entered the service of Prince Henry of Portugal and made two voyages to the northwest African coast in 1455 and 1456. His account of his adventures was first published in Venice in 1507.

Moorish dress—North African Arab style of clothing.

Adapted from Richard Henry Major, **The Discoveries of Prince Henry the Navigator** (London: Simpson Low, Marston, 1877), pp. 164–165.

Vassal: an official of the king.

Affonso, early 16th-century African king, whose letters to two successive kings of Portugal contain the earliest surviving African commentary on experiences with Europeans.

From **The African Past** by Basil Davidson, by permission of Atlantic-Little, Brown and Co., and Curtis Brown, Ltd. Copyright © 1964 by Basil Davidson, pp. 191–192.

here wishing to have the goods and wares grab our people and sell them. So great is the corruption and licentiousness that our country is being completely depopulated.

That is why we beg of Your Highness to help and assist us in this matter, commanding your merchants that they should not send here goods and wares, because it is our will in these Kingdoms there should not be any trade of slaves nor outlet for them.

The official signature of King Affonso of Kongo

A European Trader's African Journal, 1678–1682

Accra—capital of the modern African state of Ghana.

The King and chief Blacks of *Accra** were very rich in slaves and gold, through the vast trade which the natives have with the Europeans on the coast, and with the neighboring Black nations up in the country.

The trade of slaves is in a more peculiar manner the business of kings, rich men, and prime merchants, exclusive of the ordinary sorts of Blacks. The king fixes the price of every sort of European goods, as also of slaves, which is to stand between his subjects and foreigners.

A European Merchant's Summary of Goods Traded, 1682

As to the different sorts of goods the Europeans generally carry to Guinea for trade, each nation commonly supplies the coast with such as their respective countries afford, and what they lack at home for well assorting their cargo, they buy in other parts of Europe. For instance:

The French commonly carry more brandy, wine, iron, paper, and guns than the English and Dutch do, those commodities being cheaper in France. The French commonly compose their cargo to purchase gold dust and slaves with brandy mostly, white and red wines, guns, flints, iron in bars, red frieze cloth, looking glasses, glass beads, sheets, tobacco, taffetas and many other sorts of silks, shirts, linens, black hats, paper, laces, calicoes, and musket balls.

Multi-colored rugs with intricate designs woven in Turkey.

The Dutch send linen, sheets, serges, cotton pieces, *Turkey carpets,** rugs, silks, brass kettles, copper basins and pans, brass locks, brass trumpets, pewter dishes and plates, fish hooks and lines, pipes, knives, iron bars, iron hammers, brass bells, guns, gun powder, lead shot, cutlasses, and spirits.

The English, besides many of the same goods mentioned above, send many different kinds of cloth, printed calicoes from India, satins from China, Barbados rum and other spirits, colored linens, and iron bars.

The Danes and Brandenburghers obtain most of their cargoes in Holland, but add copper and silver, either in bullion or in coins. The Portuguese also make up most of their cargo in Holland, under the names of Jews residing there, which consists of what the Dutch send, to which the Portuguese add the products of Brazil as tobacco, tame cattle, rum, and other commodities.

Adapted from Donnan, **Documents,** Vol. I, pp. 287–293.

A150

2 Atlantic Slave Trade

Organization and Conduct

Introduction

Africans were carried away from their homeland under all sorts of conditions. Some were kidnapped or pirated away from coastal villages by European explorers and adventurers. Others were given to Europeans by African monarchs in exchange for horses, firearms, and military assistance against other Africans. But most of the Africans transported to the Americas—perhaps 98 out of every 100—were delivered to European ships by African kings and merchants as payment for supplies of European trade goods.

In West Africa, slavery was the fate of convicted criminals, debtors, and prisoners of war. When the Europeans arrived and the Atlantic trade developed, these traditional sources of slaves were not enough to meet the demand. Wars between African kings increased in order to catch more slaves. Slave-raiding and kidnapping by groups of Africans also increased. By the middle of the seventeenth century most of the slaves sent to the New World had been captured in war or kidnapped by slave hunters.

How the Slave Trade Worked

The organized Atlantic slave trade became a highly profitable and very involved set of operations. Cargoes of trade goods were taken aboard sailing vessels in Europe. They were shipped thousands of miles on what was known as the *Outward Passage* to several dozen places along the West African coast and exchanged for slaves. The slaves were shipped thousands of miles on the *Middle Passage* to one of many ports in the Caribbean, Brazil, Spanish or English America. There they were sold for cash, or exchanged for cargoes of Caribbean or mainland products such as sugar, molasses, rum, tobacco, or indigo. These cargoes were shipped thousands of miles on the *Inward Passage* back to Europe and sold for home consumption or re-export.

Depending on the weather and on the availability of cargoes, such a series of voyages would take anywhere from nine months to a year and a half to complete. The trade offered three separate profits: one at the end of the outward passage on the trade goods shipped to Africa, a second after the middle passage on the slaves shipped to the Americas, and a third on the sale of Caribbean or colonial products in Europe. Thus three continents were bound together in a triangular trade system* of profit and human misery.

The Atlantic slave trade was a business. Though most of the slaves came from African peoples living near the coasts, slave hunters penetrated into some of the most remote corners of Africa. No one was truly safe. Very few African peoples were lucky enough to escape without some losses to slave hunters. By the middle of the eighteenth century the slave trade was well organized. Captives from inland regions would sometimes pass through the hands of as many as five or six African slave merchants before reaching the sea.

Europeans organized trading companies to deal directly with African kings and African slave merchants. The European companies were usually allowed to establish factories, or fortified trading posts, at convenient places along the West African coast. These factories were staffed by small numbers of Europeans and headed by an employee of the trading company called a *factor*. The job of the factor was to facilitate the exchange of trade goods for slaves, to load the slave cargoes, and to get the ships underway as quickly as possible. In this way began the forced emigration of Africans from their homeland—first by hundreds, then by thousands—a journey from freedom to indentured servitude to slavery.

Ghana's "Castles"

Every European country participating in the Atlantic slave trade had factories along the West African coast at one time or another. Two of the most famous were Elmina and Cape Coast Castle located in what is now the modern African state of Ghana.

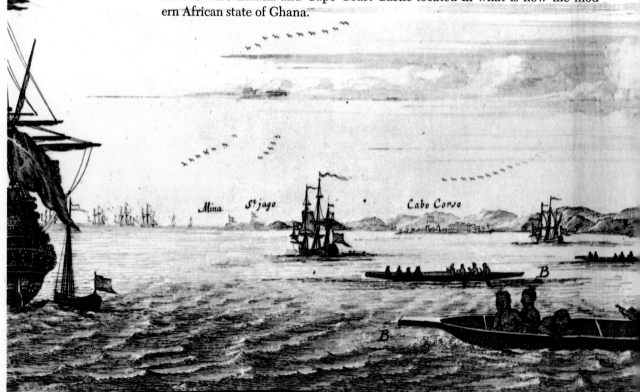

The Portuguese began building Elmina, or São Jorge da Mina, in 1481 and took eighty years to finish what was to be the strongest fort on the coast. It was a true castle with high towers, thick walls, and protected on the landward side by two deep moats cut into solid rock. Four hundred cannon protected Elmina from attack by land or by sea, and its slave pens had room for over a thousand slaves. Despite this, the Dutch starved Elmina into surrender, took it from the Portuguese in 1637, and held it for two hundred years.

Almost within gunshot of Elmina was Cape Coast Castle, which was fought over by marauding powers for three centuries. It was founded by the Swedes in 1652, captured by the Danes in 1657, taken by Africans in 1660, captured by the English in 1662, taken by the Dutch in 1663, and recaptured by the English in 1664. Cape Coast Castle was attacked by the Dutch in 1665, by the French in 1757, and by Africans several times during the eighteenth century.

Finally, along with several other monuments from a brutal and bloody past, Elmina and Cape Coast Castle were transferred to the government of the independent African state of Ghana in 1957.

The history and organization of the Atlantic slave trade is not pleasant reading. All phases of the trade (capturing slaves in Africa, the Atlantic crossing, and sale in the Americas) combined to produce an experience of brutality, horror, and degradation that is unparalleled in world history. Yet that experience is an essential part of American history. Indeed, it is a part of history that all Americans ought to know.

Objectives are to:

—Examine given testimony on the Atlantic slave trade and describe the ways slaves were bought in Africa and sold in the Americas.

—Analyze given testimony about voyages on the Middle Passage and make a judgment about life on a slave ship.

—Make hypotheses explaining the behavior of African and European participants in the Atlantic slave trade.

Manfrou   Mouree

Ghana's "Castles" were not used for royalty or affairs of state. They were built by European powers greedy for the slave trade and were used to pen unfortunate Africans until they were transferred to slave ships.

A153

4 TRADING FOR SLAVES IN DAHOMEY

By the end of the seventeenth century, trading for slaves had become highly organized on both the European and African sides. Slave trading was no business for men with consciences or for amateurs. The slightest hint of mercy had no place in a business where success depended upon supreme indifference to human suffering. Inexperienced or uninformed traders had no chance in a business where profits depended upon many factors.

Success depended on a supply of slaves at any given moment and on the number of ships likely to call. It also depended on the cost of trade goods from a dozen different European countries, and changing values of many different African standards of payment. Successful European and African traders had to be pitiless, but they could never be stupid.

As the trade expanded, the forceful kings of Dahomey developed a system of taxes and customs. The busiest traders on the entire coast, these kings made Europeans pay taxes before they could trade. They rigorously imposed this tax system on all ships calling at their great slave port of *Whydah.** Other Africans who were neither slave-owners nor slave-traders found themselves dependent upon the slave trade for their livelihoods. While reading these selections from accounts of slave-trading practices and of a slave's experiences, keep in mind these questions:

1. Who provided slaves for European traders at Whydah and who profited from that trade?

2. How was the value of slaves determined at Whydah?

3. What happened to slaves after examination and trade?

Captain Thomas Phillips Describes Slave Trading at Whydah, 1694

Our factory at Whydah stands low near the marshes about three miles from the sea side which makes it a very unhealthy place to live. The White people that the Africa Company send there from England seldom return to tell tales about the place. The factory is surrounded with a mud wall about six feet high with a gate on the south side. Within the walls is a large yard, a mud-thatched house where the Factor, Mr. Peirson, lives with the other White men. Near the house is a storehouse, a trunk or pen for the slaves, a good *forge,** several other small houses, and a place where they bury their dead White men, called very improperly, *the hog yard.*

The factory has proved highly beneficial to us. When bad weather prevents the canoes from carrying out a parcel of slaves to the ships, they are secured in the trunk and provided for. The Factor is a brisk man with a good interest with the king and with his *caboceers** and has great skill in negotiating with them. He knows when to be civil and when to be rough.

Whydah or **Ouidah** is located in the modern African state of Dahomey. As recently as 1961, the Portuguese maintained a one-man garrison in Fort St. John the Baptist which they had constructed in Whydah in 1677. In 1961, the Portuguese gave up custody of the fort to the government of the independent African state of Dahomey.

Forge: a small furnace used for metal working, in this instance making and repairing chains and shackles.

Caboceer—a word of Portuguese origin meaning **nobleman** or **chief.**

A154

As soon as the king learned of our landing, he sent two of his caboceers to greet us at our factory. They invited us to attend the king at once, which we did with samples of our goods. The king and his caboceers exacted very high prices and we had to agree to buy the king's slaves first. Then, the bell was sounded giving notice to all of the people to bring their slaves to the trunk for sale.

After four or five days of looking and examining, we selected such as we liked and agreed in what goods to pay for them. The prices had been already stated before the king how much of each sort of merchandise we would give for each man, woman, and child. Thus was saved an abundance of disputes and wrangling. We gave the owners notes signifying our agreement about the different sorts of goods they could redeem at our factory. Next, we marked the slaves we had bought with a hot iron having the letter of the ship's name on it, on the breast or shoulder. We anoint the place to be marked first with a little palm oil. The hot iron causes very little pain. The mark is usually well healed in a few days and appears very plain and white thereafter.

When our slaves were brought to the sea side, our canoes and long boat conveyed them aboard ship. All of the men were put in irons, shackled two by two together, to prevent mutiny or swimming ashore. The Negroes are so fearful of leaving their own country they often leap out of the canoes or off the ships into the sea drowning themselves rather than go to the Barbados of which they have a more dreadful apprehension than we have of hell. We have seen many of them eaten by sharks which hover about the ships anchored in this place. I have been told that sharks follow the ships all the way to the Barbados for the dead Negroes that are thrown overboard in passage. We had about twelve Negroes who willfully drowned themselves and others who starved themselves. It is their belief that when they die they shall return home to their own country and friends again.

Adapted from Donnan, **Documents**, Vol. I, pp. 399–400.

The flower of the Dahomean army was this brigade of women formed by King Trudo of Dahomey because he lacked enough men to defeat his enemies. He is shown here leading his Amazons to war.

Customs that Ships Trading at Whydah Must Pay to the King of Dahomey

For permission to trade	The value of eight slaves.
For water and washerwomen	The value of one slave.
For use of the factory house	The value of eight slaves.
For the canoes	The value of seven slaves.

SLAVES ARE VALUED AS:

6 kegs of brandy is one slave.
200 pounds of gunpowder is one slave.
25 guns is one slave.
10 long cloths is one slave.
10 blue cloths is one slave.
10 chintz cloths is one slave.
40 iron bars is one slave.

After the payments are made and they must be made as soon as possible, as traders dare not trade until the King's payments have been received, the vice roy gives you nine servants who must also be paid.

To the vice roy for himself	1 bolt of silk, 1 cask of flour, and 1 cask of beef.
To the interpreters	40 coweries* a day, a flask of brandy every Sunday, and at the end of your trade give each a keg of brandy and 1 bolt of cloth.
To the captain of the water side	1 keg of brandy on arrival and on departure. 1 bolt of cloth and 1 keg of brandy.
For every load taken from the ship	120 coweries for each keg of brandy and in proportion for lighter and heavier goods.

Coweries—Cowrie shells used as money and standards of value along the West African coast.

Adapted from Donnan, **Documents,** Vol. II (1931), pp. 531–533.

Olaudah Equiano's* Account of How He Became Enslaved, 1756

Olaudah (pronounced O-la-oo-dah) Equiano was born in the kingdom of Benin about 1745. He was kidnapped and enslaved in 1756 and sold in Virginia. He purchased his freedom in 1777, made his living as a sailor, and later became active in the antislavery movement in England. He married an English woman in 1792.

The kingdom of Benin is divided into many provinces: in one of the most fertile and most distant from the sea I was born. I was the youngest of th sons and a special favorite of my mother.

As we lived in a country where nature is good to us, our needs were few and easily supplied. Of course we had a few manufactures, for the most part, calicoes, china dishes, ornaments, tools, and arms. We also had busy markets which were frequently visited by husky brown colored men from the southwest. They generally brought us firearms, gun powder, hats, beads, and dry fish. They also carried slaves through our land and we inquired very strictly into how and where they were obtained. Sometimes we sold slaves to them, but they were only prisoners of war or such among us as had been convicted of kidnapping, or adultery, and other detestable crimes. This practice of kid-

A156

napping makes me think that despite all of our strictness about taking slaves, the principal business of these brown colored men from the southwest was to take our people.

One day when I was eleven, an event occurred that put an end to my happiness. One day when all of the grown people had gone off to the fields, two men and a woman climbed over our walls and seized me. They stopped my mouth and carried me off to the woods where they tied my hands. They took me to a small house that night. The next morning we left and travelled all day. Day after day, I travelled, sometimes by land and sometimes by water till after six months we reached the sea coast.

My first sight of the sea was that of a slave ship riding at anchor and waiting for a cargo. I was terrified when taken on board and was sure that I had been taken into a world of evil spirits. Seeing White men with horrible looks, red faces, and long hair, I feared they were going to eat me.

Adapted from the **Interesting Narrative of the Life of Olaudah Equiano or Gustavus Vassa, the African,** written by himself (London, 1789), pp. 6–7, 15–24, 25–26.

5 THE MIDDLE PASSAGE

In the seventeenth and eighteenth centuries, life at sea in the best of situations was always hard. Ships were small, accommodations were extremely cramped, and ventilation was so inadequate that the stench below decks was overpowering. Food was scarce and on long voyages such as the seven to ten week Middle Passage from Africa to the Americas, it was not fit to be eaten. Discipline was brutal, punishments excessively harsh and frequent, disease always present, and medical services were rough and incompetent.

In addition to hardships of life at sea, slave ships had other horrors. Overcrowding, disease, and abusive treatment made death routine during the Middle Passage. How many slaves died will probably never be known. On some voyages the number of slaves who died was appalling; on other voyages all survived. The length of time at sea, the sea routes taken, the treatment they received, epidemics—all affected how many slaves lived and how many died. Estimates of slave mortality in transit from Africa to the Americas range from an average of about 25 percent at the end of the seventeenth century to about 6 percent at the end of the eighteenth century.

While reading these selections from accounts of slaving voyages on the Middle Passage and studying a chart of late eighteenth-century mortality data, keep in mind these questions:

1. How were the slaves housed and treated during the Middle Passage?

2. What does John Dawson's deposition suggest to you about life aboard a slave ship during the Middle Passage?

3. What conclusion about life on a slave ship is suggested by this sample of mortality data? How do you explain it?

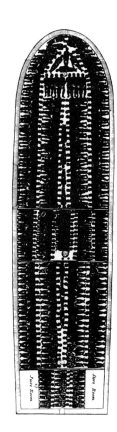

Africans in the slave ships on their forced journey to strange lands.

Descent into Slavery—The terror for Africans began with brutal capture, the first step on the long hard road to slavery. During the overland march to the coast, slaves were strung together in chains. Frequently, wooden yokes were used when costly iron chains were lacking.

Those who survived the cross-country march faced stifling imprisonment in the coastal barracoons under the blazing tropical sun. Here they were chained to posts until they were transferred to ships for the Atlantic crossing.

Jammed into ships for the Atlantic voyage, many slaves perished or were reduced to "walking skeletons" like these slaves taken from the bark "Wildfire."

On arrival, they were subjected to the indignities of close examination by traders, sale on the auction block, and final life-long servitude in the New World.

NEGROES FOR SALE AT AUCTION THIS DAY AT 1 O'CLOCK

Olaudah Equiano's Account of the Middle Passage, 1756

After I was put aboard the slave ship, I was put below deck where many men were chained together. I inhaled a stench like nothing I had ever experienced before. All about me there was crying. From the stench and crying I became so sick that I was unable to eat. I wished only for death to relieve me. Soon two of the crew offered me food and when I refused it, one of them stretched me across the *windlass** while the other flogged me severely.

I had never been treated like that in my entire life; and though I feared the water, if I could have gotten over the nettings covering the side of the ship, I would have jumped into the sea. One day, two of my companions who were chained together, preferred death to such a life of misery, plunged through the nettings into the sea and disappeared. Immediately another followed their example. Many more would have done the same if the crew had not prevented them.

While we remained on the coast I was allowed to remain on deck most of the time. The stench below deck was so intolerable and loathesome that it was dangerous to remain there for any length of time. But when the ship put to sea, we were all put below deck. We were so crowded that one could scarcely turn. The closeness of our confinement and the unbearable heat almost suffocated us. The air below deck became so foul that it was unfit for breathing. Very soon the sick and dying were all around me.

A Ship Surgeon's Account, 1785

Once during my last voyage, the port holes were shut and the gratings were covered on account of heavy weather. This tight confinement caused high fevers and losses of body fluid among the Negroes in their lodging places. While they were thus closed in, I frequently went below among them till at length below deck became so extremely hot that it was sufferable only for a very short time. But the excessive heat below was not all that rendered the situation of the Negroes intolerable. The decks of their lodging places were so covered with blood and mucus which had proceeded from them that they resembled a slaughter house. It is not within the power of human imagination to picture a situation more dreadful and disgusting. Numbers of slaves had fainted. When they were carried up to open air most were restored with some difficulty, but several died. The experience had nearly proved fatal to me as well.

*Deposition** of John Dawson, Mate of the *Rainbow*, Touching the Supposed Murders of George Crawford and Richard Kirkby, 1758

That on the high seas in a voyage from the coast of Africa to America, George Crawford, one of the mariners on board being ordered to assist in hauling up the try sail, fell in a violent manner with his head upon the deck, where he remained stunned and senseless.

Windlass—a machine for hoisting or hauling. It consists of a shaft around which rope is coiled. It has a handle to raise and lower a ship's anchor.

Adapted from **The Life of Olaudah Equiano or Gustavus Vassa, The African** (Boston: I. Knapp, 1837), pp. 30–52.

Adapted from Gomer Williams, **History of the Liverpool Privateers and Letters of Marque with an Account of the Liverpool Slave Trade** (London: William Heinemann Co., 1897), p. 587.

Deposition means an opinion or statement asserted; it is usually used in testimony.

That Captain Joseph *Harrison** at that time having a cat-of-nine tails in his hand and driving some Negroes off the deck believed that Crawford was shamming and gave him a gentle blow with the cat such as would not have hurt a child. Captain Harrison did not kick or otherwise abuse George Crawford, but when the surgeon tried to revive him the said George Crawford remained still, speechless, and died. I verily believe that George Crawford's fall on deck was the occasion of his death and not from any ill usage he received from Captain Harrison. I declare further that I know of no ill will between Captain Harrison and George Crawford at the time of his falling.

That Captain Harrison at Benin hired one *Dick,** a free Negro, as a *linguist** for the voyage.

That Richard Kirkby reported that Dick was bought as a slave by Captain Harrison and would be sold in the West Indies.

That Dick grew sulky and the slaves on board refused to eat. Captain Harrison asked Dick what was the matter and with some reluctance Dick told the Captain what he had heard. Captain Harrison inquired into the matter and discovered that Kirkby was the author of the report. Whereupon Dick demanded satisfaction from Kirkby. The Captain told him he could not give him satisfaction as he had no power to beat any white person on board. Dick stormed and raged on deck. Fearing insurrection from the slaves, Captain Harrison allowed Dick to take satisfaction of Kirkby, which he did by tying him up and giving him on two different occasions four and twenty lashes.

I verily believe that the whipping was not the occasion of Kirkby's death and that he died of the *flux** and *dropsy** which was upon him before the whipping. Nor do I believe that the whipping hastened his death because it was not severe or violent and no blood issued from the body of Kirkby by the whipping.

On this voyage from Liverpool to Benin, and Benin to Barbados, Captain Harrison lost 25 crewmen and 44 slaves. Dick was killed in an attempted insurrection of slaves.

Linguist here refers to speakers of more than one lnaguage, who know the different languages of the slaves and English. Most slave ships carried African linguists.

Flux—diarrhea or dysentery. Dropsy—a fatal condition characterized by great swelling and discoloration.

Adapted from Donnan, **Documents**, Vol. IV (1935), pp. 371–372.

Mortality of Slaves and Crew on Nine Slaving Voyages, 1766–1780

SHIP		SLAVES	DIED	%	CREW	DIED	%
Royal Charlotte	1766	120	3	2.5	17	0	0
Royal Charlotte	1767	455	10	2.2	18	0	0
Molly	1769	105	50	48.0	13	7	53.0
Ferret	1770	105	5	4.7	13	3	23.0
Surrey	1771	255	10	3.9	25	4	16.0
Three Friends	1773	144	8	5.5	12	2	16.0
Venus	1775	321	10	3.0	22	2	9.0
Harriet	1776	277	7	2.5	18	0	0
Camden	1780	580	51	8.8	65	4	6.0
Totals		2362	154	6.5	203	22	10.8

Adapted from **Thomas Clarkson,** An Abstract of the Evidence (London, 1791).

(*See page 166.)

A161

6   IN THE AMERICAS

Arrival in American waters brought the slaves a brief period of relief. The long voyage was over. Unless the weather was bad or food and water supplies exhausted, the last two or three days of the Middle Passage were usually easier. All or most of the slaves might be unchained, food and water rations would be increased, and more time would be spent on deck. In general, the captain and crew would try to improve the physical condition and appearance of the slaves. They would clean and cover up cuts, sores, abrasions, and all signs of illness and disease in order to increase the sales price of the slaves.

Procedures for selling a cargo of slaves varied from port to port, but they were always inhuman, degrading, and terrifying. While reading these accounts of slave-selling and studying ships' records, keep these questions in mind:

1. How was the manner of selling slaves in the Americas inhuman, degrading, and terrifying?

2. How were slaves sold? What was a <u>scramble</u>*?*

3. How were slaves purchased? What were some of the ways payment was made?

Olaudah Equiano's Account of Being Sold, 1756

Olaudah Equiano

At last we came in sight of the island of Barbados, and soon we anchored at Bridgetown. Many merchants and planters came on board, even though it was late in the evening. They put us into separate lots and examined us attentively. They made us jump and pointed to the land indicating that we were to go there. We thought by this that we were to be eaten by these ugly men, as they appeared to us. They sent some old slaves among us who said we were not to be eaten, but to work, and were soon to go on land where we would see many of our country people.

Sure enough, after we were landed there came to us Africans of all languages. We were conducted immediately into a merchant's yard where we were all pent up together like so many sheep without regard for age or sex. We were not many days in the merchant's yard before we were sold in the usual manner. On a signal, the beat of a drum, the buyers rushed into the yard where the slaves were confined and chose the lot of slaves they liked best. The clamor and noise were terrifying.

In this manner, relatives and friends were separated, never to see each other again. I remember several brothers who were sold in different lots and it was pathetic to hear their cries at parting.

I stayed on this island for a few days. Then I and some other slaves who were not sold with the rest were shipped off on a sloop for North America. We landed in the Virginia country, up a river and a long way from the sea. I saw few or none of our native Africans and met not one soul whose language I could understand. Unable to talk with anyone, I was constantly grieving and wishing for death rather than anything else.

Adapted from **The Interesting Narrative of the Life of Olaudah Equiano,** pp. 30–33.

Jamaica Slave Scramble, 1788

Upon arriving in port the captain and a factor went over the cargo of slaves and picked out the slaves who were maimed or diseased. These slaves were carried to a dockside tavern and auctioned off to the highest bidders. The price of these so called *refuse-slaves** was usually half of that paid for a healthy Negro. Sometimes they would be sold for a few pounds per head.

The healthy slaves remaining after the refuse had been sold off were commonly sold by scramble, that is, a standard price for each man, woman, boy, and girl in the cargo would be set with purchasers who would then scramble for the pick.

On the Emilia lately arrived in Kingston, the ship was darkened with sails and covered all around. The men slaves were placed on the main deck, and the women slaves on the quarter deck. The purchasers on shore were informed that a gun would be fired when the sale was ready to open. When the gun was fired a great number of people came on board with cards and tallies in their hands and rushed all about the ship. Some had three or four handkerchiefs tied together to encircle as many as they thought fit for their purposes.

Refuse-slaves were those who were unsaleable. Frequently, they were left to starve on the docks.

Adapted from Alexander Falconbridge, **An Account of the Slave Trade on the Coast of Africa** (London, 1788).

Account of the Sales of Negroes Sold out of the Ship *Swallow* for the Royal Africa Company, Captain Evan Says, Master, Island of Nevis, January 12, 1681

PURCHASERS	MEN	WOMEN	BOYS	GIRLS	POUNDS OF SUGAR*
Sir W. Stapleton	4	0	0	1	15,000
George Cruff	0	0	1	0	2,800
James Walker	4	3	1	0	26,600
Moses Leavermore	1	1	1	0	10,400
Edward Parsons	3	1	2	0	19,200
John Pope	0	0	1	0	2,800
John Chapman	0	0	0	1	2,000
John Williams	1	0	0	0	3,500
Thomas Weekes	1	1	1	0	9,500
John Syms	2	1	0	0	10,800
Captain Evan Says	1	0	0	0	2,560

Altogether, this list included 24 purchasers of 71 slaves (31 men, 29 women, 7 boys, and 4 girls) for a total outlay of 200,457 pounds of sugar.

Adapted from Donnan, **Documents,** Vol. I, p. 257.

Pounds of sugar represent purchase prices for the slaves.

Account of Sales of Negroes by the *Arminian Merchant*, Captain John Hosea, Master, Barbados, February 27, 1690

PURCHASERS	MEN	WOMEN	BOYS	GIRLS	£
Joseph Holdersby to pay in April	1	0	0	0	40
Eliza Ramsay to pay in three months	0	1	0	0	18
John Phillips to pay in ready money	2	0	0	0	45
John Newsam to pay in six months	1	0	0	0	26
William Dotten to pay in bills of the ship*	13	0	1	0	333
Jonathan Walker to pay 15 percent in ready money, the rest in six months	2	2	1	0	82
Edmund Scrope to pay in three months	3	2	1	1	130
Joseph Kirle to pay in ready money	2	1	0	0	40
Nicolas Handmary to pay in ready money	1	1	0	0	35
Phillip Scott to pay in six months	2	0	0	0	46
Commission to the Captain	9	6	1	0	

Altogether, this list included 90 purchasers of 431 slaves (252 men, 149 women, 19 boys, and 11 girls) for a total outlay of £5,138.

Bills of the ship meant vouchers or receipts indicating that sums of money had been deposited with the ship owners in anticipation of the delivery of cargo.

Adapted from Donnan, **Documents**, Vol. I, p. 372.

Cape Coast Castle about 1806.

Profits on Five Slaving Voyages, 1784–1805

YEAR	SHIP	SLAVES	DESTINATION	NET PROFIT	AVG. PROFIT PER SLAVE
1784	Bloom	307	—	£8,123	£26
1798	Lottery	453	Barbados	£12,091	£27
1802	Lottery	305	Jamaica	£11,039	£36
1803	Enterprize	392	Cuba	£6,428	£16
1805	Fortune	343	Bahamas	£9,487	£28

Adapted from Donnan, **Documents**, Vol. N, p. 631.

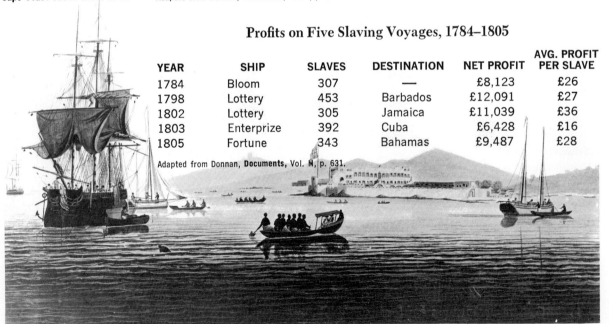

3 Atlantic Slave Trade

Resistance and Reform

Introduction

Resistance to slave trading by both free and enslaved blacks is as old as the trade itself. Nuño Tristam, one of the earliest Portuguese slavers, was killed by blacks while taking slaves on the Geba River in 1446. As early as 1522 enslaved blacks on the island of Hispaniola rose against their Spanish masters. Others in the West Indies and in North America did the same with increasing frequency during the seventeenth and eighteenth centuries. Insurrection was one of the ever-present facts of slave-trade history.

As the trade expanded in the eighteenth century, insurrections on slave ships became more frequent. Accounts of them in slave-trading company records, in dispatches from colonial officials, and in colonial newspapers increased. Attempted insurrections became so common during the eighteenth century that some trading companies prepared instructions for their ship captains and crews on how to prevent them. In addition, insurance companies in Liverpool and Bristol sold policies that would reimburse merchants and ship owners for the value of slaves lost or killed during insurrections on board ship during the Middle Passage. The business was thus sure to thrive even if its victims did not.

White protest against the Atlantic slave trade has a much shorter history than does black resistance to it. Protests against Indian slavery occurred very early, but once Africans had replaced Indians in the mines and fields of the New World, enslavement of blacks became an unquestioned fact of life. It was a matter of business, and the uninvolved had no lasting interest in it. For about 150 years this state of indifference continued. Then Englishmen entered into the trade. As they began to dominate it, and as the brutal facts of slavery became known, English consciences were stirred. With that stirring, hope for the slaves was born.

The first suggestions of doubt came from George Fox, the founder of the Quakers. He visited Barbados in 1671, saw the condition of slaves, and urged their owners not only to deal mildly and gently with them, but to set them free after a number of years of servitude. Fox's advice was not well received and resulted in laws prohibiting Quaker meetings and Quaker emigration to the West Indies. In 1688, Quakers in Pennsylvania made what was probably the first American protest against the slave trade, and in 1700 Judge Sewall published his famous pamphlet against slavery, Selling of Joseph. During the first half of the new century, Quakers in both England and America passed resolutions at their yearly meetings condemning the trade.

George Fox—founder of the Society of Friends, who lived 1624–1691, wrote various tracts on the treatment of Negroes.

A165

Thomas Clarkson, son of an English clergyman, was one of the founders of the <u>Society for the Abolition of the Slave Trade</u> in England in 1787. He was a tireless worker, researcher, and writer for the cause of abolition throughout his life.

William Wilberforce—philanthropist, became a member of the House of Commons at 21; was a tireless champion for the abolition of slavery. Through his efforts, Parliament abolished the slave trade in the British colonies in 1807.

Anthony Benezet (1713–1784), born in France, brought up in London. Became a Quaker at the age of 14. He came to Philadelphia in 1731 where his family founded a highly successful business and Anthony was a school teacher for many years. Worked to obtain justice for American Indians, African slaves, and French refugees from Nova Scotia. Campaigned against excessive use of alcohol.

Granville Sharp (1735–1813) was responsible for winning freedom for the slave, **James Somerset.** Though of modest means and obliged to work for a living every day, Sharp provided the money, time, and learning necessary to bring the Somerset case before the court for decision.

Voices for Justice

Beginning in the 1750's, *Anthony Benezet,** an American Quaker, published several pamphlets which directly inspired the launching of a full-scale campaign against the slave trade. John Wesley, the founder of the Methodist Church in England, used the first part of Benezet's <u>Some Historical Accounts of Guinea</u> as a basis for powerful sermons against slavery. Thomas Clarkson, the son of a well-to-do English parson, became a life-long crusader against slavery after reading Benezet's <u>Short Account of that Part of Africa Inhabited by the Negroes.</u> Benezet's pamphlets were also widely read in France and elsewhere in Europe with the result that he acted as a link between the growing antislavery movements on both sides of the Atlantic.

The resolutions of the Quakers, the writings of Benezet and others, and the preaching of Wesley slowly began to achieve some genuine results. In 1772, *Granville Sharp,** son of an English clergyman and a minor clerk in an English government department, succeeded in getting the case of James Somerset, a slave brought from Virginia to England, before Lord Chief Justice Mansfield. Since there were no laws that sanctioned slavery in England, Justice Mansfield decided that because slavery was such an evil in itself and no laws sanctioned it in England, no man in England could be a slave and no slave could set foot in England without becoming free.

From this success others followed. In 1783 English Quakers presented the first petition to the British Parliament for an end to England's participation in the slave trade and founded the first antislavery society. The machinery for a full-scale campaign against the slave trade was at hand. All that was needed was to find the proper men to run it.

The proper men were also available and ready. They were Thomas Clarkson, described by some as "the slave of the slaves," and by others as a "moral steam engine," and William Wilberforce, a young, wealthy, talented, and deeply religious member of the British House of Commons. Clarkson was a hard-working, meticulous collector of facts and figures, and a voluminous writer. Wilberforce was a brilliant speaker, man of influence, and personal friend of the Prime Minister.

A166

Moral Victory

In 1787 the Quakers, Granville Sharp, Thomas Clarkson, and William Wilberforce all came together. They embarked on a campaign against the Atlantic slave trade that took twenty years to complete. Despite endless disappointments, repeated failures, and even a major European war, these men succeeded in bringing about a major change in public values and morals. In 1807, the British Parliament and the United States Congress passed laws that made importing slaves into their respective territories illegal and punishable.

To be sure, enacting laws and enforcing them are frequently entirely different problems. The Abolition Laws of 1807 made the slave trade illegal, but they could not end it. Suppression of the illegal slave trade required additional laws and naval patrols to enforce them. Nevertheless, moral revolutions are fully as important as political ones, and the Abolition Laws of 1807 were the result of a major moral revolution.

Knowing how blacks resisted the slave trade and understanding how and why this moral revolution against slavery happened are the purposes of this assignment.

Objectives are to:

—Examine given testimony on the Atlantic slave trade and describe black resistance to it.

—Recognize and identify the fundamental ideas that inspired the antislave trade movement.

—Make hypotheses about the historical importance of the antislave trade movement.

7 RESISTANCE ON SLAVE SHIPS

Whether successful or unsuccessful, insurrrections on slave ships always brought death. If successful, most or all of the crew would die; if unsuccessful, some of the slaves would die—usually in a torturous manner so as to discourage other uprisings. Because successful insurrections left few or no eyewitnesses, most of what is known about black resistance to the slave trade comes from accounts of insurrections that failed.

While reading the following statements and newpaper reports of insurrections on slave ships, keep in mind these questions:

1. *Where and when were slave insurrections most likely to occur?*
2. *How did slave insurrections usually begin?*
3. *How were insurrections stopped and further attempts prevented?*

John Atkins's* Observations of the Prospect of Negro Insurrections, 1735

Once a ship has its full cargo of slaves and is at sea, it is commonly imagined that the Negroes' ignorance of navigation will be a safeguard against insurrection. Yet many of the slaves believe they have been bought to be eaten. Others believe that death will return them to their own country. There have been instances enough of slaves rising and killing a ship's company when distant from land, though not so often as when on the coast. That

John Atkins was a surgeon in the English Navy who sailed on an expedition to the West African Coast in 1721 to disperse or capture a band of pirates whose operations were disrupting the slave trade.

A167

Adapted from John Atkins, A Voyage to Guinea, Brasil, and the West Indies in His Majesty's Ships, the Swallow and Weymouth (London, 1735) in Donnan, Documents, Vol. II, p. 281–282.

such insurrections have happened when distant from land is sufficient to show that a captain's care and diligence should never be relaxed until the destination is made and the slaves delivered.

Tomba's Insurrection, 1721

One of the most thriving independent traders at Sierra Leone was John Leadstine, commonly known as Old Cracker. On looking over some of Old Cracker's slaves, I could not help taking notice of one fellow above the rest, a tall, strong man with a bold, stern appearance. As he thought we were viewing them with an intention to buy, he seemed displeased with his fellow slaves for their readiness to be examined. He refused to look at us, rise, or stretch out his limbs as Old Cracker commanded. This refusal earned him an unmerciful whipping from Cracker's own hand. Cracker would have killed him except for the money he would have lost by so doing. All of this the Negro bore without a whimper, shrinking very little under the lashes, and shedding only a tear or two which he tried to hide as if ashamed of even that modest weakness.

All of us were amazed by his courage and wanted to know how Cracker had obtained him. He told us that this brave fellow was called *Captain Tomba** and was a leader of some country villages that opposed our trade at the Nunez River. Tomba had killed some of our African friends and burned their cottages. With the help of Cracker's men, those sufferers surprised Tomba in the night, bound him, and delivered him here as he was, but not before he had killed two of his attackers. Shortly thereafter, Cracker sold Tomba in a lot of thirty slaves aboard the galley Robert out of Bristol, *Richard Harding,** Master.

What eventually happened to **Tomba** and **Captain Harding** is unknown. But in 1729, eight years after the uprising, the **Robert** was reported captured by Spanish Coast Guard in the West Indies. In 1732, under a different captain, Nathaniel Leatherland, the **Robert** landed 147 slaves at Barbados.

Some few weeks later we came upon the Robert at Jaque à Jaque on the Ivory Coast. Captain Harding gave us the following melancholy story. This Tomba conspired with three or four of his stoutest countrymen to kill the ship's company and attempt their escape while they still had a coast to fly to. With the help of a woman slave, they almost succeeded. Being more at large, she was to watch for a proper opportunity. The woman brought Tomba word one night that there were no more than five white men on deck and they were all asleep. She gave Tomba a hammer which was the only weapon she could find.

Tomba sought more accomplices, but only one more than the original conspirers and the woman followed him up on deck. He found three sailors sleeping on deck and killed two of them with single strokes on their temples. The third sailor was seized by Tomba's accomplices and quickly was dispatched in the same manner. Going aft to finish their murderous work, they found the other two on the watch already up and on their guard. Their struggle soon awakened Captain Harding who came on deck and thereupon laid Tomba flat on the deck with repeated blows from a handspike and secured all of them in irons.

A168

With matters thus secured, Captain Harding considered the stoutness and worth of Tomba and one of his accomplices and decided to do what they do to rogues of dignity. He whipped and *scarified** them only. The three other abettors of the insurrection he sentenced to cruel deaths, killing one first, and making the others eat his heart and liver before they were killed. The woman, he hoisted up by the thumbs, whipped and slashed her with knives before the other slaves until she died.

Scarify means to lacerate and scar.

Adapted from Donnan, **Documents,** Vol. II, pp. 265–266.

Voyage of the Little George, 1730

I, George Scot, Master of the sloop, Little George, belonging to Rhode Island, sailed from the coast of Guinea on the first of June, 1730, having on board ninety-six slaves, thirty-five of which were men. On June 6, at half past four in the morning, being one hundred leagues from land, the men slaves got off their irons and making their way upon deck killed four men on watch.

I, being in my cabin, took my pistol and fired up the scuttle, which made all of the slaves that were loose, except two, run foward. These two seemed to laugh at the cowardice of the rest, us being but four men and a boy. They secured the scuttle and kept us confined in the cabin.

They made sail towards land and continually heaved chunks of wood and poured water down into the cabin with the intention of disabling us or spoiling our powder. After nine days they passed the bar of the Sierra Leone river and ran ashore three leagues up the river.

The natives waded out from shore with firearms and would have overcome us except for being persuaded by the slaves that we would shoot them if they appeared in our sight. The natives encouraged the grown slaves to go ashore and drove the younger ones overboard to follow.

When the slaves had gone, we went up on deck with our arms and hoisted out our boat. The natives fired on us several times, but we made what haste we could to the other side of the river. We rowed down river about two leagues and found an English sloop riding at anchor. Captain James Collingwood took us aboard where we refreshed ourselves, having had nothing to eat for nine days but raw rice.

Adapted from Donnan, **Documents,** Vol. III (1932), pp. 119–121.

𝔑𝔢𝔴-𝔈𝔫𝔤𝔩𝔞𝔫𝔡.
The *Boʃton* Weekly News-Letter.

Boston News-Letter, September 25, 1729

From a vessel lately arrived from the West Indies, we have been informed that the Clare, having taken on board her number of slaves, departed from the coast of Guinea for South Carolina. But she did not pass ten leagues on her way before the Negroes rose and made themselves masters of the gunpowder and firearms. The captain and crew took to their long boat and got ashore near Cape Coast Castle. The Negroes ran the ship on shore within a few leagues of the said castle and made their escape.

Adapted from Donnan, **Documents,** Vol. IV, p. 274.

Report in the Boston News-Letter, June 21, 1750

From a vessel lately arrived from the West Indies, we have been informed that a ship out of Liverpool, coming from the coast of Africa with about 350 slaves on board, suffered an insurrection. When in sight of the island of *Guadeloupe,** the slaves being admitted to come upon the deck to air themselves, they seized an opportunity on May 28 and captured the ship. They killed the Captain and Mate and threw fifteen of the crew overboard. They sent a boat with two white lads and three or four slaves to discover what land was close by. Meanwhile, the ship drove down wind giving the lads an opportunity to escape and inform the Commandant of that part of the island what had happened. The Commandant raised about 100 men, put them aboard a sloop, pursued the ship, and in a few hours took and carried her into *Port Louis.**

Adapted from Donnan, **Documents**, Vol. II, p. 485.

Port Louis is located on Guadeloupe, a French possession in the West Indies.

Newport Mercury, November 18, 1765

We have learned that Captain Hopkins in a *Brig** out of Providence survived an insurrection soon after leaving the coast of Africa. The number of his crew being reduced by sickness, Captain Hopkins was obliged to permit some of the slaves to come on deck to assist the crew. These slaves contrived to release the others and the whole of them rose against the crew and tried to take possession of the vessel. They were prevented by the Captain and his men who killed, wounded, and forced overboard eighty of them, which persuaded the rest to submit.

Brig (short for **brigantine**) is a two-masted sailing vessel.

Adapted from Donnan, **Documents**, Vol. III, p. 213.

8   REFORM OF SLAVE TRADE

As the Atlantic slave trade expanded in the eighteenth century, many in both England and America viewed that expansion with alarm for a variety of different reasons. While that alarm was sufficient to persuade some colonial assemblies outside of the West Indies to prohibit or restrict slave imports, the trade continued to thrive. Such actions by colonial assemblies proved to be either reversible or ineffective, and did not lead to reform.

Great reform movements are inspired by ideas and are organized and promoted by men. Usually such ideas are powerful but simple, and such men are tireless but complicated. The movement for abolition of the slave trade after the 1750's is a case in point. While reading the following statements from reformers and persons with misgivings about the slave trade, keep in mind these questions:

1. Who profits from the slave trade? Who suffers from it?

2. Why should the slave trade be opposed and ended?

A170

3. What fundamental idea or set of ideas do you think is most responsible for the growing opposition to slave trade?

Captain *Thomas Phillips** on Color as a Basis for Enslavement, 1694

Except for the lack of Christianity and true religion (their misfortune more than fault), Negroes are as much the works of God's hands, and no doubt are as dear to him as ourselves. Nor can I imagine why they should be so despised for their color, being what they cannot help and the effect of the climate where God has been pleased to place them. I cannot think there is any intrinsic value in one color more than another, nor that white is better than black. We think so, only because we are so, and are prone to judge favorably our own case. It is the same with the blacks who say the devil is white and so paint him.

Captain Thomas Phillips was an experienced seaman who was given command of the Hannibal owned by the Royal Africa Company and made a slaving voyage to Cape Coast Castle and to the Barbados in 1693–1694.

William Byrd's** Observations on the Slave Trade and the Future of Virginia, 1736

They import so many Negroes here, that I fear this colony will some time or other be known by the name of New Guinea. I am sensible of many bad consequences from the increase of Negroes among us. They blow up the pride and ruin the industry of our white people, who seeing a rank of poor creatures below them, detest work for fear it should make them look like slaves.

Another unhappy effect of many Negroes is the necessity of being severe. Numbers make them insolent, and then foul means must do what fair will not. We have nothing like the inhumanity here that is practiced in the islands and God forbid we ever should. But they must be bridled with a tight rein or they will be apt to throw their rider. Yet even this is terrible to a good-natured man, who must submit to being either a fool or a fury. And this will be more and more our unhappy case, as Negroes increase among us.

But these private fears are as nothing when compared to the public danger. We have already 10,000 Negroes fit to bear arms and their numbers increase everyday, as well by birth as by importation. Should a man of desperate courage arise among us he might, with more advantage than *Cataline,** kindle a servile war that may tinge our rivers with blood and cost millions to end.

It is worth the consideration of the British Parliament to put an end to the unchristian traffic of making merchandise of our fellow creatures. At least the further importation of them into our colony ought to be prohibited before they prove as troublesome and dangerous as they have been recently in Jamaica where they have cost the lives of many of His Majesty's subjects. All these matters duly considered, I wonder whether the legislature will continue to allow a few ravenous traders to endanger public safety, especially when such traders would as freely sell their fathers, their elder brothers, and even their wives, if they could black their faces and get anything for them.

William Byrd (1674–1744) of Westover, Virginia, was a planter, colonial official, and author of the now famous Secret Diary.

Cataline, a Roman aristocrat, headed an unsuccessful conspiracy to organize servants and slaves and overthrow the government of Rome in 63 B.C. He and several others were put to death without trial.

Adapted from Donnan, **Documents,** Vol. I, p. 403 and Vol. II, pp. 131–132.

Anthony Benezet on the *Iniquitous** Nature of the Man-Trade, 1767

Iniquitous—wicked, unjust, evil.
Odious—deserving or provoking hatred or repugnance.
Pernicious—injurious, destructive or deadly.

Greed and pride have introduced many iniquitous practices into civil society, which though *odious** in themselves and most *pernicious** in their consequences have become adopted through custom and usage. We silence the dictates of conscience and reconcile ourselves to what otherwise would have sickened us with horror. A lamentable and shocking instance of the influence which love of gain has upon the minds of those who yield to its allurements is the Negro trade.

The evil is so deep and attended with such dreadful consequences that no well-disposed person can be a silent and innocent spectator. How many thousands of our harmless fellow-creatures have fallen in sacrifice to that selfish greed that gives life to this complicated wickedness. The iniquity of being engaged in a trade by which so great a number of innocent people are yearly destroyed is magnified by the consideration that we as a people have been particularly favored with the light of the Gospel.

From Anthony Benezet, A Short Account of That Part of Africa Inhabited by the Negroes (Philadelphia: Association of Friends, 1858), pp. 51–53.

How miserable must be our condition, if for filthy lucre, we should continue to act so contrary to the nature of God's divine call, the purpose of which is to introduce a universal and affectionate brotherhood among all of mankind. For this end the Son of God became man, suffered, and died. The whole tenor of the gospel declares that for those of us who refuse or neglect this divine call, the Son of God has suffered in vain.

Thomas Clarkson's Reasons for Getting Involved, 1808

I scarcely know of a subject, the contemplation of which is more pleasing than that of correcting or removing any of the evils of life. Men rejoice that the sufferings of our fellow creatures have been in any way relieved, and we must rejoice equally to think that our own moral condition must have been improved by the benevolent change that has happened to others.

Among the many evils corrected by the general influence of Christianity on the minds of men or by particular associations of Christians, the African slave trade appears to me to have been the greatest. The abolition of it should be accounted as one of the greatest blessings, and as such should be one of the greatest sources of our joy. Indeed I know of no evil, the removal of which should excite in us a higher degree of pleasure. Yet, we must offer thanksgiving to the great Creator for his favor in disposing our legislators to take away such a portion of suffering from our fellow creatures and such a load of guilt from our native land.

Thomas Clarkson, The History of the Rise, Progress, and Accomplishment of the Abolition of the African Slave-Trade by the British Parliament (London: Longman, Hurst, Rees, and Orme, 1808), Vol. I, pp. 2–13.

If the great evil of the slave trade has fallen prostrate before the efforts of those who attacked it, what evil of less magnitude shall not be more easily subdued? May we never cease to believe that many of the miseries of life are still to be remedied, or to rejoice that we may be permitted to heal them. The Divinity never so fully dwells in us as when we do His Will; and we never do His Will more agreeably than when we employ our time in works of charity and mercy toward the rest of our fellow creatures.

A172

4 Atlantic Slave Trade

Suppression and Liberation

Introduction

For Clarkson and Wilberforce enactment of the Abolition Law of 1807 was the end of one campaign and the beginning of another. The suppression of a legal trade in slaves inevitably gave rise to an illegal one. English ships withdrawn from the slave trade were promptly replaced by French, Portuguese, Spanish, and above all, by American. Each group flouted its country's laws against the trade. The newcomers profited greatly. The drop in the number of slave ships trading along the African coast reduced prices because traders had a surplus of slaves and not enough markets. On the other hand, prices went up in the Americas because the demand for slaves was greater than the supply. With the prospects of huge profits before them, English ships very soon returned to the slave ports of Whydah, Bonny, and Calabar and entered into the illegal trade.

Problems of Abolition

As this new situation developed, three problems became clear. First, the *Abolition Law of 1807** had to be tightened up if the illegal trade was to be suppressed. Second, some method had to be devised for curbing the trading activities of the French, Portuguese, Spanish, and Americans. Third, the evils of the slave trade would never disappear until slavery itself was abolished in every part of the world.

The courses of action required to solve these three problems did not take long to discover. Shortly after the enactment of the Abolition Law, Clarkson and Wilberforce founded the African Institution. Its purpose was to oversee the enforcement of the laws against slave trading, to recommend improvements in them, and encourage development of new products and commodities as a basis for trade between Africans and Europeans.

Two armed ships of the Royal Navy—Solebay and Derwent—were dispatched to the African coast to patrol the waters off the most-frequented slave ports. Next, the Abolition Law was amended in 1811 making slave trading a felony and punishable by five years' imprisonment. During the summer, of 1814, nearly one million Englishmen signed 772 petitions and presented them to the British House of Commons. These petitions urged *Lord Castlereagh** to insist upon including prohibition of the slave trade in international peace treaties then being negotiated to end the long war with Napoleon.

The English Abolition Law of 1807 provided that convicted slave traders would be fined £100 for every slave found on board and would suffer confiscation of the vessel and all its equipment and furnishings.

Lord Castlereagh (pronounced Cas-sel-ree) (1769–1822) was Foreign Secretary. He introduced the issue of abolition of the slave trade at the Paris Peace Conference in 1814, and again at the Congress of Vienna in 1815. His efforts led to abolition laws in Denmark, Holland, France, and Ceylon.

Sir Thomas Foxwell Buxton (1786–1845) was a deeply religious and wealthy man who was active in a variety of charitable activities. A member of Parliament since 1818, he was personally selected by Wilberforce to head the Anti-slavery Party in the House of Commons. For his services on behalf of black people, Queen Victoria knighted him in 1840.

Objectives are to:

—Draw inferences from a given chronology, set of statistical data, and filmstrip about the suppression of the illegal slave trade and the eventual abolition of legalized slavery.

—Make hypotheses about the organizations and actions most responsible for the suppression of the illegal slave trade and the eventual abolition of legalized slavery.

—Evaluate your hypotheses and make judgments upon them.

Indeed, Clarkson and Wilberforce were no longer alone. Younger men, and on occasions masses of people, became deeply involved in campaigns for more ships for the West African patrol and for the enactment of laws abolishing the institution of slavery itself. In 1823 Wilberforce and Clarkson founded the British and Foreign Anti-slavery Society and young *Thomas Foxwell Buxton** introduced the first motion in the British House of Commons calling for the abolition of slavery throughout the British Empire.

The British government countered Buxton's motion with a plan to allow their colonial legislative assemblies time to proceed against slavery on their own. The government warned the colonies that the British Parliament would most certainly intervene in cases of undue delay. It emphasized the seriousness of this warning by approving the penalty of death by hanging for captured and convicted slave traders.

Britain Leads Way in Abolition, 1833

Despite the British government's warning, progress was very slow, and public opinion in England forced the government and Parliament to support their words with actions. In 1833 Parliament enacted a law abolishing slavery in the British Empire. By 1838 all the slaves in the West Indies were set free. After some persuasion, Britain's example was gradually followed by other European states and some Latin American ones. Yet, some slave systems still remained where no steps toward emancipation had been taken: the southern United States, Cuba, Brazil, Zanzibar, and southern Arabia.

The Royal Navy undertook energetic actions in all of the oceans of the world to see that users of slaves were deprived of fresh supplies from Africa. British warships patrolled the coasts of both West and East Africa, the approaches to the Red Sea, the western reaches of the Indian Ocean, and the coasts of Brazil and Cuba. Wherever the slave ships ventured in their illegal trade, the ships of the Royal Navy pursued, except into the territorial waters of the United States. Eventually, however, British diplomatic pressure, British sea power, and the American Civil War brought slavery to an end in the Americas.*

The **last illegal shipment of slaves** to the Americas probably was landed in Cuba as late as 1880.

A174

9 THE ROYAL NAVY AND THE SUPPRESSION OF SLAVERY

The suppression of the illegal slave trade and the abolition of legalized slavery throughout the world was a long and difficult task. It required determination, diplomacy, money, bloodshed, and above all, power. The most powerful forces in the world during the nineteenth century were the ships, guns, and men of the Royal Navy. The role played by the British Navy in ending four hundred years of brutal exploitation of black people is unique in the history of armed forces.

Examination of the chronology of events and statistical data presented here will provide you with a factual basis for drawing inferences and making hypotheses about when, where, and how slave trading was suppressed, and how legalized slavery throughout the world was abolished. While studying these materials, keep in mind the following questions:

1. How did the British attempt to restrict the activities of foreign slave traders? What countries resisted the British efforts?

2. When do you think the turning point in the suppression of the illegal Atlantic slave trade occurred? Why?

3. What do you think suppression of the slave trade cost? Who paid for most of it?

Estimated Slave Imports into American Territories, 1811–1870

	UNITED STATES	CUBA	PUERTO RICO	FRENCH CARIBBEAN	BRAZIL
1811–1820	10,000	79,000	6,400	31,400	266,800
1821–1830	10,000	112,500	12,100	46,000	325,000
1831–1840	10,000	126,000	14,100	3,600	212,000
1841–1850	10,000	47,600	10,600	—	338,300
1851–1860	10,000	123,000	7,200	15,000	3,300
1861–1870	1,000	61,500	4,700	—	—
TOTAL NUMBER	51,000	550,000	55,100	96,000	1,145,000
PERCENT OF TOTAL IMPORTED	2.7	28.9	3.0	5.1	60.0

Adapted from Curtin, **The Atlantic Slave Trade**, p. 234.

Chronology of the Suppression of the Slave Trade and Slavery

1807	Great Britain abolishes slave trade. United States abolishes slave trade.
1810	Venezuela abolishes slave trade.
1811	Great Britain makes slave trade a felony, punishable by five years' imprisonment. Chile abolishes slave trade.
1812	Argentina abolishes slave trade.
1813	Sweden abolishes slave trade.
1814	Denmark and Holland abolish slave trade.
1815	France abolishes slave trade. Britain pays Portugal £300,000 for abolishing slave trade north of the Equator.
1816	Slaves in Ceylon emancipated.
1817	Portugal and Spain grant Great Britain right of search-and-seizure of suspected slave ships on the high seas or in coastal waters.
1818	Holland grants Great Britain right of search-and-seizure.
1819	United States sends four warships to participate in the West Africa anti-slavery patrol.
1820	Great Britain and Arab sheikdoms on the Red Sea, by treaty, declare slave trade to be piracy. United States Congress declares slave trading to be piracy.
1822	Spain receives £400,000 from the British government for abolishing slave trade. United States founds Liberia as a colony for liberated slaves.
1823	British and Foreign Anti-slavery Society founded. Buxton's motion in the English Parliament for emancipation of slaves in the British Empire. United States Congress appropriates $50,000 to United States Navy to suppress slave trade.
1824	Great Britain enacts law declaring slave trading is piracy, punishable by death. United States refuses to grant Britain right of search-and-seizure in American waters.*
1826	United States Congress appropriates $32,000 to United States Navy to suppress slave trade.
1829	Petitions against slavery presented to the British Parliament. Abolitionists meet in London. Mexico abolishes slavery.
1830	Brazil abolishes slave trade. Portugal abolishes slave trade.
1831	United States Congress appropriates $16,000 to United States Navy to suppress slave trade.

One of the issues in the War of 1812 between Great Britain and the United States was **freedom of the seas.** Americans were unwilling to grant by treaty what they had gone to war to protect, no matter how worthy the cause.

1833	Slaves emancipated and slavery abolished in British Empire. France grants Great Britain right of search-and-seizure.
1837	United States Congress appropriates $11,000 to United States Navy to suppress slave trade.
1841	Great Britain, Austria, Prussia, and France agree to a treaty granting right of search-and-seizure.
1842	United States Congress appropriates $10,000 to United States Navy to suppress slave trade.
1844	Independent State of Texas grants Great Britain right of search-and-seizure.
1845	Belgium and Brazil grant Great Britain right of search-and-seizure.
1847	Liberia becomes an independent Republic.
1848	Slaves emancipated and slavery abolished in all French territories.
1849	France sets up a protectorate* over Conakry-Guinea.
1850	Britain organizes the port of Accra and the Gold Coast as British colonies.
1851	British capture slave port of Lagos.
1854	United States Congress appropriates $8,000 to United States Navy to suppress slave trade.
1856	Governor of South Carolina suggests reopening slave trade. United States Congress condemns proposals to reopen slave trade.
1857	United States Congress appropriates $8,000 to United States Navy to suppress slave trade.
1858	Slavery abolished in Portuguese territories.
1860	United States Congress appropriates $60,000 to United States Navy to suppress slave trade.
1861	American Civil War begins. Confederate States of America prohibit slave trading with foreign countries. United States Congress appropriates $900,000 to United States Navy to suppress slave trade. Port of Lagos proclaimed as British territory, the first step in establishing the British African colony of Nigeria.
1862	Treaty of Washington between Great Britain and the United States grants right of search-and-seizure.
1863	France sets up a protectorate over Dahomey. Emancipation Proclamation in the United States. Holland abolishes slavery in its territories.
1865	Thirteenth Amendment prohibits slavery in the United States and its territories.
1868	Royal Navy begins antislavery patrol in Indian Ocean to suppress Arab slave trade.
1870	Emancipation of slaves begins in Cuba.
1871	Emancipation of slaves begins in Brazil. Dutch sell Elmina Castle and other ports on the Gold Coast to the British.

Protectorate—when a great power assumes political control over an independent state without formally incorporating it into its own territory.

Britain proclaims emancipation —slaves in the West Indies hear the official news of their release from bondage.

1888	Slavery abolished in Brazil.
1890	General Act of the Brussels International Conference becomes charter for international efforts to suppress slavery throughout the world.
1893	France makes Conakry-Guinea a French colony.
1894	France makes Dahomey a French colony.
1898	Slavery abolished in Cuba.
1920	Liberia becomes a member of the League of Nations.
1923	Slavery abolished in Afghanistan.
1924	League of Nations forms an International Slavery Committee. Slavery abolished in Iraq.
1926	League of Nations adopts International Slavery Convention. Slavery abolished in Nepal.
1929	Slavery abolished in Iran.
1937	Slavery abolished in Bahrain.
1942	Slavery abolished in Ethiopia.
1948	United Nations Declaration of Human Rights demands that slave trade and slavery be abolished.
1957	British colony of Gold Coast becomes the independent state of Ghana.
1958	French colony of Guinea becomes independent. French colony of Dahomey becomes independent.
1960	British colony of Nigeria becomes independent.
1962	Slavery abolished in Yemen and Saudi Arabia.

A178

5 What historians have said

Analyzing Historical Judgments

Introduction

When Englishmen first came to North America, no one intended the establishment of a labor system based on the enslavement of anybody. English law did not recognize the existence of *chattel slavery.** Yet within a hundred years, the foundation of a labor system based on the enslavement of black people was well established. Unfortunately, the details of this process whereby Englishmen in America created a legal status for blacks which ran counter to English legal concepts are very difficult to reconstruct. While there is not enough evidence to show precisely when, where, and how blacks came to be treated so differently from whites in seventeenth-century colonial America, there is just enough to make historians differ about why.

This assignment concludes your work on the Atlantic slave trade by examining selections from two well-known professional historians on the problem of why slavery in colonial America involved only blacks.

Chattel means any piece of property except real estate; hence **chattel slavery** means that in law slaves were nonpersons, pieces of property.

10 OSCAR AND MARY F. HANDLIN: LEGAL STATUS OF BLACK PEOPLE IN 17th-CENTURY AMERICA

Oscar Handlin was born in Brooklyn, New York, in 1915, and was educated at Brooklyn College and Harvard University. He received his doctorate in American history from Harvard in 1940 and has taught American history at that university since 1939. Professor Handlin has written several important books and numerous articles on many different aspects of American history, one book being The Uprooted (1951), which won the Pulitzer Prize for history in 1952. With his wife, Mary F. Handlin, Professor Handlin has co-authored several important studies of colonial American history.

The selection below is taken from an article which the Handlins published in the William and Mary Quarterly in 1950. While reading this selection, keep in mind these questions:

1. What was the meaning of the term "slave" and how did seventeenth-century Englishmen use it?

Objectives are to:

—Analyze two given historical selections on the evolution of slavery in 17th-century colonial America for differences in interpretation.

—Identify statements of fact, inferences, or judgments.

—Identify specific historical judgments in two given interpretations that have made them different.

—Make inferences about the nature of history and history-writing from your analysis of opposing historical interpretations.

2. What was the legal status of black people and how were they treated in English America between 1619 and 1660?

3. How do the Handlins account for the fact that after 1660 black people in the English colonies acquired the legal status of slaves and were treated accordingly?

Not Slaves—but Servants

Through the first three-quarters of the seventeenth century, the Negroes even in the south were not numerous; nor were they concentrated in any district. They came into a society in which a large part of the population was to some degree unfree; indeed, in Virginia under the company almost everyone, even tenants and laborers, bore some sort of *servile** obligation. The Negroes' lack of freedom was not unusual. These newcomers, like so many others, were accepted, bought and held, as kinds of servants. They were certainly not well-off. But their ill-fortune was of a sort shared with men from England, Scotland, and Ireland, and with the unlucky aborigines held in captivity. Like the others, some Negroes became free, that is, terminated their period of service. Some became artisans; a few became landowners and the masters of other men. The status of Negroes was that of servants; and so they were identified down to the 1660's.

Servile—appropriate to or relating to slaves.

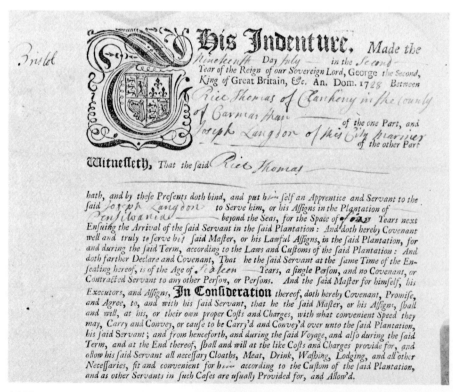

The word "slave" was, of course, used occasionally. It had no meaning in English law, but there was a significant *colloquial** usage. This was a general term of *derogation.** It served to express contempt. . . . Penal servitude too was often referred to as slavery; and the phrase, "slavish servant" turns up from time to time. Slavery had *no* meaning in law; at most it was a popular description of a low form of service.

Yet in not much more than a half century after 1660 this term of derogation was transformed into a fixed legal position. In a society characterized by many degrees of unfreedom, the Negro fell into a status novel to English law, into an unknown condition toward which the colonists unsteadily moved, slavery in its eighteenth and nineteenth century form. The available accounts do not explain this development because they assume that this form of slavery was known from the start. . . .

Finally, there is no basis for the assertion that such a colony as South Carolina simply adopted slavery from the French or British West Indies. To begin with, the labor system of those places was not yet (between 1620–1660) fully evolved. . . . The Barbadian gentlemen who proposed to come to South Carolina in 1663 thought of bringing "Negroes and other servants." They spoke of slaves as did other Englishmen, as a low form of servant. . . .

Although colonists assumed at the start that all servants would "fare alike in the colony," the social realities of their situation early gave rise to differences of treatment. . . . From time to time, regulations applied only to "those of our own nation" or to the Dutch, the French, the Italians, the Swiss, the *Palatines,** the Welsh, the Irish, or to combinations of the diverse nationalities drawn to these shores.

In the same way the colonists became aware of the differences between themselves and the African immigrants. . . . So Bermuda's law to restrain the insolencies of Negroes "who are servants" . . . was the same in kind as the legislation that the Irish should "straggle not night or dai, as is too common with them." Until the 1660's, the statutes on Negroes were not at all unique. Nor did they add up to a decided trend.

But in the decade after 1660 far more significant differentiation with regard to term of service, relationship to Christianity, and disposal of children, cut the Negro apart from all other servants and gave a new depth to his bondage.

After 1690, however, South Carolinians (and still later Georgians) turned from naval stores and the fur trade to the cultivation of rice, cotton, and indigo. In the production of these staples, which required substantial capital equipment, there was an advantage to large-scale operations. By then it was obvious which was the cheapest, most available, more exploitable labor supply. The immense profits from the tropical crops steadily sucked in slaves in ever-growing numbers into the plantation. With this extensive use . . . the price of slaves everywhere rose sharply, to the advantage of those who already held them. The prospect that the slave owner would profit not only by the Negroes' labor, but also by the rise in their unit value and by their probable increase through breeding, accounted for the spread of the plantation to

Colloquial—used in conversation.

Derogation—taking away, lessening of status or value.

Palatines were Germans from the southern Rhine River valley.

A181

the older tobacco regions where large-scale production was not, as in the rice areas, necessarily an asset.

The new social and economic context impressed indelibly on the Negro the peculiar quality of chattel with which he had been left, as other servants escaped the general degradation that had been originally the common portion of all. Not only did the concentration of slaves in large numbers call for more rigid discipline, not only did the organization of the plantation with its separate quarters, hierarchy of overseers, and absentee owners widen the gulf between black and white, but the involvement of the whole southern economy in plantation production created an effective interest against change in status. . . . The distinctive qualities of the Southern labor system were . . . the complete outcome of a process by which the American environment broke down the traditional European conception of servitude. In that process the weight of the plantation had pinned down on the Negro the clearly defined status of a chattel, a status left him as other elements in the population achieved their liberation.

From **Race and Nationality in American Life** by Oscar Handlin. Copyright © 1950 by Oscar Handlin. By permission of Atlantic-Little, Brown and Co. (1957) Chapter I.

11   CARL N. DEGLER: LEGAL STATUS OF BLACK PEOPLE IN 17th-CENTURY AMERICA

Carl N. Degler was born in Orange, New Jersey, in 1921, and was educated at Upsala College and Columbia University. He received his doctorate in American history from Columbia in 1952, and has taught American history at Washington Square College, Adelphi College, City College of New York, Vassar College, and Stanford University. Professor Degler has written several books and articles on the history of the American South and on social history, two of the more recent ones being Out of Our Past: The Forces That Shaped Modern America (1959) and The Age of Economic Revolution, 1876–1901 (1967).

The next selection is from an article by Professor Degler published in Comparative Studies in Society and History in 1959. While reading this selection, consider:

1. *What was the meaning of the term "slave" for seventeenth-century Englishmen and what did they know about slavery?*

2. *What was the legal status of black people and how were they treated in English America between 1619 and 1660?*

3. *How does Degler account for the legal enslavement of black people in seventeenth-century English America?*

A182

Facts of Slavery Without the Law

It has long been recognized that the appearance of legal slavery in the laws of the English colonies was remarkably slow. The first mention does not occur until after 1660—some forty years after the arrival of the Negroes. . . . This late, or at least slow, development complicates our problem. For if there was no slavery at the beginning, then we must account for its coming into being some forty years after the introduction of the Negro. . . .

Actually, asking why slavery developed late in the English colonies we are setting ourselves a problem that obscures rather than clarifies. . . . To ask why slavery in the English colonies produced discrimination against Negroes after 1660 is to make the tacit assumption that prior to the establishment of slavery there was none. If instead, the question is put, "Which appeared first, slavery or discrimination?", then no prejudgment is made. Indeed, it now opens a possibility for answering the question as to why slavery in the English colonies . . . led to a *caste** position for Negroes, whether free or slave. In short . . . the fact that slavery first appeared in the statutes of the English colonies forty years after the Negro's arrival, has tended to obscure the real possibility that the Negro was actually never treated as an equal of the white man, servant or free.

> **Caste** means a rigidly-fixed position in society into which persons are born and out of which they cannot move.

It is true that when Negroes were first imported into the English colonies, there was no law of slavery and therefore whatever status they would have would be the work of the future. The absence of a status for the black men . . . made it possible for almost any kind of status to be worked out. It was conceivable that they would be accorded the same status as white servants . . . it was also possible that they would not. It all depended on the reactions of the people who received the Negroes.

It is the argument of this paper that the status of the Negro in the English colonies was worked out within a framework of discrimination; that from the outset, as far as the available evidence tells us, the Negro was treated as an inferior to the white man, servant or free. If this be true, then it would follow that as slavery evolved as a legal status, it reflected and included as part of its *essence,** this same discrimination which white men had practiced against the Negro all along before any statute decreed it. . . . Slavery, when it developed in the English colonies, could not help but be infused with the social attitude which had prevailed from the beginning, namely, that Negroes were inferior.

> **Essence** means the basic underlying element or characteristic; the heart of the matter.

It is indeed true . . . that before the seventeenth century the Negro was rarely called a slave. But this fact should not overshadow the historical evidence which points to the institution without employing the name. Because no discriminatory title is placed upon the Negro we must not think that he was being treated like a white servant, for there is too much evidence to the contrary. . . .

As will appear . . . the kinds of discrimination visited upon Negroes varied immensely. In the early 1640's, it sometimes stopped short of lifetime servitude or inheritable status—the two attributes of true slavery—in other instances it included both. But regardless of the form of discrimination, the important point is that from the 1630's up until slavery clearly appears in the statutes in the 1660's, the Negroes were being set apart and discriminated against as compared with the treatment accorded Englishmen, whether servant or free.

The colonists of the early seventeenth century were well aware of a distinction between indentured servitude and slavery. This is quite clear from the evidence in the very early years of the century. . . . As early as 1623, a voyager's book published in London indicates that Englishmen knew of the Negro as a slave in the South American colonies of Spain. The book told of the trade in "blacke people" who were "sold unto the Spaniard for him to carry into the West Indies to remain as slaves either in their Mines or in any other servile uses they in those countries put them to." In the phrase "remain as slaves" is the element of unlimited service. . . .

From the evidence available it would seem that the Englishmen in Virginia and Maryland learned their lesson well. This is true even though the sources available on the Negroes' position in these colonies in the early years are not as abundant as we would like. It seems quite evident that the black man was set apart from the white. . . . An act passed in the Maryland legislature in 1639 indicated that at that early date the word "slave" was being applied to non-Englishmen. The act was an enumeration of the rights of "all Christian inhabitants (slaves excepted)." The slaves referred to could have been only Indians or Negroes, since all white servants were Christians. It is also significant of the differing treatment of the two races that though Maryland and Virginia very early in their history enacted laws fixing limits to the terms for servants who entered (the colonies) without written contracts, Negroes were never included in such protective provisions . . . in the Maryland statute (1643) it was explicitly stated: "slaves excepted." . . .

A Virginia law of 1640 provided that "all masters" should try to furnish arms to themselves and "all those of their families which shall be capable of arms" —which would include servants— "(excepting Negroes)" . . . . At no time were white servants denied the right to bear arms; indeed as these statutes inform us, they were *enjoined** to possess weapons. . . . Three different times before 1660—in 1643, 1644, 1658—the Virginia Assembly . . . included Negro and Indian women among the *"tithables."** But white servant women were never placed in such a category, inasmuch as they were not expected to work in the fields. From the beginning, it would seem, Negro women, whether free or bond, were treated by the law differently from white women servants. . . .

Concurrently with these examples of onerous service or actual slavery of Negroes, there were of course other members of the race who did gain their freedom. But the presence of Negroes rising out of servitude to freedom does not destroy the evidence that others were sinking into slavery; it merely underscores the unsteady evolution of slave status. . . .

As early as 1669 the Virginia law virtually washed its hand of protecting the Negro held as a slave. . . . In fact by 1680 the law of Virginia had erected a high wall around the Negro. One discerns in the phrase "any Negro or other slave" how the word Negro had taken on the meaning of slave. . . .

Yet it would be a quarter of a century before Negroes would comprise even

Enjoined—ordered, directed, or compelled.

Tithables—property subject to taxation for the support of church, in this case the Anglican Church.

A184

a fifth of the population of Virginia. Thus long before slavery or black labor became an important part of the Southern economy, a special and inferior status had been worked out for the Negroes who came to the English colonies. Unquestionably, it was a demand for labor which dragged the Negro to the American shores, but the status which he acquired here cannot be explained by reference to that economic motive. Long before black labor was as economically important as unfree white labor, the Negro had been consigned to a special discriminatory status which mirrored the social discrimination Englishmen practised against him. . . .

It would seem then, that instead of slavery being the root of the discrimination visited upon the Negro in America, slavery itself was molded by the early colonists' discrimination against the outlander.

By Carl N. Degler from "Slavery and the Genesis of American Race Prejudice," **Comparative Studies in Society and History,** Vol. II, 1959, pp. 49–66. By permission of Cambridge University Press, N.Y.

Additional Reading

Bennett, Lerone Jr., *Before the Mayflower: A History of the Negro in America, 1619–1964.* Baltimore, Maryland: Penguin, 1962.

Conneau, Theophile, *Captain Canot, or Twenty Years of an African Slaver,* edited by Brantz Mayer. New York: Arno, 1968.

Davidson, Basil, *The African Past.* Boston: Little, Brown & Co., 1964.

Davidson, Basil, *Black Mother: The Years of the African Slave Trade.* Boston: Little, Brown & Co., 1961.

Edwards, Paul, ed., *Equiano's Travels.* London: Heinemann Education Books, Ltd., 1967.

Jordan, Winthrop D., *White Over Black: American Atitudes Toward the Negro, 1550–1812.* Chapel Hill, N.C.: Institute of Early American History and Culture at Williamsburg, Virginia, by the University of North Carolina Press, 1968.

Mannix, Daniel, and Cowley, Malcolm, *Black Cargoes: A History of the Atlantic Slave Trade, 1518–1865.* New York: The Viking Press, 1962.

Chicago Historical Society

21 Preparing Slaves for the
Middle Passage, 1805

22 Branded and Sold, 1830

New York Public Library, Schomburg Collection

A186

Courtesy of Josiah Wedgwood
& Sons, Inc., of America

23 The Seal of the Anti-Slavery Society for the Abolition of the Slave Trade, 1787

Bettmann Archive

24 English Children Signing a Petition Against
the Slave Trade, 1805

Bettmann Archive

25 How Sweet Does Your Sugar Taste?, 1830

A187

Copyright, National Portrait Gallery,
London. Painting by Benjamin Haydon

27 HMS **Buzzard** Capturing the Spanish Slave Ship **Formidable** off Sierra Leone, 1834

28 British Sailors Raiding a Slave Station on the Gallinas River Near Monrovia, Liberia, 1849

Copyright British Museum

Copyright British Museum

29 British Sailors from the HMS **Dee** and HMS **Castor** Raid Slave Pens
on the East Coast of Africa, 1850

30

Liberated Slaves on the
Deck of the HMS **Daphne,**
Indian Ocean, 1870

Courtesy of the National Maritime Museum, Greenwich

A191

The American Revolution

ROBERT E. BURNS

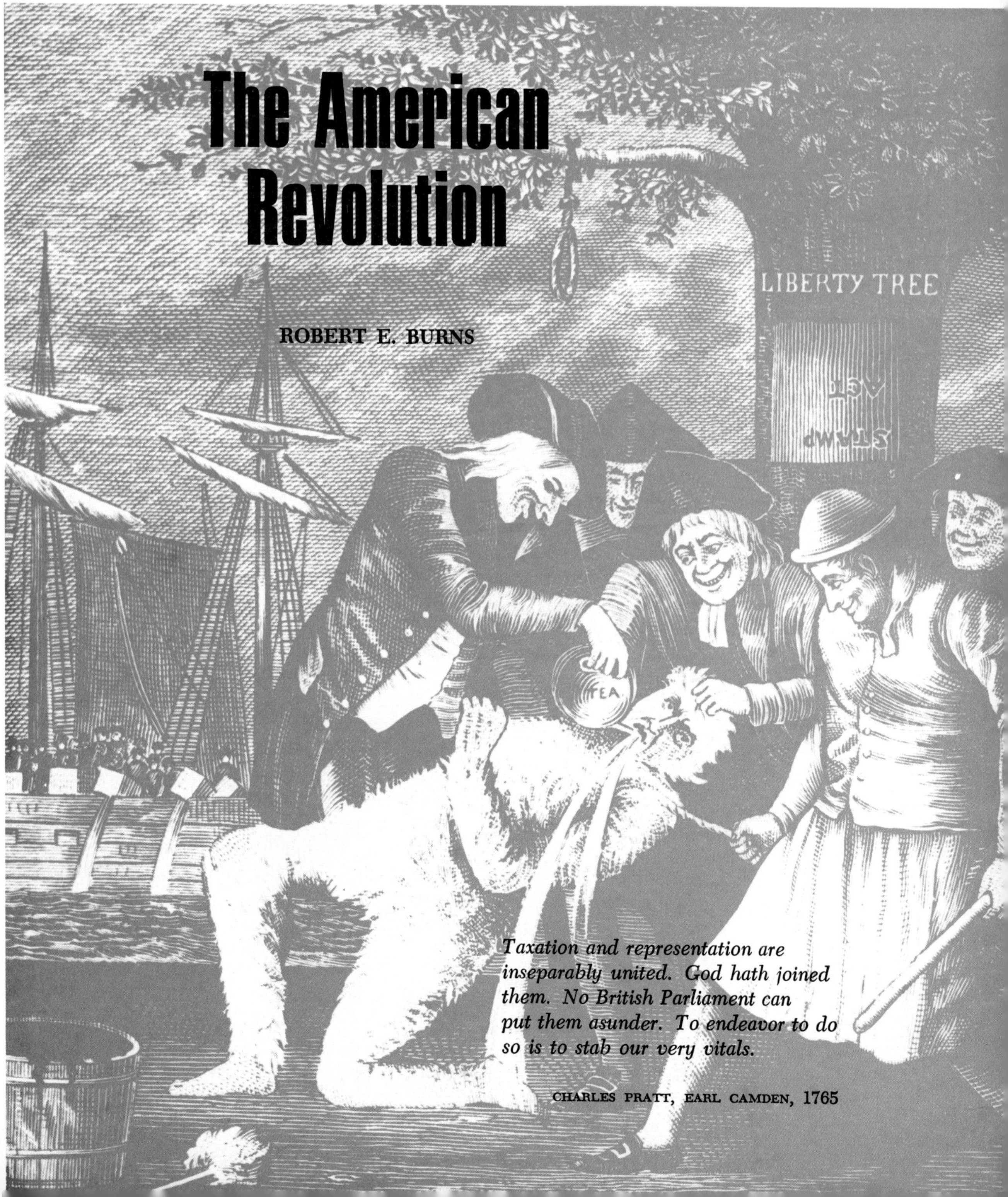

LIBERTY TREE

Taxation and representation are inseparably united. God hath joined them. No British Parliament can put them asunder. To endeavor to do so is to stab our very vitals.

CHARLES PRATT, EARL CAMDEN, 1765

1 Britain and colonial America, 1760-1770

The Gathering Storm

Objectives of this assignment are to:
—Draw inferences about financial and commercial tensions within the British Empire after 1763 from a map and chart of social and economic data.
—Identify in a chronology of political events 1760–1770 the causes of political and social protest within the British Empire.
—Identify in a chronology of events 1760–1770 the responses of the British government to protest within the empire.
—Analyze graphs of British and American identity symbols, 1760–1770, for meaning.
—Make a judgment on when and what caused the colonists to think and act as Americans rather than as Englishmen.

Connecticut, Rhode Island, Pennsylvania, Delaware, and Maryland

Introduction

Great Britain's victory over France in the Seven Years' War left her the most powerful nation in the world. The Royal Navy was master of the seas. British possessions in the New World, India, and Africa, together with the islands of Britain and Ireland made up an empire upon which the sun never set.

Managing this huge empire was a vast and complicated problem. For example, territories under British control in India and Africa were administered through incorporated trading companies. Ireland had its own elected Parliament, but was run by officials who were responsible to the British Parliament. In America, after the territories taken from France had been organized, there was a chain of thirty-one separate colonies running from Quebec to the West Indies. All but two of these colonies, Quebec and East Florida, had legislatures elected by the people. All *but five** were royal provinces with governors appointed by the Crown.

At the center of this vast empire was the king's chief minister, known as the First Lord of the Treasury, and two Secretaries of State. Distances between parts of the Empire were enormous, taking up to seven weeks for letters to pass from London to New York and up to seven months from London to the east coast of India. Furthermore the number of men actually employed by the king to govern the Empire was small. A mayor of a modern American city the size of Houston or Detroit has more clerks, assistants, specialists, and consultants at his disposal than George III had to govern his entire empire. In any case, neither the chief minister nor the secretaries of state could afford to spend very much of their time on the problems of Ireland, America, or India. They were all deeply involved in English politics and European international relations.

The chief minister and secretaries of state were appointed by the king, but remained in office only so long as they were supported by a majority in the British House of Commons. Majorities in the House of Commons were won or lost on English political issues, not on imperial ones. Neither Ireland, America, nor India had formal representation in the House of Commons.

B2

Finance and Defense

The seven-year struggle against France and her Indian allies in America had been a difficult and expensive set of military and naval operations. During the war, Massachusetts, Connecticut, and New York had contributed generously to the cost of driving the French out of Canada, but the rest of the mainland American colonies had not. The financial burden of waging war in America was borne by British taxpayers. Not only did British taxpayers have to spend great sums for the army and navy, but they were also obliged by the King to pay back to the colonial American governments approximately £2 out of every £5 raised in America for the war effort. Overall, England's financial contribution to the defeat of France was twenty times greater than that of the Americans.

By 1763, England's national debt had risen to a staggering 132 million pounds. Consequently, after the peace treaty was signed, reduction of the national debt and elimination of high wartime taxes were matters of highest priority for the British Parliament. However, before the Parliament could act, Pontiac's War added an additional 1.6 million pounds to what the government of Britain owed. The prospect of continuing heavy expenses for the defense of the western frontiers of the American colonies made financial affairs Britain's most urgent postwar problem.

The Question of Authority

Taxation was a matter of law. Counting the British Parliament, Irish Parliament, and all of the legislative assemblies in America and the West Indies, the British empire contained no less than thirty-three lawmaking bodies. Obtaining agreement from so many distant and distinct legislative bodies on tax questions within a reasonable period of time was impossible. Moreover, the financial record of the American legislative assemblies as a whole during the recent war suggested that they would be even less generous in times of peace.

More important was the fact that by 1763 the Irish Parliament and the American legislative assemblies had begun to think and act like the British Parliament, and claimed an equal status and power with it. Although such actions and claims were generally unacceptable to the government and Parliament of Britain, only with respect to Ireland had the question of legislative authority within the empire ever been faced. In 1720, the British Parliament had enacted a Declaratory Law that had asserted the authority of the British Parliament over the Irish Parliament and declared that laws enacted by the British Parliament for whatever purpose were binding in Ireland.

In the past the British Parliament had indeed enacted laws that were binding on both Ireland and America. However, such laws were invariably for the purpose of regulating the nature and direction of British, Irish, or American overseas trade. The Declaratory Law made no change in this policy. At no time before 1764 did the British Parliament impose taxes on Irish or American overseas trade for the purpose of raising money for imperial purposes. At no time before 1765 did the British Parliament impose taxes on persons, property, or trade within Ireland or America for any purpose. When it decided to implement such a policy, it did so at an unfortunate time. Not only were the Irish Parliament and the American legislative assemblies becoming increasingly self-conscious of their own legislative authority, but common people throughout England, Ireland, and America were growing increasingly suspicious of authority of any kind.

The Crisis over Authority

A crisis over authority occurs whenever a significant proportion of the population of a village, city, region, or country refuses to accept the decisions of its judges and officials or refuses to obey laws enacted by its legislative assemblies. Such conditions prevailed in several cities and regions in Britain, Ireland, and America during the period 1760–1770. The continuing authority crises were inspired by a variety of causes and circumstances. These included economic grievances, instances of public and private injustice, social prejudice, frustrated personal ambitions, and inept political leadership.

However, the authority crisis in colonial America was different from those crises occurring in England and Ireland in one important respect. Throughout the 1760's more and more of the people living in British North America began to think and speak of themselves as Americans rather than as British. That kind of change in thinking and speaking made the authority crisis in colonial America a revolutionary one.

1   BRITAIN AND NORTH AMERICA: RESOURCES AND RESPONSIBILITIES

When the Seven Years' War ended in 1763, the British government quickly discovered that they had won a continent and acquired enormous new financial responsibilities. The king's ministers in England believed that the resources of the British empire were sufficient to meet these new responsibilities, and they expected the empire as a whole, especially the Thirteen Colonies, to provide some of the resources to meet them.

The human and economic resources of Britain and the Thirteen Colonies were different and unequal. Britain had more people, more manufacturing, more ships, more money, and more debt. America had more land, more lumber, more furs, more fisheries, and more labor shortages. Furthermore, the relationship between the resources of Britain and the resources of the Thirteen Colonies was changing rapidly. In almost every area except manufacturing, the resources of the Thirteen Colonies were increasing faster than those of Britain.

While studying the following map, financial information, population estimates, and shipping data, keep in mind the following questions:

1. Why, do you think, did the acquisition of French North America create a major financial problem for the British government in 1763?

2. How did the trade patterns of the Thirteen Colonies change between 1750 and 1770?

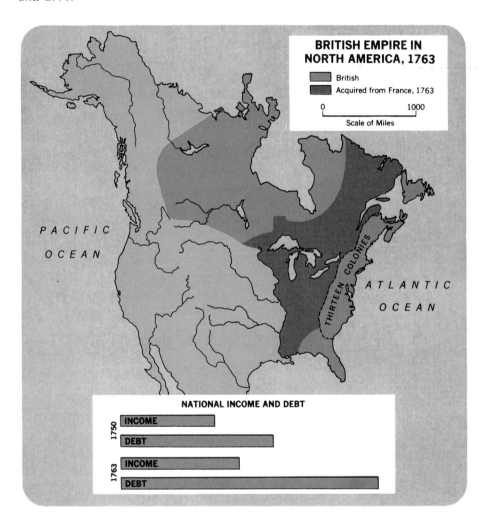

BRITISH EMPIRE IN NORTH AMERICA, 1763

☐ British
☐ Acquired from France, 1763

0 ———————— 1000
Scale of Miles

PACIFIC OCEAN

ATLANTIC OCEAN

THIRTEEN COLONIES

NATIONAL INCOME AND DEBT

1750 — INCOME
1750 — DEBT
1763 — INCOME
1763 — DEBT

Men, Money, and Shipping

	1750	1763	1770
Estimated British Population	6,200,000	6,700,000	7,100,000
Estimated American Population	1,170,000	1,700,000	2,150,000
Estimated British National Income	£56,000,000	£70,000,000	£77,000,000
Estimated British National Debt	£78,000,000	£132,000,000	£130,000,000

B5

Destinations of Ships Leaving Boston, New York, and Hampton, Virginia

	1750	1770
British Isles	19%	23%
Europe	9%	7%
West Indies	42%	29%
Ports in Colonial America	22%	30%
Other	8%	11%
	100%	100%

Ports of Origin of Ships Arriving in Boston, New York, and Hampton, Virginia

	1750	1770
British Isles	31%	26%
Europe	10%	8%
West Indies	36%	31%
Ports in Colonial America	18%	26%
Other	5%	9%
	100%	100%

Prepared from data in U. S. Bureau of the Census, **Historical Statistics of the United States, Colonial Times to 1957** (Washington, D. C., 1960), Z43–55; Z56–75.

2   ANGLO-AMERICAN POLITICS, 1760–1770

For the British Empire the years between 1760 and 1770 were extremely important ones. The period began with the coronation of an idealistic young king committed to peace and reform. It ended with the imprisonment of a popular elected official in London, military rule in Northern Ireland, and violent death in the streets of Boston. In ten short years the British Empire passed from a state of unparalleled glory to a condition of unbounded gloom. Authority had been challenged everywhere, and everywhere authority had reacted.

In 1760 political revolution was unthinkable anywhere in the British Empire. By the end of 1770 some men in Britain and America thought it possible. A very few men in America thought it desirable. Knowledge of the major events of Anglo-American politics during the 1760's will help you understand how the revolutionary movement in America began and what the conditions were that contributed to its development. While studying the following chronology, keep in mind the following questions:

1. *What were the causes of protest in England and Ireland? What forms did protest take?*

2. *How did government in England and Ireland react to them?*

3. *What were the causes of protest in colonial America? What forms did protest take?*

4. *How did government in Britain and America react to them?*

5. *What British protests were supported by colonial American Groups? What colonial American protests were supported by British groups?*

Chronology of Political Events in the British Isles and the American Colonies, 1760–1770

BRITISH ISLES	AMERICAN COLONIES

1760

Oct. —George III becomes King.

1761

Oct. —Earl of Egremont becomes a Secretary of State and responsible for Irish and American affairs.

Nov. —Troops required to suppress *White Boy** riots in southern Ireland over unemployment and high food prices.

White Boys: members of a semisecret organization of Catholic peasants in **Southern** Ireland who performed acts of violence at night as a protest against their living and working conditions. Their name was taken from their white clothing and hoods.

1762

Mar. —Earl of Bute becomes the king's chief minister and head of the government.

1763

Feb. Treaty of Paris ends the Seven Years' War.

Apr. 16 —George Grenville becomes the king's chief minister and head of the government.

Apr. —John Wilkes, British Parliament, arrested in London for publishing attack on peace treaty in Number 45 of the *North Briton.*

July —Troops required to suppress *Oak Boy** riots in northern Ireland over enforcement of the Road Act and payment of tithes.

Sept. —Earl of Halifax becomes Secretary of State responsible for Irish American affairs.

May —Pontiac's War breaks out in the West.

June —Pontiac's forces capture western forts.

Oct. —Royal Proclamation prohibits settlement beyond the Appalachian mountains.

Oak Boys: members of a semisecret organization of Presbyterian peasants and townsmen in **Northern** Ireland who committed acts of violence in order to avoid paying tithes to the Church of England and to avoid forced road building. They acquired their name from the sprig of oak leaves which they pinned to their hats.

His Majesty,   King George the Third

B7

Chronology of Political Events in the British Isles and the
American Colonies, 1760–1770

BRITISH ISLES	AMERICAN COLONIES

1764

	BRITISH ISLES		AMERICAN COLONIES
Jan.	—John Wilkes expelled from the British Parliament and flees to France.	**Mar.**	—Sugar Act increases the duty on foreign refined sugar and on other foreign goods imported from England.
Mar.	—British Parliament passes the Sugar Act (American Revenue Act) to raise money for the Crown in America.	**Mar.**	—Vice Admiralty Courts (no jury trials) given jurisdiction over trade law violations.
Apr.	—British Parliament passes the Currency Act prohibiting the issuance of paper money in colonial America.	**June**	—Massachusetts Assembly establishes a Committee of Correspondence to communicate with other colonies about grievances.
		Aug.	—Boston merchants agree not to import certain specified goods from England.

1765

	BRITISH ISLES		AMERICAN COLONIES
Mar.	—British Parliament passes the Stamp Act to raise money for the defense of colonial America.	**Mar.**	—The Stamp Act requires the purchase of tax stamps for newspapers, legal documents, pamphlets, and even playing cards wherever used or sold in the colonies.
Apr.	—Irish Parliament passes laws authorizing the death penalty for persons convicted of associating to commit acts of violence against persons or property.	**May 15**	—Quartering Act requires civil authorities to provide barracks and supplies for the British army.
May	—British Parliament passes the Quartering Act.	**May 30**	—Virginia House of Burgesses passes resolutions against the Stamp Act.
		June	—Massachusetts Assembly calls for an intercolonial meeting in New York to seek relief from the Stamp Act.
July	—Marquis of Rockingham becomes the king's chief minister and head of the government.	**July**	—Secret organizations known as the Sons of Liberty formed to resist the Stamp Act.
July	—General H. S. Conway becomes a Secretary of State and responsible for Irish and American affairs.	**Aug.**	—Records of the Vice Admiralty Courts are burned, and homes of British officials in Boston are attacked by rioters.
		Oct.	—Stamp Act Congress meets in New York and petitions the British Parliament to repeal the Stamp Act and the measures of 1764.
		Nov.	—Merchants and citizens in Boston, New York, and Philadelphia agree to boycott English goods until Stamp Act is repealed.

A British tax stamp, and a Pennsylvania publisher's reaction to direct taxation on all newspapers. William Bradford ran the skull and crossbones cartoon in his **Pennsylvania Journal and Weekly Advertiser** along with an editorial against the "fatal stamp."

BRITISH ISLES	AMERICAN COLONIES

1766

Jan. —London merchants petition the British Parliament for repeal of the Stamp Act.

Mar. —British Parliament repeals the Stamp Act.

Mar. —British Parliament passes the Declaratory Act which proclaims the British Parliament's right to make laws for America that are binding in all cases.

May —Duke of Richmond becomes a Secretary of State and responsible for Irish and American affairs.

Aug. —Duke of Grafton becomes the king's chief minister and head of the government.

Aug. —Earl of Shelburne becomes a Secretary of State and responsible for Irish and American affairs.

Aug. —Riot in New York between citizens and soldiers over the Quartering Act.

Aug. —Charles Townshend becomes Chancellor of the Exchequer and chief financial officer of the government.

Nov. —British Parliament reduces duties on molasses and sugar going to America.

Nov. —Reduction of molasses and sugar duties lowers the cost of those products.

Dec. —New York Assembly refuses to vote money for supplying the British Army.

1767

Feb. —British Parliament reduces the "war time" land tax in England by 25%.

Apr. —Scheme to raise money in Ireland for 3,000 soldiers to defend the colonies rejected by the Irish Parliament.

June 15 —British Parliament suspends the powers of the New York Assembly until they vote supplies for the British army in America.

June 6 —New York Assembly agrees to vote supplies for the British army in America.

June 29 —British Parliament passes Townshend Revenue Act to provide money for the administration of justice and the support of civil government in America.

June 29 —Townshend Revenue Act imposes duties on all imported glass, lead, paint, tea, and paper.

June 29 —British Parliament passes the Customs Collection Act.

June 29 —Customs Collection Act establishes five Customs Commissioners in Boston to collect the new duties for British Treasury.

This is the Day before the never-to-be-forgotten STAMP-ACT was to take Place in America.

New-Hampshire GꞫ R GAZETTE, AND HISTORICAL CHRONICLE,

Thursday October 31, 1765. No. 474 } Weeks since this Paper was first Publish'd.

Chronology of Political Events in the British Isles and the
American Colonies, 1760–1770

BRITISH ISLES	AMERICAN COLONIES

1767 (cont'd)

Sept. —Townshend dies and is replaced as Chancellor of the Exchequer by Lord North.

Oct. —Nonimportation agreements revived in Boston, Providence, Newport, and New York.

1768

Jan. —Earl of Hillsborough appointed to the newly created office of Secretary of State for the American colonies.

Feb. —Massachusetts House of Representatives adopts *Samuel Adams's** circular letter denouncing the Townshend Acts and urging common action by all of the colonies.

Mar. Wilkes returns from France and is elected to the British Parliament for Middlesex County.

Mar. —Governor Bernard of Massachusetts denounces the circular letter as seditious and dissolves the Massachusetts Assembly.

Apr. 21 —Hillsborough orders all colonial governors to prevent colonial Assemblies from endorsing the Massachusetts Circular Letter by dissolution if necessary.

May —The assemblies of New Hampshire, New Jersey, Connecticut, and Virginia commend the stand of the Massachusetts Assembly.

Apr. 27 —Wilkes arrested.

June 1 —Sons of Liberty of Boston protest Wilkes's imprisonment and proclaim the fate of Wilkes and America stand together.

May —Troops required to suppress riots in London over Wilkes's arrest. In St. George's Fields troops kill seven persons and wound twenty-four.

June 8 —Wilkes fined £1,000 and sentenced to prison for twenty-two months.

June 10 —After seizing the sloop *Liberty* for wine smuggling, Boston customs officials are assaulted by a mob.

Oct. —Viscount Weymouth becomes a Secretary of State responsible for Irish affairs.

Aug. —Boston merchants agree not to import any commodity bearing the Townshend duty.

Oct. —Two regiments of British soldiers sent from Halifax to Boston to enforce the customs laws.

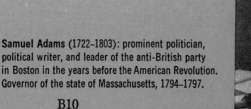

Samuel Adams (1722–1803): prominent politician, political writer, and leader of the anti-British party in Boston in the years before the American Revolution. Governor of the state of Massachusetts, 1794–1797.

Portrait by John Singleton Copley. Painted about 1770–1772. Deposited by the City of Boston. Courtesy, The Museum of Fine Arts, Boston

BRITISH ISLES	AMERICAN COLONIES

1769

Feb. —Wilkes expelled from British Parliament.

Feb. —British Parliament recommends to the king that inciters of disorder in America be brought to England for trial. The king does not accept it.

Apr.–May—While in prison Wilkes is reelected and expelled from the British Parliament four times.

May 18 —Virginia House of Burgesses adopts George Mason's resolutions protesting British policies and condemning the proposal to remove American malcontents to England for trial.

May 19 —After the governor dissolved the Virginia Assembly, the Burgesses formed the Virginia Association to encourage non-importation of English goods.

Nov. —Scheme to raise money in Ireland for soldiers to defend the colonies accepted by the Irish Parliament provided that troops sufficient to defend Ireland and maintain order remain in the country.

June–Nov.—Associations similar to the Virginia Association spread through colonies.

June–Nov.—Brawling and rioting between soldiers and citizens in the streets of Boston.

1770

Feb. —Lord North becomes the king's chief minister and head of the government.

Mar. —Lord North persuades the British Parliament to repeal all of the Townshend duties except the tax on tea and pledges no new taxes for the American colonies.

Apr. 5 —Lord North allows the Quartering Act to expire.

April 17 —Wilkes released from prison and elected an Alderman for the City of London.

July —Widespread rioting and destruction of property in northern Ireland over rent increases.

Dec. —Irish government requests permanent billeting of troops in northern Ireland to maintain order.

Jan. 17–19—The "Battle of Golden Hill" in New York where soldiers and citizens clashed over enforcement of the Quartering Act.

Mar. 5 —The "Boston Massacre" where soldiers fired on a riotous mob in Boston killing five persons.

Mar. 23 —Boston Citizens Meeting sends John Wilkes a written account of the "Boston Massacre."

Apr. —Nonimportation Associations disbanded in most of the colonies.

Oct. —Two soldiers found guilty of manslaughter in the "Boston Massacre" and were punished by being branded on the hand.

Lord North

The true Sons of Liberty

And Supporters of the Non-Importation

Agreement,

ARE determined to refent any the leaft Infult or Menace offer'd to any one or more of the feveral Committees appointed by the Body at Faneuil-Hall, and chaftife any one or more of them as they deferve; and will alfo fupport the Printers in any Thing the Committees fhall defire them to print.

**Handbill of
True Sons of Liberty**

B11

3   THE GROWTH OF AN AMERICAN NATIONAL IDENTITY, 1760–1770

During the 1760's many colonial Americans strongly opposed British policies toward them. Not only were actions by the British Parliament such as the Sugar Act, Stamp Act, and Townshend Duties deeply resented by the colonists, but they responded with counteractions of their own. Countermeasures such as Committees of Correspondence, Nonimportation Associations, Sons of Liberty, and the Stamp Act Congress all required high degrees of intercolonial cooperation.

In the past, instances of intercolonial cooperation had been rare. For example, the delegates to the Stamp Act Congress in 1765 acted together in ways that had been impossible for members of the Albany Congress in 1754. The Stamp Act Congress succeeded where the Albany Congress had failed, even though the threats to colonial American security and prosperity were far greater in 1754 than in 1765. Something had changed in colonial America in eleven years.

Some changes are obvious and easily traced. For example, colonial Americans knew more about each other in 1770 than in 1750; the number of newspapers published in colonial America increased from 12 to 29. Postal service had become more reliable and faster. Letters that took twenty days to pass from Philadelphia to Boston in 1750 were being delivered in less than ten days in 1770. Better mail service improved cooperation among the colonies.

Other changes are obvious, but not easily traced. For example, colonial American reactions to British policies during the 1760's strongly suggest that attitudes toward Great Britain had changed. Many colonial Americans no longer thought of themselves as being British. For persons of such a mind, laws enacted by the British Parliament were no more acceptable than were decrees of the Turkish Sultan or the King of Siam. A policy was wrong, a tax was unjust precisely because it was British-made. A policy was right, a tax was just only when it was American-made. Knowing when the colonists began to think of themselves as American rather than British may help us to discover why.

Indicators of American National Identity

Tracing the growth of an American national identity in the 1760's is more complicated than counting colonial newspapers or the days required to send letters from Philadelphia to Boston. Counting is involved, but computers have to do it. Knowing what to have the computers count is our problem. One solution developed by Professor Richard L. Merritt of Yale University is called symbol analysis.

Attitudes expressing national identity are in people's minds and cannot be traced or measured directly. But neither can something like the state of a person's health. Nevertheless, a physician can measure symptoms such as a patient's pulse count, body temperature, and blood pressure. From such data physicians are able to recognize changes and make a judgment about the state of a patient's health. Similarly, historians of colonial America can recognize symptoms of what people were thinking by identifying symbols of their thoughts appearing in the colonial American press. By counting the number of times symbols of American or British identity appear in the press over a period of months or years, historians can make judgments about the growth or decline of those identities.

Symbols of national identity are simple phrases or statements appearing in the press which indicate an attachment or preference for the idea of British or American. For example, references in the colonial American press describing the colonists as "British colonists" or "His Majesty's subjects" would be counted as symbols of British identity. References describing the colonists as "Virginians," "Massachusetts men," or "Americans" would be counted as symbols of American identity.

Professor Merritt's procedures were much more complicated than can be adequately explained here. But simply stated, he counted all of the identity symbols appearing in representative samples of the colonial American press between 1735 and 1775. By using a computer, he was able to compute on both a monthly and yearly basis what percentage of the total number of identity symbols appearing in his samples was British or American. The two graphs that follow have been prepared from the data collected by Professor Merritt.

While studying these graphs of British and American identity symbols for the period 1760–1770, keep in mind these questions:

1. How can the growth of an American national identity during the 1760's be traced?

2. In what year did the percentage of American symbols in the colonial American press reach their highest point?

3. In what year did the percentage of American symbols in the colonial American press first begin to rise sharply? In what part of the year?

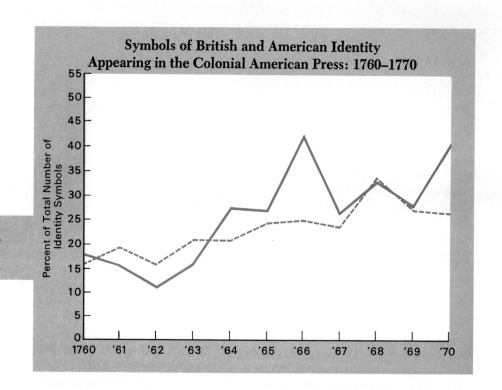

Symbols of British and American Identity Appearing in the Colonial American Press: 1760–1770

British symbols
American symbols

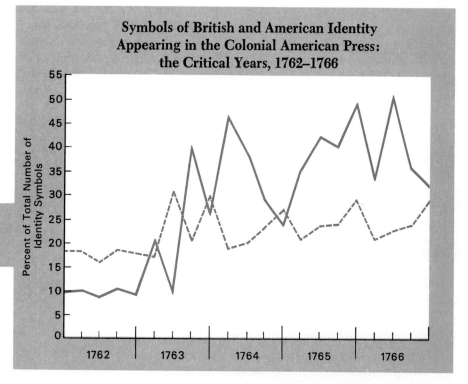

Symbols of British and American Identity Appearing in the Colonial American Press: the Critical Years, 1762–1766

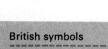

British symbols
American symbols

Prepared from data in Richard L. Merritt, **Symbols of American Community, 1735–1775** (New Haven, Conn.: Yale University Press, 1966), Appendix II, pp. 215, 260–261.

2 The Boston Massacre

Violence and Justice

Objectives of this assignment are to:
—Analyze two conflicting contemporary accounts of the shooting on King Street, March 5, 1770, known as the Boston Massacre, for meaning.
—Analyze testimony presented at the trial of the soldiers for agreement and disagreement.
—Make inferences from a recording about the fairness of the trial.
—Make a judgment on the justice of the verdicts and sentences of the trial.

Introduction

Trouble was brewing in Boston in 1768. Nonimportation associations and anti-government political organizations were very powerful. Merchants daring to import British goods subject to the Townshend Import Duties were severely treated. So were the customs officers who tried to collect them.

The harsh treatment of these offending merchants included the seizure and destruction of their property. The merchants themselves and their employees were beaten or "tarred and feathered." Customs officials were assaulted and driven from the town. Local magistrates were either unwilling or unable to arrest and punish the persons responsible for these violent actions.

Elements of five *British regiments**—approximately 2,000 soldiers—arrived in Boston during October and November of 1768. They had been sent to this town of 16,000 people to maintain order and to help local magistrates and customs officials enforce the customs laws.

Of the regiments ordered to Boston, two did not remain there very long. Disturbances in Ireland required the transfer of the 64th and 65th in August, 1769. The 59th spent most of its time in Castle William, an island in Boston harbor. The 14th and 29th were quartered in town, and within a few months relations between the townspeople and the soldiers of the 29th became very bad.

The soldiers of the 29th were typical of most British regiments in some respects and quite untypical in others. Like most regiments, the 29th included two kinds of foot soldiers: ordinary infantrymen and grenadiers. Ordinaries wore red coats and black, white-laced three-cornered hats. Grenadiers were special soldiers, always the tallest men, wearing red coats and distinctive tall mitre-shaped bearskin hats bearing the King's White Horse badge and the Latin motto: *Nec aspera terrent* (They fear no difficulty.)

Appearing like giants in their tall hats when standing beside other men, the grenadiers of the 29th were different from other grenadiers. They were mostly over thirty years old, mostly Irish, and many were Catholic. In addition, all of the drummers of the 29th, ordinary or grenadier, were black men recruited in the West Indies. In Boston in 1770, Catholics were unpopular and unwelcome; blacks were unknown except as servants, sailors, or slaves.

When the troops first landed in Boston, there were no demonstrations nor attempts to hinder the actual landing. But every conceivable kind of delaying tactic was used to prevent them from being comfortably quartered. Some

At full strength, which was rare, a British infantry regiment in 1770 mustered 484 officers and men.

B15

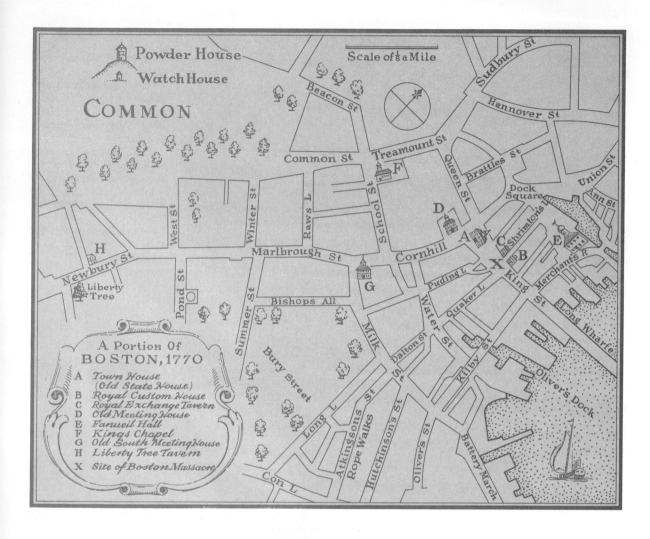

A Portion Of
BOSTON, 1770

A Town House (Old State House)
B Royal Custom House
C Royal Exchange Tavern
D Old Meeting House
E Fanueil Hall
F Kings Chapel
G Old South Meeting House
H Liberty Tree Tavern
X Site of Boston Massacre

One month after arriving in Boston, **Private Richard Ames** of the 14th Regiment was **courtmartialed** and shot for desertion. The sentence was carried out on Boston Common. The public was invited to attend, and off-duty soldiers were required to witness the execution and then march past the bullet-riddled body of Private Ames.

were housed in warehouses and public buildings, while others had to camp on the Boston Common, a public park.

Part of the Boston business community was pleased by the money which the troops spent in the town, but most Bostonians were appalled by the severe discipline under which the men lived. Public whippings of soldiers for infractions of discipline and crime became regular spectacles. Sentences by army courts of 1,000 lashes laid on over a month's time were not uncommon. Desertions were high, and groups in Boston organized to encourage and aid them.* Within a few months, however, sympathy for the soldiers turned to hatred.

Week after week, newspapers printed detailed accounts of atrocities committed by soldiers; musket butts and bayonets were their principal instruments of law enforcement. Many Bostonians became convinced that the soldiers broke the law more than they enforced it.

B16

In some instances, the behavior of the officers was more frightening than that of the men. One evening Captain John Wilson of the 59th Regiment drunkenly encountered a group of Negro slaves and told them to go home and cut their master's throats, promising that he would free them and would run his sword through the heart of anyone who opposed them. Captain Wilson was charged by the civil magistrates with drunkenness and incitement to riot. The selectmen of the Town of Boston ordered the town watch to see that good order prevailed in the town and to arrest all Negroes who were out of doors at unreasonable hours.

Soldiers versus Citizens

If the military became increasingly hateful to the townspeople, the soldiers had cause to complain about Bostonians. When the soldiers arrived, they expected to work as allies of town officials and judges. Very quickly they discovered that Boston magistrates regarded them as enemies instead of allies. If a soldier on sentry duty challenged passersby too vigorously, he might find himself facing a civil charge of disturbing the peace. In such cases Boston judges showed extreme partiality. Justice Richard Henry Dana instructed a jury in such a case to believe nothing the soldier said, and everything the accusing townsman said. In cases between townsmen and soldiers, experience taught the troops not to expect justice, they could never win. Soldiers showed their contempt for the legal process in Boston by using violence frequently to rescue comrades from arrest by town officers.*

With the soldiers and civil magistrates in a state of undeclared war, law and order became nearly unenforceable in Boston. The withdrawal of the 64th and 65th Regiments from the town in August, 1769, made no improvement. Incidents between soldiers and townsmen increased. Mob violence against customs officials, merchants importing goods from England, and government supporters reached alarming proportions.

In November, 1769, a mob tarred and feathered a former officer in the Customs Service. They put a pro-government newspaper out of business and drove the publisher out of town.

During January and February so-called importers had their shop windows smeared with tar or broken. On February 22, another former Customs Service officer, Ebenezer Richardson, was saved from being lynched by a quick arrest and indictment for murder. While defending his house from a mob attack, he fired a shot which mortally wounded a fourteen-year-old boy.

Conditions in Boston during the last week of February were intolerable. Mobs of townsmen and gangs of soldiers roamed the streets every night looking for trouble and finding it. Many townsmen and soldiers expected a showdown soon; they only wondered where and when. The showdown came on King Street in front of the Customs House near the sentry box guarded by Private Hugh White, Grenadier, 29th Regiment, on Monday evening, March 5, 1770.

On July 14, 1769, **Private John Riley** of the 14th was rescued from the Court of Justice by Edmund Quincy, an officer, and seven soldiers. The offending officer and soldiers were later arrested and tried. The officer was fined £20 and each of the soldiers £7.

A "Brown Bess" musket like the weapons used in the Boston Massacre and the Revolutionary War.

4   SHOWDOWN ON KING STREET

Rope walk: a plant where rope was manufactured by employees working on an irregular (seasonal) basis.

All accounts agree that the chain of events leading to the bloody confrontation on King Street began with an incident between Private Patrick Walker of the 29th and William Green, a rope worker, at John Gray's *Rope Walk** on Friday, March 2, 1770. Insults were exchanged. Green, aided by other rope workers, beat, humiliated, and drove away Private Walker. In a few moments, Walker returned with seven or eight other soldiers including a big grenadier private from the 29th Regiment, William Warren.

As the soldiers and rope workers squared off against each other, other workers armed with clubs joined in the fight and forced the soldiers to withdraw. Within fifteen minutes, approximately forty soldiers appeared. They were led by a very tall black drummer from the 29th, Private Thomas Walker. Though warned by Justice of the Peace Hill to stay out of white men's quarrels, the drummer joined his comrades then in the fight and also in the hospital on the following day.

The fighting was fierce. Two men, a grenadier private from the 29th, Mathew Kilroy, and a rope worker, Samuel Gray, distinguished themselves as brawlers. However, the civilians had superiority of numbers, turned the battle, and drove the soldiers away. Back at the barracks a corporal managed to get control over the soldiers and kept them indoors for the rest of the day.

On Saturday, March 3, 1770, Private John Carroll, grenadier of the 29th, and two other soldiers fought with rope workers and with James Bailey, a sailor. When the Bostonians were joined by a tannery worker armed with two large bats, the fight became unequal. Private Carroll carried away one of his comrades with a fractured skull and broken arm.

Sunday, March 4, 1770, was the Sabbath and was relatively quiet. The officers of the 29th restrained their men and spent much of the day looking for a sergeant who had missed roll call.

On Monday, March 5, 1770, incidents between soldiers and civilians occurred throughout the day. When night fell on this town without street lighting, groups of townsmen and parties of soldiers took to the streets.

Private Hugh White mounted guard at the sentry box near the Customs House on King Street. A small group of young wigmaker *apprentices** began taunting and insulting Private White. One of the young apprentices, Edward Garrick, challenged White to show his face. White stepped forward and struck Garrick on the side of the head with his musket.

Apprentice: a young man bound by a legal agreement to serve an employer a number of years while learning a craft or a trade.

Quickly a crowd of about fifty gathered around the sentry, daring him to fight and pelting him with snowballs. White loaded his musket and fixed his bayonet. Large chunks of ice were thrown. White tried to retreat into the Customs House, but could not get in. Private White shouted for assistance, "Turn out, main guard!"

Two accounts of what happened next, obituaries of the dead, and notices of the wounded, follow. The first account appeared in an anti-government newspaper seven days after the incident. The second version is an account sent to London by Captain Thomas Preston, 29th Regiment, the officer who ordered Corporal William Wemms and six grenadier privates—Warren, Kilroy, Carroll, Hartigan, McCauley, and Montgomery—to go to Private White's assistance. While reading these two accounts, keep in mind these questions:

1. *According to the testimony published in the* Boston Gazette, *who was responsible for the King Street confrontation? Who was responsible for the shooting?*

2. *According to Captain Preston's account, who was responsible for the King Street confrontation? Who was responsible for the shooting?*

3. *On what points do these two accounts agree?*

An Account of the Late Military Massacre at Boston, 5 March 1770

What happened at Mr. Gray's rope-walk on 2 March may be said to have led the way to the catastrophe of 5 March. That the rope-walk lads, when attacked by superior numbers of soldiers, should have defended themselves with so much spirit and success was too *mortifying** to be forgotten. It appears that even some of the officers were affected. Many stories were circulated among the soldiers to agitate their spirits, particular that one Sergeant Chambers, missing for a day, had been murdered by the townsmen. The following day Sergeant Chambers was found unhurt and very much alive in a house of pleasure.

Mortifying: humiliating, annoying, or depressing.

The evidence already collected shows that many threats had been made by the soldiers. Although we do not say there was any preconceived plan, we do venture to declare that from their conduct it appears that the soldiers intended to provoke the townsmen into squabbles. It appears also that the soldiers intended to make use of weapons other than canes, clubs, or bludgeons.

On the evening of Monday, 5 March, several soldiers of the 29th Regiment were seen parading the streets with drawn cutlasses and bayonets, abusing and wounding a number of inhabitants. A few minutes after nine o'clock, four youths walking down Cornhill together came upon a person armed with a club and a soldier swinging a huge broadsword against a building making sparks fly. One of the youths, Edward Archbald, cried out to the other, William Merchant, to look out for the sword. Whereupon, the soldier turned and struck Archbald on the arm. Next, he lunged at Merchant piercing his clothes and grazing his skin. Merchant retaliated by striking the soldier with a stick he happened to have. Two other soldiers entered the fray, one armed with a pair of tongs and the other with a shovel. The one with the tongs pursued Archbald through an alley, collared the youth, and beat him over the head with the tongs. The noise brought other people together. John Hicks, a young lad, coming up knocked the soldier down, but let him up again.

With more lads gathering, they drove the soldiers back to the barracks where the boys stood some time to keep them in. In less than a minute, ten or twelve soldiers came out with drawn cutlasses, clubs, and bayonets and set upon the unarmed boys and young folk. Finding their equipment unequal, the young folk dispersed.

On hearing the noise, one Samuel Attwood came up to see what was the matter. He asked a gang of ten or twelve soldiers if they intended to murder people? They answered, "'Yes, by God, root and branch!" They began beating Mr. Attwood. Retreating several steps, Mr. Attwood met two officers and asked what was the matter? They answered, "You'll see by and by."

Gangs of soldiers continued running through Dock Square attacking single and unarmed persons, insulting everyone, but avoiding conflict with groups or persons able to defend themselves. Meanwhile, thirty or forty persons, mostly lads, gathered in King Street. They were charged by Captain Preston and a party of soldiers with fixed bayonets. They cleared the area and took a position in front of the Customs House, continually harassing the people with bayonet thrusts. Because of this provocation, the people became clamorous, and, it is said, some threw snowballs. Upon this account, the Captain commanded the soldiers to fire. With more snowballs coming, he said again, "Damn you, fire! Be the consequence what it will!"

One soldier fired, and a townsman with a cudgel struck him with such force that he dropped his firelock. Rushing forward, the same townsman aimed a blow at the Captain's head which only grazed his hat but fell heavily upon his arm. The soldiers continued the fire successively till seven or eight, or as some say eleven guns were discharged. By this fatal maneuver three men were laid dead on the spot and two more struggling for life. Even more cruel were the attempts to fire and bayonet persons undertaking to remove the slain and wounded. Mr. Benjamin Leigh now came up and after some conversation with Captain Preston advised him to draw off his men, which he did.

People throughout the town were immediately alarmed by the report of this horrid massacre, the bells were set a-ringing, and great numbers soon assembled at the place where this tragic scene had been acted. The Governor soon came to the Town House, met with some of His Majesty's Council, and a number of Civil magistrates. A great body of the people made entry into the Council chamber. The Governor urged the people to retire to their houses, to let matters rest for the night, and promised to do all in his power to see that justice be done and the law have its course. Men of weight and influence with the people urged them to comply with the Governor's request and promising that on the following morning measures would be undertaken to obtain satisfaction for the blood of their fellow townsmen. At three o'clock Captain Preston was arrested as were the soldiers who had fired.

At eleven o'clock on Tuesday morning the inhabitants met in Faneuil Hall. After some animated speeches becoming the occasion, they chose a committee of fifteen respectable gentlemen to wait upon the Governor. The committee requested the Governor to order the immediate withdrawal of the troops from the town.

Adapted from **The Boston Gazette and Country Journal** (12 March 1770).

Captain Thomas Preston's Account of the Late
Disturbances in the Town of Boston

On 2 March, two men from the 29th Regiment while going through Gray's rope-walk were hailed by the rope makers and insultingly asked if they would care to empty their latrines. The desired effect was to provoke, and very soon from words they went to blows. Both parties suffered in this incident, and finally the soldiers returned to their quarters. Officers took every precaution to prevent ill consequences. However, single quarrels could not be prevented because the inhabitants constantly provoked and abused soldiers.

Insolence and hatred increased daily, and a plan was conceived for 5 and 6 March. They privately agreed upon a general engagement and several of the militia armed and came in from the country to join their friends.

On Monday night, about 8 o'clock two soldiers were attacked and beaten. But the party of townspeople determined to carry matters to extremes, broke into two Meeting Houses and rang the bells. About 9 o'clock some of the guard came and informed me that the townspeople were assembling to attack the troops and the bells were ringing for that purpose. As I was *Captain of the Day,** I went immediately to the main guard. I saw the people in great commotion and heard them use the most cruel and horrid threats against the troops. About 100 people moved toward the Customs House where the King's money is kept. They surrounded the sentry there and with clubs and other weapons threatened to take vengeance on him.

Captain of the Day: duty officer in charge of the guard and barracks area while the commanding officers are away or off duty.

I was informed by a townsman of their intention to carry off the soldier from his post and probably murder him. I sent the townsman back for further intelligence and when returning he assured me they would murder the sentry. Believing this to be a prelude to plundering the King's money, I sent a non-commissioned officer and 12 men to protect the sentry and the King's money.

Come on, you rascals . . .

Fearing that the non-commissioned officer and the men might be provoked into some rash act, I quickly joined the men. They rushed through the people, and by charging with bayonets were able to keep them at a little distance. I gave no orders to load as my intention was not to act offensively. The mob increased and became more outrageous, striking their clubs together, calling out "come on, you rascals, you bloody backs, you *lobster** scoundrels, fire if you dare, fire and be damned, we know you dare not."

Great quantities of **lobsters were eaten** by Bostonians. The brilliant red color of cooked lobsters was similar to the military coats worn by the king's soldiers.

At this time I was between the soldiers and the mob trying to persuade them to retire peaceably, but to no purpose. They advanced to the points of the bayonets, struck some, and even the muzzles of some of the pieces, and seemed to be trying to close in on the soldiers.

Some well behaved persons asked me if the guns were loaded. I replied yes. They asked me if I intended to order the men to fire. I answered, "By no means," observing to them I was in front of the muzzles and must be the first to fall if they fired.

While I was speaking thus, one of the soldiers having received a severe blow with a stick slipped a little on one side and instantly fired. As I turned to ask why he fired without orders, I was struck by a club on my arm, which for some time deprived me of the use of it. If the blow had struck my head, it most probably would have destroyed me. On this happening a general attack was made on the men by a great many heavy clubs and snowballs. All our lives were in imminent danger. Some persons at the same time from behind calling out, "Damn your bloods—why don't you fire?" Instantly, three or four soldiers fired, one after another. Directly after, three more fired in the same confusion and hurry. The mob ran away, except three unhappy men who instantly expired, among whom was Mr. Gray at whose rope-walk prior quarrels took place. One man is since dead, three others dangerously and four slightly wounded. The whole of this melancholy affair was transacted in about twenty minutes.

On my asking the soldiers why they fired without orders, they said they heard the word fire and supposed it came from me. This might be the case as many of the mob called out fire, fire. I assured the men, I had given no such order, my words were "don't fire," or "stop your firing." On the people assembling again to take away the dead bodies, the soldiers supposing them coming to attack, were making ready to fire again, which I prevented by striking up their firelocks with my arm.

Judging it unsafe to remain there any longer, I sent the party to the main guard which was more easily defended. As there were constant cries from the inhabitants of "to arms, to arms" and the town drums were beating to arms, I ordered my drummers to beat to arms and was soon joined by different companies of the 29th Regiment. I deployed them for defense and sent a sergeant with a party to Colonel Dalrymple, the commanding officer, to acquaint him with every particular.

After great difficulty the Governor persuaded the people to retire. On hearing that three Justices of the Peace had issued a warrant to apprehend me and eight soldiers, I went instantly to the Sheriff and surrendered myself. For the space of four hours, I had it in my power to escape had I the least consciousness of any guilt.

On examination before the Justices, two witnesses swore that I gave the men orders to fire. One testified that he was within two feet of me; the other testified that I swore at the men for not firing at the first word. The next day they got five or six more to swear that I gave the word to fire. So bitter are the malcontents that they are using every method to fish out evidence to prove that what happened was a concerted scheme to murder the inhabitants. Others are creating the utmost malice and revenge in the minds of people who will be my jurors, by false publications and votes of towns. A quick trial while people's minds are so inflamed can have only one termination.

Though perfectly innocent, without the prospect of a Royal pardon, I have nothing in reason to expect but the loss of life in a very ignominious manner.

Adapted from British Public Records Office, London, C. O. 5/759, **Preston's Account** (March 13, 1770).

The Dead

Samuel Gray: a rope worker, resident of Boston, killed instantly by a musket ball entering his skull. His body was taken to his brother's house.

*Michael Johnson** or Crispus Attucks: a mulatto, perhaps of mixed African and Indian ancestry, probably a sailor, over forty years of age, standing six feet three inches tall, and reported as being born in Framingham. He had come to Boston from the Bahamas and was headed for North Carolina. Attucks was killed instantly by two musket balls entering his chest. Since he was a stranger in Boston, his body was taken first to the Royal Exchange Tavern and then to Fanueil Hall.

James Caldwell: a sailor killed instantly by two musket balls entering his back. Since he was a stranger in Boston, his body was taken first to the Prison House and then to Fanueil Hall.

Samuel Maverick: a youth of seventeen, a resident of Boston, an apprentice to an ivory turner was wounded by a musket ball entering his stomach and lodging there. He was taken to his widowed mother's boarding house where in a few hours he died.

Patrick Carr: a man over thirty years of age, a recent arrival from Ireland, a resident of Boston, and employed by a leather-breeches maker on Queen Street. He was mortally wounded by a musket ball entering his hip and passing out the other side. He was taken to his employer's house where he died on March 15.

*Attucks called himself Michael Johnson. Boston officials identified him as **Crispus Attucks** after he had been killed.*

The Wounded

John Clark: a youth of seventeen from Medford, an apprentice to a sea Captain, wounded by a musket ball entering his groin and passing out through his hip.

John Green: a tailor, resident of Boston, wounded by a musket ball entering his hip and lodging there.

David Parker: a youth, resident of Boston, an apprentice to a wheelwright, wounded by a musket ball entering his thigh.

Christopher Monk: a youth of seventeen, resident of Boston, an apprentice to a shipwright, wounded by a musket ball entering his back and lodging there.

Edward Payne: a merchant, resident of Boston, wounded by a musket ball entering his arm while standing in his own doorway.

Robert Paterson: a sailor, resident of Boston, still bearing scars from the attack on Richardson's house, wounded by a musket ball passing through his arm.

Lawyer for the defense, John Adams—as he looked at the time of the Boston Massacre trial. Adams, 41 years old, was already a successful lawyer. This portrait was painted by Benjamin Blyth in 1776.

Vagrants: persons without homes or regular work who wander from place to place begging or supporting themselves in unlawful ways.

The customs officials were alleged to have fired from the upper windows and balcony of the Customs House.

Lawyer for the prosecution, Robert Treat Paine was 39 years old at the time of the trial. He is shown here at a more advanced age.

5   THE TRIALS

During the days and weeks immediately following the shooting on King Street, public outrage in Boston reached a fever pitch. Fortunately for all concerned, the officer and men in the firing party quickly surrendered themselves to the civil magistrates. The public funeral and common burial of the victims demonstrated Boston's deep sense of outrage over the killing of five of its citizens. Administrative actions by the selectmen were aimed at getting revenge. Two of the arrested soldiers—Hartigan and Montgomery—were married. The selectmen of Boston decided that Mrs. Elizabeth Hartigan and Mrs. Isabella Montgomery and her three children were *vagrants.** These women had no visible means of support because their soldier husbands were in the Boston jail. The selectmen ordered Mrs. Hartigan and Mrs. Montgomery and her three children to leave town within fourteen days or face prosecution for vagrancy.

Anti-government groups agitated for immediate trials while public feelings remained high. Pamphlets and newspapers kept the issue alive. Almost overnight a new industry was created. The message of this new industry was simple, clear, and repetitive. Men of Boston had died before the guns of British soldiers, and no punishment was too severe for those responsible. The shooting on King Street was a brutal and bloody fact which none could be allowed to forget. In the name of justice Bostonians demanded punishment.

The governor wanted the trials delayed as long as possible and succeeded in doing so until September 7, when one officer, seven soldiers, and four customs officials were indicted for murder. During the next three months the officer was tried alone, the seven soldiers were tried as a group, and the four *customs officials** were tried together.

The eminent lawyer, anti-government politician, and future second President of the United States, John Adams (1735–1826) was one of the lawyers engaged to defend the officer and soldiers. Robert Treat Paine (1731–1814), future signer of the Declaration of Independence, was one of the lawyers assigned to the prosecution. Great care and much time was given to the task of jury selection, and the outcome of the trials was virtually determined by it. The trial of the customs officials was brief and probably unnecessary. It rested on the accusations of a fourteen-year-old boy, who was himself later convicted and punished for perjury.

While reading the following selections from eyewitness testimony given at the trial of the soldiers, keep in mind these questions. According to these eyewitnesses:

1. *What happened to Montgomery? What did he do?*
2. *What happened to Kilroy? What did he do?*
3. *What happened to Attucks? What did he do?*

The Accused Murderers

Thomas Preston	Captain, 29th Regiment.
William Wemms	Corporal, ordinary, 29th Regiment.
John Carroll	Private, grenadier, 29th Regiment.
James Hartigan	Private, grenadier, 29th Regiment.
Mathew Kilroy	Private, grenadier, 29th Regiment.
William McCauley	Private, grenadier, 29th Regiment.
Hugh Montgomery	Private, grenadier, 29th Regiment.
William Warren	Private, grenadier, 29th Regiment.
Hugh White	Private, grenadier, 29th Regiment.
Hammond Green	Customs Official.
Thomas Greenwood	Customs Official.
Edward Manwaring	Customs Official.
John Munro	Customs Official.

Testimony Given at the Trial of the Soldiers, November 27–December 5, 1770

Richard Palmes, Merchant

I saw a piece of ice or snow strike Montgomery's gun. He fell back and fired his gun. Then I heard the word fire. Seven or eight guns were fired. Montgomery pushed at me, I struck him. Another soldier came at me with a bayonet and I ran.

I am sure Montgomery was not knocked down before he fired. He did not fall. I struck Montgomery and knocked him down just as the last gun was fired.

James Bailey, Sailor

Montgomery was knocked down by a club or stick by one of the inhabitants and as soon as he got up he fired his gun. That was the first gun. I cannot be certain whether the first gun killed or hurt anybody. Montgomery fired about where the mulatto man fell. It was not seven or eight minutes before the firing that I saw the mulatto man at the head of about twenty-five or thirty sailors in Cornhill, they held their sticks up in the air cheering and whistling.

John Danbrooke

I saw Montgomery and I saw him fire. I saw no blow given or struck or anything thrown at him. I saw a little stick fly over their heads. I saw two men fall as he fired and before I heard any other gun. One was the mulatto man. I did not hear Attucks say anything. He stood leaning over a long stick which he had, resting his chest upon it.

Andrew, Negro Servant of Mr. Oliver Wendell

The people seemed to be leaving the soldiers when there came a great number from Jackson's corner cheering and crying, "Damn them, they dare not fire, we are not afraid." One of these people, a big man with a long cordwood stick, threw himself in among them and struck at the officer. Whether he hit him, I know not. The big man turned around, struck the soldier's gun and immediately fell in with his club, knocking his gun away, and striking him on the head. The big man held the bayonet with his left hand, pulled at it, and cried "kill the dogs, knock them over." The people crowded in. The soldier pulled back, recovered his gun, and began to lunge at the people. I turned to go away. When I had gotten a few feet I heard the word fire. At the word fire I thought I heard the sound of a gun. I saw the same soldier swing his gun and fire it.

I thought and still think the big man who fell in and struck the soldier was the mulatto man. I then thought the soldier who was assaulted and who fired was Kilroy. I now think it was Kilroy from my best observation, but I cannot positively swear.

Edward Langford, Town Watchman

I knew Samuel Gray and he was just by me when the first gun went off. I stood so near that the soldiers might have reached me, and they did. A bayonet went through my clothes. I heard the word "fire" twice and the words "God damn you, fire!" once. I don't know who fired the first gun. I did not see anybody press on the soldiers with large cord wood sticks. I did not know the Indian who was killed.

I saw Kilroy fire and Samuel Gray fell striking my left foot. I knew Kilroy from before very well. I heard no gun but Kilroy's at that time. Gray spoke to no one but me. He had no weapons. He threw no snowballs or anything. Gray's hands were in his pockets. I was looking Kilroy right in the face and have no doubt that his gun killed Gray. I did not see that Kilroy aimed at Gray any more than at me. He intended to kill us both, I suppose.

Adapted by permission of the publishers from pp. 108–110, 115, 118, 120 and 204 of L. Kinvin Wroth & Hiller B. Zobel, eds. **The Legal Papers of John Adams,** Volume III. Cambridge, Mass.: The Belknap Press of Harvard University Press, Copyright, 1965, by The Massachusetts Historical Society.

The Verdicts and Sentences

Thomas Preston, Esq.	Not Guilty, October 30, 1770
Wemms, Carroll, Hartigan, McCauley, Warren, and White	Not Guilty, December 5, 1770
Montgomery and Kilroy	Not Guilty of Murder, but Guilty of Manslaughter, December 5, 1770
Green, Manwaring, Greenwood, and Munro	Not Guilty, December 12, 1770

On December 14, 1770, the Sheriff of Suffolk County carried out the sentence of the Superior Court upon Private Hugh Montgomery and Private Mathew Kilroy by branding the right thumb of each soldier with a hot iron.

3 From protest to rebellion

Toward War and Independence

Introduction

By the end of 1770, relations between Great Britain and colonial America appeared to be much improved. No one in Britain or colonial America wanted anything like the King Street confrontation to happen again. In Britain, the new First Lord of the Treasury, Lord North, worked for peace in both colonial America and Ireland. He stood for reform in India, peace in Europe, and tax reductions at home.

In colonial America, the atmosphere of crisis and alarm temporarily disappeared. Merchants imported vast quantities of goods to replace depleted stocks. Cargoes of American grain, meat, and fish found ready markets abroad at higher prices than usual. Business of all kinds prospered. Antigovernment agitators talked mainly to themselves.

The period of calm did not last. By the summer of 1773 the now familiar cycle of American actions and responses had returned. A mob attacked and burned the *Gaspee*, a helpless customs vessel run aground near Providence, Rhode Island. When the news reached London, tempers flared at this outrage against one of His Majesty's ships. His Majesty's government responded. A Royal proclamation offered £500 for the discovery of the attackers and authorized their transfer to England for trial. No one claimed the reward, and the attackers were never brought to court.

Within a few days of the *Gaspee* incident came an announcement from *Governor Hutchinson** of Massachusetts. Hutchinson said that henceforth he and all Superior Court judges in Massachusetts would receive their salaries directly from the king rather than from the Assembly. When coupled with the Proclamation authorizing transfer of trials to England, this announcement gave antigovernment agitators an issue that commanded attention. It was relatively easy for Sam Adams and others to alarm Bostonians with visions of unfair trials in England, or, at best, unfair trials in Massachusetts before judges in the pay of the king.

The prospects of unfair trials were serious matters indeed. But for the moment, they were only prospects, not realities. They were causes for concern, for protest, not for rebellion. What began the transformation of colonial American protestors into rebels was not a new system of unfair judicial procedures. It was tea.

When Lord North repealed the Townshend Duties in 1770, the three-penny-per-pound tax on tea was retained. Colonial Americans imported and drank large amounts of tea. Not counting the vast quantities of tea smuggled

Objectives of this assignment are to:
—Make hypotheses from a chronology and graphs explaining the sharp decline and sudden rise in American identity symbols, 1770–1775.
—Identify in a chronology the specific actions by the British government and colonists which led to war.
—Analyze selections from contemporary colonial writers on the issue of independence from England for meaning.
—Draw inferences from a filmstrip on the art work of Paul Revere about the events and actions that transformed colonial protesters into rebels.
—Make a judgment on what revolutionaries require most to transform protesters into rebels.

Thomas Hutchinson
(1711–1780): member of a prominent, wealthy Boston family whose home and library were destroyed by a Boston mob in 1765. Lawyer, judge, writer, and governor of Massachusetts, 1771–1774. He went to England in 1774 where he remained in exile until his death.

in from Holland, the colonists legally imported over 370,000 pounds of tea each year. Many people drank tea, and many merchants sold it.

The Act passed by the British Parliament in 1773 was not intended to deprive colonial Americans of their tea or make them pay more for it. The Tea Act was part of a series of reforms enacted for the East India Company. It was a measure intended to bail the Company out of financial difficulties. The Tea Act eliminated duties on tea payable in England and allowed the East India Company to sell tea directly in the American colonies through its own agents. East India Company agents were able to undersell every tea merchant in colonial America.

Merchants in all of the port towns believed themselves threatened by the East India Company's competitive advantage and held protest meetings. Sons of Liberty organized tea boycotts, and made plans to resist the landing of tea. Feelings ran high everywhere, but especially in Boston. Again confrontation was in the air.

Two mass meetings passed resolutions demanding that tea ships in Boston harbor return to England and forbidding the landing of any tea. However, Governor Hutchinson, whose two sons and a nephew happened to be East India Company tea agents, refused to allow any tea ship to leave the harbor until it could prove that its tea had been landed and the three-penny-per-pound duty had been paid. Confrontation was at hand.*

Customs regulations required that the duty on tea be paid within 20 days of arrival or the cargo could be seized. Since the time had expired, the ships could not legally leave Boston harbor without paying the duty.

What happened next is well known. After another mass meeting, Sam Adams gave an order, and a band of men disguised as Mohawk Indians boarded three ships and dumped overboard 342 chests of East Indian Company tea. This was the famous Boston Tea Party, but Boston was not alone in refusing tea. Resistance occurred also in New York, Philadelphia, and Charleston.

Once again an American action made certain a British response. This time the nature of the American action—violent destruction of property—made certain that British response would be severe. It was. The Boston Tea Party was the point of no return. After the destruction of tea in Boston, relations between Britain and colonial America were never again the same. A new and irreversible cycle of action and response began, escalating ultimately into armed conflict in 1775, and to full-scale war and independence in 1776. Between 1773 and 1776 American protestors became rebels.

6 ANGLO-AMERICAN POLITICS, 1771–1776

Between 1771 and 1776 British policy toward colonial America changed from conciliation to military repression, and colonial American leaders abandoned protest for armed rebellion. This result was not *inevitable.** Revolution might have been avoided. As a matter of fact, for a brief period Anglo-American relations seemed to be on the verge of a permanent improvement. Yet events, actions, and responses in both Britain and America combined to make reconciliation difficult, then impossible. Knowing when and why reconciliation became impossible requires knowledge of trade relations, of growth of an American *national identity*, and of the sequence of events.

Inevitable: unavoidable, certain to happen.

While studying the following graphs and chronology, keep in mind these questions:

1. How would you explain the decline of American identity symbols in the colonial American press during 1771 and 1772?

2. How did the British government respond to the Boston Tea Party?

3. How would you explain the increase of American identity symbols in the colonial American press after the Boston Tea Party?

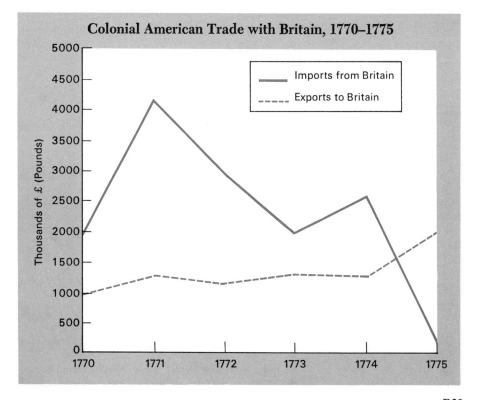

Colonial American Trade with Britain, 1770–1775

Public Records Office, **Customs 3,** London, England.

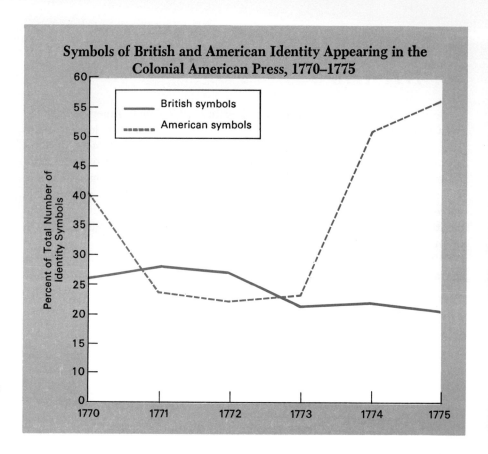

Symbols of British and American Identity Appearing in the Colonial American Press, 1770–1775

Percent of Total Number of Identity Symbols

British symbols
American symbols

Prepared from data in Richard
L. Merritt, **Symbols of American
Community, 1735–1785** (New Haven:
Yale University Press, 1966)
Appendix II, p. 215.

Chronology of Political Events in the British Isles and the American Colonies, 1771–1776

BRITISH ISLES		**AMERICAN COLONIES**
	1771	
Disorders in northern Ireland continue, and emigration to North America increases.	**May**	—Outbreak of fighting between North Carolina frontiersmen known as Regulators and North Carolina militia led by Governor Tryon.
	1772	
Jan. —Lord North cuts expenditures for modernizing the navy.	**June**	—British Revenue boat *Gaspee* burned by a mob in Narragansett Bay.
Sept. —Political crisis in Ireland between the Lord Lieutenant and Irish Parliament ended by replacement of the Lord Lieutenant.	**June**	—Governor of Massachusetts announces that his salary and those of judges will be paid by the king instead of the Massachusetts Assembly.
	Nov	—Sam Adams organizes new Committees of Correspondence in Massachusetts.

Chronology of Political Events in the British Isles and the American Colonies, 1771–1776

BRITISH ISLES	AMERICAN COLONIES

1773

Feb. —British government cuts naval and army budgets.

Mar. —Committees of Correspondence expanded from Massachusetts into other colonies.

Apr. —British Parliament passes the Tea Act repealing all British export duties on tea.

Apr. —Tea Act allows the East India Company to undersell colonial tea merchants in American markets.

May —British government reforms the East India Company's system of governing its territories in India.

Oct. —Sons of Liberty in Boston, New York, and Philadelphia threaten tea importers and pledge a tea boycott.

Nov. —Bill to tax absentee landlords defeated in the Irish Parliament.

Dec. —Sam Adams organizes the Boston Tea Party where Bostonians disguised as Indians dump East India Company tea worth £11,000 into Boston harbor.

Dec. —Benjamin Franklin illegally obtains in England private letters from the governor of Massachusetts which the Massachusetts Assembly publishes.

1774

Jan. —Lord North removes the last wartime taxes still paid by Englishmen.

Jan. —Benjamin Franklin dismissed as Deputy Postmaster General for America.

Mar. —British Parliament passes Coercive Acts (Boston Port Act, Administration of Justice Act, and Massachusetts Government Act).

Mar. —Coercive Acts closed the Port of Boston until compensation was paid for the tea, allowed trials of certain cases to be transferred out of Massachusetts, and annulled the Massachusetts Charter and the system of government it guaranteed.

May —British Parliament passes the Quebec Act legalizing Catholicism in Canada and extending the borders of Quebec to the Ohio River Valley.

May —Coercive Acts lead to calls for an intercolonial Congress.

June —British Parliament passes a Quartering Act that applies to all of the colonies.

Sept. —All colonies except Georgia represented at the First Continental Congress in Philadelphia.

Congress approves Resolves of Suffolk County, Massachusetts, protesting the Coercive Acts, urging economic sanctions against Britain, and advising military preparations.

Joseph Galloway's plan for union between Britain and the colonies presented to the Congress and narrowly rejected.

Congress adopts the Declarations and Resolves urging the British Parliament to repeal thirteen laws enacted since 1763.

Chronology of Political Events in the British Isles and the American Colonies, 1771–1776

BRITISH ISLES	AMERICAN COLONIES

1774

Nov. —George III decides that the New England colonies are in rebellion and must be suppressed by force.	Congress forms the Continental Association that requires all of the colonies to discontinue slave trading and cease all import and export trade with Britain, Ireland, and the West Indies.
	Oct. Congress adjourns but agrees to meet again on May 10, 1775, if grievances are not redressed.
	Oct. —British troops in Boston and Massachusetts militia make preparations for war.

1775

Jan. —Four regiments ordered to leave Ireland for America.	**Jan.** —Loyalist party forms in most of the colonies.
Feb. —Lord North offers plan of reconciliation promising no parliamentary taxation if colonial Assemblies will provide funds for civil government and the common defense.	**Mar.** —Patrick Henry delivers his famous "Liberty or Death" speech in the Virginia House of Burgesses.
	Apr. 18 —Midnight ride of Paul Revere and William Dawes's warning of a British advance on Concord.
Feb. —Four more regiments ordered to leave Ireland for America.	**Apr. 19** —British destroy military stores at Lexington and Concord. War has begun.

BRITISH ISLES	AMERICAN COLONIES

BRITISH ISLES

Mar. —Fighting breaks out between country people and troops in southern Ireland.

Mar. —British Parliament passes the New England Restraining Act barring New Englanders from the North Atlantic fisheries and from trading with any nation except Britain and the West Indies.

Apr. —Fighting spreads in southern Ireland.

Aug. —Five more regiments ordered to leave Ireland for America.

Aug. —George III proclaims the American colonies in a state of rebellion.

Sept. —British government rejects the Congress's petition.

Sept. —New fighting breaks out in southern Ireland.

Oct. —Some regiments in Ireland, ordered to America, mutiny.

Oct. —British government opens negotiations to hire German troops for service in Ireland and America.

Nov. —Rioters ruthlessly suppressed in southern Ireland; the leaders were hanged.

Nov. —Irish Parliament votes to support the king in the war against the American colonies.

AMERICAN COLONIES

May —Fort Ticonderoga captured from the British by Ethan Allen.

May 10 —Second Continental Congress meets in Philadelphia and resolves to put the colonies into a state of defense.

June 15 —Congress appoints George Washington chief of the Continental forces.

June 17 —British capture Breed's Hill and Bunker Hill from Continental forces but suffer heavy casualties.

July —Congress adopts *John Dickinson's** petition to the king to stop military actions and work out a reconciliation.

Aug. —Continental forces under *Richard Montgomery* and *Benedict Arnold** invade Canada.

Oct. —Congress founds a navy.

Nov. —Congress appoints a committee to seek foreign assistance.

Nov. —*Governor Dunmore** raises a Loyalist force in Virginia and by promising freedom to Negro slaves forms a Negro regiment to fight for the king.

Dec. —Governor Dunmore defeated and driven out of Norfolk.

John Dickinson (1732–1808): Maryland lawyer, writer, political opponent of Franklin, Member Second Continental Congress; advocated reconciliation with England. Once independence had been voted, he joined the Continental Army.

John Murray, Earl of Dunmore (1732–1809): a Scottish noble's son; served as governor of New York and Virginia during the 1770's. After being driven out of Norfolk, he returned and burned it to the ground. Went back to England in 1776.

Richard Montgomery (1736–1775): Irish born; served British Army during Seven Years' War; to America, 1772; delegate, First Continental Congress; Brog. Gen., Continental Army; killed leading assault on Quebec, 1775.

Benedict Arnold (1741–1801): Connecticut Revolutionary general; distinguished himself in combat, but betrayed his command to the British in 1779. Defected, 1780. Lived his last years in England.

B33

1776

BRITISH ISLES		AMERICAN COLONIES	
		Jan.	—Thomas Paine publishes *Common Sense*, first public demand for American independence.
Feb.	—Associations of armed Protestant gentlemen and farmers formed to keep order in southern Ireland.	Feb.	—British attack on Charleston fails.
		Mar.	—British troops evacuate Boston and take 1,000 Loyalists with them.
		Mar.	—Congress advises disarming all Loyalists.
Mar.	—First contingents of troops hired in Germany embarked for service in America.	Apr.	—Continental forces retreat and abandon their Canadian campaign after failing to take Quebec.
Apr.	—Seven regiments ordered to leave Ireland for America.	Apr.	—North Carolina Convention empowers its delegates to the Congress to vote for independence.
		June 7	—Richard Henry Lee of Virginia introduces a resolution in the Congress that the colonies "are, and of right ought to be, free and independent states."
		June 11	—Congress appoints Thomas Jefferson, Benjamin Franklin, John Adams, Robert Livingston, and Roger Sherman to draft a declaration of independence.
July	—New outbreaks of rioting and destruction of property in southern Ireland.	July 2	—Congress votes for independence.
		July 4	—Final version of the Declaration of Independence unanimously approved by the Congress.

7   UNION OR SEPARATION

By early 1775, many colonial Americans were convinced that Anglo-American constitutional and political relations had to change. Men could no longer live and work in the atmosphere of crisis and alarm which the present system had helped to create.

Precisely what the new arrangements ought to be were matters of great uncertainty. To be sure, some colonial leaders such as Sam Adams had been committed to the idea of separation and independence for several years. But for most colonial Americans the idea of separation and independence seemed unnatural and unrealistic. History did not support or encourage it. Switzerland had won its independence from the Holy Roman Empire in the fourteenth century, the Netherlands did the same in the sixteenth century, and that was about all. Ireland tried in the seventeenth century to win its independence, and failed. The prospect of any great power in the eighteenth century allowing dependent territories to go their own way was extremely remote.

Two of the most influential arguments for changing the existing system of Anglo-American constitutional and political relations were made by *Joseph Galloway** and *Thomas Paine.** Galloway, a native-born American, wealthy lawyer, Speaker of the Pennsylvania Assembly, and member of the First Continental Congress, argued for a closer constitutional union with Great Britain in a speech delivered before the First Continental Congress on September 28, 1774. Paine, an English-born writer, soldier, and professional revolutionary who first came to America in 1774, argued for separation and independence in his pamphlet *Common Sense* published in January of 1776.

While reading the following selections, keep in mind these questions:

1. According to Galloway, why should the colonists seek a closer constitutional union with Great Britain?

2. According to Paine, why should the colonies seek separation and independence?

3. Why do you think their respective attitudes toward the British connection are so different?

Joseph Galloway's Plan of Union, 1774

Since the proposal I intend to make has been opposed, I have waited to hear a better one. Nothing has come forward except a scheme for a general cessation of trade between Britain and ourselves. It is impossible that America can long exist under a total non-exportation. We would have thousands of people thrown upon the cold hand of charity.

I am as much a friend to liberty as anyone, and no man shall go further in risking his fortune or blood than the man who now addresses you. There must be a union of wills and strength, a state must be animated by one soul.

As we are not within the jurisdiction of the Parliament of Great Britain, we are independent states and the laws of Great Britain do not bind us in any case whatsoever.

We want aid, assistance, and protection of our mother country. Protection and allegiance are *reciprocal** duties. We must come to terms with Great Britain.

I propose this proposition. We require a constitutional arrangement where there will be two classes of laws. The first being laws of internal policy. The second being laws in which more than one colony is concerned. I propose a constitutional arrangement whereby no law would be enacted without the assent of Great Britain and no law would be enacted without the assent of America. I propose a British-American legislature.

In every government whatever its form, there must be a supreme legislature. I know of no <u>American</u> constitution. A Virginia constitution, a Pennsyl-

Joseph Galloway (1731–1803) later became a Loyalist and served the British during the war. His property was confiscated by Pennsylvania, and he spent the last 20 years of his life as an exile in England.

Thomas Paine (1737–1809): served the revolutionary cause in America, but returned to England in 1787 where he was outlawed for seditious writing. Participated in the French revolution in 1792, narrowly escaped death, and returned to the United States in 1794 where he lived in obscurity and poverty.

Reciprocal: shared or felt by both sides.

B35

vania constitution we have. We are totally independent of each other. However, it is necessary that the trade of the empire should be regulated by some power. Can the empire hold together without a supreme legislature? Who shall regulate it? Shall the legislatures of Nova Scotia or Georgia regulate it? Massachusetts or Virginia? Pennsylvania or New York? Our legislative powers extend no further than the limits of each separate colony.

There is a necessity that an American legislature be set up or else we must give the power to Parliament or to the King.

Therefore, be it resolved:

That the Congress apply to His Majesty for a redress of the grievances under which his faithful subjects in America labour.

That we assure His Majesty the Colonies abhor the idea of being communities independent of the British government and most ardently desire a political union, not only among ourselves, but with the mother state.

That as the Colonies from local circumstances and distance cannot be represented in the Parliament of Great Britain, we propose establishment of a British and American legislature in America for regulating the administration of the general affairs of America.

That the said legislature shall consist of a Grand Council chosen by the representatives of the people in their respective legislative assemblies once every three years and a President-General appointed by the King.

That assent of the President-General shall be required for all acts of the Grand Council and it shall be his office and duty to carry them into execution.

That the President-General and Grand Council shall exercise all legislative powers and authorities necessary for administering general policies and affairs in which Great Britain and any of the Colonies are concerned or in which more than one Colony is concerned.

That each Colony shall retain its present constitution and powers of regulating and governing its own internal policies in all cases whatsoever.

From Charles Francis Adams, ed., **The Works of John Adams** (Boston: Charles C. Little and James Brown, 1850), Vol. II, pp. 387–391. Chauncey Ford, ed., **Journals of the U. S. Continental Congress 1774–1789** (Washington, D.C.: U. S. Govt. Printing Office, 1904), Vol. I, pp. 48–51.

That the President-General and Grand Council shall be an inferior and distinct branch of the British legislature united with it for the aforementioned general purposes, and that any of the said general regulations may originate either in the Parliament of Great Britain or in the Grand Council and be sent to the other for approval or dissent.

That the assent of both the Parliament of Great Britain and the Grand Council shall be required for all such general acts or statutes.

Thomas Paine's *Common Sense*,* 1775

I offer nothing more than simple facts, plain arguments, and common sense.

Volumes have been written on the subject of the struggle between England and America. Men of all ranks with different motives and various designs have embarked in this controversy, but all have been ineffectual. The period of debate is closed. Arms as a last resort must decide the contest. The appeal to arms was the King's choice, and the Continent has accepted the challenge.

The sun never shone on a worthier cause. It is not the affair of a city, a country, a province or a kingdom, but of a Continent containing at least one eighth of the habitable Globe. It's not the concern of a day, a year, or an age; posterity is involved, the future will be more or less affected to the very end of time by the proceedings now.

By referring the matter from argument to arms, a new era for politics is begun, new methods of thinking have arisen. All plans and proposals made prior to the nineteenth of April are like last year's almanacs, proper and useful once but superseded and useless now.

As much has been said of reconciliation which like an agreeable dream has left us and passed away, it is right that we should inquire into the injuries suffered by the Colonies from being connected with Great Britain.

I have heard some assert that America has flourished while connected with Great Britain and that the same connection is necessary for future happiness. Nothing could be more fallacious. America would have flourished as much had no European power taken notice of her. America has been enriched by commerce, and as long as Europeans continue the custom of eating, America shall have markets for her products.

It has been asserted that the Colonies have no relation to one another except through England. Pennsylvania and New Jersey are sister Colonies only by way of England. This is a round about way of proving relationship. It is a direct way of proving enmity or enemyship. France and Spain never were our enemies as <u>Americans</u>. We become their enemies because we are subjects of Great Britain.

I challenge the warmest advocates for reconciliation to show a single advantage derived from the connection. Our corn will bring its price in any market in Europe, and our imported goods must be paid for wherever we buy them.

As to matters of government, it is not in the power of Britain to do this Continent justice. Small islands are not capable of protecting themselves and are the proper objects for government by others. There is something absurd in supposing a Continent to be perpetually governed by an island. In no instance has nature made the satellite larger than the planet. As England and America, with respect to each other, reverse the common order of nature, it is evident that they belong to different systems. England to Europe and America to itself.

No man was warmer for reconciliation than myself before the fatal nineteenth of April, 1775. The moment the events of that day were made known, I rejected the hardened, sullen-tempered *Pharaoh** of England forever. I disdain the wretch who with the pretended title of FATHER OF HIS PEOPLE can unfeelingly hear of their slaughter, and composedly sleep with their blood upon his soul.

Every spot of the old world is overrun with oppression. Freedom has been hunted round the Globe. Asia and Africa have long expelled her. Europe regards her as a stranger, and England has given her warning to depart. O! receive the fugitive, and prepare in time an asylum for mankind.

Common Sense sold over 120,000 copies in three months. Some of Paine's other writings are more memorable for the power of their language than for sales figures. Paine wrote the famous patriotic lines in his **Crisis Papers,** "These are the times that try men's souls. The summer soldier and the sunshine patriot will, in this crisis, shrink from the service of their country."

Pharaoh: title of the all-powerful ruler of ancient Egypt, meaning here that George III is a tyrant.

From **The Writings of Thomas Paine** (The Knickerbocker Press, New York, 1894).

1

Paul Revere at Work, 1768

Portrait by John Singleton Copley
USA 1768–70. Oil on canvas
Gift of Joseph W., Wm. B., and Edward H. R. Revere
Courtesy Museum of Fine Arts, Boston

2 Paul Revere's 45-Gill Liberty Bowl

Museum of Fine Arts,
Boston

3

The Bloody Massacre on
King Street, 1770

Courtesy the American
Antiquarian Society

4

No. VII Engrav.d for Royal American Magazine Vol. I

Mr. SAMUEL ADAMS.

Paul Revere's Engraving
of Samuel Adams, 1774

Both, Courtesy the American Antiquarian Society

5

No. X   Engraved for Royal American Magazine.   Vol. I.

The able Doctor. or America Swallowing the Bitter Draught.

The Able Doctor or
America Swallowing
the Bitter Draught

4 Independence and war, 1776-1783

Ideas and Events

Objectives of this assignment are to:
—Analyze the Declaration of Independence to discover the specific grievances by which the American Revolution was justified.
—Identify in a chronology of the war the decisions and actions which were most critical in determining its outcome.
—Draw inferences from a film-strip of events of the Revolutionary War about what is essential for successful colonial revolutions.
—Make a judgment on why the Americans won and the British lost the war.

Introduction

Public opinion in favor of independence and war grew very rapidly during the early months of 1776. Thomas Paine's brilliant statement of the case for independence in Common Sense forced Americans to think about the advantages of separation from Britain, while the military and diplomatic situation persuaded many that prospects for obtaining it were good. After all, by the spring of 1776, American forces had already tested British power in armed conflict in Massachusetts, Canada, Vermont, Virginia, and the Carolinas, and found it wanting. Furthermore, when British forces evacuated Boston and withdrew temporarily to Halifax in March, the British army had no permanent foothold in the colonies until they returned to New York in late summer.

A series of events brought America closer and closer to war. In April, 1776, the North Carolina convention instructed its delegates to vote for independence. Virginia followed suit in May. Also in May, France and Spain gave firm promises of arms and ammunition. The decision to avoid a final break with Great Britain was no longer possible.

The Declaration of Independence

Richard Henry Lee of Virginia offered his resolution that the United Colonies "are, and of right ought to be, free and independent States" on June 7. After some debate, the Congress decided to postpone a decision on Lee's

Signing of the Declaration of Independence—Delegates from all the colonies gathered on August 2, 1776, in Independence Hall, Philadelphia, to affix their signatures to the historic document that gave birth to a new nation.

resolution until July 1, but appointed a committee of Thomas Jefferson, Benjamin Franklin, John Adams, and Roger Sherman to prepare a declaration of independence.

Thomas Jefferson was charged with the responsibility for actually drawing up the document, and after a few changes added by Franklin and Adams it was presented to the Congress on June 28. There was opposition to independence from delegates from Pennsylvania, South Carolina, and Delaware; and New Yorkers refused to commit themselves either way. Nevertheless, independence was formally voted by the Congress on July 2, 1776, with 12 votes for, none against, and New York abstaining.

Next, Congress debated for two days the form and content of the Declaration which Jefferson had prepared, and made several changes. Finally, on July 4, 1776, the amended Declaration was approved by the Congress without a dissenting vote, though New York again abstained. The Declaration was publicly proclaimed in Philadelphia on July 8 and read before General Washington and his troops in New York City on the following day. On July 9, also, the Provincial Congress of New York voted to approve the Declaration, making the action at Philadelphia unanimous.

During those hot July days a new nation had been born. The thirteen British colonies were now the Confederation of the United States. There was little time for celebrations. The Congress which had declared independence had to establish it. Congress had governments to organize and a war to wage.

The Confederation of the United States

When Richard Henry Lee offered his resolution for independence on June 7, 1776, he also proposed that Congress prepare a plan for confederation of all the colonies. Congress appointed a committee headed by John Dickinson, composed of one member from each colony to draft such a plan. On June 12, 1776, the committee submitted its Articles of Confederation and Perpetual Union to the Congress. Debated off and on for more than a year, the Articles were not formally adopted until November 17, 1777. Ratification by the states took a long time and was not completed until March 1, 1781.

The Articles of Confederation represent the first American effort to resolve the problem of how governmental authority was to be shared among thirteen separate state legislatures. The Declaration of Independence had not solved that problem. It merely transferred the problem from London to Philadelphia. The thirteen new states and their legislatures were no more willing to give up portions of their authority to an overall American Congress than the thirteen colonies had been willing to accept the supremacy of the British Parliament.

In their final form the Articles announced a perpetual union for common defense and general welfare between the states. Each state retained full authority, or *sovereignty*,* over its own affairs, and every right and function of government not explicitly delegated to the central government. Free inhabitants in one state were to be entitled to all privileges of free citizens anywhere in the Union. Judicial records and proceedings in one state were to be honored in all of the others. Fugitives from justice were to be delivered up.

Sovereignty: from a Latin word meaning superior or above.

The Central Government

The central government consisted of a Congress of delegates chosen annually by the states. No state was to have more than seven or less than two delegates, but each state irrespective of its size, population, wealth, or number of delegates was to have only one vote in the Congress.

Management of war and foreign affairs was assigned to the national government. Costs of war and other general expenses were to be paid out of a common treasury to which each state was to contribute a share based on the value of its surveyed lands. Only the states had powers to levy and collect taxes. Payments into the common treasury were by requisition. The national government could only ask, not compel, state contributions.

Disputes between states were to be settled by a court or commission appointed by Congress whenever one state requested it to do so. Relations between states were essentially international; each state gave full faith and credit to the records and judicial actions of all other states. Citizens of one state were entitled to all of the privileges and immunities of other states. Criminals had to be be extradited. Congress could not make war or treaties unless nine of the thirteen states agreed; and no changes in the articles were possible without the agreement of all thirteen state legislatures.

Under the Articles, the distribution of powers between the states and the central government favored the states. The United States in Congress assembled was empowered to carry out the wishes of the states and not much else. State governments held the power, and lawmaking was essentially their function. Congress was hardly a <u>legislative</u> body at all. It was really an <u>executive</u> organization authorized to do only those things that nine of the thirteen states could agree were worth doing. Effective government in the United States was vested largely in the governments of the thirteen states.

State Governments

Between 1776 and 1780 every state except *Connecticut* and *Rhode Island** drew up new constitutions. Most of these new constitutions had provisions for governors with limited powers and short terms of office.

Almost all of the new state legislatures were composed of two houses and were elected for short terms. In all of the states, the legislatures were extremely powerful. Legislatures elected their governors in eight states and shared powers of appointment with them in seven states.

An appointed judiciary, property qualifications for officeholding, and voting were general. Most of the states guaranteed traditional British civil liberties such as jury trials, reasonable bail, and freedom of the press in bills of rights. Several states adopted provisions requiring reexamination of their constitutions and fundamental laws by periodic constitutional conventions.

While the new state constitutions differed in detail, taken together they suggest that Americans had some definite ideas about how they wanted to be governed. Americans wanted state officials rotated in office, and the different branches of state government separated. They also wanted protection for citizens' rights and regular procedures for changing the state constitution and state laws. This generation of Americans wanted to be the masters of their government, not the servants of it.

The War

When the Continental Congress decided for independence in July, 1776, it also decided for war. At the moment it appeared to be a war which it could not lose. The Americans controlled virtually the entire country from Quebec to Florida and from the sea to the mountains. All the Americans had to do to win was to hold on to what they already had.

For the British the military problems of waging a war in America appeared overwhelming. They had to conquer a vast territory to win, and they had to do it with troops brought and supplied by bulky, slow-moving sailing vessels that took anywhere from five to twelve weeks to cross the Atlantic. With communications over three thousand miles of ocean so uncertain, and with such long lines of supply open to the ordinary hazards of seafaring as well as attack, several British *military experts** thought the reconquest of America was hopeless from the start. Yet honor, prestige, and concern for the Loyalists in America required that the realities of ocean and wilderness be ignored. The king's ministers decided to wage a full-scale war.

Connecticut and Rhode Island continued to use their colonial charters of 1662 and 1663, simply deleting all references to the British Crown.

Lord Barrington, the Secretary of War, the Adjutant-General, and two senior Administrators of the Army all declared that military reconquest was hopeless.

B43

If Americans were as united and determined as the speeches and votes of the gentlemen in Philadelphia suggested, they might have won independence in a year. But there was so much Loyalist feeling and sheer apathy about the war that Congress found it difficult to keep an army together and to feed the soldiers. There were actually periods during the five years of fighting when British generals recruited more soldiers in America than Washington did.

Furthermore, if the Americans had vast territories into which they could retreat, they also had vast territories to defend. Troops had to be raised and trained, arms and ammunition had to be obtained, and money had to be raised. Foreign assistance was essential for survival, and as events quickly demonstrated, foreign naval support and the intervention of foreign troops in the field were necessary for victory. Without French aid, the Americans would have been badly beaten by 1780.

Apathy was no less a problem for the British. The war was never popular in Britain. Pro-American speeches were frequent occurrences in the British House of Commons. Some parts of Britain, such as Belfast in northern Ireland, were so pro-American that troops had to be quartered there to maintain order. There were so many American sympathizers in Britain that German *mercenaries** had to be hired to bring the army up to full fighting strength.

Mercenaries: hired professional soldiers. The British tried to hire 20,000 Russians in 1775, but were refused. Contracts were signed with the rulers of the German states of Hesse and Brunswick for 18,000 regular soldiers in January, 1776, to help subdue America.

Moreover, as the conflict dragged on and European powers intervened, the cost of waging war skyrocketed. The British government faced serious political and economic crises in Ireland and in the north of England in 1778 and 1779. There was uncontrollable rioting in London during June, 1780. The army which surrendered at Saratoga in October, 1777, was replaced, but the one which surrendered at Yorktown in October, 1781, was not. British public opinion demanded an end to the fighting in America. Lord North's government resigned in early 1782, and peace talks began in April, 1782.

The Peace of Paris

The Anglo-American treaty was to go into effect after Britain reached a settlement with France. Preliminary articles between Britain and France were not signed until January 20, 1783.

In Paris, Benjamin Franklin, John Adams, Henry Laurens, and John Jay met with the British negotiators, Richard Oswald and Henry Strachey. Terms of the *treaty** agreed upon in October, 1782 included recognition of American independence and establishment of the St. Croix River, the Great Lakes, and the 45th parallel as the northern boundary with Canada. The Mississippi River was the western boundary with Spanish Louisiana; the 31st parallel and Apalachicola River, the southern boundary with Spanish Florida.

The United States was given the right to fish in Newfoundland and Nova Scotia waters, and liberty to dry and cure fish on unsettled shores of those regions. All debts due creditors of either country were to be honored. Congress pledged itself to recommend to the state legislatures restoration of the rights and property of Loyalists. Finally, all hostilities were to cease on February 4, 1783, and British land and naval forces were to evacuate American territory with all convenient speed. The treaty was ratified by Congress on January 14, 1784, and the United States took its place among the nations of the world.

B44

8   THE GREAT DECLARATION

The Declaration of Independence which Congress adopted and proclaimed from New Hampshire to Georgia was neither lengthy nor complicated. Jefferson's original rough draft filled only four hand-written pages. If it was written quickly and in the language of political controversy, it was also written carefully and brilliantly. The document itself consists of four parts: a preamble, philosophical paragraph, list of charges against the king, and the actual declaration of independence from Great Britain.

The Declaration is one of the greatest and most influential documents of modern times because it was an expression of the American mind. The Declaration was at once a justification for revolution, a statement of grievances, a moral judgment on a form of government, and an expression of hope. While reading the Declaration of Independence, keep in mind these questions:

1. According to the preamble, why was the Declaration of Independence issued?

2. According to the second, or philosophical, paragraph of the Declaration of Independence, what is the purpose of government?

3. According to the Declaration of Independence, when and under what conditions are revolutions justified?

4. Do you think the grievances listed in the Declaration of Independence are sufficient cause for revolution? Do they meet the conditions set down in the Declaration justifying revolution?

Unalienable: rights that cannot be given or taken away.

Usurpation: illegal seizure of sovereign power.

Despotism: government where all power is concentrated in the hands of a single arbitrary ruler.

4 July 1776

The Unanimous Declaration of the Thirteen United States of America

When in the course of human events, it becomes necessary for one people to dissolve the political bands which have connected them with another, and to assume among the powers of the earth the separate and equal station to which the Laws of Nature and of Nature's God entitle them, a decent respect to the opinions of mankind requires that they should declare the causes which impel them to the separation.

We hold these truths to be self-evident, that all men are created equal, that they are endowed by their Creator with certain *unalienable rights,** that among these are life, liberty, and the pursuit of happiness. That to secure these rights, governments are instituted among men, deriving their just powers from the consent of the governed. That whenever any form of government becomes destructive of these ends, it is the right of the people to alter or to abolish it, and to institute new government, laying its foundation on such principles and organizing its powers in such form, as to them shall seem most likely to effect their safety and happiness. Prudence, indeed, will dictate that governments long established should not be changed for light and transient causes; and accordingly all experience hath shown, that mankind are more disposed to suffer, while evils are sufferable, than to right themselves by abolishing the forms to which they are accustomed. But when a long train of abuses and *usurpations,** pursuing invariably the same object evinces a design to reduce them under absolute *despotism,** it is their right, it is their duty, to throw off such government, and to provide new guards for their future security. Such has been the patient sufferance of these Colonies; and such is now the necessity which constrains them to alter their former systems of government. The history of the present King of Great Britain is a history of repeated injuries and usurpations, all having in direct object the establishment of an absolute tyranny over these States. To prove this, let facts be submitted to a candid world.

He has refused his assent to laws, the most wholesome and necessary for the public good.

He has forbidden his Governors to pass laws of immediate and pressing importance, unless suspended in their operation till his assent should be obtained; and when so suspended, he has utterly neglected to attend to them.

He has refused to pass other laws for the accommodation of large districts of people, unless those people would relinquish the right of representation in the legislature, a right inestimable to them and formidable to tyrants only.

He has called together legislative bodies at places unusual, uncomfortable, and distant from the depository of their public records, for the sole purpose of fatiguing them into compliance with his measures.

He has dissolved representative houses repeatedly, for opposing with manly firmness his invasions on the rights of the people.

He has refused for a long time after such dissolutions, to cause others to be elected whereby the legislative powers, incapable of annihilation, have returned to the people at large for their exercise the State remaining in the meantime exposed to all the dangers of invasion from without and convulsions within.

He has endeavoured to prevent the population of these States, for that purpose obstructing the laws for naturalization of foreigners; refusing to pass others to encourage their migration hither, and raising the conditions of new appropriations of lands.

He has obstructed the administration of justice, by refusing his assent to laws for establishing judiciary powers.

He has made judges dependent on his will alone, for the tenure of their offices, and the amount and payment of their salaries.

He has erected a multitude of new offices, and sent hither swarms of officers to harass our people, and eat out their substance.

He has kept among us, in times of peace, standing armies without the consent of our legislatures.

He has affected to render the military independent of and superior to the civil power.

He has combined with others to subject us to a jurisdiction foreign to our constitution, and unacknowl- *edged by our laws; giving his assent to their acts of pretended legislation:*

For quartering large bodies of armed troops among us:

For protecting them, by a mock trial, from punishment for any murders which they should commit on the inhabitants of these States:

For cutting off our trade with all parts of the world:

For imposing taxes on us without our consent:

For depriving us in many cases of the benefits of trial by jury:

For transporting us beyond seas to be tried for pretended offences:

For abolishing the free system of English laws in a neighbouring Province, establishing therein an arbitrary government, and enlarging its boundaries so as to render it at once an example and fit instrument for introducing the same absolute rule into these Colonies:

For taking away our Charters, abolishing our most valuable laws, and altering fundamentally the forms of our governments:

For suspending our own Legislatures, and declaring themselves invested with power to legislate for us in all cases whatsoever.

He has abdicated government here, by declaring us out of his protection and waging war against us.

He has plundered our seas, ravaged our coasts, burnt our towns, and destroyed the lives of our people.

He is at this time transporting large armies of foreign mercenaries to compleat the works of death, desolation, and tyranny, already begun with circumstances of cruelty and perfidy scarcely paralleled in the most barbarous ages, and totally unworthy the head of a civilized nation.

He has constrained our fellow citizens taken captive on the high seas to bear arms against their country, to become the executioners of their friends and brethren, or to fall themselves by their hands.

He has excited domestic insurrections amongst us, and has endeavoured to bring on the inhabitants of our frontiers the merciless Indian savages, whose known rule of warfare is an undistinguished destruction of all ages, sexes, and conditions.

In every stage of these oppressions we have petitioned for redress in the most humble terms: our repeated petitions have been answered only by repeated injury. A prince whose character is thus marked by every act which may define a tyrant, is unfit to be the ruler of a free people.

Nor have we been wanting in attention to our Brit-

ish brethren. We have warned them from time to time of attempts by their Legislature to extend an unwarrantable jurisdiction over us. We have reminded them of the circumstances of our emigration and settlement here. We have appealed to their native justice and magnanimity, and we have conjured them by the ties of our common kindred to disavow these usurpations, which would inevitably interrupt our connections and correspondence. They too have been deaf to the voice of justice and of consanguinity. We must, therefore, acquiesce in the necessity, which denounces our separation, and hold them, as we hold the rest of mankind, enemies in war, in peace friends.

We, therefore, the Representatives of the United States of America, in General Congress assembled, appealing to the Supreme Judge of the world for the rectitude of our intentions, do, in the name, and by authority of the good people of these Colonies, solemnly publish and declare, That these United Colonies are, and of right ought to be Free and Independent States; that they are absolved from all allegiance to the British Crown, and that all political connection between them and the State of Great Britain is and ought to be totally dissolved; and that as Free and Independent States they have full power to levy war, conclude peace, contract alliances, establish commerce, and to do all other acts and things which independent States may of right do. And for the support of this declaration, with a firm reliance on the protection of Divine Providence, we mutually pledge to each other our lives, our fortunes and our sacred honor.

9 THE WAR FOR AMERICAN INDEPENDENCE, 1776–1783

The major battles in the war for American independence were fought over a period of six years in widely separated theatres of operations. Most of the land battles were fought on American soil. The movement of fleets and sea battles ranged from the North American coasts to the Caribbean and from the British seas to the Mediterranean. Soldiers from virtually every country in western Europe participated in the fighting. White men, black men, red men, of every religion died fighting for or against the cause of American independence.

Battles of another kind were waged in the diplomatic chanceries of the great powers of Europe, the Parliament of England, and even on the streets of London. This great conflict not only established American independence and accounted for the only defeat Britain suffered in her hundred-year struggle with France for world leadership, but it also provided a model and inspiration for the succession of colonial revolutions that have continued into our own time. The war for American independence was as much an event in world history as it was an event in the histories of North America and Britain.

While studying the chronology of the war and examining the maps of the major campaigns, keep in mind these questions:

1. Why was the battle of Saratoga such an important victory for the Americans?

2. Why was 1779 a critical year for the British?

3. Why was 1780 a critical year for the Americans?

4. What British and French decisions made in 1781 do you think accounted for French naval supremacy at Yorktown?

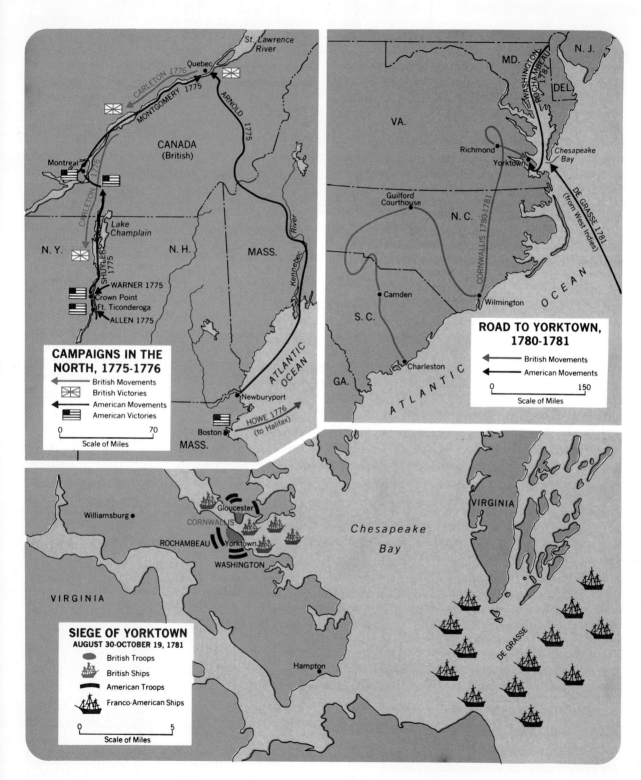

CAMPAIGNS IN THE NORTH, 1775-1776

- British Movements
- ⚔ British Victories
- American Movements
- 🏴 American Victories

0   70
Scale of Miles

St. Lawrence River

Quebec

CARLETON 1776
MONTGOMERY 1775
CARLETON 1776
ARNOLD 1775

Montreal

CANADA (British)

Lake Champlain

SHUYLER 1775

WARNER 1775
Crown Point
Ft. Ticonderoga
ALLEN 1775

N.Y.

N.H.

MASS.

Kennebec River

ATLANTIC OCEAN

Newburyport

HOWE 1776 (to Halifax)

Boston

MASS.

ROAD TO YORKTOWN, 1780-1781

- British Movements
- American Movements

0   150
Scale of Miles

MD.
N.J.
DEL.

WASHINGTON 1781
ROCHAMBEAU 1781

VA.

Richmond
Yorktown
Chesapeake Bay

Guilford Courthouse

N.C.

CORNWALLIS 1780-1781

DE GRASSE 1781 (from West Indies)

Camden

Wilmington

S.C.

OCEAN

GA.

Charleston

ATLANTIC

SIEGE OF YORKTOWN
AUGUST 30-OCTOBER 19, 1781

- British Troops
- 🚢 British Ships
- American Troops
- ⛵ Franco-American Ships

0   5
Scale of Miles

Williamsburg

Gloucester
CORNWALLIS
ROCHAMBEAU
Yorktown
WASHINGTON

VIRGINIA

Chesapeake Bay

VIRGINIA

Hampton

DE GRASSE

B48

Chronology of the War for American Independence, 1776–1783

BRITAIN AND EUROPE	AMERICA

1776

July —Independence celebrations occur throughout the states.

July —British fleet lands 32,000 men on Staten Island.

Sept. —British occupy New York City.

Oct. —Battle of White Plains; Washington retreats into New Jersey.

Dec. —Opponents of the American war in the British Parliament disrupt National Day of Fast and Sorrow by public feasting and drinking.

Dec. —Washington captures 1,000 Hessian mercenaries in a surprise attack on Trenton.

1777

Feb. —British land tax increased 33% to pay for the war in America.

Jan. —Washington checks British advance at Princeton and forces British withdrawal from eastern New Jersey.

Feb. —British plan knockout blow to isolate New England by an invasion from Canada and by a combined land and naval attack on Philadelphia.

June —7,770 British and German troops with Indian allies under General Burgoyne invade New York state from Canada.

July —Marquis de Lafayette, 20 years old, French nobleman, volunteers for service with the American army, commissioned a Major-General. Other officers from France, Poland, Prussia, and Bavaria commissioned in the American army.

Marquis de Lafayette

Sept. 11 —Lafayette wounded at Battle of Brandywine.

Sept. 26 —British occupy Philadelphia, Congress flees to Lancaster.

Oct. 7 —Benedict Arnold leads an American charge at Bemis Heights, New York, and checks Burgoyne's advance.

Oct. 17 —Burgoyne surrenders the 5,700 men remaining in his army to the Americans at Saratoga.

Nov. —States begin large-scale confiscation of the property of Loyalists. New York and Maryland raise $5 $\frac{1}{2}$ million by sale of Loyalist property.

Dec. —France recognizes American independence.

Dec. —General Washington establishes winter quarters for his army at Valley Forge.

Chronology of the War for American Independence, 1776–1783

BRITAIN AND EUROPE	AMERICA

1778

Feb.	—Alliance between France and the United States arranged.		
Feb.	—Lord North offers to repeal all legislation since 1763 to conciliate America and end the war.		
Mar.	—British Parliament partially restores civil rights to English Catholics.		
Apr.	—Peace Commissioners under Lord Carlisle sent to Philadelphia to negotiate a peace. Congress insists on recognition of independence and withdrawal of British troops as a precondition for negotiation.	**Apr.**	—John Paul Jones raids coasts of England, Ireland, and Scotland.
Apr.	—British Parliament repeals minor restrictions on Irish trade.		
		May	—Congress ratifies the French alliance.
		May	—George Rogers Clark begins a campaign against British posts north and west of the Ohio River.
June	—Britain and France go to war.	**June**	—British evacuate Philadelphia as French fleet approaches New York.
		July	—Loyalists and Iroquois Indians raid Wyoming Valley in Pennsylvania and massacre settlers.
		July	—Congress returns to Philadelphia.
Aug.	—Irish Parliament partially restores civil rights to Irish Catholics.	**Aug.**	—A French fleet of 17 ships under Comte d'Estaing fails to capture Newport, Rhode Island.
Aug.	—Protestants in Ireland form armed volunteer associations to protect Ireland from French invasion or internal disorders.		
		Dec.	—British land and naval force captures Savannah.

1779

		Jan.	—British capture fortified posts and towns in the Carolinas.
		Feb.	—George Rogers Clark captures Fort Vincennes from the British.
		May	—British garrisons driven out of New Jersey.
June	—Spain declares war on Britain and besieges Gibraltar.		
		Aug.	—General Sullivan attacks Loyalists and Indians in New York State, destroying forty Seneca and Cayuga villages and the military power of the Iroquois.

BRITAIN AND EUROPE	AMERICA
	Sept. —John Paul Jones in the *Bonhomme Richard* defeats and captures British man of war *Serapis.*
	Sept. —Spanish capture Baton Rouge and Natchez from the British.
Oct. —Irish Parliament demands free trade.	**Oct.** —Comte d'Estaing's fleet of thirty-five ships and 5,500 French and American troops fail to capture Savannah.
Nov. —Volunteer associations in Ireland demonstrate for free trade.	
Dec. —British Parliament grants Ireland free trade.	
Dec. —Associations formed in Yorkshire for extending voting rights in England.	

1780

	Mar. —Spanish take Mobile from the British.
Apr. —Irish Parliament demands that the legislative supremacy of the British Parliament over it be ended.	
Apr. —John Dunning's resolution that the power of the British Crown be diminished is passed by the British Parliament.	
May —League of "Armed Neutrality" against Britain formed by Russia, Denmark, Holland, Prussia, Austria, and Portugal.	**May** —Charleston falls to the British, and 5,600 American troops and 1,000 seamen surrender.
	May —Units of Washington's army at Morristown, New Jersey, mutiny over lack of supplies and pay. Mutineers suppressed by troops marched from Pennsylvania.
June —Lord George Gordon anti-Catholic riots break out in London and rage for ten days. Troops required to restore order in London.	
July —French complain to Americans about what the war is costing them.	**July** —Comte de Rochambeau with 5,000 French troops and a naval escort captures Newport, Rhode Island, from the British.
	Aug. —American forces defeated at battle of Camden, and British hold on Georgia and South Carolina strengthened.
	Sept. —Benedict Arnold flees to the British after his plans to betray West Point to them are discovered.
Dec. —Britain declares war on Holland.	

1781

	Jan. —Pennsylvania troops mutiny over lack of pay and supplies. Washington suppresses the mutiny and executes the leaders.
Mar. 13 —British decide to send 32 ships from the Home Fleet to supply and reinforce Gibraltar.	**Mar.** —British defeat Americans at Guilford Courthouse, but are forced to leave North Carolina for a campaign in Virginia.

Chronology of the War for American Independence, 1776–1783

BRITAIN AND EUROPE	AMERICA

1781

Mar. 22 —Admiral de Grasse's fleet of 28 French warships slips out of Brest for the West Indies without interference from the British Home Fleet.

June —De Grasse's fleet arrives in the West Indies.

June —Cornwallis establishes a main base at the small seaport, Yorktown, Virginia.

July —British send six ships from the West Indies to Britain for repairs.

Aug. 5 —British fleet defeats the Dutch at Battle of Dogger Bank.

Aug. 5 —De Grasse gambles by sending 27 ships and 3,000 soldiers from the West Indies north to Chesapeake Bay, leaving French West Indian islands unprotected.

Aug. —Protestant volunteers in Ireland increase to a force of 80,000 armed men.

Aug. 30 —De Grasse arrives in Chesapeake Bay and blockades the British Army at Yorktown.

Sept. —Combined French and Spanish fleet attacks British shipping in the English Channel.

Sept. 5 —A British fleet of 19 ships challenges De Grasse's fleet of 27. The battle is indecisive. No ships lost on either side. The British fleet withdraws, leaving De Grasse in control of Chesapeake Bay and British forces at Yorktown cut off.

The Surrender of Lord Cornwallis at Yorktown, painted by John Trumbull. Cornwallis himself was ill, so he sent a deputy to the ceremony held at Yorktown on October 19, 1781 (the general standing in the center of the picture). George Washington, out of courtesy, also sent his deputy (on the white horse).

Yale University Art Gallery

BRITAIN AND EUROPE	AMERICA

Lord Cornwallis

AMERICA

Sept. 24 —Rochambeau's 7,800 French troops, Washington's 5,800, and 3,000 Virginia militia besiege 6,000 British troops under Cornwallis at Yorktown.

Oct. 13 —American assault troops led by Alexander Hamilton and French Grenadiers led by Colonel DeuxPonts, capture two key British positions.

Oct. 18 —With ammunition exhausted and only 3,200 men fit for duty, Cornwallis surrenders his entire force to the Franco-American Army.

Oct. 24 —De Grasse's fleet leaves Chesapeake Bay for the West Indies.

Dec. —Fighting in America at a standstill.

1782

Feb. —British garrison on Minorca surrenders to Spanish fleet and army.

Feb. —Convention of Protestant volunteers in Ireland demands legislative independence for the Irish Parliament.

Mar. 5 —British House of Commons votes to stop the war in America.

Mar. 20 —Lord North is replaced as chief minister by Lord Rockingham, who opens peace negotiations with the Americans.

Apr. —Irish Parliament declares legislative supremacy of the British Parliament at an end.

Apr. 12 —British fleet under Admiral Rodney defeats De Grasse in the West Indies at the Battle of the Saints, and takes him prisoner.

Apr. 26 —British army leaves New York City with 7,000 Loyalists. This group was the last of 100,000 Loyalists who left the United States for Canada or Europe since 1776.

May —British Parliament repeals Declaratory Law and grants legislative independence to the Irish Parliament.

Oct. 19 —British fleet breaks Spanish siege of Gibraltar, Spanish withdraw.

Nov. —Preliminary peace treaty between the United States and Britain signed.

1783

Jan. —Terms of the British-Dutch peace treaty negotiated.

Sept. 3 —Final peace treaty between Britain and the United States signed in Paris.

—Peace treaties between Britain, France, and Spain signed at Versailles.

Sept. 3 —American independence recognized by all of the great powers, though Congress does not ratify the peace treaty until January, 1784.

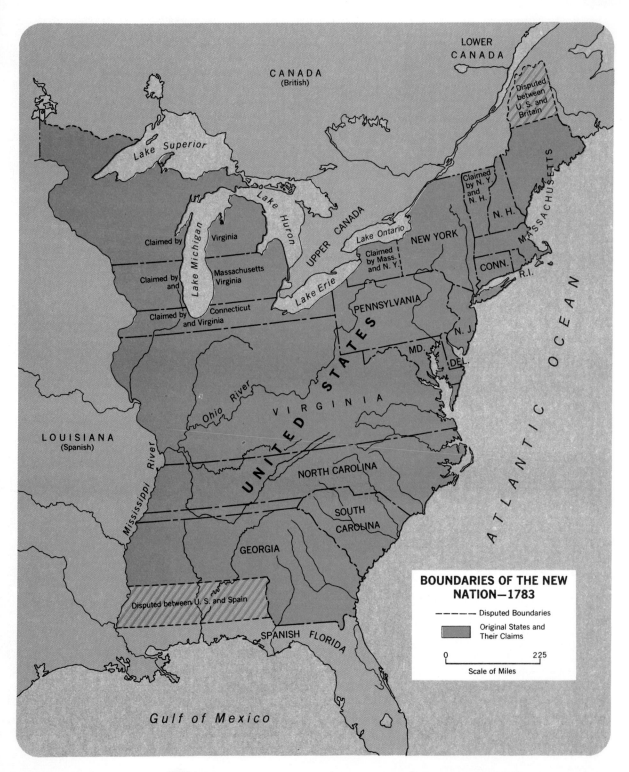

LOWER
CANADA

CANADA
(British)

Disputed
between
U. S. and
Britain

Lake Superior

Lake Huron

Claimed by
Virginia

Claimed by
and
Massachusetts
Virginia

Lake Michigan

UPPER CANADA

Lake Ontario

Lake Erie

Claimed by Mass.
and N. Y.

Claimed by N. Y
and N. H.

N. H.

NEW YORK

MASSACHUSETTS

CONN.

R.I.

Claimed by Connecticut
and Virginia

PENNSYLVANIA

N. J.

Ohio River

MD.

DEL.

UNITED STATES

LOUISIANA
(Spanish)

VIRGINIA

Mississippi River

NORTH CAROLINA

ATLANTIC OCEAN

SOUTH
CAROLINA

GEORGIA

Disputed between U. S. and Spain

SPANISH FLORIDA

Gulf of Mexico

BOUNDARIES OF THE NEW
NATION—1783

— — — Disputed Boundaries

▨ Original States and
  Their Claims

0   225

Scale of Miles

Kennedy Galleries, Inc.

6 Raising a Liberty Pole, July, 1776

7

Britannia Receives American
Loyalists in England

8 London Mob Attacks Newgate Prison, June 7, 1780

© British Museum

9

Dying Hessian Commander
Surrenders to Washington
at Trenton

Detail of **The Capture of the
Hessians at Trenton** by John
Trumbull. Courtesy of the
Yale University Art Gallery

10 Lafayette, Washington and Rochambeau at Yorktown

Colonial Williamsburg

Courtesy Gilbert Upton

11　Fourth of July Parade, Charlestown, N. H., 1830

5 What historians have said

Analyzing Historical Judgments

Introduction

Revolutions have always been easier to describe than to explain. The American Revolution is no exception. Generations of historians and students have studied the American Revolution in extraordinary detail, and yet have disagreed sharply about why it happened and what it accomplished. Part of this disagreement arises from the crucial importance of the American Revolution as the first of the great revolutions of modern history: American, French, Mexican, Russian, and Chinese. Comparisons have been inevitable if not always instructive.

The other part of this disagreement arises from uncertainty about the nature of revolution itself: what constitutes a revolution, and what has to happen in order to have one. The word "revolution" has been used to designate at least three different concepts: an overthrow of one set of political leaders by another, replacement of one form of government or set of political institutions by another, as well as social upheaval and economic changes of the most extreme sort. Uncertainty about the precise nature of revolution has led to questioning whether the colonial American war for independence from Britain was really a revolution at all.

The American Revolution was and still is a fascinating but puzzling subject of study. Yet, however interpreted or explained, there is one indisputable truth about it. All historians agree that the American Revolution changed the course of world history.

This assignment concludes your work on the American Revolution by examining historical interpretations of its meaning and accomplishments taken from the works of two well-known professional historians.

Objectives of this assignment are to:
—Analyze selections from writings of two modern historians of American Revolution.
—Suggest procedures for deciding which of two interpretations of the American Revolution is most accurate.
—Draw inferences about history and history writing from your analysis of these conflicting historical interpretations.

10 JAMESON ON ACCOMPLISHMENTS OF THE AMERICAN REVOLUTION

John Franklin Jameson was born in Somerville, Massachusetts, in 1859 and was educated at Amherst College and Johns Hopkins University. He received the first doctorate in history ever conferred by Johns Hopkins University in 1882. Professor Jameson taught American history at Johns Hopkins University,

Brown University, and the University of Chicago for many years. He was one of the founders of the American Historical Review, became its editor for a time, and served as Chief of the Manuscripts Division of the Library of Congress until his death in 1937. As a representative of the American Historical Association, Jameson took part in the organization of the American Council of Learned Societies in 1919. He played a major role in the planning of the Council's massive twenty volume *Dictionary of American Biography*. Professor Jameson wrote many articles and several books on different aspects and periods of American history.

The selection below is taken from his very influential and now classic work, The American Revolution Considered as a Social Movement, published in 1926. While reading this selection, keep in mind these questions. According to Jameson:

1. *How was the right to vote affected by the American Revolution?*
2. *How was the institution of slavery affected by the American Revolution?*
3. *How was landholding affected by the American Revolution?*

The American Revolution as a Social Movement

It is indeed true that our Revolution was strikingly unlike that of France, and that most of those who had originated it . . . would have considered their work done when political independence from Great Britain had been secured. But who can say to the waves of revolution: Thus far we shall go and no farther? . . . The stream of revolution, once started, could not be confined within narrow banks, but spread abroad the land.

Many economic desires, many social aspirations were set free by the political struggle, many aspects of colonial society were profoundly altered by the forces thus let loose. The relation of social classes to each other, the institution of slavery, the system of landholding . . . all felt the transforming hand of revolution. . . .

There are . . . some political changes that almost inevitably bring social changes in their wake. Take, for instance, the expansion of the *suffrage.** The status in which the electoral franchise was left at the end of the Revolutionary period fell far short of complete democracy. Yet during the years we are considering the right of suffrage was much extended. The freeholder, or owner of real estate, was given special privileges in four of the new state constitutions, two others widened the suffrage . . . and two others conferred it on all taxpayers. Now . . . we must take account of the fact that elevation of whole classes of people to the status of voters elevates them also in their social status. . . .

Suffrage: the right to vote.

There is no lack of evidence that . . . the analogy between freedom for whites and freedom for blacks was seen. . . . The first antislavery society in this or any other country was formed on April 14, 1775, five days before the battle of Lexington . . . in Philadelphia. . . . The New York "Society for Promoting the *Manumission** of Slaves" was organized in 1785. . . . In 1788 a society . . . was founded in Delaware and within four years there were other such in Rhode Island, Connecticut, New Jersey, Maryland, and Virginia. . . .

States also acted. Rhode Island . . . passed a law [in 1774] . . . to the effect that all slaves thereafter brought into the colony should be free. . . . A similar law was passed that same year in Connecticut. Delaware prohibited importation in 1776, Virginia in 1778, Maryland in 1783, South Carolina in 1787, . . . and North Carolina in 1786 imposed a larger duty on each negro imported. . . .

Pennsylvania in 1780 provided for gradual abolition. . . . The Superior Court of Massachusetts declared that slavery had been abolished in that state by the mere declaration in its constitution that "All men are born free and equal." In 1784 Connecticut and Rhode Island passed laws which gradually extinguished slavery. . . . Virginia passed an act . . . making private manumission easy where before it had been difficult. [It] appears to have led in eight years to the freeing of more than ten thousand slaves, twice as great a number as were freed by reason of the Massachusetts constitution. . . .

Thus in many ways the successful struggle for the independence of the United States affected the character of American society by altering the status of persons. The freeing of the community led not unnaturally to the freeing of the individual. . . .

❖   ❖   ❖   ❖   ❖

[Also], great *confiscations** of *Tory** estates were carried out by state legislatures, generally in the height of the war. . . . In Massachusetts a sweeping act confiscated at one blow the property of all who had fought against the United States or had even retired into places under British authority without permission of the American government. . . . Altogether . . . a great deal of land changed hands, and the confiscation of Tory estates contributed powerfully to break up the system of large landed properties, since the states usually sold the lands thus acquired in much smaller parcels. . . .

The *feudal ages** had discovered that, if men desired to give stability to society by keeping property in the hands of the same families generation after generation, the best way to do this was to *entail** the lands strictly, so that the holder could not sell them or even give them away, and to have a law of *primogeniture,** which in case the father made no will, would turn over all his lands to the eldest son, to the exclusion of all other children. There could not be two better devices for forming and maintaining a landed aristocracy. . . .

In ten years from the Declaration of Independence every state had abolished entails excepting two. . . . In fifteen years every state without exception abolished primogeniture . . . since which time the American eldest son has never been a privileged character. . . . Now I submit that this was no accident. . . . Such uniformity must have had a common cause, and where shall we find it if we do not admit that our Revolution, however much it differed from the French Revolution in spirit, yet carried within itself the seeds of social revolution.

Manumission: formal emancipation from slavery.

Confiscation: governmental seizure of private property without compensation.

Tory: British political party; name was applied to colonists who remained loyal to the Crown during the American Revolution.

Feudal ages: the medieval period of European history.

Entail: to settle by law precisely how property shall be inherited.

Primogeniture: under English law, the exclusive right of inheritance belonging to the eldest son.

Selections from J. Franklin Jameson, **The American Revolution Considered as a Social Movement** (copyright 1926, © 1967 by Princeton University Press; Princeton Paperback, 1967), pp. 9–38. Reprinted by permission from Princeton University Press.

11 BOORSTIN ON ACCOMPLISHMENTS OF THE AMERICAN REVOLUTION

Daniel J. Boorstin was born in Atlanta, Georgia, in 1914, and educated at Harvard, Oxford, and Yale Universities. He was a Rhodes Scholar at Oxford 1934–1937 and received his doctorate in Juristic Science from Yale in 1940. Professor Boorstin taught American history at Harvard, Swarthmore College, and the University of Chicago for many years. He has been a visiting professor in Turkey, France, India and Ceylon, Iran, and Japan. Professor Boorstin has written many articles and books on American history. He has a special interest in early American political and constitutional history.

The selection below is taken from Boorstin's *The Genius of American Politics* published in 1953. While reading this selection, keep in mind these questions. According to Boorstin:

1. What is the most obvious peculiarity of the American Revolution? Why have we been slow to recognize it?

2. What was the major issue in the American Revolution?

3. What was the major objective of the American Revolutionaries? What was their major accomplishment?

The American Revolution as a Conservative Movement

We have been slow to see some of the more obvious and more important peculiarities of our Revolution because influential scholars on the subject have cast their story in the mold of the French Revolution of 1789. Some of our best historians have managed to empty our Revolution of much of its local flavor by exaggerating what it had in common with that distinctively European struggle. . . .

The most obvious peculiarity of our American Revolution is that, in the modern European sense of the word, it was hardly a revolution at all. . . .

A number of historians . . . have pointed out the ways in which a social revolution, including a redistribution of property, accompanied the American Revolution. These are facts which no student of the period should neglect. Yet it seems to me that these historians have by no means succeeded in showing that such changes were so basic and far reaching as actually in themselves to have established our national republican institutions. . . .

The Revolution . . . is the series of events by which we separated ourselves from the British Empire and acquired a national identity. Looking at our Revolution from this point of view, what are some features which distinguish it from the French Revolution of 1789 or other revolutions to which western European nations trace their national identity? . . . .

1. First, and most important, the United States was born in a *colonial rebellion** . . . ours was one of the few conservative colonial rebellions of modern times. . . . The argument of the best theorists of the Revolution . . . has been often misrepresented and sometimes simply forgotten . . . the British by their treatment of the American colonies were being untrue to the ancient spirit of their own institutions. The slogan, "Taxation Without Representation Is Tyranny" was clearly founded on a British assumption. . . .

Boorstin refers here to **James Otis** (1725–1783) and the argument in his pamphlet **The Rights of the British Colonies** published in 1764.

According to their own account, then, the Americans were . . . forced . . . to defend the ancient British tradition; to be truer to that tradition than George III and Lord North and Townshend knew how to be. They were fighting not so much to establish new rights as to preserve old ones. . . . From the colonists' point of view, until 1776 it was the Parliament that had been revolutionary, by exercising a power for which there was no warrant in English constitutional precedent. . . .

2. Second, the American Revolution was <u>not</u> the product of a *nationalistic** spirit. . . .

Nationalistic: an exaltation of one's nation and culture over all other nations.

Perhaps never was a new nation created with less enthusiasm. . . .

In the period of the American Revolution we do discover a number of enthusiasms: for the safety and prosperity of Virginia or New York, for the cause of justice, for the rights of Englishmen. What is missing is anything that might be called widespread enthusiasm for the birth of a new nation: the United States of America. . . .

3. Our Revolution was successful at the first try. . . . There was no long drawn out agitation. . . . Thomas Paine's <u>Common Sense</u> . . . did not appear until January 10, 1776. Down to <u>within</u> six months of the break, few would have considered independence; and even then the colonists had only quite specific complaints. There had been no considerable tradition in America either of revolt against British institutions or republican theorizing.

The political objective of the Revolution, independence from British rule, was achieved by one relatively short continuous effort . . . properly speaking, 1776 had no sequel, and needed none. The issue was separation, and separation was accomplished. . . .

The proper slogan of the Revolution—if, indeed, there was a slogan—was "No Taxation Without Representation." Such words are . . . far too legalistic to warm the popular heart. But if we compare them with the "Liberty, Equality, Fraternity" of the French Revolution and the "Peace, Bread, and Land" of the Russian, we have a clue to the peculiar spirit of the American Revolution. It is my view that the major issue of the American Revolution was the true constitution of the British Empire, which is a pretty technical legal problem. . . .

The Revolution itself . . . had been a kind of *affirmation** of faith in ancient British institutions. In the greater part of the institutional life of the community the Revolution thus required no basic change. . . . This helps to account

Affirmation: to accept as true or good.

B63

From Daniel J. Boorstin, **The Genius of American Politics** (Chicago: The University of Chicago Press, 1953), pp. 66–98.

Habeas Corpus: a legal protection against unlawful imprisonment.

Act of Attainder: a law passed to abolish a person's civil rights.

Antipathy: dislike, distaste, or aversion.

for the value which we still attach to our inheritance from the British constitution: trial by jury, due process of law, representation before taxation, *habeas corpus,** freedom from *attainder,** independence of the judiciary, the rights of free speech, free petition, and free assembly, as well as our narrow definition of treason and our *antipathy** to standing armies in peacetime. . . .

Additional Reading

Alden, John R., *The American Revolution, 1775–1783.* New York: Harper, 1954. (Paperback: Harper Torchbooks)

Becker, Carl L., *The Declaration of Independence, A Study of the History of Political Ideas.* New York: Harcourt, Brace, 1922. (Paperback: Vintage Books)

Labaree, Benjamin Woods, *The Boston Tea Party.* New York: Oxford University Press, 1964.

Nelson, William H., *The American Tory.* Oxford University Press, 1962. (Paperback: Beacon Press, 1964)

Palmer, R. R., *The Age of the Democratic Revolution: A Political History of Europe and America, 1760–1800.* Vol. I: *The Challenge.* Princeton: Princeton University Press, 1969.

Shy, John, *Toward Lexington: The Role of the British Army and the Coming of the American Revolution.* Princeton: Princeton University Press, 1965.

Zobel, Hiller B., *The Boston Massacre.* New York: W. W. Norton & Company, Inc., 1970.

UNIT FIVE

The New Nation

JOHN J. LYON

*Be a nation, be Americans, and
be true to yourselves . . .*

GEORGE WASHINGTON

1 Making of the Constitution

Crisis and Compromise

Introduction

The five years following ratification of the Peace Treaty in 1783 were extremely critical ones for the American people. Many of the same old issues which the colonies had disputed with Britain before 1776 became sources of disagreement and division between the newly-independent states. The end of the war did not bring prosperity to the new nation. It brought a period of political, economic, and social turmoil.

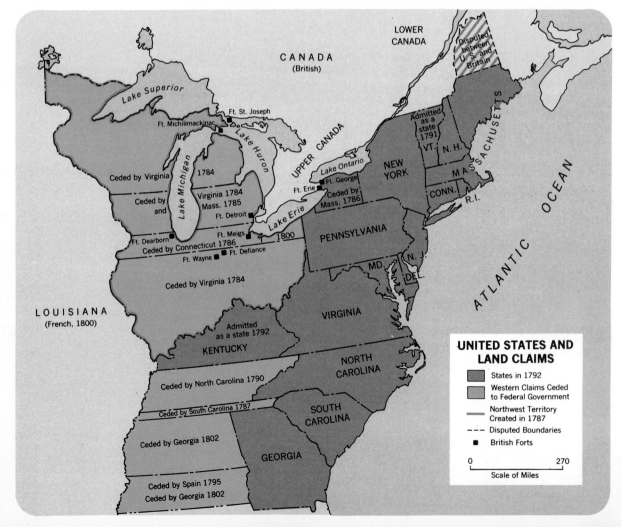

UNITED STATES AND LAND CLAIMS

- States in 1792
- Western Claims Ceded to Federal Government
- Northwest Territory Created in 1787
- – – – Disputed Boundaries
- ■ British Forts

0   270

Scale of Miles

The Critical Years

During the war Congress had borrowed large sums of money from foreign powers. *Robert Morris,** named Secretary of Finance in 1781, resigned in disgust in 1784 because Congress could not get the States to keep up even interest payments on the debt.

Before the war, American ships had freely entered ports in Britain and other parts of the empire. After 1783, Americans were no longer part of the empire, and British trade laws discriminated against them. They found themselves excluded from their once-profitable trade with the British West Indies. Without adequate power to regulate foreign commerce, Congress found it impossible to negotiate beneficial commercial treaties with *foreign nations.**

The Western Lands Controversy

The treaty of Paris in 1783 recognized the independence of the United States. It also gave the new nation control of all lands from the Atlantic coast west to the Mississippi, and from Canada to Spanish possessions in the Floridas and Louisiana.

Despite the explicit terms of the peace treaty, the British retained control of forts and fur-trading posts in lands north and west of the Ohio River. Congress was powerless to drive them out. In 1784, Spain closed the mouth of the Mississippi River to American commerce, and encouraged American frontiersmen to establish states in the west that would be dependent on Spain.

The American government tried to assert its claims to these western lands by settling and organizing them as quickly as possible. However, under colonial charters, many states claimed vast tracts of land west of the Appalachian Mountains. States without such claims—New Jersey, Rhode Island, Maryland, Delaware, New Hampshire and Pennsylvania—insisted that Congress be empowered to establish firm western boundaries of states with such claims. In fact, Maryland refused to ratify the Articles of Confederation until Virginia ceded her claims to lands north of the Ohio River to the central government.

Under the Articles of Confederation, Congress established a committee to deal with western lands, with Thomas Jefferson as chairman. In 1787 Congress passed an ordinance to organize the lands north and west of the Ohio River. Known as the Northwest Ordinance, this legislation provided for survey of lands and creation of state governments in this *territory.** Under the terms of the ordinance Congress guaranteed republican forms of government and prohibited slavery in all of the new states created out of the Northwest Territory. Under these terms the five states of Ohio, Indiana, Illinois, Michigan, and Wisconsin were eventually created. The Northwest Ordinance was the most significant achievement of the nation under the Articles of Confederation.

Internal Crisis

Not all of the new nation's difficulties were complicated by the interference of foreign powers. While commercial relations with foreign nations remained uncertain and Britain and Spain continued to interfere in the west, internal

Robert Morris (1734–1806): financier of the American Revolution, strengthened public credit, served as merchant marine agent for the Continental Congress, and as Senator from Pennsylvania after 1788.

Foreign countries believed they might have to negotiate **separate commercial treaties** with each state, rather than a single one with the United States.

Northwest Ordinance, 1787, provided that when there were 5,000 free adult males in a territory, a bicameral legislature would be established. When the population reached 60,000, the territory was eligible for admission to the Union on an equal footing with the original states.

problems were increasing. In June, 1783, approximately 100 veteran troops, in a mutinous mood over Congress' failure to pay them, actually drove the Congress out of Philadelphia. The next year Pennsylvania and Connecticut almost went to war over their conflicting claims to lands in the Wyoming Valley in eastern Pennsylvania.

Class differences broke out into social war in parts of Massachusetts. A post-war recession and increased taxes in some states caused great suffering among the poor. Land was often seized by the state when taxes on it were not paid, and those unable to make mortage payments sometimes found their property seized by their creditors. In 1786, in order to prevent such proceedings, small farmers and ex-soldiers unable to pay debts and taxes forced the courts to close in several western Massachusetts counties. Led by a former Revolutionary War soldier, Daniel Shays, one group organized as a guerrilla band and had to be dispersed by the State militia in early 1787.

Many Americans were becoming convinced that the successful revolution against Britain was being succeeded by *domestic anarchy.**

The Call for a New Constitution

Domestic: at home; here meaning one's own country.
Anarchy: absence of government; lawlessness and political disorder.

After a commercial conference between Maryland and Virginia in 1785, all the states were invited to a convention to discuss commercial problems. This convention opened at Annapolis, Maryland, on September 11, 1786, with delegates from only five states present. The delegates invited Congress to call a convention to discuss ways to make the Federal government strong enough to cope with the difficulties besetting the nation.

In February, 1787, Congress agreed to call a convention, but only for the purpose of amending the Articles of Confederation.

The Constitutional Convention

The Constitutional Convention opened in May, 1787, with a talented roster of delegates. They included George Washington (Virginia), who was named as its president; Benjamin Franklin (Pennsylvania); Alexander Hamilton (New York); *James Madison** and *Edmund Randolph** (also representing Virginia).

James Madison (1751–1836): author of several of **The Federalist Papers**, 1787–1788, and leader of the ratification forces in Virginia; introduced in Congress the first ten amendments to the Constitution; served as Jefferson's Secretary of State, 1801–1809, and as President of United States, 1809–1817.

Edmund Randolph (1753–1813) served as Attorney General and Secretary of State under President Washington.

The Convention went far beyond amending the Articles of Confederation. By September, 1787, it had drawn up a completely new form of government. The new constitution greatly strengthened the power of the central government. The Convention approved it and asked Congress to approve and submit it to the people of the states for ratification. Each state legislature was, in turn, to call a special convention of the people of its state to ratify or reject the new constitution.

The Process of Ratification

The issues raised by the proposed constitution were hotly debated. Two parties appeared. Those supporting a more powerful central government were called *Federalists*. Those championing the cause of states' rights and a weak central government were called *Anti-Federalists*.

B68

Despite heated controversies between Federalists and Anti-Federalists, conventions in nine states had ratified the new Constitution by June, 1788. Virginia and New York ratified within a month, but Rhode Island and North Carolina remained formally outside the Union until after the inauguration of Washington as the first President of the United States on April 30, 1789, in New York City. North Carolina formally ratified in November, 1789, and Rhode Island in May, 1790.

Washington addressing the delegates at the Constitutional Convention in Philadelphia

Compromise and the Constitution

The adoption of the Constitution and the rejection of the Articles of Confederation did not mean simply the exchange of a weak central government for a strong one. It was one of the most successful efforts ever devised to share governmental authority among several separate cooperating legislative bodies. The constitution was an experiment in *federalism** that succeeded.

Compromise was the life of the Constitution. Small states wanted a Federal legislature in which all the states had the same voting power. Large states wanted representation to be proportionate to population. The result was a two-house or bicameral legislature. In the upper house or Senate, each state had two votes; in the lower house or House of Representatives, representation was according to population.

Federalism: a system of government based on contracts between semi-sovereign institutions, in which each institution retains certain powers while giving up others.

B69

Some delegates wanted the Federal government to have strong taxing powers. Others feared that this power would allow the central government to discriminate against some state or sectional interests. In the end Congress was restricted to levying and collecting direct taxes only in proportion to population.

Some delegates wanted Congress to have strong control over commerce; others—particularly in the south—feared Congress's power to hurt the economy of one section of the country while helping that of another. In the end taxes on exports were prohibited and a two-thirds majority in the Senate was necessary to pass on commercial treaties.

Separation of Powers

The Constitution explicitly separated what was now called the Federal government into three branches—*legislative, executive,* and *judicial.* The powers of each branch of government were a check upon the powers of the other two. For example, Congress might pass a bill, but the President could veto it. Congress may then pass the same bill over the executive veto, but it must do so by a two-thirds majority of each house. Once a bill is enacted into law the Supreme Court has the power to decide whether such a law is constitutional or unconstitutional. If the court decides that a law is unconstitutional, the law becomes invalid. This process is called *judicial review.* The power of the Supreme Court is checked by the fact that the President appoints justices, with the advice and consent of the Senate. In addition the Senate has the power to *impeach** high officers of government such as the President or Justices of the Supreme Court. Finally, the Constitution can be amended when three-fourths of the states agree to do so.

Impeach: to charge a public official with misconduct in office and to try him before a competent tribunal; to convict and remove an official from office for misconduct.

The Bill of Rights

When the state legislatures drew up their constitutions after 1776, they included in them provisions designed to protect individuals against violations of their civil rights. Such provisions, usually called Bills of Rights, guaranteed to the citizen such things as freedom of speech and of the press, the right to jury trial, and security against unwarranted search or seizure of property.

These were all rights which Americans believed had been violated by Great Britain, and they insisted on protecting themselves against possible future violations by their own government. The new Federal Constitution, however, had no Bill of Rights, and many of those who opposed its adoption in 1787 and 1788 did so on the grounds that their indivdual liberties would be no more secure under the Constitution than under the British Parliament.

But the Constitution was a flexible instrument of government. It provided for a process of amendment. When the first Congress met in 1789, a "Bill of Rights" in the form of the first ten amendments was passed by Congress and subsequently ratified by three-fourths of the states in 1791. The new nation had a new government.

1 WE THE PEOPLE OR WE THE STATES?

All Americans agreed that the new Constitution provided a government that was quite different from what they had known under the Articles of Confederation. For some the new national Constitution appeared to be both incomplete and a step backward. It appeared incomplete because, unlike so many of the new state constitutions, when it was first adopted in 1788 it had no provisions guaranteeing traditional civil rights such as freedom of speech and assembly. The new Constitution appeared to be a step backward because the strong central government proposed in it seemed no different from the monarchical form against which the Revolutionary War had been fought.

Most Americans, however, felt a strong central government was necessary to avoid disorder and confusion in the country. The proposed new Constitution promised a national government strong enough to win respect abroad and to insure justice and prevent anarchy at home.

Famous and brilliant men argued both for and against the new Constitution. In a speech to the Virginia State Convention called in 1788 to ratify the new Constitution, the old patriot and orator, Patrick Henry (1736–1799), took the stand that the new government should be rejected. In a series of political letters written to New York newspapers in 1787 and 1788 and published later in a collection called The Federalist, the young hero of Yorktown, Alexander Hamilton (1755–1804), declared the new government should be adopted.

While studying passages from the Articles of Confederation, the Constitution, and the Bill of Rights, and reading selections from Henry's speech and Hamilton's contribution to The Federalist, keep in mind these questions:

1. According to the Articles, what was the basis of the Confederation of the United States? What powers did Congress have?

2. According to the Constitution, what was the basis of the union? What powers did Congress have?

3. Why does Patrick Henry **oppose** *the new Constitution?*

4. Why does Alexander Hamilton **support** *the new Constitution?*

5. Which Articles of the Bill of Rights are concerned with the rights of individuals? Which with the rights of states?

"We the States"?	"We the People"?
ARTICLES OF CONFEDERATION	CONSTITUTION OF THE UNITED STATES
Article III. The said states hereby severally enter into a firm league of friendship with each other, for their common defense, the security of their liberties, and their mutual and general welfare, binding themselves to assist each other, against all force offered to, or attacks made upon them, or any of them, on account of religion, sovereignty, trade, or any other pretense whatever.	We the people of the United States, in order to form a more perfect Union, establish justice, insure domestic tranquility, provide for the common defense, promote the general welfare, and secure the blessings of liberty to ourselves and our posterity, do ordain and establish this CONSTITUTION for the United States of America.

Article II. Each state retains its sovereignty, freedom and independence and every Power, Jurisdiction and right, which is not by this confederation expressly delegated to the United States, in Congress assembled.

Article I, Section 8. The Congress shall have the power. . . . To make all laws which shall be necessary and proper for carrying into execution . . . all . . . powers vested by this Constitution in the government of the United States. . . .

Article VI, Section 2. This Constitution, and the laws of the United States which shall be made in pursuance thereof, . . . shall be the supreme law of the land; and the judges in every State shall be bound thereby, any thing in the Constitution or laws of any State to the contrary notwithstanding.

Patrick Henry Argues against the New Constitution, 1788

Solicitude: care, attention.

Patrick Henry

Adapted from **Orations of American Orators** (New York: Collier & Son; 1900), pp. 62–64.

My political curiosity, exclusive of my anxious *solicitude** for the public welfare, leads me to ask who authorized them [the framers of the proposed constitution] to speak the language of "We, the People," instead of "We, the States?" States are the characteristics and the soul of a confederation. If the States be not the agents of this compact, it must be one great consolidated national government of the people of all the States. . . . The people gave them no power to use their name. That they exceedd their power is perfectly clear. Disorders have arisen in other parts of America, but here in Virginia all has been calm and tranquil.

The fate of America may depend on this question. Have they said, We, the States? Have they made a proposal of a compact between States? If they had, this would be a confederation: it is otherwise most clearly a consolidated government. The whole question turns, sir, on that poor little thing—the expression, We, the People, instead of the States of America. I need not take much pains to show, that the principles of this system are extremely pernicious, impolitic, and dangerous.

Here is a revolution as radical as that which separated us from Great Britain. It is as radical, if in this transition, our rights and privileges are endangered, and the sovereignty of the States relinquished. And cannot we plainly see that this is actually the case? The rights of conscience, trial by jury, liberty of the press, all your immunities and franchises, all pretensions to human rights and privileges, are rendered insecure, if not lost, by this change talked of so loudly by some, and inconsiderately by others. Is this same relinquishment of rights worthy of freemen? Is it worthy of that manly fortitude that ought to characterize republicans? It is said eight States have adopted this plan. I declare that if twelve States and a half had adopted it, I would, with manly firmness, and in spite of an erring world, reject it. . . .

Alexander Hamilton Argues for the New Constitution, 1787

A major weakness of our existing government is that it never was ratified by the PEOPLE. Resting on no better foundation than the consent of the several state legislatures, it has been exposed to frequent and *intricate** questions concerning the validity of its powers. Owing its ratification to the law of a State, some have contended that state legislatures might repeal the law by which the confederation was ratified. The possibility of a question of this nature arising proves the necessity of laying the foundations of our national government on something more firm than the mere consent of state legislatures. The fabric of American empire ought to rest on the solid basis of THE CONSENT OF THE PEOPLE. The streams of national power ought to flow immediately from that pure, original fountain of all legitimate authority.

Adapted from "Publius" (i.e., Alexander Hamilton), The Federalist No. 22 (originally from the **New York Packet**, Dec. 14, 1787).

Intricate: complicated, difficult

The Bill of Rights

ARTICLE I

Congress shall make no law respecting an establishment of religion, or prohibiting the free exercise thereof; or abridging the freedom of speech, or of the press; or the right of the people peaceably to assemble, and to petition the Government for a redress of grievances.

ARTICLE II

A well regulated militia, being necessary to the security of a free state, the right of the people to keep and bear arms shall not be infringed.

ARTICLE III

No soldier shall, in time of peace, be quartered in any house, without the consent of the owner; nor in time of war, but in a manner to be prescribed by law.

ARTICLE IV

The right of the people to be secure in their persons, houses, papers, and effects, against unreasonable searches and seizures, shall not be violated. . . .

ARTICLE V

No person shall be held to answer for a capital, or otherwise infamous crime, unless on a presentment or indictment of a grand jury . . . ; nor shall any person be subject for the same offense to be twice put in *jeopardy** . . . ; nor shall be compelled, in any criminal case, to be a witness against himself; nor be deprived of life, liberty, or property, without due process of law; nor shall private property be taken for public use, without just compensation.

Jeopardy: expose to death, danger, loss or injury.

ARTICLE VI

In all criminal prosecutions, the accused shall enjoy the right to a speedy and public trial, by an impartial jury . . . ; and to have the assistance of counsel for his defense.

ARTICLE VII

In suits at common law, . . . the right of trial by jury shall be preserved, and no fact tried by a jury shall be otherwise reexamined in any court of the United States than according to the rules of the common law.

ARTICLE VIII

Excessive bail shall not be required, nor excessive fines imposed, nor cruel and unusual punishments inflicted.

ARTICLE IX

The enumeration in the Constitution, of certain rights, shall not be construed to deny or disparage others retained by the people.

ARTICLE X

The powers not delegated to the United States by the Constitution, nor prohibited by it to the States, are reserved to the States respectively, or to the people.

2 INTERPRETING THE CONSTITUTION

The Constitution provided a framework for the Federal government of the United States. It also provided a body of political ideas for the guidance and proper functioning of that government. However, the Constitution did not and could not offer specific remedies for every possible governmental situation. Precisely what the Federal government could do or could not do in situations not specifically provided for in the Constitution was a problem which the new nation had to resolve.

One of these problems arose from post-war financial difficulties. Alexander Hamilton, President Washington's Secretary of the Treasury, proposed that a national bank be established to manage the financial relations of the Federal government. Since the Constitution said nothing about establishing a national bank or any other governmental corporation, the legality of Hamilton's proposal was challenged.

Washington asked for opinions from his cabinet about the constitutionality of the bank proposal. The responses of Thomas Jefferson, the Secretary of

At left, Alexander Hamilton; at right, Thomas Jefferson

The First Bank of the United States—Hamilton succeeded in persuading Congress in 1791 to charter a Bank of the United States with a capital of 10 million dollars.

State, and Alexander Hamilton went far beyond the question of whether a bank could be established or not. They raised the broader issue of how the Constitution should be interpreted and whether Congress could exercise powers that the Constitution had neither enumerated nor prohibited.

While reading these selections from the writings of Thomas Jefferson and Alexander Hamilton, keep in mind these questions:

1. *According to Jefferson, what is the <u>foundation</u> of the Constitution?*

2. *According to Hamilton, what is the <u>decisive</u> clause in the Constitution?*

3. *According to Jefferson, what does the Constitution allow Congress to do in order to carry out its enumerated powers?*

4. *According to Hamilton, what does the Constitution allow Congress to do in order to carry out its enumerated powers?*

Thomas Jefferson: Only Those Means Necessary, 1791

I consider the foundation of the Constitution as laid on this ground: that "all powers not delegated to the United States, by the Constitution, nor prohibited by it to the states, are reserved to the states, or to the people." To take a single step beyond the boundaries thus specially drawn around the powers of Congress, is to take possession of a boundless field of power, no longer *susceptible** of any definition.

✿   ✿   ✿   ✿   ✿

It would reduce the whole Constitution to a single phrase, that of instituting a Congress with power to do whatever would be for the good of the United States. And since Congress would be the sole judge of the good or evil, it would also have the power to do whatever evil it pleased.

Susceptible: receptive to any action or idea; not resisting outside stimulus or influence.

B75

The Constitution allows only the means which are "necessary," not those which are merely "convenient," for carrying out Congress's enumerated powers. The Constitution restrains Congress to the necessary means, that is to say, to those means without which the grant of power would be useless.

Can it be thought that the Constitution intended that, for a shade or two of convenience, Congress should be authorized to break down the most ancient and fundamental laws of the several states? Will Congress be too strait-laced to carry the Constitution into honest effect, unless they pass over the foundation-laws of the state governments, for their own convenience?

The veto of the President is the shield provided by the Constitution to protect against congressional invasion of the rights of the states. The case at hand involves a right that under the Constitution remains exclusively with the States. That right requires the protection of the Presidential veto.

Adapted from Albert E. Bergh, ed., **The Writings of Thomas Jefferson** (Washington: 1905), Vol. III, 146–152.

Alexander Hamilton: All Means Necessary, 1791

Premised: set forth at the start; taken for granted.

. . . In entering upon the argument it ought to be *premised** that the objections of the Secretary of State . . . are founded on a general denial of the [power of the] United States to erect corporations. . . .

Now it appears to the Secretary of the Treasury that this general principle of erecting corporations *is inherent* in the very definition of government, and *essential* to every step of the progress to be made by the United States. Every power vested in a government is in its nature sovereign, that is, it includes a right to employ all *means* necessary for the effective use of such power. The only limitations are those specified in the Constitution, those which are immoral, or those which are contrary to the *essential ends* of political society. . . .

If it would be necessary to bring proof to a proposition so clear, there is a clause of the Constitution which would be decisive. It is that which declares that the Constitution, and the laws of the United States made in pursuance of it, shall be the **supreme law of the land.** The power which can create a supreme law of the land, in any case, is doubtless sovereign in this case.

It is essential to the being of the national government, that the Secretary of State's conception of the meaning of the word *necessary* should be exploded.

It is certain that the word necessary often means no more than needful, requisite, incidental, useful, or conducive to, and this is the true sense in which the word is to be understood as used in the Constitution. Congress is empowered to make all *laws* necessary and proper for *carrying into execution* all powers vested by the Constitution in the *government* of the United States.*

See **Article I,** Section 8, paragraph 18 of the Constitution on **Powers Delegated to Congress,** page B127.

To understand the word *necessary* as the Secretary of State does would be to depart from its obvious and popular sense, and to give it a restrictive meaning—an idea never before entertained. The case at hand is not forbidden by any particular provision of the Constitution, and therefore may be safely undertaken by the Congress.

Adapted from Henry C. Lodge, ed., **The Works of Alexander Hamilton** (New York: 1885), III, pp. 180–192.

2 George Washington: man and legend

Charismatic Leader

Introduction

In nations new or old, the success of government and even the survival of the nation itself depends as much on the character of its leaders as on its natural resources and political institutions. Americans had natural resources aplenty and political institutions inherited from four hundred years of English constitutional development. The leaders of the new nation were their own, drawn largely from the same families that had given the colonies legislators, lawyers, planters, and merchants for the previous hundred years.

After 1783, had it not been for leaders of vision and ability, the United States might have fallen into civil war or disintegrated and been absorbed by Britain, France, or Spain. In truth, the leaders of the new nation had to be more than men of vision and ability. They had to be *charismatic,** possessed with qualities of personal magnetism that inspired confidence and respect. George Washington was such a man.

Although Washington was not the only charismatic leader of the Revolutionary generation, he was outstanding among them. Henry Lee of Virginia (1756–1818) summed up Washington's role in his country's history by describing him as, "first in war, first in peace and first in the hearts of his countrymen." The country had turned to Washington in 1775 to command its armies against Britain. The new nation turned once again to him for guidance and leadership through the first eight years of its life under the new Constitution.

Born February 22, 1732, in Westmoreland County, Virginia, Washington became an officer in the Virginia militia and served his colony with distinction during the French and Indian War. After holding several local offices in Virginia, Washington was named as a delegate to both the First and Second Continental Congresses. On June 15, 1775, the Second Continental Congress chose him as Commander-in-Chief of the Continental Army.

In December, 1784, with independence finally secured, Washington resigned his commission to Congress and went into what he hoped would be a peaceful retirement at his plantation, Mount Vernon. But five years later the nation called him to its service once more, unanimously choosing him first President of the United States under the new Constitution.

Washington survived the rigors of two full terms in that office, and then retired once more to Mount Vernon. His retirement was interrupted in 1798

Objectives of this assignment are to:
—Analyze a selection of contemporary accounts of George Washington's character and leadership.
—Draw inferences from a filmstrip of portraits of George Washington about the emotions and feelings which his achievements inspired.
—Identify problems encountered in making historical judgments on great national heroes.

Charisma comes from a Greek word meaning a quality or qualities which inspire confidence in a leader.

Historic Mount Vernon—Nellie Custis, left, with Martha and George Washington stroll on the verdant green lawns (the bowling green) of the Washington plantation in Virginia. The line drawings show how George Washington added to his estate until it became the Mount Vernon we know today. At the top left is Washington's bedroom which is viewed by hundreds of thousands of tourists each year.

1776

1778

1785

1787

by a call to service as the nation edged toward war with France. President John Adams made him Commander-in-Chief of the nation's armed forces once again. But war with France was avoided. He died at Mount Vernon, December 13, 1799.

3 WASHINGTON AS SEEN BY CONTEMPORARIES: MAN AND LEADER

Great men are almost invariably complex men. They appear in different lights to different people. An observer's training and background, as well as his relationship with the great man, largely determine how the observer views him. Military officers may be struck by one aspect of a man's character, whereas politicians or personal friends may be impressed by others. Good relationships with a great man may lead an observer to one sort of judgment of his character, while strained or unfriendly encounters may lead to another.

Three men who knew and observed Washington at different periods of his life have left detailed accounts of him. George Mercer knew Washington as a young officer during the French and Indian War. The Abbé Robin observed Washington while serving with the French Army in America in 1781. And Senator William Maclay of Pennsylvania recalls Washington during the early years of his first term as President.

While reading these three accounts, keep in mind the following questions:

1. According to Mercer, what kind of an appearance did Washington make in 1760?

2. According to Maclay, what kind of appearance did Washington make in 1789?

3. According to Robin, what qualities set Washington apart from most other men?

George Mercer Describes George Washington, 1760

I would describe Colonel George Washington, late Commander of Virginia Provincial Troops, as being as straight as an Indian, measuring six feet two inches in his stockings, and weighing 175 pounds when he took his seat in the House of Burgesses in 1759. His frame is padded with well-developed muscles, indicating great strength. His bones and joints are large, as are his feet and hands. He is wide shouldered, but has not a deep or round chest; Washington is *neat** waisted, broad across the hips, and has rather long legs and arms. His head is well shaped though not large, but is gracefully poised on a superb neck. His nose is large and straight rather than prominent. He has blue-gray penetrating eyes, which are widely separated and overhung by a

Neat: trim.

Countenance: appearance, or expression.

Cue here means queue, or braided hair.

Adapted from W. S. Baker, ed., Early Sketches of George Washington . . . (Philadelphia, 1894), pp. 13–14.

heavy brow. His face is long rather than broad, with high round cheek bones. He has a clear though rather a colorless pale skin, which burns with the sun, a pleasing benevolent, commanding *countenance,** and dark brown hair which he wears in a *cue.** His mouth is large and generally firmly closed, but sometimes discloses some defective teeth. In conversation he looks you full in the face and is deliberate and engaging. His voice is agreeable rather than strong. He is at all times composed and dignified. His movements and gestures are graceful, his walk is majestic, and he is a splendid horseman.

A United States Senator Describes George Washington, 1789

The Vice-President rose and addressed a short sentence to the President, indicating that he should now take the oath of office. He seemed to have forgot half what he was to say, for he made a dead pause and stood for some time in a vacant mood. The business done was communicated to the crowd by proclamation. The crowd gave three cheers, and repeated it on the President's bowing to them.

As the company returned into the Senate chamber, the President took the chair and the Senators and Representatives took their seats. He rose and addressed them. This great man was more agitated and embarrassed than he ever was by the leveled cannon or pointed musket. He trembled, and several times could scarce make out to read, though it must be supposed he often read it before. When he came to the words all the world, he made a flourish with his right hand, which left an ungainly impression. I sincerely wished that this first of men had read off his address in the plainest manner, without ever taking his eyes from the paper, for I felt hurt that he was not first in everything. He was dressed in deep brown with white stockings and carried a sword.

✦   ✦   ✦   ✦   ✦

It was a great dinner, and the best of the kind I ever was at. The room, however, was disagreeably warm. It was also the most solemn dinner ever I sat at. Not a toast was drunk and scarce a word was said until the table cloth was taken away. Then the President, filling a glass of wine, with great formality drank to the health of every individual by name round the table. Everybody imitated him, *charged glasses,** and there was a great buzz of "health, sir," and "health, madam," and "thank you, sir," and "thank you, madam." The ladies sat with us a good while. The bottles were passed about, but there was almost a dead silence. At last, Mrs. Washington withdrew with the ladies.

Charged glasses: that is, filled their glasses with wine.

I expected that now the men would begin to talk, but the same stillness remained. The President told a funny story about a New England clergyman who had lost a hat and wig while crossing a river called the Brunks. He smiled, and everybody else laughed. He now and then said a sentence or two on some common subject, and what he said was not amiss. When the table cloth was taken away the President kept a fork in his hand which I thought was for the purpose of picking nuts. He ate no nuts, however, but played with the fork, striking the edge of the table with it. We did not sit long after the ladies retired. The President rose, went up-stairs to drink coffee; the rest of the company followed. I took my hat and went home.

Quoted from **Journal of William Maclay, United States Senator from Pennsylvania 1789-1791** edited by Edgar S. Maclay, A. M. (New York: D. Appleton and Company, 1890), pp. 8-9, 137-138, 375.

A French Army Chaplain Describes George Washington, 1781

I saw Washington, the man who is the soul and support of one of the greatest revolutions that has ever happened! I gazed at him earnestly with the eagerness that is always aroused by the presence of great men. One may find in the features of such men the marks of the genius which sets them apart and places them above all others.

More than any other man Washington's features reveal the kind of man he is. He is tall, noble and well-proportioned. He has an open, kind, and calm expression, an appearance that is simple and modest but striking. He impresses everyone, friends as well as enemies.

As the head of a nation in which every individual shares in the supreme power, he knew how to impress upon his soldiers an absolute subordination and make them eager to deserve his praise. They feared even his silence. He knew how to keep up their confidence even after defeats and showed himself at all times able to find new resources in the face of adversity.

Fearless in the midst of dangers, he sought danger only when the good of the country was at stake. He chose to *temporize** and to remain on the defensive because he believed that time was on his side. He was thrifty and moderate in his own affairs, but spent money lavishly for the common cause. He conquered without fighting, and saved his country.

Temporize means to delay or postpone action.

Through all the land he appears like a benevolent god. Old men, women, children all flock eagerly to catch a glimpse of him when he travels and congratulate themselves because they have seen him. People carrying torches follow him through the cities. His arrival is marked by public demonstrations. Though Americans are a cold people who even in the midst of troubles have always tended to control their emotions, they have grown enthusiastic about Washington and have glorified him in both story and song.

Nouveau Voyage dans l' Amerique Septentrionale, en l'armee 1781: Par M. l'Abbe Robin (Philadelphia and Paris, Montard: 1782), pp. 61-64.

4 WASHINGTON AS SEEN BY CONTEMPORARIES: GENERAL AND PRESIDENT

Great men are not only complex; they are also controversial. Anyone spending a lifetime in politics will make enemies as certainly as he will make friends.

Two men who knew Washington as a politician were Thomas Paine and Thomas Jefferson. Paine had known Washington during the war and followed his career closely.

While in France during that country's revolution, Paine was imprisoned. Believing that Washington had betrayed him by not intervening with the French government on his behalf, Paine wrote his famous public letter to George Washington shortly after being released from a French jail.

Thomas Jefferson had known Washington and served with him in a variety of capacities for more than twenty years. During Washington's second term as President, Jefferson became the spokesman for the political opposition to Washington's party. In a letter written in 1814, fifteen years after Washington's death, Jefferson made a general evaluation of Washington's character and historical importance. While reading these selections from the accounts of Paine and Jefferson, keep in mind these questions:

1. *What was Paine's judgment of Washington as a general?*
2. *What was Paine's judgment of Washington as a President?*
3. *What was Jefferson's judgment of Washington as a general?*
4. *What was Jefferson's judgment of Washington as a President?*

Thomas Paine on George Washington, 1796

Had it not been for the aid received from France in men, money and ships, your cold and unmilitary conduct would, in all probability, have lost America. You slept away your time in the field till the finances of the country were completely exhausted, and you have but little share in the glory of the final event. It is time, sir, to speak the undisguised language of historical truth.

When we speak of military character, something more is understood than constancy; and something more **ought** to be understood than simply doing nothing. The successful skirmishes at the close of one campaign—matters that would scarcely be noticed in a better state of things—comprise the brilliant exploits of General Washington. No wonder we see so much *irresolution** in the President when we see so little enterprize in the General.

Elevated to the chair of the Presidency, you assumed the merit of every thing to yourself, and the natural ingratitude of your constitution began to appear. You commenced your presidential career by encouraging and swallowing the *grossest adulation,** and you travelled America from one end to the other, to put yourself in the way of receiving it.

It has for some time been known, by those who know you that you have no friendships; that you are incapable of forming any; you can serve or desert a man or a cause with cold blooded indifference; and it is this cold unfeeling faculty that has imposed itself on the world, and was credited for a while by enemies as by friends, for prudence, moderation, and impartiality.

The character which you have attempted to act in the world, is a sort of non-describable, *cameleon-coloured** thing called prudence. It is, in many cases, a substitute for principle, and is so nearly allied to hypocrisy, that it easily slides into it.

Irresolution: uncertainty as to how to act.

Grossest adulation: excessive flattery.

Cameleon-coloured means changing colors like a chameleon. A chameleon is a lizard that has the ability to take on the color of its surroundings.

B82

As to you, Sir, treacherous in private friendship, and a hypocrite in public life, the world will be puzzled to decide, whether you are an *apostate** or an *impostor;** whether you have abandoned good principles, or whether you ever had any?

Adapted from **A Letter to George Washington** . . . by Thomas Paine, Philadelphia, Benjamin Franklin Bache, 1796.

Thomas Jefferson on George Washington, 1814

I think I knew General Washington intimately and thoroughly; and were I called on to *delineate** his character, it should be in terms like these.

His mind was great and powerful, without being of the very first order. His penetration strong, though not so acute as that of a *Newton, Bacon,* or *Locke.** His judgment was slow in operation, being little aided by invention or imagination, but sure in conclusion. Hence the common remark of his officers, of the advantage he derived from councils of war, where hearing all suggestions, he selected whatever was best. Certainly no General ever planned his battles more judiciously. But if *deranged** during the course of the action, if any part of his plan was dislocated by sudden circumstances, he was slow in readjustment. The consequence was that he often failed in the field, but rarely against an entrenched enemy as at Boston and York. He was incapable of fear, meeting personal dangers with the calmest unconcern.

Perhaps the strongest feature in his character was prudence, never acting until every circumstance, every consideration, was maturely weighed. He hesitated if he had a doubt, but when once decided, he went through with his purpose, whatever obstacles opposed. His integrity was most pure; his justice the most inflexible I have ever known. No motives of interest or *consanguinity,** of friendship or hatred, were able to bias his decision. He was indeed, in every sense of the words, a wise, a good, and a great man.

His temper was naturally high toned, but he kept it well under control. If ever, however, it broke its bonds, he was most tremendous in his wrath. In his expenses he was honorable, but exact; liberal in contributions to whatever promised utility; but frowning and unyielding on all visionary projects and all unworthy calls on his charity.

His heart was not warm in its affections; but he exactly calculated every man's value, and gave him a solid esteem proportioned to it. His person, you know, was fine, his stature exactly what one would wish, his *deportment** easy, erect, and noble; the best horseman of his age, and the most graceful figure that could be seen on horseback. Although in the circle of his friends, where he might be unreserved with safety, he took a free share in conversation, his *colloquial talents** were not above mediocrity, possessing neither copiousness of ideas, nor fluency of words. In public, when called on for a sudden opinion, he was unready, short and embarrassed.

On the whole, his character was, in its mass, perfect. In nothing was it bad, and in few points was it indifferent. His was the singular destiny and merit, of leading the armies of his country successfully through an arduous war, for the establishment of its independence. He conducted its councils through the birth of a government, new in its forms and principles until it

Apostate: one who has renounced his former faith.

Impostor: one who pretends to be someone or something which he is not.

Delineate: draw or describe.

Isaac Newton (1642–1727), **Francis Bacon** (1561–1627), and **John Locke** (1632–1704) were English philosophers and scientists.

Deranged: as used here, it means if Washington's plan of operation of the war was upset by circumstances which forced change.

Consanguinity: relationship by blood.

Deportment: behavior or conduct; also, bearing or posture.

Colloquial talents: conversational ability.

Scrupulous: ethically strict.

had settled down into a quiet and orderly train. The history of the world furnishes no other example of so *scrupulous** an obedience to the laws as he gave through the whole of his civil and military career.

He has often declared to me that he considered our new constitution as an experiment on the practicability of republican government, and on how much liberty man could be trusted with for his own good. He was determined that this experiment should have a fair trial, and pledged the last drop of his blood in support of it. I do not believe that General Washington was firmly convinced that our government would last. He was naturally distrustful of men and inclined to gloomy apprehensions. I am persuaded that he expected we must at length end in something like a British constitution. For that reason he adopted the ceremonies of *levees*,* birth-days, pompous meetings with Congress, and other forms of the same character, calculated to prepare us gradually for a change which he believed possible, and to let it come on with as little shock as might be to the public mind.

Levee: a formal reception.

These are my opinions of General Washington, which I would swear at the judgment seat of God, having been formed on an acquaintance of thirty years. I felt on his death, with my countrymen, that "verily a great man hath fallen this day in Israel."

Adapted from Jefferson to Dr. Walter Jones, Monticello, January 2, 1814, Paul Leicester Ford, ed., **The Writings of Thomas Jefferson** (New York: Knickerbocker Press, 1898), Vol. IX, pp. 448–451.

Napoleon's Tribute to Washington

Order of the Day to the Consular Guard and All Soldiers of the French Republic

Washington is dead. This great man fought against tyranny and established the liberty of his country. His memory will always be dear to the people of France, as it will be to all free men of both hemispheres. This is particularly so since, like him and the American soldiers, French soldiers are fighting for equality and liberty.

The first Consul therefore orders, that, during ten days, black crepe shall be suspended from all the flags and guidons throughout the French Republic.

Paris, Pluviose 18, Year 8.

Adapted from **Moniteur.** Feb. 6, 1800.

12

The Young Washington, 1760, in his
Virginia Militia Uniform
Portrait by Charles Willson Peale (1772)

The Pennsylvania Academy of Fine Arts

Washington and Lee University

13

The General of the Revolution,
1781

George Washington at **Princeton**
by Charles Willson Peale

14

Washington: The Image of a Hero, 1784

Bust by Jean Antoine Houdon
Courtesy of the Boston Athenaeum

Independence National Historical Park

15

Washington Presiding Over the
Signing of the Constitution, 1787

Painting by Thomas Rossiter

Courtesy of the Henry Francis du Pont Winterthur Museum

3 The new nation consolidates and grows

Foreign Policy, 1788–1823

France was a much more powerful and aggressive nation than Spain.

Under the leadership of Toussaint L'Ouverture the black people of **Haiti** won their **independence from France** in 1804 by forcing surrender of a French army. All slaves were freed and whites were killed or driven out of the country.

Introduction

Once ratification of the new constitution had given the new nation domestic peace, foreign affairs became the dominant issue facing the American people.

After 1788, commercial expansion, cultural growth, and national security required the establishment and maintenance of diplomatic relations with many nations. In the decades after ratification of the Constitution, our relations with four of these nations—Spain, Russia, England, and France—were most critical.

European Wars and American Expansion

In 1789, a year after the adoption of the United States Constitution, a revolution broke out in France which was to reshape the government of that nation and to involve it in almost constant warfare with Great Britain and other European nations from 1793 to 1815. Great Britain gradually swept the French navy and merchant vessels from the seas. France destroyed the armies of British allies in Europe and came to control virtually all of the continent south of the Baltic Sea and west of Russia. The United States was slowly drawn into this great international struggle.

In 1799 Napoleon Bonaparte became First Consul of France and in 1805 Emperor of the French. As part of a plan for rebuilding a French Empire in America, he forced Spain in 1800 to cede back to France the Louisiana Territory which Spain had acquired in 1763. French reoccupation of New Orleans presented a much *greater threat** to the United States than had Spanish occupation.

But fortunately for the new nation, Napoleon's plans for a new world empire were more than he could carry out. After the failure of a French army to subdue a black rebellion in *Haiti** discouraged Napoleon, he agreed to sell the entire Louisiana Territory to the United States for approximately $15,000,000. Thus at one stroke in 1803 the territorial size of the United States doubled. The Louisiana Purchase was the greatest bargain in American History. However, in 1803 it appeared that the United States had bought a scrap of paper. No one was certain Napoleon could deliver territory controlled by Spain. Nevertheless, within a month of the agreement a Spanish governor handed Louisiana over to a French prefect, who immediately transferred it to the United States.

Spain in America

In 1788, the United States was bounded on the south and west by Spanish Florida and Louisiana. Fearing expansionist tendencies of the United States, the Spanish encouraged Indians living within United States boundaries to resist American penetration of the frontier.

They hoped to create Indian buffer states between their own possessions and American settlements. Thus the question of Indian relations on the western and southern frontiers became part of the larger problem of European conduct and diplomacy.

The *Spanish cession** of Louisiana to France and the later French sale of it to the United States removed French and Spanish influence from the western frontier and gave the United States control of the mouth of the Mississippi.

By the secret **treaty of San Ildefonso,** October 1, 1800, Spain returned Louisiana to France.

After Napoleon's armies occupied Spain in 1808, Spanish control over the rest of her new world possessions was weakened. Beginning in 1810 a series of revolutions broke out in Spanish America from Mexico to Argentina. These revolutions ultimately destroyed the Spanish empire and established Latin American independence.

West Florida was *occupied** by the United States in 1810. Nine years later Spain ceded her claim in East Florida to the United States for a small sum. By 1823 Spain had been removed as a great power in the new world.

American settlers led a revolt and established an independent republic in West Florida. President Madison then proclaimed the region part of the United States.

Russia in America

British and American vessels had charted parts of the coast of the Pacific northwest by 1792, and explorers of both nations had travelled overland to what was known later as the *Oregon Territory* by 1806.*

Russian fur traders, explorers, and missionaries had crossed the Bering Strait from Siberia earlier in the eighteenth century and had established themselves in Alaska. From there they built a chain of fur-trading posts as far south as Bodega Bay near present-day San Francisco. Because of the great distance from American settlements, the Russian presence in North America was not a threatening one. However, on September 4, 1821, the Czar of Russia officially claimed as Russian territory lands as far south as Vancouver Island and excluded the shipping of other nations from the surrounding waters. This action appeared to threaten the young republic and it could not be ignored.

For the **Americans,** Captain Robert **Gray** entered the mouth of the Columbia River by sea in 1792. Meriwether **Lewis** and William **Clark** reached the Pacific Ocean overland in 1805. For the British, Captain James Cook explored the Oregon Territory in 1778, and Captain George Vancouver did the same in 1792. Sir Alexander Mackenzie reached the Pacific coast overland in 1793.

The American Secretary of State, John Quincy Adams, responded to this sweeping Russian claim by asserting that the new world was no longer open to colonization. This principle of closing the Americas to future European colonization was restated two years later in *President Monroe's* famous message to Congress.*

Under a treaty signed in 1824 Russia agreed to limit her territorial claims to what is now the southern coastal boundary of Alaska and remove restrictions on shipping in the area.

President Monroe's message to Congress on December 2, 1823, stated the principle of closing America to future European colonization and became known as the **Monroe Doctrine.**

Britain and France

Though Spain and Russia presented only minor problems for the new nation in the period 1788 to 1823, this was not the case with Britain and France. When war broke out between those two countries in 1793, the United States had a treaty of alliance with France, binding us to defend French possessions in the West Indies against British attack.

American opinion was sharply divided over what our treaty obligations involved. One group, largely New England Federalists, insisted that all treaty obligations to France were cancelled when the French Revolutionaries overthrew the monarchy. Furthermore, the commercial interests of New England strongly favored closer and friendlier relations with Britain.

Another group, largely *Democratic-Republicans,** from the south and west, believed that our treaty obligations to France ought to be maintained. They were sympathetic to the French Revolution and to the Republican forms of government it had established.

Wanting to steer a middle course between two extremes, President Washington issued a Neutrality Proclamation on April 22, 1793. In this proclamation, the word neutrality was not actually used. Washington declared that the United States was at peace with both Britain and France, and American citizens were cautioned to avoid acts of hostility toward either country.

Democratic-Republicans: followers of Thomas Jefferson who organized themselves as a political party to oppose the Federalists during the 1790's.

The Perils of Neutrality

During their long life and death struggle, 1793–1815, both Britain and France violated American rights as neutrals. Angered by French interference with American shipping, Congress in 1798 revoked the old French alliance. An "undeclared" naval war was fought against the French by American vessels during 1798–1800.

But a much more serious threat to American shipping was presented by Britain, whose control of the seas gave her greater opportunity to *harass** American trade. The British seized American cargoes destined for French ports and *impressed** American sailors for duty in the Royal Navy. For example, on June 22, 1807, the British frigate *Leopard* attempted to impress four sailors from the American frigate *Chesapeake* off Norfolk. When the *Chesapeake* refused to give up the sailors, the *Leopard* opened fire, killing and wounding several Americans and taking the four sailors.

British interference in American affairs was not limited to naval actions. Although the British had evacuated their former forts in the Northwest territory, they continued to influence Indian politics in that region. In fact when an Indian uprising in 1811 was suppressed by American troops, the great Shawnee chief, *Tecumseh,** fled to the British in Canada and fought with them against the Americans in the War of 1812.

Presidents Jefferson (1801–1809) and Madison (1809–1817) tried various policies to avoid a showdown with either of the *belligerents.** But America was treated with disdain by both nations and her rights were disregarded.

Tecumseh (1768–1813), Shawnee Chief and British ally, formed a confederation of Indians in the Northwest territory to resist American expansion.

Harass: to worry or annoy.

Impress: to take by force for military or naval service.

Belligerents: nations at war, France and Britain

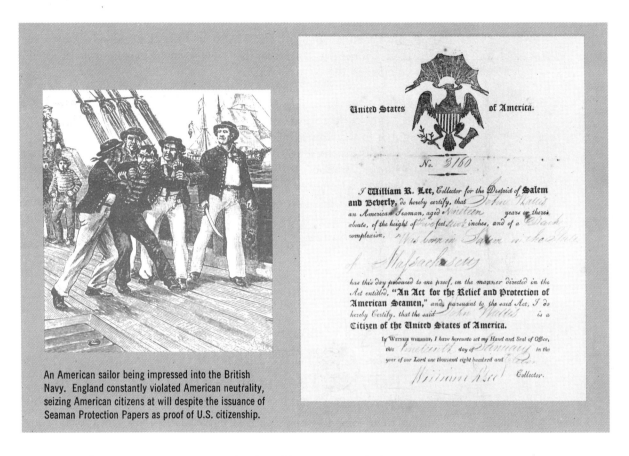

An American sailor being impressed into the British Navy. England constantly violated American neutrality, seizing American citizens at will despite the issuance of Seaman Protection Papers as proof of U.S. citizenship.

America had no army or navy to defend itself. It appeared that American independence was purely *nominal** and that America was destined to become a dependent of the victor of the great war in Europe.

Under these circumstances, war was inevitable. The only question was: who would the new nation go to war against—Britain or France? The question was answered in 1812, when the United States went to war against Britain. With the exception of a few brilliant naval encounters and Andrew Jackson's victory at New Orleans there was little military distinction for American arms during the war. A treaty signed in December, 1814, brought the war to an end with no changes in territorial boundaries and few major issues settled.

The Monroe Doctrine

After the overthrow of *Napoleon** in 1814 and the restoration of the Bourbon monarchy in France, the European nations tried to turn back the clock to the way things were before 1789. A *Holy Alliance,** consisting of Russia, Prussia, Austria, and France committed itself to suppressing revolutions wherever they might appear. Revolutions were crushed by the Alliance in

Nominal: in name only; symbolic.

Napoleon was exiled to the Mediterranean Island of Elba. He returned to France in 1815 and ruled the country for 100 days. He was finally defeated by a British and Prussian army at Waterloo in Belgium, June 18, 1815.

The **Holy Alliance** was formed on September 26, 1815, by Czar Alexander I of Russia, as a kind of religious brotherhood of monarchs. Austria and Prussia joined first, later followed by other European monarchs.

Italy in 1821 and in Spain in 1823. Also in 1823 these allied powers even considered suppressing by force the newly-won independence of Spain's former colonies in the New World.

Both Britain and the United States were horrified by such a prospect. Britain wanted her profitable trade with the new Latin American states to continue. The United States did not want another strong European power as a neighbor in the New World.

In the face of this challenge from Europe, and knowing the British position, President James Monroe (1817–1825) devoted a section of his annual message to Congress, December 2, 1823, to a declaration of United States opposition to any future European colonization of the New World. The Monroe Doctrine became the keystone of the New Nation's foreign policy. There was room enough for only one great power in the new world. It was to be the United States.

5 THOMAS JEFFERSON ON THE PROSPECTS FOR WAR AND PEACE, 1802–1812

During the presidency of Thomas Jefferson, 1801–1812, the United States became increasingly affected by the war in Europe. Relations with both France and Britain at one time or another reached the breaking point. French acquisition of Louisiana and the port of New Orleans in 1801 was regarded as an intolerable threat to American security and prosperity. The British attack on the American warship *Chesapeake* in 1807 aroused a wave of anti-British feeling throughout the country.

Both Jefferson and his successor in office, James Madison, had to respond very quickly to rapid changes in the international situation. Deciding whether France or Britain posed a greater threat to American interests was not easy. Past relationships and old fears were no help. Present realities and future possibilities had to be carefully considered.

While reading these selections from the writings of Thomas Jefferson, keep in mind these questions. According to Jefferson:

1. How will French acquisition of New Orleans affect American foreign policy?

2. What has brought the United States and Britain to the verge of war in 1807?

3. How should the United States fight a war with Britain?

Thomas Jefferson and the Prospect for Peace, 1802

The cession of Louisiana by Spain to France works most sorely on the United States. On this subject the *Secretary of State** has written to *you** fully. Yet I cannot forbear referring to it personally, so deep is the impression it makes in my mind. It completely reverses all the political relations of the United States and will form a new epoch in our political course. Of all nations of any consideration France is the one which hitherto has offered the fewest points on which we could have any conflict of right, and the most points of a communion of interests. From these causes we have ever looked to her as our *natural friend,* as one with which we never could have an occasion of difference. Her growth, therefore, we viewed as our own; her misfortunes, ours.

There is on the globe one single spot, the possessor of which is our natural and habitual enemy. It is New Orleans, through which the produce of three-eighths of our territory must pass to market, and from its fertility it will ere long yield more than half of our whole produce and contain more than half our inhabitants. By placing herself in that door, France assumes an attitude of defiance toward us. Spain might have retained New Orleans quietly for years. Her pacific disposition, her feeble state, would induce her to increase our facilities there, so that her possession of the place would be hardly felt by us. It would not perhaps be very long before some circumstance might arise which might encourage Spain to cede it to us in exchange for something of more worth to her. Not so can it ever be in the hands of France. It is impossible that France and the United States can long continue friends when they meet in so irritable a position. They, as well as we, must be blind if they do not see this; and we must be very *improvident** if we do not begin to make arrangements on that hypothesis. From the day that France takes possession of New Orleans we must marry ourselves to the British fleet and nation.

James Madison was the Secretary of State. The letter to which Jefferson refers was written by Madison to **Robert R. Livingston,** United States Minister to France.

Improvident: not providing for the future.

Adapted from Paul Leiscester Ford, ed. **Writings of Thomas Jefferson** (New York: Putnam's Sons, 1897), Vol. VIII, pp. 144–145.

Thomas Jefferson and the Prospect for Peace, 1807

*You** will receive information of the critical situation in which we are with England. An *outrage** not to be borne has obliged us to fly to arms, and has produced such a unanimous state of exasperation, as never has been seen in this country since the battle of Lexington. We have between 2000 and 3000 men on the shores of the Chesapeake, patrolling them for the protection of the country, and for preventing supplies of any kind being furnished to the British; and the moment our gun-boats are ready we shall endeavor by force to expel them from our waters. We now send a vessel to call upon the British government for reparation for the past outrage, and security for the future. Nor will anything be deemed security but a renunciation of the practice of taking persons out of our vessels, under the pretence of their being English. Congress will be called some time in October, by which time we may have an

Jefferson was writing to **John Armstrong,** United States Minister to France.

The **outrage** was the attack by the British frigate **Leopard** on the American frigate **Chesapeake,** June 22, 1807.

Adapted from Paul Leicester Ford, ed., Writings of Thomas Jefferson, Vol. IX, pp. 116–17.

answer from England. In the meantime we are preparing for a state of things which will take that course, which either the pride or the justice of England shall give it. I think she will find that there is not a nation on the globe which can gall her so much as we can.

Thomas Jefferson to General Thaddeus *Kosciusko** on the Prospects for War, 1812

Kosciusko (1746–1817) was a Polish patriot and volunteer in Washington's army during the American Revolution. He was Colonel of engineers.

Jefferson's first sentence in French translates: "We are now, my good friend, at war with England."

Iniquity: gross injustice or wickedness.

*Nous voila donc, mon cher ami, en guerre avec l'Angleterre.** This was declared on the 18th of June, thirty years after the signature of our peace in 1782. Within these thirty years what a vast course of growth and prosperity we have had! It is not ten years since Great Britain began a series of insults and injuries which would have been met with war by any European power. Britain's actions would not have been borne so long, but that France has kept pace with England in *iniquity** of principle, although not in the power of inflicting wrongs on us. The difficulty of selecting a foe between them has spared us many years of war, and enabled us to enter into it with less debt, more strength and preparation. Our present enemy will have the sea to herself, while we shall be equally predominant on land, and shall strip her of all her possessions on this continent. She may burn New York, indeed, by her ships and rockets, in which case we must burn the city of London by *hired*

Hired incendiaries: arsonists or "firebugs."

*incendiaries,** of which her starving manufacturers will furnish abundance. . . . Hunger will make them brave every risk for bread. The partisans of England here have endeavored much to goad us into the folly of choosing the ocean instead of the land, for the theatre of war. That would be to meet their strength with our own weakness, instead of their weakness with our strength. I hope we shall confine ourselves to the conquest of their possessions, and defence of our harbors, leaving the war on the ocean to our privateers. These will immediately swarm in every sea, and do more injury to British commerce than the regular fleets of all Europe would do. . . . We have nothing to fear from their armies, and shall put nothing in prize to their fleets. Upon the whole, I have known no war entered into under more favorable auspices.

Adapted from Paul Leicester Ford, ed. Writings of Thomas Jefferson, Vol. IX, pp. 361–62.

6   CRISIS AND WAR, 1810–1815

For the second time in a generation the United States went to war with Britain. Though generally popular in the South and West, the war was strongly opposed by many, especially in New England and coastal towns.

American war aims were confused and varied. Commercial interests sought an end to British interference with American shipping. Westerners blamed the British in Canada and the Spanish in East Florida for Indian troubles on the frontier and saw the war as an opportunity to seize both of those regions. Still others wanted to rid the new world of kings and colonialism.

While examining the maps of campaigns and studying the chronology of the war, keep in mind these questions:

1. *When and where did American land forces achieve their greatest successes?*
2. *When and where did American naval forces achieve their greatest successes?*
3. *What role did Indians play in the war?*

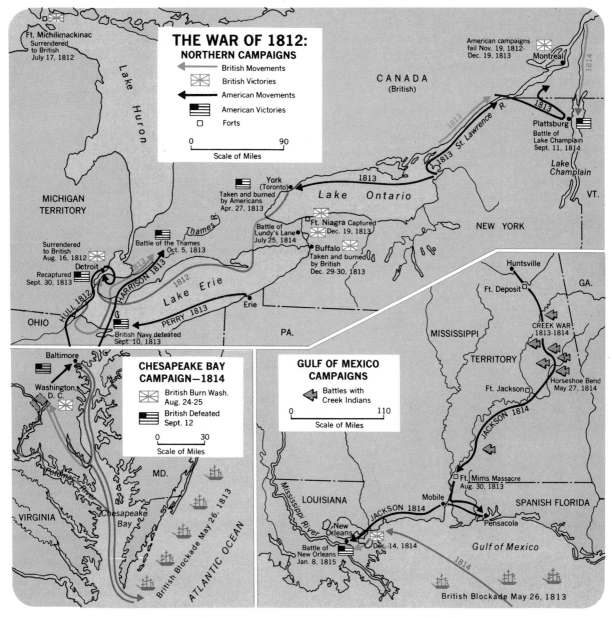

THE WAR OF 1812:
NORTHERN CAMPAIGNS

→ British Movements
British Victories
→ American Movements
American Victories
□ Forts

0   90
Scale of Miles

Ft. Michilimackinac
Surrendered
to British
July 17, 1812

Lake Huron

MICHIGAN TERRITORY

Surrendered
to British
Aug. 16, 1812
Detroit
Recaptured
Sept. 30, 1813

HULL 1812

HARRISON 1813

Battle of the Thames
Oct. 5, 1813

Thames

Lake Erie

Erie

PERRY 1813

British Navy defeated
Sept. 10, 1813

OHIO

PA.

York (Toronto)
Taken and burned
by Americans
Apr. 27, 1813

Lake Ontario

1813

Ft. Niagra Captured
Dec. 19, 1813

Battle of
Lundy's Lane
July 25, 1814

Buffalo
Taken and burned
by British
Dec. 29-30, 1813

NEW YORK

CANADA
(British)

American campaigns
fail Nov. 19, 1812-
Dec. 19, 1813
Montreal

1814

St. Lawrence R.
1813

Plattsburg
Battle of
Lake Champlain
Sept. 11, 1814

Lake Champlain

VT.

**CHESAPEAKE BAY
CAMPAIGN—1814**

British Burn Wash.
Aug. 24-25
British Defeated
Sept. 12

0   30
Scale of Miles

Baltimore

Washington,
D. C.

Potomac River

VIRGINIA

Chesapeake Bay

MD.

British Blockade May 26, 1813

ATLANTIC OCEAN

**GULF OF MEXICO
CAMPAIGNS**

Battles with
Creek Indians

0   110
Scale of Miles

Mississippi River

LOUISIANA

JACKSON 1814

New Orleans

Battle of
New Orleans
Jan. 8, 1815

Dec. 14, 1814

Mobile

Ft. Mims Massacre
Aug. 30, 1813

Pensacola

SPANISH FLORIDA

Gulf of Mexico

1814

British Blockade May 26, 1813

Huntsville

Ft. Deposit

GA.

CREEK WAR
1813-1814

Horseshoe Bend
May 27, 1814

Ft. Jackson

MISSISSIPPI TERRITORY

Chronology of Major Events, 1810–1815

DATE	EVENT
Oct. 27, 1810	President Madison annexes West Florida, claiming it was part of the Louisiana Purchase.
May 16, 1811	United States warship *President* fires on British corvette *Little Belt* in an attempt to stop British from taking American seamen.
Nov. 7, 1811	William Henry Harrison, governor of the Indiana territory, defeats confederated Indian tribes led by the Shawnee chief, Tecumseh, at the battle of Tippecanoe. Many Indians migrate to Canada.
June 18, 1812	President Madison declares war on Britain.
June, 1812	Napoleon's army invades Russia.
July 17, 1812	Americans surrender Ft. Michilimackinac to British, opening the upper Northwest territory and Great Lakes to British control.
Aug. 15, 1812	Fort Dearborn (Chicago) surrenders to the British and Indians. Indians massacre inhabitants.
Aug. 16, 1812	General William Hull surrenders Detroit to the British.
Aug. 19, 1812	United States warship *Constitution* destroys British frigate *Guerriere*.
Oct. 13– **Nov. 28, 1812**	Military campaign of U. S. Army and N. Y. State militia against British on Niagara River fails due to lack of unified command.

Jackson at New Orleans

DATE	EVENT
Oct. 18, 1812	United States warship *Wasp* captures British frigate *Frolic*.
Oct. 25, 1812	United States warship *United States* captures British frigate *Macedonian*.
Nov. 19, 1812	American military campaign against Montreal fails.
Dec. 2, 1812	James Madison is re-elected President, defeating DeWitt Clinton, the anti-war candidate.
Dec. 29, 1812	United States warship *Constitution* captures British frigate *Java*.
Jan. 22, 1813	British and Indians defeat American forces at Frenchtown near Detroit.
April 27, 1813	Americans capture and burn York (Toronto), Ontario.
May 26, 1813	British impose blockade from New York to New Orleans. New England ports left open for another year to encourage the pro-British and anti-war sentiments of the region.
June 1, 1813	United States warship *Chesapeake* captured by British frigate *Shannon* near Boston. Captain James Lawrence's last command before dying was: "Don't give up the ship."
Aug. 30, 1813	Five hundred Americans massacred by Creek Indians at Fort Mims, Alabama.

DATE	EVENT	DATE	EVENT
Sept. 10, 1813	United States fleet commanded by Oliver Hazard Perry destroys British naval power on Lake Erie in battle of Put-in-Bay.	**July 25, 1814**	Battle of Lundy's Lane stops American invasion of Canada.
Sept. 30, 1813	United States troops reoccupy Detroit which British had evacuated after Perry's victory in Lake Erie.	**Aug. 24–25, 1814**	British veterans from the European wars capture and burn Washington City.
Oct. 5, 1813	Americans defeat British at Battle of Thames in Canada. Tecumseh killed while fighting for the British. Indian power broken in the Northwest territory.	**Sept. 11, 1814**	American naval victory at Plattsburg, New York, wins control of Lake Champlain. British invasion from Canada ends.
July–Oct., 1813	Second American campaign against Montreal fails.	**Sept. 12–14, 1814**	British attack on Baltimore fails. Francis Scott Key composes "The Star-Spangled Banner."
Dec. 19, 1813	British and Indians capture Fort Niagara.	**Dec. 15, 1814– Jan. 4, 1815**	Hartford Convention of New England, opponents of the war, urge limitation of the power of the Federal government and an assertion of states rights.
Dec. 29–30, 1813	British and Indians capture and burn Buffalo.	**Dec. 24, 1814**	Peace of Ghent (Belgium) ends the war with no territorial changes.
Mar. 27, 1814	Tennessee volunteers under General Andrew Jackson defeat Creeks at Horseshoe Bend, Alabama, and break Indian power in the Southwest.	**Jan. 8, 1815**	General Andrew Jackson and frontier troops defeat a British invasion force from Jamaica at the Battle of New Orleans. British suffer 2,036 casualties, Americans, 21.
Apr. 6, 1814	Napoleon's overthrow allows British to transfer veteran troops to America.	**Feb. 15, 1815**	Treaty of Ghent unanimously ratified by the United States Senate.

7   THE MONROE DOCTRINE

In the years following the War of 1812, the United States and Britain worked out satisfactory settlements of commercial relations and boundary questions. Resolution of such past disagreements led to the discovery of points of common interest. Both the United States and Britain opposed Russian claims and expansion into the Pacific Northwest. They also agreed that interference in the affairs of the newly-independent Latin American states by European powers would endanger their interests in that part of the world.

In 1823, both George Canning, the British Secretary for Foreign Affairs, and John Quincy Adams, the American Secretary of State, suggested what ought to be done to protect their respective countries' interests in that region. While reading the following selections from the writings of George Canning and John Quincy Adams and the selection from President Monroe's message to Congress, keep in mind these questions:

1. What does Canning propose to the American minister?

2. What does Adams suggest as a response to Canning's proposal? Why?

3. What does Monroe propose as a new policy for the Americas?

George Canning, British Foreign Secretary, Discusses Latin America with the United States Minister in London,* August 20, 1823

Is not the moment come when our Governments might understand each other as to the Spanish-American colonies? And if we can arrive at such an understanding, would it not be fitting for ourselves, and beneficial for all the world, that the principles of it should be clearly settled and plainly avowed?

For ourselves we have no disguise.

1. We conceive the recovery of the colonies by Spain to be hopeless.

2. We conceive the question of the recognition of them, as Independent States, to be one of time and circumstances.

3. We are, however, by no means disposed to throw any *impediment** in the way of an arrangement between them and the mother country by friendly negotiations.

4. We aim not at the possession of any portion of them ourselves.

5. We could not see any portion of them transferred to any other Power, with indifference.

Impediment: obstacle or block.

If these opinions and feelings are, as I firmly believe them to be, common to your Government as with ours, why should we hesitate mutually to confide them to each other; and to declare them in the face of the world?

If there be any European Power which cherishes other projects, which looks to a forcible enterprise for reducing the colonies to subjugation, on the behalf of or in the name of Spain; or which considers the acquisition of any part of them to itself, by cession or by conquest; such a declaration on the part of your government and ours would be at once the most effectual, and the least offensive, mode of suggesting our joint opposition to such projects.

Nothing could be more gratifying to me than to join with you in such a work, and, I am persuaded, there has seldom, in the history of the world, occurred an opportunity when so small an effort of two friendly Governments might produce so unequivocal a good and prevent such extensive calamities.

Adapted from Richard Rush **A
Residence at the Court of London.
. . . .1819–1825,** Second Series,
Richard Bentley (London: 1845),
p. 412.

John Quincy Adams, Secretary of State, Argues for an Independent United States Foreign Policy, November 7, 1823

Cabinet meeting at the President's from half-past one till four. The subject for consideration was the confidential proposal of the British Secretary of State, George Canning, to Richard Rush, and the correspondence between them relating to the projects of the Holy Alliance upon South America. There was much conversation, without coming to any definite point. Canning's object appears to have been to obtain some public pledge from the Government of the United States, apparently against the forcible interference of the Holy Alliance between Spain and South America; but really against the acquisition by the United States of any part of the Spanish-American possessions.

We have no intention of seizing any such territory. But the inhabitants of Texas or Cuba may exercise their primitive rights, and solicit a union with us. They will certainly do no such thing to Great Britain. By joining with

John Quincy Adams, Secretary
of State in the Monroe
Administration and President of
the U. S., 1825–1828.

B98

her, therefore, in her proposed declaration, we give her a substantial and perhaps inconvenient pledge against ourselves, and really obtain nothing in return. . . . We should at least keep ourselves free to act as emergencies may arise, and not tie ourselves down to any principle which might immediately afterwards be brought to bear against ourselves.

The President was opposed to any course which should appear to take a position subordinate to that of Great Britain, and suggested the idea of sending a special Minister to protest against the *interposition** of the Holy Alliance.

I observed that it was . . . as I thought, a very suitable and convenient opportunity for us to take our stand against the Holy Alliance, and at the same time to decline the overture of Great Britain. It would be more candid, as well as more dignified, to avow our principles explicitly to Russia and France, than to come in as a *cock-boat** in the wake of the British man-of-war.

Interposition here means interference.

Cock-boat: small boat used as a tender for a larger boat.

Adapted from Charles Francis Adams, ed., **Memoirs of John Quincy Adams** (Philadelphia: J. P. Lippincott & Co., 1875), Vol. VI, pp. 177–79.

President Monroe Announces a New Policy for the Americas, Dec. 2, 1823

The occasion has been judged proper for the asserting, as a principle in which the rights and interests of the United States are involved, that the American continents, by the free and independent condition which they have assumed and maintain, are henceforth not to be considered as subjects for future colonization by any European powers. . . .

The citizens of the United States cherish sentiments the most friendly in favor of the liberty and happiness of their fellow-men in Europe. In the wars of the European powers in matters relating to themselves we have never taken any part, nor does it *comport** with our policy to do so. It is only when our rights are invaded or seriously menaced that we resent injuries or make preparation for our defense. With the movements in this hemisphere we are of necessity more immediately connected, and by causes which must be obvious to all enlightened and impartial observers. We owe it, therefore, to candor and to the friendly relations existing between the United States and European powers, to declare that we should consider any attempt on their part to extend their system to any portion of this hemisphere as dangerous to our peace and safety. With the existing colonies or dependencies of any European power we have not interfered and shall not interfere. But with the Governments who have declared their independence and maintained it, and whose independence we have, on great consideration and on just principles, acknowledged, we could not view any interposition for the purpose of oppressing them, or controlling in any other manner their destiny, by any European power in any other light than as the manifestation of an unfriendly disposition toward the United States.

It is impossible that the allied powers should extend their political system to any portion of either continent without endangering our peace and happiness; nor can anyone believe that our southern brethren, if left to themselves, would adopt Spanish rule of their own accord. It is equally impossible that we should behold European intervention in any form with indifference.

James Monroe, President of the United States, 1817–1824, and author of the Monroe Doctrine.

Comport: agree or suit.

Adapted from James D. Richardson, ed. **Messages and Papers of the Presidents, 1789–1897** (Published by Authority of Congress, 1899), Vol. II, pp. 209, 218, 219.

4 The westward movement

Settling a Continent

Objectives of this assignment are to:
—Draw inferences from maps and a chronology of the westward movement about how new territory was acquired and settled.
—Analyze selections of contemporary accounts of westward travel for meaning.
—Draw inferences from a filmstrip on westward movement about how and why people moved west.
—Make a judgment on why so much of the West was occupied and settled so quickly.

Zebulon Montgomery Pike (1779–1813) was an American soldier and explorer of the upper Mississippi region (1805–1806) and the southwestern part of the Louisiana Purchase. A Brigadier-General in the War of 1812, he was killed in the attack on York (Toronto), Canada.

Daniel Boone (1734–1820): born in Pennsylvania, Boone settled in North Carolina. In 1767 he blazed a trail through the Cumberland Gap that eventually became the Wilderness Road. He pioneered in the settlement of Kentucky.

Introduction

As soon as independence had been won from Britain, white settlers journeyed across the Appalachian barrier. Pioneers from Virginia and the Carolinas poured into Tennessee and Kentucky. Families from New England and New York moved toward the St. Lawrence River and the Great Lakes. Settlers from Pennsylvania, Virginia, and elsewhere moved into Ohio. By 1793, Americans had established small settlements across what is now Indiana and Illinois and as far west as Missouri.

The Conquest of a Continent

People moved west faster than our western political boundaries could be defined. Jefferson's purchase of Louisiana (1803) followed by the explorations by Lewis and Clark (1804–1806) and *Zebulon Pike** (1805–1807) attracted fur traders, explorers, and settlers toward parts of Minnesota, the Dakotas, Iowa, Nebraska, and Kansas. The War of 1812 removed the last obstacles to settlement east of the Mississippi, and was followed by fifty years of one of the greatest migrations of modern history.

Morris Birkbeck, an English traveller on his way to the Illinois territory in 1817, wrote "Old America seems to be breaking up, and moving westward." So it must have seemed. Americans followed the setting sun in pursuit of wide open spaces. Texas was acquired in 1845, and the Pacific Northwestern boundary with Canada was established in 1846. Two years later California, New Mexico, and Arizona territories became United States possessions. The Gadsden Purchase of land along the Mexican border was made in 1853 and Alaska was purchased from the Russians in 1867. By 1861, nine new states had been created out of lands west of the Mississippi. Never before in history were so many people on the move; never before in history had a continent been settled, populated, and organized in so short a time.

The Ways West

Americans moved west on foot, on horseback, in wagons, on rafts, flatboats, steamboats, by railroad, and on anything that would roll or float. Work on roads in the West had begun as early as 1775 when *Daniel Boone** and his men started the Wilderness Road connecting Virginia and Kentucky. The main land route west, however, was not begun until 1811. The Cumberland Road or National Turnpike began at Baltimore and when completed ran almost six hundred miles to Vandalia, Illinois. An eighty-foot-wide clearing with a twenty-foot strip of macadam paving running down the center, the National Pike became the main street of the region northwest of the Ohio. Other roads such as the Lancaster Pike from Philadelphia to western Pennsylvania and the Genesee Road from Albany across New York State opened routes west for Pennsylvanians, New Yorkers, and New Englanders.

No matter where they started, most settlers headed for the Ohio River, which was the best water route or "Grand Track" west until completion of the Erie Canal in 1825. Floating down the Ohio to river towns such as Cincinnati, settlers would proceed from there overland to their final destinations. The Erie Canal linked the Hudson River with the Great Lakes. Later canal building in Ohio, Indiana, and Illinois opened water routes from Albany to the Mississippi River. After 1830, the development of railroads enabled even more people to move west easier and faster.

The Costs of Conquest

After 1783, the United States government inherited from the British the problem of regulating white settlement of lands occupied by Indians. Although an Indian department was established by the Federal government as early as 1786 and a Bureau of Indian Affairs created in 1836, the United States Government was no more successful in preventing exploitation of Indians by white traders and land speculators than had been King George III. Indians' rights to lands which they had occupied for generations were usually ignored or denied. Often both government agents and private land speculators would negotiate land purchases from individual Indians who had no right to dispose of tribal lands. Though such land sales were *fraudulent,** they were frequently enforced by the government and upheld by the courts. In other cases, large tracts of territory were taken from Indians by force without even the benefit of a fraudulent sale.

The Case for the Cherokees

Everywhere on the frontier Indians suffered, but the case of the Cherokees was extraordinary. Ever since the 1790's the Cherokees had been recognized by the United States government in a series of treaties as a *dependent nation.** They had become extremely well adjusted to the white man's ways of living and working. They were farmers and cattle raisers. Cherokees owned sawmills, looms, cotton gins, and slaves. *Sequoyah,** a Cherokee scholar, developed a written language for Cherokee speech. They maintained their own schools and published a newspaper, The Cherokee Phoenix.

In order to prevent further encroachments upon their lands, the Cherokees

COMMERCIAL MAIL STAGE, IN THIRTY-NINE HOURS, From Boston to New York.

Thirty-nine hours from Boston to New York—in 1815 the commercial stagecoach was in the toddling infancy of modern transportation, the precurser of the swifter steamboats and railroads that helped open up the west.

Fraudulent: deceiving, tricky.

Dependent nation: in the case of **Cherokee Nation v. Georgia,** 1831, Chief Justice John Marshall decided that the Cherokees were a domestic, dependent nation, and not a foreign state.

Sequoyah (1770–1843): son of a white father and a Cherokee mother of mixed blood, By 1821 Sequoyah worked out a series of symbols for the 86 Cherokee syllables to create a written Cherokee language.

held a constitutional convention at New Echota, Georgia, on July 4, 1827. Within a month, they devised a frame of government and declared themselves a Cherokee republic. Georgians insisted that the United States constitution prohibited the creation of a new state within the territory of an existing one. State and Federal authorities descended upon the Cherokees and attempted to move them off their ancestral lands. The discovery of gold on Cherokee land in 1829 was followed by Congress's enactment of a law authorizing the forcible removal of any Indian tribe to lands west of the Mississippi river. In 1836 the Federal government began removing the *Cherokees** 1,000 miles west to a newly created Indian territory.

Cherokee removal: a dissident faction of the Cherokees signed a Treaty with the United States government in December, 1835, ceding Cherokee lands. In return the United States government made a cash payment to the tribe, and promised to provide them with free transportation to new lands in the Indian Territory. In 1838 the Army was used to force the last Cherokee out of his ancestral lands in Georgia and Tennessee.

Indians and the United States Government

Confronted by ever-mounting pressures from white settlers for Indian lands, the Federal government was at times unable and at other times unwilling to protect the Indians or honor previous treaties made with them. On the frontiers of the new nation, the right of might and the power of numbers prevailed. The human cost of conquering a continent was high. The American Indians paid most of it.

8   THE CONQUEST OF A CONTINENT, 1800–1900

In 1800 the United States was a nation of 5,308,000 people inhabiting 889,000 square miles of territory. One hundred years later, the nation had grown to 76 million people inhabiting 3 million square miles of territory. This tremendous expansion is itself a great American epic adventure. The facts and details of the American westward movement have provided the basis for some of the most important chapters of nineteenth century American history. Equally important, the experience of conquering a continent profoundly affected the way Americans thought about themselves, their past, and their future.

While examining the following maps of America's territorial expansion and studying a chronology of our westward movement, keep in mind these questions:

1. Where was the frontier in 1800?

2. How did the United States expand from the Mississippi to the Pacific coast? From whom and by what means was territory acquired?

3. What territories had not achieved statehood by 1861?

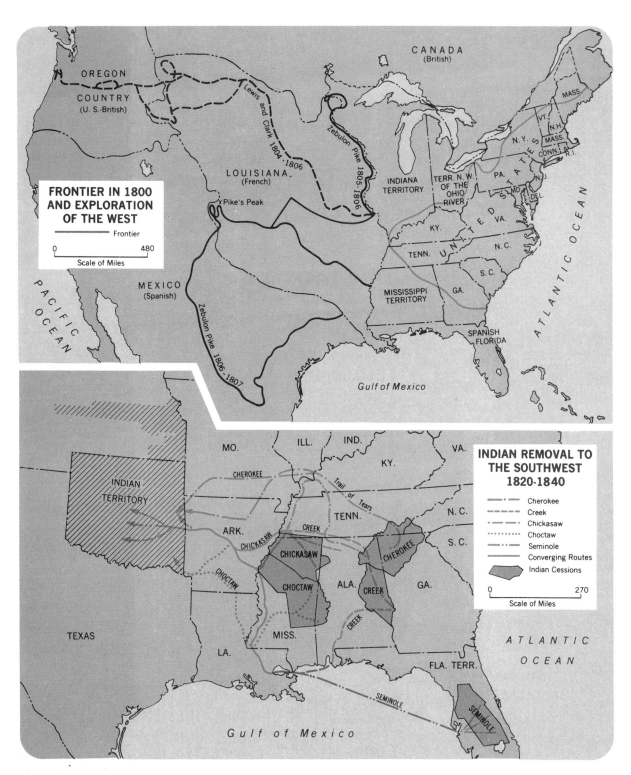

FRONTIER IN 1800 AND EXPLORATION OF THE WEST

—— Frontier

0 —— 480
Scale of Miles

OREGON
COUNTRY
(U. S.-British)

CANADA
(British)

Lewis and Clark 1804-1806

Zebulon Pike 1805-1806

LOUISIANA
(French)

x Pike's Peak

MEXICO
(Spanish)

Zebulon Pike 1806-1807

INDIANA
TERRITORY

TERR. N.W.
OF THE
OHIO
RIVER

MASS.

VT.
N.H.
N. Y.
MASS.
CONN.
R.I.
PA.
N.J.
MD.
DEL.

KY.

VA.

TENN.

UNITED STATES

N.C.

S. C.

MISSISSIPPI
TERRITORY

GA.

SPANISH
FLORIDA

Gulf of Mexico

PACIFIC
OCEAN

ATLANTIC OCEAN

INDIAN REMOVAL TO THE SOUTHWEST 1820-1840

—·—·— Cherokee
— — — Creek
—·—·— Chickasaw
·········· Choctaw
—··—··— Seminole
———— Converging Routes
▨ Indian Cessions

0 —— 270
Scale of Miles

MO.
ILL.
IND.
VA.
KY.

INDIAN
TERRITORY

CHEROKEE

Trail of Tears

TENN.

N.C.

ARK.

CHICKASAW

CREEK

CHICKASAW

CHOCTAW

CHOCTAW

ALA.

CHEROKEE

CREEK

S.C.

GA.

TEXAS

MISS.

LA.

CREEK

FLA. TERR.

SEMINOLE

SEMINOLE

ATLANTIC
OCEAN

Gulf of Mexico

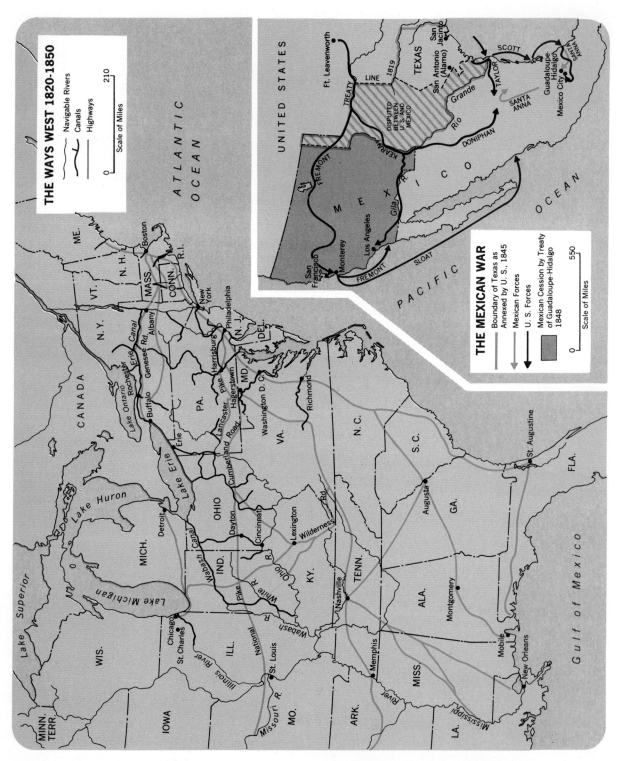

THE WAYS WEST 1820-1850

- ∿ Navigable Rivers
- ⋎ Canals
- — Highways

Scale of Miles

0   210

THE MEXICAN WAR

- Boundary of Texas as Annexed by U. S., 1845
- → Mexican Forces
- → U. S. Forces
- ▨ Mexican Cession by Treaty of Guadaloupe-Hidalgo 1848

Scale of Miles

0   550

ATLANTIC OCEAN

PACIFIC OCEAN

Gulf of Mexico

UNITED STATES

M E X I C O

TEXAS

Ft. Leavenworth

San Antonio (Alamo)

San Jacinto

SCOTT

TAYLOR

DONIPHAN

KEARNY

FREMONT

SLOAT

SANTA ANNA

Guadaloupe-Hidalgo

Mexico City

Rio Grande

Gila R.

TREATY LINE 1819

DISPUTED BETWEEN U.S. AND MEXICO

San Francisco

Monterey

Los Angeles

CANADA

Lake Superior

Lake Michigan

Lake Huron

Lake Erie

Lake Ontario

Detroit

Buffalo

Rochester

Genesee Rd.

Erie Canal

Albany

Boston

New York

Philadelphia

Harrisburg

Lancaster Pike

Cumberland Road

Hagerstown

Washington D. C.

Richmond

ME.

N.H.

VT.

MASS.

CONN.

R.I.

N.Y.

PA.

N. J.

DEL.

MD.

VA.

N. C.

S. C.

GA.

FLA.

St. Augustine

Augusta

OHIO

Dayton

Cincinnati

Lexington

Wilderness Rd.

MICH.

IND.

Wabash Canal

ILL.

Chicago

St. Charles

WIS.

IOWA

MINN. TERR.

Illinois River

Missouri R.

St. Louis

MO.

ARK.

White R.

Pike

Ohio R.

Wabash River

National Road

KY.

TENN.

Nashville

Memphis

ALA.

MISS.

Mississippi River

LA.

New Orleans

Mobile

Montgomery

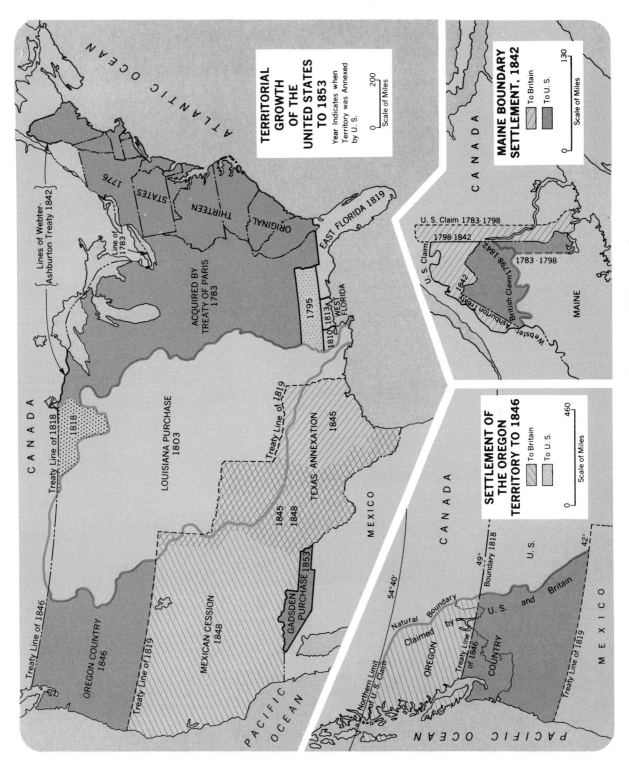

TERRITORIAL GROWTH OF THE UNITED STATES TO 1853

Year Indicates when Territory was Annexed by U. S.

0   200
Scale of Miles

ATLANTIC OCEAN

CANADA

1776

ORIGINAL

THIRTEEN

STATES

ACQUIRED BY TREATY OF PARIS 1783

Lines of Webster-Ashburton Treaty 1842

Line of 1783

EAST FLORIDA 1819

1795

WEST FLORIDA

1813

1810

Treaty Line of 1818

1818

CANADA

LOUISIANA PURCHASE 1803

Treaty Line of 1819

TEXAS ANNEXATION 1845

1845
1848

MEXICO

1845
1848

Treaty Line of 1846

OREGON COUNTRY 1846

Treaty Line of 1819

MEXICAN CESSION 1848

GADSDEN PURCHASE 1853

PACIFIC OCEAN

MAINE BOUNDARY SETTLEMENT, 1842

To Britain
To U. S.

0   130
Scale of Miles

CANADA

U. S. Claim 1783-1798

1798-1842

1783-1798

U. S. Claim 1798-1842

British Claim 1798-1842

Webster-Ashburton Treaty 1842

MAINE

SETTLEMENT OF THE OREGON TERRITORY TO 1846

To Britain
To U. S.

0   460
Scale of Miles

CANADA

U. S.

49° Boundary 1818

54°40'

Natural Boundary Claimed by

OREGON COUNTRY

U. S. and Britain

42°

Northern Limit of U. S. Claim

Treaty Line of 1846

Treaty Line of 1819

MEXICO

PACIFIC OCEAN

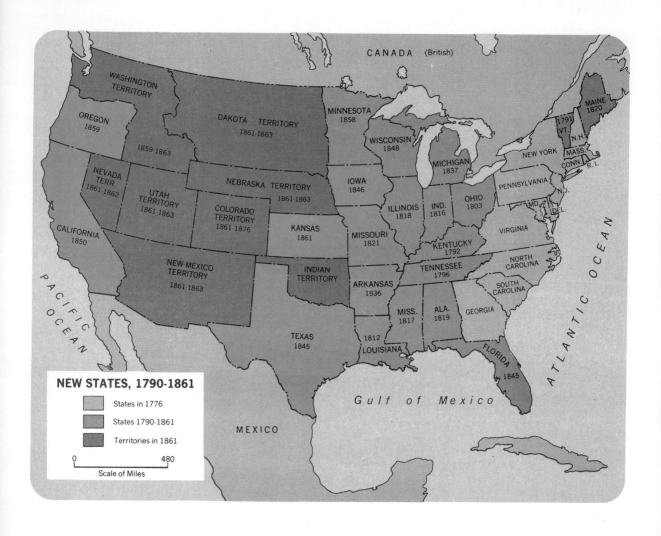

NEW STATES, 1790-1861

States in 1776

States 1790-1861

Territories in 1861

0   480
Scale of Miles

CANADA (British)

WASHINGTON TERRITORY

OREGON 1859

1859-1863

NEVADA TERR. 1861-1862

UTAH TERRITORY 1861-1863

CALIFORNIA 1850

DAKOTA TERRITORY 1861-1863

MINNESOTA 1858

WISCONSIN 1848

MICHIGAN 1837

NEBRASKA TERRITORY 1861-1863

IOWA 1846

NEW YORK

MAINE 1820

1791 VT.

N.H.

MASS. CONN. R.I.

PENNSYLVANIA

N.J.

COLORADO TERRITORY 1861-1876

KANSAS 1861

ILLINOIS 1818

IND. 1816

OHIO 1803

MD. DEL.

MISSOURI 1821

KENTUCKY 1792

VIRGINIA

NEW MEXICO TERRITORY 1861-1863

INDIAN TERRITORY

ARKANSAS 1836

TENNESSEE 1796

NORTH CAROLINA

SOUTH CAROLINA

MISS. 1817

ALA. 1819

GEORGIA

TEXAS 1845

1812 LOUISIANA

FLORIDA 1845

ATLANTIC OCEAN

PACIFIC OCEAN

Gulf of Mexico

MEXICO

Chronology: The Westward Movement, 1803–1900

DATE	EVENT
April 30, 1803	United States acquires Louisiana Territory from France for $15 million.
1804–1806	Meriwether Lewis and William Clark, sent by President Jefferson to explore the new West, reach the Pacific Ocean, Nov. 7, 1805.
1805–1807	Lieutenant Zebulon Pike explores the sources of the Missouri River, and what is now Colorado and New Mexico.
Oct. 27, 1810	President Madison annexes West Florida, claiming it was part of the Louisiana Purchase.
1811	First steamboat, *New Orleans,* navigates

DATE	EVENT
	the Mississippi from Louisville to New Orleans.
Mar., 1811	American businessman, John Jacob Astor, establishes fort at Astoria on the Columbia River as base for fur trade.
1815	Steamboat *Enterprise* navigates from Pittsburgh to New Orleans and returns.
Apr.–May, 1818	Andrew Jackson and American troops occupy East Florida to prevent Seminole Indians there from raiding the Southern frontier.
Oct. 20, 1818	United States and Great Britain sign the <u>Convention of 1818,</u> which sets the

DATE	EVENT
	boundary between British North America and the United States at the 49th parallel from Lake of the Woods to the Rocky Mountains. Oregon Territory is to be left open for the time to settlement by both British and Americans.
Feb. 22, 1819	United States and Spain sign the Adams-Onis Treaty, by which Spain renounces all claims to West Florida and cedes East Florida to the United States. The western boundary of the Louisiana Purchase is also settled by this agreement.
Mar., 1820	*Missouri Compromise** accepted by Congress. Slavery is prohibited in the lands of the Louisiana Purchase north of 36° 30′, except for the state of Missouri.
	Missouri Compromise: the number of slave and free states in the Union was equal (11 of each) in 1819. When Missouri applied for statehood as a slave state, the question of the status of slavery in the Louisiana Territory arose. Maine, a free state, was admitted to the Union to offset Missouri's statehood.
Jan., 1821	*Moses Austin** receives a charter to colonize in Texas from the Mexican government.
	Moses Austin (1761–1821), Connecticut-born merchant who moved to Missouri in the 1790's to exploit the lead deposits there.
Apr. 17, 1824	United States and Russia agree to set southern boundary of Alaska at 54° 40′.
Oct., 1825	Erie Canal links Hudson River with Lake Erie. Provides easy route for migration to the West.
July, 1829	Gold is discovered on Cherokee lands in Georgia.
1832–1834	Overland expeditions, financed by Nathaniel Wyeth of Massachusetts, reach Oregon.
Dec., 1835	Dissident faction of Cherokees surrender tribal lands in Georgia and Tennessee in return for a cash payment and new lands in the Indian Territory.
1836–1838	Cherokee nation removed to the Indian Territory.
Mar. 2, 1836	American settlers in Texas assert independence from Mexico.

DATE	EVENT
May 14, 1836	Mexican President Santa Anna recognizes Texas independence after being captured at the Battle of San Jacinto.
Aug. 9, 1842	United States and Great Britain sign the Webster-Ashburton Treaty, which establishes the boundary between the Northeastern states and Canada. The boundary line then was drawn through the middle of Lakes Ontario, Erie, Huron, and Superior, and then westward to the Lake of the Woods.
Dec. 2, 1845	President James K. Polk claims all of the Oregon Territory up to 54° 40′ for the United States, and recommends ending the joint occupancy of the Territory with Great Britain.
Dec. 29, 1845	Texas annexed and enters the Union.
June 15, 1846	Compromise Oregon treaty negotiated and signed with Great Britain limiting the boundary between British North America and the United States along the 49th parallel from the Rocky Mountains to the Pacific.
May 11, 1846	United States goes to war with Mexico over Texas boundary dispute.
July 24, 1847	First *Mormon** settlers arrive at the Great Salt Lake after migrating from Illinois.
	Mormons: members of the Church of Our Lord Jesus Christ of the Latter Day Saints, founded in New York State, 1830. They later migrated to Ohio, Missouri, and Illinois, where they were persecuted for their religious customs, which included allowing polygamy.
Jan. 24, 1848	Gold discovered in California.
Feb. 2, 1848	Treaty of Guadalupe-Hidalgo ends Mexican War. Mexico cedes all lands north of the Rio Grande River, plus her territories in California and New Mexico, to the United States.
Dec., 1849	President Polk announces to Congress that gold has been discovered in California, and the Gold rush begins.
Dec. 30, 1853	Gadsden Purchase: United States purchases land south of the Gila River from Mexico for purposes of constructing a railroad to the Pacific.
Oct. 18, 1867	Alaska purchased from Russia for 7\frac{1}{2}$ million.
April 30, 1900	Hawaii annexed and given territorial status.

9 GOING WEST: THE REASONS WHY

During the early nineteenth century, Americans from the settled regions of the original states began a massive, but orderly, move west. Moving families and household possessions hundreds of miles required planning, organization, and money. White men who decided to go west usually did so of their own free will and at their own expense. Black people and Indians who moved west during the early nineteenth century were usually taken or driven there by force.

Under the best of circumstances going west was not easy. People undertaking such a journey had to be extremely determined. For most travelers, the trek west was both an escape and an adventure. For white men, going west was an escape from misfortune or disappointment and an adventure into hope and success. For black men and Indians, going west was another adventure in hardship which only the most determined could survive.

While reading the following accounts of how and why people went west, keep in mind these questions:

1. *How did emigration from the east to the Mississippi valley proceed? What geographical patterns were followed?*

2. *By 1832, how did most emigrants travel to the West?*

3. *What was the role of river towns such as Cincinnati and St. Louis in the westward movement?*

4. *Why did emigrants from the Carolinas and Georgia rush into Alabama, Mississippi, and Louisiana?*

Patterns of Western Settlement

In traveling over the various states and territories of the West, I have been struck with a fact which is somewhat remarkable. It is the manner in which that country has been colonized. The emigration to the Valley of the Mississippi seems to have gone on in columns, moving from the east almost due west, from the respective states from which they originated. From New England the emigrating column advanced through New York, peopling the middle and western parts of that state in its progress; but still continuing, it reached the northern part of Ohio, then Indiana, and finally Illinois. A part of the same column from New England and New York is *diverging** into Michigan. It is true, also, that straggling companies, as it were, diverge to a more southerly direction, and scatter over the middle and southern parts of the Valley, and are to be found in every state, in every county and town, in greater or less numbers. The Pennsylvania and New Jersey column advanced within the *parallels of latitude** of those states into West Pennsylvania, and still continuing, advanced into the middle and southern parts of Ohio, and extended even into the middle parts of Indiana and Illinois. The Virginia column advanced first into the western part of that state and Kentucky—which was long a constituent part of it—thence into the southern parts of Indiana and Illinois,

Diverging: turning aside or moving in another direction.

Parallels of latitude: imaginary lines used by map-makers to mark off and measure distances north and south of the equator.

until it spread over almost the whole of Missouri. The North Carolina column advanced first into East Tennessee, thence into West Tennessee, and also into Missouri. And the South Carolina and Georgia column moved upon the extensive and fertile lands of Alabama, and in some degree peopled Mississippi. Louisiana was a *foreign colony*.* The American part of it is composed of emigrants from the upper part of the Valley, and from the southern and eastern states. The same remark is true of the small population of the state of Mississippi. In Arkansas the emigrating columns of Kentucky and Tennessee predominate.

Louisiana a foreign colony: that is, it was originally settled by the French and Spanish.

Adapted from Robert Baird, **View of the Valley of the Mississippi, or the Emigrant's and Travellers' Guide to the West** (Philadelphia; 1834), pp. 100–103.

The Westward Movement, 1832

As a result of the universality and cheapness of steamboat and canal passage and transport, more than half the immigrants now travel west by water. This applies to nine-tenths of those who come from Europe and the northern states. They thus escape much of the expense, slowness, inconvenience and danger of the ancient, *cumbrous** and tiresome journey in wagons.

Cumbrous: clumsy, slow-moving, heavy.

The immigrants from Virginia, the two Carolinas and Georgia, still travel west after the ancient fashion, in the southern wagon. That is a vehicle almost unknown at the north. It is strong, comfortable, and roomy. It contains not only a movable kitchen, but provisions and beds. Drawn by four or six horses, it serves all the various functions of house, shelter and transport; and is, in fact, the southern ship of the forests and prairies. The horses, that convey the wagon, are large and powerful animals, followed by servants, cattle, sheep, swine, dogs, the whole forming a primitive caravan. The strong southern hulk, with its chimes of bells, its black drivers, and its long train of followers, moves on with power in its dust.

Perhaps more than half the northern immigrants arrive at present by way of the New York canal and Lake Erie. If their destination be the upper waters of the Wabash, they debark at Sandusky, and continue their route without approaching the Ohio. The greater number make their way from the lake to the Ohio, either by the Erie and Ohio, or the Dayton canal. Emigrants from Pennsylvania will henceforward reach the Ohio on the great Pennsylvania canal, and will 'take water' at Pittsburgh. If bound to Indiana, Illinois or

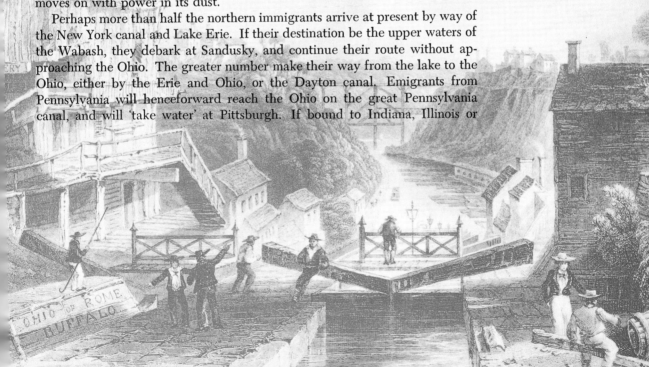

Missouri, they build or purchase a family boat. Many of these boats are comfortably fitted up, and are neither inconvenient, nor unpleasant floating houses. Two or three families sometimes fit up a large boat in partnership. We need hardly add, that a great number of the wealthier emigrant families take passage in a steam boat.

After the immigrants have arrived at Cincinnati, Lexington, Nashville, St. Louis, or St. Charles, in the vicinity of the points, where they had *anticipated**** to fix themselves, a preliminary difficulty is to determine where to go. All the towns swarm with speculating companies and *land agents,** and the chance is, that the first inquiries for information in this confusion will be addressed to them, or to persons who have a common understanding and interest with them. One advises to the Wabash, and points on the map to the rich lands, fine mill seats, navigable streams and growing towns in their vicinity. Another presents a still more alluring picture of the lands in some part of Illinois, Missouri, the region west of the lakes, and the lead mines. Another tempts him with White River, Arkansas, Red River, Opelousas, and Attakapas, the rich crops of cotton and sugar, and the escape from winter, which they offer. Still another company has its nets set in all the points, where immigrants congregate, advertising all the advantages of Texas, and the Mexican country. In Cincinnati, more than in any other town, there are generally *precursors** from all points of the compass, to select lands for companies, that are to follow. There are such here at present both from Europe and New England; and we read advertisements, that a thousand persons are shortly to meet at St. Louis to form a company to cross the Rocky Mountains, with a view to select settlements on the Oregon.

Anticipated: thought about beforehand.

Speculating companies and land agents: groups of men who bought vast tracts of land to re-sell it at a profit to settlers.

Precursors: those who have already been to a region and returned.

Adapted from Timothy Flint, **History and Geography of the Mississippi Valley** (Cincinnati: Flint & Co.; Boston: Carter, Hevdee & Co., 1833), Vol. II, pp. 188–190.

A Trip through the New Southwest, 1827

I returned to the Planter's Hotel in Charleston where I found the four daily papers as well as the conversation of the boarders, teeming with Cotton! Cotton!! Cotton!!! Thinks I to myself, "I'll soon change this scene of cotton."

I arrived in Augusta; and when I saw cotton wagons in Broad Street, I whistled! But said nothing!!!

Leaving Augusta I overtook hordes of cotton planters from North Carolina, South Carolina, and Georgia with large gangs of Negroes, bound to Alabama, Mississippi, and Louisiana, "where the cotton land is not worn out."

I went to Milledgeville, Georgia, where I found the prevailing topic of the place, "What an infernal shame it was, that such a quantity of virgin cotton land should be allowed to remain in the possession of the infernal *Creek Indians.**"

I went to New Orleans and stayed for six days. During that time there arrived more than 20,000 bales of cotton. I took a steamer up river and saw many boats loaded with cotton. At the mouth of the Arkansas river, we took on board about fifty Negroes and two overseers, who had made a very excellent crop of cotton in that territory, but found it too unhealthy a place to remain, and were going back to North Alabama.

Creek Indians: powerful Indian tribe in central Georgia and Alabama who were treacherously removed from their lands by 1829.

Adapted from **Georgia Courier,** Augusta (Oct. 11, 1827), "Documentary History of American Industrial Society" (Cleveland: Arthur H. Clark Co., 1910), Vol. I, pp. 284–287.

B110

Courtesy J. N. Bartfield Art Galleries, Inc., New York

Going West, 1800 **"Immigrating North Carolina Family"** by James Beard

18

Cumberland Road, 1815

"Fairview Inn"
or "Three Mile Inn"
by Thomas Ruckles

Courtesy of Maryland Historical Society

B113

19

Flatboat on
the Ohio River,
1820

Courtesy of Indiana University

20 The Erie Canal near Albany, 1830. Painting by Eric Schaal

The New-York Historical Society

LIFE magazine, © 1972 Time, Inc.

21   Steamboats at St. Louis, 1832

22

Railroad Meeting
a Steamboat, 1834

The "Planet"
Camden and Amboy Railroad

Courtesy of Kennedy Galleries, Inc.

B117

5 What historians have said

Analyzing Historical Judgments

Objectives of this assignment are to:
—Analyze selections from writings of three modern historians on Jacksonian Democracy for meaning.
—Suggest procedures for deciding which of three interpretations of Jacksonian Democracy is most accurate.
—Draw inferences about history and history writing from your analysis of these conflicting historical interpretations.

Raucous and indecorous: noisy, disorderly, violating good manners.

Egalitarian: believing in human equality in essential matters.

Introduction

Before the election of 1828, American Presidents had either belonged to what was called the "Virginia Dynasty" (Washington, Jefferson, Madison, Monroe), or else had come from Massachusetts (John Adams and John Quincy Adams). Despite party differences and disagreement over several major issues, all of these men had much in common. They were all from long-established regions of the East, where the influence of aristocratic British manners and social customs had long been dominant. They were all wealthy men and depended for their incomes on established forms of money-making: the plantation, banking, law, land, and trade.

But the election of 1828 brought to the White House Tennessee's best-known citizen, Andrew Jackson. His inauguration was *raucous* and *indecorous.** Thousands of people from all sections of the country, but particularly from the West, flooded into Washington to shake hands with the general, to drink punch with him in celebration, and to leave the imprint of their muddy boots and stained fingers on White House carpets and curtains. It seemed a far cry from Washington's levees and formal dinner parties.

Andrew Jackson—"The Gin'ral," or "Old Hickory"—had been well known throughout the country ever since his military victories in the War of 1812. Further military campaigns against the Seminole Indians and the Spanish in Florida established him as a national hero. Two terms as a forceful, energetic President, 1829–1837, capped his career of service to the United States and gave him a permanent place in the history and folklore of our country.

During Jackson's two terms in office, strong democratic social and economic trends appeared. Massive immigration to western lands, the growth of labor unions and workingmen's associations in the Eastern cities and the elimination of property qualifications for voting in several states were all indicators of social and economic change. A new *egalitarian** set of attitudes dominated government and society. Men came to be respected not for who they were, or what they inherited, but for what they could do. Fulfillment of dreams of great material success seemed to be within the grasp of any enterprising American. Rightly or wrongly, this spirit of enterprise and egalitarianism was associated with President Jackson. This revolution in manners and morals has been described by historians as Jacksonian Democracy.

This assignment concludes your work on the development of the New Nation. The next readings from the works of three American historians are concerned with the meaning and nature of Jacksonian Democracy.

B118

IO FREDERICK JACKSON TURNER ON JACKSONIAN DEMOCRACY

Andrew Jackson, Tennessee's great military hero, western frontiersman, and plain man of the people, put an end to the "dynasty" of aristocrats and scholars from Virginia and New England when he became President. Portrait by Thomas Sully, now a part of the Mellon Collection in the National Gallery of Art, Washington, D.C.

Frederick Jackson Turner was born in Wisconsin in 1861 and was educated at the University of Wisconsin and Johns Hopkins University. He received his doctorate in American history from Johns Hopkins in 1890 and taught American history for many years at the University of Wisconsin and Harvard University until his retirement in 1924. Professor Turner wrote several major books and articles on the significance of the western frontier in American history. One book, The Significance of Sections in American History, won the Pulitzer Prize for History in 1932. Although Professor Turner died in 1932, he was one of the most influential American historians of the twentieth century. Turner's interpretation of the role of the frontier in forming Americans and their history has become a classic.

The selection below is taken from a book, The United States, 1830–1850, published in 1935 after his death. While reading this selection, keep in mind these questions. According to Turner:

1. *What were the sources of Jacksonian Democracy?*
2. *What were the leading characteristics of Jacksonian Democrats?*
3. *How did Jacksonian Democrats view property?*

Jacksonian Democracy: A Product of the Frontier Experience

After the War of 1812, Andrew Jackson became the hero of the Mississippi Valley and of the democracy of the less densely settled regions in general.

❀   ❀   ❀   ❀   ❀

By 1830 the growth of population in the west, and the development of the frontier type of society, had gone forward to such an extent as to give these sections the balance of political power and bring about the triumph of Jacksonian Democracy.

❀   ❀   ❀   ❀   ❀

Jacksonian Democracy was based primarily upon the characteristics of the back country. Jackson was himself a product of the frontier west—that west which was born of the southern upland in the days when a sharp contrast existed between the interior farmers and the tidewater planters.

Although he grew up in this frontier society, he had become a man of property, a cotton planter, a leader who used his leadership to protect the interests of himself and conservative friends in days when all men on the frontier, in the midst of abundant opportunities, strove to build up their fortunes. . . . he was none the less the national leader to whom frontier democracy turned, who bore in his own personal experiences and qualities many of the frontiersmen's fundamental characteristics. . . .

The widening of the suffrage in the older states, by statute and by constitutional change, had been in active progress, and the newer states had, almost from their birth, reposed political power in the hands of the people, either by white manhood suffrage or by so low a tax qualification as to amount to the same thing. By 1830 there were few states that, in practice, had not come to this. The western states had also based representation, in both houses of their legislatures, on numbers rather than on a combination of property and population. This marked a revolt characteristic of the period, against the idea that property was entitled to a special representation. . . .

The election of Andrew Jackson was significant in American history for many reasons. . . .

As the outcome showed, it meant that an agricultural society strongest in the regions of rural isolation rather than in the areas of greater density of population and of greater wealth, had triumphed, for the time, over the conservative, industrial, commercial, and manufacturing society of the New England type. It meant that a new, aggressive, expansive democracy, emphasizing human rights and individualism, as against the old established order which emphasized *vested rights** and *corporate action,** had come into control.

[This new Democracy] . . . was not only a society in which the love of equality was prominent: it was also a competitive society. To . . . critics it has seemed not so much a democracy as a society whose members were "expectant capitalists." And this, indeed, is part of its character. It was based upon the idea of the fair chance for all men. . . . But, while this is true, it must also be remembered that the simplicity of life in this region . . . together with the vast extent of unoccupied land and unexploited resources, made it easy . . . to conceive of equality and competitive individualism as consistent elements of democracy. . . . The self-made man was the ideal of this society. . . .

* * * * *

On the whole, it must be said that Jackson's presidency was more representative of the America of his time than would have been that of any of his rivals. The instincts of the American people in supporting him conformed to the general drift of the tendencies of this New World democracy. [Jacksonian] Democracy . . . preferred persons to property. . . .

Vested rights: legal rights, particularly those regarding the ownership and use of property.

Corporate action: the action of organized associations.

Frederick Jackson Turner, **The United States, 1830–1850** (New York: Holt, Rinehart and Winston, Inc.: 1935), pp. 13–31.

11 ARTHUR M. SCHLESINGER, JR., ON JACKSONIAN DEMOCRACY

Arthur M. Schlesinger, Jr., was born in Columbus, Ohio, in 1917 and was educated at Harvard University. Professor Schlesinger taught American history at Harvard University from 1954–1961 and has been a Professor of Humanities at the City University of New York since 1966. He served as special assistant to Presidents Kennedy and Johnson from 1961 to 1964. Professor Schlesinger has written many important articles and books on both early nineteenth century and recent American history. One book, The Age of Jackson, won the Pulitzer Prize for History in 1945. Since the publication of that important book, most historical work on Jacksonian politics has either agreed or sharply disagreed with the interpretation presented in The Age of Jackson.

While reading the following selection from The Age of Jackson keep in mind these questions. According to Schlesinger:

1. *What were the sources of Jacksonian Democracy?*
2. *What were the leading characteristics of Jacksonian Democrats?*
3. *How did Jacksonian Democrats view property?*

Jacksonian Democracy: A Product of Working-Class Egalitarianism

The specific problem was to control the power of the capitalistic groups, mainly Eastern, for the benefit of the noncapitalist groups, farmers and laboring men, East, West, and South. The basic Jacksonian ideas came naturally enough from the East, which best understood the nature of business power and reacted most sharply against it. The legend that Jacksonian democracy was the explosion of the frontier, lifting into the government some violent men filled with rustic prejudices against big business, does not explain the facts, which were somewhat more complex. Jacksonian democracy was rather a second American phase of that enduring struggle between the business community and the rest of society which is the guarantee of freedom in a liberal capitalist state.

Andrew Jackson, 1832

❖   ❖   ❖   ❖   ❖

. . . the East remained the source of the effective expression of Jacksonian radicalism, and Eastern ideas rose to supremacy in Washington as Jacksonianism changed from an agitation into a program. The East simply had the consistent and bitter experience which alone could serve as a *crucible of radicalism.*❖

Crucible of radicalism: where radicalism was most severely tested.

The great illusion of historians of the frontier has been that social equality produces economic equalitarianism. In fact, the demand for economic equality is generally born out of conditions of social inequality, and becomes more rigid. The actual existence of equal opportunities is likely to diminish the vigilance with which they are guarded, and to stimulate the race for power and privilege. The fur capitalists of St. Louis and the land speculators of Mississippi were as characteristic of the West as Andrew Jackson.

❖   ❖   ❖   ❖   ❖

Jacksonians . . . tended to exalt human rights as a counterweight to property rights. The *Whigs,*❖ some charged . . . were seeking such an extension of "the rights of property as to swallow up and annihilate those of persons"; the Democratic party would "do all in its power to preserve and defend them."

Whigs: political party largely composed of manufacturing and business interests, formed as opposition to Jacksonian Democrats.

B121

Orestes Augustus Brownson (1803–1876): American philosopher and journalist. Involved in American Workingmen's Party.

Ideological bastion: a strong point in a system of ideas.

Jeffersonian tradition: belief that the independent small farmer led an especially virtuous life and was the backbone of the country.

From **The Age of Jackson** by Arthur M. Schlesinger, Jr., pp. 209, 307, 312, 339, Copyright 1945, by Arthur M. Schlesinger, Jr., by permission of Little, Brown and Co.

"We believe property should be held subordinate to man, and not man to property," said *Orestes A. Brownson,** "and therefore that it is always lawful to make such modifications of its constitution as the good of Humanity requires." . . . But the Democrats had surrendered an important *ideological bastion.** The right of property provided a sturdy foundation for liberalism, while talk of human rights too often might end up in sentimentality or blood.

✻   ✻   ✻   ✻   ✻

The frontal attack on capitalist domination had to be supported by the full mobilization of the noncapitalist groups. The *Jeffersonian tradition** had already rallied the farmers and the artisans. But the Jeffersonians, no less than the Federalists, looked on industrial labor as an element, fortunately small, to be regarded with mistrust and abhorrence. Without property the working classes of great cities must be without independence, factious and corrupt, the prey of demagogues and tyrants. . . .

The class thus grew, for all the disapproval of the old parties, and eventually its power commanded recognition. Jacksonian democracy acted on this new political fact.

Frontier Election, 1830—Before the secret ballot, voters lined up to cast spoken ballots, with candidates standing on the platform to greet them. The atmosphere was convivial and cider flowed freely.

12 BRAY HAMMOND ON JACKSONIAN DEMOCRACY

Bray Hammond was born in Springfield, Missouri, in 1886 and was educated at Stanford University. He taught American history at the State College of Washington from 1913 to 1916, served as a captain in the United States Army during World War I, and worked in private business from 1919–1930. He was a member of the Federal Reserve Board from 1930 to 1950, when he retired. Mr. Hammond has written several articles and a book on early nineteenth-century American political and economic history. His book *Banks and Politics in America from the Revolution to the Civil War* won the Pulitzer Prize for History in 1958. Mr. Hammond died in 1968.

While reading the next selection from *Banks and Politics,* published in 1957, keep in mind these questions. According to Hammand:

1. What were the sources of the Jacksonian Revolution?

2. What changes in social outlook had occurred in America by the time of Jackson's election to the Presidency?

3. How did Jacksonians view capitalism?

Jacksonian Democracy: A Product of Individual Enterprise

During the half century that ended with General Jackson's election, America underwent changes perhaps the most radical and sweeping it has ever undergone in so short a time.

❀   ❀   ❀   ❀   ❀

The changes in social outlook were profound. Steam was generating conceptions of life, liberty, and the pursuit of happiness that were quite alien to Thomas Jefferson's. . . . People were led as they had not been before by visions of money-making. Liberty became transformed into *laissez-faire.** A violent, aggressive, economic individualism became established. The democracy became greedy, intolerant, imperialistic, and lawless. It opened economic advantages to those who had not previously had them; yet it allowed wealth to be concentrated in new hands only somewhat more numerous than before, but less responsible, and less disciplined. There were unenterprising and unpropertied thousands who missed entirely the economic opportunities with which America was thick. There was poverty in the eastern cities and poverty on the frontier. Those who failed to hold their own in the struggle were set down as unfit.

> **Laissez-faire:** French words which have come to mean individual freedom of choice in economic affairs and opposition to government regulation of business.

❀   ❀   ❀   ❀   ❀

Socially, the Jacksonian revolution signified that a nation of democrats was tired of being governed, however well, by gentlemen from Virginia and Massachusetts . . . . Economically, the revolution signified that a nation of

B123

potential money-makers could not abide traditionary, conservative limitations on business enterprise, particularly by capitalists in Philadelphia. The Jacksonian revolution was a consequence of the Industrial Revolution and of a farm-born people's realization that now anyone in America could get rich and through his own efforts, if he had a fair chance. . . . The humbly born and rugged individualists who were gaining fortunes by their own toil and sweat, or wits, were still simple Americans, Jeffersonian, anti-monopolistic, anti-governmental, but fraught with the spirit of enterprise . . . .

[Consequently] . . . Jacksonians still employed the vocabulary of their agrarian backgrounds. The phraseology of idealism was adapted to money-making. . . . Their terms of abuse were "oppression," "tyranny," "monied power," "aristocracy," "wealth," "privilege," "monopoly"; their terms of praise were "the humble," "the poor," "the simple," the "honest and industrious." Though their cause was a sophisticated one of enterpriser against capitalist, of banker against regulation, and of *Wall Street** against *Chestnut Street,** the language was the same as if they were all back on the farm . . . . Notwithstanding [the] . . . language, therefore, the [Jacksonian Revolution] . . . was in no sense a blow at capitalism or property or the "money power." It was a blow at an older set of capitalists by a newer, more numerous set. It was incident to the democratization of business, the diffusion of enterprise among the mass of people, and the transfer of economic primacy from an old and conservative merchant class to a newer, more aggressive, and more numerous body of business men and speculators of all sorts.

Wall Street and **Chestnut Street:** Wall Street was the center of private banking and financial activity in New York. Chestnut Street in Philadelphia was the site of the Bank of the United States, which Jacksonians distrusted as a privileged corporation. The Bank's charter was not renewed by President Jackson.

Selections from Bray Hammond, **Banks and Politics in America from the Revolution to the Civil War** (copyright © 1957 by Princeton University Press; Princeton Paperback, 1967), pp. 326–329. Reprinted by permission of Princeton University Press.

Additional Reading

Beard, Charles A., *The Economic Basis of Politics.* (Paperback: Vintage Books, 1957)

Benson, Lee, *The Concept of Jacksonian Democracy: New York as a Test Case.* Princeton; Princeton University Press, 1961.

Hacker, Louis M., *The Triumph of American Capitalism.* New York: Columbia University Press, 1940.

Hartz, Louis, *The Liberal Tradition in America.* New York: Harcourt Brace Jovanovich, 1955.

Hofstadter, Richard, *The American Political Tradition.* New York: Alfred A. Knopf, Inc., 1948.

Meyers, Marvin, *The Jacksonian Persuasion, Politics and Belief.* (Paperback: Vintage Books, 1960)

Parrington, Vernon Louis, *Main Currents in American Thought.* New York: Harcourt Brace Jovanovich, 1954; Vol. II: *The Romantic Revolution in America, 1800–1860.*

Ward, John W., *Andrew Jackson, Symbol for an Age.* New York: Oxford University Press, 1955.

The Constitution of the United States of America

Preamble

We the people of the United States, in order to form a more perfect Union, establish justice, insure domestic tranquility, provide for the common defense, promote the general welfare, and secure the blessings of liberty to ourselves and our posterity, do ordain and establish this CONSTITUTION for the United States of America.

Article 1. Legislative Department

SECTION 1. CONGRESS

All legislative powers herein granted shall be vested in a Congress of the United States, which shall consist of a Senate and House of Representatives.

SECTION 2. HOUSE OF REPRESENTATIVES

1. *Election and term of office.* The House of Representatives shall be composed of members chosen every second year by the people of the several states, and the electors in each state shall have the qualifications requisite for electors of the most numerous branch of the state legislature.

2. *Qualifications for representatives.* No person shall be a representative who shall not have attained to the age of twenty-five years, and been seven years a citizen of the United States, and who shall not, when elected, be an inhabitant of that state in which he shall be chosen.

3. *Apportionment of representatives and direct taxes.* Representatives [and direct taxes] shall be apportioned among the several states which may be included within this Union, according to their respective numbers, [which shall be determined by adding to the whole number of free persons, including those bound to service for a term of years, and excluding Indians not taxed, three-fifths of all other persons.] The actual enumeration shall be made within three years after the first meeting of the Congress of the United States, and within every subsequent term of ten years, in such manner as they shall by law direct. The number of representatives shall not exceed 1 for every 30,000, but each state shall have at least 1 representative; [and until such enumeration shall be made, the state of New Hampshire shall be entitled to choose 3; Massachusetts, 8; Rhode Island and Providence Plantations, 1; Connecticut, 5; New York, 6; New Jersey, 4; Pennsylvania, 8; Delaware, 1; Maryland, 6; Virginia, 10; North Carolina, 5; South Carolina 5; and Georgia 3.]

4. *Filling vacancies.* When vacancies happen in the representation from any state, the executive authority thereof shall issue writs of election to fill such vacancies.

5. *Election of officers; impeachment.* The House of Representatives shall choose their Speaker and other officers; and shall have the sole power of impeachment.

SECTION 3. SENATE

1. *Number of senators and term of office.* The Senate of the United States shall be composed of two senators from each state, [chosen by the legislature thereof,] for six years, and each senator shall have one vote.

2. *Classification; filling vacancies.* [Immediately after they shall be assembled in consequence of the first election, they shall be divided as equally as may be into three classes. The seats of the senators of the first class shall be vacated at the expiration of the second year, of the second class at the expiration of the fourth year, and of the third class at the expiration of the sixth year, so that one-third may be chosen every second year; and if vacancies happen by resignation, or otherwise, during the recess of the legislature of any state, the executive thereof may make temporary appointments until the next meeting of the legislature, which shall then fill such vacancies.]

3. *Qualifications for senators.* No person shall be a senator who shall not have attained to the age of thirty years, and been nine years a citizen of the United States, and who shall not, when elected, be an inhabitant of that state for which he shall be chosen.

4. *President of the Senate.* The Vice-President of the United States shall be president of the Senate, but shall have no vote, unless they be equally divided.

5. *Other officers.* The Senate shall choose their other officers, and also a President *pro tempore,* in the absence of the Vice-President, or when he shall exercise the office of President of the United States.

6. *Trials of impeachment.* The Senate shall have the sole power to try all impeachments. When sitting for that purpose, they shall be on oath or affirmation. When the President of the United States is tried, the Chief Justice shall preside; and no person shall be convicted without the concurrence of two thirds of the members present.

7. *Punishment for conviction.* Judgment in cases of impeachment shall not extend further than to removal from office, and disqualification to hold and enjoy any office of honor, trust, or profit under the United States; but the party convicted shall nevertheless be liable and subject to indictment, trial, judgment, and punishment, according to law.

SECTION 4. ELECTIONS AND MEETINGS OF CONGRESS

1. *Regulation of elections.* The times, places, and manner of holding elections for senators and representatives shall be prescribed in each state by the legislature thereof; but the Congress may at any time by law make or alter such regulations, except as to the places of choosing senators.

2. *Meetings.* The Congress shall assemble at least once in every year, [and such meeting shall be on the first Monday in December,] unless they shall by law appoint a different day.

SECTION 5. RULES OF PROCEDURE

1. *Membership and sittings.* Each house shall be the judge of the elections, returns, and qualifications of its own members, and a majority of each shall constitute a quorum to do business; but a smaller number may ad-

journ from day to day, and may be authorized to compel the attendance of absent members, in such manner, and under such penalties, as each house may provide.

2. *Proceedings.* Each house may determine the rules of its proceedings, punish its members for disorderly behavior, and with the concurrence of two thirds, expel a member.

3. *Journal.* Each house shall keep a journal of its proceedings, and from time to time publish the same, excepting such parts as may in their judgment require secrecy; and the yeas and nays of the members of either house on any question shall, at the desire of one fifth of those present, be entered on the journal.

4. *Adjournment.* Neither house, during the session of Congress, shall, without the consent of the other, adjourn for more than three days, nor to any other place than that in which the two houses shall be sitting.

SECTION 6. PRIVILEGES AND RESTRICTIONS

1. *Salary and privileges.* The senators and representatives shall receive a compensation for their services, to be ascertained by law and paid out of the Treasury of the United States. They shall in all cases, except treason, felony, and breach of the peace, be privileged from arrest during their attendance at the session of their respective houses, and in going to and returning from the same; and for any speech or debate in either house, they shall not be questioned in any other place.

2. *Restrictions.* No senator or representative shall, during the time for which he was elected, be appointed to any civil office under the authority of the United States, which shall have been created, or the emoluments whereof shall have been increased, during such time; and no person holding any office under the United States shall be a member of either house during his continuance in office.

SECTION 7. METHOD OF PASSING LAWS

1. *Revenue bills.* All bills for raising revenue shall originate in the House of Representatives; but the Senate may propose or concur with amendments as on other bills.

2. *How a bill becomes a law.* Every bill which shall have passed the House of Representatives and the Senate shall, before it becomes a law, be presented to the President of the United States; if he approve, he shall sign it, but if not, he shall return it, with his objections, to that house in which it shall have originated, who shall enter the objections at large on their journal, and proceed to reconsider it. If after such reconsideration two thirds of that house shall agree to pass the bill, it shall be sent, together with the objections, to the other house, by which it shall likewise be reconsidered, and, if approved by two thirds of that house, it shall become a law. But in all such cases the votes of both houses shall be determined by yeas and nays, and the names of the persons voting for and against the bill shall be entered on the journal of each house respectively. If any bill shall not be returned by the President within ten days (Sundays excepted) after it shall have been presented to him, the same shall be a law, in like manner as if he had signed it, unless the Congress by their adjournment prevent its return, in which case it shall not be a law.

3. *Presidential approval or veto.* Every order, reso-lution, or vote to which the concurrence of the Senate and House of Representatives may be necessary (except on a question of adjournment) shall be presented to the President of the United States; and before the same shall take effect, shall be approved by him, or being disapproved by him shall be repassed by two thirds of the Senate and House of Representatives, according to the rules and limitations prescribed in the case of a bill.

SECTION 8. POWERS DELEGATED TO CONGRESS

The Congress shall have power

1. To lay and collect taxes, duties, imposts, and excises, to pay the debts and provide for the common defense and general welfare of the United States; but all duties, imposts, and excises shall be uniform throughout the United States;

2. To borrow money on the credit of the United States;

3. To regulate commerce with foreign nations, and among the several states, and with the Indian tribes;

4. To establish a uniform rule of naturalization, and uniform laws on the subject of bankruptcies throughout the United States;

5. To coin money, regulate the value thereof, and of foreign coin, and fix the standard of weights and measures;

6. To provide for the punishment of counterfeiting the securities and current coin of the United States;

7. To establish post offices and post roads;

8. To promote the progress of science and useful arts by securing for limited times to authors and inventors the exclusive right to their respective writings and discoveries;

9. To constitute tribunals inferior to the Supreme Court;

10. To define and punish piracies and felonies committed on the high seas and offenses against the law of nations;

11. To declare war, [grant letters of marque and reprisal,] and make rules concerning captures on land and water;

12. To raise and support armies, but no appropriation of money to that use shall be for a longer term than two years;

13. To provide and maintain a navy;

14. To make rules for the government and regulation of the land and naval forces;

15. To provide for calling forth the militia to execute the laws of the Union, suppress insurrections, and repel invasions;

16. To provide for organizing, arming, and disciplining the militia, and for governing such part of them as may be employed in the service of the United States, reserving to the states, respectively, the appointment of the officers, and the authority of training the militia according to the discipline prescribed by Congress;

17. To exercise exclusive legislation in all cases whatsoever, over such district (not exceeding ten miles square) as may, by cession of particular states, and the acceptance of Congress, become the seat of government of the United States, and to exercise like authority over all places purchased by the consent of the legislature of the state in which the same shall be, for the erection

of forts, magazines, arsenals, dockyards, and other needful buildings;—and

18. To make all laws which shall be necessary and proper for carrying into execution the foregoing powers, and all other powers vested by this Constitution in the government of the United States, or in any department or officer thereof.

SECTION 9. POWERS DENIED TO THE FEDERAL GOVERNMENT

1. [The migration or importation of such persons as any of the states now existing shall think proper to admit shall not be prohibited by the Congress prior to the year 1808; but a tax or duty may be imposed on such importation, not exceeding $10 for each person.]

2. The privilege of the writ of *habeas corpus* shall not be suspended, unless when in cases of rebellion or invasion the public safety may require it.

3. No bill of attainder or *ex post facto* law shall be passed.

4. No capitation or other direct tax shall be laid, unless in proportion to the census or enumeration herein before directed to be taken.

5. No tax or duty shall be laid on articles exported from any state.

6. No preference shall be given by any regulation of commerce or revenue to the ports of one state over those of another; nor shall vessels bound to, or from, one state, be obliged to enter, clear, or pay duties in another.

7. No money shall be drawn from the Treasury, but in consequence of appropriations made by law; and a regular statement and account of the receipts and expenditures of all public money shall be published from time to time.

8. No title of nobility shall be granted by the United States; and no person holding any office of profit or trust under them, shall, without the consent of the Congress, accept of any present, emolument, office, or title, of any kind whatever, from any king, prince, or foreign state.

SECTION 10. POWERS DENIED TO THE STATES

1. No state shall enter into any treaty, alliance, or confederation; grant letters of marque and reprisal; coin money; emit bills of credit; make anything but gold and silver coin a tender in payment of debts; pass any bill of attainder, *ex post facto* law, or law impairing the obligation of contracts, or grant any title of nobility.

2. No state shall, without the consent of the Congress, lay any imposts or duties on imports or exports, except what may be absolutely necessary for executing its inspection laws; and the net produce of all duties and imposts, laid by any state on imports or exports, shall be for the use of the Treasury of the United States; and all such laws shall be subject to the revision and control of the Congress.

3. No state shall, without the consent of Congress, lay any duty of tonnage, keep troops, or ships of war in time of peace, enter into any agreement or compact with another state, or with a foreign power, or engage in war, unless actually invaded, or in such imminent danger as will not admit of delay.

Article 2. Executive Department

SECTION 1. PRESIDENT AND VICE-PRESIDENT

1. *Term of office.* The executive power shall be vested in a President of the United States of America. He shall hold his office during the term of four years, and together with the Vice-President, chosen for the same term, be elected as follows:

2. *Electoral system.* Each state shall appoint, in such manner as the legislature thereof may direct, a number of electors, equal to the whole number of senators and representatives to which the state may be entitled in the Congress; but no senator or representative, or person holding an office of trust or profit under the United States, shall be appointed an elector.

3. *Election of President and Vice-President.* [The electors shall meet in their respective states, and vote by ballot for two persons, of whom one at least shall not be an inhabitant of the same state with themselves. And they shall make a list of all the persons voted for, and of the number of votes for each; which list they shall sign and certify, and transmit sealed to the seat of the government of the United States, directed to the president of the Senate. The president of the Senate shall, in the presence of the Senate and House of Representatives, open all the certificates, and the votes shall then be counted. The person having the greatest number of votes shall be the President; if such number be a majority of the whole number of electors appointed; and if there be more than one who have such majority, and have an equal number of votes, then the House of Representatives shall immediately choose by ballot one of them for President; and if no person have a majority, then from the five highest on the list the said House shall in like manner choose the President. But in choosing the President the votes shall be taken by states, the representation from each state having one vote. A quorum for this purpose shall consist of a member or members from two-thirds of the states, and a majority of all the states shall be necessary to a choice. In every case, after the choice of the President, the person having the greatest number of votes of the electors shall be the Vice-President. But if there should remain two or more who have equal votes, the Senate shall choose from them by ballot the Vice-President.]

4. *Time of elections.* The Congress may determine the time of choosing the electors, and the day on which they shall give their votes; which day shall be the same throughout the United States.

5. *Qualifications for President.* No person except a natural-born citizen, [or a citizen of the United States, at the time of the adoption of this Constitution,] shall be eligible to the office of President; neither shall any person be eligible to that office who shall not have attained to the age of thirty-five years, and been fourteen years a resident within the United States.

6. *Filling vacancies.* [In case of the removal of the President from office, or of his death, resignation, or inability to discharge the powers and duties of the said office, the same shall devolve on the Vice-President, and the Congress may by law provide for the case of removal, death, resignation, or inability, both of the President and Vice-President, declaring what officer shall then act as President, and such officer shall act accordingly, until the disability be removed, or a President shall be elected.]

7. *Salary.* The President shall, at stated times, receive for his services, a compensation, which shall neither

be increased nor diminished during the period for which he shall have been elected, and he shall not receive within that period any other emolument from the United States, or any of them.

8. *Oath of office.* Before he enter on the execution of his office, he shall take the following oath or affirmation:—"I do solemnly swear (or affirm) that I will faithfully execute the office of President of the United States, and will to the best of my ability, preserve, protect, and defend the Constitution of the United States."

SECTION 2. POWERS OF THE PRESIDENT

1. *Powers over the military and executive departments; reprieves and pardons.* The President shall be Commander in Chief of the Army and Navy of the United States, and of the militia of the several states, when called into the actual service of the United States; he may require the opinion, in writing, of the principal officer in each of the executive departments, upon any subject relating to the duties of their respective offices, and he shall have power to grant reprieves and pardons for offenses against the United States, except in cases of impeachment.

2. *Treaties and appointments.* He shall have power, by and with the advice and consent of the Senate, to make treaties, provided two thirds of the senators present concur; and he shall nominate, and by and with the advice and consent of the Senate, shall appoint ambassadors, other public ministers and consuls, judges of the Supreme Court, and all other officers of the United States, whose appointments are not herein otherwise provided for, and which shall be established by law; but the Congress may by law vest the appointment of such inferior officers, as they think proper, in the President alone, in the courts of law, or in the heads of departments.

3. *Filling vacancies.* The President shall have power to fill up all vacancies that may happen during the recess of the Senate, by granting commissions which shall expire at the end of their next session.

SECTION 3. DUTIES OF THE PRESIDENT

He shall from time to time give to the Congress information of the state of the Union, and recommend to their consideration such measures as he shall judge necessary and expedient; he may, on extraordinary occasions, convene both houses, or either of them, and in case of disagreement between them, with respect to the time of adjournment, he may adjourn them to such time as he shall think proper; he shall receive ambassadors and other public ministers; he shall take care that the laws be faithfully executed, and shall commission all the officers of the United States.

SECTION 4. IMPEACHMENT

The President, Vice-President, and all civil officers of the United States, shall be removed from office on impeachment for, and conviction of, treason, bribery, or other high crimes and misdemeanors.

Article 3. Judicial Department

SECTION 1. FEDERAL COURTS

The judicial power of the United States shall be vested in one Supreme Court, and in such inferior courts as the Congress may from time to time ordain and establish. The judges, both of the Supreme and inferior courts, shall hold their offices during good behavior, and

shall, at stated times, receive for their services a compensation, which shall not be diminished during their continuance in office.

SECTION 2. JURISDICTION OF FEDERAL COURTS

1. *General jurisdiction.* The judicial power shall extend to all cases, in law and equity, arising under this Constitution, the laws of the United States, and treaties made or which shall be made, under their authority; to all cases affecting ambassadors, other public ministers and consuls; to all cases of admiralty and maritime jurisdiction; to controversies to which the United States shall be a party; to controversies between two or more states; between a state and citizens of another state; between citizens of different states; between citizens of the same state claiming lands under grants of different states, and between a state, or the citizens thereof, and foreign states, citizens, or subjects.

2. *Supreme Court.* In all cases affecting ambassadors, other public ministers and consuls, and those in which a state shall be a party, the Supreme Court shall have original jurisdiction. In all the other cases before mentioned, the Supreme Court shall have appellate jurisdiction, both as to law and fact, with such exceptions, and under such regulations as the Congress shall make.

3. *Conduct of trials.* The trial of all crimes, except in cases of impeachment, shall be by jury; and such trial shall be held in the state where the said crimes shall have been committed; but when not committed within any state, the trial shall be at such place or places as the Congress may by law have directed.

SECTION 3. TREASON

1. *Definition.* Treason against the United States shall consist only in levying war against them, or in adhering to their enemies, giving them aid and comfort. No person shall be convicted of treason unless on the testimony of two witnesses to the same overt act, or on confession in open court.

2. *Punishment.* The Congress shall have power to declare the punishment of treason, but no attainder of treason shall work corruption of blood or forfeiture except during the life of the person attainted.

Article 4. Relations Among the States

SECTION 1. OFFICIAL ACTS

Full faith and credit shall be given in each state to the public acts, records, and judicial proceedings of every other state. And the Congress may by general laws prescribe the manner in which such acts, records, and proceedings shall be proved, and the effect thereof.

SECTION 2. PRIVILEGES OF CITIZENS

1. *Privileges.* The citizens of each state shall be entitled to all privileges and immunities of citizens in the several states.

2. *Extradition.* A person charged in any state with treason, felony, or other crime, who shall flee from justice, and be found in another state, shall on demand of the executive authority of the state from which he fled, be delivered up, to be removed to the state having jurisdiction of the crime.

3. *Fugitive slaves.* [No person held in service or labor in one state, under the laws thereof, escaping into another, shall in consequence of any law or regulation therein, be discharged from such service or labor, but

shall be delivered up on claim of the party to whom such service or labor may be due.]

SECTION 3. NEW STATES AND TERRITORIES

1. *Admission of new states.* New states may be admitted by the Congress into this Union; but no new state shall be formed or erected within the jurisdiction of any other state; nor any state be formed by the junction of two or more states, or parts of states, without the consent of the legislatures of the states concerned as well as of the Congress.

2. *Power of Congress over territories and other property.* The Congress shall have power to dispose of and make all needful rules and regulations respecting the territory or other property belonging to the United States; and nothing in this Constitution shall be so construed as to prejudice any claims of the United States, or of any particular state.

SECTION 4. GUARANTEES TO THE STATES

The United States shall guarantee to every state in this Union a republican form of government, and shall protect each of them against invasion; and on application of the legislature, or of the executive (when the legislature cannot be convened) against domestic violence.

Article 5. Methods of Amendment

The Congress, whenever two thirds of both houses shall deem it necessary, shall propose amendments to this Constitution, or, on the application of the legislatures of two thirds of the several states, shall call a convention for proposing amendments, which, in either case, shall be valid to all intents and purposes, as part of this Constitution, when ratified by the legislatures of three fourths of the several states, or by conventions in three fourths thereof, as the one or the other mode of ratification may be proposed by the Congress; provided that [no amendments which may be made prior to the year 1808 shall in any manner affect the first and fourth clauses in the Ninth Section of the First Article; and that] no state, without its consent, shall be deprived of its equal suffrage in the Senate.

Article 6. General Provisions

1. *Public debts.* All debts contracted and engagements entered into, before the adoption of this Constitution, shall be as valid against the United States under this Constitution, as under the Confederation.

2. *The supreme law of the land.* This Constitution, and the laws of the United States which shall be made in pursuance thereof, and all treaties made, or which shall be made, under the authority of the United States, shall be the supreme law of the land; and the judges in every state shall be bound thereby, anything in the constitution or laws of any state to the contrary notwithstanding.

3. *Oaths of office; no religious test.* The senators and representatives before mentioned, and the members of the several state legislatures, and all executive and judicial officers, both of the United States and of the several states, shall be bound by oath or affirmation, to support this Constitution; but no religious test shall ever be required as a qualification to any office or public trust under the United States.

Article 7. Ratification

The ratification of the conventions of nine states shall be sufficient for the establishment of this Constitution between the states so ratifying the same.

Done in Convention by the unanimous consent of the States present the seventeenth day of September in the year of our Lord one thousand seven hundred and eighty-seven and of the independence of the United States of America the twelfth. In witness whereof we have hereunto subscribed our names.

Amendment 1. Freedom of Religion, Speech, Press, Assembly, and Petition (1791)

Congress shall make no law respecting an establishment of religion, or prohibiting the free exercise thereof; or abridging the freedom of speech, or of the press; or the right of the people peaceably to assemble, and to petition the government for a redress of grievances.

Amendment 2. Right to Keep Arms (1791)

A well-regulated militia, being necessary to the security of a free state, the right of the people to keep and bear arms shall not be infringed.

Amendment 3. Quartering of Troops (1791)

No soldier shall, in time of peace, be quartered in any house, without the consent of the owner; nor in time of war, but in a manner to be prescribed by law.

Amendment 4. Searches and Seizures; Warrants (1791)

The right of the people to be secure in their persons, houses, papers, and effects, against unreasonable searches and seizures, shall not be violated; and no warrants shall issue but upon probable cause, supported by oath or affirmation, and particularly describing the place to be searched, and the person or things to be seized.

Amendment 5. Rights of Accused Persons (1791)

No person shall be held to answer for a capital, or otherwise infamous, crime, unless on a presentment or indictment of a grand jury, except in cases arising in the land or naval forces, or in the militia, when in actual service in time of war or public danger; nor shall any person be subject for the same offense to be twice put in jeopardy of life or limb; nor shall be compelled, in any criminal case, to be a witness against himself; nor be deprived of life, liberty, or property, without due process of law; nor shall private property be taken for public use, without just compensation.

Amendment 6. Right to Speedy and Public Trial (1791)

In all criminal prosecutions, the accused shall enjoy the right to a speedy and public trial, by an impartial jury of the state and district wherein the crime shall have been committed, which district shall have been previously ascertained by law, and to be informed of the nature and cause of the accusation; to be confronted with the witnesses against him; to have compulsory process for obtaining witnesses in his favor, and to have the assistance of counsel for his defense.

Amendment 7. Jury Trial in Civil Cases (1791)

In suits at common law, where the value in controversy shall exceed twenty dollars, the right of trial by jury shall be preserved, and no fact tried by a jury shall be otherwise reexamined in any court of the United States than according to the rules of the common law.

Amendment 8. Bail, Fines, Punishments (1791)

Excessive bail shall not be required, nor excessive fines imposed, nor cruel and unusual punishments inflicted.

Amendment 9. Powers Reserved to the People (1791)

The enumeration in the Constitution, of certain rights, shall not be construed to deny or disparage others retained by the people.

Amendment 10. Powers Reserved to the States (1791)

The powers not delegated to the United States by the Constitution, nor prohibited by it to the states, are reserved to the states respectively, or to the people.

Amendment 11. Suits Against States (1798)

The judicial power of the United States shall not be construed to extend to any suit in law or equity, commenced or prosecuted against one of the United States, by citizens of another state, or by citizens or subjects of any foreign state.

Amendment 12. Election of President and Vice-President (1804)

The electors shall meet in their respective states, and vote by ballot for President and Vice-President, one of whom, at least, shall not be an inhabitant of the same state with themselves; they shall name in their ballots the person voted for as President, and in distinct ballots the person voted for as Vice-President, and they shall make distinct lists of all persons voted for as President, and of all persons voted for as Vice-President, and of the number of votes for each, which lists they shall sign and certify, and transmit, sealed, to the seat of government of the United States, directed to the President of the Senate; the President of the Senate shall, in the presence of the Senate and House of Representatives, open all the certificates and the votes shall then be counted; the person having the greatest number of votes for President shall be the President, if such number be a majority of the whole number of electors appointed; and if no person have such majority, when from the persons having the highest number not exceeding three on the list of those voted for as President, the House of Representatives shall choose immediately, by ballot, the President. But in choosing the President, the votes shall be taken by states, the representation from each state having one vote; a quorum for this purpose shall consist of a member or members from two thirds of the states, and a majority of all the states shall be necessary to a choice. [And if the House of Representatives shall not choose a President whenever the right of choice shall devolve upon them, before the fourth day of March next following, then the Vice-President shall act as President, as in the case of the death or other constitutional disability of the President.] The person having the greatest number of votes as Vice-President, shall be the Vice-President, if such number be a majority of the whole number of electors appointed, and if no person have a majority, then, from the two highest numbers on the list, the Senate shall choose the Vice-President; a quorum for the purpose shall consist of two thirds of the whole number of senators, and a majority of the whole number shall be necessary to a choice. But no person constitutionally ineligible to the office of President shall be eligible to that of Vice-President of the United States.

Amendment 13. Slavery Abolished (1865)

SECTION 1. Neither slavery nor involuntary servitude, except as a punishment for crime whereof the party shall have been duly convicted, shall exist within the United States, or any place subject to their jurisdiction.

SECTION 2. Congress shall have power to enforce this article by appropriate legislation.

Amendment 14. Rights of Citizens (1868)

SECTION 1. *Citizenship defined.* All persons born or naturalized in the United States and subject to the jurisdiction thereof, are citizens of the United States and of the state wherein they reside. No state shall make or enforce any law which shall abridge the privileges or immunities of citizens of the United States; nor shall any state deprive any person of life, liberty, or property, without due process of law; nor deny to any person within its jurisdiction the equal protection of the laws.

SECTION 2. *Apportionment of representatives.* Representatives shall be apportioned among the several states according to their respective numbers, counting the whole number of persons in each state, excluding Indians not taxed. But when the right to vote at any election for the choice of electors for President and Vice-President of the United States, representatives in Congress, the executive, and judicial officers of a state, or the members of the legislature thereof, is denied to any of the male inhabitants of such state, being twenty-one years of age and citizens of the United States, or in any way abridged, except for participation in rebellion, or other crime, the basis of representation therein shall be reduced in the proportion which the number of such male citizens shall bear to the whole number of male citizens twenty-one years of age in such state.

SECTION 3. *Disability for engaging in insurrection.* No person shall be a senator or representative in Congress, or elector of President and Vice-President, or hold any office, civil or military, under the United States, or under any state, who, having previously taken an oath, as a member of Congress, or as an officer of the United States, or as a member of any state legislature, or as an executive or judicial officer of any state, to support the Constitution of the United States, shall have engaged in insurrection or rebellion against the same, or given aid or comfort to the enemies thereof. But Congress may, by a vote of two thirds of each house, remove such disability.

SECTION 4. *Public debt.* The validity of the public debt of the United States, authorized by law, including debts incurred for payment of pensions and bounties for services in suppressing insurrection or rebellion, shall not be questioned. But neither the United States nor any state shall assume or pay any debt or obligation incurred in aid of insurrection or rebellion against the United States, [or any claim for the loss or emancipation of any slave;] but all such debts, obligations, and claims shall be held illegal and void.

SECTION 5. *Enforcement.* The Congress shall have power to enforce, by appropriate legislation, the provisions of this article.

Amendment 15. Rights of Suffrage (1870)

SECTION 1. The right of citizens of the United States to vote shall not be denied or abridged by the United States or any state on account of race, color, or previous condition of servitude.

SECTION 2. The Congress shall have power to enforce this article by appropriate legislation.

Amendment 16. Income Tax (1913)

The Congress shall have power to lay and collect taxes on incomes, from whatever source derived, without apportionment among the several states, and without regard to any census or enumeration.

Amendment 17. Election of Senators (1913)

SECTION 1. *Method of election.* The Senate of the United States shall be composed of two senators from each state, elected by the people thereof, for six years; and each senator shall have one vote. The electors in each state shall have the qualifications requisite for electors of the most numerous branch of the state legislatures.

SECTION 2. *Filling vacancies.* When vacancies happen in the representation of any state in the Senate, the executive authority of such state shall issue writs of election to fill such vacancies. *Provided* that the legislature of any state may empower the executive thereof to make temporary appointments until the people fill the vacancies by election as the legislature may direct.

[SECTION 3. *Not retroactive.* This amendment shall not be so construed as to affect the election or term of any senator chosen before it becomes valid as part of the Constitution.]

Amendment 18. National Prohibition (1919)

[SECTION 1. After one year from the ratification of this article the manufacture, sale, or transportation of intoxicating liquors within, the importation thereof into, or the exportation thereof from, the United States and all territory subject to the jurisdiction thereof for beverage purposes is hereby prohibited.

SECTION 2. The Congress and the several states shall have concurrent power to enforce this article by appropriate legislation.

SECTION 3. This article shall be inoperative unless it shall have been ratified as an amendment to the Constitution by the legislatures of the several states, as provided in the Constitution, within seven years from the date of the submission hereof to the states by the Congress.]

Amendment 19. Woman Suffrage (1920)

SECTION 1. The right of citizens of the United States to vote shall not be denied or abridged by the United States or by any state on account of sex.

SECTION 2. Congress shall have power to enforce this article by appropriate legislation.

Amendment 20. "Lame Duck" Amendment (1933)

SECTION 1. *Beginning of terms.* The terms of the President and Vice-President shall end at noon on the 20th day of January, and the terms of senators and representatives at noon on the 3d day of January, of the years in which such terms would have ended if this article had not been ratified; and the terms of their successors will then begin.

SECTION 2. *Beginning of congressional sessions.* The Congress shall assemble at least once in every year, and such meeting shall begin at noon on the 3rd day of January, unless they shall by law appoint a different day.

SECTION 3. *Presidential succession.* If at the time fixed for the beginning of the term of the President, the President-elect shall have died, the Vice-President-elect shall become President. If a President shall not have been chosen before the time fixed for the beginning of his term, or if the President-elect shall have failed to qualify, then the Vice-President-elect shall act as President until a President shall have qualified; and the Congress may by law provide for the case wherein neither a President-elect nor a Vice-President-elect shall have qualified, declaring who shall then act as President, or the manner in which one who is to act shall be selected, and such person shall act accordingly until a President or Vice-President shall have qualified.

SECTION 4. *Filling Presidential vacancy.* The Congress may by law provide for the case of the death of any of the persons from whom the House of Representatives may choose a President whenever the right of choice shall have devolved upon them, and for the case of the death of any of the persons from whom the Senate may choose a Vice-President whenever the right of choice shall have devolved upon them.

[SECTION 5. *Effective date.* Sections 1 and 2 shall take effect on the 15th day of October following the ratification of this article.

SECTION 6. *Time limit for ratification.* This article shall be inoperative unless it shall have been ratified as an amendment to the Constitution by the legislatures of three fourths of the several states within seven years from the date of its submission.]

Amendment 21. Repeal of Prohibition (1933)

SECTION 1. The eighteenth article of amendment to the Constitution of the United States is hereby repealed.

SECTION 2. The transportation or importation into any state, territory, or possession of the United States for delivery or use therein of intoxicating liquors, in violation of the laws thereof, is hereby prohibited.

[SECTION 3. This article shall be inoperative unless it shall have been ratified as an amendment to the Constitution by conventions in the several states, as provided in the Constitution, within seven years from the date of the submission hereof to the states by the Congress.]

Amendment 22. Two-Term Limit for Presidents (1951)

SECTION 1. No person shall be elected to the office of the President more than twice, and no person who has held the office of President, or acted as President, for more than two years of a term to which some other person was elected President shall be elected to the office of the President more than once. [But this Article shall not apply to any person holding the office of President when this Article was proposed by the Congress, and shall not prevent any person who may be holding the office of President, or acting as President, during the term within which this Article becomes operative from holding the office of President or acting as President during the remainder of such term.]

[SECTION 2. This article shall be inoperative unless it shall have been ratified as an amendment to the Constitution by the legislatures of three fourths of the several states within seven years from the date of its submission to the states by the Congress.]

Amendment 23. Presidential Electors for District of Columbia (1961)

SECTION 1. The District constituting the seat of Government of the United States shall appoint in such manner as the Congress may direct:

A number of electors of President and Vice-President equal to the whole number of senators and representatives in Congress to which the District would be entitled if it were a State, but in no event more than the least populous State; they shall be in addition to those appointed by the States, but they shall be considered, for the purposes of the election of President and Vice-President, to be electors appointed by a State; and they shall meet in the District and perform such duties as provided by the twelfth article of amendment.

SECTION 2. The Congress shall have power to enforce this article by appropriate legislation.

Amendment 24. Poll Tax Banned in National Elections (1964)

SECTION 1. The right of citizens of the United States to vote in any primary or other election for President or Vice-President, for electors for President or Vice-President, or for senator or representative in Congress, shall not be denied or abridged by the United States or any state by reason of failure to pay any poll tax or other tax.

SECTION 2. The Congress shall have the power to enforce this article by appropriate legislation.

Amendment 25. Presidential Disability and Succession (1967)

1. In case of the removal of the President from office or his death or resignation, the Vice-President shall become President.

2. Whenever there is a vacancy in the office of the Vice-President, the President shall nominate a Vice-President who shall take the office upon confirmation of a majority vote of both houses of Congress.

3. Whenever the President transmits to the President *pro tempore* of the Senate and the Speaker of the House of Representatives his written declaration that he is unable to discharge the powers and duties of his office and until he transmits to them a written declaration to the contrary, such powers and duties shall be discharged by the Vice-President as Acting President.

4. Whenever the Vice-President and a majority of either the principal officers of the executive departments or of such other body as Congress may by law provide, transmit to the President *pro tempore* of the Senate and the Speaker of the House of Representatives their written declaration that the President is unable to discharge the powers and duties of his office, the Vice-President shall immediately assume the powers and duties of the office as Acting President.

Thereafter, when the President transmits to the President *pro tempore* of the Senate and the Speaker of the House of Representatives his written declaration that no inability exists, he shall resume the powers and duties of his office unless the Vice-President and a majority of either the principal officers of the executive department or of such other body as Congress may by law provide, transmit within four days to the President *pro tempore* of the Senate and the Speaker of the House of Representatives their written declaration that the President is unable to discharge the powers and duties of his office. Thereupon Congress shall decide the issue, assembling within forty-eight hours for that purpose if not in session. If the Congress, within twenty-one days after receipt of the latter written declaration, or, if Congress is not in session, within twenty-one days after Congress is required to assemble, determines by two thirds vote of both houses that the President is unable to discharge the powers and duties of his office, the Vice-President shall continue to discharge the same as Acting President; otherwise, the President shall resume the powers and duties of his office.

Amendment 26. Voting Age (1971)

SECTION 1. The right of citizens of the United States who are eighteen years of age or older, to vote shall not be denied or abridged by the United States or by any state on account of age.

SECTION 2. The Congress shall have power to enforce this article by appropriate legislation.

Reform: Past and Present

PHILIP GLEASON

In the history of the world the doctrine of Reform
had never such scope as at the present hour. . . .

RALPH WALDO EMERSON

1 The present and the past

Is History Relevant?

Introduction

Objectives of this assignment
are to:
—Describe purpose of studying
history by comparing episodes
from the past with those from
the present as explained in this
assignment.
—Analyze selections from
Thomas Cole's explanation of
his early nineteenth century
picture series **The Course of
Civilization.**
—Analyze selection from Jensen-
Leibmann modern parody of the
Cole picture series for meaning.
—Summarize differences and
similarities between the Cole
and Jensen-Leibmann treatment
of the same theme.
—Draw inferences from filmstrip of Cole and Leibmann
paintings about value of studying
history by comparing past and
present.

"Why do we have to study this stuff anyhow? What good is it to know
about things that happened a hundred years ago?"

History teachers have listened to such student complaints for generations.
Now these objections are more insistent than ever because of the contemporary stress on relevance. Students are not alone in their objections. They are
joined by many educators and social commentators who think we should
concentrate all our energies on solving the grave problems in our society. They
contend that we should be studying the present and the future, not the past.

According to this view, history is a distraction. It's irrelevant. Even worse,
history is said to be a burden that weighs us down. Looking back into the past
fixes our minds in the old patterns, blinds us to new realities and new opportunities, and thus unfits us for dealing with our own times. Carried to its
logical extreme, this line of thinking would lead to the conclusion that the
best thing we could do about history is forget it!

Memory and History

At this point, historians usually respond that history isn't irrelevant at all
because the present grew out of the past, and can only be understood in terms
of what went before. Let us examine the objection by asking whether it is
good advice to tell an individual to forget his past. Perhaps, in certain circumstances, it might be good advice. But would we ever advise a friend to let his
power of memory slacken and deteriorate? Would we like to find our own
memories utterly useless and unreliable? Certainly not! A person becomes less
competent mentally as he loses his power of recalling the past. Thus, *amnesia** is recognized as a serious disorder of the central nervous system. A man
who cannot remember his past cannot function properly in society.

Amnesia means partial or total
loss of memory, caused by
shock, illness, brain injury, or
psychological disturbance.

It is very much the same with history. A people who have lost contact
with their own past don't know who they are or which way they are going. If
history is irrelevant, our personal recollections are also irrelevant a good deal
of the time. Memory doesn't *always* help us solve immediate problems. But
sometimes it does. Hasn't your ability to recall the past ever steered you
around an obstacle, or helped you avoid an embarrassing situation? If you
quarrelled with a friend, wouldn't you review the steps that led up to the
quarrel? And might not this review help you decide what to do next?

In such cases, the individual depends on his memory just as society depends upon history, its collective memory. Just as society needs to know and reflect upon its history, so should an individual review and think about his past experiences from time to time. Often we find ourselves doing this when something in the present reminds us of an episode or occurrence of the past. When this happens, we can compare our memory with the current situation. Even if such a comparison does not solve anything, it can set us thinking. It can give us a new slant on both past and present and thus enrich our minds.

Why Examine Past and Present?

In history there is a parallel for this sort of remembering and comparing. It consists in thinking about the past in relation to the present. That is what we will be doing in the assignments that make up this unit. We will be comparing various aspects of the *ante-bellum** Era of Reform with our own times.

The purpose in examining past and present is not to prove that history repeats itself. Neither is it to draw lessons from history that we can apply to our problems today. The purpose is to stimulate thought by placing both past and present in a new perspective. There are both similarities and differences between the Era of Reform and the 1970's. Let us see whether thinking about these similarities and differences gives us any clues to history's relevance or irrelevance.

The impulse toward social criticism and reform in the ante-bellum generation is the broad similarity which reminds us of our own dissent-filled, reform-minded age. Before turning to any of the reform movements of the 1830's and 1840's, we will look at some evidence of the general tone or spirit of the age and will begin with the work of an artist.

Ante-bellum refers to the period before the Civil War, roughly 1830–1860. The Latin word **ante** means "before"; **bellum** means "war."

1   NATURE AND THE COURSE OF EMPIRE IN THE 1830'S

A great difference between the Era of Reform and the 1970's is that vast spaces were then an untouched wilderness, while the settled area itself was overwhelmingly agricultural. Cities were beginning to grow rapidly, but true *urbanites** were few. The great mass of the people were rural in outlook as well as life-experience. They knew nature at close range and could feel a special sympathy with the love of nature proclaimed by romantic writers like the English poet William Wordsworth.

In Ralph Waldo Emerson and Henry David Thoreau, America produced two great nature writers of her own. The book that made Emerson famous was entitled *Nature* (1836). His younger friend, *Thoreau,** described his life at Walden pond in a work that has remained a classic of American literature.

Urbanite: someone who lives in a city. The word also suggests a person of greater sophistication than one who lives in the country.

Thoreau lived at Walden Pond just outside Concord, Massachusetts, for two years (1845–1847), and in 1854 published the book, **Walden,** based on his experience.

These men and many other Americans regarded nature as more than woodland walks or inspiring scenery. They regarded it as visible evidence of the divine spirit. To be close to nature was to be in intimate contact with the source of all beauty, truth, and goodness. To lose contact with nature was to cut oneself off from the stream of life and energy flowing through the universe.

Viewed from this frame of reference, progress was bound to arouse misgivings. Progress and civilization meant overcoming nature—cutting the forests, damming the streams, spanning the prairies with steel rails, and transforming quiet villages into mighty cities. Progress was desirable, of course. But how could a people cherish nature as the source of all values and virtues while continuing to deface and destroy her?

No one better expressed the uneasiness Americans felt at this dilemma than *Thomas Cole,** the leading landscape painter of the 1830's and 1840's. In 1836—the same year Emerson's *Nature* appeared—Cole put on display five large paintings which made up a series called The Course of Empire. It made a tremendous impression at the time and was regarded as one of the masterworks of world art. Before painting the series, Cole wrote a letter describing what he intended to portray. After reading the letter and studying the paintings, try to answer these questions:

1. *How do you know Cole intended his paintings to have symbolic meaning?*
2. *Does the symbolic meaning apply to America?*
3. *How does Cole try to link changes in nature with changes in the development of society? Does he succeed?*

Thomas Cole: The Course of Empire

I have in mind to paint a series of pictures illustrating the changes in a piece of natural landscape, and at the same time giving a summary of the story of man's progress from primitive barbarism through civilization to a condition of luxury, then destruction, and finally, ruin and desolation.

The philosophy of my subject is drawn from the history of the past, wherein we see how nations have risen from the savage state to that of power and glory, and then fallen, and become extinct. Natural scenery also has its changes—the hours of the day and the seasons of the year—sunshine and storm. These will give expression to each picture of the series. It will be well to have the same location in each picture; this location may be identified by some striking object in each scene—a mountain of peculiar form, for instance. The scene must be composed so as to be picturesque in its wild state, appropriate for cultivation, and the site of a seaport. There must be the sea, a bay, rocks, waterfalls, and woods.

The First Picture, representing the savage state, must be a view of a wilderness, the sun rising from the sea and the clouds of night retiring over the mountains. The figures must be savage, clothed in skins, and occupied in the chase. There must be a flashing *chiaroscuro,** and the spirit of motion pervading the scene, as though nature were just springing from chaos.

Cole was born in England and emigrated to the United States as a young man. He is considered the founder of the Hudson River School of landscape painters.

Chiaroscuro (a word of Italian origin, pronounced Kee-yar-o-Skuro) refers to the contrast of light and dark tones in a painting. Modern artists also use this technique.

The Second Picture must be the pastoral state—the day further advanced, light clouds playing about the mountains, the scene partly cultivated, with a few peasants tending their flocks or engaged in simple amusements. The chiaroscuro must be of a milder character than in the other scene, but yet have a fresh and breezy effect.

The Third must be noonday—a great city girding the bay, gorgeous piles of architecture, bridges, aqueducts, temples, the port crowded with vessels, splendid processions, and so on. All that can be combined to show the fullness of prosperity. The chiaroscuro broad.

The Fourth should be a tempest—a battle and the burning of the city, towers falling, arches broken, vessels wrecked in the harbor. In this scene there should be a fierce chiaroscuro, masses and groups swaying about like stormy waves. This is the scene of destruction.

The Fifth must be a sunset—the mountains shattered, the city a desolate ruin, columns standing isolated amid the encroaching waters, no human figure, a solitary bird, perhaps: a calm and silent effect. This picture must be as the funeral knell of departed greatness, and may be called the state of desolation.

You will perceive what an arduous task I have set myself.

Adapted from Louis LeGrand Noble, **The Life and Works of Thomas Cole.** Edited by Elliott S. Vesell for the John Harvard Library (Cambridge, Mass.: The Belknap Press of Harvard University Press, 1964), pp. 129–130.

23 The Course of Empire: The Savage State (1836)

24 The Course of Empire: The Arcadian or Pastoral State (1836)

25 The Course of Empire: The Consummation of Empire (1836)

26 The Course of Empire: Destruction (1836)

27 The Course of Empire: Desolation (1836)

All of the Thomas Cole paintings are reproduced by courtesy of The New-York Historical Society

2   NATURE AND THE COURSE OF EMPIRE MODERNIZED

Almost a century and a half has passed since Cole painted his series. In that time, factories and shopping centers have sprawled over the landscape that Cole loved. From Walden Pond one can hear cars zipping by on a super-highway, and exhaust fumes drift through the countryside where woodsy sounds and smells once gave delight to Thoreau. America has become an urban-industrial nation with a chrome and plastic civilization. As a people, we are no longer close to nature. Many Americans today feel that the nation has also lost whatever unspoiled natural virtue it might have had in an earlier and simpler age.

These changes accompanied our national growth and, until recently, most Americans regarded them as the price of progress. They felt that damage to the landscape was compensated by greater wealth and comfort. In the late 1960's, however, this view was challenged by a new group of scientist-reform-ers called *ecologists*.* As the 1970's began, the country found itself facing an environmental crisis—the frightening prospect that overpopulation and pollu-tion of the environment might soon make life impossible.

Ecologists study the relation of living organisms to their environment.

Was it only a coincidence that Emerson and Thoreau preached the neces-sity of harmony between man and nature? Was Cole correct in foreseeing destruction at the end of the cycle that began with barbarism and progressed through civilization? Did the men of the 1830's have anything worthwhile to say to us on these matters across all those years?

Two men who believed Cole had an important message for our times were Oliver Jensen and Gerhardt Liebmann. They collaborated on an article in the magazine American Heritage not long before the ecological crisis made headlines. Mr. Jensen, a writer, and Mr. Liebmann, an artist, made Thomas Cole's Course of Empire the model for a parable on nature, progress, and civilization, which they described as "a fable for city planners." As you study the text and pictures, consider these questions:

1. *What do you think is the moral or main point of the Jensen-Liebmann fable?*

2. *Why do you think Cole's* Destruction *is included in Liebmann's painting as though held by a paper clip?*

3. *What words would you use to describe the mood of the Jensen-Liebmann fable?*

The Shape of Things Practically Here

Once upon a time there was a young republic and it Thought Big. It was located in a big new country which was almost empty of people except for a scattering of Noble Red Men. The government of the republic needed a capital, a place for its head man to live, a legislative hall for talking, and offices for the army, the navy, the treasury, and whatever else they thought of next, such as the Bureau of Urban Dislocation in the National Resources Division

B140

of the Department of Health, Wealth, and Wisdom (BUDNRDDHWW). But the government was suspicious of cities, especially old cities. . . .

And so the head man, the Father of His Country, picked out a place for a new capital. It was a *bosky** dell, very bosky in summer, by a sluggish river. It was handy to his place farther down the river. And he got a friend, a *Frenchman,** to lay out a classic town in the wilds. The Frenchman thought big, too. There he is surveying. And over at the right is an abandoned ship, which appears symbolically to show that the people of this republic have come from abroad, and mean to leave behind forever the *fetid** slums of the Old World. The Noble Red Men, however, are not as optimistic about the future. Three white men is fetid enough for them, and they are jumping off cliffs to their deaths. This was an *aboriginal** way of expressing permanent disapproval.

The city in our fable grew and grew. Of course, it was a fictional place but it came by 1966 to look more and more like Washington, D. C. Its landscape was bursting with noble memorials and great marble buildings to house the lawmakers, and demonstrators, and anti-demonstrators, and the hundreds of thousands of absolutely essential employees. We have not forgotten BUDNRDDHWW, now renamed Project Surge. You can see its temporary buildings, the row of low fifty-year-old structures abutting the reflecting pool. Planning was big business now; and the head man was running it personally. You can see him in the right foreground, waving a *western hat** at the multitude, his wife by his side. His residence has been beautified with a statue, and across the pool an iron ball is knocking down some old brick houses that block the view of a new cloverleaf out of the picture at left.

Beauty and historic preservation were the watchwords now; whole blocks of buildings were being torn down to make room for the new high-rise Save-Our-History Building and its 100-acre parking lot. Everybody drove, of course, and the traffic, as you can see, was fierce, but the new 36-lane Beauty Thruway, just coming off the boards, was expected to solve all that.

Only a rear guard, in fact, really seemed to worry about the future of the city, and they are represented in the center foreground, by our old friend, the Frenchman. There he is fighting off a lot of politicians, developers, and real-estate men.

Our fable concludes in a scene we may safely set perhaps fifty years hence. If progress means more of everything, which most people in the republic always seemed to think, then the capital is at the pinnacle. There are more buildings, more statues, more people, more demonstrators, more causes, more cars, more roads—and those durable temporary buildings. And the city has come at last to the great ultimate moment which the builders have destined for it, the moment when the cars all stop and the people have scarcely room to stand. The overcrowding, the fire, and the panic leave only room to jump. And as the nightmare of *Malthus** comes true, and Cole's <u>Destruction</u> finds a modern parallel, our poor dreamer, the Frenchman, trudges away, dragging his dream behind him, to make, somewhere, a fresh start. The moral: If you're looking for Larger Values, Think Small.

Bosky means wooded, or covered with shrubs and bushes.

The Frenchman was **Pierre Charles L'Enfant** who laid out the original plan for Washington, D. C.

Fetid means foul-smelling.

Aboriginal refers to the earliest-known native inhabitants of a region.

The President, when this article was written, was **Lyndon B. Johnson**, a Texan who sometimes wore western-style hats.

Thomas Malthus was an early 19th-century English economist who predicted that population would increase faster than the food supply, resulting in widespread starvation and misery.

Adapted from "The Shape of Things Practically Here," by Oliver Jensen. © Copyright 1966 by American Heritage Publishing Co., Inc. Reprinted by permission from the June, 1966, **American Heritage**, pp. 44–49.

28 Liebmann's Interpretation of Cole's **"The Savage State"** (1966)

29 Liebmann's Interpretation of Cole's **"The Consummation of Empire"** (1966)

30 Liebmann's Interpretation of Cole's **"Destruction of Empire"** (1966)

2 Reform and changing styles

In Past and Present

Introduction

In the preceding assignment you studied paintings from the 1830's and the 1960's and noted both similarities and differences in the way the two artists treated the relation of social progress to the natural environment. Painters can express their feelings and their vision of the world through their artistic creations. Those who lack artistic talent express feelings and attitudes in other ways, such as words and actions, clothes, and styles.

In this assignment we will examine some of the shifts in fashion during the Age of Reform, 1830–1855. By comparing them with some of the examples of stylistic changes in our own time, we may be able to see past and present in a different light.

Symbolic Importance of Fashion

Shakespeare said that "the apparel oft proclaims the man." Young people today know what he meant. Changes in styles of dress and personal adornment are often considered trivial matters. But in the 1960's long hair and beards, and certain styles of dress became important symbols of a new life-style. They proclaimed the values of those who adopted them. To many older persons—those on the far side of the "generation gap"—these new styles sometimes seemed not merely novel and surprising, but shocking or even outrageous. Some schools established a dress code and set definite limits to the length of boys' hair and the length of girls' skirts.

Once a style is widely adopted, most people follow it without giving any particular thought to its symbolic significance. They simply wish to keep up with the prevailing fashion. Eventually, the new styles are adopted even by those who found them offensive at first. But in times of rapid change or revolutionary upheaval, new styles flash a message that something deeper is happening in society.

In the English civil war of the 1640's, the opposing sides were identified by their contrasting hair styles. The parliamentary forces who executed King Charles I in 1649 wore their hair closely cropped, and were called Roundheads. The king's supporters flaunted their long aristocratic locks, and were known as Cavaliers. During the French Revolution, the poor

Objectives of this assignment are to:

—Analyze accounts of changing hair and clothing styles in the period 1830 to 1855 for meaning.

—Analyze accounts of changing hair and clothing styles during the 1960's for meaning.

—Compare hair and clothing styles in 1830–1855 with those of 1960's for similarities and differences.

—Draw inferences from your comparison of hair and clothing styles about the similarity of political and social issues in 1830–1855 and in 1960's.

—Make a judgment on effectiveness of studying history by comparing past and present.

B144

who formed the Parisian mob got the nickname of *Sans-culottes** because they did not wear the fancy knee breeches favored by the upper classes. And when Czar Peter the Great set out to modernize Russia around 1700, one of his most dramatic acts decreed that all beards had to be shaved off. Since people in up-to-date countries did not wear beards, Russian beards had to go!

More recently, the issue of dress has arisen in several African countries. In 1968 the government of Malawi took steps to ban the sale of miniskirts. The miniskirt was also under attack in Uganda as a symbol of the lingering cultural imperialism of western Europe over Africa. At the same time, however, authorities in Tanzania ordered the *Masai** tribesmen to wear trousers. The near-nakedness of their traditional costume was felt to be inappropriate for a modernizing state.

Sans-culottes literally means "without knee breeches."

The Masai are a pastoral people in the highlands of Kenya and Tanzania. The men often attain a height of seven feet.

A Philosophy of Clothes

Historians have often overlooked the importance of fashion. Thomas Carlyle was an exception. Carlyle was a native of Scotland and one of the most influential English writers of the nineteenth century. In his book, *Sartor Resartus,* Carlyle developed a "philosophy of clothes." The title means "The Tailor Retailored," and the book is one of the classics of English literature.

It is a rambling and complicated book, and Carlyle seems to be writing with tongue in cheek in some of his talk about "clothes-philosophy." But he was quite serious in likening all of external nature to clothing. Just as a man's clothing hides his body, so the body itself hides man's spirit. All of visible nature is to be understood as a garment covering the invisible spiritual principle that governs the universe.

Clothing partly hides and partly reveals the human figure. Colorful apparel can express joy; solemn dress, sadness. In the same manner, says Carlyle, everything in nature both hides and reveals something else, and can convey some symbolic message from beneath the veil of appearances. It was this symbolic quality of clothing that Carlyle stressed. "All visible things are emblems," he wrote. "Clothes, from the King's mantle downwards are emblematic, and all emblematic things are properly clothes, thought-woven or hand-woven."

If Carlyle was right and clothes can tell us something about the inner nature of the person who wears them, perhaps startling changes in fashion and personal appearance can tell us something about a society that adopts them. Carlyle's book, *Sartor Resartus,* was first published in the United States in 1836 when the country was in the midst of startling changes in fashions and when vast numbers of Americans were committing themselves to social reform movements such as temperance, antislavery, peace, nonviolence, and women's rights.

3 CHANGING FASHIONS IN THE REFORM ERA, 1830–1855

Throughout the period, 1830–1855, hair and clothing styles were closely identified with a commitment to social change. Reformers and dissatisfied young people were very serious about how they looked and dressed. It was a relatively easy, sometimes risky, but always dramatic way of demonstrating opposition to the social, political, and educational establishments of their day.

While reading the accounts and examining the pictures that follow, keep in mind these questions:

1. Why was Joe Palmer persecuted? What form did it take?

2. Why was Josiah Quincy unpopular with students?

3. Why were the disciples of The Newness *a sore trial to the community in the 1840's?*

4. Why was changing women's clothing styles thought to be important in the struggle for women's rights?

Joe Palmer's Beard

Joseph Palmer was the victim of one of the strangest persecutions in history. He was persecuted for wearing a beard. It was a magnificent growth, and just about the only one east of the Rockies at the time. When Palmer came to Fitchburg, Massachusetts, in 1830, his beard was probably the first one seen in New England for a century. The Pilgrim Fathers wore beards, but after about 1720, facial hair was gone completely. Cartoonists did not even add chin whiskers to the figure of Uncle Sam until the late 1850's.

Joe Palmer paid dearly for being a pioneer. Little boys jeered at him on the street, and rowdies broke the windows of his house. Even in church he was humiliated by being by-passed at the Communion table. When he defended himself against some ruffians who tried forcibly to shave off the offending brush, he was jailed for "unprovoked assault." Although he spent a year in jail, Joe kept his beard. He also gained sympathy far and wide as a martyr for individual rights.

After he got out of jail, Palmer became a familiar figure on the New England reform scene. He supported both the antislavery movement and temperance reform. He was also involved in one of the *utopian** communities in Massachusetts. Famous men like Emerson and Thoreau greeted him as a friend. When Palmer died in 1875 the American male was gloriously bewhiskered. But the monument at Palmer's grave reminds us that he was "persecuted for wearing the beard."

Utopian means visionary, impractical, dedicated to the view that man can create a perfect society. The word comes from Sir Thomas More's book **Utopia** (1516) describing a perfect society.

Adapted with permission of The Macmillan Company from **Lost Men of American History** by Stewart Holbrook, pp. 145–153. Copyright 1946 by Stewart H. Holbrook.

Herman Melville

Walt Whitman

James Russell Lowell

A College Student's Diary, 1830*

I begin to consider myself a man of fashion since I have purchased my bell-bottomed pantaloons, square-toed boots, patent leather *stock*,* and a pyramid formed hat. I imagine that a handsome dress actually has some tendency to elevate the mind.

A College President's View, 1835

Josiah Quincy, president of Harvard from 1829 to 1845, was quite unpopular with the students by the end of his term. In his conferences with them, he was abrupt and tactless, often committing the unpardonable sin of criticizing their dress, or the whiskers which (greatly to his disgust) began to sprout toward the end of his administration.

The author of this diary entry, **John Humphrey Noyes,** became famous in the 1840's as the founder of a utopian colony called "Oneida Community" in New York State.

Stock means a band-like collar or neck-cloth.

From George W. Noyes, ed., **The Religious Experience of John Humphrey Noyes** (New York: Macmillan, 1923), p. 23. By permission of Charlotte N. Sewall.

Adapted from Samuel Eliot Morison, **Three Centuries of Harvard** (Cambridge, Mass.: The Belknap Press of Harvard University Press, 1937), p. 251.

The **Newness** was a general term for the sense of experimentation and wonder associated with the love of nature and with new ideas in religion, literature, and society.

Adapted from Robert Carter, "The Newness," **Century Magazine**, XXXIX (1889), p. 129.

Byron collar: loose unstarched collar, worn open at the throat, with a carelessly-tied silk scarf. It was named after the English poet, **Lord Byron.**

A **sack coat** was a short coat with a straight back and no seam at the waist.

High Fashion, 1851 . . . Amelia Bloomer models the "bloomer" costume to which she gave her name.

A Reminiscence of 1840

The disciples of what was called at the time *The Newness** experimented with new ideas in religion, literature, and social relations. They also indulged in a number of oddities in respect to dress. They would not be considered strange now, but then they were a sore trial to the community. They wore their hair long, and allowed their beards to grow at a time when everybody else shaved. They also had a fondness for peculiar garments, such as felt hats with broad brims, *Byron collars,** and *sack-coats.**

Women's Dress and Women's Freedom, 1855

I am amazed that intelligent women who are striving for their rights do not see the relation between their dress and the oppressive evils they are struggling to throw off. What women need most is to change their idea of themselves. It will do them little good to gain the right to vote if they retain their present false notion of themselves, and of their relations to the opposite sex. And these false notions are emphatically represented and perpetuated in women's dress.

The woman must first fight against herself—against personal and mental habits so deep-rooted as to be mistaken for her very nature. If she succeeds

"ARABELLA MARIA. "Only to think, Julia dear, that our Mothers wore such ridiculous fashions as these!"
BOTH. "Ha! ha! ha! ha!"

Emancipated women, 1851–
Nattily attired in pantsuits,
swinging their riding crops, and
smoking cigars on street
corners, these ladies shocked
their more sedate sisters.

in this, an easy victory will follow in all the spheres of life. And what should
be the battleground for this indispensable self-conquest? You will laugh
when I answer that her dress—aye, her dress—must be that battleground.

Adapted from a letter of Gerrit Smith
to Elizabeth Cady Stanton, Dec. 1,
1855, in **History of Woman Suffrage**,
Elizabeth Cady Stanton, ed., et al.
Second edition (Rochester, 1889),
Vol. I, pp. 837–839.

4   CHANGING FASHIONS IN THE 1960'S

Styles in dress and personal appearance changed markedly during the
1960's. In some ways clothing and hair styles obscured social problems;
in other ways they accentuated them. In some instances clothing and hair
styles became matters of racial pride. All Americans were touched by the
force of fashion in the 1960's, but young people and black Americans were
especially affected.

While reading the accounts and examining the pictures that follow, keep
in mind these questions:

*1. How have clothes affected the condition of the poor in contemporary
America?*

2. What are the new hair styles for men supposed to mean?

*3. What are the new clothing styles for young men and young women sup-
posed to mean?*

4. Why are black Americans adopting new clothing and hair styles?

Love Plaques, 1820 and 1970

Affluent means prosperous or wealthy. The book **The Affluent Society** by John K. Galbraith published in 1958 popularized the term.

Adapted from Michael Harrington, **The Other America** (Baltimore: Penguin Books, Inc., 1963), pp. 12–13. By permission of Michael Harrington and The Macmillan Company, New York.

LOVE ONE ANOTHER

Clothing and the Invisible Poor, 1963

Clothes make the poor invisible, too; America has the best-dressed poverty the world has ever known. Even people with terribly depressed incomes can look prosperous.

This is an extremely important factor in defining our emotional ignorance of poverty. In Detroit the existence of social classes became more difficult to discern the day the companies put lockers in the plants. From that moment on, one did not see men in work clothes on the way to the factory, but citizens in slacks and white shirts. It almost seems as if the *affluent** society had given out costumes to the poor so that they would not offend the rest of society with the sight of their rags.

Long Hair, Beards, and Individuality, 1968

Today, hair power is second only to black power as a driving force of American life. Look at sideburns: they are creeping across America like crabgrass, each one a pennant proclaiming—however seedily—that inside the impersonal shell there still lives a person. The new styles are messengers of a revolution that is long overdue. They are hurrying the day when it will no longer be possible to tell who anybody is by the way he looks and dresses—when we will be at last liberated from snap judgments.

Reprinted by permission of William K. Zinsser, "Some Bristly Thoughts on Victory Through Hair Power," **Life,** Vol. LXIV (New York: Time-Life, Inc., January 19, 1968), p. 10. Copyright © 1968 by William K. Zinsser. (Adapted.)

Fashions, Family Roles, and Social Changes, 1966

In an earlier day, boys wished to look like their fathers. Now they do not. Since a responsible adult male is supposed to be neat, boys now cultivate the unkempt look. Fathers keep their hair trimmed neatly; sons let theirs grow wild. Heads of families dress soberly and without fancy ornamentation; their male offspring favor splashy colors and showy cuts, and they wear beads, headbands, and other ornaments that used to be exclusively feminine.

What we have is a curious cycle. Mama is imitating her daughter's styles. But daughter is imitating big brother. He in turn is revolting against Papa in the strongest way he can—by going fancy and feminine. In fact, young men now seem to dress as young women masquerading as boys.

These transferences of sexual characteristics are fever symptoms of social reconstruction. Obviously, our civilization is roiling up from the bottom. Similar periods in the past can be charted by a cyclical pattern in dress. First, wild exaggeration, followed by an abrupt return to romanticism—then revolution or war.

Reprinted by permission of Harold Ober Associates from Agnes deMille, "Whatever Has Become of Mommy?," **Horizon,** VIII (Summer, 1966), pp. 13, 15. Copyright © 1966 by American Heritage Publishing Co., Inc. (Adapted.)

Style Changes and Black Americans, 1969

All across the country now one can find blacks wearing their hair *"Afro"** style. For the girls it means they no longer go to the beauty parlor to have their hair straightened with hot combs. They wear it as it was before the hot combs and grease got to it. Howard University's Homecoming Queen of 1966 was a former SNCC worker who wears her hair *au naturel.* For the men it means letting the hair grow long. Not only is this true of young blacks directly involved in "the movement," but of teen-agers in the urban centers.

Julius Lester, **Look Out, Whitey! Black Power's Gon' Get Your Mama!** (New York: Grove Press, Evergreen Black Cat Edition, 1969), pp. 92–93. By permission of The Dial Press, N. Y.

The **"natural"** hairstyle, adopted by black Americans in the mid-1960's, was also called the **"Afro."** It ended efforts by blacks to force their hair into the straight lines of the whites.

From Newsweek, "Selling Soul Style," Copyright Newsweek, Inc. LXXII (July 1, 1968), p. 84.

Selling Soul Style, 1968

Does the black American male feel comfortable in Whitey's clothes?

Not according to New Breed, a national clothing firm specializing in threads to fit the fashion-conscious soul brother. For openers, members of the New Breed regard the three-button suit as a straight-jacket. "Our measurements are different from the white man's," explains Jason Benning, president of the Harlem-based organization. "The black male is thinner in the waist, a little heavier through the chest and has a slightly protruding backside." To fit this physique, the six-month-old firm features jackets with pinched waists, wider lapels and "peacock flares" in the back (high center vents which flare slightly over the seat).

. . . the New Breeders believe that what the black man really wants is clothes to fit his concepts. Accordingly, New Breed is introducing fashions with a philosophy—using elements from the past and present in designs for the Afro-American.

       ❖   ❖   ❖   ❖   ❖

What will happen if Whitey takes a fancy to the New Breed of fashion? "We don't care if the white man comes in and buys our clothes," says [*Howard*] *Davis.** "But if he wears a *Dashiki,** he better know what it stands for and where his mind is at."

A vice-president of the **New Breed** firm.

Dashiki is a garment of African origin consisting of a one-piece loose smock, with a hole for the head.

B151

3 Temperance crusade

A Movement That Failed

Introduction

In this assignment, we will take a closer look at one of the reform movements of the ante-bellum era—the temperance crusade. Unlike several other reforms of that era, it does not have a clear counterpart today. Indeed, most Americans in the 1970's do not even consider temperance a genuine social reform. They are troubled about the use of drugs and cigarette-smoking. But they consider drinking a matter of personal choice, regard temperance reformers as busybodies, and the Prohibition Party as a joke.

Things were very different in the Era of Reform. Temperance was then believed to be an important social reform. In fact, it had more supporters than any other reform movement, including antislavery. It was the only major reform of the period to win a substantial following in the South. The abolitionists and many other groups in society regarded drink as a great evil. People believed drunkenness caused street crime, child neglect, and wife beating. Women, for example, were prominent in the temperance crusade. Workingmen's temperance societies were formed in the 1830's in the larger cities. Similar groups sprang up on many college campuses. Members of Congress even formed their own temperance society in 1833.

The 18th Amendment to the Constitution, ratified in 1919, established Prohibition. The Volstead Act (1919) set up the enforcement machinery. Prohibition went into effect January 16, 1920. It was ended by the 21st Amendment, which repealed the 18th Amendment. The 21st Amendment was ratified in December, 1933.

Prohibition and Its Effects

Strangely enough, it was because the temperance reformers finally got what they wanted that their movement is held in such low esteem today. After almost a century of struggle, the temperance forces in 1919 pushed through a *Constitutional Amendment** prohibiting the manufacture, sale, or transportation of intoxicating liquors in the United States.

Bootlegging meant transporting and supplying liquor in violation of the law. The term probably arose from the earlier practice of concealing a liquor bottle in the leg of one's boot.

But Prohibition did not work out as its sponsors had anticipated. Americans continued to drink, even though it was illegal. *Bootlegging** became a thriving underworld industry, and gangland wars erupted over the rich spoils. Corruption spread as public officials were paid off to wink at law-breaking. A general cynicism about law and public morality infected American society.

President Herbert Hoover called Prohibition "an experiment noble in intention." The term was used scornfully thereafter.

The failure of Prohibition discredited temperance as a social reform. Looking back at the dismal reality, Americans forgot the broad social concern that inspired many of the leaders of the temperance crusade. Unable to take Prohibition seriously as a *noble experiment,** most people came to the conclusion that it must have been the work of hypocrites, puritans, or narrow-minded bigots.

B152

By the 1870's women had become the most active temperance workers. Sometimes they picketed in front of saloons, or entered them to debate the proprietor and his customers—or to pray over them. When women adopted these militant tactics in Cincinnati, they were arested for creating a public nuisance. Thomas Nast, the famous cartoonist, reacted indignantly. His cartoon, which appeared in **Harper's Weekly** June 13, 1874, was headed "Pearls Among Swine." In the 1960's, "police brutality" was a major issue in the explosive race crisis. After the militant "Black Panthers" started calling police "pigs," this abusive epithet gained wide currency among radicals.

This pervasive feeling still colors our understanding of the whole temperance movement. It therefore requires a special effort of the imagination to look at the temperance movement as men saw it in the nineteenth century—before the disaster of Prohibition.

Temperance in the Era of Reform

Drinking was a serious problem in the early nineteenth century. Foreign visitors reported with awe the quantities of alcohol consumed by Americans. According to one survey, New York City had approximately one grogshop for every forty-eight inhabitants in 1818. With general consumption at this level, every community had a sizeable quota of confirmed drunkards.

Warning voices had been raised in the eighteenth century. *Dr. Benjamin Rush,** for example, discussed the dangers of excessive drinking from the medical and scientific point of view. But the temperance movement did not really gain momentum till after the War of 1812, when it was caught up in the reawakening of evangelical Protestantism. State and local temperance societies were formed, usually under religious auspices. The founding in 1826 of a national organization, the American Temperance Society, coincided with the beginning of the greatest wave of religious enthusiasm of the century. By 1833 it had half a million members in some 4,000 local branches.

Religious revivalists did not neglect the social aspect of religion. They stressed that Christ's Kingdom was one of love. The true Christian, therefore, should act with benevolence toward his fellow men. If all men could be *converted** from their sinful lives, a truly just and righteous social order would

Benjamin Rush (1745–1813), a prominent physician in Philadelphia, was active in philanthropy as well as natural science. He was an outstanding representative of the Enlightenment in America.

To be **converted** meant to undergo a drastic spiritual change by which one renounced sin and was reborn as a new man who would live in the close friendship of God. This interior change of one's spiritual condition was believed to result from the direct action of God on the individual.

B153

Objectives of this assignment
are to:
—Analyze selections from statements by temperance reformers
in 1830's and the President's
Task Force Report on Drunkenness in 1967 on the social consequences of drunkenness for
similarities and differences.
—Make a judgment on right of
state to legislate morality.
—Make a judgment on effectiveness of studying history by
comparing past and present.

Millennium: the thousand-year
period, predicted in the Bible
(Rev. 20:1–7), during which
Christ will rule on earth. Some
believed the millennium would
follow the Second Coming of
Christ; others that it would
precede the Second Coming and
that it was beginning in the
1830's.

Total abstinence from alcoholic
drinks was referred to as
teetotalism.

come into being. Within this frame of reference, the battle against intemperance took its place as part of a larger campaign against wickedness and sin.
The rapid growth of the temperance societies seemed a proof of God's blessing. As thousands upon thousands of former sinners experienced conversion
in the revivals, many deeply religious men rejoiced that the *millennium** was
about to begin.

The religious fervor of evangelical religion, however, soon led to a split
between moderates and radicals within the temperance movement. In its
earlier phases, the drive had been against ardent spirit—that is, distilled
drinks or hard liquor. The moderate use of beer and wine was considered
acceptable. By the mid-1830's, however, *total abstinence** from all alcoholic
beverages was demanded. At the same time, much heavier emphasis was
placed upon the sinfulness of drinking. Selling liquor was also pronounced a
sin. If it were a sin, should it not be prohibited by law?

Within a decade of the founding of the American Temperance Society,
the moderates had lost their fight. They had hoped to reach the intemperate
by means of persuasion. But from the late 1830's, the thrust of the movement
was toward political pressure to change the laws governing the use of alcohol. There was still a long way to go, but the journey toward the 18th Amendment had begun.

5 THE CRUSADE AGAINST DRUNKENNESS, 1830–1840

During the 1830's the leadership of the American Temperance Society was
firmly convinced that the entire country was threatened by the curse of drunkenness and exploited by the liquor manufacturers and saloon keepers. No
cause was more sacred or more just than that of sobriety. A sober American
would be a good American, and the Society turned all of its energies and
resources to the task of keeping Americans sober and making them good.

While reading these selections from the Annual Reports of the American
Temperance Society, keep in mind these questions:

*1. According to the American Temperance Society, what were the social
consequences of drunkenness?*

2. What was the greatest obstacle in the path of temperance reform?

*3. What did temperance reformers expect would happen once temperance
goals were attained?*

The Social Consequences of Drunkenness, 1831

The Superintendent of the Albany Alms-House states that but for the use
of strong drink his institution would be empty. According to other state-

ments, ninety-five percent of the inmates of the Montgomery County (N.Y.) Poor House owe their situations to intemperance. Two-thirds of all the children sent to the New York City House of Refuge were known to be children of intemperate parents.

In Cumberland County, Pennsylvania, 48 out of 50 paupers were made such by intemperance and in Oneida, New York, no less than 246 out of 253 paupers owe their conditions to strong drink.

The Keeper of the Ogdensburg jail states that seven-eighths of the criminals and three-fourths of the debtors imprisoned there are intemperate persons. Only 36 out of 134 men in the State Prison in Columbus, Ohio, even pretend to be sober men. Drink was the cause of crimes that sent 100 out of 119 men to the State Prison in Charlestown, Massachusetts.

A distinguished physician in Massachusetts has stated that should the people of the United States renounce the use of spirituous liquors, nearly half of the diseases of the country would be prevented.

Adapted from **Permanent Temperance Documents,** Fourth Report, 1831.

Morality and the Law, 1833

From the beginning, the Society took the position that it is morally wrong to drink ardent spirit. The Society next said that it is also wicked to make or sell it. Thus it is a sin both to drink ardent spirit and to furnish it to others. Anything that helps people see the truth of this, helps the Temperance Reformation. Anything that prevents people from seeing this, hinders the Temperance Reformation.

Nothing at present so much hinders the cause in this way as the fact that the law permits the making and selling of ardent spirit. The sanction of favorable legislation is a public testimony to the world that selling and drinking ardent spirit are right and permissible actions. That, however, is a fundamental and fatal error—one that is destructive in its effects both in this life and the life to come.

✿   ✿   ✿   ✿   ✿

Let all sanctioning by law of this abominable traffic in ardent spirit be forever abandoned. And if the rising indignation of a deeply injured and long-suffering humanity does not sweep it away by force of public opinion alone, the people can undertake this righteous work of self-defense by means of legislation. As all political power is in their hands, it will be found practicable to do this.

✿   ✿   ✿   ✿   ✿

Moreover, if the laws authorizing the manufacture and sale of ardent spirit are morally wrong and if traffic in ardent spirit is immoral, then the laws authorizing that traffic are likewise immoral. If these laws are immoral, then we are immoral, too, unless we protest against them. For in a republican government such as ours, every voter has a share in making the laws. Hence we are responsible for the character of the laws.

Adapted from **Permanent Temperance Documents,** Sixth Report, 1833, and Seventh Report, 1834.

A Vision of Temperance Triumphant

Zion was the name of the hill in Jerusalem upon which the Temple was built. Zion became the symbol of the Kingdom of God, or the gathering place of all true believers.

Let the inhabitants of this land give up ardent spirit. Let them exclude from their churches those who make and sell ardent spirit. Then will *Zion** arise and shine. The glory of the Lord, brighter than the sun, will break forth. Violence will be banished from the land. Our walls will be salvation and our gates will be praise. And as others throughout the world join the Temperance Reformation, the word of the Lord will run very swiftly. Its mighty energy will be like the rains that come down from heaven and cause the earth to bud and bring forth fruit. The frost and the snows of six thousand winters will be forever dissolved. The springtime of millennial beauty and the autumnal fruit of millennial glory will open upon the world.

Adapted from **Permanent Temperance Documents,** Sixth Report, 1833.

6 THE PROBLEM OF DRUNKENNESS, 1960–1970

During the 1960's, drunkenness continued to be one of the country's most pressing social problems. In 1965, for example, two million arrests, or one out of every three arrests made in the United States, were for the offense of public drunkenness. Given the fact that police do not generally arrest everyone who is under the influence of alcohol, the dimensions of the problem of drunkenness in contemporary America are enormous.

The problem remains, but our approaches to it have changed from what they were one hundred and forty years ago. While reading these selections from the President's Task Force Report on Drunkenness, keep in mind these questions:

1. According to the Task Force Report on Drunkenness, *what are the social consequences of drunkenness?*

2. What does the Task Force Report on Drunkenness *suggest is a major cause of drunkenness in contemporary America?*

3. How does the Task Force Report on Drunkenness *propose to deal with the problem of drunkenness in contemporary America?*

The Social Consequences of Drunkenness, 1967

The evidence is overwhelming that alcohol use is strongly associated with both acute and long-term adverse physical effects, and with acute and long-term adverse social and psychological ones.

Alcoholics attempt and also complete suicide at a much higher rate than the nonalcoholic population.

Drivers who drink are more likely to be involved in traffic accidents.

Life in the Bowery—A derelict weaves his way toward a Skid Row barroom where he can escape reality through liquor. Craving for alcohol is a most damaging disease, bringing ill health, crime, misery, and destruction.

Arrests for alcohol use account for more than half of all reported offenses in the United States. Surveys of offenders reveal that the offender has more often been drinking prior to the commission of certain types of crimes than other types. For example, in big city homicides either or both victim and killer have been drinking in the majority of cases. Alcohol is also implicated in other crimes of violence, and in unskilled property crimes.

President's Commission on Law Enforcement and Administration of Justice, **Task Force Report: Drunkenness** (Washington, D. C.: U. S. Government Printing Office, 1967), pp. 36, 43, 44.

The Tasks Before Us, 1967

Our first task is to accept our own present inability to make any dramatic immediate changes in the drinking habits of Americans at large or problem drinkers in particular. The second task is to control the risks to the present generation of drinkers and those around them as much as we can. The third task is to streamline our handling of alcohol use offenders as such (chronic drunkenness and related charges). The fourth task is to embark on a long-term program aimed at preventing future excess drinking in the coming generation. Social, economic, educational, medical, and mental health improvements must be made in the metropolitan slum areas and other places where people live lives of deprivation, disorder and delinquency.

President's Commission on Law Enforcement and Administration of Justice, **Task Force Report: Drunkenness** (Washington, D.C.: U. S. Government Printing office, 1967), pp. 44–45.

4 Antislavery Movement

Colonization Movement

Introduction

Objectives of this assignment
are to:
—Analyze statement by Colonization Society in 1817 favoring
colonization of free blacks in
Africa for meaning.
—Analyze statements by black
and white opponents of colonization scheme in 1831–1832 for
meaning.
—Analyze statements by modern
black American immigrants to
Africa for meaning.
—Compare attitudes of free
blacks in 1831 about moving to
Africa with those of black
American immigrants to Africa
in 1970.
—Identify problems encountered
when history is studied by comparing past and present.

Finley's father-in-law, **Elias
Boudinot,** was the founder of
the American Bible Society.
Others among Finley's relatives
and associates were involved
in the work of the religious
benevolent societies.

In the case of temperance, the twentieth-century experience of Prohibition
makes it difficult for us to understand and sympathize with the reformers of
the 1830's and 1840's. This assignment considers a reform movement where
the effect of twentieth-century experience is just the opposite. The crucial
importance of equality for black Americans as a social issue in our own time
makes it much easier for us to appreciate the significance of the antislavery
movement, and to sympathize with its aims.

We will deal here with the first phase of the movement, up to about 1830.
The principal means by which reformers hoped to eradicate slavery during
this period was the colonization of free blacks in Africa.

Background and Course of Colonization Movement

As in the case of temperance, the beginnings of antislavery reform date
back to the closing years of the eighteenth century. The reawakening of
evangelical Protestantism sparked new interest and inspired a new approach
after the War of 1812. A Presbyterian clergyman named *Robert Finley** was
strongly impressed with the possibilities for improving society through the
religious benevolent associations being formed in those years. He therefore
determined to establish such a society for the purpose of transporting free
blacks to Africa, and settling them in a colony founded specifically to provide
a new home.

Reverend Finley lived in New Jersey. He had observed that the free blacks
there, and elsewhere in the North, lived in misery. They were poor and despised. Race prejudice excluded them from desirable jobs and kept their
children from receiving a good education. The only solution, Finley argued,
was to transport them to Africa, where they could build colonies and live
in true freedom and dignity.

Finley believed that by removing the problem of fitting the free blacks into
white society, colonization would also hasten the end of slavery. It would encourage many troubled slaveholders to free their bondsmen, since they could
be sure the former slaves would prosper as free men in Africa rather than adding to the race problem in America. Everyone would benefit. Even the civiliz-
ing of Africa would be speeded by the coming of the free blacks. They would
bring Christianity and enlightenment to the dark continent.

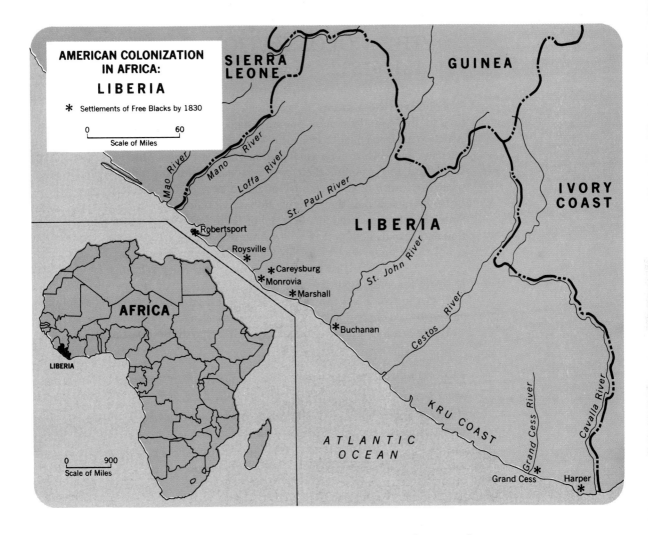

AMERICAN COLONIZATION
IN AFRICA:
LIBERIA

* Settlements of Free Blacks by 1830

0   60
Scale of Miles

The colonizationists' method for getting rid of slavery was indirect and gradual. But establishing and maintaining a colony in Africa was a most ambitious program for a private society. Hence the Colonization Society sought government assistance and tried to win important men to its cause. It did attract big-name *supporters,** but the government did not provide any financial help. The Society established Liberia with private funds. By 1830 it had transported some 1400 free blacks there as settlers. Liberia remained the private domain of the Colonization Society until 1847, when it became an independent republic.

From its founding in 1817 to about 1830, the American Colonization Society was the principal agency devoted to antislavery. After that date a more militant type of antislavery reformer appeared. Colonization came under severe criticism and declined quickly. The society's influence, though brief, was important because it put slavery and the race issue on the agenda of reform.

Henry Clay, then Speaker of the House of Representatives, was chairman of the organizational meeting of the American Colonization Society.
Judge Bushrod Washington, nephew of George Washington, was the Society's first president. **James Madison** later served as president; **James Monroe** and **John Marshall** held office in local branches of the Society.

B159

7   THE COLONIZATION CONTROVERSY, 1817–1832

Conceived by a group of prominent white Americans as a humane solution to the country's most pressing social problem, the idea of colonizing Africa with freed blacks from the United States quickly became an issue of intense controversy. The colonization scheme forced Americans, both black and white, to reexamine their own personal values and think seriously about what the future of their country ought to be.

In the selections that follow, Robert Goodloe Harper, a former United States Senator and prominent citizen of Baltimore, states the case for colonization and reveals how part of white America viewed the prospect of a free and equal multi-racial society in the United States. William Lloyd Garrison, an impatient, dedicated, twenty-five-year-old antislavery reformer from Boston, presents the case against colonization. The views of the people most concerned, the free black Americans, are represented by a series of resolutions passed by a convention of black citizens meeting in Pittsburgh in 1831.

While reading these selections, keep in mind these questions:

1. According to the colonizationist argument, what impassable barrier prevents free blacks from obtaining equality in America?

2. According to Garrison, how have freed blacks been persecuted and why are colonizationists bad Christians?

3. Why does the Convention of Free Blacks *oppose the colonizationist scheme, and how do they regard the free blacks who support it?*

A Colonizationist States the Case, 1817

Colonizing the free people of color in Africa would benefit us by ridding us of a group for the most part idle and useless, and too often vicious and mischievous. Here they are condemned to hopeless inferiority and degradation because of their color—an indelible mark of their origin and former condition. This establishes an impassable barrier between them and us.

Our habits and feelings, which perhaps it would be more correct to call our prejudices, make us recoil with horror from the idea of an intimate union with the free blacks. For this reason, there can never be the sort of equality between them and us that would make us one people. The free blacks also contribute greatly to the corruption of the slaves by setting a bad example and causing the slaves to become idle, discontented, and disobedient.

Colonization would tend very strongly to rid us, gradually and entirely, of slavery, a great moral and political evil. It is an evil which is likely to cause a great calamity in the future. This, in my opinion, is the most important reason for supporting colonization.

Colonization would have this effect because it would make *manumission** more attractive. Many persons are now reluctant to *manumit** their slaves because they believe the freed slaves would become a nuisance in this country. Such persons would gladly set their slaves free if they were then sent to a place where they might enjoy their freedom in a manner useful to themselves and to society.

Transplanted to a colony composed of themselves alone, the free blacks would enjoy real equality: in other words, real freedom. They would become landowners, master mechanics, shipowners, merchants, and eventually schoolmasters, justices of the peace, militia officers, ministers of religion, judges, and legislators. There would be no whites to remind them of their original inferiority, or to perpetuate it. Enjoying all the privileges of freedom, they would soon enjoy all its advantages and all its dignity. The whites who might visit them would visit them as equals, for the purpose of a commerce mutually advantageous. They would rise rapidly in the scale of existence, and soon become equal to the people of Europe, or of European origin, so long their masters and oppressors.

Manumission means emancipation from slavery; manumit means to release from slavery.

Adapted from Robert Goodloe Harper's letter to the American Colonization Society, as given in William H. Pease and Jane H. Pease, eds., **The Antislavery Argument** (Indianapolis: Bobbs-Merrill, 1965), pp. 19–29. Reprinted by permission.

William Lloyd Garrison's Critique of Colonization, 1832

The superstructure of the Colonization Society rests upon the following pillars:

1st. Persecution. It declares that the whole colored population must be removed to Africa. But as the free portion are almost unanimously opposed to a removal, it seems to be the determination of the Society to make their situation so uncomfortable and degraded here as to compel them to migrate. Consequently, it discourages their education and improvement in this, their native home. This is persecution.

2d. Falsehood. It stigmatizes our colored citizens as being natives of Africa, and talks of sending them to their native land. But they are no more related to Africa than we are to Great Britain.

3d. Cowardice. It avows as a prominent reason why colored citizens ought to be removed, that their continued presence among us will be dangerous to us as a people! This is a libel upon their character. Instead of demanding justice for this oppressed class, the Society calls for their removal.

4th. *Infidelity.** It boldly denies that there is power enough in the gospel to melt down the prejudices of men. It insists that so long as the people of color remain among us, we must be their enemies! Every honest man should abhor this doctrine.

Infidelity here means religious unbelief, lack of Christian faith.

Adapted from William Lloyd Garrison, **Thoughts on African Colonization** (Boston, 1832), Arno Press edition, 1968, Part I, p. 11.

Declaration of a Convention of Free Blacks, 1831

Resolved, That "we hold these truths to be self-evident: that all men are created equal, and endowed by their Creator with certain inalienable rights; that among these are life, liberty, and the pursuit of happiness"—Liberty and Equality now, Liberty and Equality forever!

Elective franchise means the right to vote. All but a handful of free blacks were denied the vote in the North. By 1840, only Massachusetts, New Hampshire, Maine, and Vermont permitted blacks to vote on the same basis as whites.

Canada and **Haiti** were often mentioned as places to which the free blacks should emigrate. "Upper Canada" was the name of a province of Canada between 1791 and 1840. It now comprises the southern part of the province of Ontario.

From William Lloyd Garrison, **Thoughts on African Colonization** (Boston, 1832), Arno Press edition, 1968, Part II, pp. 34–35.

Resolved, That it is the decided opinion of this meeting, that African colonization is a scheme to drain the better-informed part of the colored people out of these United States, so that the chain of slavery may be rivetted more tightly; but we are determined not to be cheated out of our rights by the colonization men, or any other set of intriguers. . . .

Resolved, That we . . . view the country in which we live as our only true and proper home. We are just as much natives here as the members of the Colonization Society. Here we were born—here bred—here are our earliest and most pleasant associations—here is all that binds man to earth, and makes life valuable. And we do consider every colored man who allows himself to be colonized in Africa, or elsewhere, a traitor to our cause.

Resolved, That we are freemen, that we are brethren, that we are countrymen and fellow-citizens, and as fully entitled to the free exercise of the *elective franchise** as any men who breathe; and that we demand an equal share of protection from our federal government with any class of citizens in the community. . . .

Resolved, That we, as citizens of these United States, and for the support of these resolutions, with a firm reliance on the protection of divine providence, do mutually pledge to each other our lives, our fortunes, and our sacred honor, not to support a colony in Africa, nor in Upper Canada, nor yet to emigrate to *Hayti.** Here we were born—here will we live by the help of the Almighty—and here we will die, and let our bones lie with our fathers. . . .

8 BLACK AMERICANS AND CONTEMPORARY AFRICA

Black Americans have a special interest and pride in the emergence of free African nations from former European colonial territories. They have watched with increasing interest the example of black people governing themselves. Black Americans have followed closely the efforts of blacks in places such as Angola, Mozambique, Rhodesia, and South Africa to achieve civil rights and self-determination. Many black Americans have chosen to identify themselves as Afro-Americans and accept African cultural achievements and African history as part of their own heritage. Africa's musical traditions have been long an inspiration and influence upon the extraordinary creativity of black American musicians. However, in recent years, Afro hairstyles, African clothing styles, and even African surnames have been embraced by some black Americans. A few have gone beyond embracing Africa as their spiritual home and have decided to emigrate there and make Africa their permanent home. The experience of black people who were born and raised in the United States and who moved to Africa has been varied and revealing.

While reading the following statements of three black Americans who chose to live and work in the African Republic of the Congo, keep in mind these questions:

1. *What satisfactions have been experienced by black Americans living in the Congo?*
2. *What adjustments did black Americans living in the Congo have to make?*

American Blacks Living in the Congo, 1970

KINSHASA, the Congo (AP)—At home in Detroit, Elaine Wamba considered herself as black as the next Negro. Two years ago when she came here to live the Congolese called her "mundele," a Lingala word that represents the way whites feel and act.

"I have a fairer skin than most Congolese but that was the last thing I expected to be called," she recalls.

That was the first impression for Mrs. Wamba, 24, the former Elaine Brown. At college in Michigan she met and married a Congolese student. Now she's one of the dozen or so black Americans who are here trying life African style. Ten are women.

They had very different backgrounds but the same ambition: as a black to live in a black society.

❊   ❊   ❊   ❊   ❊

"As a black I have a sense of freedom here I never had in the United States," she says. "I feel here as I never could back there. My own situation is different and I can look at things in a different way. It's changed me— for the better, I think."

Charles Robinson, a Washingtonian, has been in the Congo on and off for nine years. He has seen some of the worst of the country's crises.

"You've no idea how it feels to be a member of the majority instead of the minority," he observes. "I never felt insecure here even when the trouble was worst—when every policeman was carrying a gun, shouting at you, asking for your papers. I felt like I was one of the majority."

❊   ❊   ❊   ❊   ❊

When asked if she thinks other black Americans should try the experience of coming back to the source, Mrs. Yvonne Mococo says: "It depends on the person concerned. Black Americans come here and they say: 'Look at the squalor. No water, no electricity. Look at the children with their fat stomachs and dirty feet. How can you live like that?'

"This sounds melodramatic but you have to have a pioneering spirit. If you haven't got that you can't really come here and hope to integrate with Africans. And if you don't want to integrate totally there's no real point in coming."

The Associated Press, New York (July 20, 1970).

5 Antislavery Movement

Radical Abolitionism

Introduction

Objectives of this assignment are to:
—Analyze accounts of radical abolitionist thought and social action for meaning.
—Make a hypothesis explaining radical abolitionist attitudes toward the United States government.
—Analyze a modern account of parallels between the beginnings of radical abolitionism and the Student Nonviolent Coordinating Committee of the 1960's for meaning.
—Identify problems encountered when history is studied by comparing past and present.

In the 1820's an indirect and gradual approach to antislavery was dominant in the form of the colonization movement. In the 1830's antislavery energies intensified rapidly and crystallized around a more radical program. Immediate abolition was the rallying cry of the new antislavery organizations.

Religious inspiration played an essential role in immediate abolitionism, just as it had in the colonization movement. The immediatists believed that slavery was a great sin which had to be eliminated totally and at once. They pointed out that the gospel did not permit men to give up sin gradually. Hence the immediatists criticized those who dallied with gradual antislavery measures such as colonization.

The emergence of immediatism in the antislavery movement coincided with the climax of religious revivalistic fervor. It also coincided with the shift to the radical total abstinence position in the temperance movement. The intensity of these evangelically-inspired forces had led to splits in the temperance forces.

The new demand for immediate abolition of slavery ultimately split the ranks of those opposed to slavery. The first split separated the immediate abolitionists from the colonizationists. But within a few years, the immediate abolitionists were likewise divided into rival factions over disagreements about strategy and tactics.

Immediatism and the Formation of Antislavery Societies

Immediatism arose among English antislavery forces about the same time as it did in the United States. English and American reformers kept in close contact with each other.* The movement in England reinforced the abolitionists in this country. However, the doctrine of immediate emancipation had also been developing in the United States, and was not simply imported from abroad.

Britain's emancipation of slaves in the West Indies in 1833 greatly encouraged American abolitionists.

The most influential American champion of immediate abolition was William Lloyd Garrison. On January 1, 1831, the twenty-five-year-old Garrison began publishing in Boston his famous abolitionist newspaper, The Liberator. A year later, Garrison founded the New England Anti-Slavery Society. Under his leadership, New England remained the most militant abolitionist center right up to the Civil War.

B164

Garrison also played an important part in the formation of the American Anti-Slavery Society in December, 1833. This national society, which was committed to immediate abolition, had its headquarters in New York City. It drew on the support of a number of evangelical religious leaders who were already active in other benevolent reforms. It sent out a small army of traveling agents who adopted the techniques of revivalism in preaching the message of abolitionism. Oberlin College in Ohio became a midwestern center for this work. Charles G. Finney, the great revivalist, moved to Oberlin in 1835 to direct its theological program. But the greatest of the Anti-Slavery Society's agents was *Theodore Dwight Weld,** a speaker and organizer whose contribution to the cause of abolition rivaled that of Garrison.

Splits in the Antislavery Movement

The sudden burst of abolitionist activity resulted by 1838 in the formation of some 1,350 local antislavery societies, with about 250,000 members. It also generated a strong backlash of anti-abolitionist feeling. In the middle 1830's violent and riotous attacks on antislavery meetings were common. More damaging to the cause, however, were internal divisions within the movement.

Garrison's growing radicalism was the principal cause of division. His language often seemed harsh and abusive to those who disagreed with him. But by the late 1830's he was associating abolitionism with what others considered *ultraist** positions on such questions as women's rights, pacifism, and government. Disagreement on these points led to a split in the American Anti-Slavery Society in 1840. Garrison and his militant New England supporters gained control of the Society. But the important evangelical group centered in New York withdrew, taking most of the financial strength and membership with them.

Weld underwent religious conversion at a revival preached by **Finney** in 1825. He was won to the antislavery cause primarily through his contact with **Charles Stuart,** a British abolitionist. Other reformers included **Arthur** and **Lewis Tappan,** wealthy New York merchants who gave generously of funds, energy, and managerial skill.

Ultraism means extremism. The terms **ultra, ultraism,** and **ultraist** were widely used in the 1830's and 1840's.

The violent anti-abolition backlash brought death and destruction. First abolitionist hero and martyr was **Reverend Elijah Parish Lovejoy,** a Presbyterian minister and editor of the Alton, Illinois, **Observer,** murdered in his newspaper office in 1837 for an abolitionist editorial he had printed. The mob afterwards threw his press into the Mississippi and marched Lovejoy's corpse through the streets.

The **Liberty Party** ran James G. Birney, a former slaveholder, for President on an antislavery platform in 1840 and 1844. Thereafter its supporters combined with the **Free-Soil Party** and other groups opposed to the expansion of slavery.

In 1844 **Foster** wrote a book criticizing the churches entitled: **The Brotherhood of Thieves: or, A True Picture of the American Church and Clergy.**

Thereafter, a portion of the anti-Garrisonians carried the antislavery effort into politics.* In the 1840's and 1850's, opposition to slavery, and especially to the expansion of slavery into new territories, became bitterly fought political issues. Garrison, however, would have nothing to do with politics because he believed it would lead to compromises. He would not cooperate with a system that recognized the existence of slavery. When faced with a choice between his cause and his country, Garrison unhesitatingly chose his cause.

Ultraism and American Society

Since the abolitionists were convinced slavery was a great sin, they considered it their duty to denounce those guilty of it and to demand that they repent. Hence they attacked slaveholders as sinners in the harshest language. But it was not slaveholders alone who were guilty. Garrison once said that there were only two groups as far as slavery was concerned: anyone who did not actively oppose slavery was indirectly a supporter of slavery!

Another New England abolitionist, *Stephen S. Foster,** expressed the same view more dramatically. He made it a habit to interrupt church services in the North and accuse the clergy and congregation of all the frightful crimes associated with slavery. His reasoning was that the whole church incurred the guilt of slaveholding so long as it admitted slaveowners as members in the South. He even went to the extreme of saying the Methodist Episcopal Church was worse than a house of prostitution because it admitted slaveowners.

These extreme tactics were partially responsible for the charge of fanaticism which was often leveled against the Garrisonian wing of the abolitionists. But Garrison himself was moving toward the ultraist position that American society itself was to be rejected as inherently sinful. What was imperfect was wrong; no existing social or political institution escaped condemnation. Garrison was prodded in this direction by John Humphrey Noyes, a religious radical who believed that God demanded absolute perfection. Since God demanded it, perfection must be possible. Therefore, both individual conduct and human society in general had to be perfect.

9 ABOLITIONISTS AND THE NATURE OF GOVERNMENT, 1837

Committed as they were to their cause, and secure in the belief that they were doing God's will, the abolitionists were at first puzzled and bewildered by the opposition which they encountered. They examined and pondered the problem for some time and finally believed they had discovered the reason for the fierce opposition to their abolition efforts and the reason why slavery continued to thrive.

B166

In letters written to William Lloyd Garrison in 1837, Henry C. Wright, a well-known New England abolitionist, and John Humphrey Noyes offer an explanation why their cause has not triumphed and what is required if God's will is to be served. While reading these selections from Wright and Noyes, keep in mind these questions:

1. According to Wright, what is the relationship between government and slavery?

2. What has Noyes done? Why did he do it?

3. What words would you use to describe the attitude of Wright toward the United States government? The attitude of Noyes?

Henry C. Wright on God and Government, 1837

God, and God alone, has a right of dominion over man. . . . Every man who desires to obtain dominion over man has the slaveholding spirit, and he would become a slaveholder in fact, if he had the power. All human governments that ever did or do exist, are, in the main, only efforts of man to acquire dominion over man. The very spirit of slaveholding pervades every government on the globe. Our government, though it embody some of the truest and noblest sentiments of divine liberty, is yet a slaveholding government.

Letter of Henry C. Wright published in **The Liberator** (Feb. 25, 1837), reprinted in Louis Ruchames, ed., **The Abolitionists, A Collection of Their Writings** (New York: Capricorn paperback edition, 1964, Copyright C. P. Putnam's Sons), pp. 111–112.

John Humphrey Noyes on the Future of the United States, 1837

I am willing that all men should know that I have signed my name to a document similar to the Declaration of 1776 renouncing all allegiance to the government of the United States, and asserting the title of Jesus Christ to the throne of the world.

When I wish to form a conception of the government of the United States, I picture to myself a bloated, swaggering libertine, trampling on the Bible, on its own Constitution, on its treaties with the Indians, and on the petitions of its citizens. With one hand it is whipping a Negro tied to a *liberty-pole,** and with the other it is dashing an emaciated Indian to the ground. Then I ask myself, "What have I, as a Christian, to do with such a villain?"

As a believer in the Bible, I know that the territory of the United States belongs to God, and that it is promised to Jesus Christ and his followers.

The Son of God will overthrow those worldly governments that stand in the way of the coming of his Kingdom, and he has chosen this country for the theatre of such an assault. For this is a country which, by its boasting hypocrisy, has become the laughing-stock of the world, and by its lawlessness has fully proved that man is incapable of self-government. Therefore, my hope of the Millennium begins where *Dr. Lyman Beecher's** ends—namely, AT THE OVERTHROW OF THIS NATION.

In the years before the American Revolution, the militant patriots known as Sons of Liberty met under **liberty poles** or **liberty trees.** The custom of erecting liberty poles as symbols of the principles of the Declaration of Independence was carried on for a number of years.

Dr. Beecher, 1775–1863, was a renowned Connecticut-born preacher, temperance reformer and moderate abolitionist.

Adapted from John Humphrey Noyes' letter to William Lloyd Garrison, March 22, 1837, as given in W. P. Garrison and F. J. Garrison, **William Lloyd Garrison, 1805–1879; The Story of His Life as Told by His Children.** 4 vols. (New York: The Century Press, 1885–1889), Vol. II, pp. 145–147.

10 GARRISON AND THE AMERICAN UNION, 1844–1854

In the 1830's and 1840's reformers spoke a great deal about what they called "come-outerism." The expression was biblical in origin and based on the prophet Isaiah's exhortation to the children of Israel to "come out" from among the sinful people surrounding them so they could serve the Lord more faithfully.

Religious come-outerism flourished during the 1830's and 1840's. New churches and religious societies were founded by people who had "come out" from older ones which they believed to be corrupt and hypocritical. However, the term was also used to describe the various ultraist social movements of the time, including the Garrison wing of the abolitionists. Come-outerism was a convenient short-hand expression for the *social radicalism of the day.**

For most Americans of the period, William Lloyd Garrison was the champion come-outer of them all. While reading the following accounts of Garrison's come-outer proposals and actions published in his newspaper The Liberator, keep in mind these questions:

1. *What policy did the Anti-Slavery Society decide to adopt in 1844? Why did they adopt it?*

2. *How did the Anti-Slavery Society propose to put this new policy into effect?*

3. *What did Garrison do at the Fourth of July meeting in 1854? How did he justify what he did?*

The American Anti-Slavery Society and the Federal Union, 1844

At the Tenth [annual convention] of the American Anti-Slavery Society . . . [in] 1844 . . . it was decided, by a vote of nearly three to one, . . . that fidelity to the cause of human freedom, hatred of oppression, sympathy for those who are held in chains and slavery in this republic, and allegiance to God, require that the existing national compact should be instantly dissolved; that secession from the government is a religious and political duty; that the motto inscribed on the banner of freedom should be, NO UNION WITH SLAVE-HOLDERS.

*   *   *   *   *

Freemen! Are you ready for the conflict? Come what may, will you sever the chains that bind you to a slaveholding government, and declare your independence? Up, then, with the banner of revolution! Not to shed blood, . . . [however, nor to injure the person or property of any uprising by slaves.] No—ours must be a bloodless strife, [unless our own blood] be shed—for we

In July, 1844, Brownson's Quarterly Review, an important magazine of the period, carried an article entitled, "Come-outerism: or the Radical Tendency of the Day."

From The Liberator (May 31, 1844), as reprinted in Truman Nelson, ed., Documents of Upheaval. Selections from William Lloyd Garrison's The Liberator, 1831–1865 (New York: Hill and Wang, 1969), pp. 202, 204.

aim, as did Christ our leader, not to destroy men's lives, but to save them—to overcome evil with good—to conquer through suffering for [the sake of righteousness]—to set the captive free by the [power] of truth!

Garrison Burns the Constitution

[At a Fourth of July meeting in 1854, Mr. Garrison performed an action which would, he said, make clear to all present how he regarded the proslavery laws and deeds of the nation.] Producing a copy of the *Fugitive Slave Law,** he set fire to it and burnt it to ashes. . . . Then, holding up a copy of the U. S. Constitution, he branded it as the source and parent of all the other atrocities. [He called it] "a covenant with death, and an agreement with hell." [Thereupon, he burned] it to ashes on the spot, exclaiming: "So perish all compromises with tyranny! And let all the people say, Amen!" A tremendous shout of "Amen!" went up to heaven in ratification of the deed. [There were also] a few hisses and wrathful exclamations from some who were evidently in a rowdyish state of mind. But [they] were at once cowed by the popular feeling.

The **Fugitive Slave Law,** passed in 1850, was a harsh one, under which fugitives could be arrested and returned to their masters. Fugitives claiming to be free men were denied right of trial by jury, and their testimony could not be used as evidence. New England abolitionists resented the law and resorted to violence to protect runaway slaves.

From **The Liberator** (July 7, 1854), as reprinted in Nelson, ed., **Documents of Upheaval**, p. 216.

11 A CONTEMPORARY HISTORIAN'S PARALLEL

In the summer of 1966, Stokely Carmichael introduced the term *Black Power.** He was the newly elected Chairman of the Student Nonviolent Coordinating Committee (SNCC), an organization which soon adopted a more militant policy under his leadership. Black Power was the new goal. But what did it mean? Did it call for effective political pressure? Racial solidarity among Negroes? Or armed violence? Among those who discussed the matter was Martin Duberman, a young historian from Princeton University, who had written widely on the antislavery movement. Although he warned that history does not repeat itself, Duberman saw an enlightening parallel between the emergence of Black Power and the abolitionist movement.

While reading this selection from Professor Duberman's article, keep in mind these questions:

1. According to Duberman, how was the abolitionist movement similar to the Student Nonviolent Coordinating Committee?

2. What does Duberman regard as the main parallel between the two movements?

3. How does Duberman explain the changes that each of the two movements underwent?

The term **Black Power** was used by the distinguished black American author, Richard Wright, in 1954 as the title of a book on life in the British colony of the Gold Coast in Africa before it became the independent state of Ghana.

Abolitionism and Black Power

The parallels between the Abolitionists and the current defenders of Black Power are numerous and striking. Neither group started off with an extremist position. At the beginning, SNCC's staff was interracial, religious in orientation, committed to the American Dream, and hopeful of sharing fully in that dream. It placed its hopes in an appeal to the national conscience, which was to be aroused by examples of nonviolence and redemptive love, and by dramatic sit-ins, freedom rides, and protest marches.

The abolitionist movement began in a similarly mild and hopeful manner. It stressed persuasion, and planned to bring the iniquity of slavery before the conscience of the average American. Once the national conscience was aroused, ways and means would be found, the abolitionists felt, to bring about rapid and orderly emancipation. Even Garrison was at first willing to settle for gradual emancipation immediately begun instead of demanding that freedom itself be instantly achieved.

But this approach brought meager results. In the North the Abolitionists encountered massive apathy, in the South massive resistance. Thus thwarted, they abandoned their flexible approach. They shifted to the position that emancipation had to take place at once and without compensation to the slaveholder. They also began (especially in New England) to advocate such doctrines as "Dis-Union" and "No-Government." These stands directly parallel Black Power's recent calls for "separation" and "decentralization." These new positions produced internal division, and external criticism—both in the case of abolitionism and of Black Power.

The most important parallel between the two movements is the similarity of their evolution from "moderation" to "extremism." It is a shift that demonstrates the developmental nature of movements for social change, and also illustrates the maxim that "revolutionaries are not born, but made." And what makes a man shift from reform to revolution is the indifference of his society; that either society refuses reforms, or gives them in the form of tokens.

Thus, *if* one views the William Lloyd Garrisons and the Stokely Carmichaels as extremists, one should at least place the blame for that extremism where it belongs—on the society which scorned or toyed with their original pleas for justice. . . .

Adapted from Martin Duberman, "Black Power in America," **Partisan Review**, XXXV (Winter, 1968), pp. 40–43. Copyright © 1968 by Martin Duberman. Reprinted by permission of The Sterling Lord Agency.

Stokely Carmichael, advocate of Black Power in the late 1960's and early 1970's, and William Lloyd Garrison, fiery leader of the Abolitionist Era from the 1830's through the 1860's.

6 Antislavery Movement

Black Abolitionists

Introduction

Besides campaigning against slavery in the South, the abolitionists battled against racial prejudice in the North. Racial prejudice infected both South and North. Abolitionists realized that racism and slavery were interconnected. Their job would be only half done if slavery were done away with and racial prejudice continued. White abolitionists were therefore committed to working for real equality between the races. But there were black abolitionists, too—although they have often been overlooked in histories of the crusade against slavery. Black abolitionists were naturally more concerned than white ones about the elimination of discrimination and the attainment of equality. In fact, they felt at times that their white friends were not altogether free of prejudice themselves.

Abolitionism, Racism, and Riots

The general record of white abolitionists was excellent as far as prejudice was concerned. But the pervasive racial prejudice of white society now and then tinged their attitude and behavior. There was often a touch of condescension in their treatment of blacks. At times difficulties arose about whites and blacks belonging to the same antislavery societies.

Whites and blacks usually worked together in the same societies, however. Tactical considerations rather than prejudice might account for white abolitionists' reluctance to flaunt their belief in racial equality. For nothing inflamed the prejudices of the general populace so much as the fear of amalgamation—that is, social mixing of the races that might lead to racial intermarriage.

Fear of amalgamation played a key role in the outburst of rioting that greeted abolitionist organizing efforts in the mid-1830's.* Both white and black abolitionists behaved with great heroism when under attack by mobs. But it seemed foolhardy to invite violence needlessly. Stressing the theme of racial equality threatened to distract attention from the primary aim of abolishing slavery.

Moreover, it was the northern blacks rather than white abolitionists who bore the brunt of mob violence. Considering all these factors, it is understandable that white abolitionists were occasionally disposed to soft-pedal their commitment to racial equality. And they flatly denied the charge of promoting intermarriage.

Objectives of this assignment are to:
—Analyze selections from the writing and thought of black abolitionists for meaning.
—Make historical judgment on most effective tactic for black people in their struggle for freedom during 1830–1860.
—Analyze selections from modern statements on American racial problems for meaning.
—Compare modern statements on America's racial problems with those made by black abolitionists during 1830–1860.
—Identify problems encountered when history is studied by comparing past and present.

In July, 1834, an **anti-abolition riot** in New York City lasted three days. It resulted in the destruction of sixty dwellings and six churches, and was put down only by the National Guard.

Black Abolitionism

Being the direct victims of prejudice and discrimination, free blacks regarded equality as a matter of greater urgency than their white abolitionist friends. They therefore not only supported the regular antislavery societies —which were biracial, but dominated by whites—but also carried on independent activities of their own.

National conventions were held in the early 1830's, and again in the 1840's, at which the views of the free black community were given public expression. Another sort of activity was deliberately kept far from the spotlight of publicity—assisting runaway slaves. Free northern blacks, rather than white abolitionists, were the chief operators of the *Underground Railroad.** But once the runaway had reached freedom and some degree of security, he might be called upon as a lecturer. Several ex-slaves gained fame as abolitionist speakers. Their reports of personal experiences had a tremendous impact.

The greatest of all black abolitionists was Frederick Douglass. Born a slave about 1818, Douglass escaped at the age of twenty. He became an abolitionist lecturer in 1841 and soon enjoyed dazzling success because of his brilliant intelligence, eloquence, and impressive appearance. His autobiographical Narrative of the Life of Frederick Douglass, which told the story of his years in slavery, was a best-seller in England as well as the United States.

In addition to Douglass, many other black men and women joined the struggle for freedom and equality. For example, Harriet Tubman, an escaped slave, became very active in the Underground Railroad. She was known as the Moses of her people and made 19 trips into the South to lead more than 300 slaves to freedom. Another famous black woman, Sojourner Truth, born a slave in New York, became a celebrated abolitionist lecturer.

The **Underground Railroad** was an organization to assist slaves to escape to the North. Between 1830 and 1860, it is estimated that approximately 50,000 slaves escaped to freedom through its assistance.

Here, escaping slaves try to avoid being captured and returned to their masters.

Prominent black men in the abolitionist movement included the gentle advocate of nonviolence, lumber merchant and editor of the National Reformer magazine, William Whipper. Reverend Theodore S. Wright, Princeton graduate and pastor of the Shiloh Presbyterian Church in New York City, was very active in abolitionist activities throughout the East. Philadelphia was the base of operations for the Harvard-educated physician and author, Martin R. Delany. Champion of black self-sufficiency, Delany was once described by Frederick Douglass as "the intensest embodiment of black nationality to be met with outside the valley of the Niger." There were many others.

Black Revolutionaries

Beside the black lecturers, writers, organizers, and humanitarians in the movement, there were other black men who sought freedom through a different means. Many black Americans, both free and slave, did not shrink from advocating violence or practicing it in order to win freedom for themselves and their people.

Slave insurrections are as old as the black man's history in North America. However, they became more frequent as the eighteenth century progressed. Slave owners in Henrico County, Virginia, were terrified by the Gabriel Prosser plot in 1801 to seize the arsenal in Richmond and to arm and liberate the slaves. Prosser and 35 alleged participants in the plot were executed. A rising occurred near Camden, North Carolina, in 1816, and slaves unsuccessfully plotted to seize Augusta, Georgia, in 1819. Denmark Vesey's intended rising in Charleston, South Carolina, in 1822 was revealed by an informer and 37 alleged participants were executed.

David Walker of Massachusetts published his famous Appeal to the Slaves to rise against their masters in 1829, and in 1831 Nathaniel Turner led a bloody but unsuccessful rebellion in Southampton County, Virginia. Despite the severity with which these risings were suppressed, faith in violence as a tactic in the black man's struggle for freedom in America continued. Again in 1843, Reverend Henry Highland Garnet reminded a National Convention of Colored Citizens in Buffalo, New York, that the price of freedom for their generation would have to be paid in blood.

For white Americans as well as for black, Garnet proved to be a remarkable prophet. Twenty years later the nation paid the terrible price which Garnet had predicted.

12   TACTICS FOR FREEDOM, 1837–1843

In the 1830's and 1840's the great majority of black abolitionists were committed to nonviolent tactics in their struggle against slavery. However, progress was slow and free blacks became increasingly impatient. This impatience forced most black abolitionists to reflect and rethink what the tactics for freedom ought to be.

William Whipper, businessman, author, and one of the chief agents of the Underground Railroad, was a firm believer in the power of moral force. In an address delivered to a convention in Philadelphia, Whipper explained why he believed nonviolence was the only tactic which would insure a speedy triumph of their cause.

Reverend Henry Highland Garnet was himself a fugitive slave. He had escaped to freedom with his parents in 1824. Dissatisfied with the progress of the antislavery movement, Garnet decided to appeal to the people most concerned—the slaves themselves.

Although Garnet's speech was wildly acclaimed by those at the National Convention of Colored Citizens in Buffalo, the convention as a whole refused to adopt it. While reading the following selections from the speeches of Whipper and Garnet, keep in mind these questions:

1. According to Whipper, why must black people in America remain non-violent in their struggle for equality?

2. According to Whipper, how should black people respond to those who behave unjustly toward them?

3. According to Garnet, what is the only hope for freedom for this generation of black people?

William Whipper Urges Nonviolence in the Struggle for Justice and Equality, 1837

It is my purpose to exhibit reason as a powerful handmaid in achieving the triumph of universal peace. If there be a single class of people in these United States where use of reason is more imperative and binding than another, it is the colored population of this country, both free and enslaved. Situated as we are, among a people that recognize the lawfulness of slavery, and more of whom sympathize with the oppressor than the oppressed, it requires us to pursue our course calmly onward, with much self-denial, patience and perseverance.

We must be prepared at all times to meet the scoffs and scorns of the vulgar and indecent—the contemptible frowns of haughty tyrants and the blighting mildew of a popular and sinful prejudice. We must learn on all occasions to rebuke the spirit of violence, both in sentiment and practice. God has said, "Vengeance is mine, and I will repay it."

And now my friends, let us cease to be guided by the influence of a wild and beguiling passion—the wicked and foolish fantasies of pride, folly, and ambition—the sickly sensibility of those who from false notions of honor attempt to promote justice by spilling their fellow creature's blood. Turn away from them, for a terrible retaliation awaits them, even in this life. What would happen if those dedicated to the glorious undertaking of freeing

William Whipper was a wealthy Pennsylvania lumber merchant.

B174

2,500,000 human beings set out with the war cry of "liberty or death"? They would have been long demolished, or a civil war would have broken out. What would be our condition, together with that of the slave population? Why, we should have doubtless perished by the sword, or been praying for the destruction of our enemies, and probably engaged in the same bloody warfare.

Let us not think the world has no regard for our efforts—they are looking forward to them with intense interest and anxiety. If some continue injustice toward us, let us always decide that their reasoning powers are defective. Let us be mindful of the weaknesses of others, and for acts of wickedness against us, let us reciprocate in the spirit of kindness.

Adapted from Carter Godwin Woodson, Editor. **Negro Orators and Their Orations** (Washington: The Association for the Study of Negro Life and History, 1925, reprinted, New York: Russell & Russell, 1969), pp. 113, 115, 117–118. Copyright © by Association for the Study of Negro Life and History, Washington, D.C.

Henry Highland Garnet's Address to the Slaves of the United States, 1843

Slavery! How much misery is comprehended in that single word. No one [person] has more right to the full enjoyment of freedom than another. In every man's mind the good seeds of liberty are planted, and he who brings his fellow man down so low, as to make him contented with a condition of slavery, commits the highest crime against God and man. Brethren, your oppressors aim to do this. They endeavor to make you as much like beasts as possible. Then, and not till then, has American slavery done its perfect work.

If you would be free in this generation, here is your only hope. However much you and all of us may desire it, there is not much hope of redemption without the shedding of blood. If you must bleed, let it come all at once—rather die freemen than live to be slaves.

In the name of the merciful God, and by all that life is worth, let it no longer be a debatable question, whether it is better to choose liberty or death.

In 1822, Denmark Vesey of South Carolina formed a plan for the liberation of his fellowmen. He was betrayed by the treachery of his own people, and died a martyr to freedom. The patriotic Nathaniel Turner followed Denmark Vesey. He was goaded to desperation by wrong and injustice. Next arose the immortal *Joseph Cinque,** the hero of the *Amistad.** He was a native African, and by the help of God he emancipated a whole shipload of his fellowmen on the high seas. Next arose *Madison Washington,** that bright star of freedom, and took his station in the constellation of true heroism. He was a slave on board the Brig *Creole,** of Richmond, bound to New Orleans with a hundred and four others. Nineteen struck for liberty or death. Only one life was taken, and the whole party were emancipated.

Brethren, arise, arise! Strike for your lives and liberty. Now is the day and the hour. Let every slave throughout the land do this, and the days of slavery are numbered. You cannot be more oppressed than you have been —you cannot suffer greater cruelties than you have already. Rather die freemen than live to be slaves. Remember that you are FOUR MILLIONS!

Joseph Cinque and **Madison Washington** were leaders of successful mutinies on the slave ships **Amistad** and **Creole** in the years 1839 and 1841, respectively.

B175

Let your motto be resistance! *Resistance!* RESISTANCE! No oppressed people have ever secured their liberty without resistance. What kind of resistance you had better make you must decide by the circumstances that surround you, and according to the suggestion of expediency. Brethren, adieu! Trust in the living God. Labor for the peace of the human race, and remember that you are FOUR MILLIONS!

Adapted from Carter Godwin Woodson, Editor. **Negro Orators and Their Orations** (Washington: The Association for the Study of Negro Life and History, 1925; reprinted, New York: Russell & Russell, 1969), pp. 152–153, 155–157. Copyright © by Association for the Study of Negro Life and History, Washington, D.C.

13   SLAVERY AND THE FUTURE OF BLACK PEOPLE IN AMERICA, 1837–1852

Prejudice was an everyday experience of black people throughout the free states of the North. When set beside the harsh reality of southern slavery, the unpleasant facts of northern prejudice gave free black intellectuals pause about the future of slavery and black people in America.

Reverend Theodore S. Wright, Martin R. Delany, and Frederick Douglass, all dedicated black abolitionists, considered the future prospects for black people in a country where they would forever be a racial minority. While reading selections from the writings and speeches of Wright, Delany, and Douglass, keep in mind these questions:

1. According to Wright, how are free blacks discriminated against?

2. Why does Delany object to living among a white majority?

3. According to Douglass, how has America been false to its past? How is it false to its present?

Theodore S. Wright Protests Discrimination in the North, 1837

The prejudice which exists against the colored man, the free man, is like the atmosphere. It is felt around him everywhere. Although we are not formally held in bondage, we are still slaves. Everywhere we feel the chain galling us. It is this prejudice which the resolution condemns—this spirit of slavery that withers all our hopes and often causes the colored parent, as he looks upon his child, to wish that child had never been born. Sir, this prejudice is wicked.

A colored man can hardly learn a trade, and if he does, it is difficult for him to find anyone who will employ him. In most of our large cities there are workingmen's associations whose rules keep colored men out.

At present we find the colleges barred against our children.

I will say nothing about the inconvenience of traveling; how we are frowned upon and despised. No matter how we may demean ourselves, we find embarrassments everywhere.

But sir, this prejudice goes farther. It debars men from heaven. I know an efficient church in this State, where a respectable colored man went to the house of God. As he was going to take his seat in the gallery, one of the officers of the church stopped him and said, "You cannot go there, sir."

Adapted from Carter Godwin Woodson, Editor. **Negro Orators and Their Orations** (Washington: The Association for the Study of Negro Life and History, 1925; reprinted, New York: Russell & Russell, 1969), pp. 93–94. Copyright © by Association for the Study of Negro Life and History, Washington, D.C.

Martin R. Delany Urges Separatism, 1852

I am not in favor of caste, nor of a separation of the brotherhood of mankind. I would as willingly live among white men as black, if I had an equal possession and enjoyment of the same privileges. But I shall never be reconciled to living among them, subservient to their will—existing by mere tolerance as we, the colored people, do in this country.

The majority of white men cannot see why colored men desire more than the formally granted right of citizenship. Blind selfishness on the one hand and deep prejudice on the other, will not permit them to understand that we desire the exercise and enjoyment of these rights, as well as the name of their possession. If there were any probability of this, I should be willing to remain in this country, struggling on and fighting the good fight of faith. But I must admit that I have no hopes in this country—no confidence in the American people, with a few excellent exceptions.

Heathenism and Liberty, before Christianity and Slavery.

> Were I a slave, I would be free,
> I would not live to live a slave;
> But boldly strike for LIBERTY—
> For FREEDOM or a Martyr's grave.

Adapted from Carter Godwin Woodson, Editor. **The Mind of the Negro as Reflected in Letters Written During the Crisis,** 1800–1860 (Washington: The Association for the Study of Negro Life and History, 1926; reprinted, New York: Russell & Russell, 1969), p. 293. Copyright © by Association for the Study of the Negro Life and History, Washington, D.C.

Frederick Douglass: Thoughts on the Fourth of July, 1852

My subject, then, fellow-citizens, is *American Slavery*. I shall see this day and its popular characteristics from the slave's point of view. Standing there identified with the American bondman, making his wrongs mine, I do not hesitate to declare, with all my soul, that the character and conduct of this nation never looked blacker to me than on this 4th of July! Whether we turn to the declarations of the past, or to the professions of the present, the conduct of the nation seems equally hideous and revolting. America is false to the past, false to the present, and solemnly binds herself to be false to the future.

Standing with God and the crushed and bleeding slave on this occasion, I will, in the name of humanity which is outraged, in the name of liberty which is fettered, in the name of the Constitution and the Bible which are disregarded and trampled upon, dare to call in question and to denounce, with all the emphasis I can command, everything that serves to perpetuate slavery —the great sin and shame of America!

❊   ❊   ❊   ❊   ❊

Some will insist that what I denounce is in fact guaranteed and sanctioned by the Constitution of the United States; that the right to hold, and to hunt slaves is part of the Constitution framed by the illustrious Fathers of this Republic.

That is a slander upon their memory, at least so I believe. In the Constitution I hold there is neither warrant, license, nor sanction of the hateful thing; but interpreted as it ought to be interpreted, the CONSTITUTION IS A GLORIOUS LIBERTY DOCUMENT.

If the Constitution were intended by its framers and adopters to be a slaveholding instrument, why cannot *slavery*, *slaveholding*, or *slave* be found anywhere in it?

Taking the Constitution according to its plain reading, I defy the presentation of a single pro-slavery clause in it. On the other hand, it will be found to contain principles and purposes, entirely hostile to the existence of slavery.

Notwithstanding the dark picture of the state of the nation which I have this day presented, I do not despair of this country. There are forces in operation which must inevitably work the downfall of slavery. Its doom is certain.

Adapted from Carter Godwin Woodson, Editor. **Negro Orators and Their Orations** (Washington: The Association for the Study of Negro Life and History, 1925; reprinted, New York: Russell & Russell, 1969), pp. 206–207, 219–221. Copyright © by Association for the Study of Negro Life and History, Washington, D.C.

14 THE CONTEMPORARY CRISIS OVER RACIAL EQUALITY

During the 1960's racial tensions increased throughout the United States. Racial disorders erupted in several American cities in 1963. A major riot involving 34 deaths, hundreds of injuries, and $35 million in property damages occurred in Los Angeles in 1965. The worst came in a two-week period in July, 1967, when major riots in Newark and Detroit claimed 66 lives, destroyed $50 million worth of property, and led to more than 10,000 arrests.

Americans were shocked by what had happened and uncertain about what might happen in the future. Explanations of why the riots occurred and statements of what must be done to assure racial peace in our cities in the years ahead were numerous and conflicting. No set of readings can do justice to the variety of viewpoints about the causes of urban disorder and the complexities of race relations expressed in recent years. The selections presented below are taken from the report of the President's Advisory Commission on Civil Disorders published in 1968 and resolutions adopted by a Black Power Conference held in 1967.

While reading these selections, keep in mind these questions:

1. According to the National Advisory Commission, what was the fundamental cause of the disorders of 1967?

2. What does the Black Power Conference propose as a solution to America's present racial problems? On what grounds does the Conference justify its proposal?

B178

Report of the National Advisory Commission on Civil Disorders, 1968

In asking "Why did it happen?" we shift our focus from the local to the national scene, from the particular events of the summer of 1967 to the factors within the society at large that created a mood of violence among many urban Negroes.

These factors are complex and interacting; they vary significantly in their effect from city to city and from year to year; and the consequences of one disorder, generating new grievances and new demands, became the causes of the next. Thus was created the "thicket of tension, and extreme opinions" cited by the President.

Despite these complexities, certain fundamental matters are clear. Of these, the most fundamental is the racial attitude and behavior of white Americans toward black Americans.

Race prejudice has shaped our history decisively; it now threatens to affect our future.

White racism is essentially responsible for the explosive mixture which has been accumulating in our cities since the end of World War II.

Report of the National Advisory Commission on Civil Disorders (New York: Bantam paperback edition, 1968), pp. 9–10.

Resolutions of the Conference on Black Power, 1967

Whereas the black people in America have been systematically oppressed by their white fellow-countrymen;

Whereas there is little prospect that this oppression can be terminated, peacefully or otherwise, within the foreseeable future;

Whereas the black people do not wish to be absorbed into the larger white community;

Whereas the black people in America find that their interests are in contradiction with those of white America;

Whereas the black people in America are psychologically handicapped by virtue of their having no national homeland;

Whereas the physical, moral, ethical, and aesthetic standards of white American society are not those of black society and indeed do violence to the self-image of the black man;

Whereas black people were among the earliest immigrants to America, having been ruthlessly separated from their fatherland, and have made a major contribution to America's development, most of this contribution having been uncompensated, and

Recognizing that efforts are already well advanced for the convening of a Constitutional Convention for the purpose of revising the Constitution of the U. S. for the first time since America's inception, then

Be it resolved that the Black Power Conference initiate a national dialogue on the desirability of partitioning the U. S. into two separate and independent nations, one to be a homeland for white and the other to be a homeland for black Americans.

A Symposium by Robert S. Browne and Robert Vernon, Should the United States Be Partitioned into Two Separate and Independent Nations-One a Homeland for White Americans and the Other a Homeland for Black Americans? (New York: Merit Publishers, 1968), pp. 3–4. By permission of Pathfinder Press, Inc.

7 Peace and nonviolence, past and present

Antiwar Protest

Objectives of this assignment are to:
—Analyze selections from the writing and thought of spokesmen for the peace movement and advocates of civil disobedience in the 1840's for meaning.
—Make historical judgment on effectiveness of civil disobedience as a tactic for changing government policies in the 1840's.
—Analyze statements and accounts of anti-war groups in the 1960's for meaning.
—Compare modern anti-war statements and actions with those made or undertaken in 1840's.
—Identify problems encountered when history is studied by comparing past and present.

Colonial Pennsylvania became a haven, not only for the peaceable Quakers, but for a number of pacifist German sects such as the Mennonites.

Worcester's book was read with much interest early in the 20th century when the movement for a League of Nations and World Court was gathering momentum.

In 1840 **Ladd** called for a world organization.

Introduction

In the 1960's, dissent and protest against the American war in Vietnam became closely intertwined with social reform causes at home, especially with the cause of equality for black Americans. It is a striking parallel that the same thing happened in the Era of Reform. Americans at that time waged a war which aroused vehement internal opposition. There was also a nonviolence movement in those days. And both nonviolence and antiwar dissent were intimately linked with the great black-white issue, antislavery. We will explore some of the past and present relationships between social reform and nonviolence in this assignment.

Course of the Peace Movement

The tradition of pacifism in America stretched back into colonial times.* But an organized movement to end war did not get under way until the end of the War of 1812. The many years of conflict beginning with the American Revolution in 1775, the French Revolution, and Napoleonic wars in Europe, 1791–1815, and the War of 1812 inspired the antiwar movement.

In 1815, peace societies were organized in New York City and in Boston. The New York leader, David Low Dodge, had been writing on peace for several years. He had reached the conclusion that all war—defensive as well as offensive—was ruled out by the gospel of Christ. The Reverend Noah Worcester was the Boston leader. In 1814 he wrote a book called *Solemn Review of the Custom of War* in which he proposed a *confederacy of nations* and an *international court.*

The peace societies followed the same general pattern as the other religious benevolent organizations. They grew slowly at first, but in the 1820's, the American Peace Society was formed as a national organization. A retired sea-captain and merchant, *William Ladd,** was the chief promoter of the national organization. Eventually Ladd reached the full pacifist position, but he was a moderate man by temperament. For the first few years the American Peace Society admitted those who believed a defensive war was justifiable, as well as those opposed to all war.

Peace Groups Split

In the 1830's, however, a split occurred between these two groups. The most radical of the pacifists called themselves nonresistants. A remark of William Lloyd Garrison makes clear the similarity between the split in the peace movement and those in other reforms already studied. Garrison said: "Nonresistance is to the violence that is in the world what teetotalism is to intemperance, or immediate emancipation to slavery."* Even defensive war was unjustifiable. Even though the American Peace Society decided to exclude believers in defensive war, the extreme nonresistants withdrew to form their own society in 1838. During the 1840's, the opponents of war were reinforced by those who were critical of U. S. policy in the Mexican War. The peace groups in this country also tried to *internationalize** the movement by establishing contacts with similar groups in Europe.

One peace advocate even drew up a "teetotal peace pledge" patterned after the total abstinence pledge used in the temperance movement.

Peace Movement Declines in the 1850's

As tensions rose over slavery, many of the nonresistants who had rejected all forms of violence in the 1830's changed their minds during the next twenty years. The decline of nonviolence during the 1850's was rapid and complete. We can see the process at work among antislavery people who abandoned the cause of nonresistance.

For example, *Angelina Grimké Weld** changed her mind about violence. Wife of the great abolitionist, Theodore Weld, and dedicated to the principles of nonviolence and nonresistance in the 1830's, she professed amazement at the rapidity with which her principles changed. By 1854, she had decided that slavery was more abhorrent to Christianity than murder. "We are compelled to chose between two evils," she wrote, "and all that we can do is take the *least,* and baptize liberty in blood, if it must be so."

Another one-time firm believer in nonresistance, Charles Stearns, abandoned his peace principles during the experience of living in *Bleeding Kansas.** Stearns had endured several severe beatings by pro-slavery gangs in Kansas. Once, when struck on the face, he turned the other cheek only to be struck immediately on that side as well. After these experiences, Stearns decided that if nonresistance was not a safe principle, it could not be a true one.

For reasons such as these many one-time nonresistants became disillusioned with their principles in the 1850's and embraced violence as a proper tactic in the struggle against slavery. For persons such as Angelina Weld and Charles Stearns who held extreme views on one question, it was not difficult to adopt extreme views on another question. Hatred of slavery proved to be more powerful than love of peace. By 1861, whites and blacks, slaveholders and abolitionists, men of violence and nonresistants were ready to fight. All Americans were overwhelmed by the greatest war ever fought on the North American continent.

The person most active in internationalizing the American peace effort was **Elihu Burritt**, a self-taught man of the people, who was known as **The Learned Blacksmith**. He mastered dozens of languages while working at his forge and in his spare time.

Angelina Grimké and her sister **Sarah** were members of a slaveholding South Carolina family. They moved to the North because of their opposition to slavery and were active in a number of reform movements.

In the mid-1850's, intermittent fighting broke out in the Kansas territory between pro and antislavery factions among the settlers. Because of this conflict, it was referred to as **bleeding Kansas.**

15 PEACE AND NONVIOLENCE IN THE REFORM ERA

The most extreme leaders of the Peace movement were also deeply involved in abolitionism. William Lloyd Garrison, foremost leader of the "immediate abolitionists," was also the most uncompromising spokesman for the nonresistants. At a convention of the American Peace Society held in Boston in 1838, the intransigence of Garrison and a few of his friends split the Society and led to the foundation of the rival New England Nonresistance Society. Garrison himself drew up the Declaration of Sentiments, a statement of principles for the new organization.

While reading the following selections from Garrison's Declaration of Sentiments, keep in mind these questions:

1. What policy does Garrison advocate toward the existing governments of the world?

2. How does the policy advocated by Garrison affect the lives of individuals?

3. How should individuals behave toward the requirements of existing governments?

Garrison's Declaration of Sentiments for the New England Nonresistance Society, 1838

We cannot acknowledge allegiance to any human government; neither can we oppose any such government by resort to physical force. We recognize but one King and Lawgiver, one Judge and Ruler of mankind. We are bound by the laws of a kingdom which is not of this world; the subjects of which are forbidden to fight; in which Mercy and Truth are met together, and Righteousness and Peace have kissed each other; which has no state lines, no national partitions, no geographical boundaries; in which there is no distinction of rank, or division of caste, or inequality of sex; the officers of which are Peace, its enforcer Righteousness, its walls Salvation, and its gates Praise; and which is destined to break in pieces and consume all other kingdoms.

Our country is the world, our countrymen are all mankind. We love the land of our birth only as we love all other lands. Hence we can allow no appeal to patriotism to revenge any national insult or injury.

We conceive that if a nation has no right to defend itself against foreign enemies, no individual possesses that right in his own case. The unit cannot be of greater importance than the aggregate. If one man may take life, to obtain or defend his rights, the same license must necessarily be granted to communities, states, and nations.

We register our testimony, not only against all wars, whether offensive or defensive, but also against all preparations for war. And likewise against all armies, monuments, trophies, celebrations of victory, and all laws requiring military service of citizens.

As every human government is upheld by physical strength, and its laws are enforced virtually at the point of the bayonet, we cannot hold any office which imposes on its incumbent the obligation to do right, on pain of imprisonment or death. We therefore voluntarily exclude ourselves from any legislative or judicial body, and repudiate all human politics. If we cannot occupy a seat in the legislature, or on the judicial bench, neither can we help elect others to do so as our substitutes.

It follows that we cannot sue any man at law, to compel him by force to restore any thing which he may have wrongfully taken from us or others.

The history of mankind is crowded with evidence proving that physical coercion is not adapted to moral regeneration. The sinful disposition of man can be subdued only by love. Evil can be exterminated from the earth only by goodness.

We shall obey all the requirements of the government, except those we deem contrary to the commands of the gospel. We shall in no way resist the operation of the law, except by meekly submitting to the penalty of disobedience.

But, while we shall adhere to the doctrines of non-resistance and passive submission to enemies, we purpose, in a moral and spiritual sense, to speak and act boldly in the cause of God; to assail iniquity in high places and low places. Thus shall we hasten the time when the kingdoms of this world shall become the kingdoms of our Lord and of his Christ, and he shall reign forever.

Adapted from Wendell Phillips Garrison and Francis Jackson Garrison, **William Lloyd Garrison, 1805–1879** (New York: The Century Press, 1885–1889), Vol. II, pp. 230–234.

16   DISSENT AND NONVIOLENT RESISTANCE TO THE MEXICAN WAR

The war between the United States and Mexico (1846–1848) was one of the most unpopular ones in American history. As in the case of the Vietnam war one hundred and twenty years later, opponents charged that the United States was engaged in a war that was both unjust and immoral. Antislavery people were particularly outraged because they believed the war with Mexico was being fought to acquire new territory into which slavery could be expanded. Reverend Theodore Parker, one of the country's most distinguished churchmen and preachers, denounced the war in language that abolitionists and antislavery people everywhere applauded.

The war also inspired the eminent writer and philosopher, Henry David Thoreau, to protest the war by going to jail for nonpayment of his poll tax

General Zachary Taylor seated on a hill of skulls denoting the dead of the Mexican War—Although the Whigs violently opposed the Mexican War in which Taylor gained fame, they nominated "Old Rough and Ready" as their candidate for President. Despite the opposition campaign posters such as the one shown here which was labeled: "An Available Candidate—The One Qualification for a Whig President," Taylor won the Presidency.

and to write an essay on nonviolent resistance that has become a world classic. Thoreau explained why he went to jail and how he believed a dedicated minority could make unjust and evil laws unenforceable.

While reading these selections from Parker's speech and Thoreau's essay, Civil Disobedience, keep in mind these questions:

1. According to Parker, why is the Mexican War wrong and what should the people of Massachusetts do about it?

2. According to Thoreau, how have most people expressed their opposition to slavery and the Mexican War?

3. According to Thoreau, how can a dedicated minority change unjust government policies?

Theodore Parker on the Mexican War, 1847

We are in a war. Men needed to hew wood and honestly serve society are marching about, learning to kill other men, men who never harmed us, learning to kill their brothers. It is a mean and infamous war we are fighting. It is like a great big boy fighting a little boy—with that little boy being feeble and sick. What makes it worse is that the little boy is in the right, and the big boy is in the wrong, and tells solemn lies to make his side seem right.

The war had a mean and infamous beginning. It began illegally, unconstitutionally. The *Whigs** say, "The President made the war." But Congress also bears part of the responsibility. Why, only sixteen members of Congress voted against the war. I say this war is mean and infamous, all the more because it is being waged by a people calling itself democratic and Christian.

We have come here to talk about the war; to work against the war. It is rather late, but "better late than never." We should have objected when the President asked for volunteers to fight against Mexico. That was the time

The President at the time of the Mexican War was **James K. Polk,** a Democrat. The Whigs were the opposition party, and many of them were critics of the war. One Whig critic was Abraham Lincoln, then a Congressman from Illinois.

B184

to stand up and say in the spirit of '76, "We won't send a man, not one Yankee man, for this wicked war." That was the time for all good men to say, "This is a war for slavery, an aristocratic war, a war against the best interests of mankind."

It is time for the people of Massachusetts to instruct their servants in Congress to oppose this war; to refuse all supplies for it; to ask for the recall of the army into our own land. It is time for us to tell them that not an inch of slave territory shall ever be added to the realm. Let us remonstrate! Let us petition! Let us command!

Your President tells us it is treason to talk this way! Treason is it? Treason to discuss a war which the Government made, but which the people are made to pay for? If the people cannot discuss the war they have got to fight and pay for, why, who under heaven can discuss it? Whose business is it, if not yours and mine? If my country is in the wrong, and I know it but hold my peace, then I <u>am guilty</u> of treason, moral treason.

Adapted from Theodore Parker, **The Slave Power** (Boston: American Unitarian Association, 1916), Vol. XI, pp. 21–31.

Henry David Thoreau on Civil Disobedience, 1848

How does it become a man to behave toward this American government today? I answer that he cannot be associated with it without disgrace. I cannot for an instant recognize that political organization as <u>my</u> government which is the slave's government also.

This people must cease to hold slaves and to make war on Mexico, though it cost them their existence as a people.

There are thousands who are <u>in opinion</u> opposed to slavery and to the war, who yet in effect do nothing to end them, who sit down with their hands in their pockets, and say they know not what to do, and do nothing. They hesitate, and they regret, and sometimes they petition; but they do nothing in earnest and with effect. They will wait, well disposed, for others to remedy the evil, that they may no longer have it to regret. At most, they give only a cheap vote and a feeble smile and God-speed, to the right, as it goes by them.

Even voting <u>for the right</u> is <u>doing</u> nothing for it. It is only expressing to men feebly your desire that it should prevail. A wise man will not leave the right to the mercy of chance, nor wish it to prevail through the power of the majority. There is but little virtue in the action of masses of men.

It is not a man's duty, as a matter of course, to devote himself to the eradication of any, even the most enormous wrong; he may still properly have other concerns to engage him; but it is his duty, at least, to wash his hands of it, and, if he no longer gives it any thought, he should not give it any practical support.

How can a man be satisfied to entertain an opinion merely, and enjoy <u>it</u>? Action from principle, the perception and the performance of right changes things and relations; it is essentially revolutionary. It not only divides states and churches, it divides families; yes, it divides the <u>individual</u> separating the devil in him from the divine.

Bettmann Archive

Henry David Thoreau

Unjust laws exist: shall we be content to obey them, or shall we endeavor to amend them and obey them until we have succeeded? Or shall we transgress them at once? Men generally, under such a government as this, think that they ought to wait until they have persuaded the majority to alter them. They think that, if they should resist, the remedy would be worse than the evil. But it's the fault of the government itself that the remedy is worse than the evil.

Under a government which imprisons any unjustly, the true place for a just man is also a prison. The proper place today, the only place which Massachusetts has provided for her freer and less desponding spirits, is in her prisons. It is there that the fugitive slave, the Mexican prisoner, and the Indian come to plead the wrongs done their people. It is the only house in a slave state in which a free man can abide with honor.

Cast your whole vote, not a strip of paper, but your whole influence. A minority is powerless while it conforms to the majority; it is not even a minority then; but it is irresistible when it clogs by its whole weight. If the alternative is to keep all just men in prison, or give up war and slavery, the state will not hesitate which to choose. If a thousand men were not to pay their tax bills this year, that would not be as violent and bloody a measure, as it would be to pay them, and enable the State to commit violence and shed innocent blood. This is, in fact, the definition of a peaceable revolution, if any such is possible.

If the tax gatherer, or any other public officer, asks me, as one has done, "But what shall I do?" My answer is, "If you really wish to do anything, resign your office." When the subject has refused his allegiance and the officer has resigned his office, then the revolution is accomplished.

Adapted from the **Writings of Henry David Thoreau**, Houghton Mifflin Company: Boston and New York, 1906, pp. 360–371.

17 DISSENT AND NONVIOLENT RESISTANCE TO THE VIETNAM WAR

During the 1960's the United States military involvement in Vietnam became extremely unpopular. As in the case of the Mexican War one hundred and twenty years earlier, the causes of peace and civil rights were closely intertwined. Men and organizations prominent in civil rights activities were also prominent in the peace movement, and strategies and tactics proven successful by one group were frequently adopted by the other.

The nature of the commitment to nonviolence by civil rights and peace groups during the 1960's is perhaps best illustrated by the Statement of Purpose prepared by the Student Nonviolent Coordinating Committee Conference in 1962. An example of the actual application of nonviolent tactics to war resistance actions is the Declaration of Conscience Against the War in Vietnam, prepared and circulated by a committee of student, war resistance,

Protestors calling themselves "The Anti-Aircraft Conspiracy" face police in a demonstration against an aircraft industry producing war materials.

peace action, and socialist groups in 1965. The spread of nonviolent tactics against the war in 1968 was noted by Time magazine early in that year.

While reading the selections presented here, keep in mind these questions:

1. According to the SNCC Statement of Purpose, what is the origin of non-violent principles and what can they accomplish?

2. What policy does the Declaration of Conscience advocate toward the United States government and the war in Vietnam?

3. What does Time magazine mean by its comment "Part Way With Thoreau"?

Statement of Purpose of the Student Nonviolent Coordinating Committee,* 1962

We affirm the philosophical or religious ideal of nonviolence as the foundation of our purpose, the presupposition of our faith, and the manner of our action. Nonviolence as it grows from the Judaeo-Christian tradition seeks a social order of justice permeated by love. Integration of human endeavor represents the crucial first step toward such a society.

Through nonviolence, courage displaces fear; love transforms hate. Acceptance dissipates prejudice; hope ends despair. Peace dominates war; faith reconciles doubt. Mutual regard cancels enmity. Justice for all overcomes injustice. The redemptive community supersedes systems of gross social immorality.

Love is the central motif of nonviolence. Love is the force by which God binds man to himself and man to man. Such love goes to the extreme; it remains loving and forgiving even in the midst of hostility. It matches the capacity of evil to inflict suffering with an even more enduring capacity to absorb evil, all the while persisting in love.

By appealing to conscience and standing on the moral nature of human existence, nonviolence nurtures the atmosphere in which reconciliation and justice become actual possibilities.

More than 200 delegates representing 52 colleges and high schools in 37 communities in 13 different states founded the **Student Nonviolent Coordinating Committee** in Raleigh, North Carolina, in 1960. The nonviolent philosophy adopted by SNCC at its formation was primarily inspired by **Rev. Martin Luther King, Jr.**, the most eloquent champion of nonviolence in 20th-century America. He was killed by an assassin's bullet on April 4, 1968.

From **Nonviolence in America: A Documentary History,** edited by Staughton Lynd, copyright © 1966, by the Bobbs-Merrill Company, Inc., used by permission of the publisher, pp. 398–399.

B187

Declaration of Conscience Against the War in Vietnam, 1965

BECAUSE the use of military resources of the United States in Vietnam and elsewhere suppresses the aspirations of the people for political independence and economic freedom;

BECAUSE inhuman torture and senseless killing are being carried on by forces armed, uniformed, trained, and financed by the United States;

BECAUSE we believe that all peoples of the earth, including both Americans and non-Americans, have an inalienable right to life, liberty, and the peaceful pursuit of happiness in their own way; and

BECAUSE we think that positive steps must be taken to put an end to the threat of nuclear castastrophe and death by chemical or biological warfare, whether these result from accident or escalation—

WE HEREBY DECLARE our conscientious refusal to cooperate with the United States government in the prosecution of the war in Vietnam.

WE ENCOURAGE those who can conscientiously do so to refuse to serve in the armed forces and to ask for discharge if they are already in.

THOSE OF US who are subject to the draft ourselves declare our own intention to refuse to serve.

WE URGE OTHERS to refuse and we refuse ourselves to take part in the manufacture or transportation of military equipment, or to work in the fields of military research and weapons development.

WE SHALL ENCOURAGE the development of other non-violent acts, including acts which involve civil disobedience, in order to stop the flow of American soldiers and munitions to Vietnam.

NOTE: Signing or distributing the Declaration of Conscience might be construed as a violation of the *Universal Military Training and Service Act,* which prohibits advising persons facing the draft to refuse service. Penalties of up to 5 years imprisonment, and/or a fine of $5,000 are provided. While prosecutions under this provision of the law almost never occur, persons signing or distributing this declaration should face the possibility of serious consequences.

"Declaration of Conscience against the War in Vietnam (New York: published jointly by the **Catholic Worker,** the Committee for Non-violent Action, the Student Peace Union, and the War Resisters League, 1965).

Part Way with Thoreau, 1968

One thing about Henry David Thoreau, when he talked about civil disobedience, he wasn't kidding. Because of his opposition to the Mexican War, he refused to pay a tax and was hustled off to jail. To express their own hostility to the Viet Nam war, 448 contemporary writers and journalists went along with Thoreau last week—or rather part of the way. Quoting Thoreau's ringing challenge to the state [from his essay Civil Disobedience], the signers announced in full-page ads . . . that "1) None of us voluntarily will pay the proposed 10% income tax surcharge or any war-designed tax increase. 2) Many of us will not pay that 23% of our current income tax which is being used to finance the war in Viet Nam."

Reprinted by permission from **Time,** The Weekly Newsmagazine; Copyright Time Inc., 1968, Vol. 91, February 9, 1968, pp. 60–62.

8 What historians have said

Analyzing Historical Judgments

Introduction

In previous assignments you have studied American reform movements during the period 1820–1860 through a series of historical comparisons with events and reform movements from our own time. You have examined temperance, the antislavery movement, and peace and nonviolence from the perspectives of past and present. You have discovered in the course of your study that this approach to historical inquiry has both advantages and disadvantages. This assignment is concerned with the problem of how the past and present are related, and whether it is worthwhile studying the past to find inspiration and guidance for action in the present.

This assignment concludes your work on early nineteenth-century American reform movements. It examines selections from the work of two well-known young American historians who have addressed themselves specifically to the questions of how much of the past we can know and whether or not what we can know is really worth knowing at all.

Objectives of this assignment are to:
—Analyze selections from two modern historians on the value and usefulness of studying history for meaning.
—Make a judgment between the two points of view presented.
—Make a judgment on usefulness as a justification for studying history.

18 MARTIN DUBERMAN ON THE PAST AS A GUIDE TO THE PRESENT

Martin Duberman was born in New York City in 1930, and was educated at Yale and Harvard. He received his doctorate in American history from Harvard in 1957. Professor Duberman has taught American history at Yale and Princeton. During the past fifteen years, he has written numerous articles and books on nineteenth-century and recent American history. He has also written extensively on the American theater.

Professor Duberman's main historical interests are in intellectual history and in the history of American reformers and dissenters. The selection below is taken from a series of essays about living and working as a historian, published under the title of The Uncompleted Past, in 1969.

While reading this selection, keep in mind these questions:

1. Why does Duberman believe that today many historians are troubled about their profession?

2. Why has knowledge of the history of slavery contributed little to our understanding of the current crisis in race relations?

3. Why is Duberman dissatisfied with his "life in history"?

On Being a Historian

Many historians are today discontented with their profession. . . . Discontent can be roughly divided into two groupings. First, a large number of young historians who seem to have little doubt that the past can yield rich *relevance** for the present if only we decide that it should, and, second, a small number of older historians who find the limitations that adhere to historical investigation so decisive that they do not believe the past can yield guidelines for the present. . . .

If a historian is interested in the past primarily because of the light he hopes it will throw on present-day problems (his own or his society's), he would do better, it seems to me, to study the present itself. . . .

One can, of course, be interested in history for any number of reasons other than "problem solving" and could justify its study by any number of other rationales. One could claim, for example, that the chief reason for studying past experience is not to help us solve the problems that confront us, but only to make us aware of how those problems developed through time, how, in other words, we got into the predicament in which we currently find ourselves. Thus it could be said that we must know the history of slavery in this country before we can understand the current crisis in race relations. (A plausible *rationale,** though also a debatable one, for the fact is that historians differ so widely among themselves about the nature and effect of the slave experience that it is difficult to say precisely what contribution is made to our current dilemma.)

❋   ❋   ❋   ❋   ❋

My point in this essay is not to argue these or other possible justifications for the study of history. It is only to say that my dissatisfaction with history (as a source of insight, as a way of life) reflects my initial expectation . . . that it could help us "problem solve," and help us understand not only how we got where we are, but also where we want to go and how to get there. Like many younger historians . . . I wish we could find a way to make the past yield information of vital concern to contemporary needs. But, unlike them, I have little hope that we can. Here I join the older group . . . who feel that the limited evidence available from the past, the very different context in which past experience took place, and the clouded perspective of any historian trying to evaluate that limited evidence and changed context, all combine to keep historical study of *marginal utility** for those concerned with acting in the present. . . .

For those among the young, historians and otherwise, who are chiefly interested in changing the present, I can only say, speaking from my own experience, that they doom themselves to bitter disappointment if they seek

Relevance: bearing on or applying to the case at hand, being pertinent.

Rationale: an explanation or underlying reason.

Marginal utility: of very little usefulness.

their guides to action in a study of the past. Though I have tried to make it otherwise, I have found that a "life in history" has given me very limited information or perspective with which to understand the central concerns of my own life and my own times.

From Martin Duberman **The Uncompleted Past** (New York: Random House), pp. 336–356. Copyright © 1964, 1965, 1966, 1967, 1968, 1969 by Martin Duberman. Reprinted by permission of The Sterling Lord Agency, Inc.

19 WILLIAM M. WIECEK ON THE RELEVANCE OF STUDYING HISTORY

William M. Wiecek was born in Cleveland, Ohio, in 1938, and was educated at the Catholic University of America, Harvard Law School, and the University of Wisconsin. He received his doctorate in American history from Wisconsin in 1968. Professor Wiecek has taught American history at the University of Missouri since 1968 and has written several articles on American constitutional history.

The next selection is taken from Professor Wiecek's review of Martin Duberman's The Uncompleted Past published in the Saturday Review in 1970. While reading this selection, keep in mind these questions. Why does Wiecek:

1. *Believe that today many historians are troubled about their profession?*
2. *Believe history writing and reading is worth doing?*
3. *How does Wiecek see historical study as being useful or practical?*

On the Uses of the Past

Many historians are currently beset with doubts that history is possible or relevant. These doubts are shared by their students and readers. Prodded as much by their own concerns as by the skepticism of their public, some historians are seeking to justify their work in a society troubled by problems so pressing that recapturing the past seems at best an unprofitable diversion of the nation's intellectual resources. . . .

This view comes close to assuming that *utility** is the highest criterion for judging history's relevance. But utility has never been the sole justification for reading or writing history, which is as much worth doing for its own sake as fiction, poetry, or drama. History is one particular way of seeking truth, and the truth is worth pursuing irrespective of any practical use it might have.

Utility: being useful.

Furthermore, men bring to historical reading their own widely differing standards of relevance. Writings about the past speak to different men in different ways. Readers draw their own morals. We would be inconceivably poorer if we refused to write about the past merely because we questioned its applicability to our transient purposes.

Analogies are forms of inferences which assume that if two different things are similar in one way, they may be similar in other ways.

The Oracle of Apollo at Delphi in ancient Greece spoke in riddles. A Delphic saying, therefore, is one that is obscure, puzzling, and can be interpreted in different ways.

From William M. Wiecek's review of **The Uncompleted Past** by Martin Duberman. **Saturday Review**, Vol. LII (January 3, 1970), pp. 23–24. Adaptation from "Voice for Troubled Intellectuals," copyright 1969, Saturday Review, Inc.

Even if we demand that historical study justify itself by being useful, more can be said for it. . . . History is helpful in a negative way when it rebuts misleading *analogies*.* The late Sir Lewis Namier, possibly Britain's greatest historian in this century, once said that men "imagine the past and remember the future." He means that men read into the past the characteristics of the present, and draw on erroneous analogies from history to predict the course of events. A thorough knowledge of history is the only corrective for the dangerous effects of this backwards-and-forwards mythologizing.

Expecting history to furnish positive action programs for the present is unreasonable. History can do little more than stimulate our thinking, taking us out of ourselves and our time momentarily so that when we return we can see our difficulties in a different light. . . . It is usually a *Delphic oracle*,* whose answers to our questions can be treacherously ambiguous. But it does tell us something about men who lived outside of our times, and we can profit from their experience and learn much about the possibilities of being human.

We cannot know who we are, how we came to be where we are, or where we are going without knowing whence we came. Man is, in part at least, what he has been. He cannot escape or ignore his past, though he may overcome it. The past has shaped our present and will continue to shape the future. . . .

Additional Reading

Griffin, C. S., *The Ferment of Reform, 1830–1860*. New York: Thomas Y. Crowell, 1967.

Filler, Lewis, *The Crusade Against Slavery, 1830–1860*. New York: Harper, 1960.

Nye, Russel B., *William Lloyd Garrison and the Humanitarian Reformers*. Boston: Little, Brown, 1955.

Schlesinger, Arthur M. Sr., *The American as Reformer*. Cambridge, Mass.: Harvard University Press, 1950.

Tyler, Alice Felt, *Freedom's Ferment*. Minneapolis: University of Minnesota, 1944. (Paperback: Harper Torchbooks)

Ward, John W., *Andrew Jackson, Symbol for an Age*. New York: Oxford University Press, 1955.

Civil War and Reconstruction

JOHN J. LYON

A house divided against itself cannot stand . . . this government cannot endure permanently half slave and half free. . . .

ABRAHAM LINCOLN

1 Slavery as an American institution

Legal Background

Introduction

Objectives of this assignment are to:

—Analyze selection from English records and commentaries on legal status of slaves in eighteenth-century England for meaning.

—Analyze selection from a United States Supreme Court decision on the legal status of slaves in the United States in 1856 for meaning.

—Compare legal status of slaves in eighteenth-century England with that of early nineteenth-century America and make a hypothesis explaining the difference between them.

An **institution,** as understood here, is any fundamental part of a culture, such as a law or series of laws, or a custom which establishes a pattern of group behavior.

Slavery was the most important problem connected with the coming of the Civil War. In previous units you have seen how slaves were brought to the New World, and how they were treated once they arrived here. You also became aware of the growing opposition to slavery in the United States in the first half of the nineteenth century.

This assignment will focus on slavery as an *institution,** a major cause of the Civil War. The legal position of slavery was settled by the Civil War. But racial discrimination and the oppression of man by his fellow man continued after 1865, just as they had before.

Even before the Constitution was adopted, the Federal Congress, operating under the Articles of Confederation, debated the problem of slavery, particularly as it affected the unorganized territories northwest of the Ohio River. In 1787 Congress passed the Northwest Ordinance for the unsettled lands. The Ordinance provided that neither slavery nor involuntary servitude, except for punishment of crimes, would be legal in the states formed from the Northwest Territory. But slaves who fled into this Territory would be returned by law to their former masters.

After purchase of Louisiana from the French in 1803, more states were created in the West. Under terms of the purchase, the United States guaranteed to protect property rights (including slave ownership) of citizens of the Louisiana Territory. But there was much opposition to extending slavery to the whole of the vast Louisiana Territory, especially to that part of it where cotton could not grow and where, consequently, the economic basis for slavery would be slight. If Congress had excluded slavery from one territory (the Northwest), couldn't it exclude it from another?

After a long struggle, Congress passed the Missouri Enabling Act, March 6, 1820. This Act prohibited slavery in that part of the Louisiana Territory north of thirty-six degrees, thirty minutes north latitude. However, in Missouri and land south of it, slavery was to be permitted. This measure is known in history as the Missouri Compromise.

But did Congress have the constitutional right to regulate property-holding in all the new territories acquired by the Union? If it did, it could by majority consent deprive some property holders of some forms of property (i.e., slaves). It could reduce the slaveholding section of the country (the South)

C2

to playing a minor role in national affairs, destroy the economic basis of Southern life, and eventually abolish slavery itself.

Despite Lincoln's *rhetoric** in his famous *House Divided** speech, the United States might have remained half-slave and half-free for a long time if the admission of new states and territories to the Union had not forced the issue of slavery to the forefront.

By 1857 slavery was the most controversial institution in the United States, though it was sanctioned by custom and law. Was this controversial institution an American development, or part of our British inheritance?

Rhetoric: the art of speaking in public, including the use of exaggerated figures of speech used to impress the audience.

The "House Divided" speech in which Lincoln declared the Union could not exist half-slave and half-free, was delivered in the Illinois House of Representatives, June 17, 1858.

1   SLAVERY IN GREAT BRITAIN

Lord Mansfield

William Blackstone is the best known British legal philosopher of modern times. His Commentaries on the Laws of England, published in 1765, formed a basic part of the legal education of generations of English and American lawyers. The selection from the work cited below spells out the attitude which British courts had already taken for some time regarding slavery. A verdict given in 1772 by Chief Justice Lord Mansfield in the "Somersett Case," as quoted below, made explicit the implications of Blackstone's Commentaries regarding slavery.

When reading the following selections from Blackstone's Commentaries, and from the argument and decision in the Somersett Case as summed up by Lord Mansfield, keep the following questions in mind:

1. What difference does Blackstone assert exists between the spirit of the laws in England and the spirit of the laws in other European countries?

2. What rights does Blackstone say belong to a slave as soon as he sets foot in England?

3. Where was Somersett first enslaved?

4. Does Mansfield make any distinctions about where slavery is legal in the British Empire?

Blackstone on the Status of Slavery in Britain

English law is quite different from the laws of other states of Europe or from the spirit of Roman imperial law. The legal codes of these states and the Old Empire usually give to the government an arbitrary and despotic control over the actions of the subject. But in England, the spirit of liberty is so deeply implanted in our constitution and rooted in our very soil that the moment a slave or Negro lands in England he comes under the protection of our laws and, so far as his natural rights are concerned, he becomes immediately a free man.

Adapted from William Blackstone, **Commentaries on the Laws of England,** Thomas M. Cooley, ed. (Chicago: Callaghan and Co., 1879), Vol. I, pp. 81–82.

Lord Mansfield's Verdict in the Somersett Case

Plaintiff: one who initiates a law suit as opposed to a **defendant,** one against whom a suit is brought.

The case, as it is stated, is this: The *plaintiff,** James Somersett, is a negro who had been a slave in Africa. He was then sold as a slave, and carried into Virginia, where he was purchased by the *defendant,** Charles Steuart. In 1769 the defendant sailed for England, taking the plaintiff with him. On October 1, 1771, Somersett left Steuart's service, and refused to return, whereupon the latter had Somersett seized and imprisoned on a ship lying in the Thames near London and bound for Jamaica where, upon arrival, he would be sold once more as a slave.

Barrister: in English practice, a lawyer who has been permitted to argue cases in court.

Those *barristers** who have defended Steuart's right to do with the plaintiff as he saw fit have argued that slavery is an institution which was recognized as such in Africa and had legal existence under the laws of Virginia and Jamaica. To let the plaintiff go would deprive the defendant of his property without compensation, and would set a dangerous precedent, we are told. Therefore, though English law might not recognize slavery in England, it did recognize it in the English colonies, and the law of the colonies ought to take precedence in this case.

Those who have defended Somersett's case have contended that slavery has no legal existence in England, and that there have been no slaves in England since time out of mind. Somersett's defenders have argued that English law does not allow a man to sell himself into slavery, though they have acknowledged that British law has legalized slavery in the American colonies.

That there are statutes which legalize slavery in the American colonies is clear. And it has been argued that slavery is a necessary institution there, for the encouragement of agriculture and commerce. And contracts for the sale of slaves are honored in England. What is at question in this case is not the enforcement of a contract but the person of a slave himself. Yet this case does not involve property, but persons. If slavery be forbidden in this country, but we maintain the relation between master and slave for those who bring their slaves from other lands where the institution is legal, then we shall indeed be introducing slavery in this land despite the law.

The case, as it is stated then, is that the slave departed and refused to serve, whereupon he was kept by force to be sold abroad. Such high-handed action must be recognized as legal in the country where it takes place. The power of a master over his slave has been extremely different in different countries. No moral or political reasons could justify the introduction of slavery into a country today. Where it exists as an institution already, it does so as the result of laws passed ages ago in less civilized times. Laws regulating slavery remain in force in certain lands today even though the reasons for their passage have long since ceased to operate. Slavery is so hateful that nothing can excuse its existence except where it is already a part of the formal laws of a country. Whatever inconveniences, therefore, may follow from the decision, I cannot say that slavery is allowed or approved by the law of England. Therefore the black must be set free.

Adapted from T. B. Howell, **A Complete Collection of State Trials** (London: Hansard, 1814), XX, p. 82.

2   THE DRED SCOTT CASE AND THE STATUS OF SLAVERY IN AMERICA

In 1857 a case came before the Supreme Court in the United States which was to become a landmark in the struggle over slavery. Dred Scott, a Negro and a slave, had been taken into the free state of Illinois and the Territory of Wisconsin by his master, and was then returned to Missouri, a slaveholding state. After his master's death, Scott sued for his freedom on the ground that residence on free soil had made him free. The case was appealed from state to Federal courts, and eventually came before the Supreme Court.

The Chief Justice of the Supreme Court at this time was Roger B. Taney (1777–1864) of Maryland. Though there were several issues at stake in the case, and though there was dissent among the Justices over the resolution of these issues, Justice Taney's verdict printed below defines the problem and explains the Court's decision.

In reading the following selection, keep these questions in mind:

1. What are the issues in the Dred Scott Case to which the Supreme Court turned its attention?

2. On what grounds was Scott suing for his freedom?

3. On what grounds did the Court deny his suit?

Dred Scott

Chief Justice Taney on the "Dred Scott Case"

The question is simply this: Can a Negro, whose ancestors were imported into this country, and sold as slaves, become a member of the political community formed and brought into existence by the Constitution of the United States, and as such become entitled to all the rights, and privileges, and immunities, guaranteed by that instrument to the citizen? One of these rights, of course, is that of suing in a court of the United States in cases specified in the Constitution.

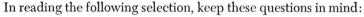

Does the Constitution of the United States act upon a man whenever he shall be made free under the laws of a State, and raised there to the rank of a citizen, and immediately clothe him with all the privileges of a citizen in every other State, and in its own courts? Does residence on free soil make a slave free, as the plaintiff contends?

The court thinks the affirmative of these propositions cannot be maintained.*

And upon a full and careful consideration of the subject, the court is of the opinion that . . . Dred Scott was not a citizen of Missouri within the meaning of the Constitution of the United States, and not entitled as such to sue in its courts. . . .

Chief Justice Roger B. Taney

By this action the Supreme Court confirmed that **Negroes could not be Federal citizens,** nor enjoy any of the rights granted in the Constitution. This did not bar freedmen from becoming citizens in their respective states.

As to the question whether Scott was made free by his residence on free soil: the right of property in a slave is distinctly and expressly affirmed in the Constitution. . . . And the Government in express terms is pledged to protect it in all future time, if the slave escapes from his owner. . . . No word can be found in the Constitution which gives Congress a greater power over slave property, or which entitled property of that kind to less protection than property of any other description. The only power conferred is the power coupled with the duty of guarding and protecting the owner in his rights.

Therefore the Constitution does not warrant the Congress' action in excluding the holding of slave property from territory acquired by the United States since the formation of the Constitution. Neither Dred Scott nor any of his family were made free by being taken into so-called free-soil territory.

Adapted from **Reports of Cases Argued and Adjudged in The Supreme Court of the U. S. December Term, 1856,** by Benjamin C. Howard (Washington, D.C.: William A. Morrison and Co., 1857), Vol. XIX, pp. 427, 453–54.

2 American sectionalism

Economic Problems

Objectives of this assignment are to:

—Draw inferences from charts of economic and social data about the patterns of early nineteenth-century economic and social development in the North and South.

—Analyze selections from contemporary accounts of the economy of the South for meaning.

—Summarize differences and similarities between economies of North and South.

Ingenuity: skillfulness, cleverness.

Introduction

Alexis de Tocqueville, a distinguished French observer of the American scene in the 1830's, wrote in his Democracy in America that it was easy to prove that all the differences in character between Northerners and Southerners had their origin in slavery. This assignment, though not specifically concerned with differences of *character*, discusses the *economic* differences between North and South and the role that slavery played in creating and maintaining these differences.

Need for New Capital and Labor

If an economy is to grow, it must have a supply of capital to draw on. Capital may be defined as wealth that is capable of producing more wealth, or, more simply, as "stored labor." It may exist in the form of buildings, machines, money, land, livestock, natural resources, or perhaps simple *ingenuity** and inventiveness.

In the 1800's, the expansion of the American economy, North and South, grew because the prices of land and natural resources were so low that they encouraged men with access to capital to expand their operations. To increase the production of goods from its farms and factories cheaply, the North needed a constant supply of free labor. This supply came partly from the stream of European immigrants, largely English, Irish, Scots, and Germans, who arrived in America in increasing numbers each decade. In theory at least, such laborers could come from anywhere, and, if their services were no longer needed, could go anywhere so far as their employers were concerned. The employer simply purchased their labor for so many hours each day.

Economic Structure of the South

In the South the situation was different. Comparatively few immigrants to the United States settled in the South. The employer of labor in the South—the plantation owner—had different expenses for his laborers (slaves) than the Northern factory owner or farmer. He not only had to provide them and their families with the necessities of life, but he also had to take care of them at a minimal level when they were ill or could not work. This was a direct expense the Northern employer did not ordinarily have.

After the abolition of the slave trade by the United States in 1808, the price paid for a slave tended to rise. Thus economically, the slave was treated as an unnatural mixture of "labor" and "machinery," just as at law he was treated as a piece of property or animated machinery.

Two different economic systems, both primarily agricultural, existed in the United States before the Civil War. One was based on the *exploitation**of free human labor assisted by machinery (in the North). The other was based on the exploitation of forced human labor-machines (in the South).

Exploitation: the process of using something or some person for one's own advantage.

"Old Virginia Labor Saving Machine"—Commentaries on the evils of slavery, such as this one, were popular in the pre-Civil War North.

TABLE I

Area and Population of Comparable Free-Soil and Slave States, 1860

STATE	TOTAL AREA IN SQUARE MILES	TOTAL POPULATION	WHITE	BLACK
Ohio*	39,964	2,339,511	2,302,838	36,673
Kentucky	37,680	1,155,684	919,517	236,167
Indiana*	33,809	1,350,428	1,339,000	11,428
Mississippi	47,156	791,305	353,901	437,404
Illinois*	55,410	1,711,951	1,704,323	7,628
Alabama	50,722	964,201	526,431	437,770

*Free-Soil States

A Statistical Abstract Supplement: Historical Statistics of the United States, Colonial Times to 1957 (Washington, D.C., 1960), p. 13, and Statistics of the United States in 1860 (Washington, D.C.: U. S. Govt. Printing Office, 1864), p. 339.

TABLE II

Agricultural Development of Comparable Free-Soil and Slave States, 1860

STATE	DATE ADMITTED TO THE UNION	STATUS (Free Soil) or Slave)	ACREAGE: Improved, in Farms, 1860 Census	ACREAGE: Unimproved, in Farms, 1860 Census
Ohio	1803	Free Soil	12,625,394	7,846,747
Kentucky	1792	Slave	7,644,208	11,519,053
Indiana	1816	Free Soil	8,242,183	8,146,109
Mississippi	1817	Slave	5,065,755	10,773,929
Illinois	1818	Free Soil	13,096,374	7,815,615
Alabama	1819	Slave	6,385,724	12,718,821
Total Free-Soil States			34,963,951	23,808,471
Total Slave States			19,095,687	35,011,803

Agriculture of the United States in 1860 (Compiled from the Original returns of the 8th census) (Washington: U. S. Govt. Printing Office, 1864), p. 184.

TABLE III

Railroad Mileage of Comparable Free-Soil and Slave States (by Region), 1860

RAILROAD MILEAGE	UNITED STATES	1860
New England States	3,669.39	
Middle Atlantic States (Maryland included)	6,321.22	These states remained "loyal" to the Union
Interior States, North (Missouri included)	11,212.38	during the Civil War.
Total:	21,202.99	
South Atlantic States	5,454.27	These states seceded
Gulf States	2,256.21	to form the Confereracy
Interior States, South	1,806.35	in 1861.
Total:	9,516.83	

Statistics of the United States in 1860 (Washington: U. S. Govt. Printing Office, 1866), p. 331.

3 FREE-SOIL AND SLAVE STATES: POPULATION, AGRICULTURE, AND INDUSTRY

Population, acreage of improved and unimproved lands, and railroad mileage are all indicators of economic and social development. Three tables on the opposite page illustrate the patterns of economic and social development in the Northern and Southern regions of the United States, 1790–1860.

Three pairs of states have been selected for comparison; each pair includes one free-soil state and one slave state admitted into the Union at approximately the same time.

While studying the tables (page 8), keep these questions in mind:

1. *Which states, free-soil or slave, had the largest population?*
2. *Which states, free-soil or slave, had more acreage in improved lands?*
3. *Which states, Northern or Southern, had greater railroad mileage by 1860?*

4 SLAVERY AND THE SOUTHERN ECONOMY AS SEEN THROUGH SOUTHERN EYES

The next set of readings includes eyewitness accounts of the economic structure of the South before the Civil War. The backgrounds of the two authors of these accounts were quite different. George Fitzhugh (1806–1881) and Hinton Rowan Helper (1829–1909) were both white Southerners. Fitzhugh was the son of a poor Virginia *Tidewater** plantation owner, and he identified himself with the interests of the slaveholding class. Helper was a North Carolinian from a largely non-slaveholding section of the state; his concern was for the "poor white," the small, independent farmer who did his own work or hired free labor to assist him.

While reading the following selections and examining the illustrations, keep these questions in mind:

1. How does Fitzhugh distinguish between "white slavery" and "black slavery"? What do the illustrations suggest about these distinctions?

2. To what cause does Helper attribute the economic backwardness of the South? Why?

In Virginia the **tidewater** region lies between the seacoast and the foothills of the Appalachian Mountains.

C9

George Fitzhugh on White Slavery and Black Slavery

Sarah Jackson, southern "poor white" (North Carolina), who washed tailings from goldmining operations to salvage gold particles.

The **British Parliament** freed all slaves in the British Empire in 1833.

Adapted from George Fitzhugh, **Cannibals All! or, Slaves Without Masters** (Richmond, Va.: A. Morris, Publisher, 1857).

We are all, North and South, engaged in the White Slave Trade, and he who succeeds best, is esteemed most respectable. It is far more cruel than the Black Slave Trade, because it exacts more of its slaves, and neither protects nor governs them. Black slavery is to a master, but White slavery is to capital. When his day's labor has ended, the White slave is free, but overburdened with the obligations of providing for his family. The Black slave has such cares taken over for him, for his master has an investment in him that the Northern employer has not in his workers.

❖ ❖ ❖ ❖ ❖

. . . The men without property in a free society are in a condition worse than that of slaves. Capitalists in a free society live in ten times the luxury and show that Southern masters do, because the slaves to capital work harder and cost less than negro slaves do.

❖ ❖ ❖ ❖ ❖

Compare Ireland and Jamaica, two fine islands both of which the British own. The Irish have become slaves to capital, for the English have come to own all the land, and the Irish must rent it or farm it for a landlord or starve. Nominally, they are the freest people in the world. In fact they are among the most depressed. Jamaica presents another picture, or did so at least until the *British emancipation* of slaves there.❖ The slaves were well cared for, and one does not read of hundreds of thousands of them dying in one year, as was the case in Ireland in the years of the famine.

Hinton Rowan Helper on Slavery as the Cause of Southern Backwardness

Subservient: acting like a servant; extremely submissive.

Muslin: plain or printed cotton cloth, such as that used for sheets.

Gewgaws: baubles, items produced for amusement.

Physic means medicine.

Cambric: closely woven cotton or linen cloth.

In one way or another we are more or less *subservient*❖ to the North every day of our lives. In infancy we are swaddled in Northern *muslin;*❖ in childhood we are humored with Northern *gewgaws;*❖ in youth we are instructed out of Northern books . . . in the decline of life we remedy our eyesight with Northern spectacles, and support our infirmities with Northern canes; in old age we are drugged with Northern *physic;*❖ and, finally, when we die, our inanimate bodies, shrouded in Northern *cambric,*❖ are stretched upon the bier, borne to the grave in a Northern carriage, entombed with a Northern spade, and memorialized with a Northern slab!

In our opinion, . . . the causes which have impeded the progress and prosperity of the South, which have dwindled our commerce, and other similar pursuits into the most contemptible insignificance; sunk a large majority of our people in galling poverty and ignorance, rendered a small minority conceited and tyrannical, and driven the rest away from their homes; entailed upon us a humiliating dependence on the Free States; disgraced us in the recesses of our own souls, and brought us under reproach in the eyes of all civilized and enlightened nations—may all be traced to one common source, and there find solution in the most hateful and horrible word that was ever incorporated into the vocabulary of human economy—*Slavery!*

Adapted from Hinton Rowan Helper, **Impending Crisis of the South: How to Meet It** (New York: A. B. Burdick, 1860), pp. 22–23, 25.

Slavery As It Exists in America

Slavery As It Exists in England

5   SOUTHERN ECONOMY SEEN THROUGH NORTHERN EYES

The following selections are taken from journals written by Frederick Law Olmsted during a series of travels through the South between 1852 and 1854. Olmsted (1822–1903) was a Connecticut-born son of a wealthy merchant. Though opposed to slavery, his reports of travels in the South were generally well received and free of exaggerated bias. After the Civil War Olmsted became nationally known as a landscape architect.

In reading the Olmsted selections, keep these questions in mind:

1. What did tobacco growing do to the ecology of the South?
2. Why did some southern employers prefer to hire Irish immigrant labor rather than use slave labor on certain jobs?

Olmsted's Reports

Mr. W. was one of the largest tobacco growers of this section of Virginia. I asked him why he did not try to grow other crops than tobacco, since it impoverished the soil so. He said that with the price of slaves being what it was, their labor could not be profitably employed on growing grains or other such crops. Tobacco required fresh land, and was rapidly exhausting, but it returned more money for the labor used on it than anything else, enough more, in his opinion, to pay for the wearing out of the land. If he was well paid for it, he did not know why he should not wear out his land.

❈   ❈   ❈   ❈   ❈

He had an Irish gang draining for him, by contract. When I asked him why he did not do the work himself, or have his slaves do it, he replied that he didn't do it for it was unhealthy work, and he did not want his slaves to do it, for a negro's life was too valuable to be risked at such work. "If a negro dies, it's a considerable loss, you know," he noted.

❈   ❈   ❈   ❈   ❈

While in Virginia, I visited a farm worked entirely by free labor. The proprietor had inherited many slaves, all of whom he freed. He was convinced that, as Jefferson had said, slavery was more pernicious to the white race than to the black. He was also confident that he had the better of the situation at the present time, for free labor was cheaper than slave labor due to the high price of slaves and the easy availability of free white immigrant labor. He pays the Irishmen he now has $120 per year plus their board, which is about $20 above the average, but these are good men, who drink very little. House maids, Irish girls, he pays $3 and $6 a month. The wages paid for slave labor that he or others might rent from their masters is the same as that paid for free labor. But the slave-employer has to provide clothing for his hired laborer, is subject to any losses caused by the carelessness or malevolence of the slave, and has to pay for him whether or not he is able to work the whole time for which his labor has been contracted.

Immigrant Miners from Ireland and Great Britain in North Carolina, 1857

Adapted from: Frederick Law Olmsted, **A Journey in the Seaboard Slave States** (New York: Dix & Edwards, 1856).

3 American sectionalism

Constitutional Problems

Introduction

The political history of the United States is unique. The original thirteen colonies were settled by people of the same stock, speaking the same language, and operating under similar forms of government. But each colony had its own special charter and was jealous of the rights and privileges included in that charter. The colonies also differed in climate and *topography.*

Such differences led to differences in the economies of the colonies. For example, the New England colonies were trading centers in the seventeenth and eighteenth centuries, and then industrialized rapidly in the nineteenth. Middle colonies such as Pennsylvania were great grain-growing regions. Southern colonies, saddled with a slave labor system, concentrated on producing cash export crops such as tobacco, rice, and *indigo.* Cotton became especially important after the invention of the cotton gin by Eli Whitney in 1793.

Though all the colonies were English, they were different from each other. The colonial legislatures were extremely careful to defend and maintain their chartered privileges. There was brisk intercolonial competition for trade, each colony trying to sell the products of its own soil, climate, and industry. The colonies also competed for trade with England and other parts of the British empire, such as the West Indies. After the Revolution the colonies of the Empire became states within a union of states. Their different characteristics made them realize that actions taken by the Federal government would not necessarily benefit all sections of the country equally.

Tariff Problems

In the first half of the nineteenth century, there developed a series of classic encounters between the South, the West, and the North over various *tariff bills.* For example, in 1828 the so-called *Tariff of Abominations* passed Congress. What it did was to widen the differences between the farming and industrial interests of the country by placing high import duties on certain manufactured goods. This tariff gave a monopoly of the American market to the manufacturers of the Middle and New England states. It forced the South and the West to purchase *domestically produced* manufactured goods at a higher price than such items cost when bought from England.

This tariff angered the agricultural South. Southerners depended for their livelihood upon being able to sell crops abroad. Now they feared that England

Objectives of this assignment are to:

—Analyze selections from Constitution of United States and Federalist Papers on rights of states and tyranny of majorities for meaning.

—Analyze selections from writings and speeches of John C. Calhoun and Daniel Webster on right of states to veto Federal legislation for meaning.

—Make judgment on the relevance of the issue of tyranny of majorities for politics today.

Topography: the "lay of the land," or characteristic surface features of a region.

Indigo: a plant from which a violet-blue dye is extracted.

Tariff bills: legislation which would impose a set of taxes on specified imports into, or exports from, a country.

Abominations: things that are hateful and disgusting.

Domestically produced means produced "at home," in the United States.

C13

and other countries would retaliate against the 1828 Tariff. They expected the English would raise their own import duties to protect sections of the British Empire which produced cotton and tobacco against Southern competition.

As a result of *discriminatory** legislation such as the Tariff of 1828, the South, especially the state of South Carolina, began complaining loudly about the way the United States government was run by certain interests, largely northern. The South felt these northern interests were promoting their own good, and not that of the general public, even though the majority of the people and of Congress seemed to support them. It seemed to South Carolina that the *tyranny** of the British monarchy had simply been replaced by the tyranny of the majority of their own countrymen.

Discriminatory: making distinctions to the disadvantage of one group and the advantage of another.

Tyranny: arbitrary use of power; despotic, absolute rule.

South Carolina Protests

In December of 1828 the South Carolina "Exposition and Protest" against the Tariff of 1828, written by *John C. Calhoun,** claimed that the Tariff of 1828 was "unconstitutional, oppressive, and unjust." In 1832 South Carolina called a state convention to consider another tariff bill of that year. The convention declared that Congress had exceeded its constitutional powers by passing a tariff which discriminated against certain states. It further stated that the Tariff Acts of 1828 and 1832 were "null, void, and no law" in South Carolina. The convention then threatened that South Carolina would secede from the Union if the Federal government tried to force her to comply.

South Carolina's threat was not carried out, thanks to a new tariff of 1833 which reduced rates—and thanks to the stern reaction of President Andrew Jackson. Jackson called nullification treason and threatened to use the army and navy to coerce South Carolina. But the issue remained: if a majority which happened to control the Federal government passed legislation which did not benefit every section and state of the Union equally, what was to be done about it? Had the Revolutionary War been fought in vain? Was there any recourse within the American system for minority rights?

John C. Calhoun (1782–1850): South Carolina lawyer, orator, and statesman, U. S. House of Representatives, Secretary of War, 1817–1825; Vice-President, 1825–1832; Senator, 1832–1850.

States' Rights and the Federal Constitution

This question had been present ever since the debates over the adoption of the Articles of Confederation. The Kentucky and Virginia Resolutions, written by Thomas Jefferson and James Madison in 1798 in opposition to the Federalist Congress' *Alien and Sedition Acts,** supported the states'-rights position that was to become so popular in the early nineteenth century. Threats of secession from the Union on the part of New England over what it felt was its diminishing influence in the Federal government were heard at the *Hartford Convention** of 1814. South Carolina's "Exposition and Protest" and its "nullification" ordinance occurred between these threats of secession and the actual secession of the Southern states in 1861. But the issue was the same: how to preserve the rights of a minority under a democratic or republican form of government.

Alien and Sedition Acts: Federal laws designed to curb freedom of speech and to control unfriendly aliens during a military crisis with France in 1798.

Hartford Convention: A meeting of dissatisfied New Englanders who spoke against the War of 1812 and endorsed states' rights and nullification of unpopular laws.

C14

6   MINORITY RIGHTS AND THE CONSTITUTION

The readings below concern the problem of *sovereignty** and minority rights as viewed by the framers of the Constitution of the United States. The first reading is a statement from the Constitution about the powers of Congress to make laws and the courts to interpret them. The second reading is a statement from The Federalist about the relationship between majority and minority rights.

While reading the selections that follow, keep these questions in mind:

1. Does the Constitution specify how disputes between states or between one or more states and the Federal government shall be settled?

2. In what ways could the majority misuse its power in a democratic republic?

3. What remedy does The Federalist *see for the threat of oppression by the majority?*

Sovereignty: ultimate or highest authority; authority from which there is no appeal.

The Constitution on Sovereignty and States' Rights

The Congress shall have power:

✿   ✿   ✿   ✿   ✿

To make all laws which shall be necessary and proper for the carrying into execution . . . all . . . powers vested by this Constitution in the government of the United States, or in any department or officer thereof. (Article I, Section 8, Constitution of the United States)

✿   ✿   ✿   ✿   ✿

The powers not delegated to the United States by the Constitution, nor prohibited by it to the States, are reserved to the States respectively, or to the people. (Article X, Constitution of the United States)

✿   ✿   ✿   ✿   ✿

The judicial power of the United States shall be vested in one Supreme Court, and in such inferior courts as the Congress may from time to time ordain and establish. . . .

The judicial Power shall extend to all cases, in law and equity, arising under this Constitution . . . to controversies to which the United States shall be a party; [and] to controversies between two or more States. . . . (Article III, Sections 1, 2, Constitution of the United States)

The Federalist on Sovereignty and the Prevention of Tyranny

What is government itself but the greatest of all reflections on human nature? If men were angels, no government would be necessary. If angels were to govern men, neither external nor internal controls on government would be necessary. In framing a government which is to be administered by men over men, the great difficulty lies in this: you must first enable the government to control the governed; and in the next place oblige it to control itself. A dependence on the people is no doubt the primary control on the government; but experience has taught mankind the necessity of auxiliary precautions.

It is of great importance in a republic not only to guard the society against the oppression of its rulers, but to guard one part of the society against the injustice of the other part. Different interests necessarily exist in different classes of citizens. If a majority be united by a common interest, the rights of the minority will be insecure. . . . In the federal republic of the United States all authority will be derived from and dependent on the society, but the society itself will be broken into so many parts, interests, and classes of citizens that the rights of individuals or of the minority will be in little danger from interested combinations of the majority.

Justice is the end of government. It is the end of civil society. It ever has been and ever will be pursued until it be obtained, or until liberty be lost in the pursuit. In a society under the forms of which the stronger faction can readily unite and oppress the weaker, *anarchy** may as truly be said to reign as in a *state of nature,** where the weaker individual is not secured against the violence of the stronger.

Anarchy: general confusion and disorder; a state without law or government.

State of nature: an imaginary state of affairs in which each man was a law unto himself.

The Federalist on The New Constitution, written in 1788 by Alexander Hamilton, John Jay, and James Madison (Washington: Thompson and Homans; Way and Gideon Printers, 1831), pp. 223–25.

7   TYRANNY OF THE MAJORITY AND RIGHTS OF MINORITIES

The two readings in this set of selections are the work of John Caldwell Calhoun and *Daniel Webster.** Calhoun was one of the most vocal and convincing of the advocates of what we would call states' rights. His distinction between the numerical majority and the concurrent majority, which is detailed in the first reading here, is rather famous. The final selection is taken from a speech delivered in the Senate of the United States in January, 1830, by Daniel Webster, one of the nation's most gifted orators.

In reading these selections, keep these questions in mind:

1. What remedy does Calhoun see for the threat of oppression by the numerical majority?

2. What is Webster's reply to Calhoun's "South Carolina Doctrine"?

John C. Calhoun on the Numerical Majority and the Concurrent Majority

The right of *suffrage** alone cannot prevent one part of a democratic republic from oppressing the others. The dominant majority for the time would really be the controlling, governing, and irresponsible rulers. The minority for the time will be as much the governed or subject portion as are the people in an aristocracy or the subjects in a monarchy. The only real difference is that, through the use of the suffrage, minority and majority can change positions without recourse to violence.

Daniel Webster (1782–1852): New Hampshire-born lawyer, orator, politician; Congressman and Senator from Massachusetts. An advocate of national, as opposed to sectional, policies, Webster became Secretary of State under Presidents Harrison, Tyler, and Fillmore.

Suffrage: the right to vote.

C16

Thus the dominant or numerical majority in our system of government is a constant threat to the rights of others. And there is only one certain way in which that threat can be prevented from being exercised. That way is the adoption of certain restrictions which will prevent the will of the majority from becoming law simply because it is numerically superior. In our system of government this can be accomplished only by giving the states a *concurrent** voice in making and executing the laws, or by giving them a veto on their execution. The right of suffrage and the rights of the states as organisms to exercise a concurrent jurisdiction over the passage and execution of the laws are sufficient to counteract the tendency of government to oppression and abuse of power. The concurrent majority, and not the numerical majority, must alone be taken as the proper way in which the sense of the community may be expressed. The numerical majority is not the people, but a portion of the people, and rule by the numerical majority is simply rule by one part of the people over another part.

Concurrent: acting together with, cooperating.

Adapted from John C. Calhoun, **A Disquisition on Government,** Richard K. Cralle, ed. **The Works of John C. Calhoun** (New York: D. Appleton & Co., 1854), Vol. I, pp. 22–31.

Daniel Webster on the "South Carolina Doctrine"

It is maintained that it is a right of the state legislatures to interfere whenever, in their judgment, the government transcends its constitutional limits, and to arrest the operation of its laws. I understand it to be insisted upon that this is a right which exists under the Constitution, and not as a right of revolution. I understand it to be said that their purpose of this right is to check an abuse of power by the general government. This is the South Carolina doctrine . . . [of John C. Calhoun].

The great question is, Whose *prerogative** is it to decide on the constitutionality or unconstitutionality of the laws? I do not admit that under the Constitution and in conformity with it there is any mode in which a state government can interfere and stop the progress of the general government by force of her own laws, under any circumstances whatever. The Constitution is the people's Constitution, made for the people, and answerable to the people. It is not a creature of the state governments. The state legislatures, however sovereign, are not sovereign over the people. The general government and the state governments derive their authority from the same source.

Prerogative: an exclusive right or privilege

✤　✤　✤　✤　✤

What sort of absurd situation would we have if each state set itself up as arbiter of which laws of government were to be obeyed! The whole Union would become a rope of sand. The Constitution makes provision for the adjudication of contentions between the states. . . . All questions of constitutional power come for a final decision to the Supreme Court of the United States.

I do not admit the competency of South Carolina or any other State to prescribe my constitutional duty, or to settle between me and the people the validity of laws of Congress for which I have voted. I have not sworn to support the Constitution according to South Carolina's construction of its clauses.

Adapted from Lindsay Swift, ed., **The Great Debate** (Boston: Houghton Mifflin and Co., 1898), pp. 182–207.

C17

4 John Brown's body

Abolition and Violence

Henry Clay (1777–1852): Virginia-born lawyer and statesman. Represented Kentucky as U.S. Representative and Senator. Three times candidate for President.

War with Mexico, 1846–1848: Ended by Treaty of Guadalupe, Hidalgo, February, 1848. U. S. acquired former Mexican lands north of Rio Grande plus California and New Mexico territories.

Bushwhacking: ambush and guerrilla warfare.

John Brown, in Kansas, 1856

Introduction

The decade of the 1850's began with compromise. It ended with violence and threats by the South that it would leave the Union.

The Compromise of 1850, worked out by *Henry Clay** and accepted by Daniel Webster, had "settled" the issue of slavery in Texas and the territories acquired by the *Mexican War* in 1848.* Under the Compromise, California was admitted to the Union as a free-soil state, and the territorial legislatures were to decide for themselves the status of slavery in other former Mexican lands.

Then in 1854, Senator Stephen A. Douglas of Illinois opened the hornet's nest once more by introducing the controversial Kansas-Nebraska Bill. Douglas's Bill provided that Congress should create two new territories, Kansas and Nebraska, and that the question of slavery be left up to the people living in the new territories. Douglas's new doctrine was called "popular sovereignty." This plainly repealed the Missouri Compromise of 1820 (page C2), because both Kansas and Nebraska were north of the line 36° 30′. The Missouri Compromise set up a dividing line between slave and free-soil land in the trans-Mississippi region of the Louisiana Purchase.

The passage of the Kansas-Nebraska Act roused the wrath of the Abolitionists in the North. It led to a rush between slave-owners and free-soilers for control of the Territorial Legislature of Kansas. Settlers from Missouri poured into the territory, as did migrants from New England and the Middle West. They turned Kansas into a battleground, where *bushwhacking** and cold-blooded murder alternated with small-scale pitched battles.

Connecticut-born John Brown made his first appearance on the national scene in Kansas. In 1856 he and six followers from a settlement at Ossawatomie butchered five men to death in a pro-slavery settlement on Pottawatomie Creek. This deed was in retaliation for the burning of Lawrence, Kansas, by pro-slavery forces.

Violence next erupted in the Senate of the United States. Representative Preston Brooks of South Carolina invaded that august chamber where he physically attacked Senator Charles Sumner of Massachusetts with a cane and knocked him unconscious in revenge for insulting remarks made in a speech by Sumner on the subject of "Bleeding Kansas."

Senator Charles Sumner fiercely opposed slavery, denounced southern "slave power," and several southern senators, including Andrew Butler of South Carolina. Butler's nephew, **Rep. Preston Brooks,** was censured and fined for beating and disabling Sumner.

Birth of the Republican Party

One noteworthy event of the decade was the birth of a new political party, the Republican. Its members were disgruntled with the stand taken by both existing national parties, the Whigs and the Democrats, on major issues such as the existence and extension of slavery.

Two of the best-known figures of the new party were Senators *William H. Seward** of New York and Abraham Lincoln of Illinois. Both gave speeches which were representative of the growing tension between North and South over the slavery issue.

In September, 1858, Seward spoke of the "Irrepressible Conflict" between the two radically different systems of labor in the country, one free and one slave. Seward forecast that the United States would eventually become either entirely a slaveholding nation or entirely free.

A few months earlier Abraham Lincoln, the Republican Party's candidate to oppose Illinois' *Senator Douglas** in the fall election of 1858, had spoken about the increased tension between the two sections of the country. In biblical phraseology, Lincoln asserted that "A house divided against itself cannot stand." He, too, forecast a crisis, after which one or another of the rival systems of labor would triumph.

William Henry Seward (1801–1872): Governor of New York, U. S. Senator, candidate for Republican nomination for Presidency, 1856, 1860, and Secretary of State under Lincoln.

Stephen Arnold Douglas, Illinois (1813–1861): served in U. S. House of Representatives and U. S. Senate; Democratic Party nominee for President, 1860; lost to Lincoln.

John Brown and the End of a Decade

Chief Justice Taney's verdict in the Dred Scott case (page C5) was given in 1857. The decision was the cause of further uproar over the slavery issue. To cap the misfortunes of the decade, John Brown and eighteen of his followers seized the Federal arsenal at Harper's Ferry, Virginia (now West Virginia) in October, 1859. Brown's aim was to free Southern slaves. Two days later Federal troops under *Robert E. Lee** and *J. E. B. Stuart** put down the insurrection. But ten of Brown's men and several townspeople were dead, and others were wounded in the violence.

A rash, daring act had been committed which threw the South into a state of fear and hatred of the North. John Brown's raid convinced some southerners that the only way to protect their "peculiar institution" (slavery) was through secession from the Union.

General Robert Edward Lee (1807–1870): soldier, superintendent of West Point, 1852–1853; Commander of the Army of Northern Virginia in the Civil War, and honored hero of the Confederacy.

James Ewell Brown Stuart (1833–1864): Confederate General in the Civil War. Commander of Lee's cavalry.

C19

Handwritten note:
Charlestown, Va, 2d December, 1859.
I John Brown am now quite certain that the crimes of this guilty land: will never be purged away; but with Blood. I had as I now think: vainly flattered myself that without very much bloodshed; it might be done.

John Brown in his beard-disguise, as he appeared at Harper's Ferry. Condemned for murder and treason, Brown was hanged December 2, 1859. John Brown's last prophecy, in his own handwriting, appears above.

8   JOHN BROWN AS SEEN BY CONTEMPORARIES

The raid at Harper's Ferry was front-page news both while it was happening and throughout the period of the trial of Brown and his followers for treason. Brown was found guilty and hanged on December 2, 1859. The surviving members of his party suffered a similar fate later.

The following set of readings contain views about John Brown as seen by three of his contemporaries. Frederick Douglass (1817–1895) was a former slave who escaped to the North and became a noted orator, journalist, and outspoken advocate of abolition and the Negro's cause. Henry David Thoreau (1817–1862), Massachusetts writer, is best known today for <u>Walden</u> and his essay "Civil Disobedience." Henry A. Wise (1806–1876) was the Governor of Virginia, the state in which John Brown's raid occurred and in which he was tried.

In reading these selections, keep the following questions in mind:

1. In what respects do Thoreau's and Douglass' accounts of John Brown agree?

2. Of the three contemporary accounts, which appraisal of Brown do you think seems the most balanced?

Objectives of this assignment are to:

—Analyze selections from contemporary accounts of John Brown for meaning.

—Analyze selections from historical and poetic accounts of John Brown for meaning.

—Analyze recording of dramatic reading of John Brown's last speech for meaning.

—Make a judgment on justice of taking the law into one's own hands.

Frederick Douglass on the Greatness of John Brown

It is an effeminate and cowardly age, which calls a man a lunatic because he rises to such self-forgetful heroism, as to count his own life as worth nothing in comparison with the freedom of millions of his fellows. . . . Are heroism and insanity synonyms in our American dictionary? Heaven help us! When our loftiest types of patriotism, our sublimest historic ideals of philanthropy, come to be treated as evidence of moon-struck madness. Posterity will owe everlasting thanks to John Brown for lifting up once more to the gaze of a nation grown fat and flabby on the garbage of lust and oppression, a true standard of heroic philanthropy, and each coming generation will pay its installment of the debt. . . .

[John Brown] believes the Declaration of Independence to be true, and the Bible to be a guide to human conduct, and acting upon the doctrines of both, he threw himself against the serried ranks of American oppression. . . . This age is too gross and sensual to appreciate his deeds, and so calls him mad; but the future will write his epitaph upon the hearts of a people freed from slavery, because he struck the first effectual blow. . . .

He has attacked slavery with the weapons precisely adopted to bring it to death. Moral considerations have long since been exhausted upon slaveholders. It is in vain to reason with them. One might as well hunt bears with ethics and political economy for weapons, as to seek to "pluck the spoiled out of the hand of the oppressor" by the mere force of moral law. Slavery is a system of brute force. It shields itself behind *might* rather than *right*. It must be met with its own weapons. Capt Brown has initiated a new mode of carrying on the crusade of freedom. . . . Like Samson, he has laid his hands upon the pillars of this great national temple of cruelty and blood, and when he falls, that temple will speedily crumble to its final doom, burying its denizens [inhabitants] in its ruins.

Douglass' Monthly, November, 1859. From The Life and Writings of Frederick Douglass, Philip S. Foner, Editor, Vol. II, pp. 458–460, Copyright © 1950. Reprinted by permission of International Publishers Co., Inc.

Henry David Thoreau on John Brown's Sanity and Divine Mission

Newspaper editors talk as if it were impossible that a man [such as John Brown] could be "divinely appointed" in these days to do any work whatever, as if vows and religion were out of date as connected with any man's daily work, and as if a man's death were a failure and his continued life, be it of whatever character, were a success. They argue that it is a proof of his insanity that he thought he was appointed to do this work which he did,—that he did not suspect himself for a moment! . . . a hero in the midst of us cowards is always so dreaded. [John Brown] is just that thing. He shows himself superior to nature. He has a spark of divinity in him.

* * * * *

Editors are still pretty generally saying that Brown's was a "crazy scheme," and their one only evidence and proof of it is that it cost him his life. I have no doubt that, if he had gone with five thousand men, liberated a thousand slaves, killed a hundred or two slaveholders, and had as many more killed on his own side, but not lost his own life, such would have been prepared to call it by another name. Yet he has been far more successful than that. They seem to know nothing about living or dying for a principle.

Governor Henry Wise of Virginia: John Brown as a Cool Fanatic

. . . they are themselves mistaken who take him [John Brown] to be a madman. He is a bundle of the best nerves I ever saw, cut and thrust, and bleeding, and in bonds. He is cool, collected, and indomitable, and it is but just to him to say, that he was humane to his prisoners. . . . [He] inspired me with great trust in his integrity, as a man of truth. He is fanatic, vain, and garrulous, but firm, and truthful, and intelligent.

From **The Journal of Henry David Thoreau,** edited by Bradford Torrey and Francis Allen (New York: Dover Publications, Inc., 1962), Vol. II, pp. 1541, 1556, 1557, (entries for Oct. 22 and Dec. 9, 1859). Reprinted through permission of the publisher.

Governor Wise, of Virginia, Speech in Richmond, Va., Friday Oct. 21, as reported in **The Richmond Enquirer,** Oct. 25, 1859. From **Incident at Harper's Ferry,** Edward Stone, ed. (Englewood Cliffs, N. J.: Prentice-Hall, Inc., © 1956), p. 191.

9   JOHN BROWN AS SEEN BY POSTERITY

In attempting to evaluate the character of such persons as John Brown and the roles which they played in history, the modern historian often turns to the insight of poetry and psychology. The two selections in this set of readings are taken from the work of the eminent historian, Allan Nevins, and that of the twentieth-century American poet and short-story writer, Stephen Vincent Benét.

In reading these two selections, keep the following questions in mind:

1. What character traits does Nevins find in John Brown?

2. What is Benét saying about John Brown in the segment of his poem cited here?

Allan Nevins on the Character of John Brown

John Brown was fifty-nine years old in May, 1859. He was no ordinary man. All who saw him, whether friends or foes, were struck by his iron will, his consuming inner fire, and his intense though erratic devotion to causes outside himself. Great as were his faults, he united a certain elevation of character with the traits of a born leader....

A man of scanty schooling, speculative, of *nomadic** tastes and marked business incapacity, he made repeated migrations in a fruitless effort to better himself. . . . He tried calling after calling; managing tanneries, land speculation, breeding racehorses, surveying, selling cattle and sheep, wool factorage, and farming. . . . His large family—for his first wife bore him seven children, his second thirteen—were reared in hand-to-mouth fashion. His character seemed full of contradictions. Usually rigidly honest, he sometimes showed a financial irresponsibility that approached dishonesty; a man of principle, he could be a provoking opportunist; kindly and philanthropic, he had a harsh vein of cruelty. All this, with his self-righteous stubbornness and utter intractability, pointed to some *psychogenic** malady.

Nomadic: wandering, aimless.

Psychogenic: of mental or nervous origin.

❁   ❁   ❁   ❁   ❁

As he grew older, as the world gave him hard buffets, as his lack of business system and foresight plunged him into failure after failure, and as his *skeptical** temper weakened his religious dogmas, his character changed. . . . His business misfortunes, combative temper, and failure to meet clear legal obligations had resulted in one controversy after another, so that between 1820 and 1845 he figured in twenty-one lawsuits in Portage County, Ohio. . . .

It was thus as a failure, a man who had lost part of his early integrity as well as his faith in organized Christianity, a soured, hardened reformer who took refuge from his own deficiencies in fighting the wrongs of others, that Brown . . . saw his sons off to Kansas, himself soon to follow. . . .

The old veins of Puritan idealism and reformative zeal were still to be found in his nature; but a vein of the ruthlessness peculiar to fanatics, and especially fanatics gnarled by failure, had asserted a dominant place. The cranky skepticism which now kept him from any formal church allegiance perhaps chiefly concerned the New Testament. It is significant that in the many religious letters of his last year he makes but one reference to Christ, and none to Christian mercy. His belief in the harsh, implacable Jehovah of the Old Testament, however, remained unchanged. Charity and forgiveness had no place in his creed.

Skeptical: uncertain or doubtful about basic religious principles.

Reprinted by permission of Charles Scribner's Sons from Volume II **The Emergence of Lincoln,** pages 5–8, by Allan Nevins. Copyright 1950 Charles Scribner's Sons.

Stephen Vincent Benét's "John Brown's Body"

No One Can Say
That the trial was not fair. The trial was fair,
Painfully fair by every rule of law,
And that it was made not the slightest difference.
The law's our yardstick, and it measures well
Or well enough when there are yards to measure.
Measure a wave with it, measure a fire,
Cut sorrow up in inches, weigh content.
You can weigh John Brown's body well enough,
But how and in what balance weigh John Brown?

From: **John Brown's Body** by Stephen Vincent Benet. Holt, Rinehart and Winston, Inc. Copyright, 1927, 1928, by Stephen Vincent Benet. Copyright renewed, 1955, 1956, by Rosemary Carr Benet. Reprinted by permission of Brandt & Brandt.

5 Americans go to war

Shiloh

Abraham Lincoln

Secession: act of formal withdrawal from a compact or contract.

Objectives of this assignment are to:

—Make inferences about Union and Confederate military objectives from maps of the Shiloh area.

—Analyze selections from reports of Union and Confederate battle preparations for meaning.

—Make a judgment on difficulty of reconstructing history of great battles.

Introduction

John Brown had been dead nearly a year, but his spirit was still alive as two long-time political foes from Illinois, Stephen A. Douglas and Abraham Lincoln, faced each other as candidates of the Democratic and Republican parties in the presidential election of 1860. In addition, a splinter group of southern Democrats nominated John C. Breckinridge of Kentucky, and a new Constitution Union Party proposed John Bell of Tennessee.

Lincoln, the winner, polled more votes than any other candidate, but less than half of the total. He was what is popularly called a "minority President." Lincoln received almost no votes from any southern state, and was thus both a minority President and the representative of only one section of the country.

In addition, though he was no fervent Abolitionist, Lincoln was mistrusted by the south. This was because he headed the Republican Party, which was opposed to the extension and continued existence of slavery. As Republican leader, Lincoln represented his party's divisive point of view. Many southerners could see no future for the South in the Union if a Republican should be elected President. They made their feelings plain before the 1860 election.

The Secession Movement

The steps to *secession** and civil war after the election of 1860 were rapid. South Carolina called a convention which repealed her ratification of the Constitution. She declared her independence in December, 1860, little more than a month after Lincoln's election. Georgia, Florida, Alabama, Mississippi, Louisiana, and Texas followed with ordinances of secession by February, 1861. On the 4th of that month a government of the Confederate States of America was begun at Montgomery, Alabama.

One month later, on March 4, 1861, Abraham Lincoln was inaugurated as President of the United States in Washington. On that important day a rival government already existed within the United States—the Confederacy —made up of seven southern states which had seceded from the Union.

South Carolina struck the first blow of the Civil War on April 12, 1861, with an attack on Fort Sumter in Charleston harbor. The fort, which was held by Federal troops, surrendered after one day of bombardment. President Lincoln promptly called for 75,000 men from state militias to suppress the rebellion.

Jefferson Davis (1808–1889):
West Point graduate, served in
Mexican War. Senator from
Mississippi; Secretary of War
under President Pierce;
President of Confederate States
of America, 1861–1865.

War fever gripped the South. Virginia, which had held back, seceded. Then the remaining states that were to compose the Confederacy—North Carolina, Arkansas, and Tennessee—followed. *Jefferson Davis** of Mississippi and *Alexander H. Stephens** of Georgia were selected as President and Vice-President of the Confederacy, and the capital was moved to Richmond, Virginia, in July, 1861.

Hard choices were forced upon men by the coming of the Civil War. Many in the South deeply loved both the Union *and* their home state. This painful conflict of loyalties is best shown in the case of Virginia's distinguished son, Robert E. Lee. When war came in 1861, Lee was a colonel in the United States Army where he had spent 32 years. He had served in the Mexican War, had been superintendent of West Point, and was in charge of the Federal troops which seized John Brown and his followers at Harper's Ferry.

Alexander Hamilton Stephens
(1812–1883): Georgia lawyer,
state legislator, member of U. S.
House of Representatives, and
Vice-President of the
Confederacy. Elected to U. S.
Senate, 1866; Governor of
Georgia, 1882.

Lee was against slavery and opposed destruction of the Union. But he refused the offer to command Union forces early in 1861. He knew he could not raise his sword against Virginia. His loyalties were first to Virginia, his home, his family, his friends. On the eve of Virginia's secession in April, 1861, Lee accepted command of her army. In February, 1865, he became General-in-Chief of all the Confederate forces.

Early Struggles, and Hopes for a Short War

Military organization and operations were typically clumsy and fumbling during the first year of the Civil War. In a sense, much of the country could not take the war seriously. The South had pious hopes of winning an overwhelming victory, after which she hoped the North would let her go her way in peace. In the North similar sentiments were present: the Confederacy was a sham; it would be crushed in one great encounter, and secession would be ended.

Even after the bloody encounter of the first battle of *Bull Run,** both sides seem to have remained unconvinced of the proportions of the war that had been launched. They reorganized their forces and prepared for that single, symbolic victory.

Bull Run, also called Manassas
Junction: site in northern
Virginia of the first big battle of
the Civil War, July 21, 1861,
where Confederate forces under
Generals Beauregard and
Johnston routed Union troops of
General Irvin McDowell.

The Battle of Shiloh

Shiloh ended such expectations. Fought by poorly organized and inadequately disciplined men on both sides, this wild encounter in southwestern Tennessee on April 6 and 7, 1862, was the bloodiest battle fought on the North American continent up to that time. More than one out of every four Confederates who went into the battle was either killed, wounded, or captured; and a third of the Union forces of the Army of the Tennessee suffered the same fate. Union losses were 13,047; Confederate, 10,699. Including Union forces of the Army of the Ohio under General Don Carlos Buell, which arrived for the second day of fighting, over 100,000 men took part in the battle. There were nearly as many casualties at Shiloh as there had been in all previous battles in the history of the United States combined.

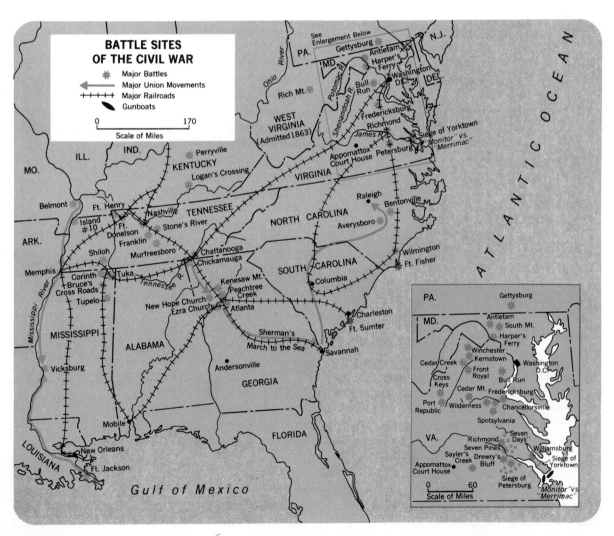

10 SHILOH: THE BATTLE AS PLANNED AND AS FOUGHT

Preceding the action at Shiloh, Union forces of the Army of the Tennessee under Major General *Ulysses Simpson Grant** had moved south up the Tennessee River after they seized the Confederate Forts Henry and Donelson in February, 1862. (See map, page C26.) Their base of operation at the ginning of April, 1862, was Pittsburg Landing on the Tennessee River, near the Mississippi border. About three miles west of the river, Union forces under Brigadier General *William Tecumseh Sherman** were encamped near Shiloh Church. (The battle would be known by both names: Shiloh and Pittsburg Landing.)

Confederate forces under their commander-in-chief, General *Albert Sidney Johnston,** were massing at Corinth, Mississippi, just twenty miles south of

Grant (1822–1885): West Point graduate, served in Mexican War. Colonel of Illinois Volunteers at outbreak of Civil War; rose to commander-in-chief of Union forces. President of U. S., 1869-1877.

Sherman (1820–1891): West Point graduate, veteran of Mexican War. Union General, noted for his march from Chattanooga through "Atlanta to the Sea" at Savannah, Georgia.

Albert Sidney Johnston was killed during the first day's fighting at Shiloh; replaced by Pierre Gustave Toutant Beauregard, who had fought at Ft. Sumter and Bull Run (July 21, 1861).

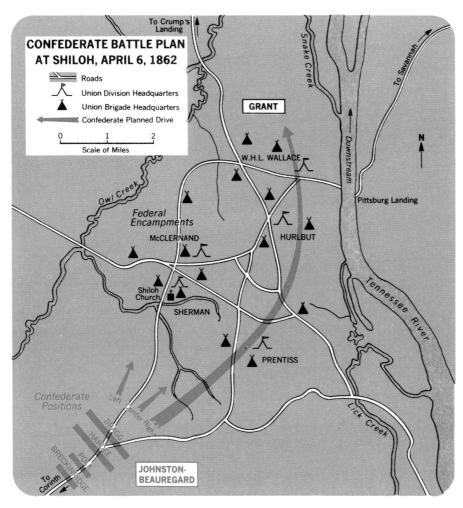

CONFEDERATE BATTLE PLAN AT SHILOH, APRIL 6, 1862

Roads
Union Division Headquarters
Union Brigade Headquarters
Confederate Planned Drive

0   1   2
Scale of Miles

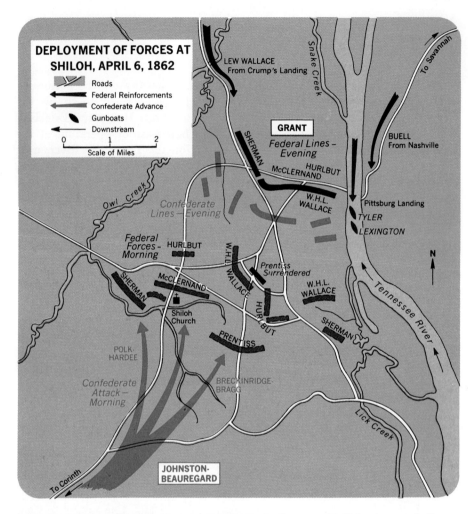

DEPLOYMENT OF FORCES AT
SHILOH, APRIL 6, 1862

Roads
Federal Reinforcements
Confederate Advance
Gunboats
Downstream

0   1   2
Scale of Miles

LEW WALLACE
From Crump's Landing

Snake Creek

To Savannah

GRANT
Federal Lines –
Evening

BUELL
From Nashville

SHERMAN

HURLBUT
McCLERNAND

W.H.L.
WALLACE

Pittsburg Landing

TYLER
LEXINGTON

Owl Creek

Confederate
Lines – Evening

Federal
Forces –
Morning

HURLBUT

W.H.L. WALLACE

Prentiss
Surrendered

N

McCLERNAND

Shiloh
Church

HURLBUT

W.H.L.
WALLACE

Tennessee River

PRENTISS

SHERMAN

SHERMAN

POLK-
HARDEE

BRECKINRIDGE-
BRAGG

Confederate
Attack –
Morning

Lick Creek

To Corinth

JOHNSTON-
BEAUREGARD

Grant's Army of the Tennessee. Johnston had some 40,000 men, and Grant slightly more; but one division of Grant's army was at Crump's Landing on the river, five miles north of the scene of the encounter. Another Union army, that of the Ohio, under General Don Carlos Buell, was approaching Pittsburg Landing from the northeast. Grant's plan was to wait for Buell and then attack the Confederates at Corinth in full strength (somewhere near 80,000 men). The Confederates planned to attack Grant before Buell could arrive and tip the balance of numbers against them.

The three maps shown on pages 27, 28, and 29 outline the Confederate plan of battle, where the major encounter took place, and how the battle was actually fought during those two terrible days in April, 1862.

While studying the maps, keep these questions in mind:

1. *What do you think was the objective of the Confederate attack at Shiloh?*
2. *How successful was the Confederate attack?*

C28

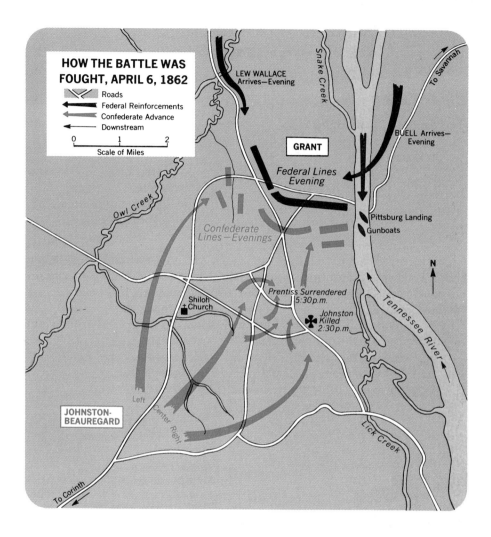

HOW THE BATTLE WAS FOUGHT, APRIL 6, 1862

Roads
Federal Reinforcements
Confederate Advance
Downstream

0   1   2
Scale of Miles

LEW WALLACE Arrives—Evening

Snake Creek

To Savannah

GRANT

BUELL Arrives— Evening

Federal Lines Evening

Owl Creek

Confederate Lines—Evenings

Pittsburg Landing

Gunboats

N

Prentiss Surrendered 5:30 p.m.

Shiloh Church

Johnston Killed 2:30 p.m.

Tennessee River

JOHNSTON- BEAUREGARD

Left

Center Right

Lick Creek

To Corinth

11   UNION AND CONFEDERATE GENERALS PREPARE FOR SHILOH

The following readings have been taken from the official records of the Union and Confederate governments. The first two short excerpts are reports made by Major General U. S. Grant and Brigadier General William T. Sherman to their superior officers the day before the battle of Shiloh erupted. Both men were extremely capable officers and were to win international reputations for their military campaigns. General Beauregard's report gives a view of the situation as seen by the Confederate staff.

In reading the next selections, keep the following questions in mind:

1. Were the Union forces ready for an attack?

2. Were the Confederates aware of the situation facing them? What did they decide to do?

General Grant Reports: No General Attack Expected

To: Maj. Gen. H. W. Halleck
    Commanding Department of the Mississippi
    St. Louis, Mo.

Headquarters District of
West Tennessee
Savannah (Tennessee)
April 3, 1862

General:

Just as my letter of yesterday to Captain McLean, assistant adjutant-general, was finished, notes from Generals McClernand's and Sherman's assistant adjutants-general were received, stating that our outposts had been attacked by the enemy, apparently in considerable force. I immediately went up, but found all quiet. . . . [The enemy] had with them three pieces of artillery and cavalry and infantry. How much cannot of course be estimated.

I have scarcely the faintest idea of an attack [a general one] being made upon us, but will be prepared should such a thing take place. . . .

I am, general, very respectfully, your obedient servant,

U. S. Grant
Major-General

From The War of the Rebellion: A Compilation of the Official Records of the Union and Confederate Armies (Washington: U. S. Govt. Printing Office, 1884), Series I, Vol. X, Part I, p. 89.

Union General Ulysses S. Grant and Confederate General Robert E. Lee. Victorious Grant went on to become President of the United States. Lee's moral character and tactical brilliance made him the best-loved and most respected Confederate figure of the war.

General Sherman Reports: No Attack Expected

Pittsburg Landing, April 5, 1862

General Grant:

Your note is just received. I have no doubt that nothing will occur today more than some picket firing. The enemy is saucy, but got the worst of it yesterday, and will not press our pickets far. I will not be drawn out far unless with certainty of advantage, and I do not apprehend anything like an attack on our position.

W. T. Sherman
Brigadier-General, Commanding

From **The War of the Rebellion: A Compilation of the Official Records of the Union and Confederate Armies** (Washington: U. S. Govt. Printing Office, 1884), Series I, Vol. X, Part II, pp. 93–94.

General Beauregard Reports Confederate Plans to Attack

It was then [April 1, 1862] determined to assume the [offensive] and strike a sudden blow at the enemy, in position under Gen. Grant, on the West bank of the Tennessee River, at Pittsburg, and in the direction of Savannah, before he was reinforced by the army under Gen. Buell, [which was approaching] from Nashville via Columbia. About the same time Gen. Johnston was advised that such an operation conformed to the expectations of President Jefferson Davis.

By a rapid and vigorous attack on Gen. Grant, it was expected he would be beaten back into his transports, and the river so captured in time to enable us to profit by the victory, and remove to the rear all the stores and munitions that would fall into our hands.

Lack of general officers, needful for the proper organization of divisions and brigades of an army brought thus suddenly together, and other difficulties in the way of an effective organization, delayed the movements until the night of the 2d instant, when it was heard from a reliable quarter that the junction of the enemies' armies was near at hand. It was then, at a very late hour, determined that the attack should be attempted at once, incomplete and imperfect as were our preparations for such a grave and momentous adventure.

Adapted from P. G. T. Beauregard, General Commanding, "Reports of the Battle of Shiloh." in **Official Reports of Battles,** published by order of the Confederate Congress at Richmond (New York: Charles B. Richardson, 1863).

Left: Union General William T. Sherman cut Confederate communications in his march from Atlanta to the sea, and completed devastation of Georgia by Christmas, 1864.

Right: Confederate General Pierre Gustave Toutant Beauregard took Fort Sumter, April 13, 1861, in the first battle of the Civil War, and served in many of the major battles.

C31

6 War and slavery

Toward Emancipation

Introduction

Objectives of this assignment are to:

—Analyze Lincoln's explanation for issuing the Emancipation Proclamation for purpose.

—Analyze resolution of Illinois State Legislature for reaction to the Emancipation Proclamation.

—Analyze judgments of a contemporary black intellectual and a distinguished black historian on the Emancipation Proclamation for meaning.

Slaves who escaped to northern lines were often treated as "Contraband," that is, enemy goods confiscated in war-time.

Alienate: to lose sympathy or support.

As they listened to the "Battle Hymn of the Republic" during the Civil War, northern Abolitionists could see the "glory of the coming of the Lord" in the "terrible swift sword" of war loosed upon the nation. To these people the war was a religious crusade against the evil institution of slavery.

Abraham Lincoln and the Federal government did not quite see the war this way—at least not at first. In the beginning, the North's main war aim was to save the Union at any cost.

Throughout the first anxious year of war, the status of slaves who had escaped or been "liberated" from their rebellious masters was a very troublesome one. Since the Confederates used their slaves at times to work on trenches and earthworks, there was little point in trying to return them to their masters once they had fallen into northern hands. Why not use them to dig northern entrenchments instead? Legally, slaves were *property;* and Abraham Lincoln had taken office to uphold the Constitution, including its provisions about slavery.

Lincoln personally hated the slave system. But he saw that any violent interference with it in the South would further divide public sentiment in the North. Abolitionists would clash with other northerners who opposed helping southern slaves. Lincoln did not want to *alienate* important segments of the population during a critical time of war and political crisis.

Lincoln and Emancipation

Lincoln himself looked to the slaveholding "border states" which had not seceded—Kentucky, Missouri, Maryland, Delaware—for the key to solving the legal problem of slaves in the states of the Union. He hoped that the legislatures of these states would emancipate the slaves. Then the Federal government would give the states financial aid to reimburse the former slaveholders.

Lincoln did not ask for immediate emancipation by the states. As he said in his address to representatives of the border states in July, 1862, he wanted "a decision at once to emancipate gradually." Then there would have to be some elaborate scheme of colonization for the freed blacks, but plenty of room for them could be found in South America.

C32

During the summer of 1862, President Lincoln changed his course of action. He saw the need of issuing some sort of declaration of emancipation. But he delayed announcing it until the North had gained military success in battle. This chance came on September 17, 1862, when the North turned back a big southern invasion threat at the Battle of Antietam in Maryland. Five days later Lincoln announced that slaves in those states in rebellion against the Union as of January 1, 1863, would be free.

Slavery Abolished

The legal basis of slavery was not finally determined, however, until the ratification of the Thirteenth and Fourteenth Amendments to the Constitution after the Civil War (December, 1865, and July, 1868). These two Amendments settled the issues raised by Justice Taney in the Dred Scott decision.

The Thirteenth Amendment provided that "neither slavery nor involuntary servitude, except as a punishment for crime, . . ." should exist under the American flag. The Fourteenth Amendment declared that all persons "born or naturalized in the United States, and subject to the jurisdiction thereof, are citizens of the United States and of the State wherein they reside. . . ." This last provision of course ended the distinction which Chief Justice Taney had made between citizenship in a state and citizenship under the Federal government.

The Emancipation of the Negroes, January, 1863. The Past and the Future. Drawing by Thomas Nast

12   THE EMANCIPATION PROCLAMATION: THE REACTION OF BLACK AMERICANS

Frederick Douglass
(1817–1895): born a slave in Tuckahoe, Md.; escaped to New York City and then to Massachusetts. After educating himself, became a leader of the Abolitionist movement and editor of his own magazine. United States minister to Haiti, 1889–1891.

W. E. Burghardt Du Bois
(1868–1963): born in Great Barrington, Mass.; received Ph.D. in history from Harvard in 1895. Taught economics, history, and sociology at Atlanta University. His book, **The Souls of Black Folk,** first published in 1903, earned national recognition. Active in Negro affairs and Civil Rights movements. Made a citizen of Ghana and spent the last years of his life there.

From **The Statutes at Large, Treaties, and Proclamations of the United States of America,** Ed. George P. Sanger (Boston: Little Brown & Co., 1863), Vol. XII, pp. 1268–1269.

The observations on the Emancipation Proclamation presented here are taken from the works of two of America's best-known authors of African descent: *Frederick Douglass** and *W. E. B. Du Bois.** Douglass' account was written at the time the Proclamation was issued; Du Bois' was written more than seventy years later (1935).

Though the Civil War was not a crusade against the moral evil of slavery, that institution was a major issue in it. How much of an issue was the question which these eminent black thinkers sought to determine. While studying the Emancipation Proclamation and the observations of Douglass and Du Bois, keep these questions in mind:

1. How does the Emancipation Proclamation justify the legal suppression of slavery?

2. What does Frederick Douglass think about the Emancipation Proclamation?

3. What does W. E. B. Du Bois think about the Emancipation Proclamation?

Emancipation Proclamation

January 1, 1863

Now, therefore, I, Abraham Lincoln, President of the United States, by virtue of the power in me vested as Commander-in-Chief of the Army and Navy of the United States in times of actual armed rebellion against the authority and government of the United States, and as a fit and necessary war measure for suppressing said rebellion, do, . . . order and declare that *all persons held as slaves* within the said designated states, and parts of states in rebellion against the government of the United States are, and henceforth *shall be free.* . . .

And I hereby enjoin upon the people so declared to be free to abstain from all violence, unless in necessary self-defense; and I recommend to them that, in all cases when allowed, they labor faithfully for reasonable wages.

And I further declare and make known that such persons of suitable condition will be received into the armed services of the United States. . . .

And upon this act, sincerely believed to be an act of justice, warranted by the Constitution upon military necessity, I invoke the considerate judgment of mankind and the gracious favor of Almighty God.

Frederick Douglass Analyzes the Emancipation Proclamation

Common sense, the necessities of war, to say nothing of the dictates of justice and humanity have at last prevailed. We shout for joy that we live to record this righteous decree. *Abraham Lincoln,* President of the United

States, Commander-in-Chief of the army and navy, in his own peculiar, cautious, forbearing and hesitating way, slow, but we hope sure, has, while the loyal heart was near breaking with despair, proclaimed and declared: [that slaves in rebellious states shall be free as of January 1, 1863]. . . .

Much as I value the present apparent hostility to slavery in the North, I plainly see that it is less the outgrowth of high and intelligent moral conviction against Slavery, as such, than because of the trouble its friends have brought upon the country. I would have slavery hated for that and more. A man that hates slavery only for what it does to the white man, stands ready to embrace it the moment its injuries are confined to the black man, and he ceases to feel those injuries in his own person. . . . I confess, if I could possibly doubt the salvation of the nation, it would not be because the traitors and Rebels are strong, but because we are weak at this vital point.

Douglass' Monthly, October, 1862. From The Life and Writings of Frederick Douglass, Philip S. Foner, Editor, Vol. III, pp. 273, 330–333, Copyright © 1952. Reprinted by permission of International Publishers Co., Inc.

❋   ❋   ❋   ❋   ❋

W. E. B. Du Bois Reflects on the Emancipation Proclamation

The slave, despite every effort, was becoming the center of war. Lincoln, with his uncanny insight, began to see it. He began to talk about compensation for emancipated slaves. . . . Lincoln then suggested that provision be made for colonization of such slaves. He simply could not envisage free negroes in the United States. What would become of them? What would they do?

❋   ❋   ❋   ❋   ❋

In August [1862], Lincoln faced the truth forward; and that truth was not simply that Negroes ought to be free; it was that thousands of them were already free, and that either the power which slaves put into the hands of the South was to be taken from it, or the North could not win the war. Either the Negro was to be allowed to fight, or the draft would not bring enough white men into the army to keep up the war.

More than that, unless the North faced the world with the moral strength of declaring openly that they were fighting for the emancipation of the slaves, they would probably find that the world would recognize the South as a separate nation; that [Southern] ports would be opened; that trade would begin, and that despite all the military advantage of the North, the war would be lost.

W. E. B. Du Bois, Black Reconstruction in America, 1860–1880 [1935] (New York: Russell & Russell, 1956), p. 82.

13   BACKLASH TO EMANCIPATION

Despite rejoicing among white Abolitionists, there is no doubt that racial prejudice and discrimination played an important part in America's reaction to Emancipation, just as they had always played a part in maintaining slavery in the South and segregation in the North. Though Lincoln was genuinely opposed to slavery, it may well be that he was not strongly opposed to racial discrimination. But this is a problem neither white nor black Americans have yet been able to solve.

While reading the Resolution of a group of Illinois legislators* and President Lincoln's letter to Horace Greeley, publisher of the New York *Tribune*, on the issuance of the Emancipation Proclamation, keep in mind these questions:

1. What does the Resolution of the Illinois legislators suggest about northern public opinion on the Emancipation Proclamation?

2. How important were Lincoln's personal feelings about slavery in issuing the Emancipation Proclamation?

Illinois Legislators Resolve the Emancipation Proclamation Unwarrantable, January 6, 1863

A group of Illinois legislators, independent of the legislature, and a group of citizens met and passed the **Resolution.**

Unwarrantable: without justification or sanction.

Usurpation: wrongful seizure of power.

Subversion: destruction by undermining principles.

Uneffaceable: permanent; unremoveable.

Resolved: That the Emancipation Proclamation of the President of the United States is as *unwarrantable** in military as in civil law; a gigantic *usurpation,** at once converting the war, professedly commenced by the administration for the vindication of the authority of the constitution, into the crusade for the sudden, unconditional and violent liberation of 3,000,000 negro slaves; a result which would not only be a total *subversion** of the Federal Union but a revolution in the social organization of the Southern States, the immediate and remote, the present and far-reaching consequences of which to both races cannot be contemplated without the most dismal foreboding of horror and dismay. The proclamation invites servile insurrection as an element in this emancipation crusade—a means of warfare, the inhumanity and diabolism of which we denounce, and which the civilized world will denounce, as an *uneffaceable** disgrace to the American people.

From **Daily State Register,** Springfield, Ill., January 6, 1863.

Lincoln to Horace Greeley, August 22, 1862

Dear Sir:

As to the policy I "seem to be pursuing" as you say, I have not meant to leave any one in doubt.

I would save the Union. I would save it the shortest way under the Constitution. My paramount object in this struggle is to save the Union, and is not either to save or to destroy slavery. If I could save the Union without freeing *any* slave I would do it, and if I could save it by freeing *all* the slaves I would do it; and if I could save it by freeing some and leaving others alone I would also do that. What I do about slavery and the colored race, I do because I believe it helps to save the Union; and what I forbear, I forbear because I do not believe it would help to save the Union. . . .

I have here stated my purpose according to my view of *official* duty; and I intend no modification of my oft-expressed *personal* wish that all men everywhere could be free. Yours,

A. Lincoln

C36

7 The New York draft riots

Protest Against Conscription

Introduction

After the fall of Fort Sumter in April, 1861, President Lincoln called for 75,000 state militia to put down the southern rebellion. (See page C24.) By the end of the Civil War two million or more men had seen service in the Union Army, while more than half this number served in the Confederate ranks. Though statistics vary considerably, it is estimated that about eight percent of the Union Army soldiers were black. There were more than one million casualties suffered by the opposing armies during that war.

War also took men out of their usual roles on the farms and in the factories and put them in noncombatant roles in the military forces. As the Union armies edged farther and farther into Confederate territory, miles of river and railroad supply lines developed behind them, running through dangerous, unfriendly lands which were open to attacks by Confederate cavalry. Sizeable forces of troops had to garrison forts and patrol strategic areas to protect Union soldiers.

The Volunteer Army

At the beginning of the Civil War, the regular United States Army consisted of fewer than 20,000 men. Those who fought actively during the first two years of the war were either state militiamen or volunteers. Their service in the Union army was limited to short enlistments. No one volunteered "for the duration," and three-year terms of enlistment were the longest.

By the time the war had ground through its third year (1863), the Federal government had to find replacements for those fighting men whose three-year terms of enlistment would end late in the spring of 1864. Such men were seasoned fighting troops, and their replacements had to be enrolled and trained well before the veterans' service ended.

The First Draft

To serve this purpose, a much-criticized law was passed. The *Conscription** Act (March, 1863) provided that all United States male citizens between the ages of 20 and 45 were subject to military service for a period of three years. This was the first forcible "draft" in American history (with the exception of the Confederate Draft Act, which was passed in April, 1862).

Conscription: forced service in the armed forces. Draft.

C37

Obnoxious: offensive; distasteful; detestable.

As expected, the Conscription Act roused great opposition. Certain provisions of it were found to be especially *obnoxious.** Particularly disliked was that part which allowed an individual whose name was called either to provide a substitute or to purchase his exemption for $300. Either way, avoiding actual service involved paying an amount of money which was far beyond the means of the average working man. The cry immediately went up that it was "a rich man's war and a poor man's fight."

Anti-draft Riots

Motives for opposition to the draft in the North were many. They ranged from simple resentment against violation of the rights of the individual, to outright sympathy with the South.

The drawing of the names of the first men to be conscripted from New York City in July, 1863, provided the spark which touched off one of the most serious riots in American history. The disturbances grew into a race riot when New York's Negro population became the scapegoats for the anger of the crowd.

For three days the city was in the grip of mob violence beyond the control of the police. Then units of the New York militia, which had just been engaged at the Battle of Gettysburg, were rushed to the scene. Pitched battles between the rioters and the militia took place, and the outbreak was soon crushed. But the destruction ran to several million dollars worth of property and more than forty human lives.

Drafting men in New York City, August, 1863

14   WHAT CAUSED THE DRAFT RIOTS?

The New York Draft Riots shocked all who witnessed them as well as hundreds of thousands more who read about them. Nearly every account of the riots, contemporary or later, insists that many issues were involved, and that the mob took to the streets for many different reasons.

The range of possible explanation of why these riots occurred is illustrated by the selections presented below from the works of Horace Greeley and W. E. B. Du Bois. Greeley was a trained newspaperman, witness to much of the actual rioting, and strongly Republican in politics. Du Bois, though he lived at a later period, was a trained historian and the most informed man of the day on the history of black Americans.

While reading these selections, keep in mind these questions:

1. How does Horace Greeley explain the outbreak of the New York Draft Riots?

2. How does W. E. B. Du Bois explain the outbreak of the New York Draft Riots?

Objectives of this assignment are to:

—Analyze accounts of New York Draft Riots by a contemporary and by a distinguished black historian for their hypotheses about cause.

—Draw inferences about causes of New York Draft Riots from filmstrip of contemporary drawings.

—Make historical judgment on causes of New York Draft Riots.

C38

Horace Greeley on the Draft Riots

The Police, though well organized and efficient, was not competent to deal with a virtual insurrection which had the great body of the foreign-born laborers of our city at its back, with nearly every one of the 10,000 *grogshops**

Grogshops: saloons; taverns.

for its block-houses and recruiting-stations. The outbreak had manifestly been premeditated and prearranged; and the tidings of its initial success, being instantly diffused throughout the city, incited an outpouring into the street of all who dreaded the Draft, hated the War, or detested Abolitionists and Negroes as the culpable causes of both.

The most revolting feature of this carnival of crime and villainous madness was the uniform maltreatment to which the harmless, frightened Blacks were subjected.

❋ ❋ ❋ ❋ ❋

It is absurd and futile to attribute this outburst of ruffianism to anything else than sympathy for the Rebels. If, as some pretend, it results from dissatisfaction with the $300 exemption, why are Negroes indiscriminately assailed and beaten almost or quite to death? Did they prescribe this exemption? On the contrary, are they not almost uniformly poor men, themselves exposed to the draft, and unable to pay $300? What single thing have they done to expose them to this infernal, cowardly ruffianism? What can be alleged against them unless it be that they are generally hostile to the Slaveholders' Rebellion?

Adapted from Horace Greeley, **The American Conflict** (Hartford: O. D. Case and Co., 1866), Vol. II, pp. 502–504.

W. E. B. Du Bois Analyzes the Draft Riots

When the draft law was passed in 1863, it meant that the war could no longer be carried on with volunteers; that soldiers were going to be compelled to fight, and these soldiers were going to be poor men who could not buy exemption.

The Democratic press had advised the people that they were to be called upon to fight the battles of "niggers and Abolitionists."

It was easy to transfer class hatred so that it fell upon the black worker. The end of the war seemed far off, and the attempt to enforce the draft led particularly to disturbances in New York City, where a powerful part of the city press was not only against the draft, but against the war, and in favor of the South and Negro slavery.

The white workers of New York declared in effect that the Negroes were the cause of the war, and that they were tired of the discrimination that made workers fighters for the rich. They, therefore, killed all the Negroes that they could lay their hands on.

This working class movement was the protest of the poor against being compelled to fight the battles of the rich in which they could conceive no interest of theirs. The just indignation of the workers was turned against the Negro laborers, rather than against *Capitalists;** and against any war, even for emancipation.

Capitalists: business owners; those who have control of "capital."

Adapted from W. E. B. Du Bois, **Black Reconstruction in America, 1860–1880** [1935] (New York: Russell & Russell, 1956), pp. 102–103.

1 Recruiting Center, New York City

Culver

2 Anti-war Mob Fights New York City Police

Library of Congress

3 Mob Chasing Negro Family Through Lexington Avenue Vacant Lots

4 Rioters Burning the Colored Orphan Asylum

Library of Congress

The New-York Historical Society, N. Y. C.

5 Looting Brooks Brothers Clothing Store

8 Problems of Reconstruction

Northern and Southern Views

Introduction

As the year of 1865 dawned, the Civil War was drawing to a close, After nearly four years of struggle, the Confederate States of America were exhausted. The ragged but defiant southern soldiers were soon to surrender to the North at Appomattox Court House, Virginia.

As early as 1863, President Abraham Lincoln had begun to plan for reconstruction of the South when the war ended. Lincoln bore no grudge toward the South. He wanted to resume working with the seceded states within the framework of the Union, as if they had never left it. Reconstructing the South was a job well within the authority of the President, Lincoln believed. His were the views of the *moderate** Republicans.

An entirely different point of view was held by a powerful group of Republican congressmen called *Radicals.** The Radical Republicans wanted to punish the South for its part in the war. They felt southern leaders were traitors who should not under any circumstances be permitted to represent the South in Congress when it finally rejoined the Union. The Radicals were afraid that if permitted to do so, southern and northern Democrats would join forces and throw the Republican party out of power in Congress.

Along this same line of thinking, the Radicals declared that southern blacks must no longer be denied equal rights, including the right to vote. This idea served both moral and practical purposes. Morally, it gave the black man citizenship and all the rights he deserved as an American and a human being. Practically, it gave him the right to show his gratitude to the Republicans for his freedom by giving them his vote.

Finally, the Radicals disagreed with Lincoln that reconstruction should be managed by the President. They regarded southern states as enemy territory, not part of the Union. The radicals argued that managing territories and admitting them as states had always been handled by Congress.

Lincoln vs. Congress

Abraham Lincoln proceeded with his plan to restore the South to the Union. He maintained that the southern states had *not* seceded and that only groups of people within those states had defied the Union. Lincoln's position was that any time the leaders of those states wanted to cooperate with the United States, they were welcome to do so.

Objectives of this assignment are to:

—Describe Lincoln's intended policy toward defeated southern states.

—Analyze selections of reconstruction legislation and contemporary comment on it for meaning.

—Discover difficulties of making historical judgment on Congressional Reconstruction policies.

Moderate: following a gentle, middle-of-the-road policy, thus avoiding extremes.

Radicals: those who believe in going to extremes and making sweeping changes.

C43

Under Lincoln's Ten Percent Plan, any southern state could regain full participation in the Union when ten percent of its voters declared their loyalty to the United States and agreed to the abolition of slavery. Three southern states (Louisiana, Tennessee, and Arkansas) which were largely occupied by northern troops set up loyal state governments in 1864.

Radical Republican congressmen opposed the plan. Whether they could have made Lincoln back down and let Congress manage reconstruction will never be known. President Lincoln was assassinated by a half-crazy actor named John Wilkes Booth five days after the South finally surrendered in April, 1865.

President Johnson vs. Congress

The martyred Lincoln was followed as President by Vice-President Andrew Johnson, a southerner who had remained loyal to the Union. Johnson, a moderate, tried to carry on for Lincoln. He collided head on with the Radicals.

Led by Thaddeus Stevens of Pennsylvania and Charles Sumner of Massachusetts, the Radicals proceeded to teach the South a "lesson" it would never forget. The Radicals were determined that the men who had led the South into secession and war would never again be in positions of responsibility and authority. Secessionists and slave holders could be neither forgiven nor forgotten. They simply had no right to any place in any government anywhere. Since each house of Congress judges the credentials of its own members, the Radicals refused to seat the representatives from the new southern state governments when they came to Washington. Instead, Congress sent a committee to the South to study charges that blacks were being mistreated and to recommend what steps to take towards reconstruction.

Thaddeus Stevens of Pennsylvania, boss of the Republican House of Representatives, 1866

The committee proposed that southern states be made to ratify the Fourteenth Amendment, which gave citizenship to blacks and barred former Confederate leaders from holding political office. After a vote by the eleven southern states, only Tennessee agreed to ratify the Amendment.

Next, over President Johnson's veto, Congress passed a series of Reconstruction Acts. The ten disobedient southern states were divided into five military districts and occupied by Federal troops. Then southern blacks were given the right to vote and told to work with white southerners to form new state governments. When these governments ratified the Fourteenth Amendment, Congress would consider readmitting them to the Union.

The new southern governments that were built under these conditions differed greatly from those of former times. The old South had been run by rich and educated white planters and businessmen. Now many of these men were forbidden to run for office, and their places were taken by black and white farmers, who lacked experience in government. The military occupation of the South caused a long-lasting bitterness in that region. Southerners were angrier about Federal occupation and the enforced ratification of the Thirteenth and Fourteenth Amendments to the Constitution than they were about losing the war itself.

15 LINCOLN'S PLAN FOR RECONSTRUCTION

Abraham Lincoln approached the problems of postwar America with the same values that had sustained him through the war: The Union must be preserved. Struck down by an assassin's bullet, Lincoln never had the chance to carry out his plan for restoring the states of the former Confederacy to the Union.

Lincoln's attitude toward what a postwar settlement ought to be was expressed in his Second Inaugural Address, March 4, 1865. The application of his ideas to the specific case of Louisiana was developed in a speech delivered on April 11, 1865, three days before his assassination.

While reading the selections which follow, keep these questions in mind:

1. According to Lincoln, were the states of the former Confederacy out of the Union?

2. Do you think Lincoln desired to punish the South—or to forgive it?

Lincoln's Second Inaugural Address, March 4, 1865

[Neither side engaged in this War expected for it] the magnitude, or the duration, which it has already attained. . . . Each looked for an easier triumph, and a result less fundamental and astounding. Both read the same Bible, and pray to the same God; and each invokes His aid against the other. It may seem strange that any men should dare to ask a just God's assistance in wringing their bread from the sweat of other men's faces; but let us judge not that we be not judged. The prayers of both could not be answered; that of neither has been answered fully. The Almighty has His own purposes. . . . Fondly do we hope—fervently do we pray—that this mighty scourge of war may speedily pass away. Yet if God wills that it continue, until all the wealth piled by the bondsman's [slave's] two hundred and fifty years of unrequited toil shall be sunk, and until every drop of blood drawn with the lash, shall be paid by another drawn with the sword . . . so still it must be said, "The judgments of the Lord are true and righteous altogether."

With malice toward none; with charity for all; with firmness in the right, as God gives us to see the right, let us strive on to finish the work we are in: to bind up the nation's wounds; to care for him who shall have borne the battle, and for his widow, and his orphan—to do all which may achieve and cherish a just, and a lasting peace, among ourselves, and with all nations.

President Lincoln's Last Public Address, April 11, 1865

We all agree that the seceded States, so called, are out of their proper practical relation with the Union; and that the sole object of the government, civil and military, in regard to those States is to again get them into that proper practical relation. I believe it is not only possible, but in fact, easier, to do this, without deciding, or even considering, whether these states have ever been out of the Union, than with it. Finding themselves safely at home, it would be utterly immaterial whether they had ever been abroad. Let us all join in doing the acts necessary to restore the proper practical relations between these states and the Union; and each forever after, innocently indulge his own opinion whether, in doing the acts, he brought the States from without, into the Union, or only gave them proper assistance, they never having been out of it.

✳　✳　✳　✳　✳

16　CONGRESS ACTS AND JEFFERSON DAVIS REFLECTS

Reconstruction involved action as well as planning. After much political maneuvering, Congress passed the First Reconstruction Act over President Johnson's veto in March, 1867. The law provided the actual basis for the Reconstruction governments in the South.

Typical of southern reaction to the Reconstruction program were the writings of the former President of the Confederacy, Jefferson Davis. Davis, who lived until 1889, published The Rise and Fall of the Confederate Government in 1881.

And yet, despite what Lincoln, Davis, or Congress wanted, new forces were at work in the nation which brought back together certain segments of the North and South in unforeseen ways. Thomas Nast's cartoon suggests what some of these segments were and how they were reunited.

While reading the selections and studying the cartoon, keep these questions in mind:

1. *What sort of government did the First Reconstruction Act provide for the states of the former Confederacy?*

2. *According to Davis, how should Reconstruction have been accomplished?*

3. *According to Thomas Nast, what had Reconstruction done for the Negro?*

Congress Legislates for the Conquered South: an Act to Provide for the More Efficient Government of the Rebel States

Whereas no legal State governments or adequate protection for life or property now exists in the rebel States of Virginia, North Carolina, South Carolina, Georgia, Mississippi, Alabama, Louisiana, Florida, Texas and Arkansas; and whereas it is necessary that peace and good order should be enforced in said States until loyal and republican State governments can be legally established: Therefore,

C46

Be it enacted by the Senate and House of Representatives of the United States of America in Congress assembled, That said rebel States shall be divided into military districts and made subject to the military authority of the United States as hereinafter prescribed. . . .

❊   ❊   ❊   ❊   ❊

Sec. 3. That it shall be the duty of each officer assigned . . . to organize military commissions or tribunals [for the purpose of administering justice] . . . and all interference under color of State authority with the exercise of military authority under this act, shall be null and void.

❊   ❊   ❊   ❊   ❊

Sec. 6. That, until the people of said rebel States shall be by law admitted to representation in the Congress of the United States, any Civil governments which may exist therein shall be deemed provisional only, and in all respects subject to the paramount authority of the United States at any time to abolish, modify, control, or supersede the same. . . .

From The First Reconstruction Act, March 2, 1867, **The Statutes at Large, Treaties, and Proclamations of the United States of America.**

❊   ❊   ❊   ❊   ❊

Jefferson Davis on Reunion through Force

When the Confederate soldiers laid down their arms and went home, all hostilities against the power of the Government of the United States ceased. The powers delegated in the *compact** of 1787 by these States, i.e., by the people thereof, to a central organization to promote their general welfare, had been used for their devastation and subjugation. It was conceded, as the result of the contest, that the United States Government was stronger in resources than the Confederate Government, and that the Confederate States had not achieved their independence.

The *compact* referred to was the Constitution which was drawn up and signed in 1787 and became effective in 1789.

Nothing remained to be done but for the sovereigns, the people of each State, to assert their authority and restore order. If the principle of the sovereignty of the people, the cornerstone of all our institutions, had survived and was still in force, it was necessary only that the people of each State should reconsider their ordinances of secession, and again recognize the Constitution of the United States as the supreme law of the land. This simple process would have placed the Union on its original basis, and have restored that which had ceased to exist, the Union by consent. Unfortunately, such was not the intention of the conqueror. . . . Henceforth there was to be established a Union of force. Sovereignty was to pass from the people to the Government of the United States, and to be upheld by those who had furnished the money and the soldiers for the war.

From Jefferson Davis, **The Rise and Fall of the Confederate Government** (New York: D. Appleton and Co., 1881), Vol. II, pp. 718–719.

C47

The New-York Historical Society, N. Y. C.

"This Is a White Man's Government."

"We regard the Reconstruction Acts (so-called) of Congress as usurpations, unconstitutional, revolutionary, and void." — Democratic Platform 1868

9 Problems of Reconstruction

Help for the Freedman

Introduction

Although many serious problems faced the United States during the Reconstruction Era, perhaps the most important one was the condition of the freedman. For him, as for his former masters, a new world of uncertainty lay ahead. In the process of reconstruction, the nation's obligations to the freedman had to be considered. What was to be done for the liberated blacks in the South?

Objectives of this assignment are to:

—Draw inferences from a chronology of Reconstruction Era, 1865–1877, about opposition to Congressional Reconstruction policies.

—Analyze a statement on functions and responsibilities of Freedmen's Bureau for meaning.

—Draw inferences from filmstrip of contemporary illustrations of Reconstruction Era about revolutionary nature of Congressional reconstruction policies.

The Problem of the Freedman

Many white Americans believed that the nation's obligations to the newly emancipated black Americans were limited. Civil rights were enough. Once the Thirteenth, Fourteenth, and Fifteenth Amendments to the Constitution had been ratified, the nation's obligations to black people would be fulfilled.

Others believed that white Americans owed black people much more. They believed that the future welfare of the country depended upon the social and economic improvement of America's black people. Acting upon this belief, concerned Americans founded a number of public and private agencies to provide social and educational services, and economic assistance, to freedmen and refugees. The most important of these agencies was the Freedmen's Bureau, established in 1865.

The Republican Congress

Though split into Moderate and Radical factions, the Republican Party controlled both houses of Congress during the Reconstruction Era. Moderates such as Senator Lyman Trumbull of Illinois favored Lincoln's approach to Reconstruction. Trumbull and others of the same mind wanted the constitutional and legal status of southern states established as soon as possible. They also wanted southern senators and representatives admitted to Congress without delay.

Radicals such as Thaddeus Stevens of Pennsylvania, Charles Sumner of Massachusetts, and Benjamin Wade of Ohio viewed the South as conquered territory. They wanted a complete reorganization of government in the South, using freedmen as officeholders as frequently as possible. Also, former Confederate leaders and conservative-minded whites were to be kept out of positions of power and influence.

The Radicals were convinced that the return of former Confederate leaders or conservative southern whites to Congress would be harmful to the country. It would prevent the total destruction of the old southern slaveholding *oligarchy*.* It would halt the integration of the freedmen into the mainstream of American social, political, and economic life.

Oligarchy: government by a small group for selfish purposes.

President Johnson

President Johnson's role in reconstructing the South was a critical one. At first the Radical Republicans thought he would support their views and policies, but his actions proved their expectations false. Though Johnson lacked Lincoln's political shrewdness and tact, he was a man of integrity and strong will. So until the Radical Republicans swept into power with the election of Ulysses S. Grant as President in 1868, Johnson and the Radical Republican leadership of Congress fought bitterly over the Reconstruction Acts. Ultimately, the Radical Republican leadership tried to remove President Johnson's resistance to their policies by *impeaching** him in 1868.

Impeachment: the process whereby public officials are accused and tried for crimes or misdemeanors in office, and removed if found guilty.

Price of Freedom

The war had been expensive and bloody, but the Union had been preserved. Approximately one soldier had died for every six slaves emancipated. Yet the peace terms were relatively easy and generous.

The war was over, but the long struggle for racial equality and justice in the United States had just begun. The whole nation, North and South, black and white, would still have to endure long periods of distrust and turmoil before that struggle was over. Freedom never comes cheaply or quickly.

Graves of Civil War Dead in Franklin, Tennessee

17 THE PROGRESS OF RECONSTRUCTION

The map and data which follow provide a chronology of events connected with Reconstruction prior to 1877, when the last Federal troops were removed from the South. By that time the states of the former Confederacy had returned to conservative white leadership.

While studying the map on readmission of seceding states to the Union, and the chronology of significant events during the Reconstruction Era, 1865–1877, keep these questions in mind:

1. During what years was most Reconstruction legislation passed?

2. What signs were there of the opposition between President Johnson and Radical Republican congressmen?

3. What was the Ku Klux Klan, and how did Congress react to its activities?

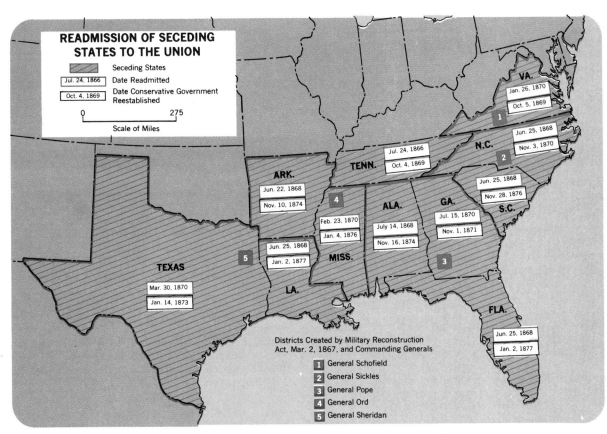

READMISSION OF SECEDING STATES TO THE UNION

- Seceding States
- Jul. 24, 1866   Date Readmitted
- Oct. 4, 1869   Date Conservative Government Reestablished

0   275
Scale of Miles

VA. Jan. 26, 1870 / Oct. 5, 1869

N.C. Jun. 25, 1868 / Nov. 3, 1870

S.C. Jun. 25, 1868 / Nov. 28, 1876

TENN. Jul. 24, 1866 / Oct. 4, 1869

ARK. Jun. 22, 1868 / Nov. 10, 1874

ALA. Feb. 23, 1870 / Jan. 4, 1876

GA. July 14, 1868 / Nov. 16, 1874

Jul. 15, 1870 / Nov. 1, 1871

MISS. Jun. 25, 1868 / Jan. 2, 1877

TEXAS Mar. 30, 1870 / Jan. 14, 1873

FLA. Jun. 25, 1868 / Jan. 2, 1877

LA.

Districts Created by Military Reconstruction Act, Mar. 2, 1867, and Commanding Generals

1 General Schofield
2 General Sickles
3 General Pope
4 General Ord
5 General Sheridan

C51

Chronology of Significant Events During the Reconstruction Era
1865–1877

EVENT	SIGNIFICANCE
1865	
Mar. 3 —Bureau of Refugees, Freedmen, and Abandoned Lands established.	—Provided necessary economic and social services for the newly freed black and for some displaced whites.
Dec. 4 —President Johnson appoints Joint Committee on Reconstruction.	—Under leadership of Thaddeus Stevens of Pennsylvania, committee investigated how to readmit southern members to Congress.
—Black Codes enacted by Legislatures of southern states.	—To prevent vagrancy by providing for black apprenticeship and by compelling blacks to remain in one place.
Dec. 18 —Thirteenth Amendment adopted.	—Prohibition of slavery.
Dec. 24 —Ku Klux Klan formed, Pulaski, Tenn.	—Originally a "fraternal organization," the Klan soon became a source of terror to the black. Its activities were designed to thwart Radical Republican policies of reconstruction.
1866	
Apr. 9 Civil Rights Act passed (over President Johnson's veto).	—To use Federal courts and forces to insure the civil rights of all persons.
May 1 —Memphis riot.	—Race riot: hatred of whites for blacks.
July 16 —New Freedmen's Bureau Bill passed by Congress (over Johnson's veto).	—Provided that military courts try those accused of depriving freedmen of civil rights.
July 30 —New Orleans riot.	—Race riot over the issue of black suffrage.
Dec. —Supreme Court decides that martial law is illegal where Civil Courts are in operation.	—Blow struck at Radical Reconstruction. Radicals refuse to comply.
1867	
Jan. 8 —Black suffrage granted in District of Columbia.	—First enfranchisement of large body of black voters by Congressional action.
Mar. 2 —First Reconstruction Act passed by Congress (over President Johnson's veto).	—Congress treated former Confederate states as conquered territory; martial law took precedence over civil law.
—Union Leagues established in the South.	—Radical Republican organizations designed to win black vote.
Mar. 23 —Second Reconstruction Act passed by Congress (over Johnson's veto).	—Federal military commanders in South authorized to prepare states under their command for readmission to Union.
July 19 —Third Reconstruction Act passed by Congress (over Johnson's veto).	—Declared existing civil governments in Southern states illegal; state officials placed under military supervision.
1868	
Mar. 11 —Fourth Reconstruction Act.	—Regulated procedures for adopting new state constitutions to prevent domination by Southern whites.
Mar. 13 —Trial of impeachment of President Johnson begins (ends May 26; acquittal).	—Radical Republicans attempted to remove the President because he opposed them on Reconstruction.
July 28 —Fourteenth Amendment adopted.	—Granted citizenship to blacks.
Nov. 3 —Gen. U. S. Grant, Republican nominee for Presidency, defeats Democratic candidate Horatio Seymour of New York.	

	EVENT	SIGNIFICANCE

EVENT   **SIGNIFICANCE**

Dec. 3 —Treason trial of Confederate President Jefferson Davis begins. (Charges dropped two months later.)

Dec. 25 —President Johnson issues proclamation of amnesty to all participants in Confederate government or military forces.

1870

Feb. 25 —First black elected to sit in Senate (Hiram R. Revels of Miss.).

Mar. 30 —Fifteenth Amendment adopted.   —Provided voting rights for blacks.

May 31 —Force Bill passed by Congress.   —Directed against activities of Ku Klux Klan and to insure enforcement of 14th and 15th Amendments. Civil rights of Southern black put under protection of Federal government.

1871

Feb. 28 —Second Force Bill passed by Congress.   —Designed to destroy Ku Klux Klan and punish acts of

Apr. 20 —Third Force Bill passed by Congress.   terrorism committed to prevent blacks from voting. Klan gradually declined.

1872

June 30 —Freedmen's Bureau phased out of existence.

Nov. 5 —U. S. Grant, Republican, defeats Liberal Republican Horace Greeley (Democrats had also nominated Greeley).

1874

Dec. 7 —Vicksburg Riots—70 blacks killed.

1875

Mar. 1 —Civil Rights Act.   —Black guaranteed equal access to and treament in public places.

1876

Nov. —Result of Presidential election between Republican Rutherford B. Hayes and Democrat Samuel J. Tilden is disputed.   —Tilden polled more popular votes than Hayes, but both candidates claimed to have won the electoral votes of South Carolina, Louisiana, and Florida.

1877

Jan. —Congress creates a special electoral commission to decide which candidate won the Presidential election.   —Republican-dominated electoral commission gave the disputed electoral votes of South Carolina, Louisiana, and Florida to Hayes.

Feb. —Hayes declared the winner of the Presidential election by the Electoral Commission.

Mar. —Congress accepts the decision of the Electoral Commission, and Hayes is inaugurated.   —Combination of Southern Democrats and Northern Republicans forced Congressional approval of the Electoral Commission's decision.

Apr. —President Hayes removes the last of the Federal troops from South Carolina and Louisiana.   —Reconstruction ended. Removal of Federal troops. Reestablishment of conservative white control of southern state governments.

Ruins of Richmond, April, 1865—Fleeing Confederates blew up the city.

18   THE FREEDMEN'S BUREAU

Disagreement over what the objectives and powers of the Freedmen's Bureau should be preceded its actual foundation. Disagreement over its accomplishments has continued ever since it was discontinued.

William Darrah (Pig Iron) Kelley (1814–1890), a Republican Congressman from Pennsylvania, was a lifelong opponent of slavery and a strong supporter of the Radical Republican program of Reconstruction. Kelley's speech, delivered on behalf of the bill establishing the Freedmen's Bureau, reveals what one of its earliest supporters hoped it would accomplish.

The text of the law establishing the Freedmen's Bureau in 1865 describes the functions and responsibilities which Congress assigned to the new agency.

While reading the following selections, keep these questions in mind:

1. According to Kelley, why was a Federal agency such as the Freedmen's Bureau necessary?

2. In what branch of government will the Freedmen's Bureau be located? Who will administer it?

3. What are the responsibilities and functions of the Freedmen's Bureau as prescribed by law?

William Darrah Kelley, Speech on Freedmen's Bureau, February 23, 1864

The future welfare of the freedmen demands their employment on confiscated lands. They must not be permitted to contract habits of idleness, indolence, and vagrancy. The welfare of the people of the North demands it. They need the commodities produced on southern lands. Northern industry is

C54

paralyzed by the want of cotton which will be produced on these fields and by the labor of the Negro freedmen.

The country, the world, humanity at large, needs the labor of these freedmen upon the broad lands abandoned by rebel owners, and I beg the house to pass this bill as the sure means of securing present blessings and future peace and national prosperity.

*Pecuniary** advantage to ourselves is a mean argument to suggest; but let me ask whether the men of the Northwest do not wish to create millions of consumers, liberal consumers, of their great staples? I know that Pennsylvania and New England will not complain if these four million Negro freedmen who have been non-consumers of Northern products shall send each fall and spring to buy the products of Northern workshops. It will do the North no harm to see these freedmen and their families in houses, rather than in dog-hutches called "slave quarters"; to know that they have carpets upon their floors, furniture in their rooms and Yankee clocks upon their mantels.

Mr. Speaker, this is not a political bill. It is required by the *exigencies** of the case. We are in the midst of a revolution, and it is no answer . . . to say that there has never been a Freedmen's Bureau before.

Pecuniary: relating to money.

Exigencies: immediate needs or demands.

Adapted from Wm. Darrah Kelley, speaking in the House of Representatives, Tuesday, February 23, 1864, on H. R. No. 51—"To Establish a Bureau of Freedmen's Affairs."

The Act to Establish the Freedmen's Bureau, March 3, 1865

An Act to establish a Bureau for the Relief of Freedmen and Refugees: Be it enacted, That there is hereby established in the War Department, to continue during the present war of rebellion, and for one year thereafter, a bureau of refugees, freedmen, and abandoned lands, to which shall be committed, as hereinafter provided, the supervision and management of all abandoned lands, and the control of all subjects relating to refugees and freedmen from rebel states, or from any district within the territory embraced in the operations of the army, under such rules and regulations as may be prescribed by the head of the bureau and approved by the President. . . .

. . . The Secretary of War may direct such issues of provisions, clothing, and fuel, as he may deem needful for the immediate and temporary shelter and supply of destitute and suffering refugees and freedmen and their wives and children, under such rules and regulations as he may direct. . . .

. . . The *Commissioner,** under the direction of the President, shall have authority to set apart, for the use of loyal refugees and freedmen, such tracts of land within the insurrectionary states as shall have been abandoned, or to which the United States shall have acquired title by confiscation or sale, or otherwise, and to every male citizen, whether refugee or freedman, as aforesaid, there shall be assigned not more than forty acres of such land, and the person to whom it was so assigned shall be protected in the use and enjoyment of the land for the term of three years. . . . At the end of said term, or at any time during said term, the occupants of any parcels so assigned may purchase the land and receive such title thereto as the United States can convey, upon paying the value of the land, as ascertained and fixed for the purpose of determining the annual rent. . . .

General Oliver Otis Howard (1830–1909): first Commissioner of the Freedmen's Bureau in 1865, provided more than twenty million rations of food to freedmen and refugees in the South.

Statutes at Large, Treaties, and Proclamations of the United States of America, Dec. 1863–Dec. 1865.

1860

Civil War and Reconstruction
Posters of Presidential Campaigns

1864

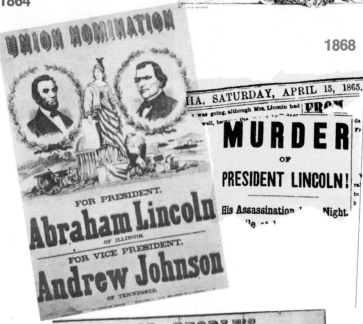

1868

1872

1876

6

Freedmen's Bureau School,
Richmond Virginia, 1866

Library of Congress

7

Political Meeting of Southern
Negroes, 1868

Library of Congress

8

The First Vote

Library of Congress

9 Jury Duty in the South, 1867

Library of Congress

Library of Congress

10 Black Congressional Delegates, 1870–1872 Standing: Representatives Robert C. De Large, South Carolina; Jefferson H. Long, Georgia. Seated: Senator H. R. Revels, Mississippi; Representatives Benjamin S. Turner, Alabama; Josiah T. Walls, Florida; Joseph H. Rainy, South Carolina; and R. Brown Elliot, South Carolina

10 What historians have said

Analyzing Historical Judgments

Introduction

Objectives of this assignment are to:

—Analyze selections from work of three modern historians of the Reconstruction Era for similarities and differences.

—Make a judgment between conflicting historical interpretations of Reconstruction Era.

—Draw inferences about nature of history and history writing from analysis of conflicting historical interpretations.

Few periods in American history have captured more attention from historians in recent years than the Reconstruction Era. Interest has focused especially on the objectives of Congressional Reconstruction policy and the motives of Radical Republicans in pursuing them.

Some historians have judged the record of Reconstruction as a genuine effort to integrate black freedmen into postwar American social, political, and economic life. Others have pronounced that record a series of halfhearted and halfway measures intended to keep the Radical Republicans in power by buying Negro votes.

The issues in this disagreement among historians are not easily resolved, because the reasons underlying political behavior are so complex. Yet complex or not, the issues involved in this disagreement among historians are so important that scholars are continually trying to resolve them.

This assignment concludes your work on the Civil War and Reconstruction by examining selections by three well-known professional historians.

19 E. MERTON COULTER ON RADICAL RECONSTRUCTION

Ellis Merton Coulter was born in North Carolina in 1890 and was educated at the Universities of North Carolina and Wisconsin. A distinguished scholar in his field, Professor Coulter taught American history for many years at the University of Georgia. He was also known as a lecturer and visiting scholar at various American universities. A respected historian of the South and of the Confederacy, who has had a particular interest in the agricultural development of his native region, Professor Coulter retired in 1958.

The selection included below is taken from Professor Coulter's "The South During Reconstruction, 1865–1877". It was published by Louisiana State University Press in 1947 as part of its series, A History of the South.

While reading this selection, keep these questions in mind. According to Coulter:

1. Who was responsible for the condition of the freedmen immediately after the Civil War?

2. What was the northern attitude toward Negro suffrage?

3. Why did Radical Republicans want to give the vote to the freedmen?

The Bankruptcy of Radical Reconstruction

The freedmen were not responsible for what they were; for what they were not the South was no more to blame than the North. The problem of the Negro was one of the greatest produced by the war, yet the North in dealing with it increased rather than diminished its difficulty. By assuming the Negro to be entirely different from what he actually was, the North acted as if there were no problem at all. . . . Instead of studying his condition—intellectual, social, and economic—and working out a five-year or a ten-year or even a lifetime program, the Radical leaders took up the Negro as a makeweight in their own political and economic schemes . . . they left the Negro worse off than when they picked him up. He was now left on the doorstep of the Southerners, who were to bear the responsibilities of his presence but were not permitted freedom in solving the riddle. . . .

Instead of helping the Negro the Radical leaders praised him. They sought to capture his sympathy and support, not by providing him with an education and land at national expense, but by telling him how civilized he already was and how well prepared he was to take over the rulership of the country he occupied. Such a program bankrupted the Radicals of their integrity, but it cost no money. . . .

To build a house without foundations was first on the Radical program. The freedmen should be given the vote to protect themselves and to guarantee the results of the war—those results being in the secret minds of the Radicals the perpetuation of their political power. . . . If the Radicals had thought that the South had been conquered sufficiently to join their party, they would have had no interest in giving the Negroes the vote. . . . The visionary reformers seemed to think that the ballot had miraculous properties, that the most ignorant and irresponsible Negroes could raise themselves by this simple device to dizzy heights of social betterment.

. . . The fact that the North "rejected and scorned" Negro suffrage for itself was considered by the Radicals insufficient reason why it should not be good for the South. There were so few Negroes in the former section that their voting could have no effect, but in the South there were great opportunities for it to work changes. Only six Northern states permitted it; Connecticut, Wisconsin, and Minnesota rejected it in 1865; and Kansas later voted it down by a 50,000 majority.

❁   ❁   ❁   ❁   ❁

Radical Reconstruction was doomed to fail. With a crass, materialistic design, it was cloaked in a garb of high idealistic justice, but its rulers were inexperienced, ignorant, and corrupt. They forgot what the world had learned

Millennium: a period of a thousand years of happiness and righteousness prophesied in the Bible.

Utopias: Unrealizable ideals about society.

From E. Merton Coulter, "The South During Reconstruction, 1865–1877", **A History of the South** (Louisiana: Louisiana State University Press, 1947) Vol. VIII, pp. 55–58, 162.

and experienced during the preceding two thousand years. *Millenniums and Utopias** might be written about, but intelligent people knew that they were never to be realized in this life.

20 CARL N. DEGLER ON RADICAL RECONSTRUCTION

Professor Carl Degler has had a special interest in the history of black Americans. You have studied his interpretation of the legal status of black people in seventeenth-century colonial America. The selection below is taken from Professor Degler's Out of Our Past, a well-received interpretive work on the forces and ideas that have shaped America, which was published in 1959.

While reading the following selection, keep these questions in mind. According to Degler:

1. What was the status of the Negro in the North when the Civil War ended?

2. What was the status of the Negro in the South when the Civil War ended?

3. What happened to the status of Negroes during Reconstruction?

Reconstruction: A Radical Achievement

As the war overturned American thinking about slavery and the nature of the Union, so the Reconstruction reeducated the American people on the place the Negro should occupy in the United States. When the war ended, the position of the newly freed black man was *ambiguous** throughout the nation. In the North, though he was a citizen, society discriminated against him, and he was denied the ballot in all states except New York and five in New England. . . . In the South, the Negro's ambiguous position was summed up in the fact that he was neither a slave nor a citizen.

But within half a decade, under the driving will of the Radical Republicans all this was reversed. The adoption of the Fourteenth and Fifteenth Amendments to the Constitution signified that the Negro was now to be a full citizen, equal in civil rights and voting privileges with white men. Insofar as modern Americans take pride from this inclusion of the Negro in the American dream of equality and opportunity, then it is to the Radicals that they are indebted. For it was solely because of the Radicals' control over the South that the requisite number of states were brought to ratify the two amendments. If not written into the Constitution then, when the conservative South was powerless to resist and the North was still *imbued** with its mission of reform, then the principle of Negro equality would probably never have been included in the national charter. This achievement of the Radicals is at least as much a part of the legacy of Reconstruction as the better-known corruption and the imposition of alien rule.

Ambiguous: doubtful, uncertain.

Imbued: inspired by, filled by.

From Carl N. Degler, **Out of Our Past,** Revised Edition (New York: Harper & Row, Publishers, 1970), pp. 209–210.

C62

21 LAWANDA AND JOHN H. COX ON THE MOTIVES OF RADICAL REPUBLICANS

LaWanda Cox was born in Aberdeen, Washington, and was educated at the Universities of Oregon and California. She received her doctorate in history from the latter institution in 1941, and has taught American history for many years at Hunter College. With her husband, John H., a Professor of History at City College, New York, Professor Cox has co-authored several important articles and a book on the Reconstruction period.

The selection below is taken from an article which the Coxes published in The Journal of Southern History in 1967.

While reading the following selection, keep these questions in mind:

1. How did the Fifteenth Amendment affect suffrage throughout the nation?

2. Why was the question of equal Negro suffrage politically dangerous to the Republican Party in the North?

3. How did the Civil War and Reconstruction affect the Democratic Party?

The Motives of Radical Republicans: A Test Case

. . . We should like to suggest that Republican party leadership played a crucial role in committing this nation to equal suffrage for the Negro not because of political *expediency*° but <u>despite</u> political risk. An incontestable fact of Reconstruction history suggests this view. Race prejudice was so strong in the North that the issue of equal Negro suffrage constituted a clear and present danger to Republicans. White backlash may be a recently coined phrase, but it was a *virulent*° political phenomenon in the 1860's. The exploitation of prejudice by the Democratic opposition was blatant and unashamed.

Expediency: advantageous to oneself or one's cause.

Virulent: dangerously powerful.

The power base of the Republican party lay in the North. However much party leaders desired to break through sectional boundaries to create a national image or to gain some measure of security from Southern votes, victory or defeat in the presidential elections of the nineteenth century lay in the Northern states.

    ✿   ✿   ✿   ✿   ✿

In short, Republican sponsorship of Negro suffrage meant flirtation with political disaster in the North, particularly in any one or all of the seven pivotal states (Ohio, Indiana, Illinois, Pennsylvania, New York, New Jersey, Connecticut) where both the prejudice of race and the Democratic opposition were strong. . . . Negroes were denied equal suffrage in every one of these critically important seven, and only in New York did they enjoy a partial enfranchisement. If Negroes were to be equally enfranchised, as the Fifteenth Amendment directed, it is true that Republicans could count upon support from an overwhelming majority of the new voters. It does not neces-

Enticing: attractive, alluring.

sarily follow, however, that this prospect was *enticing** to "shrewd politicians." What simple political computation could add the number of potential Negro voters to be derived from a minority population that reached a high of 3.4 per cent in New Jersey . . . ; determine and subtract the probable number of white voters who would be alienated [from the Republican party by their support of the Fifteenth Amendment] . . . and predict a balance that would ensure Republican victory?

✿   ✿   ✿   ✿   ✿

From whatever angle of vision they are examined, election returns in the seven pivotal states give no support to the assumption that the enfranchisement of the Northern Negroes would help Republicans in their struggle to maintain control of Congress and the Presidency. This conclusion holds for all of the North.

✿   ✿   ✿   ✿   ✿

The nature of the Fifteenth Amendment also suggests the inadequacy of the view that its purpose was to make permanent Republican control of the South. The amendment did not constitute a guarantee for the continuance of Radical Republican regimes, and this fact was recognized at the time. What it did was to commit the nation, not to universal, but to impartial suffrage. . . . A number of Republican politicians, South and North, who measured it in terms of political arithmetic, were not happy with the formulation of the amendment. They recognized that under its provisions the Southern Negro vote could be reduced to political impotence by *literacy tests** and other qualifications, ostensibly equal.

Literacy tests: many states instituted laws requiring minimal skills in reading as a requirement for voting in elections.

✿   ✿   ✿   ✿   ✿

The motives of congressmen doubtless were mixed, but in a period of national crisis when the issue of equality was basic to political contention, it is just possible that party advantage was subordinated to principle. . . . During the years of Civil War and Reconstruction, race prejudice was institutionalized in the Democratic party. Perhaps this very fact, plus the jibes of inconsistency and hypocrisy with which Democrats derided their opponents, helped to create the party unity that committed Republicans, and through them the nation, to equal suffrage irrespective of race.

From LaWanda and John H. Cox, "Negro Suffrage and Republican Politics: The Problem of Motivation in Reconstruction Historiography," **The Journal of Southern History,** XXXIII (August, 1967), pp. 303–330.

Additional Reading

Bruce Catton, *A Stillness at Appomattox.* Garden City, New York: Doubleday, 1954

Bruce Catton, *This Hallowed Ground.* Garden City, New York: Doubleday, 1956

Clifford Dowdey, *The Land They Fought For.* Garden City, New York: Doubleday, 1955

J. C. Furnas, *The Road to Harper's Ferry.* New York: W. Sloane Associates, 1959

Carl Sandburg, *Lincoln: The Prairie Years and the War Years.* New York: Harcourt Brace and Co., 1954

Bell Wiley, *The Life of Johnny Reb.* New York: The Bobbs-Merrill Co., 1943

Bell Wiley, *The Life of Billy Yank.* Indianapolis: The Bobbs-Merrill Co., 1952

UNIT EIGHT

Making of Industrial America

PHILIP GLEASON

> *The snail's pace of crawling ages has suddenly become the headlong rush of the locomotive, speeding faster and faster....*
>
> HENRY GEORGE

1 The great transformation

Industry Remakes American Society

Introduction

Objectives of this assignment are to:

—Describe concept of rational- ization as defined in this assign- ment.

—Identify a hypothesis about America's industrial advantages in given reading.

—Draw inferences from chart of economic and social data about American industrial growth, 1860–1910.

—Test your hypothesis about America's industrial advantages with the data on the chart and with the inferences you have drawn from it.

American life in the 1970's has been profoundly shaped by industrialism. Without knowing something about industrialization and its effects, we can- not possibly understand the society in which we live. The assignments in this Unit will help you gain that understanding by looking at industrialization historically. These assignments deal with the years between 1860 and 1910— a period in which industrialization took root and remade American society.

How Industrialism Shapes Our Lives

What does it mean to say that industrialization has profoundly shaped our lives? Let's see if an example can make that statement more concrete.

The book you are now reading is a typical product of industrial society. What can we learn about industrialism by looking more closely at this book and how it was made?

The first thing to note is that we take it for granted. Ordinarily you wouldn't give a second thought to how the book came into being and got into your hands. We are so accustomed to industrial civilization that we don't even stop to notice how it affects us. The same is true of many other features of industrial life. What we must do in studying industrialization is try to look into the background of familiar things like textbooks and see what has made them the way they are.

Secondly, your book was made by machines and factories. Raw materials like wood and metals have been turned into paper, ink, and print. Printing presses are large, complicated machines. Smaller, complicated machines like typewriters and cameras also played a part in the making of this book. In other words, this book and everything else we read are products of industrial technology.

But machines do not run themselves. Even computers, which we some- times call "thinking" machines, do not build and run themselves. Industrial civilization depends on a tremendous variety of human skills. The making of even a small, everyday item like this book requires the cooperation of a large number of people with different skills. For instance, historians do the research and write the story; editors make their writing more readable; artists design the layout and put the illustrations where they belong; and photographers, printers, and bookbinders contribute their skills.

C66

Cooperation by all these skilled workers points up another feature of industrial civilization: namely, that it requires a high degree of careful organization. The machine must be put together carefully if it is to operate properly. In a factory, machines that perform different parts of the manufacturing process must be positioned for efficiency. Otherwise the raw material would not move smoothly through the sequence of stages that turns it into a finished product.

Cooperation on Many Fronts

The need for organization does not stop at the factory gate. In making this book, the historians had to finish their work before the editors could begin their tasks. The layout artists must wait for the editors to finish. The printing comes after all the preceding stages. Only after this can the salesmen begin their part of the work, since the distribution of goods (including books) through marketing channels is part of the industrial system.

Thus the making of a book involves careful organization and the dovetailing of one part of the process into the next according to a strict schedule. Time and scheduling therefore take on greater importance in the industrial era than in earlier days. All of us find our lives regulated by the clock and the calendar. The primitive tribesman or peasant farmer was guided by the sun and the seasons. But we have deadlines to meet. We must be at school or at our office "on time." A bus or plane leaves on schedule. If we're not there, we miss it. Just as we miss a favorite TV program if we tune in too late. Time is vital.

Since you are reading this book, you know that all deadlines were met. That part of the organization worked. Something else had to be organized in order to produce this book—money.

It costs a great deal of money to make a textbook and get it into the hands of students. The paper and binding must be paid for. The machines that do the typing and printing must either be bought or hired. Advertising costs money. Salesmen must be paid, along with editors, artists, printers, and everybody else. Even historians like to receive some compensation for their long labor.

Where does all this money come from? In the end, of course, it comes from the sale of the book. If the books a publishing company puts out do not sell in sufficient numbers, the publisher cannot stay in business. But sales come at the end of the line, and the income from sales is not available to meet the costs incurred in making and distributing the book. The money needed along the way must come from prior income, from savings, or from borrowing.

The most common way of organizing the financial resources, called capital, (that is, bringing the necessary money together) is through the corporation. A corporation is a business organization formed to manufacture some product (e.g., automobiles) or to perform some service, such as providing life insurance. It accumulates capital by selling securities, or stocks and bonds.

In buying a share of stock in a corporation an individual is investing his money in a firm which he thinks will do a profitable business. If it does, he will share in the profits according to the amount he has invested in it. If it loses money, there will be no profits to share. In buying a bond, an individual is lending his money to the corporation. In return, he receives a fixed rate of interest rather than a share in the profits.

Ginn and Company

The firm which published this book is Ginn and Company. Ginn and Company was founded as a one-man company by Edwin Ginn in Boston in 1867. The firm soon became a partnership. The partnership was the usual form of business organization before the Civil War.

In the late nineteenth century, the corporation really came into its own. Businessmen found they could more easily bring together the capital they needed by selling shares to many investors rather than relying on a handful of partners. As the economy continued to grow, many corporations found it necessary or advisable to merge with other corporations.

These mergers were usually between firms in the same line of business. The resulting combinations were popularly called *"trusts."** Many people feared the trusts because these great combinations were so rich and powerful. They were often accused of trying to monopolize the market by eliminating competitors and of gouging the public by the high prices they charged.

In spite of public opposition, the trend toward business combinations continued in the twentieth century. Ginn and Company, which adopted the corporation form of organization in 1939, has recently become part of an even larger combination, the Xerox Corporation.

When Ginn and Company was founded in 1867, the public school system was in its infancy. But Edwin Ginn believed the market for textbooks would expand because he thought the schools would continue to grow. He was right, of course. An industrial society absolutely has to have educated people. The skills needed to make the system work must all be learned. The organization and planning that go into making a book, an airplane, or a TV program require brainwork. Industrialization demands brainpower much more than muscle power. One of the tasks of schools is to develop that brainpower.

Thus, both your textbook and the school in which you use it are part and parcel of industrialization.

One Kind of Change Leads to Another

The example of this textbook suggests that industrialization involves much more than manufacturing. The results of industrialization are all around us. Transportation, agriculture, labor, the quality of life in our cities, immigration, architecture, art, and even our school system have all been deeply affected by industrialization. Furthermore, changes in one area lead to changes in other areas. As inquirers you should try to learn as much as you can about the *connections* between these changes.

Strictly speaking, a **trust** was a specific type of business combination which brought several independent companies together under unified control. John D. Rockefeller's Standard Oil Trust of 1882 was first of the type. In common usage, trust came to mean any giant firm or group of firms having monopolistic tendencies.

For example, the development of railroads not only improved transportation but also affected agriculture and immigration. Changes in immigration affected the quality of life in our cities and required changes in our school system. The expansion of our cities forced changes in architectural styles and in our ideas of what was beautiful and useful. Industrialization affected all of society and there were links between developments that may seem, at first, to be entirely unrelated.

The Case of Chicago

The variety of changes inspired by industrialization and the interconnection between them is perhaps best illustrated by the history of Chicago from 1860 to 1910. The most obvious change in Chicago during these years was in size. Chicago's population multiplied twenty-two times between 1860 and 1910 (from 100,000 to 2,200,000).*

Many of these new Chicagoans came to the city by train, for it was a great rail center. The railroads spurred both population growth and economic growth. Because it was a hub of transportation close to rich agricultural regions, Chicago attracted new industries such as meat-packing and farm-equipment manufacturing. These and other growing firms drew multitudes of workers to the city.

The new Chicagoans came from surrounding or worn-out farms and earlier settlements, especially from the East. The railroads and technological improvements in farm machinery brought about a revolution in agriculture. Farmers who couldn't keep up with the changes often decided to move to town and look for work in factories, offices, or stores.

Other newcomers traveled longer distances. Chicago and its jobs beckoned immigrants from as far away as Sweden, Poland, and Italy. The new steamships and railroads made it easier to get there. By 1910 the city was a great melting pot of many immigrant nationalities. Thirty-six percent of its population was foreign-born, and another forty-two percent were born in this country of immigrant parents. After having been peasant farmers, these immigrants now found themselves part of an industrial society which required many changes in their way of life.

Chicago also was changed by the coming of the immigrants. No city could absorb such a tremendous influx without running into all sorts of problems, from fire-protection to education. Chicago was devastated by fire in 1871, was rebuilt, and went ahead to even faster growth. Other problems didn't stop the city, either. Reformers attacked one urban evil after another—slum housing, political corruption and poor schools. The reformers didn't always overcome the problems they tackled, but they helped to change Chicago.

In spite of all its problems the people of Chicago were proud of their city. They were proud that Chicago architects pioneered in building skyscrapers. All the great cities needed tall buildings which could bring large numbers of people together on small ground space. The "Chicago School" of architecture showed how such structures could be made beautiful as well as useful.

Only nine American cities had a population of 100,000 or more in 1860. By 1910, fifty cities were this large.

C69

Architecture was not the only form of art in which Chicago pioneered. We don't usually think of industrialism and poetry as going together, but they did in the "Windy City." Poetry, the most influential magazine of verse in the country, was established there in 1912. Four years later Carl Sandburg wrote a famous poem in which he praised Chicago as:

> Hog Butcher for the World,
> Tool Maker, Stacker of Wheat,
> Player with Railroads and the Nation's Freight
>   Handler;
> Stormy, husky, brawling,
> City of the Big Shoulders. . . .

From "Chicago" from **Chicago Poems** by Carl Sandburg. Copyright 1916 by Holt, Rinehart and Winston, Inc. Copyright 1944 by Carl Sandburg. Reprinted by permission of Holt, Rinehart and Winston, Inc.

From population growth to poetry, all these changes were linked with industrialization. What was true of Chicago was true elsewhere, so be alert for interconnections as you study this Unit.

A New Concept

Explaining the complex changes occurring in American society during the last half of the nineteenth century is not easy. Finding parallels or similarities between what happened to transportation, agriculture, labor, immigration, urban life, and education in America between 1860 and 1910 requires imagination. One such highly imaginative concept that social scientists have developed in order to explain the processes of economic and social change in a society undergoing industrialization is called *rationalization*.

We don't use the word rationalization very often in conversation. When we do, it usually means something like an excuse—that is, an explanation which sounds reasonable for some action we have taken, even though it may not be the true explanation.

This is not what rationalization means in this Unit. Here, rationalization means systematic organization according to a carefully thought-out plan.

If you look back at the discussion of the textbook as an illustration of industrial society, you will see that it mentions careful organization of skilled labor, scheduling of activities, and organization of money. Without this kind of systematic organization, industrial development in nineteenth-century America would have been impossible. Without this kind of systematic organization, life as we know it today in the United States would be much different. Systematic organization is characteristic of industrial societies throughout the world. As used in this Unit, rationalization is the process through which this systematic organization of resources, labor, and money is carried out.

The next assignment takes up the concept of rationalization in greater detail. You should try to get as clear an idea as possible of what it is and how it works, for the concept comes up again in later assignments. Rationalization does not explain everything there is to know about industrialization. But it is a very useful concept and can be applied to other areas of historical inquiry.

1 WHY DID INDUSTRIALIZATION TAKE PLACE SO RAPIDLY IN THE U.S.?

The *Industrial Revolution** began in England in the middle of the eighteenth century. A hundred years later, in 1860, Great Britain still stood at the forefront of the manufacturing nations, followed by France and Germany. The United States was in fourth place. By 1900, however, the United States had taken over first place and was producing almost twice as much as second-place England.

Natural resources, labor, and capital were of very great importance in accounting for America's rapid industrialization. Yet by themselves they would not have guaranteed rapid economic growth. Human energies had to be set in motion before that could happen. What was it that sparked the vital explosion of human energy?

Questions like this are harder to answer than questions about raw materials or the role of foreign investment. Many observers believed, however, that the social attitudes of Americans, their political system, and their cultural values played a key role.

While studying the chart of comparative social and economic statistics and reading a selection in which Edward Atkinson, a Boston cotton manufacturer, analyzes American industrial growth, keep these questions in mind:

1. Which categories show the greatest rate of increase?

2. Which categories show the least rate of increase?

3. What does Atkinson identify as America's chief industrial advantage over England?

4. How does Atkinson account for America's having such an advantage?

The term **Industrial Revolution** was coined in the 19th century by French writers. They regarded the economic changes in England as being comparable to the political changes brought about in their country by the French Revolution. The term industrialism came into use around 1830 and industrialize in the 1880's.

Comparative Statistics of American Population and Industrial Growth, 1860–1910

		1860	1910
1.	Total population	31,513,000	92,407,000
2.	Rural population	25,226,803	49,973,334
3.	Urban population	6,216,518	41,998,932
4.	Foreign-born population	4,096,753	13,344,545
5.	Farm work force	6,208,000	11,592,000
6.	Non-farm work force	4,325,000	25,779,000
7.	Bituminous coal production (tons)	20,471,000 (1870)	417,111,000
8.	Railroad mileage	30,626	240,293
9.	Applications for patents on inventions	7,653	63,293
10.	Daily newspapers	387	2,600

From Bureau of the Census, **Historical Statistics of the United States, Colonial Times to 1957** (Washington: U. S. Govt. Printing Office, 1960).

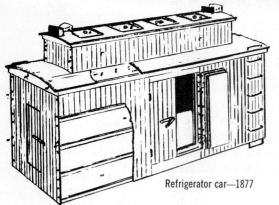

Refrigerator car—1877

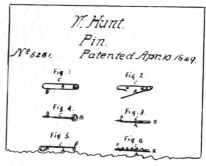

Sewing machine—1846

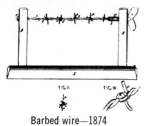

Barbed wire—1874

Telephone—1876

The early inventions on this page show how American technology began. The inventions gained popularity because they made life easier for everyone, reaching the stage of advancement and refinement we know today.

Adapted from Edward Atkinson, "Report on the Cotton Manufacturers of the United States," in **Tenth Census of the United States, 1880, Manufactures** (Washington: U. S. Govt. Printing Office, 1883), pp. 949–951.

Edward Atkinson Explains Why American Industry Has Grown, 1880

In our industrial competition with England it is often said that our chief advantage lies in our versatility and our capacity for adapting means to ends. Another way of putting it is to say that our working people are very quick to see the desirability of using new processes or inventions and are equally quick to adopt them.

If it is true that we have this advantage, there must be special causes for it. I would suggest the following explanation:

First, our system of common and purely secular schools which are attended by the children of rich and poor alike. The schools are thoroughly democratic. In them each pupil learns that it depends on himself alone what place he may take in life. The habits of cleanliness, order, and respect for authority which are developed in the schools also help to make good workmen. In addition, the schools give every pupil some knowledge of the geography and resources of the country. This knowledge tends to make working people more willing to move from place to place—every boy believes he can achieve success somewhere else, if not at home.

Second, the system of manhood suffrage which gives every man the right to vote. In spite of its abuses, this system of self-government works distinctly in the direction of safety, stability, and order in the community.

Third, the ease with which land may be acquired. This provides an incentive to economy and induces habits of saving that are of great importance in their effect on society.

Fourth, the great number of small savings banks which encourage industriousness and thrift.

Fifth, the absence of a standing army. Because of this, the proceeds of taxation are, on the whole, usefully and productively expended. And very few of our young men are withdrawn from productive labor to serve in the army.

It is obvious that even the least imaginative will be affected by these influences. Versatility and readiness to adopt laborsaving devices will be promoted by them. Indeed, such attitudes will be absolutely forced into action, when such vast areas are to be occupied, and when even the dullest boy is educated in the belief that he is one of those who are to build up this nation to the full measure of its high calling.

2 Rationalization

*The Concept and Its Application
to Industrialization*

Introduction

You were introduced to the concept of rationalization in the preceding assignment. Here we shall look into it more closely and see how it applies to the development of an industrial society.

Suppose your class were called upon to present a program on ecology, or pollution and the environmental crisis. How would you go about it?

At first there would probably be a certain amount of rather confused and aimless discussion. The problem of industrial wastes would come up, no doubt. Someone would mention automobile exhaust fumes. Another might talk about the dangers of massive application of pesticides. But eventually someone would say: "We could go on talking forever. It's time to get this thing organized!" To get your program moving you would have to organize it systematically according to a carefully thought-out plan. This systematic organization which we will describe here is termed *rationalization*.

To organize systematically, you would have to do some hard thinking. For instance, you would have to decide just what kind of program you wanted. Would it focus on the local community or would it try to cover the national scene? Would you bring in guest experts, or use students as speakers? Would you want to use slides or films?

If the class chose to focus on pollution as a national issue, it would have to decide how to proceed. The tasks required to put on your program would have to be identified, and the responsibilities for performing them assigned to individuals. In other words, you would have to work out a *division of labor*.

Perhaps certain individuals would develop a knack for setting up effective visual displays. Others might build special equipment to show how pollution affects living things. Still others might prepare or distribute literature to your audience. By performing only one kind of task each person would become a *specialist*, increasing productivity and efficiency.

Suppose your class were asked to provide teams to present your ecology program to several other schools. Written procedures, or guidelines, would have to be prepared to ensure that each team would cover the same subject matter in its presentation. In other words, your materials, such as script, slides, or films, would have to be *standardized*.

Your presentation teams may discover through feedback that their audiences prefer learning about local, rather than national, pollution problems.

Objectives of this assignment are to:

—Recall and describe the concept of rationalization learned in the previous assignment.

—Describe six aspects of concept of rationalization defined in text which help explain industrial growth.

—Draw inferences about rationalization of industrial enterprises from filmstrip of industrial activities.

—Summarize effect of rationalizing activity on mass production and mass distribution.

C73

You would then have to *recombine* and *coordinate* the elements of your presentation to emphasize local concerns.

In a modest way you have rationalized the organization, preparation, and presentation of your ecology program much the same as nineteenth-century American industrialists and managers rationalized their business problems. *Like them, you analyzed your capabilities, assigned a division of labor, encouraged specialization, standardized the elements making up your program, and recombined and coordinated them into a new presentation that more people wanted to hear.*

The Scope of Rationalization

The basic notion of rationalization—the application of reason to the organization of human activities—is in itself fairly simple and straightforward. However, it can get rather complicated when we begin to apply it.

The fact that rationalization is such a general concept is something else that it makes it more difficult to grasp fully. Because it is such a broad and inclusive idea, we do not see all its applications immediately. In fact, the longer one works with the idea of rationalization, the more areas he will discover in which rationalization may be applied.

Max Weber lived from 1864 to 1920. His most famous work concerns the relationship between Protestantism and the development of capitalism.

The man who first identified the concept of rationalization and called attention to its importance was the great German sociologist, *Max Weber.* He saw rationalization as a key concept in understanding the development of Western civilization. He traced its operation in economic life, in politics, and even in such improbable areas as music.

Our concern is much more limited. In this assignment, we will try to clarify the concept as it relates to the manufacture and distribution of goods in American industrial society. As we take up other topics later, rationalization will come up again in a variety of applications and contexts.

As we noted earlier, rationalization does not explain everything. But it is a useful concept for analyzing and understanding industrialization and its effects on society. It should also help you to tie together developments in different areas and to see connections that you might otherwise have missed.

2   RATIONALIZING THE METHODS OF PRODUCTION

The replacement of small shops and household manufactures by the factory system is one of the hallmarks of industrialism. The factory system was introduced in England, but was carried to its highest degree of perfection in the United States in what we know as mass production.

Mass production is much more complicated than merely increasing the quantity of production. It involves coordinating the division of labor and standardization with the *moving assembly line.* It involves also the further coordination of standardization with *scheduling,* or the timing of different parts of the manufacturing process.

Although no single individual invented mass production, Henry Ford made a greater contribution to it than anyone else.

While reading Ford's description of how the assembly-line technique was introduced to automobile manufacturing, keep these questions in mind:

1. Where did the idea of a moving assembly line for automobile manufacturing come from?

2. How many aspects of Henry Ford's rationalization of automobile manufacturing can you identify?

3. How did Henry Ford's rationalization of magneto assembling and motor assembling affect production?

Henry Ford Describes the Assembly Line

Along about April 1, 1913, we first tried the experiment of an assembly line. We tried it on assembling the fly-wheel *magneto.* ° . . .

I believe that this was the first moving line ever installed. The idea came in a general way from the overhead trolley that the Chicago packers use in dressing beef. We had previously assembled the fly-wheel magneto in the usual method. With one workman doing a complete job he could turn out from thirty-five to forty pieces in a nine-hour day, or about twenty minutes to an assembly. What he did alone was then spread into twenty-nine operations; that cut down the assembly time to thirteen minutes, ten seconds. Then we raised the height of the line eight inches—this was in 1914—and cut the time to seven minutes. Further experimenting with the speed that the work should move at cut the time down to five minutes. In short, the result is this: by the aid of scientific study one man is now able to do somewhat more than four did only a comparatively few years ago. That line established the efficiency of the method and we now use it everywhere. The assembling of the motor, formerly done by one man, is now divided into eighty-four operations—those men do the work that three times their number formerly did. In a short time we tried out the plan on the *chassis.* ° . . .

It must not be imagined, however, that all this worked out as quickly as it sounds. The speed of the moving work had to be carefully tried out. . . . The chassis assembling line, for example, goes at a pace of six feet per minute; the front axle assembly lines goes at one hundred eighty-nine inches per minute. In the chassis assembling are forty-five separate operations or stations. . . . Some men do only one or two small operations, others do more. The man who places a part does not fasten it—the part may not be fully in place until after several operations later. The man who puts in a bolt does not put on the nut; the man who puts on the nut does not tighten it. On operation number thirty-four the budding motor gets its gasoline; it has previously received lubrication; on operation number forty-four the radiator is filled with water, and on operation number forty-five the car drives out. . . .

Magneto: small generator used in the ignition system of the Model-T Ford, the manufacture of which Henry Ford describes.

Chassis: rectangular steel frame to which the motor and body of the automobile are attached.

Samuel Crowther and Henry Ford, **My Life and Work** (Garden City, New York: Doubleday & Company, Inc., 1922), pp. 81–83.

3 RATIONALIZING THE METHODS OF DISTRIBUTION

The great increases in production brought about by industrialization went hand in hand with drastic changes in distribution. In fact, changes in these two areas were dependent on each other. Mass production could not be carried on unless there was a mass market, and a mass market could not be reached except through improved methods of distribution. Two new methods of mass distribution—the mail-order house and the department store—were developed in the late nineteenth century.

One of the earliest mail-order houses was Montgomery Ward founded in the 1870's. In the next twenty years other firms entered the field, and by the 1890's Sears, Roebuck and Company had become a major competitor.

Aiming at the rural market and making use of low-cost rail transportation and an efficient post office, mail-order companies flooded the countryside with their catalogues. These colorful books pictured the goods that could be purchased by sending pre-paid orders to the company.

The department store was a more important innovation in marketing than the mail-order house. Growing out of the traditional general store, which sold everything for which there was a demand, department stores began appearing in the 1850's. Aimed at the growing urban markets, these stores quickly became the centers of retail trade in most of our large towns and cities.

While reading the following account of the operating methods of Sears, Roebuck and Company in 1906 and the selection comparing a general store with a department store, keep these questions in mind:

1. How many aspects of the rationalization of order-handling by Sears, Roebuck can you identify?

2. Where did general stores flourish longest? Why?

3. How many aspects of the rationalization of department-store operations can you identify?

How Sears, Roebuck Handled Orders, 1906

The great expansion of business around the turn of the century made the task of handling orders much more difficult. In 1906, the company moved into a new forty-five acre plant which had all sorts of equipment to facilitate the movement of goods. There were miles of railroad track, elevators, moving sidewalks, gravity chutes, and pneumatic tubes running around and through the building. A scheduling system was also worked out to put the filling of orders on a strict timetable. As soon as an order was received, it was assigned a fifteen-minute slot within the next forty-eight hours. When the appointed time arrived, the shipment had to be ready to go.

The mailbags containing orders were weighed when they came in. Experience had shown that there were usually forty orders per pound of mail.

The letters were opened at the rate of about 27,000 per hour, by automatic mail-openers developed by the company. Each letter containing an order was given a number. The time the merchandise was due in the shipping-room was stamped on the order, and a bin in the shipping-room was simultaneously reserved for that order for the specified fifteen-minute period.

Orders were then checked to make sure the catalogue number tallied with the description of the goods ordered and to see that the payment enclosed was correct. Notation was made of the manner of remittance; whether by cash, check, or money order. Labels were made out, and tickets for each item in the order were sent to the departments concerned.

All this was done by workers on the early shift before the main body of employees arrived at 8:00 A.M. By that hour, each department manager would have an estimate of the number of orders he would probably have to handle that day. Clerks then selected the specified items of merchandise on any given order from shelves numbered to correspond with the catalogue numbers. Gravity chutes and conveyor belts carried the merchandise to assembly points where it was dropped through chutes into the shipping rooms. There, mechanical conveyors carried the packed orders to loading platforms; precanceled stamps were attached; and the goods were ready to load on the adjacent railhead. Heavy goods shipped from factories owned wholly or partially by the company were, in many instances, shipped on the same or a similar schedule system. The new assembly-line technique aroused great interest. Among those who came to inspect it was Henry Ford.

Adapted from Boris Emmet and John E. Jeuck, **Catalogues and Counters: A History of Sears, Roebuck and Company** (Chicago: The University of Chicago Press, 1950), pp. 132–136.

The General Store and the Department Store

A century ago most Americans did their shopping at a *general store.* These retail outlets flourished longest in rural areas where the local market was too small to support specialized shops carrying only one line of goods.

As its name implied, the general store carried a highly miscellaneous stock —everything from eggs and tablecloths to hardware, rubber boots, and axle grease. The merchandise came from local suppliers and from wholesalers in the nearest city. It was displayed in helter-skelter fashion—in boxes, bins, and glass-fronted counters, on shelves, hanging from hooks, and stacked on the floor.

The proprietor ran the place himself, sometimes with the help of his family or a hired clerk. He waited on trade, kept the books, inspected the samples displayed by traveling salesmen, and put out the cat at closing time. He liked to pass the time of day with his customers, for the general store was a friendly and informal place. Two symbols of its sociable atmosphere entered into the folklore of the "good old days"—the pot-bellied stove and the cracker-barrel philosopher.

The first real department store was founded by R. H. Macy in the 1850's. By 1900 department stores dominated retail selling in the cities and larger towns. The most successful were located in the heart of great urban centers such as New York, Philadelphia, and Chicago.*

Macy's store was in New York, John Wanamaker's in Philadelphia, and Marshall Field's in Chicago.

The department store resembled the general store in the variety of goods it carried. But everything was on a bigger scale and better organized. Each department specialized in a particular line of goods. Each had its own chief, who was called a *buyer*.

The work as well as the merchandise was differentiated and organized for efficiency. The clerks, of course, dealt directly with customers. Specialized functions such as bookkeeping and shipping were the responsibility of separate departments. Various levels of management coordinated the overall operation.

11 Beginning of the Mail-Order Business, Montgomery, Ward, & Co., Inc., 1878   Montgomery, Ward

The department store's success was based on volume sales and rapid turnover. Since it required vast amounts of goods, the department store purchased directly from manufacturers. This eliminated the middlemen, reduced costs, and meant savings for the consumer through lower prices.

Department stores did not have the homey air of the general store. The leisurely gossip around the pot-bellied stove gave way to hurrying crowds of shoppers. The floorwalker replaced the cracker-barrel philosopher. But many shoppers found enjoyment as well as bargains in the bustle, excitement, and many different riches which the department store displayed.

12 Wanamaker's Store, Philadelphia, 1865

13

Hog Butchering and
Packing Cincinnati,
1873

1   2   3   4

8   9

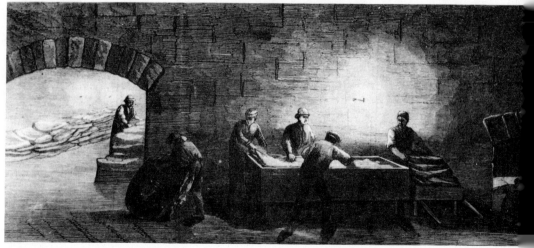

12

5   6   7

10   11

13   14   15

14 Henry Ford's Magneto Assembly Line, 1913

Both photos Courtesy of the Ford Archives, Henry Ford Museum, Dearborn, Michigan

15 Henry Ford's Motor Assembly Line, 1913

3 The railroad age

Interrelationships of an Industrial Society

Introduction

Did you ever notice how often the "ages" we talk about in history take their names from the principal means of transportation used in that period? We speak, for example, of the *Age of Sail,* the *Age of the Automobile,* or the *Air Age.* Most recently, mankind crossed the threshold of the *Space Age.*

We don't usually realize it, but in using terms like these we are proclaiming the social importance of transportation. Getting from place to place seems a very everyday matter. But the means by which we do it can shape the character of an era. This fact was never made clearer than in the *Railroad Age* in the United States.

The great days of the railroad are long past. We must stretch our imaginations to recapture their revolutionary impact and importance. But consider how our society would be changed if land travel and the movement of goods depended either on horse-drawn vehicles or the railroads. Imagine how a society that had known nothing but horse-drawn transportation would respond to the railroad!

In this assignment, we will examine the growth of the railroads and their place in American history in the late nineteenth century.

The Railroad Empire

Railroads were well established in the Northeast before the Civil War. But the great age of expansion came in the quarter-century following the war. Track mileage increased more than fivefold between 1860 and 1890, from 30,626 to 166,703.

The most spectacular achievement was the forging of rail connections between the Pacific Coast and the Mississippi Valley. On May 10, 1869, the Union Pacific and Central Pacific met near Promontory Point, Utah.

By 1893, several additional transcontinental lines had been built.* During the same years, the rail network in the older-settled areas was filled in, and obstacles to efficient use—such as unbridged rivers, or differences in the *gauge of track*—were removed.

The vast distances and tremendous engineering problems of railway construction in the western plains and mountains gripped the imagination of the American people. So did the epic struggles for control of a region between the different roads and their colorful masters. The railroads produced in men

Objectives of this assignment are to:

—Analyze readings on impact of railroads on agriculture, manufacturing, immigration, and growth of cities.

—Draw inferences from picture series on impact of railroads on Indian life.

—Make a judgment on effect of rationalizing activity on railroad management.

The **Great Northern** was completed in 1893. In the 1880's the Northern Pacific reached Portland, Oregon; the Atchison, Topeka & Santa Fe reached Los Angeles; and the Southern Pacific linked California and New Orleans.

The **gauge** of railroad tracks refers to the distance between the rails. The Erie Railroad, for example, had been originally built with a broad gauge of 6'. In the 1870's it shifted to the standard gauge of 4' 8½''.

The Gilded Age (1873) was a novel by Mark Twain and Charles Dudley Warner which satirized the scramble for wealth and influence in post-Civil War years. Its title, "Gilded Age," became a label for the whole era.

A **rebate** was a refund of a portion of the shipping charge which railroads often made to their best customers. Another form of **rate-discrimination** involved charging much more to haul freight in areas where there was no competition.

like Commodore Vanderbilt of the New York Central, and James J. Hill of the Great Northern, the typical empire-builders of the era. More famous fortunes were made in railroading during the *Gilded Age** than in any other single field.

The railroad giants were not always fair in their methods of moneymaking. The temptations offered by huge fortunes to be made led to scandals in the construction and financing of railroads. As competition between the fast-multiplying lines grew more intense, railroads made use of *rebates** and other forms of *rate-discrimination** to win a larger share of the business. Complaints against these and other monopolistic practices led to a widespread demand for government regulation of railroads.

Earlier the attitude of the government, and of the people, had been enthusiastic support for railroad-building. Thus the Federal government and the states had granted vast tracts of land to the railroads to encourage them

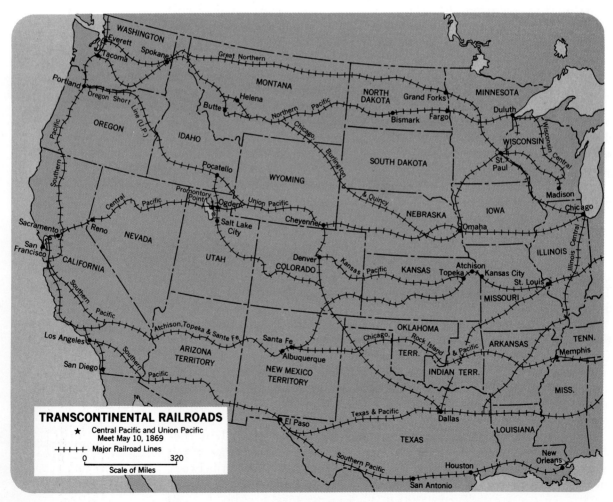

TRANSCONTINENTAL RAILROADS
★ Central Pacific and Union Pacific Meet May 10, 1869
+++++ Major Railroad Lines
0   320
Scale of Miles

to build through unpopulated regions.* But in 1887, Congress passed the Interstate Commerce Act, outlawing specific abuses and creating the Interstate Commerce Commission to police the railroads. The Government's attitude had changed from promotion to restraint.

The railroads received **131.4 million acres** of land from the Federal government and **48.9 million acres** from the states. There has been much controversy over the extent of these land grants ever since the 1870's.

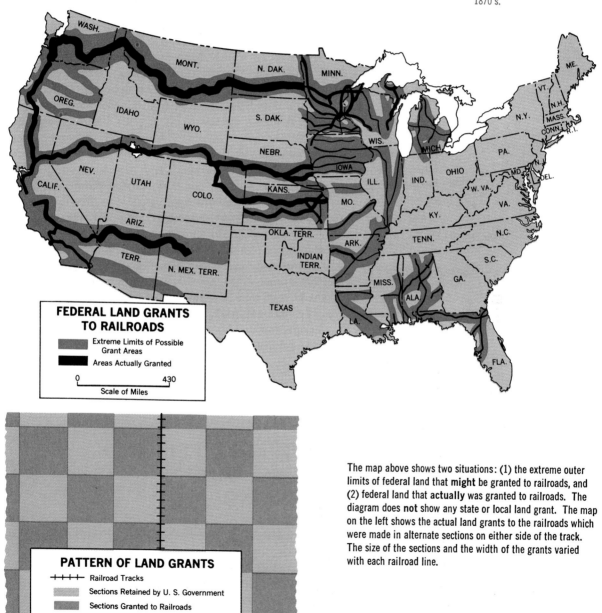

FEDERAL LAND GRANTS TO RAILROADS

Extreme Limits of Possible Grant Areas

Areas Actually Granted

0   430
Scale of Miles

PATTERN OF LAND GRANTS

Railroad Tracks

Sections Retained by U. S. Government

Sections Granted to Railroads

The map above shows two situations: (1) the extreme outer limits of federal land that **might** be granted to railroads, and (2) federal land that **actually** was granted to railroads. The diagram does **not** show any state or local land grant. The map on the left shows the actual land grants to the railroads which were made in alternate sections on either side of the track. The size of the sections and the width of the grants varied with each railroad line.

C85

The Crucial Place of Railroads in the Industrial Era

Railroads occupied the center of the political stage during much of the post-Civil War generation. This showed their vital importance to society as a whole. No enterprises approaching the same magnitude had ever before been undertaken in America. The railroads were the first big business. They experienced needs and faced difficulties that other industrial giants were to meet later.

The railroads' need for capital played an important role in the rise of Wall Street as the nation's financial center. The strategic function of the investment banker in the world of finance linked the fortunes of such institutions as the banking house of *J. P. Morgan** to the railroads.

Morgan's greatest contribution to railroading was to revive and reorganize **railroads** which went bankrupt in hard times of 1870's–1890's.

The construction and operation of the railroads brought heavy demands for labor. This not only stimulated immigration from Europe but prompted the importing of Chinese laborers on the West Coast. Railroad workers organized some of the most important unions of the period. Several of the most violent outbursts of labor unrest also occurred in railroading.

The vast size and complexity of the railroads led to new techniques of management and administration which were later carried over into other fields. The requirements of efficient rail transportation also affected society in ways so subtle that they are easy to overlook. Thus, for example, the division of the country into the standard time zones that we still use was brought about by the desirability of a uniform basis for scheduling trains.

The railroads touched practically every area of national life. They brought the different parts of the country into new relationships with each other. Because they reduced the cost of transportation, railroads stimulated regional specialization and created a national market for raw materials, foodstuffs, and manufactured goods. By opening up the vast farming and mining regions of the West, they changed the relative position of the United States in the world market.

4 HOW RAILROADS AFFECTED AGRICULTURE AND MANUFACTURING

Both agriculture and manufacturing were deeply affected by the development of railroads. By welding the nation together into one economic unit, railroads greatly expanded and developed the potential markets for agricultural products and manufactured goods. As one of the country's largest employers of men and an enormous consumer of industrial products, railroads were at once a product of industrialization and a promoter of it. Railroads brought a new way of life to nineteenth-century America.

While reading selections from the U.S. Census Report of 1860 and from a history of manufacturing about the impact of railroads on American economic development, keep these questions in mind:

1. How did railroads benefit agriculture?

2. How did railroads affect the lumber industry of the upper Mississippi valley?

3. How did railroads affect the iron and steel industry?

Railroads and Agriculture in 1860

Agriculture has benefited greatly by the construction of railroads. So great are these benefits that farmers would have gained immensely even if they had paid the entire cost of building the railroads between the Atlantic coast and the western states. As an example, consider the ways in which the railroads have benefited the grain-growing states especially.

1. First, the trade that now exists between the Atlantic cities and the central western states simply could not be carried on by any other means of transportation than the railroads. Without the railroads, there would be no point in raising more grain than the people in the immediate vicinity could use. The surplus beyond local needs would perish in the fields. In fact, this was exactly the state of things in the West before the general introduction of railroads.

2. Second, the railroads have raised the prices received by western farmers much nearer to the prices that prevail in eastern cities. They did this by reducing the cost of transportation. It is the producer, rather than the consumer, who gets the benefit of this reduction in transportation costs. Prices tend to remain high in cities along the Atlantic because they are growing rapidly and are demanding increasing quantities of food from the West. When the cost of transportation is reduced, the price the western farmer receives approximates more closely the price his products will bring in eastern markets.

3. Third, because they give the farmer the benefit of the best markets and the highest prices, railroads have stimulated agricultural production beyond anything before known in the world.

Indeed, railroads are the only means by which the distant parts of this country could have been commercially united; thus the railroad has become a mighty means of WEALTH, UNITY, and STABILITY.

Adapted from **Agriculture of the United States in 1860** (Washington: U. S. Govt. Printing Office, 1864), pp. clxv-clxix.

Railroads and Manufacturing

Improvements in transportation influenced the geography of our manufacturing industries in a revolutionary way. They opened new markets and tapped new sources of raw materials. Improved transportation facilities also brought small establishments which served local markets into competition with larger rivals from industrial centers.

The history of lumbering in the Upper Mississippi Valley illustrates how railway construction caused markets to expand. In 1857, this region produced about 300 million feet of lumber. This level of output exceeded the demand in those days, and the sawmilling business was depressed. Ten years later, however, sawmillers were doing a very good business even though their output had doubled. According to an observer at the time, "The extension of the railroads in the adjoining states and the construction of the Union Pacific are assigned as the causes of this unusual prosperity."

The completion of the Union Pacific had a decided effect on many branches of manufacturing. The demand for iron to build it, for example, was sufficient to have a steadying effect on the whole iron market.

The business depression that began in 1873 also illustrated the connection between railroad construction and prosperity in the iron and steel industry. Railroad construction fell off by almost one-half in 1873. At that time the railroads consumed approximately half the iron and steel produced in the United States. When their consumption declined so markedly, the decrease in demand completely upset market conditions and caused heavy overproduction of iron and steel.

One of the earliest indications of better times after the Panic of 1873 was an increased demand for railway equipment. In 1878, orders for locomotives and rails came in more freely than for several years previously. The building of the New York Elevated Railway also created a new demand for structural iron, large enough in itself to give a tone of optimism to the market.

Adapted from **History of Manufactures in the United States, 1860–1893**, Vol. II, pp. 149, 288–290, by Victor S. Clark. Published for the Carnegie Institution, Washington, 1929. Used with permission of McGraw-Hill Book Company.

5 RAILROADS AND AMERICAN SOCIAL GEOGRAPHY

The influence of railroads on American life was more than just economic. Railroads determined where new communities would be located, whether older towns would live or die, and where immigrants would settle.

Railroads were agents of social, as well as economic, change. They were colonizers as well as carriers. As colonizers of the West, railroads also affected Indians as well as whites.

While (1) reading the following selections from modern historical accounts of the influence of railroads on the growth of cities and western migration and (2) examining the picture series on the impact of railroads on the Indian way of life, keep these questions in mind:

1. How did railroads affect the growth of cities?

2. How did railroads try to encourage settlement of lands granted to them by the Federal government?

3. What inferences about the impact of railroads on Indian life are suggested by these pictures?

Railroads and the Growth of Cities

In large measure, the location and initial growth of important cities . . . was tied to the building of a national system of transportation. In the early part of the nineteenth century, the outcome of struggles for transportation had drastically affected the rank and importance of the cities of the East. . . . The rivalry among city promoters and real estate speculators to win railroads for their communities in newly developed regions supplied one of the most dramatic chapters in the history of American urbanization. Earlier rivalries had been limited by nature—by the location of rivers and lakes.

But railroads were not bound by topography, by the paths of river commerce, or by natural trade patterns. Railroads could be built anywhere, creating cities where they chose. Since the building of railroads was dependent to a considerable extent on subsidies from local communities, railroad leaders were willing to bargain with competing towns to obtain the best possible deal in stock subscriptions, bond issues, and right-of-ways. It was sometimes possible, therefore, for towns with few natural advantages to triumph over better situated rivals for the prize of regional dominance. . . .

From early in the railroad era, railroad officials were well aware of the possibilities of profit in urban growth in the West. The *platting** of town sites and the sale of town lots became an established aspect of the process of building railroads into new regions. The techniques of town development and the system of bargaining with competing communities were perfected by the Illinois Central Railroad, chartered in 1851 to build southward from Chicago through the heart of the state. The company used the threat of building new towns or running its tracks through neighboring places in order to force local officials in established communities to offer concessions of right-of-ways, railroad station site donations, or stock purchases.

To **plat** a town means to draw up a map showing the layout of streets, lots, and business sites.

Centralia, Kankakee, Champaign, and La Salle were established as competing towns by the Illinois Central when agreements could not be effected with Central City, Bourbonnais, Urbana, and Peru. . . . The company's concern with town promoting contributed to considerable urbanization along the line of the Illinois Central. In 1850, there were only ten towns in the immediate vicinity of the railroad's route; ten years later there were forty-seven; in 1870, eighty-one. The combined population of these urban places, excluding Chicago, rose from 12,000 in 1850, to 70,000 in 1860, and to 172,000 by 1870.

Charles N. Glaab and A. Theodore Brown, **A History of Urban America** (London: The Macmillan Company, 1967), pp. 112-113.

Railroads and Immigration

The railroads that received land grants from the Federal government or the states wanted to have it settled as soon as possible. Accordingly, many of them spent large sums of money in efforts to attract immigrants, both from Europe and from longer-settled regions in the United States.

The first road to carry on this colonizing work was the Illinois Central. It began its promotional campaign as early as 1855. But the heyday of railroad colonization did not come until the seventies and eighties. By then the Northern Pacific, Burlington and Missouri, Santa Fe, Southern Pacific, and many other roads were operating land and immigration departments.

Among the inducements the railroads held out to prospective land-purchasers were free "land-exploring" tickets, reduced steamship and railroad fares, liberal sales policies, and long-term financing plans. Many of the roads built immigrant houses on the plains where buyers could stay free of charge while they selected suitable tracts. Some, like the Great Northern, offered to educate settlers in plains-farming techniques. A few roads even went so far as to build churches and schools for the communities they planted. Altogether the colonization activities of the railroads were marked by a benevolence which contrasted strangely with some of their other contemporary practices.

Railroad colonization tended to establish compact groups of immigrants together in the same place. As a result, it did more than a little to determine the ethnic pattern of the trans-Mississippi West.

The Burlington planted numerous German, British, and Scandinavian colonies in Nebraska and Iowa. The Northern Pacific fathered an even greater number in Minnesota, Dakota, and the Pacific Northwest; and the Santa Fe was responsible for bringing to Kansas thousands of Russo-German Mennonites. Each of these colonies, moreover, acted in succeeding decades as a *lodestone** for immigrants of similar background.

Lodestone means magnet. Once established, any settlement of immigrants attracted more settlers of the same nationality who wished to be close to friends, relatives, or persons of the same language and culture.

Adapted from Maldwyn Allen Jones, **American Immigration** (Chicago: The University of Chicago Press, 1960), pp. 188–189.

Indians Destroying Railroad Tracks Near Russell, Kansas, 1867—The Indians realized that the railroad meant the end of their world, and they resisted its coming. To the right is the scene as the artist, I. Gogolin, imagined it.

Slaughter of the Buffalo, 1871—As railroads penetrated the West, trainloads of sportsmen came for big game hunting. In a few short years the buffalo was almost exterminated.

Indians Staging a Performance for Tourists

C91

6 RAILROADS AND IMPROVEMENTS IN BUSINESS MANAGEMENT

Running a railroad is an immensely complicated business. Someone has to know where the rolling stock is at all times—how much of it is idle, how much is carrying a payload, how much is returning empty, and how much is being loaded or unloaded. Decisions must be made affecting schedules and rates over hundreds of miles of track and covering many types of freight.

These managerial problems could not be handled by the techniques of administration used in less complicated enterprises in the early nineteenth century. Because they were facing novel demands, the railroad men had to work out new and more systematic patterns of administration.

While reading the following historical account, consider:

1. How did McCallum try to improve the management of the Erie Railroad?

2. What new uses did McCallum make of the telegraph?

The Erie Railroad's System of Statistical Reporting

By the end of 1853, the directors had split the Erie into five geographic divisions, each about a hundred miles long. . . . In 1854 they picked Daniel C. McCallum, at the time superintendent of one of the new divisions, to be the general superintendent. McCallum, the inventor of an inflexible truss bridge and an able engineer, approached the Erie's management in much the same way as he designed bridges. His great strength was in sharpening lines of authority and communication and in stimulating the flow of the minute and accurate information which top management needed for the complex decisions it was increasingly being called upon to make. Hourly, daily, and monthly reports . . . provided this essential information.

The hourly reports, primarily operational, gave by telegraph the location of each train and the reasons for any delays or mishaps. The information thus received was tabulated and proved vital in the elimination of bottlenecks and other trouble spots. McCallum's use of the telegraph impressed other railroad managers because it demonstrated that wires were more than a means to make trains safe—they were also a device to improve co-ordination and better administration.

Daily reports, the real basis of the system, were required from both conductors and station agents. They covered all important matters of train operation, and the handling of freight and passengers. These reports provided information from two different sources on train movements, car loadings, damages, and misdirected freight, and acted as a valuable check on the honesty and efficiency of both conductors and agents. . . .

Besides assisting in operations, these statistical data were essential in rate making; for only analysis of these reports could provide the information necessary to determine what were the costs of carrying an item, and whether, therefore, the charges produced a profit or not.

Alfred D. Chandler, Jr., and Stephen Salsbury, "The Railroads: Innovators in Modern Business Administration," in Bruce Mazlish, ed., **The Railroad and the Space Program: An Exploration in Historical Analogy** (Cambridge, Mass.: The M.I.T. Press, 1965), pp. 138–139. Reprinted from **The Railroad and the Space Program** by permission of the American Academy of Arts and Sciences, Boston, Massachusetts.

4 Dislocations and adjustments

Farmers in the Industrial Age

Introduction

Industrialization affected the lives of millions who lived far from the shriek of factory whistles. The story of the American farmer in the late nineteenth century makes this very clear. It also shows the mixed reaction of the American people to the changes brought about by industrialization. For some Americans, these changes were a blessing; for others, they were a curse. But for all, the changes were facts to be faced. There was no going back.

In many ways, late nineteenth-century agriculture was a great success story. Farmers filled up the western plains so rapidly that in 1890 the Bureau of the Census declared that there was no longer any clear frontier line between settled and unsettled lands. More acreage was brought under cultivation between 1870 and 1900 than in the previous two-and-one-half centuries dating back to the founding of Jamestown.

Agricultural production soared. Between 1870 and 1900, output of four leading crops (corn, wheat, cotton, and livestock) increased between 130 and 150 percent. This spurt in production took place without a corresponding increase in the *agricultural work force.** In 1870, every farmer was feeding seven other Americans; by 1900, he was feeding ten.*

The skyrocketing growth of American cities accounted for part of the demand, but the farmer was also sending more and more of his products overseas. Yearly exports of wheat multiplied fivefold between the 1860's and 1900. Exports of cotton and pork tripled or quadrupled in the same period. Agricultural commodities accounted for three-quarters or more of the nation's total exports throughout the last half of the century. Without these riches of the earth to export, Americans would have been unable to import the manufactured goods they needed from Europe.

None of this could have taken place without the *Communications Revolution.* This term has been coined by historians to designate the changes made by the widespread use of railroads, ocean steamships, the telegraph, the transatlantic cable, and improvements in economic institutions such as commodity markets.*

The combined effect of these changes was to create a genuine world market. Farmers in Nebraska were brought within the same system as growers in Argentina, Australia, and central Europe. This meant, of course, that their prosperity was greatly affected by what happened ten thousand miles away.

Objectives of this assignment are to:

—Analyze contemporary account of Grange movement and a Grange picture in order to discover the objectives of the Grange movement.

—Analyze contemporary account of development and use of machinery in agriculture for meaning.

—Draw inferences from recording of Granger protest song about the social attitude of farmers toward themselves and the rest of society.

—Make a judgment about the attitude of farmers toward industrialization.

—Make a judgment on effect of rationalizing activity on farming.

The **agricultural work force** increased only 69 percent during these years.

Farm productivity and **efficiency** has continued to improve at fantastic rates. In 1969, every farmer was providing food and fiber for 45 persons.

Several of these **improvements** in transportation and communication were introduced before the Civil War. But the full impact of their widespread use was not felt until after the war.

The Farmer's Discontent

The uncertainties of the world market and the unexplainable shifts in rising and falling prices had much to do with farm unrest. Thus it appeared to the farmer that his marvels of production were not bringing him a proportionate reward. When the bottom fell out of his prices, he still had to keep on paying the freight rates set by the railroads. He also had to meet mortgage payments for the additional land he was buying and for new machinery to farm in the modern way.

When times were really bad, farm discontent turned into anger; angry men looked for someone to blame for their troubles. The railroads were the natural target. For although railroad rates actually declined in these years, farmers' prices sometimes declined even more. Moreover, rates varied widely in different localities, and charges of unfair discrimination and other shady practices were often justified.

The Patrons of Husbandry, or the Grange, was the organization used by the farmers to battle against the railroads in the 1870's. The *Granger laws** in states like Illinois were an important landmark in governmental control of big business, but within ten years, the Supreme Court threw out several of the Granger laws as unconstitutional. However, farmers were among the groups supporting the passage of the Federal Interstate Commerce Act in 1887 which replaced the Granger laws by giving the Federal government power to regulate the railroads.

In the 1880's the Alliance movement replaced the Grange as the most politically active network of farm organizations. In the early 1890's, the various Alliances merged into the People's Party. The Populists, as they were usually called, elected five United States senators and ten members of the House of Representatives in 1892. This was clearly the most significant third-party movement in years, and the Democrats soon moved to capture the Populists' support. Thus, in 1896, the Democrats and Populists united behind William Jennings Bryan from Nebraska, a presidential candidate who spoke for the farmer and *free silver.**

The 1896 election brought to a climax the farmers' "Thirty-Years' War" against the plutocrats and monopolists. Bryan was defeated by William McKinley, after a hard-fought campaign. The following year the long depression lifted, and farmers forgot some of their complaints as American agriculture entered its golden age of prosperity.

The **Granger laws** set up state railroad commissions to regulate the roads and to set limits on passenger fares, freight rates, and warehousing charges. They also prohibited specific abuses such as the long-haul, short-haul discrimination.

Many farmers believed **inflation** would improve their situation. Hence they supported the movement for free coinage of silver which was aimed at expanding the currency.

"The Grange Awakening the Sleepers"—The Grange attempts to arouse unwary countrymen to the perils of railroad power.

A Grange meeting in session.

7   THE FARMERS ORGANIZE

The first major farm organization, the *Grange*, or *Patrons of Husbandry*, was founded in 1867.° It grew very rapidly in the 1870's, when farmers in the Mississippi Valley were hard hit by falling prices and high railroad rates.

The Grange was supposed to be a non-political association. But no one could stop farmers from talking politics when they got together, and a meeting of the local Grange was a natural occasion for such a discussion. Its members often formed pressure blocs or allied themselves to independent political parties.

After the depression of the 1870's, however, the Grange confined itself more closely to social and educational activities. By doing so, it outlived the more politically-oriented farm organizations of the period.

While reading the following contemporary account of the Grange movement and examining the Grange illustration, consider these questions. According to this account:

1. What did the Grange offer the farmers of the United States?

2. Who victimized the farmers? How did the Grange propose to deal with them?

3. How did the Grange propose to improve the social life of the farmers?

4. What words would you use to describe the image of farm life suggested by the Grange print?

The Purposes of the Patrons of Husbandry

In the first place, the Grange offers to the farmers of the United States a means of combination, of harmony of action such as they have never before possessed. It offers them the means of expressing their views and wishes as a body, and of enforcing them.

The Grange recognizes the plain fact that the American farmer is the victim of certain evils, and it proposes to correct these. It recognizes that the farmer is robbed of his fair reward by the extortions of the railroad companies. It seeks to bring about a more liberal state of affairs in which the railroads, while earning a just return on their investments, shall allow the farmer a more generous and less ruinous rate of freight.

This is a task of great magnitude, for the power of the corporations is immense and they will not easily surrender it. But the Grange has taken a lesson from them. It has observed that they have achieved their power to plunder by combination and unity of action, and it proposes to fight them with the same weapons.

The *Order*° seeks no affiliation with any of the political parties of the present day. It has nothing to do with what men usually call politics. It is devoted to the interests of the farmers and leaves political questions to its individual members.

The founder of the Grange was **Oliver H. Kelley,** Washington Agriculture Bureau clerk. He took a three-month trip through the war-ravaged southern states in 1866, which impressed him with the need for a social organization for farmers. Except for a fruit-grower, all of Kelley's original co-founders were government employees.

These were the years when secret societies and **fraternal orders,** such as the **Masons** and the **International Order of Odd Fellows,** were most popular. Kelley was a Mason, and he modeled the Patrons of Husbandry on that fraternal society. Hence, the Grange was a sort of fraternal order for farmers, with rituals, degrees of membership, secrecy, and so on.

C95

C96

There is another feature of the Grange that alone makes it invaluable to the farmers of America. It is the best means that has yet been devised of cultivating social relations among them. In its social aspects, it is a success.

Before the Grange was organized in Iowa, for example, farmers lived quite isolated from each other. The dull monotony of their existence was broken only by an occasional wedding or funeral. They met together seldom, and read little. In fact, they transformed themselves into corn- and wheat-producing machines. Of business methods they knew almost nothing. It was a rare farmer who could tell you how much it cost him to make a bushel of wheat, or a pound of butter, or a ton of hay.

The condition of the farmer's wife was even worse. Her work began earlier and ended later than that of her husband. It was a slavish life, with nothing to give it variety or to lift the woman out of the deep rut of her daily drudgery.

Grange meetings also feature prepared talks or discussion of topics of special interest to farmers. Any matter which tends to make better farmers can be considered. The women too have their own sessions where they learn to be better housewives. Sometimes the Grange takes up social and moral questions, and sometimes its exercises are of a literary character. The discussion of political and religious questions is strictly forbidden by the constitution of the Order.

From such Grange activities, the farmer is taught that the world does not end at the boundaries of his farm. He learns of hopes, fears, joys, and sorrows beyond his domain in which it is his duty to take an interest.

Adapted from Edward Winslow Martin, **History of the Grange Movement** (Philadelphia: National Publishing Company, 1873), pp. 440–444, 450–461.

8 NEW MACHINERY AND NEW METHODS OF PRODUCTION

Farmers are a traditionally conservative group—they generally prefer the old tried-and-true methods. But American farmers faced new problems in a rapidly changing society. There were always enough venturesome men to assure that new inventions and methods would get a trial. When something was shown to be a workable improvement, other farmers adopted it quickly. The U.S. Department of Agriculture played an important role in communicating information about the application of machinery to farming.

While reading the following selections from the U.S. Department of Agriculture Yearbook, 1899, reviewing agricultural progress and studying the picture series of farm machinery, keep these questions in mind:

1. What is the difference between a reaper and a self-binding harvester?

2. What is a combine? What was the result of widespread use of these machines?

3. What are creameries? What influence did they have on the dairy industry?

McCormick Reaper of 1831— Grain was cut by a moving sickle bar and pushed onto the platform by an overhead reel. A man walked beside the reaper, raking grain off the platform so other workers could tie it into sheaves.

Self-raking Reaper— First reapers with mechanical arms (A) came on the market in 1850. They eliminated need for men to rake grain off the platform.

C98

Marsh Harvester, 1860—Two endlessly-moving canvas aprons replaced the mechanical raking arm. The grain fell back on one apron and was carried along the second to the men who bound the sheaves. This machine saved several bushels of grain per acre by binding the grain before it touched ground. It saved much backbreaking labor.

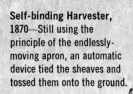

Self-binding Harvester, 1870—Still using the principle of the endlessly-moving apron, an automatic device tied the sheaves and tossed them onto the ground.

Mechanization of Grain Harvesting

The most prominent feature in the development of agriculture is the immense improvement that has taken place in agricultural methods and machines. Indeed, the word <u>improvements</u> is not adequate to express the change that has taken place in the methods of agriculture in this country. The implements and machines are creations rather than improvements, and their mission has been radical and far-reaching.

In the case of the grain reaper, for example, the first patent was issued to Obed Hussey in 1833. *Cyrus McCormick** took out his first patent in 1834, although he had constructed and tested a machine in 1831 with some success. The world heard little of reaping machines for some twenty years. By 1855, however, about 10,000 mowers and reapers had been built by different makers. At an international exposition held that year in France, an American reaper proved to be more efficient than its English and French competitors. The French machine did the allotted work in 72 minutes, the English in 66, and the American in 22.

The earlier reapers cut the grain and a man raked it onto the ground, bunched up in the proper size for a sheaf. The sheaves were then tied by hand and set in shocks by workers who followed the reaper on foot. The harvester was an improvement on this because it had a place for one or two men to ride while they tied the grain into sheaves as fast as it was cut. But the self-binding harvester went beyond that. It had a mechanical attachment which tied the cut grain into sheaves without the aid of human labor. It was not until 1870 that the self-binder was a mechanical success.

But the self-binder was not the end of invention in constructing machines to harvest wheat. It remained for the ingenuity of man to make a combined reaper and thresher. This machine combines the two operations of cutting the grain and of separating the kernels of grain from the stalk and chaff. The farmer needs only to drive it across the wheat field in order to obtain the grain ready for transportation to the elevator or elsewhere.

It is one of the marvels of the age that these inventions have cut the labor time necessary to produce a bushel of wheat to 10 minutes. In 1830, it took 3 hours and 3 minutes! In the same period, the cost of human labor required to produce this bushel of wheat declined from 17¾ cents to 3⅓ cents.

New Methods in Dairying

The beginning of the twentieth century will find the dairy industry established on a plane far above the crude and variable domestic art of three or four generations ago. The milch cow itself, upon which the whole business rests, is almost as much a machine as a natural product. By virtue of systematic breeding for milk production, today's cow is a very different creature from the average animal of olden times.

Marvelous new inventions—such as the *centrifugal separator**—have replaced the homely and inconvenient implements formerly in use. Long rows of shining tin pans no longer adorn rural dooryards. The factory system of

McCormick combined mechanical inventiveness with great business ability. He moved to Chicago and opened a factory in 1847 to manufacture farm implements which later merged with other companies to form International Harvester Corporation.

Adapted from **Yearbook of the United States Department of Agriculture, 1899** (Washington: U. S. Govt. Printing Office, 1900), pp. 314, 318–319, 332.

Since cream is lighter than skimmed milk, rapid circular motion tends to separate the two by causing the cream to fly off faster and farther. The **centrifugal separator,** based on this principle, was a highly efficient device for extracting cream rapidly from fresh whole milk.

C100

cooperative or concentrated manufacture has so far taken the place of home dairying that, in many areas, the farm churn has become as rare as the spinning wheel.

St. Albans in northern Vermont provides an example of the radical changes that have taken place in dairying.

In the middle of the century, farmers from miles around brought their country-made butter to market in St. Albans every Tuesday. The average weekly supply of 30 to 40 tons was quite varied in quality. After being classified into three grades, it was sent on to the Boston market, 200 miles away. Between 1850 and 1875 some 65 million pounds of butter, worth $20 million, passed through this little town. All of it was produced on a thousand or so individual farms.

In 1880 the first creamery was built in the county; ten years later there were fifteen. Now, a creamery company located at St. Albans has fifty-odd skimming or separating stations distributed through this and adjoining counties. Milk from 30,000 cows in the area is brought to these stations, run through the machines which separate cream and skimmed milk, and tested for butter content.

From the skimming stations, the separated cream is carried by rail and wagon—largely the former—to the central factory. There, in one room, from ten to twelve tons of butter are made every working day. A single churning place for a whole county!

All of this butter is of standard quality, called "extra creamery," and is sold on its reputation, upon orders from different points received in advance of its manufacture. The price is relatively higher than the average for the product of the same farms fifty years ago. This is mainly because of better average quality and greater uniformity—two important advantages of the creamery system.

Adapted from **Yearbook of the United States Department of Agriculture, 1899** (Washington: U. S. Govt. Printing Office, 1900), pp. 397–398.

An early mechanized creamery. The large vats are churning out butter and the workers are packaging it by hand.

5 Workingmen in an age of industrialization

More Dislocations and Adjustments

Evils of Child Labor—Young girl in a Carolina cotton mill, 1909.

In 1870 there were 6.4 million gainfully employed in farming; by 1910, the figure was 11.6 million. Non-farm occupations employed 6.0 million in 1870; 25.8 million in 1910.

In 1870 there were only about 354,000 women over the age of ten engaged in these industries.

In 1904 reformers organized the **National Child Labor Committee** to combat the evils of child labor.

Introduction

The preceding assignment showed how farmers were affected greatly by industrialization, and how their reactions to it were mixed. Urban workingmen were even more directly affected than farmers by industrialization. In some ways their reactions were like those of the farmers. Other parts of their experience were quite different. This assignment will look more closely at the worker's situation.

After the Civil War, the industrial work force grew at a much faster pace than the agricultural. Between 1870 and 1910, the number of persons employed in non-farming jobs quadrupled, while those in farm occupations increased by only *80 percent.*

Most of these workers were men. But a special Census Bureau investigation in 1900 showed that more than a *million women* over the age of sixteen were employed in manufacturing and mechanical industries.* Textiles and dressmaking accounted for most of these women workers.

The textile industry was also the largest single industrial employer of children. In 1900, children between the ages of ten and fifteen made up 13 percent of the total number of wage earners in textiles. By that date, there was much concern over the abuses connected with women's and children's labor. After 1900 many reformers turned their attention to the special needs of these two groups of workers.*

Rationalizing the Worker's Tasks

In mill and factory the number of workers increased dramatically. In 1879, for example, the average size of the labor force in an individual steel plant or rolling mill was 220 men; twenty years later the average was 412 men.

This rapid growth, along with increasing mechanization and other changes, tended to reduce the status of the individual worker. The gap widened between the owners and managers, on the one hand, and the workers on the other. The older informality of the small workshop was lost. The worker no longer owned his own tools; they were issued to him when he came to work and checked in when he went home. More systematic and formal methods of assigning tasks and controlling performance were gradually introduced. Often a man had to adjust the pace of his work to that of the machine he operated.

For example, after 1900 a new group of industrial engineers or *efficiency experts** appeared on the industrial scene. These experts would observe a worker very closely, timing all his moves with a stop-watch. On the basis of this time-and-motion study, the job would be reorganized and the worker told exactly what to do in order to perform it more efficiently.

All this was part of conforming the worker to what has been called the *industrial discipline*—that is, adjusting human labor to the requirements of new machines and new methods. The workers resented it, just as they resented the terrific difference between their wages and the salaries of top management or the fabulous wealth of the great captains of industry.

But the workers also benefited from the new machines and methods. These innovations multiplied the productivity of labor. What this means is that a given amount of human effort resulted in the creation of vastly more goods under the new industrial system than under the older handicraft system. The sale of the enlarged product brought in more money. Increased productivity meant a larger pie to be shared in the form of dividends for the owners, salaries for management, and wages for the workers.

Wages did go up with the spread of industrialization. A modern scholar estimates that *real wages** increased by about 50 percent between 1860 and 1890. This was certainly a genuine improvement for the worker; but considering the increases in productivity, it was a moderate gain. Another improvement was the shortening of the working day. In 1860 the 11-hour day was the general rule. By the end of the century, the president of the American Federation of Labor estimated the average working day at *9 to 9½ hours.**

Labor's Response to Industrialization

The improvements in wages and hours were gradual and quite unspectacular. Far more dramatic were the explosions of discontent on the part of the workers—strikes, demonstrations, and other acts of violence.

In 1877 the great railroad strikes seemed to threaten a new civil war. They were marked by riots from Baltimore to St. Louis, and Federal troops had to be called out to restore order in Martinsburg, West Virginia, and Pittsburgh.

Strikers fought a pitched battle with 300 *Pinkerton agents** at the Homestead Steel mill near Pittsburgh in 1892. Two years later there was more violence at the Pullman strike in Chicago. Smaller work stoppages—both strikes and lockouts by employers—numbered between one and two thousand a year from 1886 to 1900, and higher than that for the next five years.

Labor also responded to industrialism by taking part in the union movement. The individual worker was powerless before the might of the corporation, just as the isolated farmer could do nothing to protect his interests against the railroads. Both farmers and workers had to *form organizations* of their own if they were to deal effectively with the challenges of industrial-

Frederick W. Taylor, an industrial engineer, launched the "scientific management" movement in the 1890's.

Real wages means wages in terms of purchasing power. Not all workers shared equally in wage advances. There were wide variations between different regions of the country, different industries, and between skilled and unskilled workers.

Larger employers led the way in reducing the hours of labor. Small operators often had to work their men longer in order to compete. Farmers and agricultural labor worked the longest hours of all, but their work was seasonal.

The Pinkerton Private Detective Agency, founded in 1850, did intelligence work for the North in the Civil War. In the 1870's they went into the industrial field, tracing embezzlers and robbers, guarding property, and spying on labor organizers and agitators. At the Homestead strike, they were used as strikebreakers.

Railroad workers were among the first to form large **unions** after the Civil War and to fight for mutual insurance because of their work hazards.

ization.* Only a small minority of the industrial work force was unionized by 1900. But the movement continued to grow in the 20th century. A closer look at the labor movement will help us gain an insight into the worker's adjustment to the great social and economic changes of the industrial era.

Certificate of Membership in the Brotherhood of Locomotive Firemen, 1878

9 THE LABOR MOVEMENT: TWO ORGANIZATIONS AND TWO PHILOSOPHIES

The Knights of Labor and the American Federation of Labor were the two principal labor organizations of the late nineteenth century. The *Knights of Labor** was founded in Philadelphia in 1869, but remained small and local in scope till 1878. Uriah Stephens was the founder and first Grand Master Workman. Terence V. Powderly led the Knights in the 1880's when they numbered some 700,000 members. The Knights of Labor soon declined when attempts to gain benefits for labor by strikes and alleged violence failed. After 1893, the Knights disappeared.

The Knights of Labor organization was not based on the trade-union principle. Rather it attempted to bring all kinds of workers under one central association. All the workers in a given geographical area were supposed to belong to the same local assembly of the Knights of Labor, no matter what their trade. The Knights defined *worker* very broadly—any *producer* could join, and that included everyone except saloon-keepers, stockbrokers, and a few others regarded as drones of society.

The *American Federation of Labor,** or A. F. of L. began later, grew slower, and lasted longer. It was founded in 1886 as a federation made up of trade unions, each of which represented workers in a different line of work, such as carpenters, printers, and machinists. *Samuel Gompers** from the Cigarmakers' Union was elected president—an office he held except for one term until his death in 1924.

The Knights of Labor began as a secret society, patterned after popular fraternal societies, with elaborate rituals and high-flown titles. Secrecy was dropped in the late 1870's.

The A. F. of L. grew out of the Federation of Organized Trade and Labor Unions, established in 1881. In 1887, the A. F. of L. had 160,000 members; in 1900, just over half a million; and in 1910, 1.5 million.

Samuel Gompers was born in London in 1850 and emigrated to the U. S. as a boy of thirteen. Socialist opposition to his policies caused his only defeat for A. F. of L. president, in 1895.

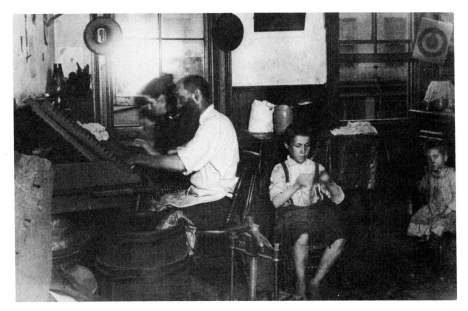

Cigar-making in a Tenement Sweatshop—Men, women, and children worked endless hours in dirt, tobacco stench, and confusion, suffering the sweat-shop system.

Objectives of this assignment are to:

—Analyze contemporary accounts of Knights of Labor and American Federation of Labor to discover overall objectives of both organizations.

—Analyze statements by Terence V. Powderly and Samuel Gompers on strikes and decide whether their views are consistent with overall objectives of their respective labor organizations.

—Make a judgment on effect of rationalizing activity on American labor movement.

Amalgamation: a solid, unified mixture.

Adapted from Terence V. Powderly, **Thirty Years of Labor** (Columbus, Ohio: Excelsior Publishing House, 1890), pp. 167–168.

Adapted from Carroll D. Wright, "An Historical Sketch of the Knights of Labor," **Quarterly Journal of Economics**, I (Jan., 1887), pp. 159–160.

Adapted from Powderly, **Thirty Years of Labor**, pp. 464–465.

These organizational differences between the two unions reflected different goals and philosophies. While reading the following selections from Knights of Labor theorists and from Samuel Gompers' explanation of the American Federation of Labor's goals, keep these questions in mind:

1. Why was the Knights of Labor organization founded? What were its goals?

2. Why were the trade unions of the American Federation of Labor founded? What were the goals of the A. F. of L.?

3. How were the goals of the Knights of Labor and the American Federation of Labor reflected in the way each was organized?

The Work of the Knights of Labor

The work to which our fraternity addresses itself is one of the greatest ever attempted in the history of the world. Its work is the knitting up into a compact and homogeneous *amalgamation** of all the world's workers into one universal brotherhood. Its work is the complete emancipation of the wealth-producers from the thraldom of wage-slavery, and the annihilation of the great anti-Christ of civilization—the idolatry of wealth.

The Nature and Mission of the Labor Local Assembly

The Local Assembly is not a mere trade union. It is something more and higher than that. It gathers into one fold all the branches of honorable toil. It assists its members in bettering their condition morally, socially, and financially. It educates its members to rely, not on strikes, but on thorough organization, cooperative undertakings, and political action—through these means the wage system will be abolished.

Our mission cannot be accomplished in a day or a generation. Agitation, education, and organization are all necessary. In short, any action that will advance the cause of humanity, lighten the burden of toil, or elevate the moral and social conditions of mankind is the proper scope and field of operation of a Local Assembly.

The Goals of the Knights of Labor

Organization once perfected, what must we do? I answer, study the best means of putting the organization to some practical use by embarking on a system of CO-OPERATION which will eventually make every man his own master, his own employer. Cooperation is to be the lever of labor's emancipation. There is no good reason why labor cannot, through cooperation, own and operate mines, factories, and railroads. By cooperation alone can a system of COLONIZATION be established through which men may band together to place the man who is willing to toil on his own homestead.

C106

Samuel Gompers Explains the Nature and Mission of the American Federation of Labor

Working people have too great a need of immediate improvements to allow them to devote their energies to some idealistic end, no matter how beautiful it may be to contemplate. In the language of that foremost of economic and social thinkers, *Ira Steward*,° "The only way out of the wage system is through higher wages. . . ."

It is my firm conviction that trade unions pure and simple are the natural organizations of the wage-earners. Such unions are best designed to secure the workers' present material improvement, and to achieve their final emancipation.

Gompers on the Wage System and the A. F. of L. Approach

We are operating under the wage system. As to what system will ever take its place, I am not prepared to say. As long as the wage system lasts, it is our purpose to secure a continually larger share for labor. Whether the time will ever come when the wage system will be abolished, I am perfectly willing to leave to the future to work out.

I regard all these schemes as very remote and far removed—such plans as those offered by the Populists, socialists, anarchists, *single-taxers*,° and the preachers of harmony of interests between capital and labor. All of these ready-made, patent solutions to our social problems are equally unsatisfactory. One would imagine from the way people sometimes talk that the solution is going to fall among us all at once—that we will go to bed one night under the present system, wake up next morning to find a revolution in full blast, and the next day organize a heaven on earth.

That is not the way progress is made. That is not the way social evolution is brought about. We are solving the problem day after day. As we get an hour's more leisure every day it means millions of golden hours to the human family. As we get 25 cents a day higher wages it brings us nearer to that time when a greater degree of justice and fair dealing will prevail among men.

Ira Steward (1831–1883) promoted the movement for the eight-hour day. He believed a shorter working day and higher wages would increase the worker's leisure time and his capacity to consume goods and services.

Adapted from **Proceedings of the American Federation of Labor, 1890**, pp. 13, 17.

The reformer, **Henry George** (1839–1897), argued that the ownership of land was the fundamental problem in society and that a single tax on land-owners could solve this problem and lead to a better social order.

Adapted from the testimony of Samuel Gompers in **Report of the Industrial Commission** (Washington: U. S. Govt. Printing Office, 1901), Vol. VII, pp. 645, 655.

10   TWO VIEWS ON STRIKES

The Knights of Labor and the A. F. of L. differed not only on overall aims, but also on the tactics labor should use. One of the key differences in this area concerned the role of strikes in the workingman's struggle. The first selection below is from a secret order that Terence V. Powderly sent out to the membership of the Knights of Labor in 1886 shortly after a major strike, unauthorized by the national officers of the Knights, had broken out against several railroad lines. The second statement on strikes and the workingman's use of them was made by Samuel Gompers before the U.S. Industrial Commission in 1901. While reading these selections from Powderly and Gompers, keep these questions in mind:

1. *What does Powderly propose as an alternative to strikes?*
2. *Why does Gompers insist that the right to strike must be preserved?*
3. *According to Gompers, who usually benefits from strikes?*

Powderly's Don't Strike Order, 1886

It has always been, and is at the present time, my policy to advocate conciliation and arbitration in the settlement of disputes. No matter what advantage we might gain by striking, a strike only medicates the symptoms. It does not penetrate the system, and therefore it fails to bring about a cure. The natural consequence is a relapse, which means more medicine and a weaker patient than before.

The word **order** here means organization, i.e., the **Knights of Labor.** Even after dropping secrecy, the Knights preserved much of the trappings and terminology of a fraternal order.

We must not fritter away our strength in the struggle against capital by rushing into useless strikes. To the cardinal principles of our *order** we must add another—patience. You have had patience for years, and had not the Knights of Labor appeared on the scene you would still be waiting. Your scale of wages must remain what it is if you cannot raise it by any other means than a strike. You must patiently submit to injustice at the hands of your employer for a while longer. Bide well your time. Make no display of organization or strength until you have every man and woman in your department of industry organized. Even then, do not strike, but study—not only your own condition, but also that of your employer. Find out how much you are justly entitled to, and a tribunal of arbitration will settle the rest.

Adapted from **The New York Times,** March 27, 1886.

Gompers on Strikes, 1901

From the earliest history of man there has been a struggle between those who possess wealth and those who work to produce it. The struggle takes different forms in different periods and different countries. We have our own particular form of that struggle. It is unpleasant; it is inconvenient. We do not like these things. But there it is, and we cannot overcome it so long as men's interests are as diverse as they are today. Men are going to combine for the purpose of protecting their interests against those who have opposing interests. We must understand the strike against this background.

Organized labor does not desire strikes, and we recognize that peaceful industry is necessary to civilized life. But we insist on maintaining the right to strike. We also claim that this right, and our being prepared to strike, actually has the effect of preventing many strikes.

No matter how just a cause is, it will be crushed if it is not backed up by sufficient power. When England has a dispute with a weak country like Afghanistan, she immediately proceeds to bombard them until they give in to her demands. But when England has a dispute with the United States, she says, "Let us arbitrate this question"!

It is the same way with employers and workers. If the unorganized railroad laborers give the managers any trouble, the managers simply throw them off the job. But when it comes to the engineers, firemen, and other railroad men who have well-organized unions, the managers act in quite a different way. Why, they meet them in conference, pat them on the back sometimes, and say they are jolly good fellows!

Strikes are costly and they teach both workers and employers to be more cautious and tolerant of each other. We begin to recognize each other's rights. We get around the table and chaff each other. But we all recognize that we were not so reasonable in the beginning.

The economic results are invariably beneficial to the workers. Strikes have convinced employers of the economic advantages of reduced hours and higher wages. The strike has taken the place of the dagger and the club, which were used in earlier times in the struggle between the possessors of wealth and the workers. Strikes in the modern sense can occur only in civilized countries.

Adapted from Gompers' testimony in **Report of the Industrial Commission,** Vol. VII, pp. 606–608, 641.

Samuel Gompers at his desk in Washington headquarters of the A.F. of L., 1923. Gompers was elected president of the union every year except one from its foundation in 1886 to his death in 1924.

6 The American melting pot

Immigrants in Industrial America

Introduction

The most widely used expression in the American language associated with immigration is *the melting pot*. America is thought of as an enormous pot where many races and nationalities of people were blended into one new and distinctive nationality. This figure of speech came into general use after a play with that title appeared on Broadway in 1909.*

Many people have denied that the melting pot really works. But in spite of its drawbacks, the "melting pot" is the best expression that has yet been found for the interaction of a multitude of different *ethnic groups** in American society.

The melting pot suggests industry in action. It brings to mind an image of molten metals being blended into a new alloy. It was introduced just as the industrial transformation of American society was reaching a climax before World War I. Industrialization had a great deal to do with bringing so many different nationalities together in America. This assignment will explore some of the connections between immigration and industrialization.

The Immigrant Tide

Immigration is as old as American history, but the century of the great mass movement of peoples to the United States was from the 1820's to the 1920's. Beginning as a trickle, the immigrant stream reached flood stage in the era of industrialization. Three times as many immigrants came in the period 1870–1920 as in the previous fifty-year span.* The volume did not expand evenly, however, for the immigrants came in a series of great waves. The graph of immigration clearly shows this succession of crests and troughs.

Why were these millions of people on the move? First, Europe was going through a population explosion. Its population more than doubled between 1800 and 1900. Multitudes had to seek homes in less crowded places. Second, changes in landholding and farming patterns forced many peasant farmers to look elsewhere for a living. Religious persecution and political repression played a lesser part in stimulating *emigration.**

The points mentioned above are often called *push factors,* since they tended to push the emigrants out of their original homelands or to make it easier for them to migrate. But *pull factors* were also at work. America was

Before the play by **Israel Zangwill,** an English Jew, people spoke of "fusion" of different nationalities in America, or of a "melting process." Zangwill's play popularized the term **melting pot.**

Ethnic group: a group of people set apart by their distinctive language, religion, nationality.

Between 1820 and 1870 some **7.4 million immigrants** came to America; from 1870–1920, 26.3 million.

When people leave their homeland to settle permanently elsewhere, the movement is called **emigration.** When people reach the country where they intend to live, they are called **immigrants.**

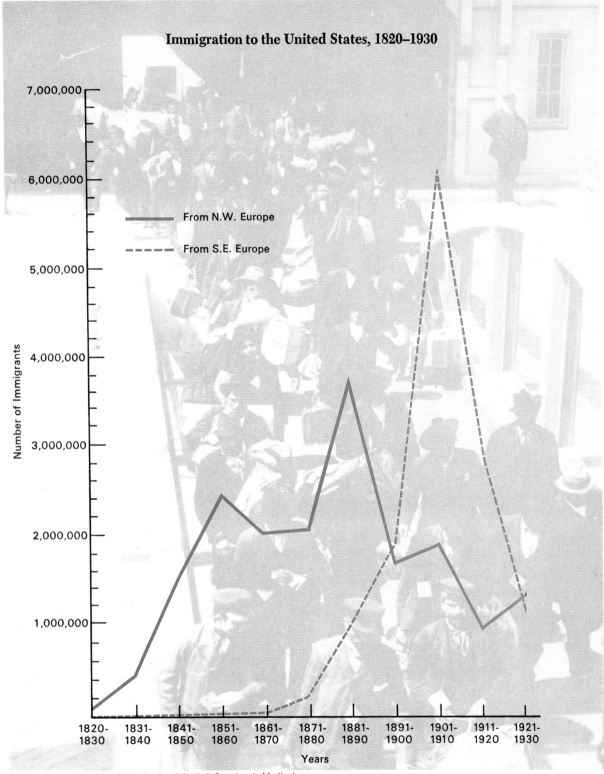

Immigration to the United States, 1820–1930

From N.W. Europe

------- From S.E. Europe

Number of Immigrants

7,000,000
6,000,000
5,000,000
4,000,000
3,000,000
2,000,000
1,000,000

1820-1830 | 1831-1840 | 1841-1850 | 1851-1860 | 1861-1870 | 1871-1880 | 1881-1890 | 1891-1900 | 1901-1910 | 1911-1920 | 1921-1930

Years

(From Immigration and Naturalization Service of the U. S. Department of Justice.)

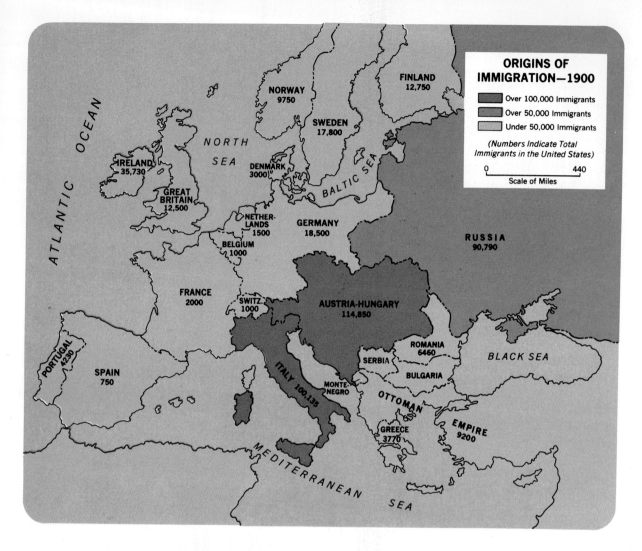

ORIGINS OF IMMIGRATION—1900

- Over 100,000 Immigrants
- Over 50,000 Immigrants
- Under 50,000 Immigrants

(Numbers Indicate Total Immigrants in the United States)

0 ———— 440
Scale of Miles

ATLANTIC OCEAN

NORTH SEA

BALTIC SEA

NORWAY 9750

SWEDEN 17,800

FINLAND 12,750

IRELAND 35,730

GREAT BRITAIN 12,500

DENMARK 3000

NETHER-LANDS 1500

BELGIUM 1000

GERMANY 18,500

RUSSIA 90,790

FRANCE 2000

SWITZ. 1000

AUSTRIA-HUNGARY 114,850

ROMANIA 6460

SERBIA

BULGARIA

BLACK SEA

PORTUGAL 4230

SPAIN 750

ITALY 100,135

MONTE-NEGRO

OTTOMAN

GREECE 3770

EMPIRE 9200

MEDITERRANEAN SEA

a great magnet drawing immigrants to itself. Although the prospect of political and religious liberty exerted a powerful attraction, the great mass of immigrants were drawn by opportunities for economic advancement. America was better known as "the land of unlimited opportunities" than as "the land of the free."

Immigrants in an Industrial Society

In colonial times and the early nineteenth century, cheap land drew the immigrants most powerfully. Many of the earlier immigrants—such as *Germans, Scots-Irish, and Scandinavians**—went into farming. But the construction of canals and railroads required an enormous force of unskilled laborers. First the Irish and later the Chinese supplied this labor. Italian immigrants performed much of the heavy construction labor in the building up of city transit systems, bridges, and tunnels.

These groups, along with the **Irish,** made up the so-called "old immigration."

C112

Skilled *immigrant workers,** especially from Great Britain (where the Industrial Revolution began), played a key role in the beginnings of American manufacturing. Even before the Civil War, the textile industry in New England depended on Irish immigration, for it had exhausted the native American labor supply of the region. Later in the century, immigrants from French Canada furnished another important source of labor for New England's mills.

The tremendous industrial growth of the late nineteenth century created an unprecedented demand for workers. Hence practically all the *new immigrants** from southern and central Europe found jobs in transportation, mining, and manufacturing industries. Without this supply of labor, America's industrial expansion could not have taken place.

In 1911, for example, 58 percent of the nation's iron and steel workers were foreign-born, and an additional 13 percent were *second-generation immigrants.** In the manufacture of clothing—which employed much sweatshop labor—the proportions were even higher. More than 95 percent of the workers were either foreign-born or second-generation immigrants, mainly Jewish and Italian. Across the range of twenty leading industries, fully six out of ten workers were first-generation immigrants.

Most of the immigrants were peasant farmers or villagers. Hence they were inexperienced as workers in mine or factory. Few could speak English. In order to make use of this immigrant labor, jobs had to be simplified. One way of doing this was by devising machines which could handle complex tasks, yet required little training on the part of the operator. Thus immigration played a role in hastening the mechanization of labor. The Immigration Commission's Report in 1911 noted that this process had taken place in bituminous coal mining, in cotton textile factories, in glass-making, in iron and steel plants, and in a number of other industries.

A few exceptional immigrants rose to positions of wealth and power.* For them the "rags-to-riches" myth was a reality rather than a dream. But for the great mass of immigrants, success meant something much more limited. It meant better wages, money in the bank, ownership of a home, and the prospect of a brighter future for their children. Although limited, this social advancement was real. It opened the way for further gains by later generations, who owe much to their immigrant ancestors.

The Movement to Restrict Immigration

Although American workers were indirectly benefited by immigration, they tended to regard the newcomers as competitors for their jobs. This is understandable, not only because of fluctuations of the economy which caused unemployment, but because recent immigrants were often used as strikebreakers. It was also widely believed—although incorrectly—that immigration drove down the wages of American workers. The unions also found it difficult to organize the new immigrants, who seemed so foreign in their speech and customs. For these reasons, the A. F. of L. advocated a literacy test for immigrants in 1897 and supported the movement to restrict easy entry of immigrants thereafter.

The most famous example is **Samuel Slater,** a skilled English textile worker, who emigrated to the United States in 1789 and constructed from memory the machinery used in English cotton mills.

The **new immigrants** consisted mainly of Italians, Slavs, and Jews.

The American-born children of immigrants are called **second-generation** immigrants; the grandchildren are the **third generation,** and so on.

The most spectacular example is **Andrew Carnegie** who emigrated from Scotland as a boy of twelve and became one of the most famous "captains" of industry.

C113

Social reformers tended to agree with labor on the need for immigration restriction and believed limitation was necessary to improve the situation of American workers. The throngs of immigrants in the cities were associated in the reformers' minds with a host of problems—slum housing, drunkenness, and political corruption. Without some stemming of the immigrant tide, reformers did not believe these problems could be dealt with successfully.

Reformers were not the only people worried about what immigration was doing to American society. Many Americans of old stock were made uneasy by the immigrant colonies and ghettos with their babble of tongues and conspicuously foreign atmosphere. Moreover, there were so many of these foreigners!

In times of prosperity and national self-confidence, the threat posed by immigration seemed manageable. But when a depression struck, when society was rocked by industrial warfare, or when some other great crisis divided the country, public opinion shifted. Then it seemed almost reckless to allow the immigrant flood to pour on unchecked, aggravating all of society's existing problems.

In such times, bigots played on ancient religious prejudices against Catholics and Jews. Fears of immigrant political radicalism grew more intense. By the outbreak of World War I, a racial theory had been worked out supposedly proving that the new immigrants sprang from inferior stock compared to the old immigrants.

The outbreak of war in Europe in 1914 proved decisive for the future of American immigration policy. The war revealed almost immediately the depth and intensity of old-world ties among immigrant groups in this country. As the crisis grew worse, and the United States was eventually drawn into the conflict, these ethnic loyalties became equated with disloyalty to America. The literacy test for immigrants became law in 1917. After the war a policy of permanent and drastic restriction ended the century of mass immigration.

11 THE PERSONAL SIDE OF IMMIGRATION

Objectives of this assignment are to:

—Analyze readings on reasons for emigrating to America and on immigrant experience in America for meaning.

—Analyze readings on immigrant aid societies to identify the services they performed.

—Draw inferences about difficulties of immigrant experience from filmstrip of contemporary illustrations.

—Make a judgment on effect of industrialization on immigrant experience.

Although immigration was a mass movement, it was also a highly personal matter for the individuals involved. The decision to leave for America was never easy. Emily Greene Balch, a professor of economics at Wellesley College, traveled to Austria-Hungary in 1905 to study the background of immigrants to America from that region and the reasons why they decided to leave. Her book, Our Slavic Fellow Citizens, is a classic in immigration studies.

The lives of immigrants were profoundly changed by the experience of living and working in America. The famous "Pittsburgh Survey," an investigation of social conditions in that industrial city, published in 1914, revealed how different that experience could be. While reading these selections from American immigrant history, keep these questions in mind:

1. *What were the phases of Slovak immigration?*

2. *What kinds of people were most apt to emigrate?*

3. *Which of the immigrants to Pittsburgh do you think had the greatest success? Which had the least success?*

Slavic Immigration: A European Perspective

At Bartfeld, a Slovak town in *Hungary,** we had an interesting talk with one of the earliest emigrants, a hatter who went to the United States about 1880. He told us that the first emigrant from this town was a Jewish dealer in cloth. When this man returned home, his account of America induced others to emigrate, among whom was the hatter. He hoped to find work as a hatter, but no one he met could tell him where hats were made, so he worked as a longshoreman, a miner, and so on. He was first in New York, then Pennsylvania, then Cleveland, and later Boston, where he did find work at hatmaking. He reported that in those days miners earned from $1.25 to $2.00 a day. Passage to America was cheap—$20 from Hamburg to New York.

Slovak emigration, and other movements like it, develop through well-defined phases. First the man goes alone and returns with his earnings, as he had planned to do originally. Then he goes again, and this time decides to settle or at least to remain for some time, and returns to bring his wife and children to America.

At a later phase, when the routes are better known and parties are frequently starting, the man often sends for his wife to come and join him, without going himself to get her. She is not always eager to begin life again under strange conditions. Often she fears to face the long and difficult journey alone with a family of little children. We met one woman just starting out, waiting at the home railroad station with baby and bundles. Her husband, after vainly urging her to come to him, had finally cut off supplies and sent a *prepaid ticket,** and willy-nilly she was going.

A still later phase is when the unmarried girls begin to go over independently, as the Irish girls have done for so long. They go mainly into domestic service as housemaids. To them America is even more of an *El Dorado** than to the men. Their wages are much higher than what they would earn at home, and they are often treated with greater respect and kindness.

An important question regarding any stream of immigration is, are we getting the failures who cannot succeed at home—as people say, "the dregs, the scum"? Among the Slovaks, those most apt to emigrate are the ones who are ambitious and whose credit is good—for they commonly go on borrowed money. They are usually physically strong, for they expect (and are expected) to make "big money" in America by undertaking what is known to be very hard work. There are exceptions, of course, but my conclusion is that on the whole we get the pick of the peasant class from which most of the immigrants are drawn.*

Before World War I, the **Slovak** homeland was part of the **Austro-Hungarian Empire. Czechoslovakia** was made an independent state as part of the Versailles settlement after the war. Czech and Slovak immigrants in the United States played an important role in promoting its creation.

A **prepaid ticket** was usually purchased in the United States by an immigrant, who then sent it home to be used by a relative or friend.

El Dorado was the name of a mythical treasure city sought by the early Spanish explorers in South America. The name came to be applied to any fabulously wealthy place.

Miss Balch explained elsewhere that a **peasant** was "far from being at the bottom of the social ladder" in the traditional agrarian society of Europe. Rather, the peasant was "a landholder, more nearly comparable to the American farmer than to any other class among us."

From Emily Greene Balch, **Our Slavic Fellow Citizens** (New York; Charities Publication Committee, 1910), pp. 100-101, 106-108.

Three Slavic Immigrants in Pittsburgh

Palinski, Mlinek, Antonik

There was no Polish national state in the 19th century. It had been divided among Prussia, Austria, and Russia. Hence, a **Russian Pole** was a Pole who came from the area controlled by Russia.

Palinski, a *Russian Pole** of forty-five who had been in America eighteen years, was an excellent example of that sizeable group of low-paid workmen who have made a small success—if owning a home and having a happy family and feeling contented is counted as success. The highest pay Palinski ever got was $1.65 a day. And yet, though he had five children, he had managed to buy in conjunction with his brother the house in which they both lived. They paid $1,600 for the property and expected to sell it for at least $3,000. The oldest child, a girl of fifteen, was in the public school, and his three other children of school age were being sent to the parochial school where tuition must be paid for. The house was strikingly clean and well arranged. Palinski seemed to be well satisfied with himself, his family, and his work.

A man who succeeded in the accepted American meaning of success was John Mlinek. On first meeting him, I did not suspect he was a Slav, so well dressed and thoroughly conventionalized did he seem, and such good English did he speak. He came to America at fifteen and worked in the mines of eastern Pennsylvania. Then he went to New Jersey to an iron works, and later became a riveter in a plant in Pittsburgh. He made $3.00 to $4.00 a day in the last place and saved up considerable money because he did not drink or indulge in other forms of dissipation. He married an American-born girl of Slovak background. She had worked as a clerk in a store where foreign customers traded and was respected and ambitious. She induced her husband to start a cigar and candy store. They have been doing very well and must have saved several thousand dollars. They are well liked and are active in social affairs in the Slovak community. Mlinek was, I should say, at the beginning of a considerable success.

Andrew Antonik was less fortunate. He was the victim of an industrial accident. Such men are met everywhere in Pittsburgh—they are so common as to excite no comment. Antonik's job was to run a "skull-cracker" in the Homestead Mill. This is a contrivance to break up scrap metal so that it can be more easily melted. Its main feature is a heavy pear-shaped iron ball which is hoisted into the air, then dropped on the scrap which has been heaped up beneath it. The crash of this ball throws pieces of metal in all directions. The work is very dangerous, especially at night. One Monday night, while he was working a *twenty-four-hour shift,** Antonik was hit by a chunk of scrap weighing four or five hundred pounds. His leg was crushed and had to be amputated.

The **usual working day** for the steelworker in this era was 12 hours; however, for technical reasons, the steelworkers had to work a 24-hour shift once every two weeks.

When I saw Antonik a year after the accident, the only work he could do was take care of his landlady's children. He had been paid $150 by the company at the time of the accident. That money was now gone. The company promised him an artificial leg and light work as soon as he was able to get around, but his stump was not yet entirely healed. His wife in Hungary was begging him for money, since she had the care of their five children. Antonik was worried.

Adapted from Russell Sage Foundation, **Wage-Earning Pittsburgh** (New York: Survey Associates, Inc., 1914), p. 66, 70, 73–74.

12   IMMIGRANT SOCIETIES

When the immigrants reached the United States, they naturally sought out their relatives, friends, and fellow-countrymen and settled near them. Many native Americans regarded the immigrants as "clannish" and vaguely resented their numerous "nationalistic" organizations, newspapers, and other institutions. Perhaps the most universal form of immigrant organization was the mutual-aid society or benevolent society. While reading these accounts of immigrant-aid societies, keep these questions in mind:

1. *Why were the German mutual-aid societies founded?*
2. *What services did the Italian mutual-aid societies perform?*
3. *What services did the Jewish fraternal societies perform?*

A German Immigrant Explains the Origin of Mutual-Aid Societies, 1860

All of us have been transplanted from our native soil to a strange land, just as Israel was removed from Zion to the waters of Babylon. And did not many of us *hang our harps on a weeping willow tree* when we landed on this foreign shore?* True, a man could earn a better living here than in the old homeland. But we ate our bread among strangers, and in a state of pervasive insecurity.

At home we had around us a world we knew, and in which we were known. We grew up bound together with that world by a thousand ties of blood and social belonging. Whether we were rich or poor, this familiar world enveloped us. None felt the loneliness and insecurity that assail the solitary stranger in a foreign land.

Things were different here, especially for those who immigrated some years ago. In those days, even the parish life of our churches was scarcely established. There was hardly any trace of those social relations which develop only through years of association. The feeling of being lost and forsaken gripped a man's heart, and made everything seem more discouraging than it actually was. This created a great need for communal support and solidarity in times of sorrow and need. Our mutual-aid societies were formed to meet this need. Such is the general explanation for the origin of these societies.

In Psalm 137 of the Old Testament the Israelites recall their sorrow in captivity in Babylon. In their sadness, they hung their harps on the trees and refused to sing. In the King James version the Psalm begins: "By the rivers of Babylon there we sat down, yea, we wept, when we remembered Zion. We hanged our harps upon the willows in the midst thereof."

Translated and adapted from **Central-Blatt and Social Justice** (St. Louis, Missouri: July, 1917), Vol. X, p. 73.

Mutual-Aid Societies Among Italian Immigrants

The Italians of Chicago have 110 mutual-aid societies. The membership is generally from the same Italian province and frequently from the same village. The most popular, the *Unione Siciliana*, has 28 lodges. Sick benefits in this order range from $8 to $12 per week, and a death benefit of $1,000 is paid. The average cost of membership is from $12 to $15 per year. Funeral expenses ranging from $50 to $90 are paid, and every member makes a contribution of $2 to the family of the dead member. During the sickness of a member all

Adapted from Robert A. Park and Herbert A. Miller, **Old World Traits Transplanted** (New York: Harper & Row, Publishers, 1921), p. 129.

other members are obliged to visit and assist him if he lacks a family. All members are obliged to attend the funeral, under penalty for absence. A band of musicians is always provided.

The Value of Jewish Fraternal Societies

The Jewish fraternal orders constitute a valuable and important factor in our communal life. One important consideration is that the recipient of benefits from the lodge or order does not lose his self-respect, nor his standing in the organization, as is often the case of recipients of public charity.

These lodges are the most valuable schools through which our immigrated Jews pass. Many have learned their English at their lodge meetings. Others have acquired there their knowledge of parliamentary procedure and decorum at public meetings. Many of our best-known public men and speakers have begun their careers by filling an office in their lodge or joining the debates at the meetings. In fact most of our people gain their connection with and knowledge of American Jewish activities through their affiliation with the Jewish fraternal orders.

Adapted from Park and Miller, **Old World Traits Transplanted**, pp. 129–130.

13   IMMIGRATION AND THE GENERATION GAP

Adjustment to American life was filled with trials for the immigrant. In spite of the sort of support given by immigrant societies, it was a wrenching experience to leave one's homeland and find a new home among strangers. What carried many an immigrant along was the hope that his children would enjoy advantages denied to their parents. Because so much was focused upon the children, there was a special sadness about the split that often grew up between immigrants and their American-born sons and daughters. The following letter reveals how parents and children sometimes found themselves in different worlds, isolated from each other. This letter was written to the Yiddish-language newspaper, the Jewish Daily Forward, in 1938. While reading this selection, keep these questions in mind:

1. What did this immigrant father do for his family?

2. Why do you think this immigrant father is disappointed?

An Immigrant Parent's Lament

Dear Editor,

I am a man in my fifties, and I came to America when I was very young. I don't have to tell you how hard life was for a greenhorn in those times. But I harnessed myself to the wagon of family life and pulled with all my strength.

My wife was faithful, and she gave me a hand in pulling the wagon. The years flew fast, and before we looked around we were parents of four children who brightened and sweetened our lives. The children were dear and smart, and we gave them an education that was more than we could afford. They went to college, became professionals, and are well settled.

And suddenly I feel as if the ground has collapsed under my feet. I don't know how to express it, but the fact that my children are well-educated and have outgrown me makes me feel bad. I can't talk to them about my problems, and they can't talk to me about theirs. It's as if there were a deep abyss between us that divides us.

People envy me my good, fine, educated children, but (I am ashamed to admit it) I often think it might be better for me if they were not so well-educated, but ordinary workingmen, like me. Then we would have more in common. I have no education because my parents were poor, and in the old country they couldn't give me the opportunities that I could give my children. Here, in America, I didn't have time, and my mind wasn't on learning in the early years when I had to work hard.

That is my problem. I want to hear your opinion about it. I enclose my full name and address, but please do not print it. I will sign instead as—

Disappointed

From **The Bintel Brief** by Isaac Metzker, copyright © 1971 by Isaac Metzker and Doubleday & Company, Inc. Reprinted by permission of the publisher.

16 Embarkation in Europe, 1874

Museum of the City of New York

17

Museum of the City of New York

18

Map of an Italian Neighborhood in New York City Showing Points of Origin in Italy and Sicily

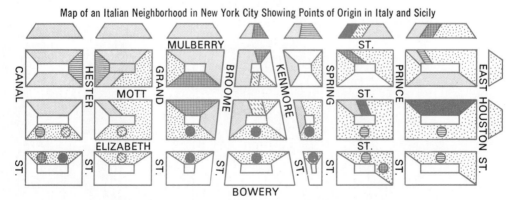

ITALIAN PROVINCES

NAPLES   BASILICATA   APUGLIA

CALABRIA   ABRUZZI   SICILY

SICILIAN TOWNS

 PALERMO   GIRGENTI

SIACCA   MESSINA

19

Immigrant Boarding House
Pittsburgh

Russel Sage Foundation: **Wage Earning Pittsburgh**

Brown Brothers

20

Immigrant Coal Miners

7 Cities in an industrial age

Crossroads of a New Civilization

Introduction

Men lived in cities for centuries before the first factory smokestacks darkened the urban skies. Indeed, cities date back to the very dawn of *civilization.** But in the nineteenth century, industrialization created a new kind of city. Most of us now live in cities partially formed by that age. Perhaps we can understand our own situation better by looking at those cities in an earlier stage of their development.

Between 1860 and 1910, the urban percentage of America's population more than doubled, jumping from 20 percent to 46 percent. The largest cities were growing fastest of all. Long before the urban population outstripped the rural population, the city had become the pacesetter and center of influence in American society.*

The new city dwellers came from American farms and villages, and as immigrants from foreign countries. The internal migration of native Americans was probably more important, but the immigrants were concentrated in the great cities, and their *polyglot** variety lent distinctive character to the urban scene. They flocked to the cities because jobs existed there. By 1910, more than one-third of the people of Chicago were foreign-born.

The fact that the words **city** and **civilization** both come from the **same Latin root** suggests how close the relation is between urban life and the growth of human culture.

Urban dwellers did not make up 51 percent of the population until 1920.

Polyglot literally means many-tongued. The word was often applied to American cities during the height of immigration.

Ethnic Ghettos

To many contemporaries, immigrants were one of the major urban problems. Packed in ethnic ghettos and clinging to their inherited languages and customs, they threatened to make the cities foreign territory within the American nation. Immigrants were associated in many people's minds with radicalism and violence. Added to this, they lived in slums that were festering sores endangering the health of the whole social body.

Looking back today we can see that the problems were real enough, but that it was a mistake to blame the immigrants, whose miseries in the slums encompassed rats, cold, and hunger. Overcrowded and substandard housing in the tenement canyons was practically inevitable. After all, hundreds of thousands of people were brought together in a few short years, and crammed into a very small land area. Density of population aggravated scores of other urban problems, ranging from sanitation and waste removal to fire protection and education.

C122

Critics and Reformers

By the 1880's many Americans were deeply troubled by what they saw around them in the cities. Some of these critics had an invincible rural bias. To them the city would always seem a diseased place! But even sympathetic observers were disturbed. They might enjoy the city's excitement, but that did not blind them to the city's flaws. From many viewpoints, then, the city came in for critical examination and suggested improvements. Between 1900 and 1917 a major campaign to improve urban life through social and political reforms took place.

During these same years social scientists began to turn their attention to the city. Sociologists at the University of Chicago played a pioneering role in the scholarly analysis of the urban scene. But historians lagged behind. The study of urban history did not really attract much interest until the 1950's. As a result, it is still rather difficult to give a connected historical account of the development of American cities.

Nevertheless, we have learned a great deal about the problems of urban life in the past, and every day we are learning more about the difficulties of living and working in American cities in the present. Knowledge of the past may help us realize that many problems that seem new are in reality old problems and their solution will be neither simple nor cheap. Making America's cities liveable was a great challenge in the 1890's, and all indications suggest that it will continue to be so in the 1990's.

Objectives of this assignment are to:

—Analyze nineteenth-century map of urban growth and selections from readings on mechanization of urban transportation and handwriting.

—Draw inferences from recording of a popular song about how urban employment and living changed social attitudes.

—Analyze contemporary accounts of urban politicians and reformers for meaning.

—Make a judgment on effect of rationalizing activity on urban reformers.

14 TRANSPORTATION AND MECHANIZATION IN THE INDUSTRIAL CITY

Improved transportation was the heart of nineteenth-century industrialization. Railroads not only bound urban areas together in a network of commerce and communication, they also played a key role in providing for the internal transportation needs of cities. Improved transportation within cities enabled them to expand in both area and population.

First came the horse-drawn street railway in the 1850's. Next, after the Civil War, the largest cities built elevated railways powered by steam locomotives. However, neither horses nor steam engines proved to be satisfactory power sources for urban transportation.

The great breakthrough came in 1887 when *Frank Sprague,* an electrical engineer, devised a practical way to use electric power to drive streetcars. Introduced first in Richmond, Virginia, the electric streetcar, or trolley, quickly displaced the horse-drawn car. Electric streetcars remained the principal means of urban mass transportation in American cities until the 1930's.

Frank Sprague was an engineer who worked with Thomas A. Edison before establishing himself in business independently.

As bustling centers for the exchange of goods and services, cities provided employment opportunities for all kinds of people—unskilled laborers, skilled tradesmen, salesmen, teachers, and especially clerks, accountants, stenographers, and secretaries. Commerce requires careful record keeping; and expanding commerce generates mountains of paper work. Consequently, white-collar jobs or office work turned out to be the most characteristic kind of urban employment.

No less than factory and farm work, white-collar jobs were also profoundly affected by technological change. The introduction of the typewriter increased output fully as much as the combine and moving assembly line.

While examining the following map of Boston's expansion into a metropolitan center and reading the description of improvements in urban transportation and in the mechanization of office work, keep the next questions in mind:

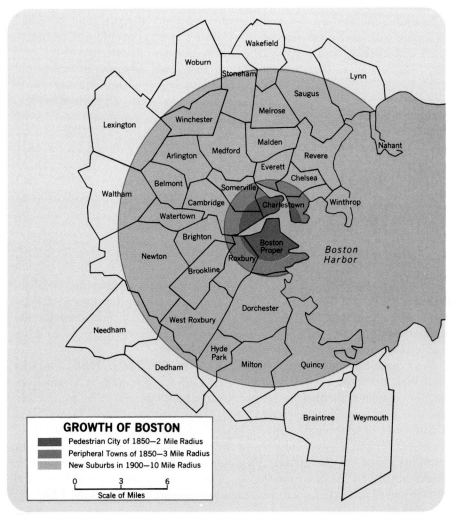

GROWTH OF BOSTON

- Pedestrian City of 1850—2 Mile Radius
- Peripheral Towns of 1850—3 Mile Radius
- New Suburbs in 1900—10 Mile Radius

0   3   6
Scale of Miles

1. *Why was the central part of Boston in 1850 called the "pedestrian city" on the map?*

2. *Why were large cities compressed into very small quarters?*

3. *What was the effect of the electrified street railway on urban growth?*

4. *What advantages did typewriting have over handwriting? Who was the first to recognize them?*

Transportation Improvement and City Growth

At the close of the century an observer accurately described past and future patterns: "When a pair of legs was the only vehicle of locomotion which the ordinary man could afford, large cities were unavoidably compressed into very small quarters. The horse-car and the *bus** added a mile or two to this area, but did not dispense with the necessity of severely economizing space. The trolley has stretched it out several miles farther, while future improvements in the machinery of transit may well make any spot within fifty miles of the center of an important city available as a place of residence for its wage earners. The extent to which the urban population may be distributed will be restricted only by the means of transit."

Bus here refers to **omnibus**, meaning a large, horse-drawn vehicle for carrying passengers. Unlike the horse-drawn street-car, the omnibus did not run on rails.

Adapted from Charles N. Glaab and A. Theodore Brown, **A History of Urban America** (London: The Macmillan Company, 1967), pp. 153–154.

Traffic Congestion in Pre-automobile Era, Chicago Loop, 1910

The Introduction of the Typewriter, 1874–1900

A number of men worked on a writing machine, but **Christopher L. Sholes** is usually considered the principal inventor. **E. Remington and Sons,** gun manufacturers of New York State, put the first commercially-practical type-writers on the market.

It was not until 1874 that the *typewriter** was placed on the market for general sale. At first it met with public skepticism. The use of the machine involved such radical changes in certain methods of business that its advantages had to be clearly demonstrated before the business world would accept it. But the typewriter had a usefulness which was not to be ignored.

Among the first to recognize this fact were court stenographers, who found that with the aid of the typewriter several copies of the record could be turned out at once with neatness and speed. Seeing its advantages, lawyers began to adopt the typewriter for their private use.

The large business houses, which have an extensive correspondence and are always ready for improvements and time-saving methods, were next to adopt the typewriter. The commercial world in general soon followed their example. In fact, there is now not a single business or profession in which the typewriter has not established its usefulness.

An experiment carried out by the U.S. Department of Labor demonstrates the advantages of the typewriting machine over hand labor. The experiment involved the copying of 1,000 words of statute law. This was accomplished by the typewriter in 19.5 minutes, or at a rate of 51 words per minute. A copyist with a pen required 1 hour and 14.8 minutes, or about four times as long.

Adapted from **Twelfth Census of the United States, 1900, Manufactures, Part IV** (Washington: U. S. Census Office, 1902), p. 443.

The rise of the typewriter has been most remarkable. Looked upon at first as an article of amusement, it promises soon to become, if it is not already, the universal writing machine.

Mechanization of White Collar Workers

C126

15 THE URBAN POLITICAL SCENE

With their great masses of potential voters, cities developed a distinctive style of political life. The era of rapid urban growth was also the era of the political boss.

Urban political power was a rich prize. Cities had numerous elective and appointive offices to be filled. Political control of a city usually carried with it the right to decide who received valuable contracts for public works and franchises for municipal services such as street railways.

Many Americans believed political bosses were corrupt. This belief was correct in many instances. Public payrolls were padded, kickbacks were paid for municipal contracts, and sometimes public funds simply disappeared. Throughout the late nineteenth century, reformers waged fierce campaigns against the evils of bossism and the corruption they bred. Yet, despite an extraordinary amount of unfavorable publicity and some ceremonial prosecutions, bossism survived. It seemed to be a necessary and vital institution of urban life.

While reading the following selection describing a day in the life of George Washington Plunkitt, a minor boss in the New York City Democratic political organization known as *Tammany Hall,*° keep these questions in mind:

1. What kinds of services did Plunkitt provide for his constituents?

2. Do you think Plunkitt's activities on behalf of his constituents were corrupt or questionable?

Tammany Hall was the name of the Democratic political organization in New York City. It was founded as a fraternal benevolent society in 1789, and named after a 17th-century Delaware Indian chief.

A Political Boss's Day

2 A.M.: Aroused from sleep by the ringing of his door bell; went to the door and found a bartender, who asked him to go to the police station and bail out a saloon-keeper who had been arrested for violating the excise law. Furnished bail and returned to bed at three o'clock.

6 A.M.: Awakened by fire engines passing his house. Hastened to the scene of the fire, according to the custom of the Tammany district leaders, to give assistance to the fire sufferers, if needed.

8:30 A.M.: Went to the police court to look after his constituents. Found six "drunks." Secured the discharge of four by a timely word with the judge, and paid the fines of two.

9 A.M.: Appeared in the Municipal District Court. Paid the rent of a poor family about to be dispossessed and gave them a dollar for food.

11 A.M.: At home again. Found four men waiting for him. Spent nearly three hours arranging employment for them in city departments or for companies doing business under municipal franchises.

3 P.M.: Attended the funeral of an Italian. Hurried back to make an appearance at the funeral of a Jewish constituent.

7 P.M.: Went to district headquarters and presided over a meeting of election district captains. Each captain submitted a list of all the voters in his

district, reported on their attitude toward Tammany, suggested who might be won over, and so on. District leader took notes and gave orders.

8 P.M.: Went to a church fair. Purchased chances on everything. Bought ice-cream for the young girls and the children. Kissed the little ones, flattered their mothers, and took their fathers out for something down at the corner saloon.

9 P.M.: At the political club-house again. Spent $10 on tickets for a church excursion. Bought tickets for a baseball game to be played by two teams from his district. Listened to the complaints of a dozen push-cart peddlers who said they were persecuted by the police and assured them he would go to police headquarters in the morning and see about it.

10:30 P.M.: Attended a Jewish wedding reception. Had previously sent a handsome wedding present to the bride.

12 P.M.: In bed.

Adapted from William L. Riordan, **Plunkitt of Tammany Hall** (New York, 1905), pp. 167–183.

16   TWO APPROACHES TO REFORM

Reformers in the late nineteenth century tried a number of different approaches in their efforts to deal with urban problems. One of the most appealing was the settlement-house movement.

The idea was that young people of middle-class background would "share the lives of the poor"* by establishing *settlement houses* in tenement districts and living there. The settlement was to serve as an educational and recreational center, and a headquarters for neighborly assistance and social work. Settlement workers also became spokesmen for the needs of the poor. They argued for reforms before municipal boards, publicized their cases in the press, and battled political bosses and grasping landlords.

Settlement houses originated in England. The first one in the United States was established in New York City in 1886. Most settlement workers were college students or recent graduates, who formed the "College and University Settlement Movement."

A visiting nurse takes a shortcut over tenement rooftops in making her calls. Sometimes these nurses and other social workers lived at settlement houses.

The most famous of the settlements was Hull House founded by *Jane Addams** in Chicago in 1888.

A second approach to urban reform emphasized the need for professionally trained specialists in city government. Such reformers insisted that housing and health problems could not be resolved or adequate municipal services provided without scientific study by trained professionals.

The belief that city government ought to be professionalized led to the development of two plans: the *city commission* and *city manager.** Under both plans, men with special technical qualifications were given responsibility for managing municipal services. At the same time, the power and responsibilities of mayors and city councils were reduced.

While reading the following selection from Jane Addam's recollections of her years at Hull House, and Henry Bruère's recommendations for municipal reform, keep these questions in mind:

1. *How did Jane Addams try to bridge the immigrant generation gap?*

2. *According to Bruère, what are the responsibilities of a good administrator?*

3. *Where did city government reformers get some of their ideas for making city government more efficient?*

Hull-House and the Immigrant Generation Gap

I recall a certain Italian girl who came every Saturday evening to a cooking class in the same building in which her mother spun in the *Labor Museum** exhibit; and yet Angelina always left her mother at the front door while she herself went around to a side door because she did not wish to be too closely identified in the eyes of the rest of the cooking class with an Italian woman who wore a kerchief over her head, uncouth boots, and short petticoats. One evening, however, Angelina saw her mother surrounded by a group of visitors from the School of Education, who much admired the spinning, and she concluded from their conversation that her mother was "the best stick-spindle spinner in America." When she inquired from me as to the truth of this deduction, I took occasion to describe the Italian village in which her mother lived, something of her free life, and how . . . she and the other women of the village had . . . developed a skill in spinning beyond that of the neighboring towns. I dilated somewhat on the freedom and beauty of that life—how hard it must be to exchange it all for a two-room tenement, and to give up a beautiful homespun kerchief for an ugly department-store hat. I intimated it was most unfair to judge her by these things alone, and that while she must depend on her daughter to learn the new ways, she also had a right to expect her daughter to know something of the old ways. . . .

It was easy to see that the thought of her mother with any other background than that of the tenement was new to Angelina and at least two things resulted; she allowed her mother to pull out of the big box under the bed the beautiful homespun garments which had previously been hidden away as

Jane Addams (1860–1935) grew up in a small town in Illinois. Her book, **Twenty Years at Hull-House,** is a classic in the literature of social reform.

The **City Commission** plan was pioneered in Galveston, Texas, following a disastrous hurricane and tidal wave. Staunton, Virginia, introduced the **City Manager** plan. These plans were most popular in small and medium-sized cities.

The **Labor Museum** was established at Hull-House so that immigrants could demonstrate handicraft methods of workmanship, and the products of pre-industrial craftsmanship.

Jane Addams, **Twenty Years at Hull-House** (Signet paperback ed., 1961), pp. 176–177. Copyright held by Macmillan Co.

uncouth; and she openly came into the Labor Museum by the same door as did her mother, proud at last of the mastery of the craft which had been so much admired.

Organizing for Efficiency in City Government

Wise administrators know that scientific organization is every bit as important as "scientific management."

The administrator must put the right man in the right place. He must organize the work according to its character and purpose. He must assign subordinate workers, and make clear the lines of authority between them and their superiors. He must also spell out what is expected of each employee in terms of the work to be done, and the time of its being done.

If the existing organization were diagrammed clearly, and the actual duties of each segment were described, few cities would continue with their present organizational structure. An honest picture of the prevailing situation in the average city department would generally cause an efficient department head to take one or more of the following steps:

1. Group and centralize control over similar functions (for example, purchasing).
2. Put together activities that belong together.
3. Place emphasis upon important work now carried on as a "side issue."
4. Divide work now done by one employee among two or more (this would be rare).
5. Give to one employee work now done by two or more (this would happen more frequently).
6. Abolish unnecessary processes and positions, old-fashioned habits, irresponsibility in subordinates, laxity or duplication in supervision, and conflicts in authority.

Such terms as *unifying, standardizing, systematizing, clarifying, coordinating,* and *controlling* are the watchwords of the efficient city government movement. They represent the processes now employed to make graft unprofitable because of sure detection.

New York City now has an accounting system equal to that of the Pennsylvania Railroad. Having learned the art of standardization of supplies from the Union Pacific Railroad, New York is setting an example for every American city. In its new municipal building it will conduct a testing laboratory unexcelled in the United States. All these steps have been taken to insure accuracy and economy in purchases in a city where only a few years ago every supply contract was an invitation to exploiters to gouge the public.

By substituting methods of precision for guesswork, the New York City budget has become an effective instrument of progressiveness and efficiency. And efficient budget methods automatically save millions a year whose waste in the grab-bag era never even came to light.

Adapted from Henry Bruère, **The New City Government** (New York & London: D. Appleton and Company, 1916), pp. 115–118.

C130

8 Schools in a changing world

The Beginnings of Modern Mass Education

Introduction

Just reading the newspapers for a few days would impress a visitor from Mars with the importance of education in today's America. Besides the dozens of routine items (like sports events, PTA meetings, and school building), the visitor would surely be struck with all the space and headlines devoted to education and the public controversy it arouses. He would find reports of teacher strikes, student unrest, racial disturbances, debates over bussing and integration, and widespread criticism of the general performance of the schools.

The sheer size of American education accounts in part for the amount of public attention it gets. Everyone knows that education is a massive thing in the United States. But the knowledge becomes more vivid when we discover that by the end of the 1960's the number of students in our elementary and secondary schools was roughly equal to the *total combined populations* of Argentina, Canada, and Austria—51.3 million. Besides that, the number of our college and university students—7.5 million in 1968—constituted a population almost as great as that of Sweden.

Anything that big cannot help being immensely important to society. But what makes education even more crucial as a public concern is its key role in the American system of values, and in the expectations of the people. Historically, schools in the United States have been regarded as a principal means of opening the gates of opportunity for the individual. Their mission is to make equality a reality, not just a promise.

Besides making the American dream come true for individuals, the schools are expected to fulfill broad social purposes. Americans have always believed that to shape the mind of youth is to shape the future of society. Thus *Thomas Jefferson* and *Horace Mann** argued that republican government demanded an educated citizenry. Whenever new social problems emerge, reformers have turned to the schools as a chief instrument in overcoming them. That was as true in the past as it is in the present.

Educational Developments in the Industrial Age

The big social and economic changes of the industrial era affected education in two ways. First, they brought about a rapid increase in the numbers

Objectives of this assignment are to:

—Analyze statements by three contemporary educators about role and mission of American education for meaning.

—Analyze statements by contemporary educational spokesmen for minority groups about role and mission of education for similarities and differences.

—Make a judgment on persistence of similar educational problems from one generation to the next.

Thomas Jefferson devoted much thought to education and was the founder of the University of Virginia. **Horace Mann** was the leading educational reformer and promoter of public schools in the pre-Civil War era.

C131

of students, teachers, institutions, and the overall complexity of the educational system. Second, the larger social and economic changes gave rise to new social problems which the schools were called upon to meet—even while they were in the midst of dizzying change themselves.

Educational Statistics, 1870–1910

	Total enrollment public elementary and secondary schools	Enrollment, grades 9–12 and postgraduates (public schools)	Percent of population 17 years old graduating from high school	Bachelors, or first professional degrees awarded by institutions of higher education
1870–71	6,871,522	80,277	2.0%	9,371
1880	9,867,505	110,277	2.5%	12,896
1890	12,722,581	202,963	3.5%	15,539
1900	15,503,110	519,251	6.4%	27,410
1910	17,813,852	915,061	8.8%	37,199

The growth that marked the beginnings of modern mass education came just at this time for a number of reasons. First, the population was shooting upward at a record pace. Second, a larger percentage of the people lived in the cities, and it was easier to reach them through the schools. Moreover, the demands of urban life made it essential for children to receive longer and more systematic formal training. They needed it to function effectively as workers, and to take advantage of new opportunities for personal development offered by a more advanced society and greater leisure.

A new educational institution developed as it became clearer that basic verbal and mathematical skills were not enough to prepare young people for the complex urban-industrial world. This institution was the public high school. The number of students in these secondary schools quadrupled between 1890 and 1910. But even in 1910, fewer than one-tenth of the seventeen-year-olds in the population graduated from high school. Public secondary education was solidly begun. But it did not become the normal expectation for another generation.

When it was introduced, the high school was called "the people's college." But the regular colleges were also attracting increasing numbers of students. Colleges were affected by the prevailing educational ferment in other ways, too. Their days of massive growth were still many years in the future,* but already colleges were being called upon to reform their curricula, allow students greater freedom of choice in their studies, and involve themselves more actively in the new world taking shape around them.

In 1900, for example, the **University of Wisconsin,** one of the largest and most progressive state universities, had only 2,619 students. In 1969, it had 35,549 students on its Madison campus alone.

Problems and Reforms

The frantic pace of growth and change filled the educational world with excitement. And with confusion. There was a pressing need to bring some order out of the chaos—to fix the place of the high school between the elementary and collegiate levels, to define its curriculum, to set up standards for teacher preparation, for college admission, and many other problems.

Educators attacked these problems through numerous committees and organizations. A new institution, the *accrediting agency,** came into being to assist in establishing standards and in enforcing them.

This work of *standardizing** and rationalizing the educational system was vitally necessary. But the widespread enthusiasm for scientific management in the early twentieth century sometimes carried educators too far in their quest for "efficiency." They often tended to make a *fetish** of statistics, and to decide educational questions solely on the basis of per-pupil costs. But the efficiency approach was regarded as a reform at the time. Even the most forward-looking progressive educators believed that "social efficiency" should be a goal of democratic education.

Just as the efficiency movement in education reflected a broader trend in American society, so the Progressive Education Movement was part and parcel of the overall impulse toward reform that dominated American society in the period between 1900 and 1917.

Practically every kind of reformer looked to the schools to aid in the removal of social evils and the creation of a "society which is worthy, lovely, and harmonious."* Business and labor spokesmen expected great things from vocational and technical education. Farm groups supported vocational training in agriculture. Urban reformers like Jacob Riis and Jane Addams saw the schools as the only hope for "the children of the poor."* Everyone recognized the crucial role education was to play in the assimilation of the immigrants into American life. Education was everybody's concern; it was everybody's business.

Accrediting agencies were usually called **standardizing** bodies around the turn of the century. North Central Association of Colleges and Secondary Schools, established in 1895, was the most influential accrediting body.

Fetish: an object that is worshipped unreasonably.

John Dewey, great philosopher of Progressive Education, wrote these words in his classic work, **The School and Society,** published in 1899.

Jacob Riis, who was best known for his book, **How the Other Half Lives** (1890), devoted much attention to the schools in his **Children of the Poor** (1892).

Laboratory of Carpentry— Around 1900 this was considered as a school to dignify labor, a school of the future.

17 IMMIGRATION, EDUCATION, AND AMERICANIZATION

We have already seen that immigration played an essential role in America's economic development, and that it was deeply enmeshed in the major social problems of the age. For educators, too, immigrants were central figures to be taught more than the English language. They had to learn the importance of safety regulations on the job, and the basic responsibilities of civic life. Above all, they had to be made *good Americans.* They had to develop new loyalties to replace those they had brought with them across the sea.

Evening courses and *Americanization* classes were arranged for the adults.* But the task of molding the children of immigrants into good Americans fell to the public schools. Thus educators found it necessary to try to define what American nationality involved, and how it might be inculcated in the children of the melting pot. While reading these selections from prominent educational theorists of the period, keep these questions in mind:

1. According to Cubberly, what is the role of the schools in the Americanization process?

2. According to Lenz, how do the public schools promote the Americanization of immigrant children?

3. According to Dewey, what is the American nationality and how should it be taught in the schools?

Adult-education programs were carried on by many employers and private groups, as well as by public schools. **Americanization** programs fostered American patriotism while teaching the English language and American government.

Ellwood P. Cubberly on the Process of Americanization

About 1882, the character of our immigration changed in a very remarkable manner. Immigration from the north of Europe dropped off rather abruptly, and in its place immigration from the south and east of Europe set in and soon developed into a great stream. . . .

These southern and eastern Europeans are of a very different type from the north Europeans who preceded them. Illiterate, docile, lacking in self-reliance and initiative, and not possessing the Anglo-Teutonic conceptions of law, order, and government, their coming has served to dilute tremendously our national stock, and to corrupt our civic life. . . . Everywhere these people tend to settle in groups or settlements, and to set up here their national manners, customs, and observances. Our task is to break up these groups or settlements; to assimilate and amalgamate these people as part of our American race, and through the schools to implant in their children, so far as can be done, the Anglo-Saxon conception of righteousness, law and order, and popular government; and to awaken in them a reverence for our democratic institutions and for those things in our national life which we as a people hold to be of abiding worth.

Adapted from Ellwood P. Cubberly, **Changing Conceptions of Education** (Boston: Houghton Mifflin Co., 1909), pp. 14–16.

C134

Frederick P. Lenz on the Assimilative Activities of the Public School

1. The school at once throws the children of various nationalities into mutual relationships. This breaks up the standards and habits of any one nationality and, in order to progress, the child finds that he must adopt a common way of thinking and acting, which means that he must adopt the American standard. A newcomer to foreign colonies sees very soon that his friends become partly Americanized, and he will learn American customs and habits from his foreign brother.

2. The public school teaches the child the English language, which enables him to associate with Americans and various other nationalities, even outside of the school and his own district.

3. The school tends to break up hostilities between nationalities. The teacher prevents hostilities in the schoolroom and this does away with strife on the playgrounds.

4. It teaches American traditions and the history of our institutions under which comes a growth of patriotism. Race ties are broken up, and a social solidarity is secured.

5. The public schools, by the introduction of manual training, not only give the child some idea of American industrial methods, but teach him that manual work is here the universal rule and not a stamp of inferiority.

From Frederick B. Lenz, "The Education of the Immigrant," **Educational Review,** LI (1916), p. 475.

John Dewey on Nationalizing American Education

I want to mention only two elements in the nationalism which our education should cultivate. The first is that the American nation is itself complex and compound. The second is that the ideal of the nation is equal opportunity for all. Strictly speaking, it is interracial and international in its makeup. It is composed of a multitude of peoples speaking different tongues, inheriting diverse traditions, cherishing varying ideals of life. This fact is basic to our nationalism as distinct from that of other peoples.

Such terms as Irish-American or Hebrew-American or German-American are false terms because they seem to assume something which is already in existence, called America, to which the other factor may be externally hitched on. The fact is, the genuine American, the typical American, is himself a hyphenated character. This does not mean that he is part American and that some foreign ingredient is then added. It means that he is international and interracial in his makeup. He is not American plus Pole or German. But the American is himself Pole-German-English-French-Spanish-Italian-Greek-Irish-Scandinavian-Bohemian-Jew- and so on. The point is to see that the *hyphen connects instead of separates.* And this means at least that our public schools shall teach each factor to respect every other, and shall take pains to enlighten all as to the great contributions of every strain in our composite make-up.

. . . To nationalize American education is to use education to promote our national idea, which is the idea of democracy. This is the soul, the spirit, of a nationalized education.

The highly vocal support given by German-Americans to their embattled homeland in the years 1914 to 1917 angered many Americans. They felt that the **hyphen** in terms like **German-American** betrayed **divided loyalties.** Thus "hyphenation" was a hot issue when Dewey spoke to the NEA in 1916.

Adapted from John Dewey, "Nationalizing Education," in National Education Association, **Addresses and Proceedings of the Fifty-Fourth Annual Meeting . . .** 1916, pp. 184, 185, 188.

Class being held in a condemned schoolroom in New York City in the early 1890's. Note the heating stoves at the far end and the gas jets for illumination.

18 THE SCHOOLS OF MINORITY GROUPS

Native Americans saw a clear connection between education and the assimilation of immigrants. Most of them wanted the schools to break down the group loyalties and group consciousness of immigrant children and to foster in them a strong American consciousness and American loyalty.

Leaders of immigrant groups were equally aware of the connection between education and group identity. But they did not always see eye to eye with native Americans on what cultural traditions the schools should transmit or what group loyalties they should implant. Immigrant leaders had their own ideas about how they wanted the lives of their children molded.

If an immigrant group differed from the American majority in religion, as well as in language and nationality, the group might turn away from the public schools and establish school systems of its own. Both Catholic and Lutheran immigrants did just that on a large scale.

Americans wanted the schools to aid in the assimilation of immigrants. But that did not hold true for members of another minority group—American blacks. On the contrary, white Americans wanted the schools to help prevent the assimilation of blacks.

The *separate-but-equal** system of racial segregation received the Supreme Court's stamp of approval in 1896. In 1954 the Court reversed itself and called for the integration of schools to proceed "with all deliberate speed." But the pattern of racially segregated education has not been completely eliminated even yet.

A Supreme Court case in 1896 established the **separate-but-equal** doctrine regarding segregated transportation facilities rather than education. However, it was applied to schools. This doctrine was overthrown by a Supreme Court decision of 1954.

C136

Although black Americans were keenly sensitive to the injustice of the segregated system, at the turn of the century they were also concerned with other educational issues. There was, in fact, a sharp disagreement between two great black leaders on the type of education most useful for blacks.

Booker T. Washington argued for "industrial education" for blacks. Industrial education was very popular at the time, and Washington had carried it on for years at *Tuskegee Institute.** Industrial education was really the same as vocational training and included such things as dressmaking, saw-milling, plastering, printing, and even beekeeping as well as technical training.

W. E. B. Du Bois disagreed with Washington. He criticized too great a reliance on industrial education. Instead, he insisted that blacks should receive the traditional sort of higher education offered by the college or university. While reading these selections about education for minority groups, keep these questions in mind:

1. Why did the Czech Catholics build their own school in St. Louis?

2. Why did Booker T. Washington advocate a system of industrial education for blacks?

3. Why did W. E. B. Du Bois advocate a system of higher education for blacks?

Tuskegee Institute in Alabama was founded as an industrial-education school in 1881. Booker T. Washington (1856–1915), its first president, had himself attended an industrial school where he later taught—Hampton Institute in Virginia.

Immigrant Czech Catholics and Their Schools

In 1869, Father Joseph Hessoun, a great early leader of the Czech Catholics in St. Louis, wrote to a friend in Bohemia: "We have erected a school which ranks with the best in the city. The building is indeed a surprise to St. Louis. . . . The Bohemians here did not have a good name. They were considered incapable of progress. Now, suddenly, the poor Czechs build a school which compares favorably with the best in our town."

The building of such a school tested the mettle of each Bohemian Catholic parish and revealed the depth of its spirituality. The school was a parish investment for the future both religiously and ethnically. It was considered the promoter and conservator of the values which the immigrant brought with him from the old world and which he thought worth perpetuating in the new.

The school served a social and cultural need. It bound the parent and child together. It did something the Anglo-Saxon, puritanically orientated, public school could never hope to do. It was able to help the child of Czech Catholic parents adapt to the American way of life, while at the same time teaching him to respect old world manners and customs which were preserved in the home.

By 1905, there were more than fifty parochial schools, with some 11,500 students, in which the Bohemian language was studied and also used in teaching certain subjects. The first secondary school for Czech Catholics was opened up in 1887. Eventually it became St. Procopius College, but in the beginning it covered only the first two years of high school.

In 1901, this academy was moved from Chicago to Lisle, Illinois. At that time its curriculum was intended to accomplish four things for the students. First, it strove to preserve their ethnic consciousness or nationality. Second, it aimed to prepare them for the pursuit of higher learning. Third, it trained them in business subjects. And fourth, it helped those who needed it to complete the upper years of elementary school.

Not only the academy, but also the four-year college and seminary which evolved from it were considered by the Bohemian Catholics as necessary institutions for the promotion of religious faith and ethnic feeling.

Adapted from Joseph Cada, **Czech-American Catholics, 1850-1920** (Lisle, Illinois: Center for Slav Culture, 1964), pp. 38, 53-57, 61-62

Booker T. Washington Advocates Industrial Education

Some years ago, when we decided to make tailoring a part of our training at the Tuskegee Institute, I was amazed to find that it was almost impossible to find in the whole country an educated colored man who could teach the making of clothing. We could find numbers of them who could teach astronomy, theology, Latin or grammar, but almost none who could instruct in the making of clothing. . . .

I would not confine the race to industrial life, not even to agriculture, for example, although I believe that by far the greater part of the Negro race is best off in the country districts and must and should continue to live there, but I would teach the race that in industry the foundation must be laid—that the very best service which anyone can render to what is called the higher education is to teach the present generation to provide a material or industrial foundation. On such a foundation as this will grow habits of thrift, a love of work, economy, ownership of property, bank accounts. Out of it in the future will grow practical education, professional education, positions of public responsibility. Out of it will grow moral and religious strength. Out of it will grow wealth from which alone can come leisure and the opportunity for the enjoyment of literature and the fine arts. . . .

"Industrial Education for Negroes" by Booker T. Washington from **The Negro Problem:** A Series of Articles by Representative American Negroes of Today (James Pott & Company, 1903).

. . . I plead for industrial education and development for the Negro not because I want to cramp him, but because I want to free him. I want to see him enter the all-powerful business and commercial world.

W. E. B. Du Bois Advocates Higher Education

There must be teachers, and teachers of teachers, and to attempt to establish any sort of a system of common and industrial school training without *first* (and I say *first* advisedly) without first providing for the higher training of the very best teachers, is simply throwing your money to the winds. . . .

There was a time when any aged and wornout carpenter could teach in a trade school. But not so today. Indeed the demand for college-bred men by a school like Tuskegee, ought to make Mr. Booker T. Washington the firmest friend of higher training. Here he has as helpers the son of a Negro senator, trained in Greek and the humanities, and graduated at Harvard; the son of a Negro congressman and lawyer, trained in Latin and mathematics, and graduated at Oberlin; he has as his wife, a woman who read Virgil and Homer in

At Tuskegee Institute, Alabama, Booker T. Washington instituted a variety of courses, from chemistry to experience in actual road building for students. In this way, thousands of blacks became self-supporting in trades and industry. Below road builders develop Tuskegee campus.

the same classroom with me* . . . indeed some thirty of his chief teachers are college graduates. . . . And yet one of the effects of Mr. Washington's propaganda has been to throw doubt upon the expediency of such training for Negroes, as these persons have had.

Men of America, the problem is plain before you. Here is a race transplanted through the criminal foolishness of your fathers. Whether you like it or not the millions are here, and here they will remain. If you do not lift them up, they will pull you down. Education and work are the levers to uplift a people. Work alone will not do it unless inspired by the right ideals and guided by intelligence. Education must not simply teach work—it must teach life. The Talented Tenth of the Negro race must be made leaders of thought and missionaries of culture among their people. No others can do this work and Negro colleges must train men for it. The Negro race, like all other races, is going to be saved by its exceptional men.

W. E. B. Du Bois (1868–1963) studied at Fisk, a black university in Nashville, Tennessee, and at Harvard University. He earned his Ph.D. in history from Harvard in 1895.

"The Talented Tenth" by W. E. B. Du Bois from **The Negro Problem.**

C139

9   What historians have said

Analyzing a Historical Judgment

Objectives of this assignment are to:

—Analyze selections from two modern historians of the era of American industrialization for similarities and differences.

—Make a judgment on extent to which these two conflicting historical interpretations have been influenced by concept of rationalization.

—Make a judgment on extent to which value judgments on American social and political behavior account for differences in interpretation.

—Draw inferences about history and history writing from your analysis of these conflicting historical interpretations.

Introduction

The great period of American industrialization, 1870 to 1910, was complex and many-sided. As we have seen, Americans responded to its opportunities and challenges in different ways. Yet, however different were the responses of businessmen, farmers, workers, or educators to industrialization there was a set of ideas and activities common to all of them. In one way or another, the great American response to the opportunities and challenges of industrialization was *rationalized* activity. But as Max Weber himself pointed out many years ago, there was a fundamental paradox within the concept of rationalization itself. The systematic, rational pursuit of a goal might lead to unanticipated and even irrational results. For example, money making might become an end in itself. Rather than being spent on human needs, money might be "rationally" used to acquire even more money.

Precisely such unanticipated and irrational results of industrialization have led to disagreements among historians of the period. One group of historians writing under the influence of the early twentieth-century reformers found little to praise and much to blame. They saw America's political and business leaders as men devoted almost solely to the accumulation of wealth and power. Their actions are represented as being selfish, irresponsible, and antisocial.

Another group writing during the 1950's emphasized the accomplishments of the American industrial system and was much more sympathetic to the business leaders who had made those accomplishments possible. Analysis of two different interpretations of the age of American industrialization conclude your work on nineteenth-century American history.

19   SAMUEL P. HAYS ON AMERICA'S RESPONSE TO INDUSTRIALIZATION

Samuel P. Hays was born in Indiana in 1921. He was educated at Swarthmore College and received his doctorate in American history from Harvard in 1953. He has taught American history for several years at the Universities of Illinois, Iowa, and Pittsburgh. Professor Hays has written several articles and books on nineteenth-century American social and political history and has been one of the pioneers in using statistical analysis and computers in historical research.

The selection below is taken from his book The Response to Industrialism, 1885–1914, published in 1957. While reading this selection, keep these questions in mind:

1. *Why did American social and political movements between 1885 and 1914 attack business leaders?*

2. *Why does Hays reject an interpretation of the period which emphasizes a struggle of poor against rich?*

3. *How does Hays explain American political and social behavior between 1885 and 1914?*

Adjusting to Industrial Change

The unifying theme of American history between 1885 and 1914, so many historians have argued, was a popular attack against corporate wealth. Through their state and Federal governments, according to this interpretation, the discontented sought to curb corporations and thereby to promote greater economic opportunity for all. This analysis . . . is a far too simple explanation.

Industrialism did create disparities in wealth and class divisions beyond our comprehension today. But the social, economic, and political movements of those thirty years reveal something more fundamental and more varied than an attempt by the dispossessed to curb the wealthy. They comprised a reaction not against the corporation alone but also against industrialism and the many ways in which it affected the lives of Americans. The people of that era sought to do much more than simply to control corporations; they attempted to cope with industrial change in all its ramifications. True, they centered their fire on the business leader, but he was a symbol of change which they could conveniently attack, rather than the essence of change itself. A simple interpretation of the discontented poor struggling against the happy rich does violence to the complexity of industrial innovation and to the variety of human striving that occurred in response to it.

In a number of instances . . . Americans responded to industrialism in ways far different from those described by many historians. Reforms frequently arose from the well-to-do themselves; the social-justice movement, for example, grew up among those who had sufficient leisure to be concerned with education, parks, and the working conditions of women and children. On the other hand, the "people" often opposed the measures which, according to historians, were designed to curb corporate influence. Urban immigrants, for example, resenting the attack on the city political machine, opposed urban civic reforms. . . .

Although industrial innovation was the common American experience between 1885 and 1914, not all were aware of or concerned with the same facets of this change. Manufacturers, merchants, farmers, and workers were most disturbed by the new, impersonal price-and-market economy. The individual enterpriser now felt engulfed by a tidal wave of world-wide influences which he could scarcely understand, let alone control. Those concerned with personal values, on the other hand—religious leaders, women active in public affairs, the new middle class, and the rising group of intellectuals excitedly searching for knowledge about human life—were most impressed with the materialistic bent of industrial society and its hostility to the human spirit.

For the millions of people torn from accustomed rural patterns of culture and thrust into a strange, urban environment, the meaning of industrialism lay in a feeling of uprootedness; in the disintegration of old ways of life; and the loss of familiar surroundings. Those left behind on the farms experienced the new forces through the expansion of urban culture and its threat to the nation's agrarian traditions. They feared that metropolitan influences would reach out and drastically change the life they knew. Finally, those in the South and West lived under the shadow of a far more highly developed area which, they felt, deliberately imposed restraints upon the economic growth of their regions.

Industrialism increased the desire for material gain among all Americans; but economic motivation does not wholly explain the behavior of the American people during these years. Industrialism was less important in changing the motives of Americans than in profoundly altering the environment, the setting within which men and women strove for many different goals. Whether one was most concerned with the life of the spirit, with social institutions, or with economic gain, he had to come to terms with the vastly new society brought about by industrialism. The way in which Americans made this adjustment varied according to the positive goals they wished to achieve.

Samuel P. Hays, **The Response to Industrialism, 1885–1914** (Chicago: The University of Chicago Press, 1957), pp. 188–190.

20   RAY GINGER ON THE AGE OF EXCESS

Ray Ginger was born in Tennessee in 1924. He was educated at the University of Michigan and received his doctorate in American Civilization from Western Reserve University in 1951. He has taught American history at Western Reserve, Harvard, Brandeis, and Wayne State Universities. Professor Ginger has written many articles and several books on late nineteenth-century American social and political history. The selection below is taken from his book Age of Excess: The United States from 1877 to 1914 published in 1965. While reading this selection keep these questions in mind:

1. According to Ginger, what has been the basis of American prosperity during the past 100 years?

C142

2. Why did corporate bureaucracies develop?

3. How does Ginger explain American political and social behavior between 1877 and 1914?

The Price of Material Progress

The upsurge in the productive capacity of the American economy from 1877 to 1914 was awe-inspiring. It contributed to a standard of physical comfort that might serve as the basis for the most deeply human society in world history. But the price paid for material progress was great.

The American economy was tied to government outlays for nonproductive purposes, especially to military expenditures. It is hardly an exaggeration to say that for a century we have enjoyed sustained prosperity only in times of war, preparation for war, or recovery from war.

By the end of the period, the old society of independent men, which still existed in great degree in 1877, was being changed into a world of bureaucracy. As the president of the National Association of Manufacturers told its convention in 1911: "We are living in an age of organization; an age when but little can be accomplished except through organization; an age when organization must cope with organization."

Power was being gathered into fewer hands. Fewer persons had scope to exercise their personal preferences or private judgment in economic affairs. To some extent, of course, the new corporate bureaucracies were essential to economic efficiency. They were needed to make use of the possibilities of modern technology.

But it was no contribution to the public welfare for a handful of men to direct such a huge portion of the total resources of America. The Du Ponts had a whole collection of empires. So did the banking firm of J. P. Morgan. So did Henry Ford. The earnings of Standard Oil moved hither and yon across the economic scene. This concentration of control was not needed for efficiency. It came about because wealth meant power, and gave men of wealth the chance to get more power. And they did.

The problem went deeper than just a few evil men. The problem was that the typical American had no far-reaching vision of what kind of society he wanted. The ideal of abiding by the rules of the game was weakened. Only success counted, and the game had no rules. To contend for fair play was to expose yourself as weak and effeminate.

Americans had been absorbed in the pursuit of wealth for so long that they could not abandon themselves to any other values. They were more ignorant of history than any people had ever been. Ideals moved them to distrust and dislike. The mind of the times is revealed in the remark of the writer, Hamlin Garland, after he met Henry Ford: "He is a colossal genius, I am merely an industrious writer of obscure books; and yet he did not appear to despise me for my failure to make money."

The craving to "get ahead" was manifested in geographical mobility and in lust for wealth as the tool of social mobility. Men who prospered changed

Reprinted with permission of The
Macmillan Company from **Age of
Excess: The United States from
1877 to 1914** by Ray Ginger. Copyright © by Ray Ginger, 1968,
pp. 319–323. (Adapted.)

their religions. Episcopalianism was the creed of the wealthy. City-dwellers scorned their ancestors still on the farm. Second-generation Americans felt contempt and shame for the outlandish ways of their immigrant parents.

The United States became a country of men in flight, running over unmarked fields without traditions to guide them or visions to serve as beacons. They had no havens for rest, no end but the grave, and no goal but wealth. And of wealth there was never enough.

Additional Reading

Cochran, T. C. and Miller, W., *The Age of Enterprise,* Revised ed. New York: Harper, 1961.

Degler, Carl, *The Age of Economic Revolution, 1876–1900.* Glenview, Illinois: Scott, Foresman, 1967.

Garraty, John A., *The New Commonwealth, 1877–1890.* New York: Harper, 1968.

Klein, Aaron E., *The Hidden Contributors: Black Scientists and Inventors in America.* New York: Doubleday & Company, Inc., 1971.

Weisberger, Bernard A. and the Editors of LIFE, *The Age of Steel and Steam.* New York: Time Incorporated, 1968.

Wiebe, Robert H., *The Search for Order, 1877–1920.* New York: Hill & Wang, 1967.

UNIT NINE

20th Century America

The U.S. At Home and Abroad

JAMES E. O'NEILL

CHARLES J. TULL

*Those who cannot remember the past
are condemned to repeat it . . .*
GEORGE SANTAYANA

1 Becoming a great power

Spanish-American War

Introduction

Objectives of this assignment are to:

–Identify reasons justifying United States foreign policy in the Far East and Caribbean at turn of century.

–Make credibility judgment on justifications for United States foreign policy identification.

–Make historical judgments on United States foreign policy in Far East and Caribbean at turn of century.

What does it mean to be a "great power"? What advantages does it entail? What dangers and responsibilities? Is it inevitable that a large and wealthy nation like the United States be a great power? Or can such a nation remain aloof from involvement in the affairs of other parts of the world?

Americans have rarely posed these questions in such general and abstract terms. Instead, at different moments in the twentieth century they have asked and debated the answers to much more specific questions: Should the Philippine Islands be annexed? Should the United States join the League of Nations? Should it expand its war effort in Vietnam, or should it withdraw from that area altogether?

Even while they have debated such specific issues, however, most Americans have been aware that broader, general issues of America's conduct as a great power have been involved. They have also been aware that sometimes what they regarded as national ideals of liberty and self-government for all peoples have been in conflict with what they regarded as genuine national interests. This conflict (real or apparent) between national ideals and national interests is not unique to Americans. But in the twentieth century it has affected them more than it has other peoples, and it has helped turn America's relations with the rest of the world into a series of national crises.

This unit deals with a number of such crises in the twentieth century. It examines what happened when Americans had to reach policy decisions affecting the outside world, or when they had to adjust to a problem presented by the outside world.

The United States Becomes a Great Power

Whether the United States could be called a great power before 1898 depends on how one would define those words. Some Americans of the day, such as *William Jennings Bryan,*° argued that the moral impact of American democracy had long given the United States an influence in world affairs much greater than colonies or striking military victories could supply.

To the great powers of Europe like Britain, France, or Germany, such an argument was meaningless. Power was based not upon ideals or examples, but upon such tangible things as warships and armies. It meant the ability of a nation to obtain what it wanted (or to prevent what it did not want) through the use of tangible force or through the threat of its use. By that def-

William Jennings Bryan (1860–1925) was the Democratic Party candidate for President in 1896, 1900, and 1908, and opposed acquiring colonies. He served as Secretary of State under President Woodrow Wilson.

D2

inition America became a great power only in 1898 with its swift and decisive victory against Spain in the Spanish-American War.

Throughout the nineteenth century Americans looked with favor on revolutions in Latin America against Spain and the other European colonizing nations. The Monroe Doctrine of 1823 was an endorsement of the recently won independence from Spain of most South American countries and a warning that Spain should not seek to regain her lost colonies.* Most Americans looked favorably on the revolution against Spanish rule that broke out in Cuba in 1895 and hoped that the Cuban insurgents would win independence for their island.

That hope was disappointed. In response to the guerrilla-like war waged by the insurgents, Spain developed a system of *reconcentration camps** and prevented an insurgent victory. In the United States large-circulation newspapers like the <u>New York Journal</u> and <u>New York World</u> played up Spanish atrocities against Cuban insurgents and pressed for American intervention. Similarly, *jingoes** in Congress and in government urged American action. Congress declared war against Spain on April 11, 1898.

The following portion of an editorial from Joseph Pulitzer's *New York World* of February 13, 1897, illustrates some of the pressures on President McKinley.

The **Monroe Doctrine,** announced by President James Monroe in a message to Congress in 1823, stated that the Western Hemisphere was no longer to be used for colonization by European powers and threatened that the United States would fight to prevent any European interference in the Americas.

The **reconcentration camps** involved locking up large numbers of civilians in barbedwire enclosures to control them.

Jingoes were those who favored an aggressive policy and war with Spain. A later age would call them **hawks.** The word came from an English music-hall song of the 1870's.

How long are the Spaniards to drench Cuba with the blood and tears of her people?

How long is the peasantry of Spain to be drafted away to Cuba to die miserably in a hopeless war, that Spanish nobles and Spanish officers may get medals and honors?

How long shall old [Cuban] men and women and children be murdered by the score, the innocent victims of Spanish rage against the patriot armies they cannot conquer?

How long shall the sound of rifles in Castle Morro at sunrise proclaim that bound and helpless prisoners of war have been murdered in cold blood?

How long shall Cuban women be the victims of Spanish outrages and lie sobbing and bruised in loathsome prisons?

How long shall women passengers on vessels flying the American flag be unlawfully seized and stripped and searched by brutal, jeering Spanish officers, in violation of the laws of nations and of the honor of the United States?

How long shall American citizens, arbitrarily arrested while on peaceful and legitimate errands, be immured in foul Spanish prisons without trial?

How long shall the navy of the United States be used as the sea police of barbarous Spain?

How long shall the United States sit idle and indifferent within sound and hearing of rapine and murder?

How long?

War with Spain, 1898

In September, 1897—six months before the Spanish-American War—the young Assistant Secretary of the Navy, Theodore Roosevelt, advocated that the American naval squadron in the Far East attack the Spanish fleet in Manila if war should come. On February 25, 1898, Roosevelt, in the absence of his superior, Secretary John D. Long, ordered Commodore George Dewey to take offensive action in the Philippines "in the event of a declaration of war."

Shortly after midnight on May 1, 1898, Admiral Dewey's squadron slipped into Manila Bay past the guns of the Spanish fortress at Corregidor. At dawn Dewey's ships opened fire, and by noon the entire Spanish fleet had been silenced or destroyed. Dewey's victory in a far-off land (10,000 miles from Cuba) unleashed an outburst of joy and pride among patriotic Americans. Theodore Roosevelt wired Brooks Brothers for a tailor-made lieutenant-colonel's uniform and dashed off to Cuba with his "Rough-Rider" volunteers.

Troops were sent to occupy Manila, and in New York City a magnificent (but temporary) Dewey triumphal arch was raised on Fifth Avenue.

In the Caribbean, too, American victory was rapid. By the Fourth of July the United States Navy had blockaded Cuba and, in the battle of Santiago, had destroyed the Spanish naval squadron. By that date the United States had also landed troops in Cuba and had won decisive victories at El Caney and San Juan Hill (where Theodore Roosevelt and his Rough Riders played a leading role). On July 17, the main Spanish forces in Cuba surrendered.

In the words of one contemporary, the Spanish-American War was a *splendid little war.** It ended in less than three months, with very few American casualties, and made the United States a great power in the Far East, Central Pacific, and the Caribbean. The Philippines were acquired from Spain and the Hawaiian Islands were annexed. To these new possessions were added Guam, Wake Island, and a portion of the Samoan Islands.

Not all these countries welcomed the United States. In the Philippines, for instance, an independence movement was already underway, led by Emilio Aguinaldo, before the U.S. arrived. When Admiral Dewey and his squadron aborted this nationalist uprising, Aguinaldo and his Filipino insurgents fought a bitter war against their new American masters. But their independence movement was finally crushed by American troops in 1902.*

In the Caribbean, the United States acquired Puerto Rico from Spain. The Panama Canal Zone was leased in 1903, and in 1916 several of the Virgin Islands were purchased from Denmark. However, in the Caribbean, American power was not exerted primarily by acquisition of colonies. It was exerted, instead, by a combination of financial investment in Caribbean countries, along with periodic intervention to assure political order or to force financial reforms on incompetent governments. The United States became the policeman of the Caribbean by periodically placing small countries of that area under its "protection." Political and economic interests of the United States required that the governments of the Caribbean countries be stable and act responsibly. The U.S. Marines were to enforce stability and responsibility.

John Hay, Secretary of State, in 1898 wrote to Theodore Roosevelt:
"It has been a splendid little war; begun with the highest motives, carried on with magnificent intelligence and spirit, favored by that fortune which loves the brave."

Emilio Aguinaldo (1869–1964) lived to see the independence of his homeland. On July 4, 1946, he was the guest of honor when the Philippine Republic was established.

D4

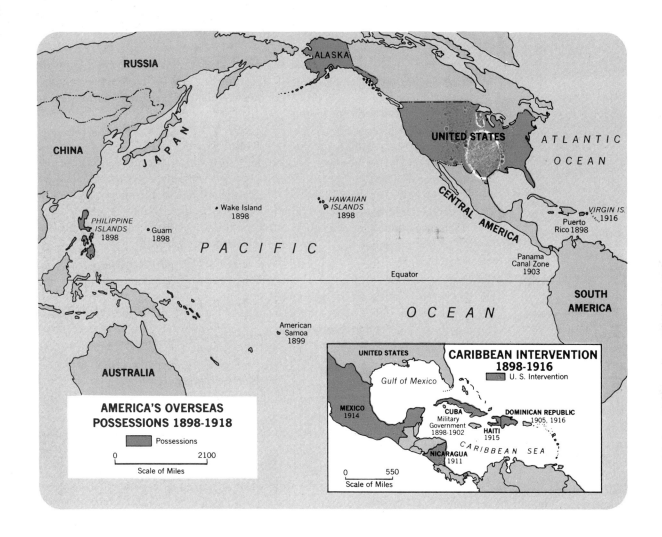

AMERICA'S OVERSEAS
POSSESSIONS 1898-1918

Possessions

0   2100
Scale of Miles

CARIBBEAN INTERVENTION
1898-1916
U. S. Intervention

0   550
Scale of Miles

1   DECISION ON CUBA

The growing clamor for armed intervention in Cuba was personally distasteful and troublesome to President McKinley. He was much more concerned about domestic issues than with foreign affairs, and only slowly and reluctantly did he come to accept the need for action. In his message to Congress on April 11, 1898, McKinley carefully analyzed the courses of action open to the United States government in the present situation and asked for war. While reading this statement of President McKinley, keep in mind these questions:

1. *Why did the United States go to war with Spain in 1898?*
2. *Why was McKinley opposed to annexing Cuba?*

McKinley Asks for Intervention in Cuba, 1898

In my annual message of last December I said: "Of the untried measures there remain only: Recognition of the insurgents as belligerents; recognition of the independence of Cuba; and intervention. I speak not of forcible annexation, for that can not be thought of. That, by our code of morality, would be criminal aggression."

Recognition of belligerence is not warranted by the facts.

Nor from the standpoint of expediency do I think it would be wise or prudent for this Government to recognize at the present time the independence of the so-called Cuban Republic. Such recognition is not necessary in order to enable the United States to intervene and pacify the island.

There remains the alternative of intervention to end the war. The grounds for such intervention may be briefly summarized as follows:

First. In the cause of humanity and to put an end to the barbarities, bloodshed, starvation, and horrible miseries now existing in Cuba, which the parties to the conflict are either unable or unwilling to stop or mitigate. It is no answer to say this is all in another country, belonging to another nation, and is therefore none of our business. It is specially our duty, for it is right at our door.

Second. We owe it to our citizens in Cuba to afford them that protection and indemnity for life and property which no government there can or will afford, and to that end to terminate the conditions that deprive them of legal protection.

Third. The right to intervene may be justified by the very serious injury to the commerce, trade, and business of our people* and by the wanton destruction of property and devastation of the island.

At this time, the United States had **$50 million invested** in sugar and tobacco plantations in Cuba, and it carried on an annual $100 million in trade.

Fourth, and which is of the utmost importance. The present condition of affairs in Cuba is a constant menace to our peace and entails upon this Government an enormous expense.

The object for which Spain has waged the war can not be attained. The fire of insurrection may flame or may smolder with varying seasons, but it has not been, and it is plain that it can not be, extinguished by present methods. The only hope of relief and repose from a condition which can no longer be endured is the enforced pacification of Cuba. In the name of humanity, in the name of civilization, in behalf of endangered American interests which give us the right and the duty to speak and to act, the war in Cuba must stop.

In view of these facts and of these considerations I ask the Congress to authorize and empower the President to take measures to secure a full and final termination of hostilities between the Government of Spain and the people of Cuba, and to secure in the island the establishment of a stable government, capable of maintaining order and observing its international obligations, insuring peace and tranquility and the security of its citizens as well as our own, and to use the military and naval forces of the United States as may be necessary for these purposes.

Adapted from **A Compilation of the Messages and Papers of the Presidents, 1789–1905,** edited by James D. Richardson (Washington, D.C.: Bureau of National Literature and Art, 1907), Vol. X, pp. 61–67.

2 DECISION ON THE PHILIPPINES

Six months later President McKinley had to make another decision. American arms had been victorious everywhere. The stars and stripes floated over Manila, and the President had to decide whether it should remain there. On November 1, 1898, the United States Peace Commissioner acting under the President's instructions demanded from Spain the cession of the Philippines. McKinley explained the basis of his decision to keep the Philippines to a group of Methodist ministers visiting him at the White House.

Most people applauded McKinley's decision as they had applauded Dewey's victory. But some Americans did not applaud. Senator George Frisbie Hoar, for instance, led the anti-imperialists who considered it un-American to annex and rule a foreign country. Another one of those who was not carried away by acquisition of the Philippines was a Chicago newspaperman named Finley Peter Dunne. Through the voice of his fictitious Irish-American bartender, "Mr. Dooley," Dunne had often gently ridiculed the pompous or pretentious with the weapon of political satire. While reading these selections, keep in mind these questions:

1. *How did McKinley decide what to do with the Philippines?*
2. *Why did McKinley decide to keep the Philippines?*
3. *Do Mr. Dooley and Mr. Hennessy agree about annexing the Philippines?*

Why McKinley Decided to Keep the Philippines

I have been criticized a good deal about the Philippines, but I don't deserve it. The truth is I didn't want the Philippines, and when they came to us, as a gift from the gods, I did not know what to do with them. When the Spanish War broke out, Dewey was at Hong Kong, and I ordered him to go to Manila and capture or destroy the Spanish fleet. He had to because, if defeated, he had no place to refit on that side of the globe. If the *Dons** were victorious, they would likely cross the Pacific and ravage our Oregon and California coasts. And so he had to destroy the Spanish fleet, and did it! But that was as far as I thought.

Dons was a popular word in the United States for the Spanish.

When next I realized that the Philippines had dropped into our laps I confess I did not know what to do with them. I sought counsel from all sides—Democrats as well as Republicans—but got little help. I thought first we would take only Manila; then Luzon; then other islands, perhaps, also. I walked the floor of the White House night after night until midnight; and I am not ashamed to tell you, gentlemen, that I went down on my knees and prayed Almighty God for light and guidance more than one night.

And one night late it came to me this way—I don't know how it was, but it came; (1) that we could not give them back to Spain—that would be cowardly and dishonorable; (2) that we could not turn them over to France or Germany—our commercial rivals in the Orient—that would be bad business and discreditable; (3) that we could not leave them to themselves—they were unfit for self-government—and they would soon have anarchy and misrule there worse than Spain's was; and (4) that there was nothing left for us to do but to take them all, and to educate the Filipinos, and uplift and civilize and *Christianize** them, and by God's grace do the very best we could by them, as our fellow-men for whom Christ also died.

And then I went to bed, and went to sleep, and I slept soundly, and the next morning I sent for the chief engineer of the War Department (our map-maker), and I told him to put the Philippines on the map of the United States [pointing to a large map on the wall of his office], and there they are, and there they will stay while I am President.

Most Filipinos were **already Roman Catholics** and many had long before adopted the ideas and attitudes of Western "civilization" from Spain.

From C. S. Olcott, **The Life of William McKinley** (Boston: Houghton Mifflin Company, 1916), pp. 621–622.

What "Mr. Dooley" Thought About the Philippines

"I know what I'd do if I was Mack," said Mr. Hennessy. "I'd hist a flag over th' Ph'lippeens, an' I'd take in th' whole lot iv thim."

"An' yet," said Mr. Dooley, " 'tis not more thin two months since ye larned whether they were islands or canned goods. If yer son Packy was to ask ye where th' Ph'lippeens is, cud ye give him anny good idea whether they was in Rooshia or just west iv th' thracks?"

"Mebbe I cudden't," said Mr. Hennessy, haughtily, "but I'm f'r takin' thim in, annyhow."

"So might I be," said Mr. Dooley, "if I cud on'y get me mind on it. Wan if the worst things about this here war is th' way it's makin' puzzles f'r our poor, tired heads. Whin I wint into it, I thought all I'd have to do was to set up here behind th' bar with a good tin-cint see-gar in me teeth, an' toss dinnymite bombs into th' hated city iv Havana. But look at me now. Th' war is still goin' on; an' ivry night, when I'm countin' up th' cash, I'm askin's mesilf will I an-nex Cubia or lave it to the Cubians? Will I take Porther Ricky or put it by? An' what shud I do with th' Ph'lippeens? Oh, what shud I do with thim? I can't annex thim because I don't know where they ar-re. I can't let go iv thim because some wan else'll take thim if I do. They are eight thousan' iv thim is-lands, with a population iv wan hundherd millyon naked savages; an' me bed-room's crowded now with me an' th' bed. How can I take thim in, an' how on earth am I goin' to cover th' nakedness iv thim savages with me wan shoot iv clothes? An' yet 'twud break me heart to think iv givin' people I niver see or heerd tell iv back to other people I don't know. An', if I don't take thim, Schwartzmeister down th' sthreet, that has half me thrade already, will grab thim sure.

"Hinnissy, I dinnaw what to do about th' Ph'lippeens. An' I'm all alone in th' wurruld. Ivrybody else has made up his mind. Ye can find out fr'm th' paper; an', if ye really want to know, all ye have to do is to ask a prom'nent citizen who can mow all th' lawn he owns with a safety razor. But I don't know."

"Hang on to thim," said Mr. Hennessy, stoutly. "What we've got we must hold."

Adapted and reprinted by per-mission of Charles Scribner's Sons from **Mr. Dooley at His Best** by Finley Peter Dunne. Copyright 1938 Charles Scribner's Sons; renewal copyright © 1966.

3　A NEW POLICY FOR THE CARIBBEAN

After assuming the role of a great power, the United States was not slow to act as one. In order to insure that stable governments would prevail in Cuba and in other Caribbean countries, the Congress of the United States passed a law, and the President of the United States issued a declaration.

In 1901, Senator Orville Platt of Connecticut introduced an amendment to an Army Appropriations Bill which Congress accepted. Acting on behalf of Elihu Root, the Secretary of State, Senator Platt's amendment was intended to establish a special relationship between the United States and Cuba. Provisions of the Platt Amendment were added to the Cuban Constitution in 1902 and to the treaty between the United States and Cuba in 1903.

In 1905, the idea of a special relationship between the United States and Cuba expanded to include other Caribbean countries, and President *Theodore Roosevelt's** annual message stated the policy known as the *Roosevelt Corollary** to the Monroe Doctrine. While reading selections from the Platt Amendment and the Roosevelt Corollary, keep in mind these questions:

1. What advantages did the United States retain in Cuba by the Platt Amendment?

2. On what grounds did Theodore Roosevelt assert the right of the United States to intervene in the Caribbean?

Theodore Roosevelt, after achieving national prominence with the "Rough Riders" in Cuba, became Governor of New York in 1898. In 1900 he was elected Vice-President, and, after McKinley was assassinated in 1901, he became President.

Platt Amendment

The Government of Cuba shall never enter into any treaty or other compact with any foreign power or powers which will impair or tend to impair the independence of Cuba, nor in any manner authorize or permit any foreign power or powers to obtain by colonization or for military or naval purposes, or otherwise, lodgment in or control over any portion of said island.

The Government of Cuba consents that the United States may exercise the right to intervene for the preservation of Cuban independence, the maintenance of a government adequate for the protection of life, property, and individual liberty, and for discharging the obligations with respect to Cuba imposed by the Treaty of Paris on the United States, now to be assumed and undertaken by the Government of Cuba.

To enable the United States to maintain the independence of Cuba, and to protect the people thereof, as well as for its own defense, the Government of Cuba will sell or lease to the United States lands necessary for coaling or naval stations, at certain specified points, to be agreed upon with the President of the United States.

Adapted from **Treaties, Conventions, International Acts, Protocols and Agreements between the United States of America and Other Powers, 1776–1909,** compiled by William M. Malloy (Washington, D.C.: U.S. Government Printing Office, 1910), Vol. I, pp. 362–364.

The "Roosevelt Corollary"

It is not true that the United States feels any land hunger or entertains any projects as regards the other nations of the Western Hemisphere save such as

A **corollary** is something that follows naturally from a circumstance; it is a result derived from a proposition. For instance, given a sound economy, the result (corollary) is prosperity.

are for their welfare. All that this country desires is to see the neighboring countries stable, orderly, and prosperous. Any country whose people conduct themselves well can count upon our hearty friendship. If a nation shows that it knows how to act with reasonable efficiency and decency in social and political matters, if it keeps order and pays its obligations, it need fear no interference from the United States.

Chronic wrongdoing, or an impotence which results in a general loosening of the ties of civilized society, may in America, as elsewhere, ultimately require intervention by some civilized nation; and in the Western Hemisphere the adherence of the United States to the Monroe Doctrine may force the United States, however reluctantly, in flagrant cases of such wrongdoing or impotence, to the exercise of an international police power.

Our interests and those of our southern neighbors are in reality identical. We would interfere with them only in the last resort, and then only if it became evident that their inability or unwillingness to do justice at home and abroad had violated the rights of the United States or had invited foreign aggression to the detriment of the entire body of American nations.

Adapted from **A Compilation of the Messages and Papers of the Presidents, 1789–1905,** edited by James D. Richardson (Washington, D.C.: Bureau of National Literature and Art, 1907), Vol. X, pp. 831–832.

2 Twentieth-century political reform

The Progressives

Objectives of this assignment are to:

–Draw inferences about emotional climate of United States, 1900 to 1917, from pictures, a reading, and selections of ragtime music.

–Analyze readings on slum conditions and political reform for meaning.

–Make historical judgment on effectiveness of Progressive reform movement.

Progressives worked for labor reforms, limiting monopolies, conservation, and a greater voice in government by the people.

Introduction

The last assignment examined the steps that led the United States to become a world power in the dawning twentieth century. This assignment deals with the great social and economic problems of twentieth-century America at home. It deals with *Progressivism,** the first response of reformers to these problems, and with the demand of a growing urban industrial society for more government intervention in every-day affairs. We shall examine here government response to that demand and the role reformers have played in the lives of twentieth-century Americans.

4 THE CONTENTED AMERICANS

At the turn of the century Americans worked hard but still found time to enjoy themselves. Entertainment was very much a part of American life. Organized sports, church socials, family outings at parks, lakes, and beaches were common experiences for most Americans. But the most popular pastime was dancing.

At the end of the nineteenth century the most popular dances were the *waltz** and the *Sousa two-step.** However, when a new style of music called *Ragtime** swept the country during the early years of the new century, the stately waltz and two-step quickly gave way to a host of more lively syncopated steps with exotic names such as the fox-trot, crab-step, kangaroo-dip, camel-walk, lame-duck, grizzly-bear, and turkey-trot.

Ragtime originated with Negro musicians in New Orleans in the 1890's and worked its way north where it became the *rage** before 1910, when Irving Berlin composed Alexander's Ragtime Band and Everybody's Doin' It Now. Here are samples of the lyrics:

ALEXANDER'S RAGTIME BAND
"Come on and hear, come on and hear
Alexander's Ragtime Band,
Come and hear, come on and hear,
It's the best band in the land . . ."

EVERYBODY'S DOIN' IT NOW
"Honey, honey, can't you hear? Funny, funny
music, dear

✻ ✻ ✻ ✻ ✻

Can't you see them all, swaying up the hall

✻ ✻ ✻ ✻ ✻

Ev'rybody's doin' it, doin' it, doin' it.

✻ ✻ ✻ ✻ ✻

Ev'rybody's doin' it now"

The new dance steps and the enthusiasm with which young people performed them amazed and shocked many of their elders. In the minds of some parents, many clergymen, and a few public officials, Ragtime dancing was vulgar and indecent.

While examining the pictures and reading the selection, Ragtime Goes to Court, keep in mind these questions:

1. *What words would you use to describe the people in these pictures?*
2. *Why was Miss Williams in court?*
3. *How did the lawyer defend her?*

Waltz: a smooth, gliding dance in three-quarter time; Johann Strauss (1804–1849) composed and popularized waltz music in 19th-century Vienna.

Sousa two-step: a sliding step-close-step in march time popularized by March King, John Philip Sousa (1854–1932), American bandmaster and composer of "Stars and Stripes Forever."

Ragtime, first departure from the staid, honeyed music of the 19th century, was internationally popular until jazz replaced it in 1920's.

Rage in this sense meant the **fad** of the times.

" 'Alexander's Ragtime Band' by Irving Berlin, © Copyright 1911 Irving Berlin. © Copyright Renewed. Reprinted by Permission of Irving Berlin Music Corporation."

" 'Everybody's Doin' It Now' by Irving Berlin. © Copyright 1911 Irving Berlin. © Copyright Renewed. Reprinted by permission of Irving Berlin Music Corporation."

Wedding Party, Omaha, 1912

"On with the dance. why stop to eat?"

"By the Beautiful Sea" Ocean Grove, N. J., 1905

THE GOOD OLD DAYS

Ragtime Goes To Court

At Millwood, N.Y., Miss Grace Williams, eighteen years old, was arraigned on complaint of former Justice of the Peace Ogden S. Bradley, who charged that she was guilty of disorderly conduct in frequently singing "Everybody's Doin' It Now" as she passed his house, and dancing the turkey trot. "Squire" Bradley said that he and his wife thought that both the song and dance were highly improper and that they had been greatly annoyed. Lawyer Stuart Baker demanded a jury trial. Miss Williams said she sang the song because she liked it, and danced because she could not help it when she heard the catchy tune. Lawyer Baker volunteered to sing the song in court. The prosecuting attorney objected, stating this would make a farce of the trial. Judge Chadeayne overruled him and told Baker to go ahead. The lawyer, who had a good baritone voice, sang the ditty. When he reached the chorus, "Everybody's doin' it, doin' it, doin' it," spectators joined in. The jurors called for an encore. Taking out his tuning fork to pitch the key, the lawyer sang the second stanza with more feeling and expression, and as he sang he gave a mild imitation of the turkey trot. The jurymen clapped their hands in vigorous appreciation, and after five minutes' deliberation found Miss Williams not guilty.

Adapted from Mark Sullivan's **Our Times, 1900–1925,** (New York: Charles Scribner's Sons, 1936), Vol. IV, pp. 256–258.

5 THE OTHER AMERICANS

Unfortunately, there was another side of American life. It was estimated that one out of eight Americans lived in crowded slum tenements. Ugly *company towns** marred the landscape of several states. Child labor was commonplace. Working conditions were often both inhuman and dangerous. Political corruption was widespread. Pollution choked the major cities. Crime was rampant in the large population centers. Wealth was concentrated in the hands of a few financiers and industrialists. There was frequent labor violence. Some *anarchists** and *socialists** openly advocated revolution. But the vast majority of Americans considered revolution unthinkable. Instead, they supported the moderate reforms of the Progressives.

Typical of the conditions which inspired the rise of the Progressive movement were those described by Jacob Riis in How the Other Half Lives. Riis, a Danish immigrant, was one of the earliest and most influential critics of American slums. He wrote about a typical two-acre block in New York's Lower East Side in which 2,781 people lived in 1588 rooms. One third of these rooms were dark and had no access to outside air.

While reading the following selection, keep these questions in mind:

1. What words would you use to describe conditions in a typical New York slum?

2. Who or what created these living conditions?

Company town: a community owned and operated by a business enterprise for the purpose of housing workers near the job site. These towns were very common in the coal and steel industries.

Anarchists: people who employ violent means to overthrow the established order.

Socialists: people who advocate various economic and political theories of collective or governmental ownership and administration of the means of production and distribution of goods.

Jacob Riis Describes a Typical New York Slum Tenement

Suppose we look into one? Number—Cherry Street. Be a little careful, please! The hall is dark and you might stumble over the children pitching pennies back there. Not that it would hurt them; kicks and cuffs are their daily diet. They have little else. Here where the hall turns and dives into utter darkness is a step, and another, and another. A flight of stairs. You can feel your way, if you cannot see it. Close? Yes! What would you have? All the fresh air that ever enters these stairs comes from the hall-door that is forever slamming, and from the windows of dark bedrooms that in turn receive from the stairs their sole supply of the elements God meant to be free, but man deals out with such *niggardly** hand.

That was a woman filling her pail by the hydrant you just bumped against. The sinks are in the hallway, that all the tenants may have access—and all be poisoned alike by their summer stenches. Hear the pump squeak! It is the lullaby of tenement house babies. In summer, when a thousand thirsty throats pray for a cooling drink in this block, it is worked in vain. But the saloon, whose open door you passed in the hall, is always there. The smell of it has followed you up. Here is a door! Listen! That short hacking cough, that tiny helpless wail—what do they mean? They mean that the soiled bow of white you saw on the door downstairs will have another story to tell—Oh! a sadly familiar story—before the day is at an end. The child is dying with measles. With half a chance it might have lived; but it had none. That dark bedroom killed it.

Niggardly: stingy, miserly.

Adapted from Jacob Riis, **How the Other Half Lives** (New York: Charles Scribner's Sons, 1890), pp. 43–44.

Italian mother and baby, New York City, c. 1899.

6 POLITICAL REFORM

Many Americans were appalled by the poverty, human misery, and political corruption of their society. Some decided to take constructive political action to make the American reality correspond more closely with the American dream. These activists soon became known as Progressives.

Progressives had great faith in the ability of the people to govern themselves honestly and effectively. Thus they advocated reform measures intended to place more political power in the hands of the voters where they believed it rightfully belonged.

The leaders of the Progressive movement were predominantly white, middle-class Protestant Americans who had very little personal experience with the evils they chose to combat. They learned about the hardships and misery of the other Americans from journalists known as *muckrakers** who exposed graft, corruption, dishonest business practices, and abuse of the poor in a series of hard-hitting articles in magazines such as McClures, Cosmopolitan, and Colliers.

One of the muckrakers, Lincoln Steffens, wrote a brilliant exposé of American politics entitled The Shame of the Cities. Steffens saw political corruption as the greatest evil of his day.

While examining the chart on Progressive Political Reforms and reading the selection from Steffens, keep in mind the following questions:

Muckrakers: in addition to Steffens, leading muckrakers were Ida Tarbell (History of the Standard Oil Company); Ray Stannard Baker (Following the Color Line); and Upton Sinclair (The Jungle).

1. *In what way are these Progressive political reforms similar?*
2. *How did Steffens learn about the realities of American political life?*
3. *Who does Steffens blame for the political corruption of his day?*

Progressive Political Reforms, 1900–1920

REFORM	PURPOSE AND FUNCTION
Secret Ballot	To allow people to vote for candidates of their choice without fear of reprisal.
Direct Primary	To allow voters to select candidates rather than have selection by party committees or conventions.
Initiative	To enable a specified number of voters to offer a law to the electorate or legislature for approval.
Referendum	To allow voters to approve or disapprove laws.
Recall	To allow voters to remove corrupt public officials from office.
Seventeenth Amendment (1913)	Required U.S. Senators to be elected by the voters rather than by state legislatures.
Nineteenth Amendment (1920)	Gave women the right to vote.

Lincoln Steffens Explains the Realities of American Politics

. . . The misgovernment <u>of</u> the American people is misgovernment <u>by</u> the American people. . . .

When I set out on my travels, an honest New Yorker told me honestly that I would find that the Irish, the Catholic Irish, were at the bottom of misgovernment everywhere. The first city I went to was St. Louis, a German city. It was corrupt. The next was Minneapolis, a Scandinavian city, with a leadership of New Englanders. It was corrupt. Then came Pittsburgh with Scotch Presbyterians and they were corrupt. The next city was Philadelphia, the purest American community of all, and the most hopeless. And after that came Chicago and New York, both mongrelbred, but the one a triumph of reform, the other the best example of good government that I had seen. The foreign element as a cause of corruption is one of the hypocritical lies that saves us from the clear sight of ourselves.

I wish I could tell you more about these practical politicians; how they have helped me; how candidly and unselfishly they have assisted me to facts and an understanding of the facts, which, as I warned them, as they knew well, were to be used against them. If I could—and I will some day—I should show that one of the surest hopes we have is the politician himself. Ask him for good politics; punish him when he gives bad, and reward him when he gives good; make politics pay. Now, he says, you don't know and you don't care, and that you must be flattered and fooled—and there, I say, he is wrong. I did not flatter anybody; I told the truth as near as I could get it, and instead of resentment there was encouragement. After "The Shame of Minneapolis," and "The Shamelessness of St. Louis," not only did citizens of these cities approve, but citizens of other cities, individuals, groups, and organizations, sent in invitations, hundreds of them, "to come and show us up; we're worse than they are."

Adpated from Lincoln Steffens, **The Shame of the Cities** (New York: McClure, Phillips and Co., 1904), Introduction.

In his article "The Shame of Minneapolis" written in 1903, Lincoln Steffens reproduced these pages from the notorious "big mitt" ledger, recording pay-offs to the mayor and the chief of police, and to the crime ring that ran Minneapolis.

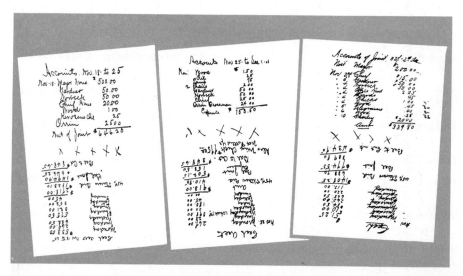

3 Theodore Roosevelt

Progressive activist in the White House

Introduction

At 4:07 P.M. September 6, 1901, *Leon Czolgosz** stepped out of the presidential reception line in the Temple of Music at the Pan American Exposition in Buffalo and fired two shots at President McKinley from a revolver concealed in his bandaged right hand. Mortally wounded, the popular Ohio President tenaciously clung to life until September 14. Vice-President Theodore *Roosevelt** received the news of McKinley's death while mountain-climbing in the Adirondacks. He hurried at once to Buffalo and was sworn in as the twenty-sixth President.

When McKinley's assassination brought Roosevelt to the White House in 1901, both houses of Congress were controlled by solid Republican majorities led by conservative men such as Senator Nelson W. Aldrich of Rhode Island and Congressman Joseph Cannon of Illinois, who were closely allied with big business. So closely was the Republican leadership of Congress tied to business interests that J. P. Morgan, the Wall Street tycoon, was reputed to be even more powerful than the President of the United States. Like it or not, Roosevelt had to work with such men in order to accomplish anything.

The nation as a whole was deeply concerned about the rapid growth of trusts or large industrial combinations, which decreased competition among businesses, raised prices, and consolidated enormous wealth in the hands of a few financiers.

The *Sherman Anti-Trust Act** had been the law of the land since 1890, but it had been rarely enforced. Roosevelt decided to enforce it. Wall Street was outraged. The stock market plummeted when Roosevelt's Attorney General, Philander C. Knox, announced that the government was taking legal action against the *Northern Securities Company,** a J. P. Morgan corporation.

Wall Street's reaction was not typical of the nation at large. Most Americans cheered Roosevelt on. For example <u>The Detroit Free Press</u> observed with tongue in cheek, "Wall Street is paralyzed at the thought that the President of the United States could sink so low as to try to enforce the law."

After two years in the courts, the government won and the Northern Securities Company was dissolved. Roosevelt did not stop with this single victory. He went on to prosecute forty-four more trust cases before he left office in 1909.

Roosevelt's activities were by no means limited to trust-busting alone. He intervened in the Anthracite Coal strike of 1902 and forced mine owners to accept reasonable *arbitration.**

Objectives of this assignment are to:

–Examine two readings on industrial dispute and identify different approaches to a solution.

–Analyze two statements by President Theodore Roosevelt on America's racial and ethnic minorities and describe his attitude toward prejudice.

–Make historical judgment on effectiveness of Theodore Roosevelt as a national leader.

Leon Czolgosz, a Detroit iron-monger, killed President McKinley in 1901 because he wished to destroy all government. Sentenced to death 12 days after the President's death, he was speedily executed.

Theodore Roosevelt: youngest man ever to become President; Harvard graduate; New York State Legislature, 1881; Assistant Secretary of the Navy, 1897; served in the Spanish-American War with the Rough Riders; Governor of New York, 1898; Vice-President, 1900.

The **Sherman Act** was a weak anti-trust law which was passed in 1890. It attempted to regulate business by outlawing all trusts, conspiracies and monopolies in restraint of trade, but it failed to define any of the above terms.

The **Northern Securities Company** formed a monopoly of the three major northwestern railroads.

Arbitration is the process for settling disputes between labor and management by impartial mediators.

A **moralist** is one who sets up and follows certain values he believes are <u>right</u>, regardless of the consequences. To be **pragmatic** means to be able to manipulate affairs skillfully in order to accomplish certain desirable ends.

He was one of the first public figures to recognize the importance of conserving our country's natural resources. By *executive* action alone, he created five national parks, 51 wild life refuges, and set aside 50 million acres of land in forest, coal, and oil reserves. His vigorous action as President on behalf of conservation was among his most lasting achievements. Just as important were his efforts to diminish problems of racial, ethnic, and religious prejudice in America by appointments and public statements. Roosevelt was a rare combination of *moralist** and *pragmatic** politician.

Major Events of Theodore Roosevelt's Political Life, 1881–1909

1881 Elected to the New York Legislature.

1889 Appointed to the United States Civil Service Commission.

1895 Appointed to the Board of Police Commissioners in New York City.

1897 Appointed Assistant Secretary of the Navy.

1898 Served with the Rough Riders in Cuba during the war with Spain.

Elected Governor of New York.

1900 Elected Vice-President of the United States.

1901 Becomes President of the United States following McKinley's assassination.

1902 Roosevelt's Attorney General begins legal action against the Northern Securities Company under the Sherman Anti-Trust Law.

Roosevelt signs the Newlands Reclamation Act for irrigation projects.

Roosevelt intervenes in the Coal Strike.

1903 Roosevelt signs <u>Elkins Act</u> outlawing secret refunds by railroads to privileged customers.

1904 Campaigns for election to the Presidency on a platform of a "Square Deal" for all Americans and defeats the Democratic candidate, Judge Alton B. Parker of New York, by a huge majority.

1906 Roosevelt signs the Hepburn Act giving the Interstate Commerce Commission limited powers to set railroad rates.

Roosevelt signs the <u>Pure Food and Drug Act</u>.

1907 By Presidential order, Roosevelt sets aside 16 million acres of land in twenty-one new forest reserves.

1908 Calls White House Conference on Conservation.

Submits an inventory of the United States' natural resources to Congress.

Persuades the Republican Party to nominate William Howard Taft for the Presidency.

1909 Calls North American Conference on Conservation.

7 COAL STRIKE, 1902

The fuel shortage caused by the prolonged coal strike of 1902 threatened to close many schools, hospitals, and factories, and leave millions of American homes without heat. As winter approached, Theodore Roosevelt decided that the deadlock between the miners and mine operators had to be broken.

He proceeded to break the deadlock, but not with troops as had been done in the past. Through arbitration he tried for a settlement that both sides would accept. The idea of arbitrating industrial disputes was new, and the mine operators had to be persuaded to undertake it.

While reading the following letter from the spokesman for the mine operators and the selection from Theodore Roosevelt's autobiography, keep in mind these questions:

1. According to George Baer, who should protect the rights and interests of working people?

2. What condition did the mine operators demand before arbitration? The miners?

3. How did Roosevelt get both sides to accept his choice of arbitration commissioners?

George Baer explains why arbitration is unnecessary

PHILADELPHIA & READING RAILWAY COMPANY

Reading Terminal, Philadelphia

PRESIDENT'S OFFICE

My dear Mr. Clark: —

                        17th July 1902

    I have your letter of the 16th instant. I do not know who you are. I see that you are a religious man; but you are evidently biased in favor of the right of the working man to control a business in which he has no other interest than to secure fair wages for the work he does there. I beg of you not to be discouraged. The rights and interests of the laboring man will be protected and cared for — not by the labor agitators, but by the Christian men to whom God in His infinite wisdom has given the control of the property interests of the country, and upon the successful Management of which so much depends. Do not be discouraged. Pray earnestly that right may triumph, always remembering that the Lord God Omnipotent still reigns, and that His reign is one of law and order, and not of violence and crime.

                Yours truly,
                Geo. F. Baer
                President

Adapted from **Report of the Anthracite Coal Strike Commission**, Bulletin 46, U.S. Department of Labor (May, 1903).

Roosevelt on Why Arbitration Is So Difficult

As long as I could avoid interfering [in the strike] I did so; but I directed the head of the Labor Bureau . . . to make a thorough investigation and lay the facts fully before me. As September passed without any sign of weakening either among the employers or the striking workmen, the situation became so grave that I felt I would have to try . . . something. The thing most feasible was to get both sides to agree to a commission of arbitration. . . . the miners . . . agreed, stipulating only that I should have the power to name the commission. The operators, however, positively refused. They insisted that all that was necessary for the State to do was to keep order, using the militia as a police force. . . .

Finally, on October 3, the representatives of both the operators and the miners met before me. . . . The representatives of the miners included as their head and spokesman, John Mitchell, who kept his temper admirably and showed to much advantage. The representatives of the operators, [with Mr. Baer as their spokesman,] on the contrary, came down in a most insolent frame of mind, refused to talk of arbitration or accommodation of any kind. . . . [Mr. Baer] . . . used language that was insulting to the miners and offensive to me. . . . [He was] curiously ignorant of the popular temper; and when they went away from the interview, . . . with much pride, [he] gave their own account of it to the papers, exulting in the fact that they had "turned down" both the miners and the President.

❖ ❖ ❖ ❖ ❖

. . . They insisted upon my naming a Commission of only five men, and specified the qualifications these men should have. . . . They made the condition that I was to appoint one officer of the engineer corps of the army or navy, one man with experience of mining, one "man of prominence, eminent as a sociologist," one Federal judge of the Eastern District of Pennsylvania, and one mining engineer.

❖ ❖ ❖ ❖ ❖

. . . I endeavored to make the operators . . . see that the country would not tolerate their insisting upon such conditions; but in vain. . . .

Then, suddenly, after about two hours' argument, it dawned on me that they were not objecting to the thing, but to the name. I found that they did not mind my appointing any man, whether he was a labor man or not, so long as he was not appointed *as* a labor man. . . . I shall never forget the mixture of relief and amusement I felt when I thoroughly grasped the fact that while they would heroically submit to anarchy rather than have Tweedledum, yet if I would call it Tweedledee they would accept it with rapture; it gave me an illuminating glimpse into one corner of the mighty brains of these "captains of industry." . . . With this understanding, I appointed the labor man I had all along had in view, Mr. E. E. Clark, the head of the Brotherhood of Railway Conductors, calling him an "eminent sociologist"—a term which I doubt whether he had ever previously heard.

Adapted and reprinted from **Theodore Roosevelt: An Autobiography,** by permission of Charles Scribner's Sons, pp. 466–469. Copyright 1913 Charles Scribner's Sons; renewal copyright 1941 Edith K. Carrow Roosevelt.

8 THEODORE ROOSEVELT AND THE MINORITY QUESTION

Racial, ethnic, and religious prejudices were much stronger in the early twentieth century than they are today. Racial equality and religious tolerance were not highly valued by most Americans. In this respect as in so many others, Theodore Roosevelt was different. Catholics and Jews served in his Cabinet. He appointed a prominent black to the post of Customs Collector in Charleston, South Carolina, and he invited the distinguished black educator Booker T. Washington to dine in the White House.

Roosevelt revealed his deep concern over the social and economic status of minorities in America in personal correspondence with friends. While reading statements by Roosevelt about racial, ethnic, and religious prejudice taken from his private letters, keep in mind these questions:

1. Why did Theodore Roosevelt invite Booker T. Washington to dinner at the White House?

2. According to Theodore Roosevelt how should black people, ethnic, and religious minorities in America be treated? How did he intend to treat them?

Roosevelt on Prejudice against Black Americans, 1901

I too have been at my wits' end in dealing with the black man. . . . When I asked Booker T. Washington to dinner at the White House, I did not devote very much thought to the matter one way or the other. I respect him greatly and believe in the work he has done. I have consulted so much with him it seemed to me that it was natural to ask him to dinner to talk over this work and the very fact that I felt a moment's qualm on inviting him because of his color made me ashamed of myself and made me hasten to send the invitation. I did not think of its bearing one way or the other, either on my own future or on anything else. As things have turned out, I am very glad that I asked him, for the clamor aroused by the act makes me feel as if the act was necessary.

I have not been able to think out any solution of the terrible problem offered by the presence of the Negro on this continent, but of one thing I am sure. . . . The only wise and honorable and Christian thing to do is to treat each black man and each white man strictly on his merits as a man, giving him no more and no less than he shows himself worthy to have.

I say . . . I am "sure" (that) this is the right solution. . . . If I am (wrong,) then all my thoughts and beliefs are wrong, and my whole way of looking at life is wrong. At any rate, while I am in public life, however short a time that may be, I am in honor bound to act up to my beliefs and convictions. I do not intend to offend the prejudices of anyone else, but neither do I intend to allow their prejudices to make me false to my principles.

Adapted from **The Letters of Theodore Roosevelt** edited by Elting E. Morison (Cambridge, Mass.: Harvard University Press, 1951) Vol. III, pp. 190–191. © President and Fellows of Harvard College.

Roosevelt on Prejudice against Ethnic and Religious Minorities, 1908

The **Magyars** are the people of ancient Hungary, now mostly scattered through central and southeastern Europe. After World War I, Hungary was detached from Austria and became a constitutional monarchy. In 1949 the Communist Party set up a People's Republic.

Adapted from **The Letters of Theodore Roosevelt** edited by Elting E. Morison and John M. Blum (Cambridge, Mass.: Harvard University Press, 1952) Vol. IV, pp. 1042–1043. © President and Fellows of Harvard College.

I grow extremely indignant at the attitude of coarse hostility to the immigrant taken by (a certain type of native Americans.) I have never had much chance to deal with the Slav, *Magyar,** or Italian, but wherever I have had the chance I have tried to do with them as with the German and the Irishman, the Catholic and the Jew, and that is, treat them so as to appeal to their self-respect and make it easy for them to become enthusiastically loyal Americans as well as good citizens. I have one Catholic . . . and a Jew in the Cabinet and part of my object in each appointment was to implant in the minds of our fellow-Americans of Catholic or of Jewish faith, or of foreign ancestry or birth, the knowledge that they have in this country just the same rights and opportunities as everyone else, just the same chance of reward for doing the highest kind of service. . . . In short, we have acted on principles of straight Americanism.

4 Woodrow Wilson

Southern Scholar in the White House

Objectives of this assignment are to:

–Analyze selections from speeches by Theodore Roosevelt and Woodrow Wilson for similarities and differences.

–Examine chart of Wilson's legislative accomplishments and decide which American social groups benefited from them.

–Make judgments on historical importance of Theodore Roosevelt's concept of "New Nationalism" and Woodrow Wilson's concept of "New Freedom."

William Jennings Bryan had been defeated by William McKinley in 1896 and 1900.

Introduction

Theodore Roosevelt dramatically expanded the role of the Federal government and vastly increased the executive power of the President. To ensure the continuation of his Progressive programs Roosevelt carefully selected his good friend, William Howard Taft, as the Republican candidate in 1908. Taft easily defeated Democrat *William Jennings Bryan,** who ran for the third and last time. Taft failed to carry forward the Progressive cause. As a result, the Republican ranks split, and the mantle of Progressive leadership fell to a Democrat, Woodrow Wilson. The question arises: How did Wilson differ from Theodore Roosevelt and how well did he respond to the needs of the American people?

Taft Succeeds Roosevelt

*Big Bill** Taft, as the less reverent journalists referred to him, was a very able individual who had served well as Secretary of War and as the first civil

President-elect Wilson and President Taft leaving for the inaugural ceremonies, March, 1913.

governor of the Philippines. He had seemed an enthusiastic supporter of the reform policies of Theodore Roosevelt. However, he was actually a good-humored conservative who believed that the President of the United States could exercise only those powers specifically delegated to him by the Constitution. This was exactly the reverse of what Theodore Roosevelt believed, namely that the President could do anything not specifically prohibited by the Constitution.

It was inevitable that the supporters of the two men would clash. Roosevelt's followers were almost fanatical in their loyalty to their chief. They compared Taft with their idol and found the former wanting on every count. Taft angered the Progressive Republicans by refusing to support the *insurgent revolt** against the tyrannical Speaker of the House, "Uncle Joe" Cannon. The reformers were also dismayed when Taft appeared to have violated a Republican campaign pledge to lower the tariff by supporting the compromise of the higher *Payne-Aldrich Tariff.**

The most immediate cause of the actual rift between Theodore Roosevelt and Taft, however, was the Ballinger-Pinchot controversy. At Roosevelt's insistence Taft had retained Gifford Pinchot, Roosevelt's close friend and adviser on conservation, as chief of the Forestry Service. Pinchot publicly criticized Taft's Secretary of the Interior, Richard Ballinger, for betraying the cause of conservation by releasing certain Alaskan lands to private interests.

Taft was a huge man, 6 feet tall, 332 pounds.

Insurgent Revolt: the successful attempt of Progressive Congressmen, led by Representative George Norris of Nebraska, to curb the dictatorial Cannon, who used his vast power as Speaker to control committee appointments and flow of legislation.

During the 1908 presidential campaign the Republican platform called for a reform of tariff and lower rates. When Taft signed the **Payne-Aldrich Tariff**, raising duties on hundreds of items, Progressive Republicans were outraged.

In the public uproar that followed, Taft fired Pinchot for disloyalty to his administration. This was the last straw for Roosevelt's followers. They demanded that Roosevelt return to active political life and seek the Presidency again in 1912.

Election of 1912

The election of 1912 was one of the most interesting in United States history. Theodore Roosevelt easily defeated Taft in the Republican primaries, but the Republican convention, completely dominated by the party regulars, renominated Taft for a second term anyway. The outraged supporters of Roosevelt bolted the Republican Party and formed a new Progressive Party. When Theodore Roosevelt was reported to have pounded his chest and boasted that he felt "as strong as a bull moose," the new party was nicknamed the "Bull Moose" Party. Elated by the Republican split, the Democrats nominated the scholarly Progressive Governor of New Jersey, Woodrow Wilson. Unfortunately for Roosevelt, Democratic Progressives refused to desert Wilson, and the Democrats won the close election with 42 per cent of the vote.

Emergence of Woodrow Wilson

Woodrow Wilson enjoyed one of the quickest rises to political prominence in American history. As president of Princeton he earned a reputation as one of the leading educators in America. But in 1910 a bitter feud with the Dean of Princeton's Graduate School, Andrew West, made Wilson decide to leave Princeton. At this point he was offered the Democratic nomination for Governor of New Jersey. The political bosses who nominated him thought they were dealing with a political innocent who would lend prestige to the ticket, but who could be easily managed once in office.

Wilson won the election as planned, but refused to cooperate with the bosses. As Governor he enacted a sweeping Progressive program which included a *workmen's compensation law,** the direct primary, and the regulation of railroads and other public utilities.

Woodrow Wilson and his wife on the campaign trail in 1916. The New York Times front pages chronicle his narrow victory.

The New York Times. EXTRA

ELECTION CLOSE, WILSON 264, HUGHES 251; TWO STATES IN DOUBT; HOUSE MAY BE A TIE

The New York Times.

ELECTION UNSETTLED; WILSON 251, HUGHES 247; DEPENDS ON CALIFORNIA AND MINNESOTA

The New York Times.

WITH 272 ELECTORAL VOTES, WILSON WINS; GETS CALIFORNIA, NORTH DAKOTA, NEW MEXICO

9 NEW NATIONALISM VERSUS NEW FREEDOM

The great issue in the election of 1912 was not the personalities of Roosevelt and Wilson, but rather their different concepts of Progressivism: Roosevelt's New Nationalism and Wilson's New Freedom. Both men believed that American society required a major reformation from top to bottom. But each man had different ideas about the role of the Federal government in bringing about reform.

Roosevelt's ideas were developed before the election campaign began. As early as 1910 in a speech at Osawatomie, Kansas, Roosevelt introduced his concept of *New Nationalism*. Wilson's concept of *New Freedom* was developed in a series of speeches delivered during the election campaign of 1912.

While reading the selections presented below, keep in mind:

1. According to Roosevelt what is the Square Deal?

2. According to Roosevelt, who should carry out the programs of the New Nationalism?

3. According to Wilson, how can individuals be assured of fair play in an industrial society?

4. According to Wilson, what kinds of measures are required to assure the New Freedom?

Roosevelt on *The New Nationalism*

I stand for the **square deal.** But when I say that I am for the square deal, I mean not merely that I stand for fair play under the present rules of the game, but that I stand for having those rules changed so as to work for a more substantial equality of opportunity and of reward for equally good service. When I say I want a square deal for the poor man, I do not mean that I want a square deal for the man who remains poor because he has not tried to make good. The man who wrongly holds that every human right is secondary to his profit must now give way to the advocate of human welfare, who rightly maintains that every man holds his property subject to the general right of the community to regulate its use to whatever degree the public welfare may require it.

But I think we may go still further. The right to regulate the use of wealth in the public interest is universally admitted. Let us admit also the right to regulate the terms and conditions of labor, which is the chief element of wealth, directly in the interest of the common good. The fundamental thing to do for every man is to give him a chance to reach a place in which he will make the greatest possible contribution to the public welfare. Give him a chance, do not push him up if he will not be pushed. Help any man who stumbles; if he lies down, it is a poor job to try to carry him; but if he is a worthy man, try your best to see that he gets a chance to show the worth that is in him.

Also, friends, in the interest of the working man himself we need to set our faces like flint against mob-violence, just as against corporate greed; against violence and injustice and lawlessness by wage-workers, just as much as against lawless cunning and greed and selfish arrogance of employers.

I do not ask for overcentralization; but I do ask that we work in a spirit of broad and far-reaching nationalism when we work for what concerns our people as a whole. We are all Americans. Our common interests are as broad as the continent. The betterment which we seek must be accomplished, I believe, mainly through the National Government.

Impotence: weakness, ineffectiveness.

The New Nationalism puts the national need before sectional or personal advantage. It is impatient of the utter confusion that results from local legislatures attempting to treat national issues as local issues. It is still more impatient of the *impotence** which springs from overdivision of governmental powers, the impotence which makes it possible for local selfishness or for legal cunning, hired by wealthy special interests, to bring national activities to a deadlock. This New Nationalism regards the *executive power as the steward of the public welfare.* It demands of the judiciary that it shall be interested primarily in human welfare rather than in property, just as it demands that the representative body shall represent all the people, rather than any one class or section of the people.

Adapted from Theodore Roosevelt, The New Nationalism (New York: The Outlook Company, 1910), pp. 3–33.

Wilson on *The New Freedom*

One of the interesting things that Mr. Jefferson said in those early days of simplicity which marked the beginnings of our government was that the best government consisted in as little governing as possible. And there is still a sense in which that is true. It is still intolerable for the government to interfere with our individual activities except where it is necessary to interfere with them in order to free them. But I feel confident that if Jefferson were living in our day he would see what we see: that the individual is caught in a great confused web of all sorts of complicated circumstances, and that to let him alone is to leave him helpless as against the obstacles with which he has to contend; and that, therefore, law in our day must come to the assistance of the individual. It must come to his assistance to see that he gets fair play; that is all, but that is much. Without the watchful interference, the resolute interference, of the government, there can be no fair play between individuals and such powerful institutions as the trusts. Freedom today is something more than being let alone. The program of a government of freedom must in these days be positive, not negative merely.

Business we have got to unshackle by abolishing tariff favors, and railroad discrimination, and credit denials, and all forms of unjust handicaps against the little man. Industry we have got to humanize, not through the trusts, but through the direct action of law guaranteeing protection against dangers and compensation for injuries. We must guarantee sanitary conditions, proper hours, the right to organize, and all the other things which the conscience of the country demands as the working-man's right.

We have got to set the energy and the initiative of this great people absolutely free, so that the future of America will be greater than the past, so that the pride of America will grow with achievement, so that America will know as she advances from generation to generation, that each brood of her sons is greater and more enlightened than that which preceded it, know that she is fulfilling the promise that she has made to mankind.

Adapted from Woodrow Wilson, The New Freedom (New York: Doubleday Co., 1913), pp. 283–294.

10   THE WILSON RECORD

Though Wilson never lost an election, he never really enjoyed participating in them. He loved mankind but was too aloof and reserved to have the common touch. However, once in office, Wilson proceeded to enact one of the most constructive and far-reaching legislative programs in the history of the Presidency.

While examining this chart of legislative landmarks of Wilson's Presidency, consider these points:

What groups were restrained by Wilson's legislative program? What groups were assisted?

Legislative Landmarks of Woodrow Wilson's Presidency, 1912–1917

1912   Defeats Roosevelt and Taft and is elected President of the United States.

1913   Signs the Underwood-Simmons Tariff which reduced tariff rates for the first time since the Civil War and introduced the Federal income tax.

Signs the Federal Reserve Act which established the Federal Reserve Board and a system of Federal Reserve Banks to supervise private banking practices.

1914   Signs Clayton Anti-Trust Act which outlawed many unethical business practices that encouraged the growth of monopolies.

Signs Federal Trade Commission Act which established a five-man Commission with authority to issue "cease and desist" orders against corporations guilty of unfair business practices.

1916   Signs Adamson Act which gave railroad employees an eight-hour work day.

1916   Signs Keating-Owen Child Labor Act which outlawed employment of children under fourteen. This act was declared unconstitutional by the Supreme Court in 1918.

Signs Federal Farm Loan Act which established a system of twelve Federal banks to make low-interest loans to farmers.

Wins reelection to a second term by defeating Republican Charles Evans Hughes of New York in a close election.

Signs Federal Highways Act which provided Federal funds for, and Federal control of, interstate highways.

1917   Signs Smith-Hughes Act which provided Federal funds for public school instruction in agricultural, commercial, and industrial arts.

1924   Wilson dies in Washington, D.C.

5 Experience of war

United States in World War I, 1917–1918

Introduction

In the first assignment you studied how the United States emerged from the Spanish-American War as a great power. But the quick and easy victory in that "splendid little war" was hardly a fair test of America's ability or willingness to play the role and accept the obligations of a great power. Even by comparison with the Civil War, the war with Spain was small-scale. In comparison with the war which broke out in Europe in 1914, it was *infinitesimal.** Not the Spanish-American War but World War I, into which the United States was drawn in 1917, drove home to most Americans just what being a great power could involve.

Infinitesimal: so small it can scarcely be seen.

The Road to War

When war broke out in the summer of 1914 few people anticipated the kind of struggle it would become. Thinking of the relatively brief and limited wars of the nineteenth century, most people (and most leaders) looked for a short war followed by peace treaties that would adjust the European power system without serious dislocation. They were wrong, for technological developments (particularly the machine-gun and the railroad) had changed the character of warfare. As a result, the war soon bogged down in a grim struggle of massive armies facing each other from complex networks of trenches and fortified positions. Between the autumn of 1914 and the spring of 1918 several million French, Belgian, and British soldiers fought several million Germans along a line which curved from the North Sea to Switzerland. Hundreds of thousands died in vain attempts to break through their opponents' defenses.

At the beginning of the war, President Woodrow Wilson proclaimed American neutrality and worked to prevent the United States from being drawn into the war.* American sympathies were divided. Many Americans, particularly those of English and Scottish ancestry, hoped for an Allied victory. Others, particularly German-Americans and many Irish-Americans (who disliked England's rule of Ireland) supported the German cause.

As the war dragged on, however, neutrality became more difficult to maintain. The Allies were more successful than the Germans in presenting their case to the American public through news stories, pictures, and books. In addition, while the English naval blockade of Germany practically eliminated all trade between the United States and Germany, the British and French

Objectives of this assignment are to:

—Analyze selections from three war memoirs for different perceptions of the war experience.

—Make inferences from a filmstrip about ways war was justified to the American people.

—Summarize your findings on the impact of war on the American people.

Woodrow Wilson, a Democrat, was elected President in 1912 and re-elected in 1916.

D28

The New York Times.

LUSITANIA SUNK BY A SUBMARINE, PROBABLY 1,000 DEAD; TWICE TORPEDOED OFF IRISH COAST; SINKS IN 15 MINUTES; AMERICANS ABOARD INCLUDED VANDERBILT AND FROHMAN; WASHINGTON BELIEVES THAT A GRAVE CRISIS IS AT HAND

placed more and more orders with American businessmen for the war supplies they needed. By 1916 most Americans had become strongly pro-Allied, and a significant portion of the American economy was occupied with supporting the British and French war efforts.

What finally brought the United States into the war was the conflict between President Wilson's ideas of Americans' right to travel and trade and the determination of the Germans to blockade Britain with submarines. In 1915 more than a hundred Americans died when a German submarine sank the British passenger liners *Lusitania* and *Arabic*. The American government protested, and for a time the Germans carefully refrained from sinking such vessels so as not to antagonize the United States. In early 1917, however, the German government concluded that it could not win the war unless it completely blockaded the British Isles. "Unrestricted submarine warfare" was resumed. Both British vessels carrying Americans and American vessels sailing in British waters were sunk. As a result, in April, 1917, the United States declared war on Germany and joined the Allies.

Different Experiences of War

There is an old story about several blind men standing next to an elephant and trying to decide what it was. One touched the trunk and decided the elephant was like a snake. Another, touching the leg, decided it was like a tree. The third, who touched the tail, decided it was like a rope. As a poet put it, "each was partly in the right and all were in the wrong," because none could see the elephant as a whole.

For most Americans the experience of such a large historic event as World War I was similar to the blind men and the elephant. While the war was going on it was impossible to see it as a whole. Each American experienced only a part of it, and experienced it in a rather different way. To some it was glory; to some it was death. Some read of it in their parlors; others made decisions that affected it in their offices, or tents, or trenches.

The readings which follow represent the different war experiences of three men: a government official, a general, and an ordinary soldier.

11 A GOVERNMENT OFFICIAL

Bernard M. Baruch (1870–1965) was a skillful and successful financier. He was named by President Wilson to run the already established War Industries Board, the government's agency in charge of mobilizing American industry to support the war effort. The President gave Baruch sweeping powers to harness America's industrial machinery to meet the enormous demands of war and insure victory. While reading Baruch's description of the way he and the War Industries Board worked, keep in mind these questions:

1. What methods were used by Baruch and the War Industries Board to mobilize production for war?
2. How did Baruch view the war?

Mr. Baruch's War

It would take a volume to tell the full story of the War Industries Board, how it went about the gigantic and unprecedented task of converting industrial America from peace to war, and how, in the process, it came to exercise such great control over the nation's industry that in the view of many I became a virtual dictator.

Such a view of my power is exaggerated. The truth is, the eventual effectiveness of the WIB was due to our recognition of the fact that the requirements of war—of survival—demanded a drastic redirection of the nation's resources. . . . In peacetime the free working of the market place can be trusted to keep the economy in balance. The law of supply and demand has time in which to operate. But in war that equilibrium must be achieved by conscious direction—for war, with its ravenous demands, destroys the normal balance and denies us time. And time means lives. . . .

In the WIB we constantly sought the wartime equivalent of supply and demand. Everything we did we tried to do in harmony with that law. Instead of allowing prices to determine what would be produced and where it would go, we decided, on the basis of need, how our resources would be employed, so that first things would come first. . . . Thus, when steel was in short supply we refused to permit the building of a theater in St. Louis, saved over 2,000 tons by reducing bicycle designs, and garnered enough metal for two warships by taking the stays out of women's corsets. When the demand for woolen fabric grew acute we induced the tailors to reduce the size of their sample swatches, thus saving 450,000 yards of cloth.

How did we in WIB go about controlling the industrial output of the United States? Actually, our specific powers were few and, considering the scope of the task confronting us, rudimentary. . . .

The most important instrument of control was the power to determine priority—the power to determine who gets what and when. . . .

Bernard M. Baruch, 1919.

The administration of priority was a complex and delicate task. Should locomotives go to Pershing to carry his army to the front or should they go to Chile to haul nitrates needed to make ammunition for Pershing's troops? Should precedence be given to destroyers needed to fight the U-boats or to merchant ships whose numbers were being decimated by the German subs? Should nitrates be allocated to munitions or to fertilizer? Should the Railroad Administration or the Fuel Administration get the tank cars both were claiming? We were not always as wise as Solomon in deciding these questions, but we did succeed in synchronizing American industry to the needs of war through the priority power. . . .

We also relied on our power of persuasion to elicit the cooperation from industry which success of the war program required. When priorities and persuasion failed, we had one instrument of last resort to enforce our will—the power of commandeering—the power to seize property. . . .

For example, WIB moved early to curtail the production of pleasure cars. We had no intention of allowing their production while we scrounged for steel for tanks, guns, locomotives, and ships. At first we tried to rely upon voluntary agreements under which the automobile producers pledged to cut production by two-thirds. But we soon found that these agreements were not self-enforcing. . . .

So, in 1918 we called representatives of the automobile industry to Washington. The heads of all the great companies were present, with the exception of Henry Ford. They listened with ill-concealed impatience as we explained WIB's plans to curtail immediately the production of automobiles, and employ the facilities thus freed for war production. . . . *John Dodge* led their attack by giving me a personal dressing down. He did not want any white-haired, white-faced Wall Street speculator telling him how he ought to conduct his business, he said among other things. . . .

The other auto manufacturers, in terms less emotional than Dodge, made it equally clear that they were prepared to ignore WIB. They informed us that they had stocked all the steel and coal they needed and could proceed in spite of us. During the lull in the argument I made up my mind on what had to be done to meet this challenge to our authority .

"Just a moment, gentlemen," I said as I picked up the phone and put in a call to *McAdoo* at the Railroad Administration. With the auto people listening to me, I said, "Mac I want you to take down the names of the following factories, and I want you to stop every wheel going in and going out."

The automobile men looked at me, astonished and outraged, as I read off the names of Dodge, General Motors, Ford, and other plants. This effect was heightened as I put in a call to *Secretary of War Baker.* "Mr. Secretary, I would like you to issue an order to commandeer all the steel in the following yards," I said. Then I called Fuel Administrator Garfield and asked him to seize the manufacturers' coal supplies.

That did it. Billy Durant, head of General Motors, said, "I quit." The others capitulated soon after. . . .

Women, like the girl above working on the punch press, joined the war effort in World War I munitions factories.

John Dodge, like Henry Ford with whom he was associated for a time, was a pioneer automobile maker. He headed the firm which made the Dodge car.

William G. McAdoo, President Wilson's son-in-law, director-general of railways, 1917–1919, spent $500 million to create an efficient nationwide railway system.

Newton D. Baker, Secretary of War, 1916–1921, was awarded "services to humanity" medal in 1933 by National Institute of Social Sciences.

Condensed from **BARUCH: THE PUBLIC YEARS** by Bernard M. Baruch. Copyright © 1960 by Bernard M. Baruch. Reprinted by permission of Holt, Rinehart and Winston, Inc.

12　A GENERAL

While Bernard Baruch was fighting automobile-makers, General John J. Pershing (1860–1948) was battling both Germans and other Allied generals. A West Point graduate who had served as a cavalry officer in the American West, Pershing was named to command all of the American troops in France —a force that eventually totalled nearly 2 million men. While reading his description of the Battle of St. Mihiel (where the Americans fought as a distinct army for the first time), keep in mind the following questions:

1. *What was the main objective of the Battle of St. Mihiel?*
2. *How did Pershing view the war?*

General Pershing's War

Beginning at the end of August, the battle concentration was started, when all combatant units were quietly moved to their battle positions.

The aviation force, consisting of nearly 1,400 planes, under *Colonel Mitchell,** was the strongest that had been assembled up to that time. Unfortunately, we could obtain no heavy tanks and only 267 light tanks, which were all of French manufacture, and of these 154 were manned by American troops. In addition to the American divisions, four French divisions were assigned to our army for the operation. The total strength of the First Army when ready for battle was about 550,000 American and 110,000 French troops.

The St. Mihiel *salient** lay between the Meuse and the Moselle Rivers. During the period of four years' occupation, the Germans had strengthened the natural defensive features by elaborate fortifications and by a dense network of barbed wire that covered the entire front. The salient was practically a great field fortress. It had, however, the characteristic weakness of all salients in that it could be attacked from both flanks in converging operations. Our heaviest blow was to be from the south where there were no great natural features to be overcome, while the secondary attack was to come from the west and join the main drive in the heart of the salient.

There was no doubt the enemy was aware that an American attack was impending. Therefore, it was possible that he might increase his strength on our front. In that case, our task would be more difficult and as anything short of complete success would undoubtedly be seized upon to our disadvantage by those of the Allies who opposed the policy of forming an American army, no chances of a repulse in our first battle could be taken.

The attack on the southern face of the salient started at 5:00 o'clock on the morning of September 12th, and before that hour I went with several staff officers to Old Fort Gironville, situated on a commanding height overlooking the battlefield from the south. A drizzling rain and mist prevented us from getting a clear view, but the progress of our troops could be followed by the artillery barrage which preceded them.

The sky over the battlefield, both before and after dawn, aflame with exploding shells, star signals, burning supply dumps and villages, presented a

General Pershing arriving by ship at Boulogne, France, June 13, 1917.

Colonel "Billy" Mitchell (1879–1936) later became the most aggressive American spokesman for the future of military airpower. His criticisms of the War and Navy Departments led to his court martial in 1925.

Salient: a place where a battle line juts out sharply. As the map (opposite page) shows, the St. Mihiel salient was shaped almost like an arrowhead pointed into the heart of France.

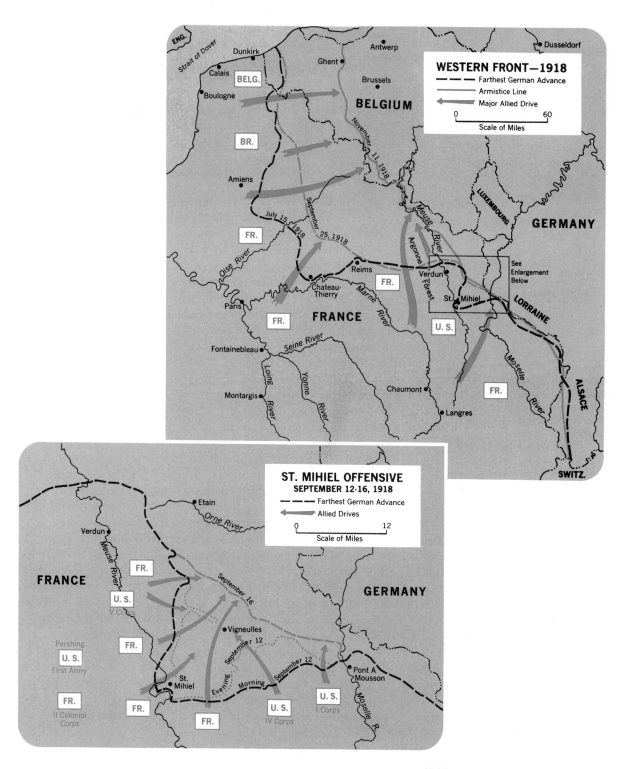

WESTERN FRONT—1918
- - - Farthest German Advance
——— Armistice Line
➤ Major Allied Drive

0   60
Scale of Miles

ENG.
Strait of Dover
Dunkirk
Calais
Boulogne
BELG.
Ghent
Antwerp
Brussels
BELGIUM
• Dusseldorf
BR.
GERMANY
November 11, 1918
Amiens
LUXEMBOURG
FR.
July 15
September 25, 1918
September 1918
Oise River
Meuse River
Argonne Forest
See Enlargement Below
Reims
Verdun
FR.
Chateau-Thierry
St. Mihiel
Marne River
LORRAINE
Paris
FR.
FRANCE
U.S.
Fontainebleau
Seine River
Loing River
Yonne River
Chaumont
FR.
Moselle River
ALSACE
Montargis
Langres
SWITZ.

ST. MIHIEL OFFENSIVE
SEPTEMBER 12-16, 1918
- - - Farthest German Advance
➤ Allied Drives

0   12
Scale of Miles

Etain
Orne River
Verdun
FR.
FRANCE
Meuse River
U.S.
V Corps
September 16
GERMANY
Pershing
U.S.
First Army
FR.
Vigneulles
September 12
FR.
II Colonial Corps
St. Mihiel
FR.
Evening
Morning
September 12
FR.
U.S.
IV Corps
Pont A Mousson
U.S.
I Corps
Moselle R.

World War I—Americans wore gas masks in the trenches in France to protect themselves against deadly poison gas which killed or maimed thousands.

Corps: in military language, a part of an <u>army</u>, made up of two or more <u>divisions</u>; each division, in turn, was made up of <u>brigades</u> and <u>regiments</u>.

From the book, **My Experiences in the World War**, Vol. II, pp. 260–273 by John J. Pershing. Copyright 1931. Renewal © 1959 by F. Warren Pershing. Abridged and adapted by permission of the publishers, J. B. Lippincott Company.

scene at once picturesque and terrible. The exultation in our minds that here, at last, after seventeen months of effort, an American army was fighting under its own flag was tempered by the realization of the sacrifice of life on both sides, and yet fate had willed it thus and we must carry through. Confidence in our troops dispelled every doubt of ultimate victory.

By afternoon the troops had pushed beyond their scheduled objectives and by evening had reached the second day's objective on most of the southern front. On that afternoon, learning that the roads leading out of the salient between the two attacks were filled with retreating enemy troops, with their trains and artillery, I gave orders to push forward without delay. Using the telephone myself, I directed the commander of the *V Corps** to send at least one regiment toward Vigneulles with all possible speed. That evening, a strong force pushed boldly forward and reached Vigneulles at 2:15 A.M. on September 13th. It immediately made dispositions that effectively closed the roads leading out of the salient west of that point. In the IV Corps a brigade advanced in force about dawn of the 13th, its leading elements reaching Vigneulles by 6:00 A.M. The salient was closed and our troops were masters of the field.

The reduction of the St. Mihiel salient completed the first task of the American Army. We had restored to France 200 square miles of territory and had placed our army in a favorable situation for further operations.

This striking victory completely demonstrated the wisdom of building up a distinct American army. No form of propaganda could overcome the depressing effect on the enemy's morale of the fact that a new adversary had been able to put a formidable army in the field against him which, in its first offensive, could win such an important engagement. This result, after nearly a year and a half of working and waiting, must have tremendously heartened our people at home, as it gave them a tangible reason to believe that our contribution to the war would be the deciding factor. It inspired our troops with unlimited confidence which was to stand them in good stead against the weary days and nights of battle they were to experience later on. The St. Mihiel victory probably did more than any single operation of the war to encourage the tired Allies. After the years of doubt and despair, of suffering and loss, it brought them assurance of the final defeat of an enemy whose armies had seemed well-nigh invincible.

D34

13 A "DOUGHBOY"

Baruch and Pershing ran large-scale war efforts and both became famous. By contrast, Private Jesse Maxey was an ordinary *Doughboy** from Virginia. In a letter to his wife he described his participation in the Meuse-Argonne Campaign, the massive American drive which began in late September, 1918, and ended only when the war itself ended on November 11, 1918. While reading Private Maxey's letter (which contains misspelled words and is sometimes ungrammatical), try to answer the following questions:

Doughboy: army slang for an ordinary American soldier in World War I.

1. *What was Private Maxey's role in the war?*
2. *How did Private Maxey view the war?*

Private Maxey's War

The night of September 24th we moved out to our right and went into some old open trenches which was wet and muddy. We staid thair until the night of the 25th and was issued more ammunition and hand grenades. So we pulled out when it got dark going through our front line trenches out into no mans land and thair we laid down to wait for our artillery to open up which opened up at 2:30 o'clock that night.

Well, the time came for us to go ahead so we got up and gave a loud yell and away we went. Our machine guns went too clicking away and our shells singing over our heads. It was not light good when we started and the smoke and fog was so thick we couldnt see more than three or four yards ahead of us. We went a few hundred yards and would drop in old shell holes and lay thair and try and listen and look ahead of us to see if *Jerry** was trying to come over to meet us.

Jerry: army slang for Germans; they were also called "Huns." Both words were borrowed from British soldiers.

We came to an old trench that was full of watter and thair wasent any way to cross it but to wade it or swim so we plunged into it and the watter came up about to our waists. It was cold believe me, we went a little farther and captured two Huns. They were under an old bridge, they had started out when we first saw them they were about 50 yards ahead of us. We dropped and leveled our rifles on them and they came on out with thair hands up scared to death.

We kept going. Finly we came to thair trenches and thair we got lots of prisiners, another fellow and myself got 13 out of one little dugout. We crawled on up to the dugout and got up and hollered for them to come out and here they came with thair hands up hollowing 'Kamerad,' 13 of them.

I never new the boys name that was with me, as we soon got mixed up with some of the rest of the fellows and you know when we was relieved that thair wasnt very many of us left.

Well, we all moved on pretty quick. We came to another line of trenches and thair I saw an awful sight. When we got in about 200 yards of the trenches an old man came running out hollowing and crying with his hands up. Well, some hollowed shoot him, shoot him we all had our guns on him so

1

I WANT YOU
FOR U.S. ARMY
NEAREST RECRUITING STATION

2

LIFE

His Mother. HERE HE IS, SIR

3

HALT the HUN!

BUY U.S. GOVERNMENT BONDS
THIRD LIBERTY LOAN

D36

4

The Smithsonian Institution

"The Sentry"
by Harvey Dunn
1918

Curtis Publishing Company

5

Homeward Bound
1919

I guess he thought we was going to kill him anyway so he just dropped down on his knees when he was about 50 yards from us and stretched his hands up and turned his face to the skye seemed that he was praying. About this time one of our officers ran out to whare he was and hollowed not to shoot. I think he was an old Priest that is, we always thought so any way, he had a long beard on his face and looked to be 60 years old.

Well, we got lots of prisiners out of them trenches and got several of our boys wounded thair as the Germans was now shooting at us from on ahead. Thair at that line of trenches in one of the dugouts one of the boys on my left threw a hand granade in on a Hun as he started to come out without his hands up and killed him. The one that he killed was an old man with mustache seemed to be at least 40 years old.

We stopped in an old trench at the edge of the woods which we had just come through, an open hill laying before us and thair was a town just over the hill. While we were stopped, of course, the Germans could get thair guns in operation which they didnt fail to do, machine guns and artillery. With this they opened fire on us. In a short while we got orders to move forward so we started to advance and by that time Jerry was sending shells over in a jiffy. But we never reached the top of the open hill, we crawled up as far as we could. Right thair was when I saw what war really was. I got covered with dirt, rocks and pieces of falling shells, I thought every minute that I would get mine. The fellow on my right got hit, I dont know how bad and I dont know what became of him. What few minutes we were up there we had one Sergeant killed and two corporals and several privates, I think we lost about 15 men.

The next morning we were relieved by some other company and we fell back into support. Thair is lots of days that I have no recollection of as I saw so many boys get killed and so many wounded right by my side that I cannot explain it. We had 250 men when we started over the top on the 26th of Sept. and when we came out thair want but about 80 of us left. Gee, I did feel lucky, which all of us did that were still alive.

Adapted from a copy in the Records of the Virginia World War I History Commission, Archives Division of the Virginia State Library.

6 Advice and consent

President Wilson, the Senate, and
The League of Nations, 1919–1920

Introduction

In the previous assignment you explored the different ways in which Americans experienced World War I. Although their experiences differed, the great majority of Americans were united in supporting American participation in the war. When the war ended, however, that unity disappeared. Different attitudes on the role of the United States in world affairs were expressed, and the rivalry of political leaders and political parties reappeared. These can be seen in the debate on whether the United States should join the new League of Nations in 1919 and 1920. The attitudes expressed in the political rivalry of those years lasted for the next generation and can still be found today.

Objectives of this assignment are to:

–Analyze readings and political cartoons on the League of Nations issue for meaning.

–Identify values underlying debate over United States membership in League of Nations.

–Make historical judgment on why the United States refused to join League of Nations.

Road to Peace

On the morning of November 11, 1918, the guns in France fell silent. An exhausted Germany, torn by revolution, had agreed to make peace. The German soldiers laid down their arms, and the troops of the victorious Allies entered Germany as an army of occupation.

The "Great War" was over. It had taken the lives of more than 10 million people. It had brought incalculable destruction and hardship. It had produced the collapse of four extensive empires and had unleashed forces of revolution with which the world has been coping ever since.* It was, beyond question, one of the great watersheds in human history.

The **German, Austro-Hungarian, Russian,** and **Turkish** empires all disappeared in the war. From the Russian Revolution of 1917 emerged Communist control of Russia.

Little wonder, then, that the eyes of the world were soon trained on Paris, where the leaders of the Allies met to write the treaty of peace, and to devise a scheme to prevent such wars from ever again ravaging mankind. And little wonder that most people's hopes rested on the American President, Woodrow Wilson. Even before the United States entered the war, Wilson spoke of the need for a just peace and for a "league of nations" to prevent future wars. He had repeated these ideas during the war, particularly in his "Fourteen Points" peace program of 1918.

It took six months to produce the peace treaty. In the process many of Wilson's ideals of what constituted a just peace were watered down or ignored. Wilson himself knew this. But he still felt that the *Treaty of Versailles,** despite its defects, was a good one. On the day it was signed, Wilson told the American people the treaty was "a great charter for a new order of affairs," a source of "deep satisfaction, universal reassurance, and confident hope."

The **Treaty of Versailles** between the Allies and Germany received its name from the Palace of Versailles, near Paris, where it was signed.

Paris, May 27, 1919—left
to right: Lloyd George,
Great Britain; Orlando,
Italy; Clemenceau, France;
and Wilson.

Covenant: a word used in the
Old Testament; it means
agreement. Its use here was
intended to suggest the
solemn nature of the League
agreement.

Internationalist describes one
who favors close cooperation
with other nations in world
affairs, and isolationist describes one who opposes such
close cooperation. Both words
came to carry strong emotional
overtones.

The basis of Wilson's "confident hope" was one particular part of the Treaty of Versailles, the part establishing a League of Nations. This *Covenant** of the League of Nations was to serve as the constitution of a world organization to which all nations, great or small, would belong. Through the League's machinery, it was hoped, small wars could be stopped and great wars prevented. This was to be accomplished principally by arbitration and by an independent World Court which would hear the cases of countries in conflict. If these failed, the members of the league would take joint action, even to the point of war, against a trouble-making aggressor nation.

14   THE TREATY GOES TO THE SENATE

President Wilson knew that while most Americans had been united in support of the recent war, some would be opposed to the United States becoming involved in such a world organization as the League. He knew that his own *internationalist* outlook would be opposed by those with an *isolationist* outlook.* In placing the Treaty before the Senate for approval he explained why he felt the United States should accept the Covenant and join the League. Read his message to the Senate and try to answer the following questions:

1. How did President Wilson claim the United States conducted itself as a Great Power?

2. Why did President Wilson believe the United States had to join the League of Nations?

D40

President Wilson's Plea for the League

America may be said to have just come of age as a world power. It was almost exactly twenty-one years ago that the results of the war with Spain put us unexpectedly in possession of rich islands on the *other side of the world** and brought us into association with other governments in the control of the West Indies. It was regarded as a dangerous thing by the statesmen of more than one European government that we should have extended our power beyond the confines of our continental dominions. They were accustomed to think of new neighbors as a new menace, of rivals as watchful enemies.

Wilson was referring to places like the Philippines, Hawaiian Islands, Guam, Wake Island, Samoa, Puerto Rico.

There were persons amongst us at home who looked with deep disapproval on such extensions of our national authority over distant islands and over peoples whom they feared we might exploit, not serve and assist. But we have not exploited them. We have been their friends and have sought to serve them. And our dominion has been a menace to no other nation. Our isolation was ended twenty years ago; and now fear of us is ended, also; our counsel and association sought after and desired. There can be no question of our ceasing to be a world power. The only question is whether we can refuse the moral leadership that is offered us, whether we shall accept or reject the confidence of the world.

The war and the Conference of Peace seem to me to have answered that question. Our participation in the war established our position among the nations and nothing but our own mistaken action can alter it. The stage is set, the destiny disclosed. We cannot turn back. We can only go forward, with lifted eyes and freshened spirit, to follow the vision. It was of this that we dreamed at our birth. America shall in truth show the way. The light streams upon the path ahead, and nowhere else.

From Woodrow Wilson's message to the United States Senate (July 10, 1919).

15   REJECTION BY THE SENATE

The Constitution of the United States gives to the President the power to make treaties, but only "by and with the advice and consent of the Senate." The Senate's consent, adds the Constitution, requires approval by "two thirds of the Senators present." From the beginning of the nation the Senate has always taken most seriously this power to accept or reject a treaty. As a result, the Senate has frequently been the forum for public debate on the great issues of American foreign policy. So it was in 1919–1920 when the Senate debated the Treaty of Versailles and the question of America's entry into the League of Nations. In the end, the Treaty failed to receive the necessary votes of "two thirds of the Senators present." The United States did not join the League.

The accompanying political cartoons indicate the judgment of two important newspapers on the Senate's rejection of the Treaty of Versailles. John

T. McCutcheon's "Interrupting the Ceremony" appeared in the Chicago Tribune. Rollin Kirby's "The Accuser" was printed in the New York World. Examine each cartoon carefully. Then see if you can answer the following questions:

1. How would you put into words the "scene" or "story" told by McCutcheon's "Interrupting the Ceremony"? By Kirby's "The Accuser"?

2. What was the judgment of each of the newspapers on the rejection of the Treaty and League?

Interrupting the Ceremony

Cartoon by John T. McCutcheon
The Chicago Tribune

The Accuser

Cartoon by Rollin Kirby
New York World

Behind the Rejection

The two newspaper cartoons present sweeping, general judgments on the Senate's action, one from an "isolationist" point of view and one from an "internationalist" point of view. But the story of the rejection of the Treaty is much more complicated.

It involved *constitutional tension** between a strong-willed President and a Senate jealous of its treaty-approving power. Since that Senate was controlled by the Republican Party while President Wilson was a Democrat, the rejection also involved party politics. To this must be added the mutual dislike between Wilson and the leader of the Republicans in the Senate, Henry Cabot Lodge. Finally, both the debates and the rejection involved a small band of Senators, mostly Republicans, who were totally opposed to any kind of participation in the League. These men, called the *Irreconcilables,** found their principal spokesman in Republican Senator William E. Borah of Idaho.

The readings and the chart which follow reflect the attitudes of the main participants in the debate on the League. The first deals with Senator Lodge's (and the Senate Foreign Relations Committee's) *"Reservation"** on the crucial Article 10 of the League's Covenant. The second indicates Wilson's view of the Lodge Reservation. The third, from a speech by Senator Borah, represents the attitude of the Republican "Irreconcilables." The chart shows the way the different groups of Senators voted. While reading the selections and studying the chart, keep in mind these questions:

1. What was the purpose of the Lodge Reservation?

2. What was Wilson's view of the Lodge Reservation?

3. Why did Senator Borah object to the United States joining the League of Nations?

4. Which groups were consistent in their voting? Which were not?

5. Do you think that Senators voted on the League of Nations issue according to party politics?

Senator Lodge's "Reservation"

[This] reservation dealt with the famous article 10, which was the provision of the League of Nations upon which the controversy centered more than upon any other. This article as it stands in the treaty, in the League covenant, is as follows:

"The Members of the League undertake to respect and preserve as against external aggression the territorial integrity and existing political independence of all Members of the League. In case of any such aggression, or in case of any threat or danger of such aggression, the Council shall advise upon the means by which this obligation shall be fulfilled."

. . . The statement in the [Senate] Committee report alluded to this reservation as follows:

"This reservation is intended to meet the most vital objection to the league

Constitutional tension is caused by conflict between Executive (President) and Legislative (Congress) branches of the government. Each branch attempts to assert its authority over the other through constitutional interpretation, resulting in a power struggle.

Irreconcilables: a group of diehard, isolationist senators who refused to allow the United States to join the League of Nations, and who defeated the Treaty of Versailles which created the League. They refused to make concessions or compromises, not even to Lodge's Reservation (see next note).

Lodge's Reservation: Senator Henry Cabot Lodge, chairman of the Senate Foreign Relations Committee, wasn't keen about the United States joining the League of Nations, but was willing to go along, providing the League's 14 provisions were weakened. His "Reservation" aimed to keep the United States out of foreign conflicts without specific Senate approval.

covenant as it stands. Under no circumstances must there be any legal or moral obligation upon the United States to enter into war or to send its Army and Navy abroad or without the unfettered action of Congress to impose economic boycotts on other countries. Under the Constitution of the United States the Congress alone has the power to declare war, and all bills to raise revenue or affecting the revenue in any way must originate in the House of Representatives, be passed by the Senate, and receive the signature of the President. These constitutional rights of Congress must not be impaired by any agreements such as are presented in this treaty, nor can any opportunity of charging the United States with bad faith be permitted. No American soldiers or sailors must be sent to fight in other lands at the bidding of a league of nations. American lives must not be sacrificed except by the will and command of the American people acting through their constitutional representatives in Congress."

In a general way this statement in the report sums up the objections to Article 10. . . . I personally went over this reservation to Article 10 again and again with groups of Senators and with individual members. Finally, I asked *Senator McCumber*° . . . to come to my house and lunch with me alone. At that time we took up the reservation which had been already brought to a point where I thought I could secure all the Republican votes for it if I could get the assent of Senator McCumber. After much discussion he and I agreed upon the reservation in the form in which it was presented to the Senate and finally adopted. The reservation was as follows:

"3. The United States assumed no obligation to preserve the territorial integrity or political independence of any other country or to interfere in controversies between nations—whether members of the league or not—under the provisions of Article 10, or to employ the military or naval forces of the United States under any article of the treaty for any purpose, unless in any particular case the Congress, which, under the Constitution, has the sole power to declare war or authorize the employment of the military or naval forces of the United States, shall by act or joint resolution so provide."

President Wilson on the Lodge "Reservation"

The Lodge reservation is a rejection of the Covenant. That is an absolute refusal to carry any part of the same responsibility that the other members of the League carry. Does the United States want to say to the nations with whom it stood in this great struggle, "We have seen you through on the battlefield, but now we are done. We are not going to stand by you." Article 10 is an engagement on the part of all the great fighting nations of the world, because all the great fighting nations are going to be members of the League, and they will respect and preserve against external aggression the territorial integrity and the existing political independence of the other members of the League. That is cutting at the heart of all wars. Every war of any consequence that you can cite originated in an attempt to seize the territory or interfere with the political independence of some other nation. This is the

Porter J. McCumber was a Republican Senator from North Dakota. He was later the only Republican who voted for the League Covenant exactly as Wilson presented it.

Adapted from Henry Cabot Lodge, **The Senate and the League of Nations** (New York: Charles Scribner's Sons, 1925), pp. 182–184.

heart of the Covenant, and what are these gentlemen afraid of? Nothing can be done under that article of the treaty without the consent of the United States.

These gentlemen say, "We do not want the United States drawn into every little European squabble." Of course, we do not, and under the League of Nations it is entirely within our choice whether we will be or not.

If the fight is big enough to draw the United States in, I predict that they will be drawn in anyhow, and if it is not big enough to bring them in inevitably, they can go in or stay out according to their own decision. Why are these gentlemen afraid? There is no force to oblige the United States to do anything except moral force.

There is no necessity for the last part of this reservation. Every public man, every statesman in the world knows that in order that the United States should go to war it is necessary for the Congress to act. They do not have to be told that, but that is not what this resolution says. This resolution says the United States assumes no obligation to preserve the territorial integrity or political independence of any other country—washes its hands of the whole business; says, "We do not want even to create the presumption that we will do the right thing. We do not want to be committed even to a great principle, but we want to say that every time a case arises the Congress will independently take it up as if there were no Covenant and determine whether there is any moral obligation; and after determining that, determining whether it will act upon that moral obligation or not, it will act." In other words, that is an absolute withdrawal from the obligations of Article 10. That is why I say that it would be a rejection of the Covenant.

From Woodrow Wilson, speech at Salt Lake City, Utah (September 23, 1919).

Senator Borah's Objections

"Entertain no compromise; have none of it." That states the position I occupy at this time and which I have, in an humble way, occupied from the first contention in regard to this proposal.

My objections to the league have not been met by the reservations.

We have said that we would not send our troops abroad without the consent of Congress. Pass by now for a moment the legal proposition. If we create executive functions, the Executive will perform those functions without the authority of Congress. The treaty authorizes the league, a member of which is our representative, to deal with matters of peace and war, and the league through its council and its assembly deals with the matter, and our accredited representative joins with the others in deciding upon a certain course, which involves a question of sending troops. What will the Congress of the United States do? What right will it have left, except the bare technical right to refuse, which as a moral proposition, it will not dare to exercise?

What is the result of all this? We are in the midst of all of the affairs of Europe. We have entangled ourselves with all European concerns. We have joined in alliance with all the European nations which have thus far joined the league, and all nations which may be admitted to the league. We are sitting there dabbling in their affairs and intermeddling in their concerns. In other words we have forfeited and surrendered, once and for all, the great policy of "no entangling alliances" upon which the strength of this Republic has been founded for 150 years.

My friends of reservations, tell me where is the reservation in these articles which protects us against entangling alliances with Europe?

Sir, we are told that this treaty means peace. But your treaty does not mean peace—far, very far, from it. If we are to judge the future by the past, it means war.

William E. Borah's speech to the Senate, November 19, 1919, adapted from the **Congressional Record,** 66th Congress, First Session, pp. 8781–8782.

Voting Patterns

In the end it was not cartoons or speeches that defeated the League, but votes—the votes of the 49 Republicans and 47 Democrats in the Senate. The acccompanying table indicates those votes on the three critical occasions when the League issue was voted upon.

The first column shows the vote on accepting the League "Covenant" exactly as it was presented by President Wilson. The second column shows the vote on accepting the "Covenant" but with Senator Lodge's "Reservations," the most important being the "Reservation" on Article 10 described above. The third column shows still a second vote, on accepting the "Covenant" four months later, after some minor changes had been made in the "Reservations." On all three votes Senator Lodge worked hard to have all Republicans vote alike and President Wilson insisted vigorously that Democratic Senators should vote for the original "Covenant" and vote against any "Reservations."

Senate Votes on Joining the League of Nations

	JOIN LEAGUE WITHOUT ANY "RESERVATIONS" (11/19/1919)		JOIN LEAGUE, BUT WITH LODGE "RESERVATIONS" (11/19/1919)		JOIN LEAGUE, BUT WITH MODIFIED LODGE "RESERVATIONS" (3/19/1920)	
	Yes	No	Yes	No	Yes	No
Regular Republicans	1	33	35	0	28	0
"Irreconcilable" Republicans	0	13	0	13	0	12
Democrats	37	7	4	42	21	23
TOTALS	38	53	39	55	49	35
Needed to pass*	61		63		56	
Result	Defeated by 23 votes		Defeated by 24 votes		Defeated by 7 votes	

Votes of **two-thirds** of the Senators present were needed for the U.S. to join the League of Nations.

7 America in the 1920's
The Long Weekend

Introduction

From President Theodore Roosevelt in 1901 until President Warren G. Harding in 1920, the American people had lived under a series of national administrations which sincerely, however imperfectly, attempted to improve the quality of American life. By 1920 Americans had tired of the high moralism of Woodrow Wilson and the other Progressives. They needed a rest. They needed a change. They needed a long weekend.

In many ways the decade of the 1920's was one long weekend. Americans pursued pleasure and personal gain with the same zest they had formerly shown for social reform. The results were startling. Automobiles changed the life-style of many young people. The sedate atmosphere of the front-porch swing or the old-fashioned parlor was replaced by the more daring, totally unchaperoned privacy of the closed car. A new breed of young uninhibited pleasure-seeking girls known as "flappers" appeared on the social scene and dominated it. They wore extremely short skirts, used make-up recklessly, smoked cigarettes in public, drank along with the boys, and, in short, mocked all of the traditional standards of female social behavior.

In politics, as well as in social life, standards changed dramatically. The scholarly, internationalist-minded Woodrow Wilson was succeeded by the more earthy and provincial Warren G. Harding. Anticipating four years of peace and prosperity, the nation received instead the most scandal-ridden administration in half a century.

Even more scandalous than grafting politicians was the extraordinary increase of intolerance. Serious race riots occurred in *Chicago,** Washington, Omaha, and Knoxville. A wave of anti-Communist hysteria swept the country. On one day alone, January 2, 1920, government agents in thirty-three cities arrested 4,000 suspected radicals and eventually deported 556 foreign-born members of the Communist Party. Two Italian anarchists, Nicola Sacco and Bartolemeo Vanzetti were arrested for murder in Massachusetts, tried under extremely unfair conditions, and eventually executed.

The decade also witnessed the rebirth of the *Ku Klux Klan** on a massive scale. Composed exclusively of white, native-born Protestants, the Klan spread into the North gaining a membership of four to five million by 1924. It was especially strong in the Midwest and Far West where Catholics were its principal targets. Most Klansmen were frightened by the spectre of an America dominated by foreigners, Catholics, Jews, and Blacks.

Objectives of this assignment are to:

—Analyze readings on American social life during the 1920's and identify areas where social attitudes have changed.

—Draw inferences about American social behavior from a filmstrip on the 1920's.

—Make historical judgment on the quality of American social life during the 1920's.

Most serious of the race riots after World War I were in **Chicago** where a young Negro boy, who accidentally floated into a white area of a Lake Michigan beach, drowned. Blacks claimed he had been stoned and accused the whites of murder. Thirteen days of bloody riots followed in which 38 persons were killed, 537 injured.

Ku Klux Klan: the Klan was revived in 1915 by William Simmons of Georgia.

In sharp contrast to the hatred directed toward minorities was the adulation which Americans heaped upon their heroes. The decade had heroes aplenty, especially athletes and fliers. Everyone knew Babe Ruth's batting average and how many yards Red Grange had gained. The Four Horsemen of Notre Dame were better known than President Coolidge's Cabinet. Jack Dempsey gave boxing its first million-dollar gate. The first woman ever to swim the English Channel was an American, Gertrude Ederle. Bobby Jones and Bill Tilden made golf and tennis spectator sports. But the greatest hero of them all was the shy, retiring flier from the Midwest, Charles A. Lindbergh.

The decade was a time of pygmies and giants, of confusion, and contrasts.

16 REVOLUTION IN LIFE-STYLES

For young people the post-war years were a time for reexamination of traditional social attitudes and values. Out of this examination came a new and more spontaneous life-style. Some of the older generation lamented that young people had lost all sense of the true meaning of life.

In August of 1920, Mrs. Katherine Fullerton Gerould, a well-known writer, severely rebuked the younger generation in an article published in The Atlantic Monthly, August, 1920. The September issue of the same magazine carried a very spirited reply by John F. Carter, Jr., a recent Yale graduate, entitled "These Wild Young People by One of Them." While reading selections from these two articles, keep in mind these questions:

1. According to Mrs. Gerould, what was most responsible for the new life-style of young people?
2. According to John Carter, what was most responsible for the new life-style of young people?
3. How does John Carter justify the new life-style?

Mrs. Gerould Lectures the Younger Generation

Granted—all of it. "It is the war, I believe," said one mother, the other evening. "It is the mothers," say other women who keep a proper tab on their own girls. "It is the motor-car," says a man who does not give his debutante daughter a car of her own. "It is the girls: they want you to make love to them," say the boys. "It is the men: they won't dance with you if you wear a corset," say the girls.

But it is really—is it not?—more than this. It is everything. Give the motor-car its due share of responsibility. Give the movie more blame, please, than it has hitherto received. Give the war some—but not too much; for all this antedates the war. Give the radical intellectuals a little, for their tendency to howl down everything that has ever, anywhere, been of good repute. Give a lot of it to the luxury of the *nouveaux riches:** a luxury which inevitably, at first, finds expression in pampering the body. Give <u>Prohibition</u> a little, if only as a down-payment on the vast blame it is going to have to shoulder in the next decade or two. And give all you can heap up to the general abandonment of religion.

For the abandonment of religion is probably most responsible of all, since it bears a *causal** relation to most of these other facts. When we had religion, we may have been vulgar, but our vulgarity was not so vital. The type of religion by which we were for the most part influenced in America did not necessarily give us manners, but it did necessarily give us morals. It called certain things sins: it stuck to the Ten Commandments. It forbade exploitation of the senses. Perhaps it forbade too much. That is not for me to say. By objecting to all music, to all dancing, to all plays, to most fiction, to a hundred forms of art and beauty, it brought about—you may believe—an inevitable and legitimate revolt. No one, I have heard it said, is wilder than the Quaker turned worldly. But the fact remains that, as a social group, we threw over—probably without meaning to—most of our everyday moral sanctions.

Nouveaux riches: newly rich people without the social graces that traditionally accompany great wealth.

Causal here means being responsible for contributing to the problems of the younger generation.

Adapted from Mrs. Katharine Fullerton Gerould, "Reflections of a Grundy Cousin," **The Atlantic Monthly** (August, 1920), pp. 158–159.

John F. Carter Defends the Younger Generation

I would like to say a few things about my generation.

In the first place, I would like to observe that the older generation had certainly pretty well ruined this world before passing it on to us. They give us this Thing, knocked to pieces, leaky, red-hot, threatening to blow up; and then they are surprised that we don't accept it with the same attitude of pretty, decorous enthusiasm with which they received it, 'way back in the eighteen-nineties, nicely painted, smoothly running, practically fool-proof. "So simple that a child can run it!" But the child couldn't steer it. He hit every possible telegraph-pole, some of them twice, and ended with a head-on collision for which <u>we</u> shall have to pay the fines and damages.

Now, with loving pride, they turn over their wreck to us; and, since we are not properly overwhelmed with loving gratitude, shake their heads and sigh, "Dear! dear! We were so much better-mannered than these wild young people. But then we had the advantages of a good, strict, old-fashioned bringing-up!" How intensely <u>human</u> these oldsters are, after all, and how fallible! How they always blame us for not following precisely in their eminently correct footsteps!

Now my generation is disillusioned, and, I think, to a certain extent, brutalized, by the *cataclysm** which <u>their</u> complacent folly engendered. The acceleration of life for us has been so great that into the last few years have been crowded the experiences and the ideas of a normal lifetime. We have in our unregenerate youth learned the practicality and the cynicism that is safe only in unregenerate old age. We have been forced to become realists overnight,

Cataclysm: a momentous and violent event marked by overwhelming upheaval and demolition, a disaster.

instead of idealists, as was our birthright. We have seen man at his lowest, woman at her lightest, in the terrible moral chaos of Europe.

We have been forced to question, and in many cases to discard, the religion of our fathers. We have seen hideous *peculation,** greed, anger, hatred, malice, and all uncharitableness, unmasked and rampant and unashamed. We have been forced to live in an atmosphere of "to-morrow we die," and so, naturally, we drank and were merry. We have seen the rottenness and shortcomings of all governments, even the best and most stable. We have seen entire social systems overthrown, and our own called in question. In short, we have seen the inherent beastliness of the human race revealed in an infernal *apocalypse.**

Peculation: embezzlement.

Apocalypse: a mystical or supernatural vision.

Adapted from John F. Carter, Jr., "These Wild Young People," **The Atlantic Monthly** (September, 1920), pp. 302–303.

17 THE EXCITING TWENTIES: A DECADE TO REMEMBER

Post-war Americans had their fill of noble causes and international crusades. Harding's campaign slogan of a "Return to Normalcy" matched the mood of the country. Though Progressive idealism survived in the speeches and actions of such men as Senator George Norris of Nebraska and Senator Robert LaFollette of Wisconsin, all three Presidents of the 1920's—Harding, Coolidge, and Hoover—were political conservatives. They assumed that what was good for big business was good for the American people.

Normalcy turned out to be the relentless pursuit of pleasure and personal gain, the greatest outburst of intolerance in our history, and a compulsive search for popular heroes. While examining the chart of major events and reading the selections presented here, keep in mind these questions:

1. According to Allen, what assets and liabilities did Harding bring to the Presidency?

2. According to Coughlan, what did the Grand Dragon say and what did his audience do?

3. According to Rice, why was the Notre Dame-Army game of 1924 so great? How did Notre Dame win?

4. According to Mary Mullett, why was Lindbergh's flight so important? What had he done for Americans?

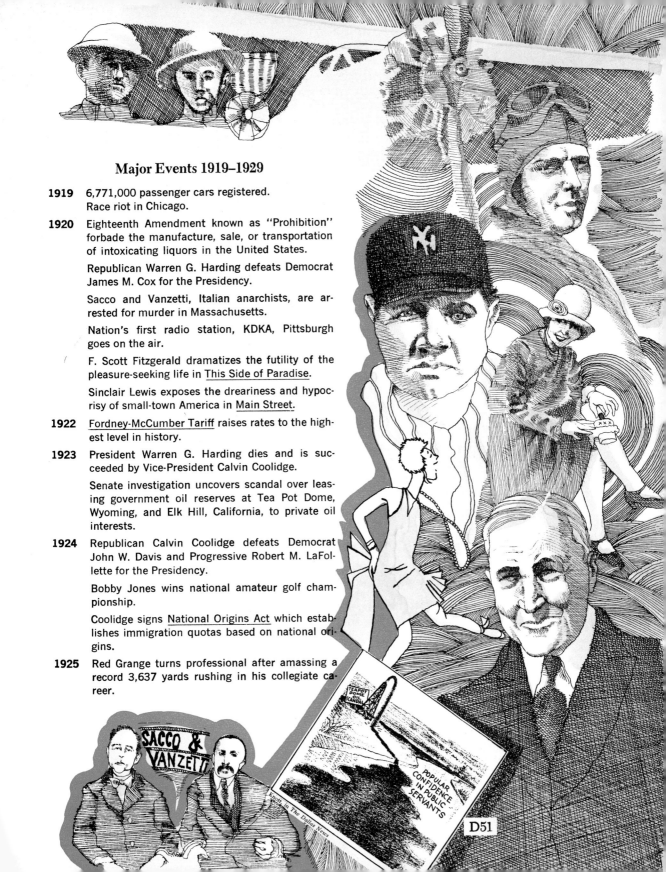

Major Events 1919–1929

1919 6,771,000 passenger cars registered.
Race riot in Chicago.

1920 Eighteenth Amendment known as "Prohibition" forbade the manufacture, sale, or transportation of intoxicating liquors in the United States.

Republican Warren G. Harding defeats Democrat James M. Cox for the Presidency.

Sacco and Vanzetti, Italian anarchists, are arrested for murder in Massachusetts.

Nation's first radio station, KDKA, Pittsburgh goes on the air.

F. Scott Fitzgerald dramatizes the futility of the pleasure-seeking life in This Side of Paradise.

Sinclair Lewis exposes the dreariness and hypocrisy of small-town America in Main Street.

1922 Fordney-McCumber Tariff raises rates to the highest level in history.

1923 President Warren G. Harding dies and is succeeded by Vice-President Calvin Coolidge.

Senate investigation uncovers scandal over leasing government oil reserves at Tea Pot Dome, Wyoming, and Elk Hill, California, to private oil interests.

1924 Republican Calvin Coolidge defeats Democrat John W. Davis and Progressive Robert M. LaFollette for the Presidency.

Bobby Jones wins national amateur golf championship.

Coolidge signs National Origins Act which establishes immigration quotas based on national origins.

1925 Red Grange turns professional after amassing a record 3,637 yards rushing in his collegiate career.

SACCO & VANZETTI

Knott in The Dallas News

TEAPOT DOME OIL SCANDAL

POPULAR CONFIDENCE IN PUBLIC SERVANTS

D51

Coach Knute Rockne of Notre Dame and the Four Horsemen cap three brilliant years of football glory by defeating Stanford in the Rose Bowl.

1926 Ernest Hemingway glorifies the search for adventure for its own sake in The Sun Also Rises.

Gertrude Ederle swims English Channel in record time of 14 hours 31 minutes.

1927 Charles Lindbergh makes first non-stop solo flight from New York to Paris.

Babe Ruth hits 60 home runs.

Sacco and Vanzetti executed in Massachusetts.

Gene Tunney defeats Jack Dempsey before a crowd of 104,000 in Chicago.

Coolidge vetoes the McNary-Haugen Bill which would have subsidized farmers through government purchases of surplus products.

Henry Ford replaces his famous Model T with a more stylish and faster Model A car.

Jack Johnson ends boxing career after winning 66 bouts and losing 5.

1928 Republican Herbert C. Hoover defeats Democrat Alfred E. Smith for the Presidency in a campaign marked by an outburst of bigotry over Smith being a Catholic.

1929 23,121,000 passenger cars registered.

Capone gang murders seven rivals in a Chicago garage on Saint Valentine's Day.

Immigration quotas reduced.

Stock market crashes.

Bill Tilden wins the United States men's tennis championship for the seventh time.

Thomas Wolfe describes coming of age in a small North Carolina town in Look Homeward Angel.

Frederick Lewis Allen Describes President Harding

Warren Harding had two great assets, and these were already apparent. First, he looked as a President of the United States should. He was superbly handsome. His face and carriage had a Washingtonian nobility and dignity, his eyes were benign; he photographed well and the pictures of him in the rotogravure sections won him affection and respect. And he was the friendliest man who ever had entered the White House. He seemed to like everybody, he wanted to do favors for everybody, he wanted to make everybody happy. His affability was not merely the forced affability of the cold-blooded politician; it was transparently and touchingly genuine. "Neighbor," he had said to Herbert Hoover at their first meeting, during the war, "I want to be helpful." He meant it; and now that he was President, he wanted to be helpful to neighbors from Marion, Ohio, and neighbors from campaign headquarters, and to the whole neighborly American public.

His liabilities were not at first so apparent, yet they were disastrously real. Beyond the limited scope of his political experience he was "almost unbelieveably ill-informed," as William Allen White put it. His mind was vague and fuzzy. . . .White tells of Harding's coming into the office of one of his secretaries after a day of listening to his advisers wrangling over a tax problem, and crying out: "John, I can't make a damn thing out of this tax problem. I listen to one side and they seem right, and then—God!—I talk to the other side and they seem just as right, and here I am where I started. I know somewhere there is a book that will give me the truth, but, hell, I couldn't read the book. I know somewhere there is an economist who knows the truth, but I don't know where to find him and haven't the sense to know him and trust him when I find him. God! what a job!" His inability to discover for himself the essential facts of a problem and to think it through made him utterly dependent upon subordinates and friends whose mental processes were sharper than his own.

If he had been discriminating in the choice of his friends and advisers, all might have been well. But discrimination had been left out of his equipment. He appointed *Charles Evans Hughes** and *Herbert Hoover** and *Andrew Mellon** to Cabinet positions out of a vague sense that they would provide his administration with the necessary amount of statesmanship, but he was as ready to follow the lead of *Daugherty** or *Fall** or *Forbes.** He had little notion of technical fitness for technical jobs. Offices were plums to him, and he handed them out like a benevolent Santa Claus—beginning with the boys from Marion.

Charles Evans Hughes: Secretary of State for Presidents Harding and Coolidge, 1921–1926.

Herbert Hoover: Secretary of Commerce for Presidents Harding and Coolidge.

Andrew Mellon: Secretary of Treasury for Presidents Harding, Coolidge, and Hoover (1921–1932).

Harry Daugherty, President Harding's close friend and political advisor. Supposedly involved in several scandals, but never convicted.

Albert B. Fall, Harding's Secretary of the Interior, convicted for taking bribes from private oil interests to lease them government oil reserves (Teapot Dome).

Charles Forbes, director of the Veterans Bureau under Harding, convicted for illicit sale of government property and misconduct in office.

From Frederick Lewis Allen, **Only Yesterday** (New York: Harper & Row, 1931), pp. 126–127.

The Klan in Indiana, 1923

On a hot July day in central Indiana, a great crowd of oddly dressed people clustered around an open meadow. They were waiting for something, their faces, framed in white hoods, were expectant, and their eyes searched the bright blue sky. Suddenly they began to cheer. They had seen it: a speck that came from the south and grew into an airplane. As it came closer it glistened in the sunlight, and they saw that it was gilded all over. It circled the field slowly and seesawed in for a bumpy landing. A bulky man in a robe and hood of purple silk hoisted himself up from the rear cockpit. As he climbed to the ground, a new surge of applause filled the country air. White-robed figures bobbed up and down; parents hoisted their children up for a view. A small delegation of dignitaries filed out toward the airplane, stopping at a respectable distance.

The man in purple stepped forward.

"Kigy," he said.

"Itsub," they replied solemnly.

"My worthy subjects, citizens of the Invisible Empire, Klansmen all, greetings! It grieves me to be late. The President of the United States kept me unduly long counseling upon vital matters of state. Only my plea that this is the time and place of my coronation obtained for me release from his prayers for guidance." The crowd buzzed.

The Grand Dragon paused, inviting the cheers that thundered around him. Then he launched into a speech. He urged his audience to fight for "one hundred per cent Americanism" and to thwart "foreign elements" that he said were trying to control the country. As he finished and stepped back, a coin came spinning through the air. Someone threw another. Some were throwing rings, watch charms, anything bright and valuable. At last when the tribute slackened, he motioned to his retainers to sweep up the treasure. Then he strode off to a nearby pavilion to consult with his attendant Kleagles, Cyclopses, and Titans.

The Klan had a weird and unintelligible system of ceremonies, signs, signals, and words. Local dens were governed by an Exalted Cyclops. Klansmen sang "Klodes," held "Klonvocations," swore blood oaths, burned crosses, muttered passwords, and carried on "Klonversations" or exchanges of code words formed from the first letters of sentences.

> Ayak: Are you a Klansman?
> Akai: A Klansman am I.
> Capowe: Countersign and password or written evidence.
> Cygnar: Can you give number and realm?
> Kigy: Klansman, I greet you.
> Itsub: In the sacred, unfailing bond.

They would then Klasp left hands (Klan loyalty a Sacred Principle). If a known non-member approached, the one who spied him first would break off the klonversation with a warning, "Sanborg" (Strangers are near. Be on guard).

A member's duties included absolute obedience to the Imperial Wizard, who was described in the Kloran or book of rules as "The Emperor of the Invisible Empire," a wise man, a wonder worker, having power to charm and control.

Adapted from Robert Coughlan "Konklave in Kokomo," in **The Aspirin Age 1919–1941,** edited by Isabel Leighton (New York: Simon & Schuster, Inc., copyright © 1949), pp. 105–106, 119–120.

The Four Horsemen of Notre Dame

Outlined against a blue-gray October sky, the Four Horsemen rode again. In dramatic lore they are known as Famine, Pestilence, Destruction and Death. These are only aliases. Their real names are Stuhldreher, Miller, Crowley and Layden. They formed the crest of the South Bend cyclone before which another fighting Army football team was swept over the precipice at the Polo Grounds yesterday afternoon as 55,000 spectators peered down on the bewildering panorama spread on the green plain below.

A cyclone can't be snared. It may be surrounded, but somewhere it breaks through to keep on going. When the cyclone starts from South Bend, where the candle lights still gleam through the Indiana sycamores, those in the way must take to storm cellars at top speed. Yesterday the cyclone struck again as Notre Dame beat the Army, 13 to 7. . . .

We doubt that any team in the country could have beaten *Knute Rockne's** array yesterday afternoon, East or West. It was a great football team, brilliantly directed, a team of speed, power and team play. The Army has no cause for gloom over its showing. It played first-class football against more speed than it could match.

Those who have tackled a cyclone can understand.

Knute Rockne, an immigrant boy from Norway, became head football coach at Notre Dame and did more than any other individual to popularize the game. His teams amassed an incredible record of 105 victories, 12 defeats, and 5 ties, before his death in a plane crash in 1931.

Grantland Rice, **New York Herald Tribune** (October 19, 1924).

The Lone Eagle

Ever since the war there has been an outcry against "modern" character, ideals, and morals; especially against those of the younger generation. Most of us have contributed our share to this chorus of denunciation. All of us have had to listen to it.

You hear it in every stratum of society. The high-brows talk of the "moral degeneration of the age." The low-brows say: "Ain't it perfectly awful!" The old folks raise their eyebrows in horror—and the young folks defiantly raise Cain! The professional reformers bewail the passing of "the good old days." The professional cynics shrug their shoulders and reply: *Autres temps, autres mœurs."** Or, if they don't speak French, they say: "Get it into your bean that times have changed, old thing!"

And this is the big thing Lindbergh has done: He has shown us that this talk was nothing <u>but</u> talk! He has shown us that we are <u>not</u> rotten at the core, but morally sound and sweet and good!

At the time Lindbergh made his flight, a particularly atrocious murder was the leading front-page story in the New York newspapers. They were giving columns to it every day. There were other crimes and scandals on the front pages.

Lindbergh banished these to almost complete oblivion. Not exactly that, either. We ourselves banished them! For if it had not been for the things <u>we</u> did, the Lindbergh news would not have demanded much space.

There wouldn't have been much to write about, if there had been no public demonstrations; no parades, dinners, receptions; no tidal wave of letters and

"Autres temps, autres moeurs": a French expression meaning <u>other times, other customs.</u>

Charles A. Lindbergh, first to make solo flight—New York to Paris—1927.

telegrams; no truck-loads of gifts; no reams of poetry; no songs; no cheers and shouts; no smiles of pride; no tears of joy; no thrill of possessing, in him, our dream of what we really and truly want to be!

When, because of what we believe him to be, we gave Lindbergh the greatest ovation in history, we convicted ourselves of having told a lie about ourselves. For we proved that the "things of good report" are the same today as they were nineteen hundred years ago.

We shouted ourselves hoarse. Not because a man had flown across the Atlantic! Not even because he was an American! But because he put ethics above any desire for wealth; because he was as modest as he was courageous; and because—as we now know, beyond any shadow of doubt—*these are the things which we honor most* in life.

To have shown us this truth about ourselves is the biggest thing that Lindbergh has done.

Mary B. Mullett, "The Biggest Thing That Lindbergh Has Done," **The American Magazine** (October 1927), p. 106.

D56

New School for Social Research, Peter Moore photo

6 The Roaring Twenties
Mural by Thomas Hart Benton

Ohio State Historical Society Library

7 A Harding Campaign Poster, 1920

8
The Ku Klux Klan Parades in
Washington, D.C. in 1920

UPI

9 The Four Horsemen of Notre Dame, 1922–1924

UPI

UPI

10
Traffic Jam on North Michigan Avenue
Chicago, 1926

8 Herbert Hoover and the Great Depression

The Morning After

Introduction

In the 1920's the spirit of the Progressives was replaced by an almost child-like confidence in the ability of the American business community to manage the nation's affairs with a minimum of interference from the Federal government. For several years this confidence seemed justified. But in 1929 the stock market crashed, and the United States entered the longest and most severe economic depression in its history.

Emergence of Herbert Hoover

Herbert Clark *Hoover** entered the White House a very happy man on March 4, 1929. To the nation, Hoover was a symbol of permanent prosperity. As Secretary of Commerce from 1921 to 1929, he received a great deal of credit for the prosperity of the 1920's, enabling Republican publicists to represent him as the "architect of prosperity." He was nominated by the Republicans for the Presidency in 1928 and defeated Alfred E. Smith of New York by a huge majority. Hoover's problems began a year later.

The Great Depression

The stock market crash of 1929 ushered in the most severe domestic crisis since the Civil War. Billions of dollars of stock values were wiped out, millions of people lost their life savings either in the stock market crash or in one of the 5000 banks which closed in the first three years of the depression. Factories slashed production or closed down entirely. Unemployment steadily mounted, approaching 15 million by 1932.

Hoover's initial response to the crisis was to hold a series of conferences with business and industrial leaders in 1929 and 1930 to persuade them to maintain steady employment at regular wages. Hoover worked hard to turn back the depression. He increased Federal spending for public works projects and urged the states and cities to do the same. He ordered the newly established Federal Farm Board (1929) to support farm prices by buying great quantities of wheat and cotton. Hoover established the Reconstruction Finance Corporation in 1932 as an independent Federal agency to loan money to banks, railroads, and large businesses.

Objectives of this assignment are to:

–Analyze a policy statement on Federal government's role in the relief crisis for meaning.

–Analyze a journalist's account of unemployment for meaning.

–Make inferences about social effects of Great Depression from a filmstrip of contemporary news pictures.

OUR NEXT PRESIDENT

HERBERT C. HOOVER

Herbert Clark Hoover, born into a poor family in West Branch, Iowa, in 1874; orphaned at the age of nine; worked his way through Stanford University and became a rich and successful mining engineer. During World War I he served with distinction as director of relief operations for Belgium and as Wilson's Food Administrator.

Although he vetoed the Wagner-Garner Relief Act of 1932, which would have provided $2.3 billion in Federal relief funds, he signed the Federal Relief Act of that same year which authorized the Reconstruction Finance Corporation to loan $300 million to the states for relief purposes. He also encouraged the establishment of national voluntary committees to aid the unemployed.

18   RELIEF CRISIS

As the national economic crisis deepened, more and more Americans demanded that the Federal government take direct action to provide adequate food, clothing, and housing for depression victims. Despite enormous pressure from Congress, social workers, and the press, President Hoover refused to go beyond his policy of loaning Federal money to the states for relief purposes. He remained firmly opposed to any form of direct Federal relief to the unemployed.

The reasons underlying Hoover's approach to the relief crisis were revealed in an official statement delivered to the press on February 3, 1931.

The dimensions of the problems confronting the nation were set out in great detail by the staff of the conservative business-oriented magazine Fortune in September, 1932. While reading Hoover's statement and selections from Fortune, keep in mind these questions:

1. Why was Hoover opposed to direct Federal relief?
2. According to Fortune, why was there a relief crisis?
3. What words would you use to describe the relief crises in New York, Philadelphia, and Chicago?

Hoover on Responsibility of Federal Government for Relief

This is not an issue as to whether people shall go hungry or cold in the United States. It is solely a question of the best method by which hunger and cold shall be prevented. It is a question as to whether the American people on one hand will maintain the spirit of charity and mutual self-help through voluntary giving and the responsibility of local government, as distinguished on the other hand from appropriation out of the Federal Treasury for such purposes. My own conviction strongly is that if we break down this sense of responsibility of individual generosity to individual and mutual self-help in the country in times of national difficulty, and if we start appropriations of this character we have not only impaired something infinitely valuable in the life of the American people but have struck at the roots of self-government. Once this has happened it is not the cost of a few score millions but we are faced with the abyss of reliance in the future upon government charity in some form or other. The money involved is indeed the least of the costs to American ideals and American institutions. . . .

I have spent much of my life in fighting hardship and starvation both abroad and in the southern states. I do not feel that I should be charged with lack of human sympathy for those who suffer but I recall that in all the organizations with which I have been connected over these many years, the foundation has been to summon the maximum of self-help. I am proud to have sought the help of Congress in the past for nations who were so disorganized by war and anarchy that self-help was impossible. But even these appropriations were but a tithe (tenth) of that which was coincidently mobilized from the public charity of the United States and foreign countries. There is no such paralysis in the United States and I am confident that our people have the resources, the initiative, the courage, the stamina, and kindliness of spirit to meet this situation in the way they have met their problems over generations.

I will accredit to those who advocate federal charity a natural anxiety for the people of their states. I am willing to pledge myself that if the time should ever come that the voluntary agencies of the country together with the local and state governments are unable to find resources with which to prevent hunger and suffering in my country, I will ask the aid of every resource of the federal government because I would no more see starvation amongst our countrymen than would any senator or congressman. I have faith in the American people that such a day will not come.

Adapted from Press Statement, February 3, 1931.

FORTUNE Reports on Plight of Unemployed

"No One Has Starved"

. . . which is not true. "Twenty-five Millions in Want"—which may be true before the winter is over. "America Faces the Facts"—which is true today for the first time, as a result of the Federal Relief Act of 1932. Under these headlines FORTUNE presents the whole story of unemployment relief: the story of an industrial problem which charity has attempted unsuccessfully to solve.

The theory was that private charitable organizations and semi-public welfare groups, established to care for the old and the sick and the indigent, were capable of caring for the unemployed in a world-wide economic disaster. And the theory in application meant that social agencies manned for the service of a few hundred families, and city shelters set up to house and feed a handful of homeless men, were compelled by the brutal necessities of hunger to care for hundreds of thousands of families and whole armies of the displaced and the jobless. And to depend for their resources upon the contributions of communities no longer able to contribute, and upon the irresolution and *vacillation*° of state legislatures and municipal assemblies long since in the red on their annual budgets. The result was the picture now presented in city after city and state after state—*heterogeneous*° groups of official and semi-official and unofficial relief agencies struggling under the earnest and

Vacillation: uncertain or wavering.

Heterogeneous: more than one kind; mixed; dissimilar or diverse.

Christmas Day breadline, New York City, 1931.

untrained leadership of the local men of affairs against an inertia of misery and suffering and want they are powerless to overcome.

Food only, in most cases, is provided and little enough of that. Rents are seldom paid. Shoes and clothing are given in rare instances only. Money for doctors and dentists is not to be had. And free clinics are filled to overflowing. Weekly allowances per family have fallen as low as $2.39 in New York with $3 and $4 the rule in most cities and $5 a high figure. And even on these terms funds budgeted for a twelve-month period have been exhausted in three or four. While city after city has been compelled to abandon a part of its dependent population.

New York City

Malnutrition: a condition of undernourishment caused by inadequate diet that lacks essential nutrients. In severe cases, malnutrition can cause serious disease in bodily organs and can retard growth.

About 1,000,000 out of the city's 3,200,000 working population are unemployed. Last April 410,000 were estimated to be in dire want. Seven hundred and fifty thousand in 150,000 families were receiving emergency aid while 160,000 more in 32,000 families were waiting to receive aid not then available. Of these latter families—families which normally earn an average of $141.50 a month—the average income from all sources was $8.20. Of families receiving relief, the allowance has been anything from a box of groceries up to $60 a month. . . . It is impossible to estimate the number of deaths in the last year in which starvation was a contributing cause. But ninety-five persons suffering directly from starvation were admitted to the city hospitals in 1931, of whom twenty died; and 143 suffering from *malnutrition,** of whom twenty-five died. . . .

Philadelphia

The situation in Philadelphia was described by its Community Council in July, 1932, as one of "slow starvation and progressive disintegration of family life" . . . . And by May, 1932, the total of unemployed was 298,000. In the following month the Governor of the state estimated that 250,000 persons in Philadelphia "faced actual starvation." Over the state at large the same conditions held. . . ." Malnutrition had increased in forty-eight counties—27 per cent of school children being undernourished (216,000 out of a school population of 800,000). New patients in the tuberculosis clinics had doubled.

Chicago

Unemployed in Chicago number somewhere between 660,000 and 700,000 or 40 per cent of its employable workers while the number for the state at large is about one in three of the gainfully employed. . . . Rents are not paid by the relief agencies and housing is, in certain sections, unspeakably bad. The situation of city employees is tragic. Teachers in May, 1932, had had only five months cash for the last thirteen months, 805 had borrowed $232,000 from loan sharks at rates adding up to 42 per cent a year, and 759 had lost their homes. The city at one time undertook to sell for tax default the houses of its employees unable to pay taxes because of its own default in wages.

"No One Has Starved," **Fortune,** VI (September, 1932). Reprinted from the September 1932 issue of Fortune Magazine by special permission; © 1932 Time Inc., pp. 19–29.

11

Home Is a Pipe. Oakland, California, 1932

Wide World

12

A "Hooverville" on the Waterfront, Seattle, Washington, 1931

Wide World

13

For Sale—$1200. Nebraska Farm, 1930

U.S. Dept. of Agriculture

14

Wisconsin Farmers Dumping Milk, 1933

Wide World

15

Tear Gas Used to Disperse a
Demonstration against Unemployment
in McKeesport, Pennsylvania, 1932

UPI

9 Franklin D. Roosevelt and the *New Deal*

Origin of the Welfare State

Introduction

Objectives of this assignment are to:

–Analyze a statement of Franklin D. Roosevelt's concept of Federal government's role in economic affairs for meaning.

–Examine chart of New Deal legislation and decide which American social groups benefited from it.

–Decide whether Roosevelt's concept of Federal government's role in economic affairs was reflected in New Deal legislation.

–Make historical judgment on whether New Deal solved the unemployment problem of the Great Depression.

As the 1932 presidential election rolled around, the nation was still in the depths of the Great Depression. The Republicans had no choice but to nominate Herbert Hoover for a second term; to do otherwise would be to admit failure. Sensing victory for the first time since 1916, the Democrats gathered in Chicago and nominated the popular Governor of New York, *Franklin D. Roosevelt.** Roosevelt easily defeated Hoover and launched a sweeping program of relief, recovery, and reform which he called the New Deal.

After an inspiring inaugural address in which Roosevelt assured the American people that they had "nothing to fear but fear itself," the new President swung immediately into action. The first "100 Days" of the New Deal saw a flurry of legislative action seldom equalled in the annals of government.

Unemployed workers, distressed farmers, and businessmen all sought and quickly received assistance from the *first* New Deal programs which provided immediate help to as many depression victims as possible.

By the end of 1934 the first New Deal had run its course. Depression victims had been cared for, but the rate of economic recovery was much too slow. Many Americans were attracted to the ideas and programs of agitators like *Senator Huey Long,** *Father Charles E. Coughlin,** and *Dr. Francis Townsend.**

In early 1935, Roosevelt, impatient with the rate of economic recovery, began the *second* New Deal, which was intended to remove what New Dealers believed to be causes of the depression. However, the reforms came to a standstill when the Supreme Court decisions in 1935 and 1936 declared major New Deal laws unconstitutional.

Franklin D. Roosevelt: member of a prominent New York family and fifth cousin of former President Theodore Roosevelt. Served in N.Y. State Legislature; Wilson's Assistant Secretary of the Navy. Crippled by polio in 1921, governor of New York, 1928–1932. Aided by James Farley, Democratic National Committee Chairman, he won the nomination, overwhelmed Hoover in 1932.

(*See margin opposite page.)

Mandate from the People

In the Presidential election of 1936, Roosevelt won a landslide victory over the Republican candidate, Governor Alfred M. Landon of Kansas. Carrying every state except Maine and Vermont, Roosevelt interpreted his victory as a mandate from the American people to continue the New Deal.

Fearing that new programs would be declared unconstitutional by the Supreme Court, the President attempted to change the attitude of the Court toward his programs by enlarging it and appointing New Dealers to it.

Roosevelt's "Court Packing Scheme" as opponents described it was firmly rejected by Congress. However, in the midst of the "Court Packing" controversy, members of the Court appear to have changed their minds about the constitutionality of New Deal programs. In a series of 5 to 4 decisions in 1937, the Court upheld a number of New Deal laws.

The Roosevelt recovery program received an even greater setback in the fall of 1937 than had been delivered by the Supreme Court in 1935. Beginning in August, 1937, the economy suddenly faltered and within three months all of the gains since 1935 were wiped out. This Roosevelt recession was checked by renewed spending on New Deal programs, but full recovery was delayed until the enormous defense spending of World War II.

19   GENESIS OF *THE NEW DEAL*

During the campaign of 1932, Franklin D. Roosevelt did not spell out his concept of a New Deal in detail. As he developed his program, he took many of his ideas from a group of young university professors and lawyers known as his *"brain trust."* In a speech before the Commonwealth Club of San Francisco on September 23, 1932, he explained his concept of the Federal government's role in economic affairs and suggested how his administration would respond to the Depression crisis.

While reading these selections from Roosevelt's campaign speech and examining a chart of his administrative and legislative actions, 1933–1938, keep in mind these questions:

1. According to Roosevelt what had been the Federal government's role in economic affairs in the nineteenth century?

2. What role should the Federal government play in economic affairs at the present time?

3. What New Deal measures were concerned with workers? With farmers? With business?

FDR on the Role of Government in the Present Crisis, September 23, 1932

The issue of government has always been whether individual men and women will have to serve some system of government or economics, or whether a system of government and economics exists to serve individual men and women. . . . On questions relating to these things men have differed, and for time immemorial it is probable that honest men will continue to differ. . . .

It was in the middle of the 19th century that a new force was released and a new dream created. . . . The dream was the dream of an economic machine,

Huey Long, Governor and Senator from Louisiana, advocated a "Share the Wealth" program. A potential rival of Roosevelt for the 1936 presidential election, he was assassinated in September, 1935.

Father Charles E. Coughlin, famed "Radio Priest" of Royal Oak, Michigan, attracted a radio audience of millions to his 16-point social justice program.

Dr. Francis Townsend, an elderly Long Beach, California, physician advocated a pension of $200 a month for all Americans over sixty provided they spent it within thirty days.

Brain Trust advisors: Raymond Moley, professor of public law at Columbia and associate editor of Newsweek; Rexford G. Tugwell, economics professor at Columbia; and Adolph Berle, specialist in corporation law and finance.

able to raise the standard of living for all; to bring luxury within reach of the humblest; to annihilate distance by steam power and electricity, and to release everyone from the drudgery of the heaviest manual toil. . . .

There was equal opportunity for all and the business of government was not to interfere but to assist in the development of industry. This was done at the request of business men themselves. The tariff was originally imposed for the purpose of "fostering our infant industry," a phrase I think the older among you will remember as a political issue not so long ago. The railroads were subsidized. . . .

Some of my friends tell me that they do not want the Government in business. With this I agree; but I wonder whether they realize the implications of the past. For while it has been American doctrine that the government must not go into business in competition with private enterprises, still it has been traditional particularly in Republican administrations for business urgently to ask the government to put at private disposal all kinds of government assistance.

The same man who tells you that he does not want to see the government interfere in business—and he means it, and has plenty of good reasons for saying so—is the first to go to Washington and ask the government for a prohibitory tariff on his product. When things get just bad enough—as they did two years ago—he will go with equal speed to the United States government and ask for a loan; and the Reconstruction Finance Corporation is the outcome of it. Each group has sought protection from the government for its own special interests, without realizing that the function of government must be to favor no small group at the expense of its duty to protect the rights of personal freedom and of private property of all its citizens. . . .

Dearth: scarcity; inadequate supply.

Every man has a right to life; and this means that he has also a right to make a comfortable living. He may by sloth or crime decline to exercise that right; but it may not be denied him. We have no actual famine or *dearth;** our industrial and agricultural mechanism can produce enough and to spare. Our government formal and informal, political and economic, owes to every one an avenue to possess himself of a portion of that plenty sufficient for his needs, through his own work.

Roosevelt was referring to the need for insuring savings in banks. Part of the New Deal program included the establishment of the Federal Deposit Insurance Corporation.

Every man has a right to his own property; which means a right to be assured, to the fullest extent attainable, in the safety of his savings.* By no other means can men carry the burdens of those parts of life which, in the nature of things, afford no chance of labor; childhood, sickness, old age. In all thought of property, this right is paramount; all other property rights must yield to it. If, in accord with this principle, we must restrict the operations of the speculator, the manipulator, even the financier, I believe we must accept the restriction as needful, not to hamper individualism but to protect it. . . .

The government should assume the function of economic regulation only as a last resort, to be tried only when private initiative, inspired by high responsibility, with such assistance and balance as government can give, has finally failed. As yet there has been no final failure, because there has been no attempt; and I decline to assume that this nation is unable to meet the situation.

The Public Papers and Addresses of Franklin D. Roosevelt

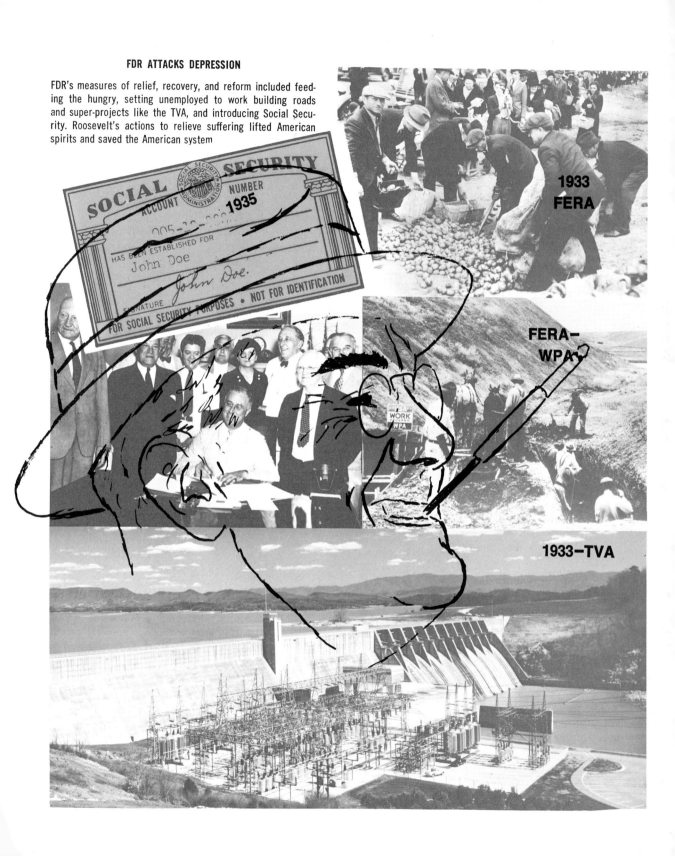

FDR ATTACKS DEPRESSION

FDR's measures of relief, recovery, and reform included feeding the hungry, setting unemployed to work building roads and super-projects like the TVA, and introducing Social Security. Roosevelt's actions to relieve suffering lifted American spirits and saved the American system

SOCIAL SECURITY
ACCOUNT NUMBER 1935
005-16-000
HAS BEEN ESTABLISHED FOR
John Doe
John Doe.
SIGNATURE
FOR SOCIAL SECURITY PURPOSES • NOT FOR IDENTIFICATION

1933
FERA

FERA–
WPA

U.S.A.
WORK
WPA

1933–TVA

The First New Deal, 1933–1935

	NEW DEAL MEASURES	NEW DEAL ADMINIS-TRATORS	SUPREME COURT DECISIONS
1933			
March 9	Emergency Banking Act provided for Federal inspection of private banks and authorized the Federal Reserve Banks to loan money to any state-chartered private bank.		
March 31	Civilian Conservation Corps (CCC) established to provide 250,000 jobs in reforestation and flood-control projects for unemployed youth 18–25.	Administered by the U.S. Army	
May 12	Federal Emergency Relief Administration (FERA) established to provide $500 million in direct Federal grants for relief to states and cities.	Harry Hopkins	
	Agricultural Adjustment Administration (AAA) established to curtail surplus production and subsidize farm prices.	George Peek	Declared unconstitutional in U.S. v. Butler, 1936
	Emergency Farm Mortgage Act provided for the refinancing of farm mortgages at lower interest rates.		
May 18	Tennessee Valley Authority (TVA) established to direct the economic development of the Tennessee River Valley through a series of dams and electric power-generating stations.	David Lilienthal	Constitutionality upheld in Ashwander v. T.V.A., 1936
May 27	Federal Securities or Truth-in-Securities Act required full disclosure of information when new stocks and bonds were issued.		
June 13	Home Owners Loan Corporation (HOLC) established to re-finance non-farm home loans at lower interest rates.		
June 16	National Industrial Recovery Act established the National Recovery Administration (NRA) to encourage business recovery by limiting competition through industrial self-regulation.	General Hugh Johnson	Declared unconstitutional in the Schechter Poultry Corporation v. U.S., 1935
	National Industrial Recovery Act established the Public Works Administration (PWA) to increase employment and stimulate business by spending $3.3 billion on public works projects.	Harold Ickes	
	Glass-Steagall Banking Act established the Federal Deposit Insurance Corporation (FDIC) to insure bank deposits up to $5,000 and greatly increased the powers of the Federal Reserve Board.		
1934			
June 6	Securities and Exchange Commission (SEC) established to regulate the operations of stock exchanges and to correct unfair practices in the buying and selling of stocks.	Joseph P. Kennedy	
June 28	Federal Housing Administration (FHA) established to in-sure loans for home repairs and improvements and new home construction.		

The Second New Deal, 1935–1938

	NEW DEAL MEASURES	NEW DEAL ADMINIS-TRATORS	SUPREME COURT DECISIONS
1935			
April 8	Emergency Relief Appropriation Act replaced the FERA with the Works Progress Administration (WPA) marking a shift from direct relief to a large-scale Federal job program. Between 1935 and 1942 the WPA employed 8½ million people.	Harry Hopkins	
April 27	Soil Conservation Service established for the control and prevention of soil erosion.		
May 11	Rural Electrification Administration (REA) established to loan money at low interest rates to bring electric power into rural areas.		
June 26	National Youth Administration (NYA) established to provide work for unemployed youth from relief families and part-time work for high school and college students. At its peak the NYA employed 750,000 students.	Aubrey Williams	
July 5	National Labor Relations Act (Wagner Act) established National Labor Relations Board (NLRB) which guaranteed workers the right to collective bargaining through the union of their choice.		Constitutionality upheld in National Labor Relations Board v. Jones and Laughlin Steel Co., 1937
Aug. 14	Social Security Act established a Federal program of unemployment insurance and old-age pensions financed by contributions from both employers and employees. It also provided Federal grants to states for the welfare of blind people and dependent children.		
Aug. 23	Banking Act of 1935 greatly increased the powers of the Federal Reserve Board over the nation's banks.		
Aug. 28	Public Utility Holding Company Act provided for strict government regulation of gas and electric companies.		
Aug. 30	Revenue Act of 1935 or Wealth Tax Act sharply increased taxes on high income groups.		
1937			
Sept. 1	National Housing Act, or Wagner-Steagall Act, established the U.S. Housing Authority (USHA) to provide for slum clearance, housing projects, and rent subsidies.		
1938			
Feb. 16	Agricultural Adjustment Act of 1938 revived earlier AAA in form modified to comply with Supreme Court decision.		
June 21	Emergency Relief Appropriation Act provided $3 billion to combat recession.		
June 25	Fair Labor Standards Act established a minimum wage of 40 cents per hour, a 40-hour work week, and forbade labor by children under 16.		

WPA workers build dikes at Richmond, Virginia, in 1935 as part of the New Deal efforts to put a large share of the millions of unemployed back to work.

20   NEW DEAL IN ACTION

In 1935, Congress replaced the Federal Emergency Relief Administration (FERA) with the Works Progress Administration (WPA). The head of the FERA, Harry Hopkins, continued on as the director of the WPA. Congress appropriated $4.3 billion for the new agency. Charges of waste, loafing on the job, and political influence made the WPA and its director highly controversial.

While reading Harry Hopkins' defense of the WPA, case histories of two WPA workers, and examining charts of unemployment and government spending statistics, keep in mind these questions:

1. How does Harry Hopkins defend the WPA against charges of waste and chiseling?

2. What is Mr. Wheeling's judgment on his WPA work experience? Mr. Krause's judgment?

3. What inferences are suggested by the unemployment and government spending statistics for 1937 and 1938?

Harry Hopkins Defends the WPA

I am getting sick and tired of these people on the W.P.A. and local relief rolls being called chiselers and cheats. It doesn't do any good to call these people names, because they are just like the rest of us. They don't drink any more than the rest of us, they don't lie any more, they're no lazier than the rest of us—they're pretty much a cross section of the American people. . . .

I want to finish by saying two things. I have never liked poverty. I have never believed that with our capitalistic system people have to be poor. I think it is an outrage that we should permit hundreds and hundreds of thousands of people to be ill clad, to live in miserable homes, not to have enough to eat; not to be able to send their children to school for the only reason that they are poor. I don't believe ever again in America that we are going to permit the things to happen that have happened in the past to people. We are never going back again, in my opinion, to the days of putting the old people in the *alms houses*,* when a decent dignified pension at home will keep them there. We are coming to the day when we are going to have decent houses for the poor, when there is genuine and real security for everybody. I have gone all over the moral hurdles that people are poor because they are bad. I don't believe it. A system of government on that basis is fallacious. . . .

I am proud of having worked for the Government. . . . I have signed my name to about $6 billion in the last three and a half years. None of it has stuck to the fingers of our administrators. You might think some of it has been wasted. If it has been wasted it was in the interest of the unemployed. You might say we have made mistakes. I haven't a thing to apologize for about our so-called mistakes. If we have made mistakes we have made them in the interests of the people that were broke.

> **Alms houses:** poor house or county home for the impoverished aged.

From Robert E. Sherwood, **Roosevelt and Hopkins** (New York: Harper & Row, 1948), pp. 83–84.

WPA Workers Discuss Their Jobs

No. 24—Mr. Wheeling is forty-eight years old and has a wife and six children, the oldest being a son of twenty-six years. He is a varnisher by trade earning $35 a week on the average. He lost his job in July 1930 and applied for assistance six months later. His work relief consisted of house painting and labor work at which he earned about $40 a month. He secured a private job for several months and when he had to return for relief he was assigned to a WPA job as a grader on a recreation field project. He earns $55 a month. He can see "no d – – – – sense in the project" and "the $150,000 being spent on the field house is a waste of money." According to Mr. Wheeling the men on the job do not work and so it may be at least two years before the job is finished. He does not believe that any of the men are placed correctly —that none of the men were placed at their own trade. This, in Mr. Wheeling's estimation, confirmed his claim that the whole project was crooked and that the "higher-ups" were getting most of the money instead of allowing the men to receive a higher wage. He had gone to the Democratic ward committeeman for assistance in getting a better-paid job but this was not successful.

No. 39—Mr. Krause is just twenty-three years old and his mother is dependent upon him as his father died fifteen years ago. He graduated from high school, where he had taken a science course together with aviation mechanics, but he has always done clerical work, earning $15 a week until he and his mother had to apply for assistance in 1932. He worked irregularly on work relief. He was at a CCC camp for six months and liked it very much and would like to return, but the $25 a month which he earned in camp is insufficient for his mother to live on, and they find that the two of them can live more comfortably on the $55 which he earns on WPA. For the first ten months he did street-repair work and then was transferred to a gardening project in Lincoln Park. This latter job is preferable to the first for he believes it to be more useful and necessary. According to Mr. Krause, WPA work has helped his morale, for he was "pretty discouraged when WPA came along and steady work has helped me to be self-respecting once again."

Adapted from Margaret C. Bristol, "Personal Reactions of Assignees to WPA in Chicago," Social Service Review (March 1938), (Chicago: The University of Chicago Press, 1938), pp. 84–87, 94, 95.

WPA Projects 1935–1943

Total Number of Projects	1,410,000
Total Cost of Projects	$11 billion
Total Number of Employees	8,500,000
Miles of New Highways	651,087
Bridges Improved or Built	124,031
Public Buildings Constructed	125,110
Public Parks Constructed	8,192
Airports Improved or Built	853

Unemployment and Government Spending

	% OF WORK FORCE UNEMPLOYED	GOVERNMENT SPENDING IN BILLIONS
1929	3.2	$ 3.3
1930	8.7	3.4
1931	15.9	3.6
1932	23.6	4.7
1933	24.9	4.6
1934	21.7	6.7
1935	20.1	6.5
1936	16.9	8.4
1937	14.3	7.8
1938	19.0	6.8
1939	17.2	8.9
1940	14.6	9.1
1941	9.9	13.3

10 Pearl Harbor

United States and Japan, 1941

Introduction

America's economic problems were not limited to the home front. The country also faced problems abroad in regions where the employment of American marines and gunboats had long been linked to American economic interests. Although President Roosevelt had changed the nation's course from "gunboat diplomacy" to freedom of trade and being a *good neighbor* on one front —Latin America—older policies continued in other areas, especially in eastern Asia. There Japan confronted an American policy in support of China, which she opposed. The result was war.

In this assignment you will study the confrontation between the United States and Japan and the coming of that war.

Day of Infamy—Explosion of USS Destroyer Shaw after attack by Japanese bombers at Pearl Harbor, December 7, 1941.

"This Is No Drill"

At 7:58 A.M. on Sunday, December 7, 1941, a Navy radio at Pearl Harbor, Hawaii, crackled the message:

"Air raid, Pearl Harbor—This is no drill."

Three minutes earlier the first bomb of the Japanese surprise attack had exploded. By the time the attack ended 18 U.S. Navy ships (including all 8 battleships in Pearl Harbor) had been sunk or badly damaged; more than 300 warplanes had been destroyed or damaged; and more than 2,400 Americans were dead. America was once again at war.

How did it happen?

Americans were angered and shocked. Their immediate reaction was to strike back vigorously, not only at Japan, but also at Germany and Italy, Japan's allies who declared war on the United States several days later. Yet, even while Americans united to fight the war, that question—how did it happen?—remained. Many felt that somehow Pearl Harbor shouldn't have happened. They felt that somehow the tragedy could have been prevented.

Japanese-Americans

Unfortunately, Japanese-Americans were the victims of American anger following the Pearl Harbor attack. In a shameful chapter in our national history, more than 110,000 of them were hastily forced to leave their homes and businesses on the West Coast early in 1942. They were confined in "relocation" camps in the west for the duration of the war.

Bent on proving their loyalty to America, Japanese-Americans enlisted in the armed forces by the thousands in World War II. One of the most famed and most decorated fighting units of the war, the 442nd Infantry Regiment, whose motto was *Go for Broke*, was made up of Nisei (second-generation Japanese-Americans).

Attached to the 36th (Texas) Division, they fought in the fiercest battles in the invasion of Italy—from the Salerno and Anzio beachheads to Monte Cassino. In their bloodiest battle, the 442nd rescued the 1st Battalion of the 141st Regiment known as *The Lost Battalion*, which was trapped behind enemy lines. For this feat, the men of the 36th Division later made all the fighting Nisei of the 442nd "Honorary Texans" and presented them with a plaque. The Nisei soldiers suffered enormous casualties, made tremendous sacrifices, and came out of the war with 18,000 individual decorations for valor, plus many battalion citations.

On January 2, 1945, the long exile from the West Coast ended for Japanese-Americans when the Supreme Court determined it was a violation of their constitutional rights to keep them in confinement. Many of them had been swindled out of their holdings or had lost their businesses. The Federal Reserve Bank estimated the long-term economic losses at about $400 million. The U.S. Government later paid out a compensation of about $38 million in evacuation claims, less than ten cents for every dollar lost.

Despite the bitterness of the war years, less than 4 percent of the Japanese left the United States for Japan. The rest chose to stay.

Background to Conflict

The United States and Japan had both become great powers in the Far East at the beginning of the twentieth century. Both developed a strong interest in trade with China. For the United States that interest had long been expressed by the ideal of an "Open Door" in China—a phrase meaning that all nations should be allowed to trade with the Chinese on equal terms. For Japan, commercial interest in China was expressed in securing exclusive control of important trading areas and special privileges for Japanese business. Because of Chinese trade, both were interested in the kind of government that would emerge to rule that vast and troubled land.

Until the 1930's the United States and Japan lived in peace with one another, although both recognized the possibility of conflict. In the decade before Pearl Harbor that possibility became increasingly likely. The Japanese had extended their power in parts of China. In 1931 they took control of Manchuria. In 1937 they began sending troops into the heart of China where they were opposed by both the Chinese government of Chiang Kai-shek and the Chinese Communists, led by Mao Tse-tung. In 1941 Japan, unable to settle the "China Incident" (as their leaders called it) after four years of bitter warfare, occupied portions of *French Indo-China** to the south. Danger to China increased. The Philippines and important rubber, tin, and oil-producing areas of Southeast Asia controlled by the British and Dutch were also threatened.

American reaction to this Japanese expansion began with diplomatic denunciation. It gradually escalated into an attempt at economic pressure. By the summer of 1941 the United States had cut off trade with Japan, including trade in scrap metal and oil, which were essential to Japanese industry.

Objectives of this assignment are to:

–Identify policy objectives of United States and Japan in East Asia from selected contemporary policy statements.

–Examine a selection of intercepted Japanese secret messages and make inferences about Japanese intentions in November and December, 1941.

–Make historical judgment on inevitability of war between United States and Japan.

–Analyze principles on which Japanese secret code was based and decipher a simulated Japanese message.

Indochina was the name given to the region between India and China, comprising the present states of North and South Vietnam, Laos, Cambodia, and Thailand. Except for Thailand (Siam) this area became a French colony in the 19th century.

21 POLICIES IN CONFLICT

By late 1941 the United States and Japan appeared to be approaching a confrontation. The position of each country was set forth in September, 1941. On September 1 the American Ambassador in Japan, Joseph C. Grew, described the American position in a letter to a Japanese friend who had criticized the actions of the United States. Five days later, a conference of the leaders of the Japanese government produced a secret policy statement describing the Japanese position.

While reading Ambassador Grew's letter and the Japanese policy statement, keep in mind these questions:

1. *What were the objectives of United States policy in East Asia?*
2. *What were the objectives of Japanese policy in East Asia?*
3. *Do you think war was inevitable? Why or why not?*

Ambassador Grew's Letter

You write of the desirability of our recognizing Japan's legitimate interests and aspirations. Indeed, our Government has time and time again expressed its full appreciation of Japan's legitimate interests and aspirations, realizing that Japan, restricted as she is in her islands, must have access to raw materials, markets for the products of her industries, and a free flow of trade and commerce.

Nevertheless, unless Japan is willing to abandon aggression by force there can be no hope for an improvement in our relations. We know by sad and bitter practical experience that Japan's so-called "New Order in East Asia" and "Co-Prosperity Sphere" visualize no neighborly relations on the basis of free give-and-take, but rather an order in which Japanese interests are to be predominant and to be exercised to the exclusion of the legitimate interests of other countries.

We have watched the gradual elimination of our own legitimate interests over these past several years, our long-standing and patiently-established business, commercial, industrial, banking and cultural interests, all legitimate and cooperative activities, progressively ousted first from Manchuria, and then, in turn, from North China, the ports, the Yangtze, and now they are in process of being excluded from Indochina, in spite of the most *categorical** assurances and promises that the Open Door and equal opportunity would be *scrupulously** observed everywhere.

As you know, I am no defeatist. I believe that in spite of present difficulties we can still guide our relations into healthy channels, and for that high purpose I am constantly thinking and working. Below are four points which my Government regards as essential for our future good relations. We confidently believe that Japan would achieve the greatest happiness, security, prosperity, and contentment by following a policy of peaceful and productive expansion based on the principle of free and equal treatment for all nations, a policy which would have the full support of the United States, while we believe that the continued use of armed force will lead eventually to social, economic and financial disaster. These are the points:

1. Respect for the territorial integrity and the sovereignty of each and all nations.

2. Support of the principle of noninterference in the internal affairs of other countries.

3. Support of the principle of equality, including equality of commercial opportunity.

4. Nondisturbance of the *status quo** in the Pacific except as the status quo may be altered by peaceful means.

If Japan will mould her policy and actions on the basis of the foregoing four points and will abandon aggression, I see a happy outlook for the development of a new era in Japanese-American relations.

Categorical: absolute or binding. Here it refers to Japan's pledge that she would honor the Open Door policy—freedom of trade for all nations in the Far East. She broke that pledge.

Scrupulously: in the sense of adhering strictly to ethical or moral standards. A scrupulous person is upright, clings to good principles rigidly.

Status quo (Latin) means the **existing arrangement,** in this case the existing states and governments in the Pacific. These four points were first stated to the Japanese as the basic American position in April, 1941.

Adapted from Joseph C. Grew, **The Turbulent Era,** edited by Walter Johnson (Boston: Houghton Mifflin Company, 1952), Vol. II, pp. 1235 and 1243.

Japanese Policy Statement

Is war with Great Britain and the United States inevitable?

Our Empire's plan to build a New Order in East Asia—the central problem of which is the settlement of the China Incident—is a firm policy based on the national principle of *Hakko Ichiu.* The building of the New Order will go on forever, much as the life of our State does.

However, it appears that the policy of the United States toward Japan is based on the idea of preserving the status quo; in order to dominate the world and defend democracy, it aims to prevent our Empire from rising and developing in East Asia. Under these circumstances, it must be pointed out that the policies of Japan and the United States are mutually incompatible; it is historically inevitable that the conflict between the two countries, which is sometimes intense and sometimes moderate, will ultimately lead to war.

It need not be repeated that unless the United States changes its policy toward Japan, our Empire is placed in a desperate situation, where it must resort to the ultimate step—namely, war—to defend itself and to assure its preservation. Even if we should make concessions to the United States by giving up part of our national policy for the sake of a temporary peace, the United States, its military position strengthened, is sure to demand more and more concessions on our part; and ultimately our Empire will have to lie prostrate at the feet of the United States.

What are the aims of a war against the United States, Great Britain, and the Netherlands?

The purposes of war with the United States, Great Britain, and the Netherlands are to expel the influence of these three countries from East Asia, to establish a sphere for the self-defense and self-preservation of our Empire, and to build a New Order in Greater East Asia. In other words, we aim to establish a close and inseparable relationship in military, political, and economic affairs between our Empire and the countries of the Southern Region, to achieve our Empire's self-defense and self-preservation, and to build up at the same time the New Order of co-existence and co-prosperity in Greater East Asia. Accordingly, we must resolutely expel the hostile powers of the United States, Great Britain, and the Netherlands, which interfere with the above purpose.

Hakko Ichiu literally means bringing "the eight corners of the world under one roof." By 1941 this phrase had come to be a motto for Japanese control of East Asia.

Some of the reference material for answering questions at the Imperial Conference held on September 6, 1941, reprinted with permission of the publisher from **Japan's Decision for War: Records of 1941 Policy Conference,** translated and edited by Nobutaka Ike (Stanford: Stanford University Press, 1967), pp. 152–153.

22   "MAGIC" MESSAGES

Whether war was inevitable or not, American leaders in Washington quickly came to believe it was likely. In November, 1941, the Japanese submitted a series of proposals touching on most of the points at issue between the two countries. The American Government found them unacceptable. On

November 26 the United States, in turn, presented its proposals for a settlement, emphasizing the four points mentioned by Ambassador Grew and insisting on better guarantees of Japanese good will in China and Indochina.

Yet the American military leaders (Admiral Harold R. Stark and General George C. Marshall) felt the chances of a peaceful settlement were slim. Their belief that war could break out at any moment was so strong that on November 27 they sent special "war warning" messages to their commanders in the Pacific, including those at Pearl Harbor.

The main reason why Admiral Stark and General Marshall sent their special "war warnings" was that they had seen a number of secret Japanese messages. American code experts had discovered the keys to many of the Japanese secret codes. They painstakingly decoded and translated into English thousands of Japanese diplomatic and military messages from all parts of the world —a project referred to as "Magic" by those few who knew of it. As a result, American intelligence officers and leaders in Washington knew of Japanese troop and naval movements towards the Philippines, the Dutch East Indies, Thailand, and British Malaya. They knew Japanese agents were reporting on ships passing through the Panama Canal, ships in Pearl Harbor and Manila, and ships at Bremerton, Washington. They knew, also, the instructions sent from Tokyo to the Japanese Ambassador in Washington.

In November and early December, 1941, the air was filled with messages. After December 7, and ever since, men have debated the inferences that might (or should, or could—depending on one's point of view) have been drawn from them. Eight of the more important "Magic" messages are printed here. While studying these messages, keep in mind these questions:

1. Do you think that any of the messages (or all of them collectively) indicate that the Japanese were going to launch a surprise attack on Pearl Harbor just after dawn on December 7?

2. What inferences about Japanese intentions would you have drawn from these messages?

3. Do you think General Tojo was right in regarding Message G as equivalent to a declaration of war? Would you regard it that way?

Tokyo to the Japanese Ambassador in Washington

Message A, November 4

Conditions both inside and outside our Empire are so tense that no longer is delay possible. We have decided to gamble once more on the continuance of the negotiations, but this is our last effort. Both in name and in spirit this counter-proposal of ours is, indeed, the last. If through it we do not reach a quick accord, I am sorry to say talks will certainly be ruptured. Then, indeed, will relations between our two nations be on the brink of chaos. I mean that the success or failure of the discussions will have an immense effect on the destiny of the Empire of Japan. In fact, we gambled the fate of our land on the *throw of this die.**

Die is the singular of **dice**. Japanese play games with a single die, unlike Americans who play with two or more dice. The phrase used here means something determined by chance.

Message B, November 5

Because of various circumstances, it is absolutely necessary that all arrangements for the signing of an agreement be completed by the 25th of this month. I realize that this is a difficult order, but under the circumstances it is an unavoidable one.

Message C, November 22 (available on November 22)

It is awfully hard for us to consider changing the date we set in my November 5th message. There are reasons beyond your ability to guess why we wanted to settle Japanese-American relations by the 25th, but if within the next three or four days you can finish your conversations with the Americans; if the signing can be completed by the 29th (let me write it out for you—*twenty-ninth*); if everything can be finished, we have decided to wait until that date. This time we mean it, that the deadline absolutely cannot be changed. After that, things are automatically going to happen.

Message D, November 19 (available on November 28)

In case of emergency (danger of cutting off our diplomatic relations), and the cutting off of international communications, the following warning will be added in the middle of the daily Japanese language short wave news broadcast.

(1) In case of Japan-U.S. relations in danger: EAST WIND RAIN.＊
(2) Japan-U.S.S.R. relations: NORTH WIND CLOUDY.
(3) Japan-British relations: WEST WIND CLEAR.

When this is heard please destroy all code papers, etc.

This became famous as the **Winds Code** message. American intelligence officers alerted both their men and those of commercial radio firms to listen for such an East Wind Rain message. However, there is no evidence that such a message was ever sent.

Tokyo to the Japanese Ambassador in Berlin

Message E, November 30 (available on December 1)

The conversations begun between Tokyo and Washington last April now stand ruptured—*broken.* In the face of this, our Empire faces a grave situation and must act with determination. Therefore, immediately interview Chancellor Hitler and Foreign Minister Ribbentrop and confidentially communicate to them a summary of the developments. Say to them that lately England and the United States have taken a provocative attitude, both of them. Say very secretly to them that there is extreme danger that war may suddenly break out between the Anglo-Saxon nations and Japan through some clash of arms and add that the time of the breaking out of this war may come quicker than anyone dreams.

Tokyo to the Japanese Ambassador in Washington

Message F, December 6 (available December 6, 3:00 P.M.)

The Government has deliberated deeply on the American proposal, and as a result we have drawn up a memorandum for the United States contained in a separate message.

D81

The first thirteen parts of the reply were actually received in Washington late on December 6. The American experts had them decoded and circulated them to the President and other leaders that night. These thirteen parts consisted of a lengthy repetition of the Japanese position and the Japanese criticism of the American position. **Part fourteen makes up Message H.**

This separate message is a very long one. I will send it in fourteen parts and I imagine you will receive it tomorrow. However, I am not sure. The situation is extremely delicate, and when you receive it, I want you to please keep it secret for the time being.

Concerning the time of presenting this memorandum to the United States, I will wire you in a separate message.

Message G, December 7 (available at 10:00 A.M., Washington time, 4:30 A.M., Pearl Harbor time)

Obviously it is the intention of the American Government to conspire with Great Britain and other countries to obstruct Japan's efforts toward the establishment of peace through the creation of a New Order in East Asia, and especially to preserve Anglo-American rights and interests by keeping Japan and China at war. This intention has been revealed clearly during the course of the present negotiations. Thus, the earnest hope of the Japanese Government to adjust Japanese-American relations and to preserve and promote the peace of the Pacific through cooperation with the American Government has finally been lost.

The Japanese Government regrets to have to notify hereby the American Government that in view of the attitude of the American Government it cannot but consider that it is impossible to reach an agreement through further negotiations.

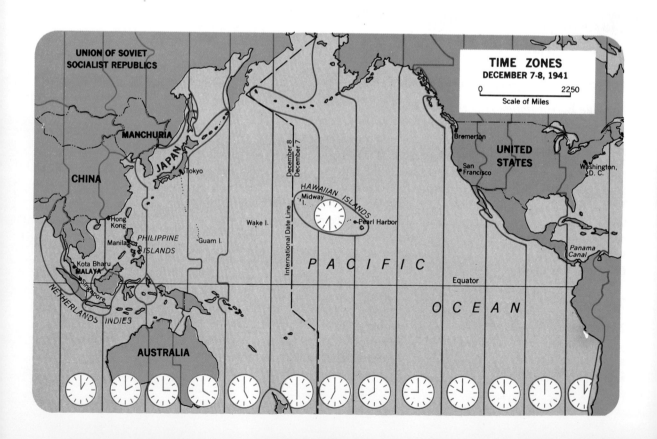

Message H,* *December 7 (available at 10:45 A.M., Washington time, 5:15 A.M., Pearl Harbor time)*

Will the Ambassador please submit to the United States Government (if possible to the Secretary of State) our fourteen-part reply to the United States at 1:00 P.M. on the 7th, your time.

Adapted from **Pearl Harbor Attack** (Washington: U.S. Government Printing Office, 1946), part 12, pp. 92–93, 100, 154, 165, 204, 238–239, 245, 248.

Japanese Coded Message Sent From an Agent in Honolulu to Tokyo on December 4, 1941. The message was decoded by the Americans on the night of December 7. It reads: "On 4th at 1 P.M. Light Cruiser (Honolulu Class) Departed Hastily."

From **Pearl Harbor Attack**, part 38, item no. 226.

Eve of Tragedy

At about 9:30 on the evening of December 6, 1941, Lieutenant Robert L. Schulz, a naval officer on duty in the White House, brought to President Roosevelt six *Magic messages.** One consisted of the first 13 parts of the Japanese message foreshadowed in *Message F*—a long repetition of the Japanese arguments. The President read the message and handed it to his close aide, Harry Hopkins.

"This means war," said the President.

As Lieutenant Schulz later recalled it, "Mr. Hopkins then expressed the view that since war was undoubtedly going to come at the convenience of the Japanese, it was too bad that we could not strike the first blow and prevent any sort of surprise. The President nodded and said, 'No, we can't do that. We're a democracy and a peaceful people.' Then he raised his voice, and this much I remember definitely. He said, 'We have a good record.'"

Sixteen hours later at 8 A.M. Pearl Harbor time, 1:30 P.M. Washington time, the first Japanese bombs hit Pearl Harbor.

As **Message H** indicated, these were to be presented formally to the United States government at 1:00 P.M. Washington time (7:30 A.M. Pearl Harbor time). But the Japanese staff in Washington had trouble getting them translated and typed. As a result the **Japanese Ambassador, Kichisaburo Nomura,** and his colleague, **Saburo Kurusu,** did not reach the State Department until after 2:00 P.M.—more than thirty minutes after the Japanese attack began. Nomura and Kurusu had no knowledge of the Pearl Harbor attack.

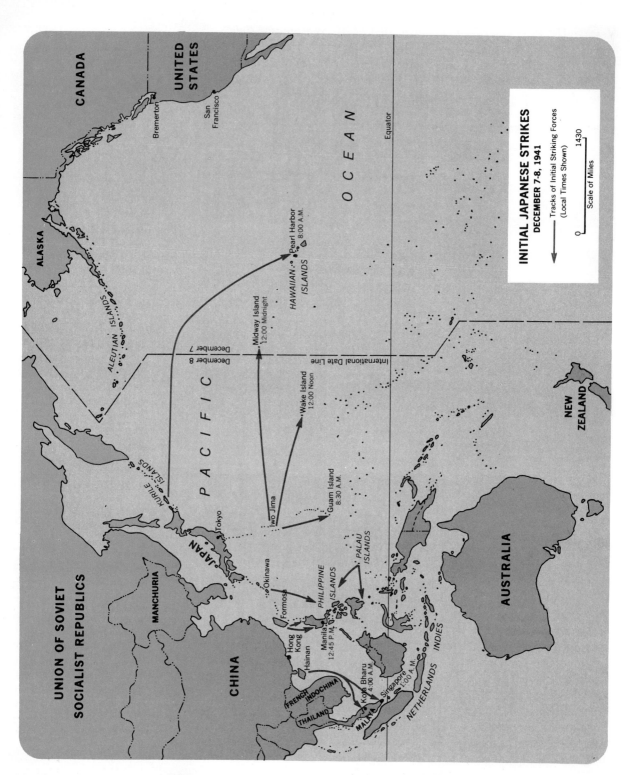

INITIAL JAPANESE STRIKES
DECEMBER 7-8, 1941

→ Tracks of Initial Striking Forces
(Local Times Shown)

0   1430
Scale of Miles

UNITED STATES

CANADA

ALASKA

UNION OF SOVIET
SOCIALIST REPUBLICS

MANCHURIA

CHINA

JAPAN

Tokyo

Okinawa

Formosa

Hong Kong
Hainan

Manila
12:45 P.M.

FRENCH INDOCHINA
THAILAND
Kota Bharu
4:00 A.M.
MALAYA
Singapore
1:00 A.M.

NETHERLANDS INDIES

AUSTRALIA

NEW ZEALAND

PACIFIC

OCEAN

KURILE ISLANDS

ALEUTIAN ISLANDS

Bremerton

San Francisco

Midway Island
12:00 Midnight

December 7
December 8

International Date Line

Equator

Pearl Harbor
8:00 A.M.

HAWAIIAN
ISLANDS

Wake Island
12:00 Noon

Iwo Jima

Guam Island
8:30 A.M.

PHILIPPINE
ISLANDS

PALAU
ISLANDS

D84

11 Strategy of global war

United States in World War II, 1941–1945

Introduction

Pearl Harbor brought the United States into World War II. In the next three-and-three-quarter years more than 16 million men were mustered into the armed forces. American industry mobilized for total war and produced warplanes, tanks, guns, and ammunition in phenomenal quantities. Places like Iwo Jima and Bastogne, and commanders like Admiral "Bull" Halsey and General George C. Patton took their places next to Bull Run and St. Mihiel, Dewey and Pershing, in the annals of American military history.

Earlier, you read of the different ways in which Americans <u>experienced</u> World War I. In this assignment you will explore ways in which they <u>shaped</u> World War II. You will study two basic decisions that determined the course of the war, affecting the lives and deaths of millions of people, and leaving permanent marks upon American and world history. These decisions were:

1. To concentrate first on the defeat of Germany and Italy, rather than on the defeat of Japan.
2. To drop the atomic bomb on Japan.

Objectives of this assignment are to:

–Analyze an account of the United States strategic decision to concentrate war effort in Europe first and discover reasons for the decision.

–Analyze an account of the United States strategic decision to use atomic bombs against Japan and discover reasons for making it.

–Make inferences about American attitudes toward Germans and Japanese in 1945 from selections of wartime oratory and popular music.

–Make judgment on popular acceptance of decision to use atomic bombs against Japanese in 1945.

23 WHERE SHOULD WE FIGHT?

The basic American decision on grand strategy was made months before the Japanese attack on Pearl Harbor. It was made in answer to the question: If war comes, how should the United States distribute its military resources against its enemies so as to achieve victory? Or, as an Admiral put it more briefly: "Where should we fight?"

The answer to this question was given by no single man. Nor was the answer given quickly. Instead, the basic decision on where to fight emerged slowly in the years 1939–1941 out of the work and thoughts of dozens of men —generals, admirals, and citizens.

In developing the answer to this question American planners were guided by what they judged to be some basic facts.

The Brigadier General was **Dwight David Eisenhower,** who later became the Supreme Allied Commander of all forces in Europe and, in time, President of the United States. His note is in: **The Papers of Dwight David Eisenhower,** edited by Alfred D. Chandler (Baltimore: The Johns Hopkins Press, 1970), Vol. I, p. 75.

The name **Plan Dog** comes from the military jargon of the day. To avoid misunderstanding the letters of the alphabet, A, B, C, and D, were given names: Able, Baker, Charlie, and Dog.

One of these, by the summer of 1940, was the fact that Hitler's Germany with its Italian ally controlled all of western and central Europe and seemed determined to bomb Britain into submission, to invade it, and to conquer it. Europe and North Africa seemed on the verge of total domination by an all-powerful and aggressive Germany.

The second fact that had to be considered was the likelihood that if the United States was drawn into the war it would have to fight a "two-ocean" war: against the Germans and Italians in Europe and the Atlantic; and, at the same time, against the Japanese in the Far East and Pacific.

The third fact was that, despite America's large population and great industrial potential, its power was limited—too limited to wage a maximum-effort type of warfare everywhere at once. As a relatively unknown *Brigadier General** put it shortly after Pearl Harbor: "We can't win by sitting on our fannies giving out stuff in driblets all over the world."*

The reasoning behind the basic decision of where to fight (or, how best to allocate American resources) is reflected in the so-called *Plan Dog"** Memorandum* prepared in November, 1940, by Admiral Harold C. Stark, the Chief of Naval Operations. Intelligence information on comparative naval strength of the major powers and the vulnerability of the Western Hemisphere to German long-range bomber attack are shown on the chart and map presented here. While reading the selection from the "Plan Dog" Memorandum and studying the chart and map, keep in mind these questions:

1. Which of the alternative strategies did Admiral Stark recommend? Why?

2. On the basis of the naval strength, do you think either Britain or the United States fighting alone could have defeated the three Axis powers—Germany, Italy, and Japan?

3. What inferences about the vulnerability of the Western Hemisphere to German air attack are suggested by the map?

The "Plan Dog" Memorandum

The strong wish of the American government and people at present seems to be to remain at peace. In spite of this, we must face the possibility that we may at any moment become involved in war. With war in prospect, I believe our every effort should be directed toward the prosecution of a national policy that will ultimately best promote our own national interests. We should seek the best answer to the question: "Where should we fight the war, and for what objective?"

(A) Shall our principal military effort be directed toward hemisphere defense, and include chiefly those activities within the Western Hemisphere which contribute directly to security against attack in either or both oceans? An affirmative answer would indicate that the United States, as seems now to be the hope of this country, would remain out of war unless pushed into it. If and when forced into war, no major effort would be exerted overseas either to the east or the west; the most that would be done for allies, besides providing material help, would be to send detachments to assist in their defense.

Under this plan, our influence upon the outcome of the European War would be small.

(B) Shall we prepare for a full offensive against Japan, assuming assistance from the British and Dutch forces in the Far East, and remain on the strict defensive in the Atlantic? If this course is selected, we would be placing full trust in the British to hold their own indefinitely in the Atlantic, or, at least, until after we should have defeated Japan. The length of time required to defeat Japan would be very considerable.

If we enter the war against Japan and then if Great Britain loses, we probably would in any case have to reorient towards the Atlantic.

(C) Shall we plan for sending the strongest possible military assistance both to the British in Europe, and to the British, Dutch, and Chinese in the Far East? The naval and air detachments we would send to the British Isles would possibly ensure their continued resistance, but would not increase British power to conduct a land offensive. The strength we could send to the Far East might be enough to check the southward spread of Japanese rule for the duration of the war. Should Great Britain finally lose, or should Malaysia fall to Japan, our strength might then be found to have been seriously reduced, relative to that of the Axis powers. Under this plan, we would be operating under the handicap of fighting major wars on two fronts.

On neither of these distant fronts would it be possible to execute a really major offensive. Strategically, the situation might become disastrous should our effort on either front fail.

(D) Shall we direct our efforts toward an eventual strong offensive in the Atlantic as an ally of the British, and a defensive in the Pacific? The least that we would do for our ally would be to send strong naval light forces and aircraft to Great Britain and the Mediterranean. Probably we could not stop with a purely naval effort. The plan might require military and naval bases in Africa and possibly Europe; and even involve undertaking a full scale land offensive. Under Plan (D) we would be unable to exert strong pressure against Japan. Full national offensive strength would be exerted in a single direction, rather than be expended in areas far distant from each other.

I believe that the continued existence of the British Empire, combined with building up a strong protection in our home areas, will do most to ensure the status quo in the Western Hemisphere, and to promote our principal national interests. As I have previously stated, I also believe that Great Britain requires from us very great help in the Atlantic, and possibly even on the continents of Europe or Africa, if she is to be enabled to survive. In my opinion, Alternatives (A), (B), and (C) will most probably not provide the necessary degree of assistance, and therefore, if we undertake war, that Alternative (D) is likely to be the most fruitful for the United States.

If Britain wins decisively against Germany, we could win everywhere; if she loses, the problem confronting us would be very great; and while we might not lose everywhere, we might, possibly, not win anywhere.

Adapted from the "Memorandum of Admiral Harold C. Stark to the Secretary of the Navy" (November 12, 1940), **President's Secretary's File, Navy**, Franklin D. Roosevelt Library.

On this chart **Germany and Allies** includes not only German, Italian, and some captured warships, but those belonging to the Vichy government of France which it was felt the Germans could control any time they wished. **Britain and Allies** includes a few Free French, Dutch, Greek Norwegian, Polish, and Yugoslavian vessels that had escaped from the Germans.

Adapted from **Pearl Harbor Attack** (Washington: U.S. Government Printing Office, 1946), Part 15, pp. 1901–1903.

Comparative Naval Strength—May 1, 1941

	GERMANY AND ALLIES*	JAPAN	AXIS TOTAL	BRITAIN AND ALLIES	U.S.	ALLIED TOTAL
Battleships	17	10	27	20	15	35
Carriers	1	7	8	8	6	14
Cruisers	38	36	74	70	38	108
Destroyers	160	100	260	227	145	372
Submarines	294	70	364	103	108	211

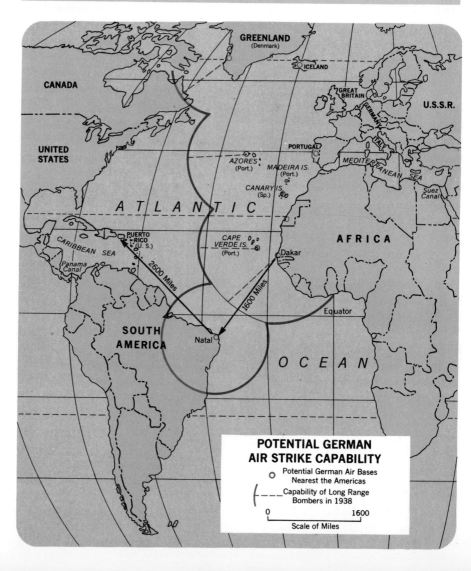

POTENTIAL GERMAN AIR STRIKE CAPABILITY

○ Potential German Air Bases Nearest the Americas

- - - Capability of Long Range Bombers in 1938

0   1600

Scale of Miles

24 COURSE OF THE WAR

The *Europe First* (or *Germany First*) decision was basic to the course of World War II. Against the Japanese the United States conducted a war that was, at first, wholly defensive and later, marked by only limited offensive action. America's principal military resources were directed against the Germans and Italians. And in that struggle, the basic *Europe First* decision provided the framework for other decisions by the Americans and British which were effective in defeating Germany by the spring of 1945. The most important of these other decisions were:

> Invasion of North Africa in 1942.
> Invasion of Italy in 1943.
> Mass bombing offensive against Germany begun in 1943.
> Invasion of France in 1944.
> Massive invasion of Germany, in cooperation with the Russians, in 1945.

In the Pacific and Far East where British resources were more limited, the United States carried most of the burden of the war. To a great extent the war in these areas hinged on America's naval recovery and its eventual attainment of naval supremacy. The significant American naval victory in the *Battle of Midway** (June, 1942) gave the opportunity for the United States to switch to the offensive in the Pacific. Eventually, this led to the regaining of the Philippine Islands and brought American forces to the doorstep of the Japanese home islands by 1945.

(See page 91.)

While examining these maps, keep in mind these questions:

1. What military developments not considered by the "Plan Dog" Memorandum do you think contributed to the defeat of Germany?

2. What words would you use to describe the pattern of the war in the Pacific after the Battle of Midway?

American assault troops land on Omaha Beach, Northern France, June 6, 1944. Smoke from naval guns supports the long line of troops moving inland from the beachhead.

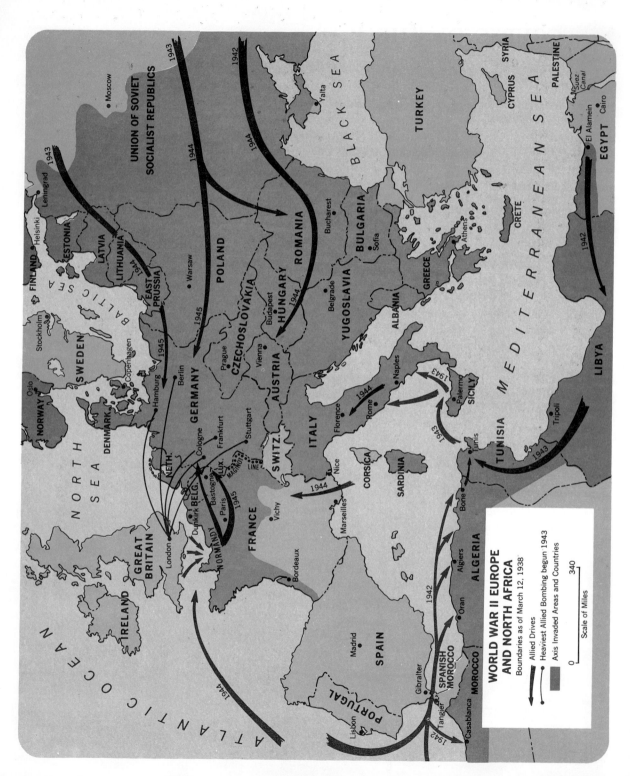

WORLD WAR II EUROPE
AND NORTH AFRICA
Boundaries as of March 12, 1938

Allied Drives
Heaviest Allied Bombing begun 1943
Axis Invaded Areas and Countries

0   340
Scale of Miles

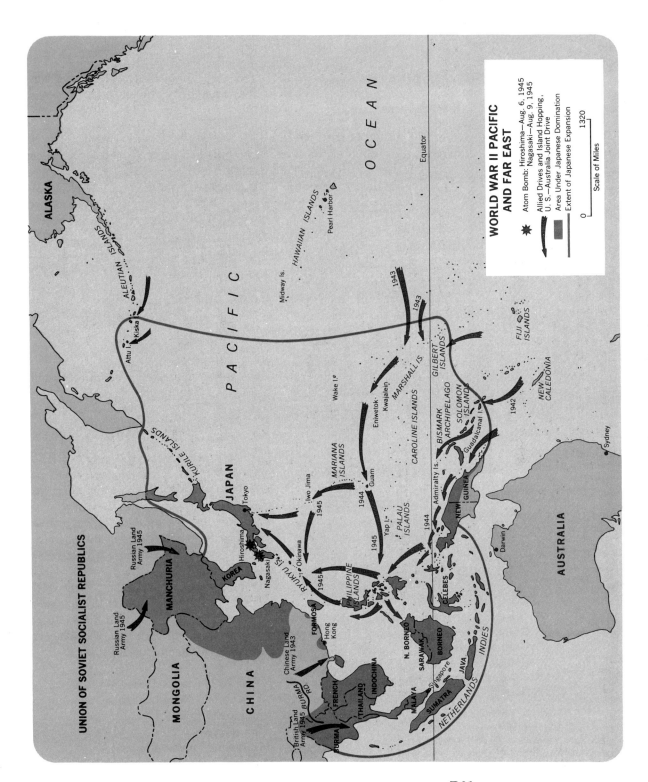

UNION OF SOVIET SOCIALIST REPUBLICS

MONGOLIA

CHINA

MANCHURIA

KOREA

JAPAN

ALASKA

ALEUTIAN ISLANDS

Attu I.
Kiska

KURILE ISLANDS

Tokyo

Hiroshima
Nagasaki

RYUKYU IS.

Okinawa

FORMOSA

Hong Kong

BURMA RD.

FRENCH INDOCHINA

THAILAND

MALAYA

Singapore

SUMATRA

BURMA

British Land Army 1945

Chinese Land Army 1943

Russian Land Army 1945

Russian Land Army 1945

N. BORNEO

SARAWAK

BORNEO

JAVA

NETHERLANDS INDIES

CELEBES

NEW GUINEA

PHILIPPINE ISLANDS

Yap I.
PALAU ISLANDS

Iwo Jima

MARIANA ISLANDS

Guam

CAROLINE ISLANDS

Admiralty Is.

BISMARCK ARCHIPELAGO

SOLOMON ISLANDS

Guadalcanal I.

GILBERT ISLANDS

MARSHALL IS.

Kwajalein

Eniwetok

Wake I.

FIJI ISLANDS

NEW CALEDONIA

Darwin

Sydney

AUSTRALIA

Midway Is.

HAWAIIAN ISLANDS

Pearl Harbor

PACIFIC OCEAN

Equator

1942

1943

1943

1944

1944

1945

1945

1945

1945

1945

1942

WORLD WAR II PACIFIC
AND FAR EAST

Atom Bomb: Hiroshima—Aug. 6, 1945
Nagasaki—Aug. 9, 1945

Allied Drives and Island Hopping,
U. S.—Australia Joint Drive

Area Under Japanese Domination

Extent of Japanese Expansion

0   1320

Scale of Miles

D91

25 ATOMIC HOLOCAUST

Estuko Fujioka was in the fifth grade. Her father was away in the Navy. She was in Hiroshima on August 6, 1945, when her world exploded. Later, she wrote how she felt:

"At the instant of the flash, I turned around and saw a weird light. I tried to get to my room. I had almost reached it when parts of the ceiling, the central pillar of the house, and pieces of glass and other things came falling on top of my small self. My little body was buried under a pile of all sorts of things. The man from the lumber yard, who is our neighbor, came and rescued me. At that time I had injuries over half my body and the flesh was even gouged away. The city is a sea of flames, it burns with a frightful roaring sound. Shrieks can be heard here and there.

"The scars from my wounds will be visible all my life. Everyone has begun to tease me by saying 'A-bomb Scar-face.' And calling me names.

"I feel sorrowful at being separated by death from my dear friends and my teachers, but on the other hand I am envious of them. I feel as though it would have been better if I had died as I was, caught there under the house."

Adapted from **Children of the A-Bomb** edited by Arata Osada. Copyright © 1959 by Dr. Arata Osada. Reprinted by permission of G. P. Putnam's Sons, pp. 172–175.

The use of the atomic bomb against the Japanese cities of Hiroshima (August 6, 1945) and Nagasaki (August 9, 1945) devastated both cities, killed close to 200,000 people, and ended World War II.

Why was it used?

The development of the bomb that scarred and shamed Estuko Fujioka began in 1939. In that year Albert Einstein, speaking for a group of fellow scientists (many of them, like himself, had fled from the threat of Hitler's persecution) wrote to President Roosevelt to tell of the possibility of such a weapon and the fear that the Germans were developing it. The ablest scientists in America and Britain were marshalled to develop the new weapon. By the spring of 1945, as the war in Europe was ending, they felt they had succeeded. On July 16, 1945, the first test bomb was exploded in a remote area of New Mexico.

But making the bomb was not the same as using it in warfare. Some of the same scientists who had labored so hard to create the weapon to use against Germany decided that it would be best not to use it against Japan. Since 1945 many persons have expressed their agreement with that position, even to the point of condemning the United States as immoral for using it.

Why, then, was it used?

*Henry L. Stimson,** Secretary of War in the years 1941–1945, summarized the reasoning of those who made the decision. Read his explanation and answer the following questions. According to Stimson:

Henry L. Stimson had a long and important career in government. He served as Secretary of War under President Taft in 1911–1913 and as Secretary of State under President Herbert Hoover in 1929–1933. He was one of several Republicans in President Roosevelt's cabinet and continued to serve under President Truman.

1. *What was the objective of dropping atomic bombs on Japan?*
2. *What role was the Japanese Emperor to play in ending the war?*

D92

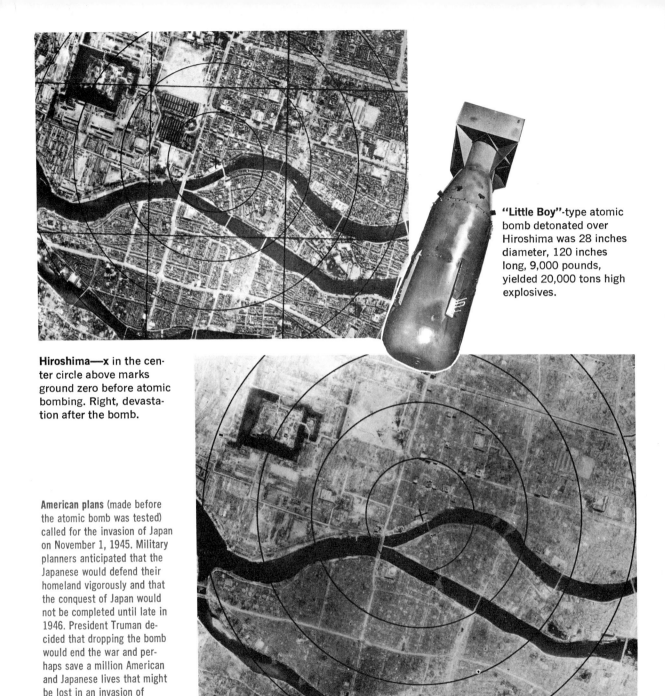

"**Little Boy**"-type atomic bomb detonated over Hiroshima was 28 inches diameter, 120 inches long, 9,000 pounds, yielded 20,000 tons high explosives.

Hiroshima—x in the center circle above marks ground zero before atomic bombing. Right, devastation after the bomb.

American plans (made before the atomic bomb was tested) called for the invasion of Japan on November 1, 1945. Military planners anticipated that the Japanese would defend their homeland vigorously and that the conquest of Japan would not be completed until late in 1946. President Truman decided that dropping the bomb would end the war and perhaps save a million American and Japanese lives that might be lost in an invasion of Japan.

Secretary Stimson's Explanation

Two great nations were approaching contact in a fight to a finish which would begin on November 1, 1945.* Our enemy, Japan, commanded forces of somewhat over 5,000,000 armed men. Men of these armies had already inflicted upon us, in our breakthrough of the outer perimeter of their defenses, over 300,000 battle casualties. Enemy armies still unbeaten had the strength to cost us a million more. As long as the Japanese government refused to surrender, we should be forced to take and hold the ground, and smash the Japanese ground armies, by close-in fighting of the same desperate and costly kind that we had faced in the Pacific islands for nearly four years.

In the light of the formidable problem which thus confronted us, I felt that every possible step should be taken to compel a surrender of the homelands, and a withdrawal of all Japanese troops from the Asiatic mainland and from other positions, before we had commenced an invasion. We held two cards to assist us in such an effort. One was the traditional veneration in which the Japanese Emperor was held by his subjects and the power which was thus vested in him over his loyal troops. It was for this reason that I suggested in a memorandum of July 2 to the President that his dynasty should be continued. The second card was the use of the atomic bomb in the manner best calculated to persuade the Emperor and the counselors about him to submit to our demand for what was essentially unconditional surrender, placing his immense power over his people and his troops subject to our orders.

In order to end the war in the shortest possible time and to avoid the enormous losses of human life which otherwise confronted us, I felt that we must use the Emperor as our instrument to command and compel his people to cease fighting and subject themselves to our authority through him, and that to accomplish this we must give him and his controlling advisers a compelling reason to agree to our demands. This reason, furthermore, must be of such a nature that his people could understand his decision. The bomb seemed to me to furnish a unique instrument for that purpose.

My chief purpose was to end the war in victory with the least possible cost in the lives of the men in the armies which I had helped to raise. In the light of the alternatives which, on a fair estimate, were open to us I believe that no man, in our position and subject to our responsibilities, holding in his hands a weapon of such possibilities for accomplishing this purpose and saving those lives, could have failed to use it and afterwards looked his countrymen in the face.

As I read over what I have written, I am aware that much of it, in this year of peace, may have a harsh and unfeeling sound. It would perhaps be possible to say the same things and say them more gently. But I do not think it would be wise. As I look back over the five years of my service as Secretary of War, I see too many stern and heart-rending decisions to be willing to pretend that war is anything else than what it is. The face of war is the face of death; death is an inevitable part of every order that a wartime leader gives. The decision to use the atomic bomb was a decision that brought death to over a hundred thousand Japanese. No explanation can change that fact and I do not wish to gloss it over. But this deliberate, premeditated destruction was our least abhorrent choice. The destruction of Hiroshima and Nagasaki put an end to the Japanese war. It stopped the fire raids, and the strangling blockade; it ended the ghastly specter of a clash of great land armies.

Beginning in November, 1944, the Japanese home islands were subjected to a steadily increasing campaign of **bombing by B-29's.** In March, 1945, after high-level selective bombing had proved ineffective, the B-29's began low-level night raids, dropping fire-bombs on the flimsy buildings of Japanese cities. The **fire-bomb raid** on Tokyo on the nights of March 9 and 10 killed 83,000 people, injured 40,000 more, left 1,000,000 people homeless, and totally burned out 15 square miles of Tokyo. Such fire-bomb raids struck 66 Japanese cities and killed 330,000 Japanese civilians.

Abridged from pp. 631–633 **On Active Service in Peace and War** by Henry L. Stimson and McGeorge Bundy. Copyright 1947 by Henry L. Stimson. Reprinted by permission of Harper & Row, Publishers, Inc.

12 The cold war

United States and Russia Since 1945

Introduction

You have just examined America's role in World War II. With the defeat of the Axis Powers in 1945, the Grand Alliance of the United States, Great Britain, and the Soviet Union broke down. It was replaced by a struggle between the two super-powers, the United States and the Soviet Union. By 1949 both had developed an atomic bomb, and the possibility of nuclear war became a reality. Since the struggle was generally carried on by all means short of a shooting war, it was labelled the **Cold War.** You will now examine the American position in three of the major Cold War confrontations between the United States and Russia after 1945: the Korean War of 1950–1953; the "Eisenhower Doctrine" of 1957 for the Middle East; and the Cuban Missile Crisis of 1962.

The "Containment" Policy

As far as the United States was concerned, after 1945 the Soviet Union was not honoring its wartime agreements concerning Europe and Asia. Instead it was using its position to promote Russian Communist expansion. In Eastern Europe, Russia imposed Communist regimes rather than permit the creation of broadly representative governments as it promised at *Yalta.** It supported Communist regimes in China and North Korea and encouraged Communist parties of war-torn Europe in their struggle to attain power. When Russian expansion threatened Greece and Turkey in 1947, President Harry S. Truman told Congress that the United States had to provide needed economic and military aid to nations threatened by a Communist takeover, if the peace and security of the world were to be preserved. Congress endorsed this "Truman Doctrine" and voted more than 600 million dollars to preserve Greece and Turkey from Russian domination.

(See page 98.)

The principle behind the Truman Doctrine and the American Cold War policy in general was *containment.* To restrain Russian expansion in Europe, massive amounts of foreign aid were injected into her economic bloodstream under the *Marshall Plan** to reconstruct European business and industry which had suffered so badly during the war. In addition, to offset the Soviet military threat to the West, the United States established the first of many military alliances, the North Atlantic Treaty Organization (NATO) in 1949. These activities helped "contain" the Russians and communism in Europe.

In Asia the story was different. In June, 1950, the Cold War suddenly

Secretary of State George C. Marshall first presented the idea of assisting European economic recovery in a commencement address which he delivered at Harvard University in June, 1947. Thus the program was named after him.

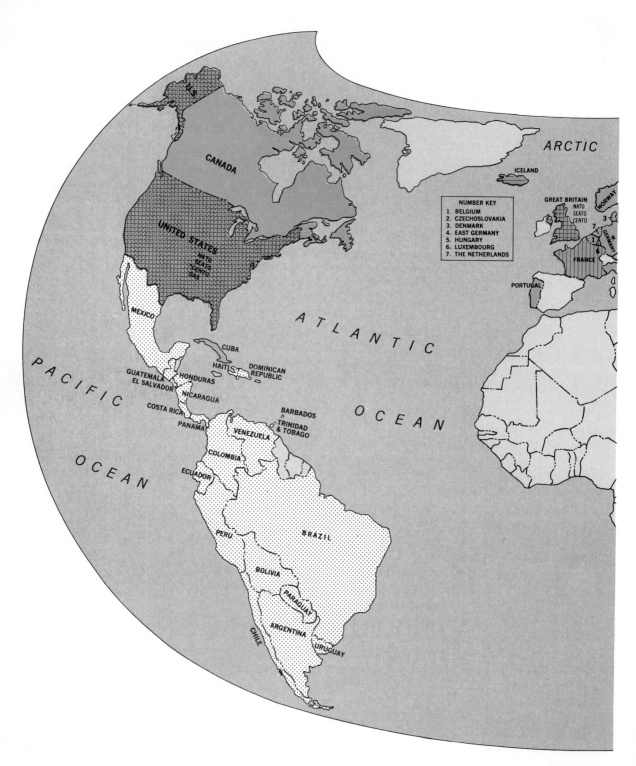

ARCTIC

ICELAND

GREAT BRITAIN
NATO
SEATO
CENTO

NORWAY

3

NUMBER KEY
1. BELGIUM
2. CZECHOSLOVAKIA
3. DENMARK
4. EAST GERMANY
5. HUNGARY
6. LUXEMBOURG
7. THE NETHERLANDS

7
1
6

W. GERMANY

FRANCE

PORTUGAL

CANADA

UNITED STATES
NATO
SEATO
CENTO
OAS

MEXICO

CUBA

HAITI

DOMINICAN
REPUBLIC

GUATEMALA
EL SALVADOR

HONDURAS

NICARAGUA

COSTA RICA

PANAMA

BARBADOS

TRINIDAD
& TOBAGO

VENEZUELA

COLOMBIA

ECUADOR

PERU

BRAZIL

BOLIVIA

PARAGUAY

CHILE

ARGENTINA

URUGUAY

ATLANTIC

OCEAN

PACIFIC

OCEAN

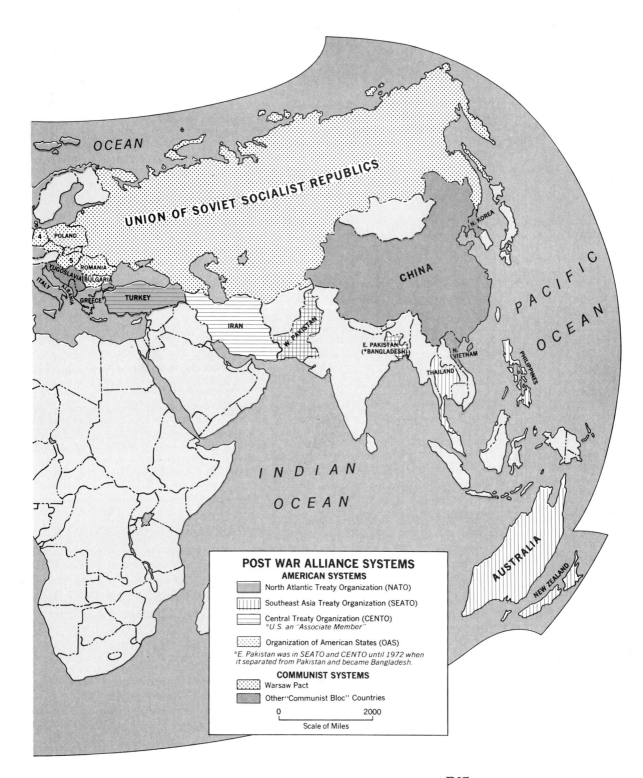

OCEAN

UNION OF SOVIET SOCIALIST REPUBLICS

POLAND

4

5

ROMANIA

YUGOSLAVIA

BULGARIA

ITALY

ALBANIA

GREECE

TURKEY

IRAN

W. PAKISTAN

CHINA

N. KOREA

PACIFIC

OCEAN

E. PAKISTAN
(*BANGLADESH)

N. VIETNAM

THAILAND

PHILIPPINES

INDIAN

OCEAN

AUSTRALIA

NEW ZEALAND

POST WAR ALLIANCE SYSTEMS
AMERICAN SYSTEMS

North Atlantic Treaty Organization (NATO)

Southeast Asia Treaty Organization (SEATO)

Central Treaty Organization (CENTO)
*U.S. an "Associate Member"

Organization of American States (OAS)

*E. Pakistan was in SEATO and CENTO until 1972 when
it separated from Pakistan and became Bangladesh.

COMMUNIST SYSTEMS

Warsaw Pact

Other "Communist Bloc" Countries

0   2000

Scale of Miles

At the **Yalta Conference** held in February, 1945, President Roosevelt, Prime Minister Winston Churchill of Great Britain and Marshal Josef Stalin of the Soviet Union met to decide on how to end the war and, especially, how to arrange the peace. Their agreements touched on almost all parts of the world.

Objectives of this assignment are to:

—Analyze two presidential policy statements about Korea and the Middle East and identify arguments on which United States policy in each region was based.

—Analyze an account of decision making during the Cuban missile crisis and identify and describe arguments which prevailed.

—Draw inferences from filmstrip about reaction of world opinion to Cuban missile crisis.

—Make historical judgment on effectiveness of the containment policy.

heated up when Communist North Korea attacked South Korea. The United States immediately brought the issue before the United Nations Security Council, which recommended that members of the United Nations furnish assistance to South Korea to repel the armed attack and restore peace and security in the area. At first the war went well for the Communists; but the tide turned in favor of the United Nations when General Douglas MacArthur surprised the North Koreans by an amphibious landing behind their lines. MacArthur drove them out of South Korea and was permitted to attack the North in an effort to unite the country, if possible. As MacArthur's forces came closer to the Chinese-North Korean border, the Red Chinese became alarmed and entered the war, driving the United Nations (mostly American) forces back. The war became a stalemate and dragged on for two more years until an armistice was signed in July, 1953, under President Eisenhower.

Alliances. During the presidential election campaign of 1952, the Republican Party had attacked the Democrats for being "soft" on communism. They criticized "containment" as too negative a policy. The new Secretary of State, John Foster Dulles, who was appointed following President Eisenhower's election, periodically talked of "liberating" the nations of Eastern Europe from Russian and Communist control.

In practice, however, containment remained the basic American policy under Republican President Eisenhower as it had been under the Democratic President Truman. Once again, it expressed itself in the formation of alliances: the Southeast Asia Treaty Organization (SEATO) and the Central Treaty Organization (CENTO). The Russians countered with their own Warsaw Pact among the Communist states of Eastern Europe. As the maps on pages 96 and 97 indicate, the superpowers—neither of which wished nuclear war—seemed intent on dividing the world into two alliance systems.

26 TWO CRISES: KOREA AND THE MIDDLE EAST

President Truman and President Eisenhower both faced Cold War crises.

For Truman the most serious crisis came in 1950 and 1951, at the time of the Korean War, and was made more difficult by General MacArthur's desire to end the war by using atomic bombs.

For Eisenhower, a particularly difficult crisis developed in 1956 and 1957 in the Middle East.

Limited resources forced the withdrawal of the two Western colonial powers, Britain and France, from this area, leaving behind what an earlier age of diplomats would have called a *power vacuum.** Between the new state of Israel and its Arab neighbors there was constant friction, which flared into warfare in 1948–1949 and in 1956. Both sought outside assistance, in particular the assistance of the United States and Russia, who thus faced the danger of being drawn into a hot war in an area where neither had a significant national interest at stake.

The **power-vacuum** idea always implied that sooner or later some great power or other would rush in (like air) to fill the vacuum.

Each President responded to these crises. In a radio broadcast to the nation on April 11, 1951, President Truman explained his policy in Korea and the Far East in general. In a formal message to Congress in 1957, which he later recalled in his memoirs, President Eisenhower set forth his "Eisenhower Doctrine" for the Middle East. While reading these selections keep in mind the following questions:

1. According to President Truman, when was the best time to meet the threat of Communist aggression?

2. Why did Truman insist on fighting a limited war in Korea?

3. Why did Eisenhower think it necessary for the United States to intervene in Middle East affairs?

President Truman's Address

The Communists in the Kremlin are engaged in a monstrous conspiracy to stamp out freedom all over the world. If they were to succeed the United States would be numbered among their principal victims. It must be made clear to everyone that the United States cannot, and will not, sit idly by and await foreign conquest. The only question is: *When* is the best time to meet the threat and *how?*

The best time to meet the threat is in the beginning. And the best way to meet the threat of aggression is for peace-loving nations to act together. If the free countries had acted together from the beginning in the 1930's to crush aggression of the dictators when it was small, there probably would have been no World War II.

If history has taught us anything, it is that aggression anywhere in the world is a threat to peace everywhere in the world; and, if supported by cruel and selfish rulers of a nation bent on conquest, it becomes a danger to the security and independence of every free nation. Most people in this country have learned this lesson thoroughly. That is why we joined the United Nations and why we have been working with other free nations to check the aggressive designs of the Soviet Union before they can result in a third world war.

The aggression against Korea is the boldest and most dangerous move the Communists have yet made. It is part of a greater plan for conquering and controlling all Asia from the Kremlin. The question is whether the Communist plan of conquest can be stopped without a general war. Our Government and the United Nations believe that the best chance of stopping it without general war is to meet the attack in Korea and defeat it there.

But you may ask: Why can't we take other steps to punish the aggressor? Why can't we bomb Manchuria and China itself? Why don't we assist the Chinese Nationalist troops to land on the mainland of China? If we were to do these things we would be running a very grave risk of starting a general war, the very thing we are trying to prevent. We would become entangled in a vast conflict on the continent of Asia. And what would suit the ambitions of the Kremlin better than for our military forces to be committed to a full-scale war with Red China?

It would be tragically wrong for us to take the initiative in extending the war. The dangers are great. Behind the North Koreans and Chinese on the front lines stand additional millions of Chinese soldiers. And behind the Chinese stand the forces of the scheming rulers of the Soviet Union.

I believe that we must try to limit the war in Korea to make sure that the lives of our fighting men are not wasted; to see that the security of our country and the free world is not needlessly jeopardized; and to prevent a third world war. Our military objective is to repel attack and restore peace.

Adapted from "An Address by President Truman, April 11, 1951" in **United States Department of State Bulletin**, Volume XXIV, No. 615 (April 16, 1951), pp. 603–605.

'DOUBLE-BARREL'

MID-EAST DEFENSE PROGRAM

MID-EAST ECONOMIC PROGRAM

IKE

Wood in the Pittsburgh Press

The Eisenhower Doctrine, 1957

Following the Suez Canal difficulties of late 1956 and the withdrawal of French and British forces from Egypt, the Middle East remained highly unstable. In this situation, one danger loomed above all others: the leaders of the Soviet Union, like the Czars before them, had their eyes on the Middle East. The Soviet goal was by no means merely the right to move ships through the Suez Canal, for less than 1 percent of the Canal traffic was Russian. Neither was the goal Middle Eastern oil; the Soviet Union had no need for it and, indeed, exported oil herself. The Soviet objective was, in plain fact, power politics: to seize the oil, to cut the Suez Canal and pipelines of the Middle East, and thus to seriously weaken Western civilization.

On New Year's Day, 1957, I met with leaders of both parties in the new Congress to ask their support for a new declaration of American policy in the Middle East. The existing vacuum in the Middle East must be filled by the United States before it is filled by Russia. Time was of the essence. I believed the new Congress, as its first order of business, should authorize a spe-

President Dwight D. Eisenhower (right) with his Secretary of State John Foster Dulles. Though Eisenhower made the important foreign policy decisions, Dulles was a strong personality and one of the most forceful Secretaries of State in history.

cial economic fund and the use of military force if necessary in the Middle East. I told the leaders that should there be a Soviet attack I could see no alternative to an immediate United States move to stop it.

I delivered my message to a joint session of Congress on January 5. The action I proposed would authorize the United States to assist any nation or group of nations in the Middle East to develop economic strength to maintain their national independence. It would also authorize the President to undertake programs of military assistance and cooperation with any Middle Eastern nation desiring them, such programs to include United States military aid when requested, against armed aggression from any nation controlled by international Communism.*

The members of Congress did not move as one man to endorse the administration's proposal. Far from it. Some thought it would confer on the President constitutional authority belonging to the Legislative branch. Others, friends of Israel, did not like helping any Arab nation. Overseas, Britain and France favored the plan; Turkey, Pakistan, Lebanon, and Iran saw the doctrine as the best possible guarantee of peace. With the help of statesmen of both parties, the Middle East Resolution, which proclaimed the administration's resolve to block the Soviet Union's march to the Mediterranean, the Suez Canal and the pipeline that fueled the homes and factories of Western Europe, obtained the consent of Congress.

Invoking the **Eisenhower Doctrine** on July 15, 1958, President Camille Chamoun of Lebanon requested U.S. troops to aid in suppressing an armed rebellion. When a revolt threatened King Hussein in nearby Jordan as a result of the American intervention, Great Britain sent military forces in to help him, also.

Adapted from **The White House Years: Waging Peace, 1956–1961** by Dwight D. Eisenhower, copyright © 1965 by Dwight D. Eisenhower. Reprinted by permission of Doubleday & Company, Inc., pp. 177–183.

27   CUBAN MISSILE CRISIS, 1962

In 1961 President Eisenhower was succeeded by President John F. Kennedy. The latter inherited both the Cold War and the American policy of containment as the way to conduct it.

He also inherited the problem of Cuba, where a social and political revolution had brought Fidel Castro to power in 1959. Castro seized American holdings (a not uncommon practice among Latin-American rulers) and made it clear that in his opposition to "Yankee Imperialism" he welcomed Russian and Chinese Communist aid. Nikita Khrushchev and the Russians responded favorably. Their response quickened in 1961 and 1962 after an American-supported invasion of Cuba by anti-Castro Cubans failed. MIG jet fighters and military technicians appeared in Cuba, flaunting Communist power and Russian technical skill only a few air-minutes from the show-place hotels of Miami Beach. Once again the Cold War heated up.

In the fall of 1962 photographs taken by American reconnaissance aircraft showed that Soviet technicians were installing offensive missiles in Cuba, contrary to Russian promises and despite American warnings by President Kennedy. Why the Russians chose to do this remains a mystery. It is possible, however, that Premier Khrushchev judged President Kennedy to be an inexperienced leader. Misunderstanding the reason for President Eisenhower's decision not to intervene in Hungary in 1956,* Khrushchev may have felt that Kennedy would do nothing about Russian missiles in Cuba.

But Cuba was not Hungary, and while President Kennedy and his advisers had no desire to begin a third world war, they were determined to get the Russian missiles out of Cuba. The three days of secret discussion by the President's advisers and their conclusions on how to remove the Russian menace from the very doorstep of the United States were reconstructed four years later by a skilled journalist, Elie Abel. The policy adopted proved effective. The Russian missiles were removed. Read Abel's account and answer the following questions:

1. What different approaches were suggested for dealing with Russian missiles in Cuba?

2. How were American policy makers influenced by lessons from the past?

3. What arguments determined the final decision?

Cuban Policy Debate

In the debate on the best way to remove the Russian missiles, George Ball, the Under-Secretary of State, argued that if the United States launched a surprise attack on Cuba it would be violating its own traditions and doing itself irreparable harm, regardless of the military outcome. Robert Kennedy picked up Ball's argument. Recalling Pearl Harbor, he said passionately: "My brother is not going to be the Tojo of the 1960's."

*In 1956 an **anti-Russian uprising** occurred in **Hungary.** While American sympathy lay strongly with the Hungarian "freedom-fighters," President Eisenhower concluded that there was no way for the United States to give any military assistance to the distant Hungarians without immediately bringing on a third World War.*

Moreover, the President's brother doubted that a surprise air strike, by itself, would take out all the missiles. An invasion would have to follow, taking a horrendous toll of innocent Cuban lives. A decent regard for humanity ought to rule out any surprise attack, he said.

The challenge to young Robert Kennedy came from a man old enough to be his father. Dean Acheson, sixty-nine, former Secretary of State, chief architect of the Truman Administration's cold war policies, disagreed sharply, rejecting the Pearl Harbor analogy with majestic scorn. For more than a century the Monroe Doctrine had made clear to all the world that the United States would not tolerate the intrusion of any European power into the Americas, Acheson said. Both the President and Congress had warned that the United States would be forced to act "by whatever means necessary, including use of arms," if the Russians installed offensive weapons in Cuba. Surely this was warning enough, Acheson said.

The following day discussion of policy goals continued. Should the President limit his objective to the simple removal of Soviet missiles, or use the occasion to get rid of Castro at the same time. The first alternative could perhaps be accomplished by a naval blockade. The second would certainly demand a full-scale invasion. The lawyers—Ball and Acheson the most prominent among them—argued the legality of each alternative.

Acheson took the position that legal niceties were so much pompous foolishness in a situation where the essential security of the United States was threatened. Cuba did not belong to the Warsaw Pact and therefore an attack on Cuba would not necessarily bring the Soviet Union into a state of war with the United States. Ball argued that a naval blockade, though traditionally regarded as an act of war, would have more "color of legality." It was suggested that the blockade might better be called a defensive quarantine, the phrase being borrowed from Franklin D. Roosevelt's "quarantine-the-aggressor" speech of 1938. By noon that day, it began to appear that the blockade advocates might prevail. Legalities had less to do with this than the practical argument that a naval blockade would avoid killing Russians and give the Kremlin time to reflect.

When debate resumed the next day, Acheson continued to maintain that if the President failed to order an armed strike against the missile bases, he would be imperiling the security of the United States and the whole free world. Again Robert Kennedy challenged him, not on legal, but on humane grounds. Returning to the Pearl Harbor-in-reverse argument, the Attorney General said his brother simply could not order an air strike. A great deal more was at stake than the Soviet missiles in Cuba and the threat they represented. The ideals and convictions of the American people made such an attack repugnant. For the United States to attack a small country like Cuba without warning, he argued, would damage beyond repair both America's standing in the world and its own conscience.

By nightfall there was broad agreement that the blockade would be the fittest, least provocative response open to the President. In effect, the naval blockade was the first option, the list of forbidden goods limited at the start to offensive weapons. If that failed, the President could decide to deny the Cubans other kinds of cargo or he could move up the scale to an air strike or even to an invasion. If one form of pressure failed in its purpose—to get the Russians to remove the missiles—then another, more severe pressure could be applied. Nothing would be lost by starting from the bottom of the scale. The clinching argument in favor of the blockade was that it could be applied without losing the option to launch an air strike later. The President approved this approach and on Monday, October 22, the day on which he was to speak to the nation on the crisis, he adopted the suggestion that the naval blockade be styled a "defensive quarantine" because the word "blockade" carried such ugly, warlike overtones.

From the book, **The Missile Crisis,** by Elie Abel. Copyright ©, 1966, by Elie Abel. Abridged and adapted by permission of the publisher, J. B. Lippincott Company, pp. 64–65, 72–73, 81, 88–89, 115.

16

A West German View

Lang in Suddeutsche Zeitung, Munich

"Now that's enough!"

17

A Mexican View

Car in El Universal, Mexico City

"The block"

18

A Swedish View

Anders in Svenska Dagbladet, Stockholm

"The Chess Game"

D104

19
A Soviet View
(Latvian)

20 Shadow Across the World (La Sombre) Painting by Juan Genovese

Photo courtesy of A. Rafael Bonache Garcia

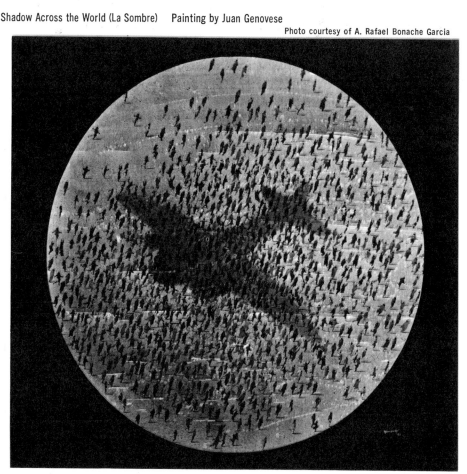

13 Truman-Eisenhower years, 1945–1960

Problems of Postwar America

Harry S. Truman, taking the oath of office while his wife, Bess, looks on, was born in Lamar, Missouri, 1884; never had the opportunity to attend college. During World War I, rose to the rank of Captain. U.S. Senator from 1934–1944. His popularity with labor brought him the vice-presidential nomination in 1944.

Nearly all polls predicted victory for **Dewey**. A Boston Globe reader survey said Dewey would get 56 per cent of the vote; Truman, 28 per cent. A Newsweek poll of 50 Washington correspondents the day before election gave Dewey 366 of the 531 electoral votes, and Truman only 126.

Welch was elderly, genteel, mannerly, and beguiled TV viewers by artfully balancing his grasp of legal intricacies with unexpected rapier thrusts of dry wit.

Introduction

On April 12, 1945, President Franklin D. Roosevelt died suddenly of a cerebral hemorrhage at Warm Springs, Georgia, after serving more than twelve years in the Presidency. Vice-President *Harry S. Truman** was immediately sworn in as his successor.

The Truman Presidency

For three years Truman continued existing New Deal programs but was unable to expand them after the great Republican congressional victories in 1946. His prospects for election in 1948 were very poor. However, he astonished friend and foe alike by upsetting Governor Thomas E. Dewey of New York in the presidential election of 1948.* During Truman's famous whistle-stop campaign he travelled over 30,000 miles and gave 351 speeches, most of them from the rear platform of his train.

Despite this great triumph, Truman was able to enact only a small portion of his Fair Deal program. Americans seemed more concerned about the Cold War and the Korean War than about social and economic reform. The great domestic issue of the Truman Presidency was Communist subversion.

Senator Joseph R. McCarthy

From 1950 to 1954 Senator Joseph R. McCarthy of Wisconsin was the most controversial political figure in America. He filled the air with charges of widespread treason and Communist subversion in the American government. So great was the public fear of communism that both Truman and Eisenhower seemed powerless to curb excesses of the brash Wisconsin senator.

Finally in the spring of 1954, McCarthy overreached himself and attacked the U.S. Army for giving an honorable discharge to a dentist with Communist sympathies. The Army counterattacked by charging that McCarthy had demanded preferential treatment for one of his young assistants, G. David Schine, who had recently been drafted. During the month-long televised inquiry known as the Army-McCarthy hearings, the Wisconsin senator at last met his match in the person of *Joseph Welch,** a nimble-tongued New England attorney who represented the Army. What little prestige McCarthy still enjoyed was destroyed later in the year when he was officially censured by his Senate colleagues by a 67–22 vote.

D106

The Democrats in Disarray

By 1952 the Truman Administration had clearly lost its momentum. Americans blamed Truman for the stalemated Korean War. And charges of Communist subversion were widely believed.

To make matters worse the Truman Administration was plagued with a number of minor but politically damaging scandals involving government officials taking bribes to secure preferential treatment for favored clients. In March, 1952, Truman publicly announced that he would not seek reelection.

At the Democratic convention in July, Governor Adlai Stevenson of Illinois defeated Senator Estes Kefauver of Tennessee for the presidential nomination. The Republicans nominated General Dwight D. Eisenhower, who had served as Supreme Allied Commander in World War II.

Dwight D. Eisenhower

The rise of Dwight D. "Ike" *Eisenhower** to fame and prominence is one of the great American success stories.

Throughout his long military career Eisenhower had never made a political statement, yet both the Democrats and the Republicans wanted him as their presidential candidate simply because he was a very popular war hero and the polls showed he could win the election easily. Early in 1952 Eisenhower clarified the political confusion by announcing that he considered himself a Republican, although he had never voted. After a bitter convention fight Eisenhower defeated the conservative favorite, Senator Robert A. *Taft** of Ohio.

The popular Kansas General went on to easily defeat Governor Stevenson in the November election by a margin of 33 million to 27 million. As President, Eisenhower quickly revealed himself to be a moderate conservative who was greatly concerned about balancing the budget and curbing inflation.

Though now a Republican politician, Eisenhower tried to stand above partisan battles and be a father image to all of the people. In this he was very successful and was unquestionably one of the most popular Presidents ever to occupy the White House. There is little doubt that he gave a majority of the American people exactly what they wanted in a President.

Dwight D. Eisenhower: born in Denison, Texas, 1890; brought up in Abilene, Kansas; appointed to West Point in 1911. World War II Supreme Commander in Europe. Chief of Staff of U.S. Armed Forces, 1945–1948. While serving as President of Columbia University (1948–1953), also became Supreme Commander of the North Atlantic Treaty Organization (1950–1953).

Robert Taft came into the convention with a slight majority of the delegates. However, several states sent both Eisenhower and Taft delegations, and the credentials committee of the convention seated the Eisenhower delegations.

28　THE TRUMAN YEARS

Harry Truman was not a New Deal insider, but he had loyally supported the New Deal and was dedicated to its continuance and expansion. On September 6, 1945, Truman announced a comprehensive twenty-one point program of social reform known as the *Fair Deal*, but Congress enacted very little of it. In January, 1949, fresh from his stunning defeat of Governor

Objectives of this assignment are to:

–Analyze policy statements by Presidents Truman and Eisenhower on Federal government's role in social and economic affairs for similarities and differences.

–Make historical judgment on effectiveness of Federal government's response to social and economic needs of Americans during Truman and Eisenhower years.

Dewey, Truman recommended to Congress even more sweeping reforms, covering practically every aspect of American life. Congress responded to Truman's extraordinary upset election victory by enacting a substantial part of his legislative program in 1949. However, in 1950 the combination of the Korean War and Senator McCarthy's widely publicized charges of Communist subversion in the State Department diverted public attention from further domestic reform.

While reading the following selection from the Truman years and studying the chart of major events, keep in mind these questions:

1. What did Truman think the Federal government's role in social and economic affairs ought to be?

2. What social and economic problems does Truman identify as requiring solution in 1949?

Truman Argues for More Reform, January 5, 1949

In this society, we are conservative about the values and principles which we cherish; but we are forward looking in protecting those values and principles and in extending their benefits. We have rejected the discredited theory that the fortunes of the nation should be in the hands of a privileged few. . . .

The American people have decided that poverty is just as wasteful and just as unnecessary as disease. We have pledged our common resources to help one another in the hazards and struggles of individual life. We believe that no unfair prejudice or artificial distinction should bar any citizen of the United States from an education, or from good health, or from a job that he is capable of performing.

. . . The Government must work with industry, labor, and the farmers in keeping our economy running at full speed. The Government must see that every American has a chance to obtain his fair share of increasing abundance.

. . . As we look around the country many of our shortcomings stand out in bold relief: We are suffering from excessively high prices . . . Our minimum wages are far too low . . . Our farmers still face an uncertain future. . . .

Some of our natural resources are being wasted. We are acutely short of electric power although the means for developing such power are abundant.

Five million families are still living in slums and firetraps. Three million families share their homes with others.

Our health is far behind the progress of medical science. Proper medical care is so expensive that it is out of the reach of the great majority of our citizens.

Our schools, in many localities, are utterly inadequate. Our democratic ideals are often thwarted by prejudice and intolerance.

Each of these shortcomings is also an opportunity—an opportunity for the Congress and the President to work for the good of the people. . . .

Adapted from **Public Papers of the Presidents of the United States,** Harry S. Truman (1949), pp. 1–7.

Major Events of the Truman Presidency

1945 January 22—Full Employment Bill introduced which requires the Federal government to guarantee and maintain full employment through government spending if necessary.

April 12—Franklin D. Roosevelt dies—Truman becomes President.

May 7—War against Germany ends.

August 14—War against Japan ends.

September 6—Truman proposes a twenty-one point Fair Deal reform program. Wave of strikes sweeps the nation—116 million man-hours lost.

1946 February 20—Full Employment Bill rejected and replaced by the Maximum Employment Act which established a three-man presidential advisory council and a congressional joint committee on economic affairs.

July 1—Wartime Office of Price Administration expires, prices on 28 basic commodities rise 25% in 16 days.

July 25—Congress enacts a weak price control law but prices continue to rise.

August 1—Atomic Energy Act is passed creating a five-man civilian commission with control over research and development of atomic energy.

November 5—Republicans win Congressional elections and take control of both houses of Congress for the first time since 1928.

1947 March—Truman Loyalty Program begins. All employees of the Executive branch are investigated by the FBI.

June 23—Taft-Hartley Act is passed over Truman's veto. The new law replaced the Wagner Act of 1935, and authorized the President to issue temporary injunctions to prevent strikes.

July 26—The National Security Act creates the new post of Secretary of Defense, overhauls the defense structure and establishes the National Security Council and the Central Intelligence Agency. James Forrestal is named first Secretary of Defense.

1948 July 26—Truman issues executive orders desegregating the Armed Forces and banning racial discrimination in the hiring of Federal employees.

August 3—Whittaker Chambers accuses Alger Hiss, a former State Department employee, of having been a Communist in the 1930's.

August 5—Truman labels House Un-American Activities Committee investigation of Alger Hiss a red herring.

November 2—Truman upsets Dewey in presidential election.

1949 Desegregation of the Armed Forces intensified.

January 5—Truman calls for sweeping social reforms in his State of the Union message to Congress.

March 4—Judith Coplon, a Justice Department employee, arrested in the act of passing secret documents to a Russian spy.

July 15—National Housing Act is passed providing for the construction of 810,000 public housing units for lower income families.

August 29—Russia explodes an atomic bomb.

October 26—Minimum wage is raised to 75 cents an hour.

October—Brannan Plan requiring a major overhaul of the farm program is rejected, but high price supports for farm products are continued.

October—Congress adjourns without taking action on Federal compulsory health insurance and Federal aid to education bills.

December—China falls under Communist control, Chiang-Kai-shek flees to Formosa.

1950 January 21—Alger Hiss is convicted of perjury.

February—British government arrests Klaus Fuchs for passing United States atomic secrets to the Russians.

February 9—Senator McCarthy begins his campaign against Communists in government with a speech in Wheeling, West Virginia.

June 1—Senator Smith attacks Senator McCarthy's tactics.

June 24—Korean War begins.

August 28—Social Security benefits increased and 10 million more people are extended coverage.

September 23—McCarran-Walter Internal Security Act is passed over Truman's veto. It provided for the registration of all Communists and Communist-front organizations and authorized the arrest of Communists in times of national emergencies.

November 1—Two Puerto Rican nationalists unsuccessfully attempted to assassinate President Truman in Washington.

November 7—Republicans make gains in Congressional elections.

1952 June 27—McCarran-Walter Immigration Act is passed over Truman's veto. It retained the quota system based on the national origin of Americans in 1920 and provided for the deportation of subversive aliens.

29 THE EISENHOWER YEARS

As the first Republican President in twenty years, Eisenhower did not try to turn the clock back. New Deal and Fair Deal legislation was not repealed. In fact he extended Social Security coverage to groups hitherto not covered and raised the minimum wage from 75 cents an hour to $1.00 an hour. Eisenhower explained his interpretation of "Modern Republicanism" in a Presidential Message delivered to Congress in February, 1953.

While reading the following selections from the Eisenhower years and studying the chart of major events, keep in mind these questions:

1. What did Eisenhower think the Federal government's role in social and economic affairs ought to be?

2. How did Eisenhower use the power of the Federal government in social and economic affairs?

Eisenhower on His Political Philosophy

Message to Congress, February 2, 1953

Our immediate task is to chart a fiscal and economic policy that can:

First, reduce the planned deficits and then balance the budget, which means among other things, reducing Federal expenditures to the minimum.

Second, meet the huge costs of our defense.

Third, properly handle the burden of our inheritance of debt and obligations.

Fourth, check the menace of inflation.

Fifth, work toward the earliest reduction of the tax burden.

Sixth, make constructive plans to encourage the initiative of our citizens.

The first order of business is the elimination of the annual deficit. This administration is profoundly aware of two great needs born of our living in a complex industrial economy. First the individual citizen must have safeguards against personal disaster inflicted by forces beyond his control; second, the welfare of the people demands effective and economical performance by the Government of certain indispensable social services.

Adapted from **Public Papers of Presidents of the United States, Dwight D. Eisenhower** (1953), pp. 12–34.

Brannan Plan: agricultural program designed by Charles Brannan, Truman's Secretary of Agriculture, which continued price supports but required sale of perishables at market prices.

Socialized medicine: a program of Federal compulsory health insurance recommended by Truman, but rejected by Congress.

Campaign Speech at Cleveland, Ohio, October 1, 1956

Now let there be no mistake. There are deep and essential differences in the beliefs and convictions of the two major parties as established by the words of their candidates and by their records in office.

Speaking simply and directly to the problem, one of the most vital of these differences is that a dominant element in the other party believes primarily in big government and paternalistic direction by Washington bureaucrats of important activities of the whole nation. Those people have in the past sponsored the *Brannan Plan** and price controls in time of peace. They have flirted with *socialized medicine.** In general, they preach continuous extension of political control over our economy.

On the other hand, we of this administration and party believe that the great American potential can be realized only through the unfettered and free initiative, talents, and energies of an entire people.

We believe that the government has the function of insuring the national security and domestic tranquility, and beyond this, has to perform in Lincoln's phrase—"all those things which individuals cannot well do for themselves."

But we emphatically reject every unnecessary invasion into the daily lives of our people and into their occupations, both industrial and on the farm. . . .

Adapted from **Public Papers of Presidents, Dwight D. Eisenhower** (1956), pp. 828–837.

Major Events of the Eisenhower Presidency

1952   November 4—Eisenhower defeats Stevenson in presidential election.

1953–1954   Mild recession hits the American economy.

1953   April 11—Department of Health, Education and Welfare is created.

July 27—Korean War ends.

1954   May 13—St. Lawrence Seaway wins Congressional approval.

September 1—Social Security benefits increased, extended to 7½ million more workers; unemployment benefits broadened.

April 22–June 16—Army-McCarthy hearings are nationally televised.

May 17—Supreme Court rules segregation in public schools unconstitutional in Brown v. Board of Education of Topeka.

November 2—Democrats sweep Congressional elections.

1955   July 11—Dixon-Yates contract to supply electrical power to the TVA is cancelled. The contract had been written by a government official who also was vice-president of the firm financing the project.

August 12—Minimum wage is raised from 75 cents to $1.00 an hour.

September 24—Eisenhower suffers a severe heart attack at Denver, Colorado.

1956   May 28—Agricultural Act of 1956 establishes Soil Bank concept which paid farmers for taking land out of cultivation.

June 29—Federal Highway Act authorizes biggest road-building program in U.S. history. Costs $26 billion in Federal funds.

November 6—Eisenhower again defeats Stevenson in presidential election, but Democrats retain control of Congress.

1957–1958   Serious recession hits American economy.

1957   September 9—Civil Rights Act establishes Civil Rights Commission. It prohibits attempts to intimidate blacks from voting in Federal elections, empowers Attorney General to take legal action when a citizen is deprived of his right to vote, and authorizes district courts to consider civil action to recover damages in cases of civil-rights violations.

September 24—Eisenhower sends Federal troops to Little Rock, Arkansas, to protect black children trying to attend all-white Little Rock Central High School.

October 4—Russia launches Sputnik I and takes lead in space technology.

1958   July 7—Alaskan statehood act is signed.

September 2—National Defense Education Act provides $1 billion for student loans and subsidies for science and languages.

September 22—Sherman Adams, Eisenhower's chief aide, is forced to resign after admitting that he took gifts from a Boston industrialist, Bernard Goldfine.

November 4—Democrats sweep Congressional elections.

1959   January 3—Eisenhower officially proclaims Alaska the 49th state.

March 18—Hawaiian statehood act is signed.

August 21—Eisenhower officially proclaims Hawaii the 50th state.

1960   May 6—Civil Rights Act of 1960 expanded 1957 Civil Rights Act; required voting records and registration papers for Federal elections be preserved 22 months.

14 Blacks in Twentieth-Century America

Black People Struggle for Equality

Booker T. Washington, American black educator, born of a plantation slave in 1856, major spokesman for his race. At 25, appointed instructor at Tuskegee Institute in Alabama, which became foremost black institution of higher education in the nation under his leadership.

Introduction

As the twentieth century began, blacks numbered 8,833,994 or 11.6% of the population. They had been legally emancipated from slavery since 1863, but the vast majority lived as second-class citizens in 1901. Throughout the South voting rights were denied to them. In every aspect of social and economic life blacks suffered discrimination. They were forced to take the lowest-paying jobs, live in the worst housing, and attend the poorest schools.

Blacks bitterly resented the degraded conditions which white Americans had imposed on them. However, they were also deeply divided over how to improve their situation. *Booker T. Washington** believed that blacks should concentrate on economic improvement and for the time being tolerate existing political and social discrimination. *W. E. B. Du Bois** disagreed. He would tolerate no discrimination of any kind. Du Bois demanded immediate political, social, and economic equality for all black Americans.

Blacks Organize for Civil Rights

Under Du Bois' leadership a group of young black intellectuals met at Niagara Falls, Canada, in 1905 and drew up a sweeping manifesto demanding freedom of speech, manhood suffrage, and the abolition of all racial discrimination in America. Known as the Niagara movement, this group was the beginning of the black civil rights movement in twentieth-century America.

In 1908 an unusually vicious race riot broke out in Springfield, Illinois, within a short distance from Abraham Lincoln's former home. This race riot so shocked a number of prominent white reformers that they invited members of the Niagara movement to join with them in forming a new interracial organization to work for the cause of black equality. Consequently, in 1909 the *National Association for the Advancement of Colored People* (*NAACP*) was founded. W. E. B. Du Bois was selected as Director of Publicity and Research. Two of its most famous leaders were Walter White and Roy Wilkins. Two years later, 1911, another important interracial organization, the *National Urban League* was founded to help blacks migrating to cities to find jobs and adjust to living in an urban environment. Whitney Young served as its executive director from 1961 until his death in Nigeria in 1971.

William E. B. Du Bois, first black to receive a Ph.D. from Harvard University, taught for many years at Atlanta University. Losing faith in America, Du Bois joined the Communist Party in 1957, moved to Ghana in 1960, and died there August 28, 1963, at 95.

World War I

Despite very poor treatment by the Wilson Administration which practiced racial discrimination in Federal employment, black Americans patriotically sprang to the nation's defense in World War I. Over 350,000 blacks served in the Army of whom 40,000 saw combat duty and 1,408 were officers. The 369th U.S. Infantry Regiment, serving with the French Army, won the *Croix de Guerre.* Despite the important black contribution to the war effort, discrimination was widespread throughout the U.S. Army, and racial incidents were common on most military installations.

Croix de Guerre: French decoration for heroism in combat.

Nevertheless, black soldiers came back from the war with a renewed pride in themselves, hopeful that their loyalty and patriotism had earned them a right to educational and job opportunities, better housing, and political equality. Their hopes were denied. A great migration of blacks to northern cities had taken place during the war years. As hundreds of thousands of soldiers returned to civilian life from the war, competition for jobs and housing between whites and blacks in urban areas put a great strain on race relations. Serious race riots broke out in several cities including Chicago, Knoxville, and Omaha.

Blacks between the Wars

During the 1920's blacks were subject to the brutal terrorism of the newly revived Ku Klux Klan. Some Southern whites formed gangs to terrorize blacks through beatings and hangings and sometimes through murdering black leaders. Many blacks in their disillusionment with America joined *Marcus Garvey's* United Negro Improvement Association, which advocated a back-to-Africa movement. Disillusionment with the condition and prospects of blacks in America continued into the 1930's. Many blacks were attracted to Elijah Muhammad's *Black Muslim movement,* which rejected integration and favored complete separation from the white community.

(See page 118.)

Blacks were especially hard hit by the Great Depression because they were already on the bottom of the economic ladder. New Deal agencies provided vast amounts of aid for blacks but did not challenge local segregation practices. President Roosevelt's refusal to press openly for civil rights legislation was a great disappointment to black leaders. Roosevelt believed there was no real possibility of civil rights laws passing Congress. He did not want to risk losing Southern support for the New Deal by advocating them. However, on June 25, 1941, Roosevelt issued an executive order forbidding employment discrimination in government and in defense industries. In addition, he appointed a great many blacks to important government offices. So numerous were his appointments that blacks in key government jobs were called by the press the "Black Cabinet." The two New Dealers who did most for the cause of black equality were the First Lady, Mrs. Eleanor Roosevelt, and Harold Ickes, Secretary of the Interior.

Upon becoming **Black Muslims** converts changed their names. The most famous Black Muslim leader was **Malcolm X** (Malcolm Little) who was converted to the Black Muslim religion while serving a ten-year prison term for burglary. He clashed with Elijah Muhammad and was expelled from the movement. He then travelled to the Middle East to study the Moslem religion. Upon returning to the United States he founded the Organization of African Unity. Malcolm X was assassinated by a group of blacks in New York City in 1965.

World War II

The 332nd Fighter Group was commanded by Colonel Benjamin O. Davis, Jr. who later became the first black Air Force General.

When World War II broke out, blacks once again served their country in great numbers. A million black men and women served in the armed forces. Although discrimination was still widely practiced, blacks were given greater opportunities than ever before. For example, 600 blacks were trained as pilots, and two all-black combat air units, the 99th Pursuit Squadron and the *332nd Fighter Group,** served in Europe with great distinction.

Civil Rights Movement Comes of Age

President Dwight D. Eisenhower signs the Civil Rights Bill, September 9, 1957. This was a landmark—the first Federal civil rights legislation since 1875.

(See page 119.)

In large measure the modern civil rights movement began with the 1954 Supreme Court decision which outlawed segregation in the public schools (Brown v. Board of Education of Topeka). The next steps came during Eisenhower's Presidency with the passage of the Civil Rights Act establishing the Civil Rights Commission in 1957 and the sending of Federal troops to Little Rock to protect black children. The nation's school districts were extremely slow to comply, but from that decision integration of the public schools became the law of the land.

The first major civil rights action to receive national publicity occurred in Montgomery, Alabama, in December, 1955. Mrs. Rosa Parks, a black seamstress, refused to give up her seat on a city bus to a white man and was promptly arrested. The Montgomery chapter of the NAACP organized a very effective bus boycott under the leadership of a young black minister *Doctor Martin Luther King, Jr.** As a result of the bus boycott King and others founded the Southern Christian Leadership Conference (SCLC) in 1957 to work for total integration through nonviolent means.

Sit-Ins Begin

James Farmer was a young divinity student who founded the Congress of Racial Equality (CORE) and served as first director from its foundation in 1942 to 1966. In 1969 Farmer became Assistant Secretary of the Department of Health, Education, and Welfare.

In 1960 the nation's first sit-in took place in Greensboro, North Carolina, when four students from the Negro Agricultural and Technical College demanded service at a Woolworth store lunch counter and refused to leave when service was denied to them. Soon sit-ins were held all over the country. Thousands of arrests were made, but swimming pools, restaurants, hotels, and facilities of all kinds formerly barred to blacks were opened up to them. Another important civil rights action during the 1960's was the Freedom Rides. Beginning in 1961, groups of young blacks under the leadership of *James Farmer** successfully challenged segregation in interstate buses and bus terminals. Freedom Riders were frequently attacked by irate whites. The worst incident occurred in Montgomery, Alabama, on May 20, 1961, when President Kennedy sent 600 U.S. Marshals into that city to protect the Freedom Riders from harassment.

Despite the initial successes of the SCLC, the Kennedy Administration was slow to press for new civil rights legislation. Kennedy believed that there was very little chance of Congress passing meaningful laws at this time. Instead, he

D114

preferred to make broad use of <u>Executive</u> powers. Nevertheless, after a confrontation with Governor Wallace of Alabama over admitting black students to the State University the Kennedy Administration sponsored a new Civil Rights Bill in June, 1963. The bill got nowhere and remained bogged down in Congressional committees.

Against Kennedy's advice, black civil rights leaders organized a gigantic rally in Washington, D.C. Over 200,000 people at the site and millions more through television heard King deliver his famous "I Have A Dream Speech." John Kennedy was assassinated before the Civil Rights Bill was passed, but the Johnson Administration steered it through Congress in 1964.

The high-water mark of cooperation between blacks and whites came in the following year at Selma, Alabama, when several thousand people of both races came from all over the United States to support Martin Luther King's efforts to register black voters. The Selma spirit of unity and brotherhood did not last. Many whites thought blacks were demanding too much too soon and became increasingly irritated with sit-ins and demonstrations. Despite the gains of recent years, many young blacks grew increasingly impatient and demanded full equality at once.

March from Selma to Montgomery, Alabama— March 25, 1965, whites and blacks, including many dignitaries active in civil rights, came from all over the U.S. to join Martin Luther and Coretta King (center front) to build up voter registration.

what a 𝒜!

D115

Rise of Black Power

SNCC: an independent student civil rights organization which was established in 1960 to coordinate student participation in sit-ins and voter registration drives. The best-known leader was James Forman.

In August, 1965, one of the worst riots in the nation's history occurred in the Watts section of Los Angeles. A succession of bloody riots swept the nation in 1966, 1967, and 1968. Also in 1966, Stokely Carmichael, the newly elected chairman of the *Student Nonviolent Coordinating Committee (SNCC)** expelled all whites from the organization and called for a new approach which he called Black Power. Shortly thereafter, Huey Newton and Bobby Seale founded the Black Panther Party for Self-Defense in Oakland, California.

As a sizeable minority of blacks took to violence, many whites turned against the Civil Rights movement. Tragedy struck the entire nation in April, 1968, when the country's most influential black leader, Martin Luther King, was murdered in a Memphis motel. A great man had been killed, but the ideals he represented lived on. The SCLC under the direction of Reverend Ralph Abernathy has remained committed to nonviolence.

Despite many tragedies and numerous disappointments, seventy years of black civil-rights activities have brought results. In 1971 the condition of black people in America is far different from what it was in 1901. Job and educational opportunities have greatly increased, housing is improved but is still largely segregated and inadequate. The most striking advances have been in politics. The black politician has come into his own and is a power to be reckoned with.

Objectives of this assignment are to:

–Analyze policy statements by black American leaders for similarities and differences.

–Draw inferences from recording of Martin Luther King's speech about tactics in struggle for racial equality.

In 1971, one black man sits on the Supreme Court and another sits in the Senate. Twelve black men and one black woman have been elected to Congress. Mayors of three major northern cities are black, and there are no less than 105 black elected officials in the state of Alabama. There are four black men wearing general's stars in the United States Army and one black man with an admiral's stripe in the United States Navy. Progress has been made, but racial equality still remains an unrealized ideal.

30   BLACKS IN POST WORLD WAR I AMERICA

Black Americans had fought in World War I to make the world safe for democracy. Upon returning from France they expected to find at home what they had risked their lives to win abroad.

W. E. B. Du Bois, editor of The Crisis, the official journal of the NAACP, defines the problem of the black's future in America by speaking out forcefully on behalf of returning black war veterans.

Marcus Garvey, a Jamaica-born immigrant and founder of the Universal Negro Improvement Association, sees the black's future in America in a different way. Garvey explains how he thinks black Americans should face the future in a speech delivered in New York City in 1922. While reading these selections, keep in mind these questions:

1. *According to Du Bois, how has white America treated black people?*
2. *According to Du Bois, what should blacks do about their situation?*
3. *Why does Garvey advocate a back-to-Africa movement?*

W. E. B. Du Bois Demands Justice for Black Veterans, 1919

We are returning from war! The Crisis and tens of thousands of black men were drafted into a great struggle. For bleeding France and what she means and has meant and will mean to us and humanity and against the threat of German race arrogance, we fought gladly and to the last drop of blood; for America and her highest ideals, we fought in far-off hope; for the dominant southern oligarchy entrenched in Washington, we fought in bitter resignation. For the America that represents and gloats in lynching, disfranchisement, caste, brutality and devilish insult—for this, in the hateful upturning and mixing of things, we were forced by vindictive fate to fight also.

But today we return! We return from the slavery of uniform which the world's madness demanded us to don to the freedom of civil garb. This country of ours, despite all its better souls have done and dreamed, is yet a shameful land.

It lynches.

It disenfranchises its own citizens.

It encourages ignorance.

It steals from us.

It insults us.

This is the country to which we *Soldiers of Democracy* return. This is the fatherland for which we fought! But it is our fatherland. It was right for us to fight. The faults of our country are our faults. Under similar circumstances, we would fight again. But by the God of Heaven, we are cowards and jackasses if now that that war is over, we do not marshal every ounce of our brain and brawn to fight a sterner, longer, more unbending battle against the forces of hell in our own land.

We return.

We return from fighting.

We return fighting.

Make way for Democracy! We saved it in France, and by the Great Jehovah, we will save it in the United States of America, or know the reason why.

Quoted from **The Crisis**, XVIII (May 1919), pp. 13–14.

Marcus Garvey Explains Goal of Universal Negro Improvement Association, 1922

The Universal Negro Improvement Association stands for the Bigger Brotherhood; the Universal Negro Improvement Association stands for human rights, not only for Negroes, but for all races. The Universal Negro

Marcus Garvey established a branch of the UNIA in Harlem in 1917. In 1922 he was indicted for mail fraud and sentenced to five years in prison. President Coolidge commuted his sentence in 1927, and Garvey was deported to Jamaica. Marcus Garvey died in London in 1940 without ever seeing the Africa that he loved so deeply.

By permission of Jacques-Garvey, Amy, editor, **Philosophy and Opinions of Marcus Garvey.** Vol. II (New York: Arno Press, 1968).

Improvement Association believes in the rights of not only the black race, but the white race, the yellow race, and the brown race. In view of the fact that the black man of Africa has contributed as much to the world as the white man of Europe, and the brown man and yellow man of Asia, we of the Universal Negro Improvement Association demand that the white, yellow, and brown races give to the black man his place in the civilization of the world. We ask for nothing more than the rights of 400,000,000 Negroes. We are not seeking, as I said before, to destroy or disrupt the society or the government of other races, but we are determined that 400,000,000 of us shall unite ourselves to free our motherland from the grasp of the invader. We of the Universal Negro Improvement Association are determined to unite 400,000,000 Negroes for their own industrial, political, social, and religious emancipation.

We of the Universal Negro Improvement Association are determined to unite the 400,000,000 Negroes of the world to give expression to their own feeling; we are determined to unite the 400,000,000 Negroes of the world for the purpose of building a civilization of their own. And in that effort we desire to bring together the 15,000,000 of the United States, the 180,000,000 in Asia, the West Indies, and Central and South America, and the 200,000,000 in Africa. We are looking toward political freedom on the continent of Africa, the land of our fathers.

The Universal Negro Improvement Association is not seeking to build up another government within the bounds or borders of the United States of America. The Universal Negro Improvement Association is not seeking to disrupt any organized system of government, but the Association is determined to bring Negroes together for the building up of a nation of their own. And why? Because we have been forced to it. We have been forced to it throughout the world; not only in America, not only in Europe, not only in the British Empire, but wheresoever the black man happens to find himself, he has been forced to do for himself.

31   TWO PATHS TO RACIAL EQUALITY

During the 1960's Civil Rights activities intensified. Black leaders were in general agreement over the ultimate goals but differed over how these goals could be most effectively attained.

In reply to eight local clergymen who had criticized his leadership of massive demonstrations in Birmingham, Alabama, Dr. Martin Luther King, Jr. explained his path to racial equality. He made the explanation from his cell in the Birmingham jail after his arrest for participating in nonviolent demonstrations in that city. The now famous letter King wrote the clergymen is quoted here.

In the second selection, Stokely Carmichael, a young graduate of Howard University, Civil Rights activist, and chairman of the Student Nonviolent Coordinating Committee from 1966–1967, explains his path to racial equality in an article published in the New York Review of Books in 1966. While reading these selections, keep in mind these questions:

1. *According to King, what are the two opposing forces within the black community?*

2. *Why was King disappointed with white moderates?*

3. *Why was Carmichael disappointed with the voice of the Civil Rights movement?*

4. *What does Carmichael mean by Black Power?*

Martin Luther King on Nonviolence, 1963

❖ ❖ ❖ ❖ ❖

I must make two honest confessions to you, my Christian and Jewish brothers. First, I must confess that over the past few years I have been gravely disappointed with the white moderate. I have almost reached the regrettable conclusion that the Negro's great stumbling block in his stride toward freedom is not the White Citizen's Counciler or the Ku Klux Klanner, but the white moderate, who is more devoted to "order" than to justice; who prefers a negative peace which is the absence of tension to a positive peace which is the presence of justice; who constantly says: "I agree with you in the goal you seek, but I cannot agree with your methods of direct action"; who paternalistically believes he can set the timetable for another man's freedom; . . .

❖ ❖ ❖ ❖ ❖

You speak of our activity in Birmingham as extreme. At first I was rather disappointed that fellow clergymen would see my nonviolent efforts as those of an extremist. I began thinking about the fact that I stand in the middle of two opposing forces in the Negro community. One is a force of complacency, made up in part of Negroes who, as a result of long years of oppression, are so drained of self-respect and a sense of "somebodiness" that they have adjusted to segregation; and in part of a few middle-class Negroes who, because of a degree of academic and economic security and because in some ways they profit by segregation, have become insensitive to the problems of the masses. The other force is one of bitterness and hatred, and it comes perilously close to advocating violence. It is expressed in the various black nationalist groups that are springing up across the nation, the largest and best known being Elijah Muhammad's Muslim movement. Nourished by the Negro's frustration over the continued existence of racial discrimination, this movement is made up of people who have lost faith in America, who have absolutely repudiated Christianity, and who have concluded that the white man is an incorrigible "devil."

I have tried to stand between these two forces, saying that we need emulate neither the "do-nothingism" of the complacent nor the hatred and despair of the black nationalist. For there is the more excellent way of love and nonviolent protest. I am grateful to God that, through the influence of the Negro church, the way of nonviolence became an integral part of our struggle.

Martin Luther King gives his famous "I Have a Dream" speech to thousands gathered in Washington, D.C., August 28, 1963.

Martin Luther King, Jr. was born in Atlanta, Georgia, in 1929. After attending Morehouse College and Crozier Theological Seminary he earned a Ph.D. in Theology from Boston University. In 1954 he became minister of the Dexter Avenue Baptist Church in Montgomery, Alabama. In 1959 King moved back to Atlanta to be co-pastor with his father of the Ebenezer Baptist Church. He received the Nobel Peace prize in 1964.

Abridged from pp. 87, 90–91 "Letter from Birmingham Jail—April 16, 1963" in Why We Can't Wait by Martin Luther King, Jr. Copyright © 1963 by Martin Luther King, Jr. Reprinted by permission of Harper & Row, Publishers, Inc.

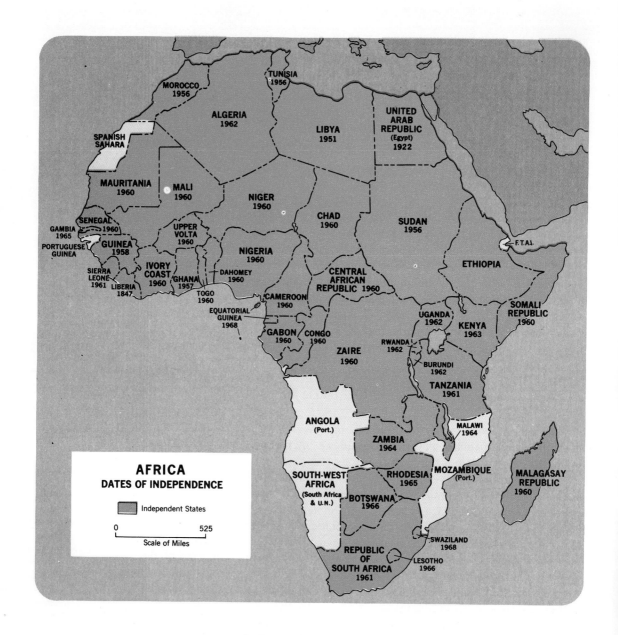

AFRICA
DATES OF INDEPENDENCE

Independent States

0 — 525
Scale of Miles

MOROCCO 1956
TUNISIA 1956
ALGERIA 1962
SPANISH SAHARA
LIBYA 1951
UNITED ARAB REPUBLIC (Egypt) 1922
MAURITANIA 1960
MALI 1960
NIGER 1960
CHAD 1960
SUDAN 1956
GAMBIA 1965
SENEGAL 1960
PORTUGUESE GUINEA
GUINEA 1958
SIERRA LEONE 1961
LIBERIA 1847
UPPER VOLTA 1960
IVORY COAST 1960
GHANA 1957
DAHOMEY 1960
TOGO 1960
NIGERIA 1960
CENTRAL AFRICAN REPUBLIC 1960
ETHIOPIA
F.T.A.I.
CAMEROON 1960
EQUATORIAL GUINEA 1968
GABON 1960
CONGO 1960
ZAIRE 1960
RWANDA 1962
BURUNDI 1962
UGANDA 1962
KENYA 1963
SOMALI REPUBLIC 1960
TANZANIA 1961
ANGOLA (Port.)
ZAMBIA 1964
MALAWI 1964
MOZAMBIQUE (Port.)
MALAGASAY REPUBLIC 1960
SOUTH-WEST AFRICA (South Africa & U.N.)
BOTSWANA 1966
RHODESIA 1965
SWAZILAND 1968
REPUBLIC OF SOUTH AFRICA 1961
LESOTHO 1966

Stokely Carmichael on "Black Power," 1966

One of the tragedies of the struggle against racism is that up to now there has been no national organization which could speak to the growing militancy of young black people in the urban ghetto. There has been only a civil rights movement, whose tone of voice was adapted to an audience of liberal whites. It served as a sort of buffer zone between them and angry young blacks. None of its so-called leaders could go into a rioting community and be listened to.

D120

For too many years, black Americans marched and had their heads broken and got shot. They were saying to the country, "Look, you guys are supposed to be nice guys and we are only going to do what we are supposed to do—why do you beat us up, why don't you give us what we ask, why don't you straighten yourselves out?" After years of this, we are at almost the same point—because we demonstrated from a position of weakness. We cannot be expected any longer to march and have our heads broken in order to say to whites: come on, you're nice guys. For you are not nice guys.

. . . The concept of "black power" is not a recent or isolated phenomenon: It has grown out of the ferment of agitation and activity by different people and organizations in many black communities over the years. Where black men have a majority, they will attempt to use it to exercise control. This is what they seek: control. Where Negroes lack a majority, black power means proper representation and sharing of control. This is what they seek: control.

. . . Integration speaks not at all to the problem of poverty, only to the problem of blackness. Integration today means the man who "makes it," leaving his black brothers behind in the ghetto as fast as his new sports car will take him. . . . As a goal, it has been based on complete acceptance of the fact that *in order to have* a decent house or education, blacks must move into a white neighborhood or send their children to a white school. This reinforces, among both black and white, the idea that "white" is automatically better and "black" is by definition inferior. This is why integration is a subterfuge for the maintainance [sic] of white supremacy.

Only black people can convey the revolutionary idea that black people are able to do things themselves. This is one reason Africa has such importance: The reality of black men ruling their own natives gives blacks elsewhere a sense of possibility, of power, which they do not now have.

This does not mean we don't welcome help, or friends. But we want the right to decide whether anyone is, in fact, our friend. We want to decide who is our friend, and we will not accept someone who comes to us and says: "If you do X, Y, and Z, then I'll help you." We cannot have the oppressors telling the oppressed how to rid themselves of the oppressor. . . .

We can build a community of love only where we have the ability and power to do so: among blacks.

Quoted from "What We Want" in the New York Review of Books (September 22, 1966).

Stokely Carmichael, in sunglasses and dashiki, talks with dedicated young blacks at a Nonviolent Coordinating Committee fund-raising in Philadelphia.

15 Vietnam

United States and Indochina

Introduction

You have already studied an analysis of the Cold War and the American policy of "containment," Cold War language for restraining Communism. As it pursued this policy, the United States found itself increasingly involved in a distant and hitherto unknown land—Indochina, especially Vietnam.

In this present assignment you will study how its involvement brought first a trickle, then a stream of money, equipment, and men to support the anti-Communist struggle in that area. In time it also brought a bitterness to American public life, as Americans debated whether and how to disengage their nation from the Indochina tangle.

How We Got Into Vietnam

Until the end of World War II, Americans knew little of Indochina—less, in fact, than they knew of Africa. Except for Thailand, or Siam (whose king once offered elephants to Abraham Lincoln to fight the Civil War), the entire region was composed of British and French colonies. The latter were conveniently lumped together as "French Indochina," a title which made things easier for map-makers and geography teachers, but which obscured the long history of the area and the differences among its peoples. Only slowly in the 1950's and early 1960's did most Americans become aware of the "new" nations of Indochina—Cambodia, Laos, and Vietnam—as they emerged from French rule. And almost before they could locate these lands on newer maps, they were involved in their troubles. Or so it seemed.

How the United States became involved in Indochina to the point of waging large-scale warfare is not a simple story. Basically, it is the story of what one historian (and former adviser to Presidents Kennedy and Johnson) has called "the policy of 'one more step'."* By this he meant that the United States committed herself, and deepened her commitment in Indochina, through a series of separate decisions, each of which was regarded as the "one more step" that would bring success to American policy.

President Truman supported with money and weapons the unsuccessful French struggle against the Vietnamese forces of Ho Chi Minh. After the French defeat and the partition of Vietnam into North and South, President Eisenhower decided to support the government of Ngo Dinh Diem in the South against the North Vietnamese government of Ho Chi Minh. President Kennedy decided to build up the force of American military advisers in South

Arthur M. Schlesinger, **The Bitter Heritage: Vietnam and American Democracy, 1941–1966** (Boston: Houghton Mifflin, 1967), p. 31.

Vietnam. President Johnson decided first to use American airpower against the North Vietnamese and then to commit regular American ground troops in increasing numbers until, in 1968, they totalled over half-a-million men. President Nixon decided to send American forces on a raid into Cambodia and to use American forces to support a South Vietnamese raid into Laos. Each of these decisions was made after careful consideration and in the belief that it would either achieve America's goal fully, or at least bring the achievement closer.

Getting Out of Vietnam

Even while American involvement in Indochina was growing, opposition to that involvement had emerged. Organized and semi-organized "anti-War" groups appeared to challenge American support for successive South Vietnamese governments and to oppose the American military presence in Indochina. In 1965 this opposition took the form of "teach-ins" among some college professors and students. The teach-in was followed, in turn, by the protest march and the public demonstration. Popular feeling, especially among young people and academics, became aroused over an issue of American foreign policy as it had never before been aroused. Nor, in time, was opposition to American policy confined to the young and to college teachers. Public

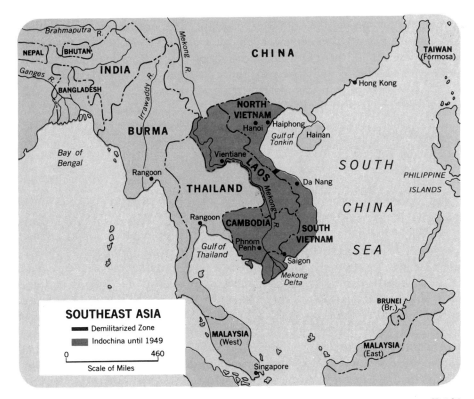

Vietnam—At Tam Ky, 350 miles north of Saigon, a U.S. Air Cavalry G.I. signals "all clear for landing" to a troop-carrying helicopter.

SOUTHEAST ASIA
- Demilitarized Zone
- Indochina until 1949

0   460
Scale of Miles

The **Gallup Poll** has periodically asked Americans: "Do you think the United States made a mistake in sending troops to fight in Vietnam?" The replies given in August, 1965, and May, 1971, were:

	August 1965	May 1971
Yes	24	61
No	61	28
No opinion	15	11

From **The New York Times,** June 6, 1971. Copyright © 1971 by The New York Times Company. Reprinted by permission.

opinion polls, representing all groups in the population, at first gave strong support to the escalation of America's commitment in Vietnam. The polls then showed a shift against such commitment.

By 1971 substantially more than half of those questioned favored withdrawal of U.S. forces, even if it meant the collapse of the South Vietnamese government, and regarded America's entry into the struggle as a mistake.* This view was strengthened in 1971 when major portions of a 7,000-page study known as the "Pentagon Papers" were published in The New York Times and other large newspapers. The papers were leaked to the press by Daniel Ellsberg, a college professor, who had worked on the study on the Vietnam war for the Defense Department.

The Pentagon Papers created a furor because they disclosed events which seemed to show that the government of the United States had secretly involved the country in deep military commitment in Vietnam without telling Americans the truth about the situation. The secret Pentagon documents revealed various clandestine operations, such as U.S. involvement in the political affairs of the South Vietnam government, and use of underground agents to harass North Vietnam.

This kind of shift in popular feeling affected government leaders as early as 1968 and led to several decisions aimed at the ultimate disengagement of the United States from the Indochina war. In March of that year President Johnson announced that henceforth only limited bombing of North Vietnam would take place, a decision which gave way to an almost complete end of bombing in November, 1968. In May peace negotiations between the United States and the North Vietnamese began in Paris. The size of the American forces in Indochina was gradually reduced, and American governments, led by Presidents Johnson and Nixon sought a peaceful, negotiated settlement of the struggle. Partly with this idea in mind, President Nixon decided to visit Communist China in 1972.

32   WHY ARE WE IN VIETNAM?

No single document can adequately explain decisions made and actions taken over twenty years. Each President since Truman (bolstered by his advisers) made his decisions in a different set of specific circumstances. Yet, there has been a basic pattern of thought in all of these decisions that deepened American involvement in Indochina. Dean Rusk, the Secretary of State under both Presidents Kennedy and Johnson, expressed it most clearly when he testified before the Foreign Relations Committee of the United States Senate in 1966.

While reading his testimony and examining the Vietnam Chronology, keep in mind the following questions. According to Secretary of State Rusk:

1. *What was the underlying general reason for American involvement in Vietnam?*

2. *What was the basis for the specific American commitment to fight in Vietnam?*

Objectives of this assignment are to:

–Analyze a policy statement on United States involvement in Vietnam and discover reasons underlying it.

–Analyze two policy statements on withdrawing from Vietnam and discover reasons justifying them.

–Make historical judgments on effectiveness of United States cold war foreign policy and Vietnam involvement.

Secretary Rusk's Explanation, 1966

Why are we in Vietnam? Certainly we are not there merely because we have power and like to use it. We do not regard ourselves as the policeman of the universe. We do not go around the world looking for quarrels in which we can intervene. We are in Vietnam because the issues posed there are deeply intertwined with our own security and because the outcome of the struggle can profoundly affect the nature of the world in which we and our children will live.

What are our world security interests involved in the struggle in Vietnam? They cannot be seen clearly in terms of Southeast Asia only. We must view the problem in perspective. We must recognize that what we are seeking to achieve in South Vietnam is part of a process that has continued for a long time—a process of preventing the expansion and extension of Communist domination by the use of force against the weaker nations on the perimeter of Communist power. This is the problem as it looks to us. Nor do the Communists themselves see the problem in isolation. They see the struggle in South Vietnam as part of a larger design for the steady extension of Communist power through force and threat. What we face in Vietnam is what we have faced on many occasions before—the need to check the extension of Communist power in order to maintain a reasonable stability in a precarious world.

In order to give support to the nations of Southeast Asia the United States took the lead in the creation of an alliance embodied in a treaty and reinforced by a collective security system known as SEATO, the Southeast Asia Treaty Organization. In joining SEATO, the United States took a solemn treaty obligation of far-reaching effect. It is this fundamental SEATO obligation that has from the outset guided our actions in South Vietnam. If the United States determines that an armed attack has occurred against any nation to whom the protection of the Treaty applies, then it is obligated "to act to meet the common danger" without regard to the views or actions of any other Treaty member.

We have sent American forces to fight in the jungles of South Vietnam because that beleaguered country has, under the language of the SEATO Treaty, been the victim of "aggression by means of armed attack." The war is clearly an "armed attack" cynically and systematically mounted by the *Hanoi** regime against the people of South Vietnam. The North Vietnamese regime has sought deliberately to confuse the issue by seeking to make its aggression appear as a native revolt. But we should not be deceived by this subterfuge.

In meeting our commitments in South Vietnam, we are using substantial

Hanoi is the capital of North Vietnam.

military forces. At the same time we are making it quite clear to North Vietnam and to the world that our forces are being employed for a limited and well-defined objective. We wish only that the people of South Vietnam should have the right and opportunity to determine their future in freedom without coercion or threat from the outside.

We have done everything possible to make clear to the regime in Hanoi that a political solution is the proper course. If that regime were prepared to call off the aggression in the South, peace would come in almost a matter of hours.

Adapted from the Statement of Secretary of State Dean Rusk before the Senate Committee on Foreign Relations, February 18, 1966, in **The Vietnam Hearings.**

Vietnam Chronology

1858–1887: Independent country of Vietnam taken over by France.

1941–1945: Japanese occupy Vietnam; Viet Minh (League for the Independence of Vietnam), led by Ho Chi Minh, oppose Japanese.

1945—Ho Chi Minh proclaims independence of Vietnam.

1946—War between Viet Minh and French begins.

1950—President Truman provides money and arms to the French to fight the Viet Minh.

1954—President Eisenhower refuses French request for direct military intervention, but proclaims importance of Vietnam in struggle with Communism.

—France suffers major defeat by Viet Minh at Dien Bien Phu, and agrees in Geneva Convention to withdraw from Vietnam.

—Vietnam is divided between North and South pending elections to be held in 1956.

—South Vietnam and United States do not sign Geneva Convention.

1955—Some American military advisers sent to Vietnam.

1956—Elections which were agreed to in Geneva Convention are not held; South Vietnam government opposes them.

1957—Large-scale infiltration of North Vietnam forces into South Vietnam begins.

1960—President Eisenhower increased U.S. military advisers in South Vietnam to 685 by May.

1961—President Kennedy expands number of U.S. military advisers in South Vietnam to 3,200.

1963—President Diem of South Vietnam ousted by South Vietnam officers and killed, November 2; President Kennedy assassinated November 22.

1964—President Johnson asks Congress for authority "to take all necessary measures" against North Vietnam, following incidents between North Vietnamese gunboats and U.S. destroyers. Congress votes Gulf of Tonkin Resolution giving President Johnson authority.

1965—U.S. launches bombing raids against North Vietnam, following Viet Cong attacks on American installations in South Vietnam.

—Large build-up and use of American ground troops in South Vietnam begins; 160,000 Americans in South Vietnam by end of year.

1966—Secretary Rusk explains administration policy to Senate Foreign Relations Committee.

1968—"Tet" (Vietnamese New Year) offensive by North Vietnam and Viet Cong. U.S. and South Vietnam forces win battle despite heavy casualties.

—U.S. forces in Vietnam exceed 500,000.

—President Johnson drops out of presidential election race.

—Preliminary peace talks with North Vietnam begin in Paris.

—Bombing of North Vietnam halted.

1969—President Nixon announces policy of **Vietnamization,** turning fighting over to South Vietnamese.

—President Nixon begins gradual withdrawal of U.S. forces.

1970—Death of Ho Chi Minh.

—U.S. and South Vietnam troops enter Cambodia to strike at Viet Cong and North Vietnamese.

1971—South Vietnamese, with indirect U.S. support, enter Laos to attack North Vietnamese installations.

—Pentagon Papers, classified government documents on development of U.S. policy in Vietnam, published by The New York Times and other large newspapers.

33 HOW SHOULD WE GET OUT OF VIETNAM?

By the end of the 1960's, there was general agreement even among public officials that American policy in Indochina needed changing and that, some-how or other, the United States must withdraw from the fighting in Vietnam.

But deciding that the United States *should* get out of Vietnam was not the same as deciding *how* to get out. And as the 1970's began, the debate on how to withdraw from Vietnam dominated American thinking on foreign affairs. The two readings below demonstrate the two basic approaches advocated by different public officials. The first is from a book by Townsend Hoopes, a high-level official in the Defense Department from 1965 to 1969, and one who originally supported the American policy. (Mr. Hoopes' position was widely shared both inside and outside of the government.) The second is from President Nixon's televised press conference of June 1, 1971.

While reading these selections, keep in mind the following questions:

1. How does Mr. Hoopes suggest that the United States get out of Vietnam?

2. How does President Nixon suggest that the United States get out of Vietnam?

Townsend Hoopes on Vietnam, August 1969

The choice, basically, is between trying yet again to strengthen and salvage the South Vietnamese regime of President Thieu for the sake of a gradual, far from complete, but hopefully honorable disengagement from a war that might, in such circumstances, continue for years to come; and casting that government aside for the sake of a fairly quick, probably unpalatable political settlement which would however permit—indeed require—the prompt and complete withdrawal of American forces.

The Nixon offer of mutual withdrawal plus elections may be indeed gener-ous by past U.S.-South Vietnamese standards, but it depends for success on reciprocal action by the Hanoi government. But Hanoi gives no indication that it feels the need to make significant concessions (like promising to with-draw its forces) in order to achieve large-scale U.S. troop withdrawals or avoid resumption of the bombing against North Vietnam. This position is no doubt based on Hanoi's quite accurate assessment that American public opin-ion more than ever favors and expects a liquidation of the U.S. war effort. The evidence strongly suggests that Hanoi intends simply to wait us out.

The alternative of *Vietnamization** suffers from similar frailties, for its ef-fectiveness as a threat to the enemy depends far less on increased material support for the South Vietnamese Army, than on the long-term retention of significant U.S. combat power (air and ground). Should the U.S. government pursue a course of partial withdrawal, while leading the American public to believe all will end well, I am afraid a number of unpleasant shocks, surprises,

Vietnamization became a term used to describe turning the war over to the South Viet-namese Army and government. It implied building up and training that Army to the point where it could deal with its enemies without American assistance.

In September 1970 and again in June 1971 the Senate voted on a resolution introduced by Senators Mark O. Hatfield (Republican from Oregon) and George McGovern (Democrat from South Dakota) which expressed substantially this position, calling for **complete withdrawal** of American forces by the end of 1971. It was defeated in 1970 by a 55–39 vote.

Bite-the-bullet: a slang phrase meaning that one tackles the problem and tries to solve it no matter how hard or painful it might be. It is said that before anesthesia some doctors had their patients bite a bullet during surgery to keep them from biting their tongues in the midst of pain.

Adapted from **The Limits of Intervention** by Townsend Hoopes. Copyright © 1969 by Townsend Hoopes (New York: David McKay Company, Inc.), pp. 230–237. Reprinted by permission of the publisher.

and politically dangerous consequences would arise. For at best such a course is a prescription for interminable war; partially disguised by the declining level of U.S. participation, it would in fact require our country to sustain a continuing burden of war casualties and heavy dollar-cents. Sooner or later, and probably sooner, the American people would reawaken to the fact that they were still committed to the endless support of a group of men in Saigon who represented nobody but themselves, preferred war to the risks of a political settlement, and could not remain in power for more than a few months without our large-scale presence.

Deliberate, orderly, but complete *withdrawal** has become, in my judgment the only practical course open to the United States, if we are to restore our foreign policy to coherence, regain our psychological balance, alleviate the deep-seated strife in our society, and reorder our national priorities in ways that will win the support of a large majority of our own people.

If we can forthrightly acknowledge the basic, unpalatable truth—that our intervention in 1965 was misconceived, that viewed through cold, clear eyes it could not be justified on the grounds that a vital national interest was at stake—then we can *bite the bullet** in Vietnam. We can acknowledge past failure and the inevitability of some degree of defeat. We can move to a phased, unilateral, and total withdrawal of forces, not as a means of pretending we have discovered a painless way to achieve partial victory or even a settlement consistent with our original objectives, but as a means of liquidating an enterprise that is beyond retrieval and a condition that is poisoning the bloodstream of our society.

President Nixon on Vietnam, June 1971

Question: Mr. President, much of the debate about Vietnam seems to have shifted from the question of practicality of policy to the questions about morality of U.S. involvement. Some of the people who have been demonstrating against the war have contended that your administration is responsible for war crimes, not only speaking of certain face-to-face encounters between U.S. soldiers and civilians, but speaking of the policy of massive bombing in large areas in Southeast Asia.

How do you respond to the suggestions that the bombing constitutes immoral, criminal conduct?

Answer: Well, my views with regard to war are well known. I grew up in a tradition where we consider all wars immoral. My mother, my grandmother on my mother's side, were Quakers, as I have often pointed out to this press corps, and very strongly disapproved of my entering World War II. As far as Vietnam is concerned, like all wars it involves activities that certainly would be subject to criticism if we were considering it solely in a vacuum.

But when we consider the consequences of not acting, I think we can see why we have done what we have. To allow a takeover of South Vietnam by the Communist aggressors would only result in the loss of freedom for 17 million people in South Vietnam; it would greatly increase the danger of that

Press Conference at the White House, June 1971—This is how it looked when President Nixon faced the battery of newspaper, radio, and television correspondents to discuss the Vietnam problem and changes in American policy.

kind of aggression and also the danger of a larger war in the Pacific and in the world. That I believe. That is why I have strongly supported ending this war, ending our involvement as we are, withdrawing Americans, but ending it in a way that we do not turn the country over to the Communists, ending it in a way that we give the South Vietnamese a reasonable chance to defend themselves against Communist aggression. And that is why I believe that kind of an ending will contribute to the peace that we all want.

Question: Mr. President, in view of your continually reducing troops in Vietnam, bringing more American troops home all the time, how do you account for the fact that two major public-opinion polls now show that about two-thirds of the American public believe they are not being told the truth with regard to the war?

Answer: I am not surprised by the polls. I think the people—and the war has been going on for a long time—are tired of the war. We are an impatient people. We like to get results.

On the other hand, if all the problems that I have in this government could be as easily solved as this one, I would be very happy, because the answer to whether or not the American people believe that I am ending the American involvement in war is in the fact. We have already brought home half. We will have brought home two-thirds, and we are going to bring all home, and bring them home—and this is what is vitally important—in a way that will not be inconsistent with two other objectives: In a way that will secure the release of our prisoners of war; and also in a way that will give the South Vietnamese a chance to avoid a Communist takeover, and thereby contribute to a more lasting peace.

That fact, the very fact that we accomplish that goal, will end the credibility gap on that issue once and for all.

From the text of President Nixon's Press Conference of June 1, 1971.

16 New Frontier, Great Society, and New Federalism

The Troubled Sixties

John F. Kennedy: born in Brookline, Mass., 1917; son of millionaire Joseph P. Kennedy; graduated from Harvard in 1940; served with distinction as a P.T. boat commander during World War II. Elected to the U.S. House of Representatives in 1946 and to the U.S. Senate in 1952.

Two days later **Oswald** was killed in the Dallas city jail by **Jack Ruby,** a Dallas nightclub operator, while millions of television viewers watched in horror.

Introduction

Since Eisenhower was barred by law from seeking a third term in 1960, the Republican nomination went to Vice-President Richard Nixon. The Democratic nomination was eagerly sought by Senators Hubert Humphrey, Lyndon Johnson, Stuart Symington, and John F. Kennedy. Kennedy won the key primary fights against Hubert Humphrey in Wisconsin and West Virginia and went on to win the nomination at the Los Angeles convention on the first ballot. Kennedy stunned most of his supporters by offering the Vice-Presidency to his bitter rival, Lyndon Johnson, who in turn astounded most of his supporters by accepting it. In a very eloquent acceptance speech Kennedy promised the American people a *New Frontier.*

The Kennedy Years

In an exciting campaign Kennedy won a narrow victory, defeating Nixon by only 118,550 votes. At forty-three, *Kennedy** was the youngest man ever to be elected President, and the first Catholic to hold that office.

The young President had outlined a comprehensive domestic reform program during his campaign, which he called the New Frontier. However, only a small part of his program was actually enacted. A powerful coalition of northern Republicans and rural Democrats had blocked most social legislation since 1938, and they continued to do so in the Kennedy Administration. Kennedy suffered major setbacks with the defeat of his education bill, his agricultural reform bill, and Medicare, a plan to provide health insurance for the aged.

Death in Dallas

Although Kennedy recognized that his legislative accomplishments had been minimal, he was greatly encouraged by his party's performance in the Congressional elections of 1962. He confidently expected to win a genuine mandate for his programs from the voters in the presidential election of 1964.

It was the need for mending his political fences in Texas for the election in 1964 that brought President Kennedy to Dallas, Texas, on November 22, 1963. The President never left Dallas alive. He was murdered by *Lee Harvey Oswald,** a young, emotionally disturbed, left-wing malcontent.

D130

Johnson Takes Command

Vice-President Lyndon B. Johnson of Texas was immediately sworn in as the 36th President of the United States. A shrewd political veteran of twenty-three years in Congress, Johnson had served as the Democratic majority leader in the Senate from 1955 to 1960.

In an emotional television address to the nation Johnson pledged himself to carry through the Kennedy legislative program. In 1964 he secured enactment of a *Civil Rights law*, a major tax reform, and the *Economic Opportunity law.* *

In his State of the Union speech on January 8, 1964, Johnson stated what were to be the objectives of his Presidency. He declared a "war on poverty" in America and pledged himself to eradicate it forever. A few months later in a speech delivered at the University of Michigan, Johnson gave a name to his vision of an America without poverty. He called it the "Great Society."

President Lyndon B. Johnson

Election of 1964

As the presidential election of 1964 approached, the Democratic National Convention unanimously nominated Lyndon B. Johnson for President. Johnson selected *Senator Hubert H. Humphrey* of Minnesota as his Vice-Presidential running mate.* The Republican National Convention chose Senator Barry Goldwater of Arizona, a likeable, handsome conservative as their candidate. Goldwater selected Congressman William Miller of New York as his Vice-Presidential candidate. Johnson and Humphrey campaigned for the Great Society, and Goldwater and Miller promised to end big government and return to individual self-reliance. When the election was over, Johnson had won with a plurality of 16 million votes, and had the biggest majority in both houses of Congress since 1936.

Economic Opportunity Act was passed in 1964. It created the Office of Economic Opportunity (OEO) and authorized the expenditure of almost a billion dollars for a wide variety of programs aimed at helping the poor, establishing the Job Corps, and community action programs.

Robert Kennedy and **Eugene McCarthy** had both wanted the Vice-Presidential nomination. Johnson rejected them in favor of Hubert Humphrey.

The Great Society

Johnson interpreted the election of 1964 as a mandate from the people for his Great Society. Congress agreed and voted bill after bill of the Johnson program into law. When Congress adjourned in October, 1965, Johnson's legislative accomplishments were the most impressive since Franklin Roosevelt's "Hundred Days." In a single session of 1965, Congress passed:

1. The **Appalachia Redevelopment Act** which authorized $1.1 billion to rehabilitate the mountainous area running from Pennsylvania to northern Alabama.
2. The **Housing Act** which authorized $2.9 billion for urban renewal.
3. A law creating a new cabinet-level department of **Housing and Urban Affairs.**
4. The **Medicare Act** which established a comprehensive system of medical insurance for the elderly.

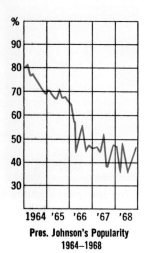

Pres. Johnson's Popularity 1964–1968

The worst act of violence occurred at the **University of Wisconsin** in 1970 where a revolutionary group blew up a science building, killing a young graduate student.

Johnson was only a write-in candidate and did not campaign; yet he received 48% of the votes.

Humphrey

Robert Kennedy

McCarthy

5. The **Elementary and Secondary Education Act** which authorized $1.3 billion in Federal aid to the nation's public schools.
6. The **Higher Education Act** which provided partial scholarships for 140,000 needy college students and created several new Federally supported teacher training programs.
7. The **Civil Rights Act** which authorized Federal supervision of voter registration in the states.

Johnson had planned on expanding and enlarging his Great Society programs in 1966. However, escalation of the Vietnam War turned both money and attention away from domestic reform. Johnson's popularity steadily declined, and with it his extraordinary ability to manage Congress disappeared.

Johnson's popularity among youth, especially college-age youth, fell drastically. Throughout 1966 and 1967 college campuses were in turmoil. In 1968 demonstrations and disruptions on college campuses reached an all-time high.* Much like Wilson's *New Freedom*, and Roosevelt's *New Deal*, Johnson's *Great Society* became a casualty of war.

Election of 1968

As opposition to Johnson's Vietnam policy increased, disenchanted Democrats rallied around Senator Eugene McCarthy of Minnesota as their choice to head a "Stop Johnson! movement." McCarthy did extremely well in the New Hampshire Presidential Primary election on March 12, 1968, when he received 42 per cent* of the votes cast. Four days later Senator Robert Kennedy of New York announced that he also intended to challenge Johnson for the Democratic presidential nomination. Johnson astonished friend and foe alike on March 31 by announcing that he would not seek renomination for the Presidency. Johnson and most of the regular Democratic organization announced their support for Vice-President Hubert Humphrey as the Democratic presidential candidate.

During a politically exciting spring, thousands of idealistic students worked long hours for McCarthy and Kennedy. But two terrible tragedies suddenly shocked a nation not yet psychologically recovered from the assassination of John Kennedy. On April 4 Dr. Martin Luther King, Jr. was murdered in Memphis, Tennessee, by a white criminal, James Earl Ray, who foolishly hoped to win fame and notoriety by this cowardly act. Then, on June 5, Senator Robert Kennedy was assassinated in a Los Angeles hotel by a young Jordanian immigrant, Sirhan Sirhan, who was enraged by Kennedy's strong support of Israel against the Arab nations.

With Kennedy dead, a distracted and divided Democratic Party then nominated Vice-President Humphrey at a Chicago convention marked by violent protest demonstrations and charges of police brutality. They also nominated Senator Edmund Muskie of Maine for Vice-President.

Sensing victory over the badly divided Democrats, the Republicans met in a more serene atmosphere at Miami Beach and nominated Richard M. Nixon, who had come out of political retirement to win a number of impressive primary victories. Governor Spiro T. Agnew of Maryland was Nixon's choice for Vice-President. Adding further confusion to an already hectic election year was the third-party candidacy of George C. Wallace, former governor of Alabama, who ran on the American Independent Party ticket. The polls showed Nixon far in the lead in the early weeks of the campaign, but Humphrey made impressive gains as the election neared, and Nixon won by a narrow margin of 510,000 votes. Wallace received almost 10,000,000 votes.*

Wallace carried the states of Alabama, Louisiana, Mississippi, Arkansas, and Georgia.

Richard M. Nixon

The new President was a native of California who had attended Whittier College and Duke Law School. He served in the Navy in World War II and entered Congress in 1946, the same year as John Kennedy. In 1950 he was elected to the Senate, but served only two years before being nominated as Eisenhower's running mate in 1952. As Vice-President from 1953–1961 Nixon served as the principal Republican political spokesman, since Eisenhower chose to remain out of party politics as much as possible. Though defeated for the Presidency in 1960 and for the governorship of California in 1962, Nixon campaigned vigorously for all Republican candidates in 1964 and 1966. By 1968, he was the most popular man in the Republican Party.

Nixon Administration

With the nation deeply divided over the Vietnam War and troubled by poverty, urban decay, student unrest, racial tensions, and an increasing crime rate, Nixon assumed the Presidency at a critical time.

In his inaugural address of January 20, 1969, Nixon wisely counseled the American people to "stop shouting at one another" and get on with solving the problems before us.

President Nixon's most important legislative recommendation came in a special address to the nation on August 8, 1969, when he announced a *New Federalism* and called for the overhaul of an *archaic** welfare system, establishment of a minimum family income, and sharing Federal tax revenues with states.

Archaic: obsolete; outdated; old-fashioned; of other times.

Americans and Scientific Leadership

Though Congress did not respond immediately to the President's recommendations, the Nixon Administration's place in history is secure. Our country's finest hour came on July 20, 1969, when astronauts Neil Armstrong and Edwin Aldrin became the first humans to walk upon the surface of the moon. Scientists and ordinary citizens the world over hailed the American accomplishment as the greatest scientific achievement in the history of man.

However, at home, once the enthusiasm inspired by the moon walk had passed, critics questioned whether or not the achievement was worth the cost. They argued that space program funds would be better spent improving the quality of life on earth.

For the first time a significant number of Americans doubted that scientific leadership, technological and industrial superiority, or being first in anything was worthwhile. In 1969 and 1970 government financial support of scientific research and space programs was drastically cut back.

Only historians writing in the next century will be able to judge how wise these cut-backs were and whether the United States could give up being first in science and technology and still survive as a great power and a free nation.

The 1960's also saw the revival of a strong ethnic consciousness in America. An increasing number of Americans doubted both the desirability and the success of the Melting Pot theory that held that all races and nationalities should be assimilated into one homogenized new American nationality. Americans of many ethnic groups took new pride in belonging to a particular race or nationality. Indians were no longer content to be ridiculed as the uncivilized savages who had to be defeated in the name of progress. They took renewed pride in their tribal culture and in many cases took direct action to reclaim land they alleged to have been illegally seized by the Federal government.

Alcatraz Island—In November, 1969, 78 young Indians crossed San Francisco Bay before dawn and occupied the former Federal penitentiary. They held it for 19 months before the final remnant of 15 men, women, and children were removed on June 11, 1971.

Cesar Chavez leads jubilant grape workers in California—With his United Farm Workers Organization, Chavez used strikes and boycotts to win union contracts with 90 percent of grape farmers. UFWOC efforts then turned to other crops.

Aroused Mexican-American farm laborers vented longtime grievances and demanded full social, political, educational, and economic equality. The leader of the Chicanos, as many Mexican-Americans wish to be called, was Cesar Chavez, who achieved great success in organizing the migrant farm workers of California. Young Japanese-Americans bitterly criticized the harsh treatment their parents had endured from the government in the World War II relocation camps and took new pride in maintaining a Japanese culture. Italian-Americans became increasingly sensitive to the bad publicity frequently given their nationality because of the Mafia. Polish-Americans protested vigorously against the derogatory nature of the Polish jokes that swept across the nation in the 1960's. The future remains uncertain, but it is obvious that far greater efforts must be made to treat every race and nationality with the full dignity and respect that our common humanity demands if the American dream of a stable, pluralistic society is ever to be realized.

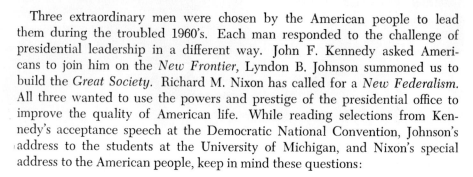

34 PRESIDENTIAL LEADERSHIP IN THE 1960's

Objectives of this assignment are to:

—Analyze selections of policy statements by Presidents Kennedy, Johnson, and Nixon for similarities and differences.

—Analyze journalist's report of disturbances at Columbia University for meaning.

—Analyze statement by aerospace industry spokesman about value of space exploration for meaning.

—Make judgment on historical importance of 1960's.

Three extraordinary men were chosen by the American people to lead them during the troubled 1960's. Each man responded to the challenge of presidential leadership in a different way. John F. Kennedy asked Americans to join him on the *New Frontier*, Lyndon B. Johnson summoned us to build the *Great Society*. Richard M. Nixon has called for a *New Federalism*. All three wanted to use the powers and prestige of the presidential office to improve the quality of American life. While reading selections from Kennedy's acceptance speech at the Democratic National Convention, Johnson's address to the students at the University of Michigan, and Nixon's special address to the American people, keep in mind these questions:

1. *According to Kennedy, what were the challenges of the* <u>New Frontier</u>?

2. *According to Johnson, what is the* <u>Great Society</u>?

3. *According to Nixon, what is the* <u>New Federalism</u>? *How does he propose to begin it?*

Kennedy: The New Frontier, 1960

Today our concern must be with the future. For the world is changing. The old era is ending. The old ways will not do. . . . The New Deal and the Fair Deal were bold measures for their generations—but this is a new generation.

A technological revolution on the farm has led to an out-put explosion—but we have not yet learned to harness that explosion usefully . . . An urban population revolution has overcrowded our schools, cluttered up our suburbs, and increased the squalor of our slums.

A peaceful revolution for human rights—demands an end to racial discrimination in all parts of our community life. . . .

A medical revolution has extended the life of our elder citizens without providing the dignity and security those later years deserve. And a revolution of automation finds machines replacing men in the mines and mills of America.

Too many Americans have lost their way, their will and their sense of historical purpose.

It is time, in short, for a new generation of leadership—new men to cope with new problems and new opportunities. . . .

For I stand tonight facing west on what was once the last frontier. From the lands that stretch 3,000 miles behind me, the pioneers of old gave up their safety, their comfort, and sometimes their lives to build a new world in the west. . . .

Today some would say that the struggles are all over—that all the horizons have been explored—that all the battles have been won—that there is no longer an American frontier.

But I trust that no one in this vast assemblage will agree with those sentiments. For the problems are not all solved and the battles are not all won—and we stand today on the edge of a new frontier—the frontier of the 1960's—a frontier of unknown opportunities and perils—a frontier of unfulfilled hopes and threats.

Woodrow Wilson's <u>New Freedom</u> promised our nation a new political and economic framework. Franklin Roosevelt's <u>New Deal</u> promised security and *succor**° to those in need. But the New Frontier of which I speak is not a set of promises—it is a set of challenges. It sums up not what I intend to offer the American people, but what I intend to ask of them. It appeals to their pride, not their pocketbook—it holds out the promise of more sacrifice instead of more security.

But I tell you the New Frontier is here, whether we seek it or not. Beyond that frontier are uncharted areas of science and space, unsolved problems of peace and war, unconquered pockets of ignorance and prejudice, unanswered questions of poverty and surplus. . . .

I am asking each of you to be a new pioneer on that New Frontier. My call is to the young in heart . . . to all who respond to the scriptural call: "Be strong and of good courage, be not afraid, neither be thou dismayed."

Succor: aid or help.

Quoted from **The New York Times** (July 16, 1960). "© 1960 by The New York Times Company. Reprinted by permission."

Johnson: The Great Society, 1964

I have come today from the turmoil of your Capitol to the tranquility of your campus to speak about the future of our country. . . . The challenge of the next half century is whether we have the wisdom to use our wealth to enrich and elevate our national life, and to advance the quality of American civilization.

Your imagination, your initiative, and your indignation will determine whether we build a society where progress is the servant of our needs, or a society where old values and new visions are buried under unbridled growth. For in your time we have the opportunity to move not only toward the rich society and the powerful society, but upward to the <u>Great Society</u>. The Great Society rests on abundance and liberty for all. It demands an end to poverty and racial injustice, to which we are totally committed in our time. But that is just the beginning. . . . It will be the task of your generation to make the American city a place where future generations will come, not only to live, but to live the <u>good</u> life. . . .

A second place where we begin to build the Great Society is in our countryside. We have always prided ourselves on being not only America the strong and America the free, but America the beautiful. Today that beauty is in danger. The water we drink, the food we eat, the very air we breathe, are threatened with pollution. Our parks are overcrowded. Our seashores overburdened. Green fields and dense forests are disappearing. . . .

A third place to build the Great Society is in the classrooms of America. There your children's lives will be shaped. Our society will not be great until

every young mind is set free to scan the furthest reaches of thought and imagination. We are still far from that goal. . . .

The solution to these problems does not rest on a massive program in Washington, nor can it rely solely on the strained resources of local authority. They require us to create new concepts of cooperation, a creative federalism, between the national capital and the leaders of local communities. . . .

For better or for worse, your generation has been appointed by history to deal with those problems and to lead America toward a new age. You have the chance never before afforded to any people in any age. You can help build a society where the demands of morality, and the needs of the spirit, can be realized in the life of the nation. So will you join in the battle to give every citizen the full equality which God enjoins and the law requires, whatever his belief, or race, or color of his skin? Will you join in the battle to give every citizen an escape from the crushing weight of poverty? . . . .

Quoted from **Public Papers of the Presidents, Lyndon Johnson, 1963–1964** (U.S. Government Printing Office, 1965), Vol. I, pp. 704–707.

There are those timid souls who say this battle cannot be won, that we are condemned to a soulless wealth. I do not agree. We have the power to shape the civilization that we want. But we need your will, your labor, your hearts, if we are to build that kind of a society.

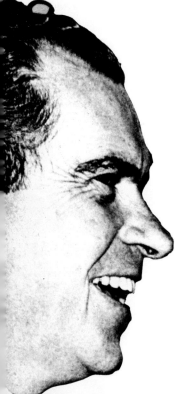

Skepticism: doubt or uncertainty.

Nixon: The New Federalism, 1969

We face an urban crisis, a social crisis—and at the same time, a crisis of confidence in the capacity of government to do its job.

A third of a century of centralizing power and responsibility in Washington has produced a bureaucratic monstrosity, cumbersome, unresponsive, and ineffective.

A third of a century of social experiment has left us a legacy of entrenched programs that have outlived their time or outgrown their purposes.

A third of a century of unprecedented growth and change has strained our institutions and raised serious questions about whether they are still adequate to the times.

It is no accident, therefore, that we find increasing *skepticism**—and not only among the young, but among citizens everywhere—about the continuing capacity of government to master the challenges we face.

Nowhere has the failure of government been more tragically apparent than in its efforts to help the poor, and especially in its system of public welfare. . . .

My purpose tonight, however, is not to review the past record, but to present a new set of reforms—a new set of proposals—a new and drastically different approach to the way in which government cares for those in need, and to the way the responsibilities are shared between the state and federal governments. . . .

After a third of a century of power flowing from the people and the states to Washington, it is time for a New Federalism in which power, funds, and responsibility will flow from Washington to the states and the people. . . . this nation became great, not because of what government did for the people, but because of what the people did for themselves.

It aims at getting everyone able to work, off welfare rolls and onto payrolls.

It aims at ending the unfairness in a system that has become unfair to the welfare recipient, unfair to the working poor, and unfair to the taxpayer.

This new approach aims to make it possible for people—wherever in America they live—to receive their fair share of opportunity. It aims to insure that the people receiving aid, and who are able to work, contribute their fair share of productivity.

This new approach is embodied in a package of four measures: first, a complete replacement of the present welfare system; second, a comprehensive new job training and placement program; third, a revamping of the Office of Economic Opportunity; and fourth, a start on the sharing of the federal tax revenues with the states.

Quoted from **Public Papers of The Presidents, Richard Nixon, 1969** (U.S. Government Printing Office, 1970), pp. 637–645.

35 A TROUBLED AND CREATIVE DECADE

The 1960's was one of the most troubled and yet creative decades in recent American history. Americans were confused and angered by student unrest and overwhelmed and amazed by the accomplishments of space exploration.

Beginning with the so-called free speech movement at the University of California at Berkeley in 1964 and culminating with the tragic shooting of students at Kent State and Jackson State Universities in 1970, student protests both violent and nonviolent spread across the country. Though causes of protest varied from campus to campus, student power or participation in the decision-making processes of their universities was a major one. Other prominent causes were the war in Vietnam, inadequate financial assistance for minority students, the lack of black and ethnic studies programs, and the universities' involvement in military research and recruitment.

America's space exploration programs became matters of both pride and concern. Pride in the American technology that could safely put the first men on the moon and concern over how much it cost to put them there.

While reading this account from Newsweek magazine of the student revolt at Columbia and a statement about space exploration from a spokesman for the aero-space industry, keep in mind these questions:

1. *What did student leaders demand from Columbia University officials?*

2. *How did university officials respond to these demands?*

3. *How has the space program benefited people?*

4. *What future benefits for people may come from the space program?*

Columbia University, 1968

The End of a Siege—And an Era   The seven-day siege of Columbia University ended last week, but the battle for control of the institution has really just begun.

The reoccupation was brief and at times brutal. Acting on a request from University President Grayson Kirk, 1,000 New York City police cleared students from five "liberated" campus buildings, including Kirk's own office. In three predawn hours, they arrested 720 demonstrators; the injured included 132 students, four faculty members, and twelve policemen.

The real meaning of the struggle, however, lay not in ugly statistics but in the fact that Columbia, with its extensive real estate and $390 million endowment, is no longer simply the property of the administration or of its trustees. President Kirk and his 26 trustees are being forced to share power with the faculty and the students. "Columbia," said Tom Hayden, 28, a founder of the militant Students for a Democratic Society, who (though not a student) was arrested in the Mathematics Building, "puts things at a new stage in this country. Universities will reform or be destroyed." . . .

*   *   *   *   *

The original student demands that triggered the confrontation were, in SDS Chairman Mark Rudd's eyes, "not very radical." The students demanded that Columbia halt construction of a gymnasium on public-park land separating the university from Harlem; that it sever its ties with the Institute for Defense Analysis, a consortium of twelve universities performing secret research for the Pentagon; that it lift its prohibition against indoor demonstrations—and finally that it grant amnesty to the students who sat in.

Grievances: Amnesty was crucial to the student militants—not so much because they feared suspension but, they said, because they were enunciating a new principle. "The students," says Rudd, "must have rights to change unjust policies, to redress grievances. Our position is akin to saying that people have a right to jobs or that students in effect have a right to be students in an institution that's rational." But to the administration, a grant of amnesty was a concession to anarchy—in effect turning the university entirely over to the students.

Thus the lines were drawn. After two or three days of sit-in, the administration yielded ground: it halted construction of the gym temporarily, pending a review with community organizations and its trustees. But negotiations on the other issues bogged down almost completely over the weekend of April 28.

*   *   *   *   *

. . . Kirk once more said he could not give in on amnesty; Rudd once again said "amnesty must be a precondition for negotiations." At 5 p.m. Monday University Vice-President David B. Truman "started the clock ticking" for police action that night.

*   *   *   *   *

At 1:30 squads of police deployed through the campus. . . .

Condensed from **Newsweek** (May 13, 1968). Copyright Newsweek, Inc., 1968, pp. 59–60.

Karl G. Harr, Jr. Says Space Exploration Is Worth the Cost

Most thoughtful men and women everywhere must still retain some of the feeling of awe they experienced when Apollo 11 Commander Neil Armstrong cautiously placed a foot upon the moon's surface in that "one small step for man—one giant leap for mankind"* . . .

Some very tangible and direct benefits to mankind have been and are being accomplished through our unmanned satellites in orbit around the Earth. Meteorological satellites have greatly enhanced our ability to forecast the weather around the globe. Communications satellites have not only vastly increased available channels for private and business communication, but have made it possible to transmit television pictures instantaneously around the world with, among other things, enormous implications for education. . . .

Within three years, first launches will be made of Earth resources survey satellites. It is expected that these spacecraft alone will produce benefits that within a few decades will cover the cost of the entire space program. They will locate sources of water, oil, and minerals that were previously undetected. They will spot forest fires and crop blights, track the movements of concentrations of fish, and aid in control of pollution. It is estimated that savings in agriculture and forestry will amount to more than $2 billion annually in the United States alone.

Another rich area of economic benefits is familiarly known as spinoffs—new products, materials, and processes that have come into existence as a result of space research and development and have quickly found application in non-space activities. Whole new families of alloys and plastics, microminiaturized electronics, revolutionary fabrication techniques, previously unattainable standards, tolerances, and degrees of quality control—all of these have grown out of space-related work and found their way into other areas of manufacturing. And this story has barely begun. . . .

Why then do some people so violently oppose this program? The fact is, they do not really oppose the exploration of space *per se.** They oppose it simply because they mistakenly view it as a competitor for national resources with programs to which they ascribe a high priority. . . .

These were the **first words** spoken from the surface of the moon and broadcast around the world.

From Karl G. Harr, Jr., "Space and Tomorrow's Society," **Space World** (December 1970), pp. 30–33.

Per se: a Latin expression meaning "in itself."

Some of the many spinoffs from space research . . .

Teflon non-stick coatings for cookware

Dehydrated and freeze-dried foods

Solid-state miniaturized equipment: radios, TV, cameras

Monitoring equipment used in auto repair shops, laboratories, hospitals, industry

Safer firemen's suits

17 The decades ahead

Some Thoughts about the Future

You have examined episodes in American history ranging in time from the first human migration into North America thousands of years ago to the recent landing of the first Americans on the surface of the moon. Knowing both historical facts and historical judgments made about our past provides us with a basis for making inferences about our future.

The statements presented below are intended to provide a basis for discussing what America might be like in the decades ahead. While studying these statements keep in mind these questions:

Do you agree with the author's inferences about the decades ahead as they concern American:

1. Life styles?

2. Political issues?

3. Technological positions?

4. Power of education?

Why or why not? On what do you base your judgment?

Life Styles in the Decades Ahead

Because of a sharp drop in the birth rate since 1960, population in the 1970's and 1980's will be young adults, not teenagers. Young adults—age 21 to 35—especially the young adult women tend to be the most conventional group in the population, the ones most concerned with the everyday problems of getting and spending. During the next decade Americans may be more concerned with jobs, mortgage payments, and savings than they were in the 1960's. Life support rather than life style may well be the slogan of the next decade.

Political Issues of the Decades Ahead

Destruction of our environment and the problems caused by pollution and over-population are likely to have such a commanding urgency in the next decade that all other issues will be overshadowed.

The cause of the environment may become no less political in the future than has been the cause of social justice in the past. The political alignments of the future may be as different from those of the 1960's as the 1960's were different from the 1920's.

Objectives of this assignment are to:

—Make critical judgments on four statements about America's future.

—Make judgment on the value of studying and writing history.

D142

America's Technological Position in the World in the Decades Ahead

For half a century the United States has led the world in scientific technology. Suddenly mounting evidence suggests that our technological world position is not only stagnant but deteriorating. The shoe industry is about gone. So is the typewriter industry, the sewing machine and electronics industries. Our fishing industry is gone. Ship building and textiles may have to go overseas to survive. United States exports of high technology products such as computers and aircraft have stagnated since the mid-1960's. If present trends continue, we will shortly be a nation of salesmen and consumers rather than technicians and producers.

Education as Power in the Decades Ahead

The uneducated man is in a very weak social position. He is forced to conform his life to the requirements of others. The man of education is in a much stronger social position. He may exercise control over the lives of others. The power once held by landowners, industrialists, and union leaders is now passing to the man of knowledge. Learned men are being asked to make the kind of important social decisions formerly made by men of wealth. Educated men decide how national resources are to be used, how our natural environment is to be preserved, and how our cities are to be made more liveable. In the future, neither property nor money will be the chief source of power for individual Americans. It will be education.

Space Station Concept—How man might live in space some future day, with four levels of living quarters and laboratories for the crew. Two specialized experiment modules are attached to the space station and one floats free nearby. Winglike arrays of solar cells provide electric power.

Additional Reading

Allen, Frederick Lewis, *Only Yesterday*. New York: Harper & Row, 1931.

American Heritage Publishing Company, Inc., *The American Heritage History of World War I*. New York: Simon and Schuster, 1964.

Bailey, Thomas A., *Woodrow Wilson and the Great Betrayal*. New York: Macmillan Company, 1945.

Eisenhower, Dwight David, *Crusade in Europe*. Garden City, New York: Doubleday & Company, Inc., 1948.

Farago, Ladislas, *The Broken Seal: The Story of Operation Magic and the Pearl Harbor Disaster*. New York: Random House, Inc., 1967.

Freidel, Frank, *The Splendid Little War*. Boston: Little, Brown and Company, 1958.

Goldman, Eric F., *The Crucial Decade—And After: America, 1945–1960*. New York: Vintage Books, 1961.

Goldman, Eric, *The Tragedy of Lyndon Johnson*. New York: Alfred A. Knopf, 1969.

Harbaugh, William H., *Power and Responsibility: The Life and Times of Theodore Roosevelt*. New York: Farrar, Straus, 1961.

Kalb, Marvin, and Abel, Elie, *Roots of Involvement: The U.S. in Asia, 1784–1971*. New York: W. W. Norton, 1971.

Leuchtenberg, William, *Franklin D. Roosevelt and the New Deal, 1932–1940*. New York: Harper & Row, 1963.

Link, Arthur, *Woodrow Wilson and the Progressive Era, 1910–1917*. New York: Harper & Row, 1954.

Lomax, Louis, *The Negro Revolt*. New York: Harper & Row, 1962.

Lord, Walter, *The Good Years; from 1900 to the First World War*. New York: Harper & Row, 1960.

Nixon, Richard, *Six Crises*. Garden City, New York: Doubleday, 1962.

Perkins, Dexter, *A History of the Monroe Doctrine*. Boston: Little, Brown and Company, 1963.

Schlesinger, Arthur Jr., *A Thousand Days: John F. Kennedy in the White House*. Boston: Houghton Mifflin, 1965.

Truman, Harry S., *Memoirs*. Garden City, New York: Doubleday & Company, Inc., 1955–1956. 2 vols.

Warren, Harris G., *Herbert Hoover and the Great Depression*. New York: Oxford University Press, 1959.

INDEX

Economic Opportunity Act, 131d
Education, 131–139c
  adult, 134c
  Americanization classes, 134c
  Federal support of, 132d
  mass education, beginnings of, 131–132c
  minority groups and, 136–139c
  power of, 143d
  Progressive Education movement, 133c
  vocational training, 133c, 137c
  See also Schools.
"Efficiency experts," 103c
Egalitarianism, 118b, 121b
Egremont, Earl of, 7b
Eighteenth Amendment, 152b
Einstein, Albert, 92d
Eisenhower, Dwight D., 98d, 99–101d, 102d, 107d, 110–111d, 114d, 130d, 133d
  Vietnam policy of, 122d, 126d
Eisenhower Doctrine, 95d, 99–101d
Elizabeth I, Queen of England, 91a
Elkins Act, 18d
Ellsberg, Daniel, 124d
Elmina, Africa, 152–153a
Emancipation, 164b
Emancipation Proclamation, 33c
  reactions to, 34–36c
Emergency Banking Act, 70d
Emergency Farm Mortgage Act, 70d
Emergency Relief Appropriation Act, 71d
Emerson, Ralph Waldo, 135b, 136b, 140b, 146b
Emigration from Europe, 110–112c
England
  antislavery movement in, 156a, 187a, 188a, 189a
  exploring N.A., 89–94a
  political and economic conditions in, 104–105a
  See also English, English colonies, Great Britain.
English
  Indian relations with, 44a, 45a
  numbers in N.A., 50a, 53a, 62a
  as slave traders, 142a, 147a, 148a, 150a, 151a, 153a
English colonies in America
  government of, 94a, 111–113a
  importance to England (chart), 116a

migration, causes of, 99–110a, 111a
  non-English elements in, 120a
  population of, 116a, 120a
  relations with England, 113a, 114–119a
  See also Colonial America.
Environmental crisis, 140b
Equiano, Olaudah, 156–157a, 160a, 162–163a
Erie Canal, 101b, 107b, 109b
Evaluation, defined, 2a, 5a
Evangelicalism, 153b, 158b, 164b, 165b
Explorations to America (1492–1609)
  English, 89–94a
  list, 95a
Exports (1860–1900), 93c
Extremism, 170b
  See also Antislavery movement, Temperance movement.

"Factors" in slave trade, 152a, 154a, 163a
Fair Deal, 106–107d, 109d, 110d, 136d
Fair Labor Standards Act, 71d
Fall, Albert B., 53d
Family
  positions and land inheritance, 61b
  roles and fashion, 150b
Faneuil Hall, Boston, 20b
Far East, 4d, 77d, 86d, 87d, 89d, 99d
Farm machinery, development of, 97–101c
Farmer, James, 114d
Farmers
  industrialization affecting, 93–101c
  machinery adopted by, 97–101c
  numbers of, 102c
  organization of, 94–97c
  railroads and, 94c
Fashion
  reform in nineteenth century and, 146–149b
  reform in twentieth century and, 149–151b
  symbolic importance of, 144–145b
Federal Bureau of Investigation (FBI), 109d
Federal Congress, on slavery, 2–3c
Federal Deposit Insurance Corporation (FDIC), 70d

Federal Emergency Relief Administration (FERA), 70d, 71d, 72d
Federal Farm Board, 59d
Federal Farm Loan Act, 27d
Federal Government
  expansion of role of, 22–24d, 30–31d, 71d, 109d, 110d
  relief and, 60–61d
  role of: F.D.R.'s view, 67–68d; Truman's view, 108d
Federal Highway Act, 27d, 111d
Federal Housing Administration (FHA), 70d
Federal Interstate Commerce Act, 85c, 94c
Federal Relief Act of 1932, 60d, 61d
Federal Reserve Act, 27d
Federal Reserve Board, 70d, 71d
Federal Securities Act, 70d
Federal Trade Commission Act, 27d
Federalist, The, 71b, 15–16c
Federalists, 68–69b, 90b
Federation of Organized Trade and Labor Unions, 105c
Field, Marshall, 77c
Finley, Robert, 158b
Finney, Charles, 6b, 165b
Firearms, Indians' use of, 44a, 47a, 48a, 50a, 56a
Fitzgerald, F. Scott, 51d
Fitzhugh, George, 9c, 10c
Five Nations, 29a
Florida, 118b
  East, 2b, 94b, 106b, 107b
  West, 89b, 96b, 106b, 107b
Food prices in England, 105a
Food-gathering of early man, 21a, 23a, 24a
Ford, Henry, 75c, 143c, 31d, 52d
Fordney-McCumber Tariff, 51d
Foreign policy of U.S., 88–99b
Formative culture stage, 16a, 24–28a
Forrestal, James, 109d
Fort Ancient, 25a
Fort Christina, 50a
Fort Dearborn, 96b
Fort Detroit, 66a, 67a, 68a
Fort Donelson, 27c
Fort Duquesne, 62a, 63a, 66a
Fort Frontenac, 63a
Fort Henry, 27c
Fort LaBaye, 66a
Fort LeBoeuf, 66a
Fort Miami, 66a

Missouri Compromise, 107b, 2c, 18c
Missouri Enabling Act, 2c
Mitchell, "Billy," 32d
Mohawks, 3–4a, 26a, 29a, 32a, 46a, 63a
Mohegans, 51a
Moley, Raymond, 67d
Monk, Christopher, 23b
Monroe, James, 89b, 92b, 118b, 159b
Monroe Doctrine, 89b, 91–92b, 97–99b, 3d, 9–10d, 103d
Montgomery, Hugh, 19b, 25b, 26b
Montgomery, Isabella (Mrs. Hugh), 24b
Montgomery, Richard, 33b
Montgomery Ward, 76c
Montreal, Canada, 52a, 63a, 96b, 97b
Morgan, J. P., 86c, 143c, 17d
Mormons, 107b
Morris, Robert, 67b
Mound-building in early N.A., 25–26a
Muckrakers, 15d
Muhammad, Elijah, 113d, 119d
Munro, John, 25b, 26b
Munsee Indians, 29a, 31a
Muskie, Edmund, 132d
Mutual-aid societies, 117–118c

Nagasaki, 92–94d
Nanticokes, 29a
Nantucket Island, 93a
Napoleon, 88b, 89b, 91b, 96b, 97b
    tribute to George Washington, 84b
Narraganset, 26a, 51a
Narrative of the Life of Frederick Douglass, 172b
Narvaez, Panfilo de, 95a
Nast, Thomas, 46c, 48c
Natchez, Miss., 51b
National Association for the Advancement of Colored People (NAACP), 112d, 116d
National Association of Manufacturers, 143c
National bank, 74–75b
National Child Labor Committee, 102c
National Convention of Colored Citizens, 173b, 174b
National Defense Education Act, 111d
National Housing Act, 71d, 109d
National identity, 12–14b, 30b, 62b
National Industrial Recovery Act, 70d
National Labor Relations Act, 71d

National Labor Relations Board (NLRB), 71d
National Origins Act, 51d
National parks, creation of, 18d
National Recovery Administration (NRA), 70d
National Reformer, 173b
National Security Act, 109d
National Security Council, 109d
National Turnpike, 101b
National Urban League, 112d
National Youth Administration (NYA), 71d
Natural hairstyle, 151b
Natural resources, 18d, 108d
Nature, 135b, 136b
Nature and progress, 135–141b
    nineteenth century view, 135–137b
    twentieth century view, 140–141b
Naval Stores Act, 115a
Navigation Laws, 114–116a
Nebraska, 100b
Negroes (Blacks), 180–185a, 47d
    citizenship granted to, 52c
    colonization plans, 32c
    equal rights in public places guaranteed, 53c
    equality, struggle for, 111d, 112–121d
    positions held, 21d, 116d
    schools and, 136–137c, 138–139c
    Senator, first elected, 53c
    vote, gaining right to, 43–44c, 52c, 53c
    See also Afro-Americans, Blacks.
Netherlands, 27–28b, 34b, 51b, 52b, 53b
Neutrality, 90–91b
Nevins, Allan, 22–23c
New Amsterdam, 102a, 120a
New Deal, 66–74d, 106d, 107d, 110d, 113d, 132d, 136d
    Supreme Court decisions, 66d, 67d, 70–71d
New England Anti-Slavery Society, 164b
New England Nonresistance Society, 182b
    sentiments, declaration of, 182–183b
New England Restraining Act, 33b
New Federalism, 133d, 136d, 138–139d

New Freedom, 25d, 26–27d, 132d, 137d
New Frontier, 130d, 136–137d
New Hampshire, 100a, 10b, 162b
New Jersey, 102a, 10b, 49b, 50b, 108b
New Mexico, 106b, 107b
New Nationalism, Roosevelt on, 25–26d
New Netherlands, 50a, 52a
New Orleans, 88b, 91b, 92b, 106b, 110b
New Orleans, Battle of, 97b
New York, 102a, 112a, 3b, 8b, 9b, 10b, 11b, 28b, 31b, 40b, 41b, 69b, 100b, 101b
New York City, 49b, 69b, 165b, 130c
New York Elevated Railway, 88c
Newfoundland, 89a, 91a, 92a, 44b
Newlands Reclamation Act, 18d
"Newness," 148b
Newport, Christopher, 94a, 95a, 97a
Newport, R.I., 10b, 50b, 51b
Newton, Huey, 116d
Nicholson, Francis, 117a
Nigeria, 143a
Nisei, 76d
Nixon, Richard M., 130d, 132–133d, 136d, 138–139d
    Vietnam policies, 123d, 124d, 126d, 127d, 128–129d
    visits Communist China, 124d
"No-Government," 170b
Nomura, Kichisaburo, 83d
Nonimportation associations, 10b, 11b, 12b, 15b
Nonresistance, 181b, 182–183b
Nonviolence, 170b, 173b, 180–188b
Norris, George, 23d, 50d
North, Lord, 10b, 11b, 27b, 30b, 31b, 32b, 43b, 50b, 53b
North Africa, 86d, 89d
North Atlantic Treaty Organization (NATO), 95d
North Carolina, 30b, 34b, 40b, 51b, 69b, 100b, 109b, 25c
North Central Association of Colleges and Secondary Schools, 133c
North Dakota, 100b
Northern Securities Company, 17d, 18d
Northwest Ordinance, 67b, 2c
Northwest Passage, 89–91a
Northwest Territory, 96b, 2c
Nova Scotia, 89a, 44b

CDEFGHIJ 07654
PRINTED IN THE UNITED STATES OF AMERICA